D0771357

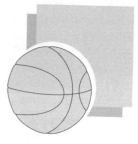

The Men of March

A Season Inside the Lives of
College Basketball Coaches

BRIAN CURTIS

TAYLOR TRADE PUBLISHING

Lanham • NewYork • Oxford

Bill Self photos courtesy of University of Illinois, Division of Intercollegiate Athletics. Steve Alford photos courtesy of University of Iowa, Office of Sports Information. Steve Lavin photos courtesy of ASUCLA and University of California, Los Angeles, Department of Intercollegiate Athletics. Mike Brey with Mike Krzyzewski courtesy of Sam Roberts; all others courtesy of Lighthouse Imaging.

Published by Taylor Trade Publishing
A Member of the Rowman & Littlefield Publishing Group
4720 Boston Way
Lanham, Maryland 20706

Distributed by National Book Network

Library of Congress Cataloging-in-Publication Data

Curtis, Brian, 1971–
    The men of March : a season inside the lives of college basketball coaches
/ Brian Curtis.
        p. cm.
    ISBN 0-87833-313-4 (hardcover : alk. paper)
    1. Basketball—Coaching—United States. 2. Basketball coaches—United States.
    3. Basketball—Tournaments—United States. 4. College sports—United States. I. Title.
    GV885.3.C87 2003
    796.323'07'7—dc21
                                                                            2002151821

⊗™ The paper used in this publication meets the minimum requirements of American National Standard for Information Sciences—Permanence of Paper for Printed Library Materials, ANSI/NISO Z39.48–1992.
Manufactured in the United States of America.

For Mom and Dad,

                    Who Never Stopped Believing

For Tamara,

                    Who Made Me Believe

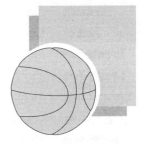

Contents

Acknowledgments

W HEN I FIRST DECIDED TO WRITE THIS BOOK, I HAD NO IDEA HOW MUCH TIME, work, and effort it would require, and I certainly did not realize all of the help that I would need along the way. This book is really a team effort from those individuals who believed in me and in my project. From the inception of the idea in the summer of 2001, to the final touches before publication in 2003, many eyes, ears, and hands helped me write this book, too many to recognize here. So, in a traditional disclaimer, let me thank everyone who contributed to this book, or to my life, in some way.

First, I must thank the four coaches, without whom this book would not be possible. From our first meetings last fall, these four men took me into their confidences and allowed me to take an intimate look at them, their families, and their programs, with great risk. They did not know me then, but they certainly know me now. Steve Alford, Mike Brey, Steve Lavin, and Bill Self let me come into their lives and be a part of their families, and did so with patience, trust, and graciousness. They sat down for lengthy interviews, let me into their practices and locker rooms, and invited me to their homes. In all of my time with the four, on only one occasion did a coach request that I leave a room, something that I had indicated from the start that I would be more than willing to do. They trusted me, and for that I am eternally grateful. I consider them all friends. I also must thank their partners in life, Tanya Alford, Tish Brey, Cindy Self, and Treena Camacho, for their understanding and time.

As evident from my research and the resulting book, a head coach is only strong with a solid supporting cast. I want to thank the assistants and staff members who welcomed me into their programs and gave me everything I needed. At Notre Dame, Sean Kearney, Anthony Solomon, Lewis Preston, Rod Balanis, Jim Phillips, Skip Meyer, and Stephanie Reed. At Iowa, Greg Lansing, Rich Walker, Sam Alford, Brian Jones, Shelly Deutsch, Pam Culver, Jerry Strom, and Phil Haddy. At Illinois, Billy Gillispie, Norm Roberts,

Wayne McClain, Jeff Guin, and Cindy Butkovich. At UCLA, Jim Saia, Gerald Madkins, Patrick Sandle, Dana Martin, Jamie Angeli, Doug Erickson, and Matt Geniesse. Of course, the four Sports Information professionals were instrumental to my work, and are the best at what they do: Bernie Cafarelli, Bill Bennett, Steve Roe, and Kent Brown.

I want to thank the players from the four teams, who never questioned my presence and who answered my questions honestly. A thank you to the many coaches, athletic directors, and media members around the nation who gave me five minutes or five hours to provide me with an honest look at the profession.

It was key for me to follow what the local press was saying throughout the season so I thank the *South Bend Tribune*, the *Los Angeles Times*, *The Daily News*, *Iowa City Press Citizen*, *Cedar Rapids Gazette*, *Des Moines Register*, *Decatur Herald & Review*, and the *Springfield State Journal-Register*.

Writing a book takes time, and there are so many people that helped me. My transcriber Kara Lawton, researcher Hamed Jones, fact-collector and information man extraordinaire Mike Douchant, and copy editor Susan Olsen. A big thank you to Steve Ackerman, Brian Matthews, and Mike Barnett. Your input was priceless. My editor at Taylor Trade, Jill Langford, is an inspiration and a shining example of what is right about this world. I am also indebted to Taylor's publicist Tracy Miracle and production editor Terry Fischer.

On the personal front, I want to thank those who have been role models, mentors, and friends over the years: Dan Markim, Janie Kleiman, Kevin Harlan, Dennis Young, Bob Costas, and Joe Wisniewski.

I owe a debt of gratitude to my new bride, who spent many nights alone as I spent cold nights watching games throughout the winter far away from home. Tamara is my inspiration and my love. I want to thank my parents, Shelly and Marty Mand, who have given me unconditional support and love throughout my life, and who believed in this project and in me. My in-laws, Claire and Don Marks, for being the best promoters in the world. Finally, I want to thank my brothers, Greg and Mike, who have set the bar high for their little brother.

After spending time with so many coaches over the past year, after talking to them, their families, and those in the game, after sitting with them after heartbreaking losses, after watching a last-minute play diagrammed in a timeout result in a game-winning shot, after the daily crises and the nights on the road, I can only conclude this about a college basketball coach: He is an amazing man, but I could never do it.

Brian Curtis
Los Angeles, 2003

Introduction

I WAS SITTING AT A TABLE IN THE BUDWEISER BREWHOUSE AT THE INDIANAPOLIS International Airport on Selection Sunday, March 10, adhering to my strict diet of a plate of nachos—no peppers—and a bottle of water. I watched a television set mounted on a wall with no sound, trying to read the lips of Greg Gumbel and Clark Kellogg as they analyzed the just-released brackets on the CBS Selection Show. As I feverishly scribbled incomprehensible pen marks on a note pad, trying to write the names of the Tournament-bound on the paper, two guys at another table noticed what I was doing. "So what are you doing? Getting ready to make your picks?" asked one of the men, a college-age looking fellow with an Indiana University baseball cap.

"Not really," I responded. With further probing by my two new friends, I proceeded to fill them in on my six-month odyssey in the college basketball world, a story that seemed to both impress and perplex them.

"That's a hell of a lot of flying," said the IU guy's buddy. Well, yes, it is. And then came the inevitable question. The one that I have heard many times throughout my journeys around America: "So which coach was the most interesting?"

If by interesting the curious man implied funny, probably Steve Lavin, Pete Strickland, or Mike Brey fit the mold. If by interesting he meant candid, then the answer could have been Bill Self, Bob Huggins, Mike Davis, Tim Carter, or John Chaney. If by interesting he meant full-throttle, then surely Tom Crean and Bobby Gonzalez come to mind. Classy? Lute Olson, John Wooden, and Paul Hewitt. Outgoing? Phil Martelli, Tim O'Shea, Billy Bayno (really, all coaches). Basketball smarts? Steve Alford, Dave Faucher, and John Beilein. I guess I could have answered the question in a hundred different ways, because *every* coach is interesting.

They are lawyers and bankers. High school teachers, Domino's pizza deliverymen, and engineers. Some majored in business and labor relations, others in phys ed. Most have a master's degree and a few have PhDs. Some have recorded CDs. Many played college ball; some simply watched as team managers. There are professional baseball players among them and decorated war veterans. Some were born in the cornfields of Iowa while others come from the blacktops of Harlem or the summer heat of Louisiana. Many remember the days of Reagan, a few remember the days of Eisenhower. They are black, they are white. They are separated by wins and losses.

There are 321 Division I schools that play college basketball, and with an average coaching staff size of four, there are 1,300 men whose lives revolve around the game, and whose futures are dictated by the talents, work ethics, and moods of 18-year-olds. Some are better known than others, referred to as Coach K, Roy, Tark, Bobby, and Lute. There is a new crop of coaches, whose names are becoming just as familiar: Quin, Matt, Rick, Tommy, and Steve(s).

You can blame the media, the money, the NCAA, the players, coaches, parents, fans, and just about everyone else for our inaccurate perceptions about coaches. The reality is that we get most of our information from the media, and the media shows us what they *think* we want to see, hear, or read. Most Americans would prefer to see a matchup between Duke and Maryland than a tough Southland Conference meeting between Northwestern State and Texas-San Antonio. *SportsCenter* would rather show you Rick Pitino in an Armani suit than Grambling's Larry Wright. You can't really blame the television guys. They are showing the best teams in the country with arguably the best players who are perceived to be coached by the best coaches.

Imagine that you are a college basketball coach for a moment. You have probably moved five times by the time you are 42. You may make a tremendous amount of money, but can rarely take off a few days to enjoy it or the upscale home your wife designed. You are in the office by 9:00 A.M. and don't leave until the games you are watching on Direct TV have finished. And when you finally do get home, your kids are asleep and your wife is busy paying bills. You eat dinner alone as you pop in a tape of your next opponent and fall asleep somewhere around 1:00 A.M. During the day, you make and receive close to 100 calls and write letters to kids encouraging them that you and your school are for them. You pick up the papers, read about how awful you are at your chosen profession, and listen to the talk radio guys rip your last coaching move. In the midst of the mayhem, you plan for the future, talk to the trainer bearing bad news, field questions from an often unfriendly media, speak to booster clubs, deal with academics and, of course, breathe.

There is so much to coaching and to the men who coach that the public never sees. In the past six months, I have been in the locker rooms at halftime during heated and crucial conference games; in the 8:00 A.M. coaches' meetings breaking down film of an opponent; in the extravagant homes of coaches eating the rare meal as a family; on the set of the weekly television coach's show; in the postgame press conferences; sitting courtside at practices and games watching these men orchestrate; listening in during timeouts and locker-room speeches; spending time in the offices as coaches write letter upon letter to prospective players. I have seen them at their best, and perhaps at their worst, and I have watched some of the game's greats struggle in their vocation. I have traveled the nation, watched more games than I can remember and talked to hundreds of coaches, players, athletic directors, conference commissioners, television analysts, family members, and, of course, the men themselves.

What has emerged from my time with these men is a rather complicated picture of their role as a coach. Today's college coaches are CEOs running a business—a big business. They are cordial with their competitors, but are willing to rip their hearts out to get

ahead. They are held accountable for their players graduating, for fund-raising and for gar-
nering community support, yet they are put to the test by the bottom line—wins. For these
responsibilities, most are compensated handsomely, often with performance incentives.

They are as different in their backgrounds as they are in their methods. They teach differently, talk to the media in varying tones, recruit in many ways unique to their personalities, and treat education with different degrees of seriousness. The game of college basketball
has changed, as coaches now are defined by success and failure in March. Indeed, everything they do during the year is geared toward peaking when it counts—in March.

There is an underlying paradox in everything that coaches do, and all that they are
about. They work incredible hours *but* they make a great deal of money. They are chastised by the media *but* that same spotlight makes them into stars. There is great whining
when they are fired *but* they give little sympathy to their colleagues who are. *They* are
"clean" and ethical in recruiting *but* there are *others* that cheat. The university and community demand so much of them *but* that same community endorses them with dollars.

My goal in researching and writing this book was to take a look at the lives of college
coaches to find out who they are, what they do and perhaps, most importantly, why they
do it. I figured the best way to understand life as a college coach was to experience a season with one—or better yet, four. A quartet of remarkable coaches granted me access to
their programs and lives throughout the 2001–2002 season: Steve Alford at Iowa, Mike
Brey at Notre Dame, Steve Lavin at UCLA, and Bill Self at Illinois. Beginning with the
preseason and ending at the Final Four, these coaches gave me unprecedented access to
their offices, locker rooms, practices, staff meetings, and homes. They accepted me into
their lives graciously, and answered my questions even when they didn't want to.

The result is a story of one season with four men and four teams, the jubilant upsets
and the crushing defeats, the daily crises, and the sacrifices of families. The profiles pre-
sented here are but a sliver of each man's life. My approach was intense and in-depth but it
did not permit me the scope with which to write complete biographies of these coaches.
My intent was to capture the moments in a season that make up coaching, and I have tried
my best to provide the details. But this book is more than a narrative of one season in college basketball. It takes a look at some key issues involving coaches: recruiting, media,
fund-raising, education, hirings and firings, race, religion, and age among others. These discussions are enhanced by contributions from interviews with coaches, athletic directors,
conference commissioners, players, and other key people in the college basketball world.

Because of the limitations of travel and time, it was impossible to witness firsthand
every game played by the four teams. But through frequent phone conversations with the
coaches, interviews with assistants and players, and some diligent research, I felt like I was
at every game.

The biggest obstacle in attempting a project of this magnitude was travel. I logged over
60,000 flight miles, staying nights at Marriotts and Red Roofs from Maui to New York City.
I almost ended the book—and my life—on a snowy Interstate 94 outside of Milwaukee en
route to interview Marquette coach Tom Crean. Two months earlier I landed in
Indianapolis in November, but could not rent a car—my driver's license had expired two
days prior and no rental car company would rent to me. It was only after numerous phone
calls, while sitting on my luggage in a parking lot at the airport, that a very nice woman in
the California Department of Motor Vehicles pulled some strings for me. Then there were
the crazy 96 hours during conference tournament play in March when I went from Los
Angeles to New York to Indianapolis and back to L.A., via taxis, trains, subways, and planes.

Every coach has his own story about when he first knew he wanted to coach. Some knew in elementary school while others did not find their calling until they had careers in other professions. Their stories of how they got their first job are as different as their personalities. But almost universally, every coach loves working with kids, enjoys teaching and probably would be doing this even if there weren't large sums of money involved.

"I'd never really thought about doing anything other than coaching and teaching," Arizona coach Lute Olson explains. "I had made that decision by the time I was a sophomore in high school. It never changed. I've never even thought about what I would do if I weren't coaching." Olson speaks from experience, having been in the game for over 40 years and having earned the respect of his peers. He started out coaching seven years at the high school level making $3,200 and teaching six classes a day, coaching basketball, baseball, and even assisting with football.

Many coaches were drawn to the profession by a parent or a former coach or teacher. For Marquette's Tom Crean it was a high school coach; for Pepperdine's Paul Westphal it was an elementary school gym teacher. Drexel's Bruiser Flint got into the game by accident. His father worked as a commissioner in the famed Sonny Hill League in Philadelphia, and one day as a freshman at nearby St. Joe's, Flint's father asked him to drive some kids over to a gym for a game. "The other team's coach didn't show up so I coached the team and I loved it." He has never stopped coaching.

Arizona State coach Rob Evans has seen his share of players through the years, but keeps it all in perspective. "I love the camaraderie with the kids. Seeing them be successful off of the court. Look, coaching to me is fun. If I ever got to be where it wasn't fun, I wouldn't do it. My degree is in English. I thought I was going to teach English in high school."

A coach is driven by a love for the game, a passion for teaching, and the challenge of sport. The material rewards are obvious, but coaches also gain self-satisfaction and the comfort of knowing they are shaping lives.

ESPN analyst and former Duke player Jay Bilas sees a disheartening trend growing in the game. "The good coaches really love the game and respect the game. That's the common thread that I see. Now you see some coaches getting into it for the money, because there is a lot of money available. You can spot those guys." Bilas poses a good question: Would many of these coaches be coaching if the money wasn't good? Every coach will tell you yes, that the love of teaching is more motivation than money. In reality, however, it seems there are some coaches who get into the profession because the lure of the fame and fortune is great.

Big Ten Commissioner Jim Delany has been an outspoken critic of college basketball but has a certain level of respect for the men coaching. The lucrative coaching profession drives many young teachers and coaches into the game, but that isn't so bad according to the former North Carolina player. If there are more people wanting to get in, just like in the college admissions process, then the quality of candidates will be better.

Delany also understands that coaching today is not like it used to be. "The coach has three parts to him. He is part teacher, part coach, and part marketer. I think in the old days they were more the teacher, coach, then marketer. Now they are more marketers than anything else. Everybody is selling something," he continues. "None of these guys would trade $750,000, five-year contracts for a seven-year, $57,000 a year contract. The guys that I am more concerned about are the guys who are making $50,000 a year and getting fired after three years. I'm not very concerned much about a guy making a half a million or a million dollars a year who is having to produce on a regular basis. By that I mean multitask production, not just winning. Graduation compliance, being a spokesman. If you are going to make that kind of money, it is not unusual to expect a person to deliver on a number of levels. If they do, it's not unusual for them to be rewarded."

When Purdue assistant Jay Price was a single man, coaching at the University of Oklahoma, he met a woman one day and asked her out to lunch in the middle of the season. She agreed to the date and asked Price when. "Whenever I can find the time," he responded. "What do you mean, you've got to find the time? All you do is sit in your office and draw up plays," the woman retorted. And so the perception of the public, from the movies, from television, and from not-so-great representatives of the coaching world, is that coaches don't do much but draw up plays on a chalkboard. They go to practice; then go home.

Many coaches will tell you that in today's game, of all of their duties as the CEO, diagramming plays, conducting practices, and coaching in games are the *least* of what they do. Most coaches assert that only 20 to 30% of their time is now spent on practice, scouting, or game coaching. So what about the rest of their time? There is the time-consuming recruiting, fund-raising, media commitments, office management, speaking engagements, and so much more.

"I'm just a teacher and have never worked in business, but I know that being a CEO is all about people management," Mike Brey explains. "I have to deal with people above me, my bosses and AD, and with people below me, my assistants, office staff and, most of all, the players. Attitudes, chemistry, recruiting, putting out fires, PR. People would be shocked at how little basketball is talked about by coaches. Just shocked."

Certainly coaches at lesser-known schools have fewer of these commitments, but then they may have added duties like driving the team van, setting up a gym for games, or doing some of the team laundry. But at the major schools like Kansas, UCLA, Duke, and Michigan, the demands from external sources, the fans, media, and university are a lot greater than those at Niagara, Monmouth, and Texas Southern. The work level is the same for all Division I coaches, but how they spend their time differs.

Perhaps Jay Price had a response to that woman back in Oklahoma who wanted a date, or perhaps he didn't even know how to begin to respond. Coaches are doing much more than drawing up plays, to their dismay and perhaps to the detriment of the game, but college basketball is no longer just a game. It is a multibillion-dollar business that demands strong personalities, an unrelenting work ethic, and coaches willing to face the pressures and demands. The benefits are great but only a select few are willing, and able, to do what coaches do.

The experience of writing this book was a memorable one, and I hope that you enjoy reading this book as much as I enjoyed writing it. My hope is that you come away with a better understanding of college coaches, of what they do, and why they do it, so the next time you are ready to question a substitution, scream an obscenity, or make your NCAA Tournament pool picks, you might just think twice about the men at the center of it all.

Self-Expectations

H UFF HALL WAS PACKED IN A SEA OF ORANGE AND BLUE BY 9:15 P.M. ON FRIDAY, October 12. The grungy, old gymnasium was the former home of Illinois basketball from 1925 to 1963, but was now relegated to intramural pickup games, gymnastics, wrestling, and volleyball matches, and an occasional concert for the Champaign faithful. On this night in the early fall, there was something different in the air that turned the old gym into a spectacle of hope. The 4,000-plus fans were crammed in, and the university police closed the doors by 9:30 P.M., fearing a visit by the local fire marshal. The Illini pep band played some catchy tunes, and the cheerleaders tried to grab the attention of the students in attendance, but to no avail. It was Midnight Madness at Illinois, the magical season lay just ahead.

There was a makeshift boxing ring sitting at midcourt and the *Rocky* theme was played loudly by the pep band. As a large screen at one end of the building showed a video of the previous season's highlights for the fans, the Illinois players and coaches joked around in the dilapidated locker rooms underneath the floor in Huff Hall. There was a heightened sense of excitement, not only because these guys were still just kids, but also because of the preseason speculation and expectations that this team could finish the season as national champions. So as they playfully hit each other with gloves, laughed with huge smiles, and joked with one another, the man in charge was more subdued—a general ready to put his plan into action.

Since the explosion of Midnight Madness celebrations in the mid-1990s, thanks in large part to ESPN, many school's marketing departments have attempted to create a huge kick off to the season with the late-night revelry. Technically, college teams cannot begin practice until 12:00 A.M. on the Saturday in October closest to October 15 (a date set by the NCAA), so someone got the idea of holding that first official practice at midnight on the first permissible day, and inviting students and fans to come and watch. Former Maryland coach Lefty Driesell is credited with the concept of Midnight Madness, dating back to

1971, when he had his Maryland players run around the football field at midnight on the first allowable day—illuminated by car headlights—attracting a crowd. But as the tradition has grown, practice is the last thing that fans see, if at all, during these "practices."

The lights in Huff Hall went out and a spotlight descended on the pep band as they played the theme from *Rocky*. The Illinois players and coaching staff were introduced through a tunnel of smoke to the frenzied crowd. Frank Williams got a loud roar, followed closely by a limping Lucas Johnson on crutches, hobbled by a torn ACL. One of the biggest cheers of the night was for Bill Self, the man who could lead the team to the championship. The festivities continued, with the presentation of the previous season's Big Ten Championship rings to players and coaches, including former stars Sergio McClain and Marcus Griffin. Self then walked out of the gym with assistants Wayne McClain, Norm Roberts, and Billy Gillispie. According to NCAA rules, they could not even be in the gym as their team takes part in a three-point shootout and dunk contest because it was not yet midnight. They lingered in the hallway, talked to some parents, and looked eager and excited. In the three-point contest, Brett Melton beat big man Damir Krupalija in the final round, 17-16. There was a roar from the fans as the P.A. announcer emphatically announced a self-alley-oop, one-handed dunk attempt by freshman Luther Head in the dunk contest.

The 2000–2001 version of Illini basketball had a successful year, finishing sixth in the final Associated Press poll in March. In his first year at Illinois, Self led the team to a 27-8 overall record, 13-3 in the Big Ten Conference, and a share of the Big Ten title. In the postseason, the Illini were a No. 1 seed and made a trip to the Elite Eight, losing to Arizona. The team was led by then sophomores Frank Williams and Brian Cook, junior Cory Bradford, and seniors McClain and Griffin. Johnson came off the bench with toughness as did classmate Robert Archibald, who was an inside presence, while Sean Harrington and Krupalija gave Illinois a deep bench. It was a team that went undefeated at home in Assembly Hall. It was a team that could have gone farther in the Tournament.

As the 2001–2002 season approached, it was natural that the local and national media liked Illinois' chances in the upcoming season. Starters Williams, Bradford, and Cook all returned, as did Johnson, Archibald, Harrington, and Krupalija. They would be joined by a highly touted recruiting class including 7'2" redshirt freshman Nick Smith, junior college transfer Blandon Ferguson and high school stars Luther Head and Roger Powell. Nine players in all returned for the 2001–2002 season and the Illini were loaded and, at least on paper, looked like they would give Duke a run for the national championship.

Every top program has its star. This year, Duke had Jason Williams; Maryland had Juan Dixon; Memphis had Dajuan Wagner. For Illinois, there was no doubt about who the man was. Frank Williams. The Peoria, Illinois, native was the reigning Big Ten Player of the Year and an All-American. He was on the 2001 Wooden Award team and was a nominee for the 2002 Wooden Award, given to college basketball's most outstanding player. He led Illinois in scoring (14.9 ppg), assists (148), and steals (67) in his sophomore campaign, scoring in double digits 27 times. His freshman season, 1999–2000, Williams started 29 games and ranked second on the team in scoring. He redshirted as a partial qualifier in 1998–1999.

Coming out of Peoria's Manual High School, Williams was "Mr. Basketball" for the state of Illinois in 1998. A McDonald's All-American, he was coached by Wayne McClain, then the head coach of Manual, father of Sergio, and now an assistant at Illinois. Williams brought high expectations with him to Illinois back in 1998, and the stage was now set for him to lead them to the promised land. But the star also had his issues. Criticized for a shoddy work ethic, and not known for his prowess in the classroom, Williams struggled in the spotlight at Illinois, on and off the court. After his phenomenal sophomore season, he had flirted with the riches of the NBA draft, but ultimately decided to return to Champaign, no doubt impressed by the billboards in town sponsored by a bank that read, "Stay, Frank, Stay!"

For Self, having a talent like Williams on the floor makes his job much easier. An experienced playmaker, known for his clutch performances, Williams could take Illinois all the way and Self knew it. But the coach was also smart enough to know that it would take a delicate coaching job to see Williams through it. That process started months earlier, when the coach met with his star player in his office. "I told him he needed to step up as a leader," Self remembers, "that the younger guys would be watching him and emulating his attitude. He agreed and understood. Frank is never going to be vocal, but he is the leader of this team."

In addition to Williams, Bradford returned to the starting lineup, the 1999 Big Ten Freshman of the Year and an All–Big Ten selection in 1999 and 2000. A seasoned veteran, Bradford was a three-point specialist, holding the NCAA record for consecutive games with a three-pointer with 88. He was a man's man playing a man's game, and though quiet like his backcourt mate, he did not shy away from the pressure. If the game was on the line, Bradford wanted the ball in his hands. He had been criticized in the 2000–2001 season for occasional shooting slumps and did not have a good assist to turnover ratio, as he recovered from a surgically repaired knee. In fact, Bradford had more turnovers (67) than assists (63). Still, he was a cornerstone of the Illini lineup and Self was counting on him to play a huge role. Headed into his senior season, Bradford also knew that he needed a strong showing to help his chances of playing in the NBA.

In the front court, 2000 Big Ten Co-Freshman of the Year Brian Cook returned and he joined Williams as a preseason Wooden Award nominee. Big things were expected of Cook, a versatile forward who could hit a three, bring the ball up, and grab a rebound. This finesse and touch, however, were substitutes for toughness and physicality and Cook was often pushed around in the post in rough Big Ten play. But with the loss of seniors Sergio McClain and Griffin, "Cookie" needed to fill some large shoes inside.

Lucas Johnson is the type of player that every team hates to play against and every player wants to have on his team. Accused of being a "dirty player" by more than one opposing coach, Johnson is often in the air, on the floor, or somewhere in between fighting for a rebound or loose ball. He has an intimidating expression and an even tougher resolve. Though he would never be a big scoring threat, his inside play and rebounding would be key. Cerebral off the court, Johnson is a business major and spent a summer working as a runner at the Chicago Board of Trade—not a place you were likely to find a college basketball player during vacation. Joining Johnson down low would be the big men, Krupalija and Archibald, two seniors with size and strength (and also the two best looking on the team according to their popularity with the coeds). Krupalija had a midseason knee injury the previous year while Archibald came back last season from back surgery in 1999–2000. Redshirt freshman Nick Smith would be able to give Self ten minutes a game, and at 7'2", could be a defensive presence.

Sean Harrington was a nice balance in the backcourt between Williams and Bradford, a shooting guard with long range who could also bring the ball up at the point guard slot. And then there were the newcomers. Freshman Roger Powell from Joliet, Illinois, was an all-state selection in high school and at 6'6", 215 lbs., looked to help the Illini front court in his first season. Luther Head was from Chicago, with "hops" as big as his own expectations, but he needed refinement of his game to play at the college level. Junior college transfer Blandon Ferguson from the College of Southern Idaho, also looked to fit in the mix.

So with Williams as the centerpiece, the table was set for a run at the national title. The 2001–2002 *The Sporting News* season preview cover had a picture of Williams. Superimposed over his picture was this headline: *Illinois is No. 1!* Other newsmags had the Illini pegged anywhere from second to fifth, but all had them as a national title contender. All 11 head coaches in the Big Ten picked Illinois to finish first in the conference in the preseason coaches' poll, followed by Iowa. Williams was the unanimous pick for Player of the Year.

"I could care less about being ranked No. 2," Self bemoans. "I really liked it about two weeks ago, because I thought it was a great recruiting tool in the middle of recruiting season." One of Self's assistants, Norm Roberts, agrees with his boss' assessment and sees rankings as simply a "great recruiting mail out." They may not put much stock in *The Sporting News* cover, but it sure came in handy when they mailed it out to hundreds of potential Illini players. New assistant Wayne McClain takes the philosophical approach. "Do I like expectations? I'd rather have people expecting you to win than expecting you to lose. As long as you are doing something positive, that beats negative all of the time."

Most coaches would be lying if they told you they don't look at the rankings or don't care. It may not directly affect what they are doing, but they, and their players, know darn well whether they are third or thirteenth. Coaches know how their teams stack up against opponents—but rarely express their true feelings. "I've always thought that the best thing you can do is be as honest as possible," Self says. "Most coaches with the exception of 2 or 3% will downplay their team more than they would build them up. It looks a lot better to win and not predict it than to predict it, and not do it. I think with your team you can say we're better than these guys and we're going to win if we play with passion tonight. You can tell that to your team. You can *never* tell that to the press."

Just because the season was kicking off at Midnight Madness for Illinois didn't mean it was just starting for Self. In fact, the previous season never ended, so there really was no beginning to this next one. There were individual workouts with Illinois players from the first week of school; he logged his time on the road recruiting for the next year's class; made speaking engagements; gave media interviews; attended academic meetings; and perhaps, most importantly, made daily decisions that would affect his team's chances. In the days leading up to Midnight Madness, Self was already in midseason form.

It was a rare day off a week earlier on October 4 when the coach found himself on a golf course at a fund-raiser in Decatur. He was playing a round with some alumni and boosters when his cell phone rang. He ignored it. Driving home later, he checked his voice-mail and heard a message from team trainer Rod Cardinal. Illinois captain Lucas Johnson, the team's leader and heart and soul, had injured himself in a pickup game that day. "I felt something pop," Johnson recalls. "I cut to the lane and planted my right foot trying to score and it just popped." (Johnson denied published reports that teammate Robert Archibald had shoved him causing the injury.)

"How bad is it?" Self asked. They didn't know at that point, but it didn't look good. It must have been severe, Self thought to himself, because Johnson is one of the toughest guys in college basketball: if he is hurting, it must be bad. He called Johnson from his cell phone to check on his status.

"He said some words that I can't say here," Johnson reflected later. "He was disappointed. I think that he was more upset than me, because he's a player himself. And he knows the thought process of a player, he knows how much I've looked forward to this season."

Further tests would reveal a torn anterior cruciate ligament in his right knee, and normal rehabilitation for that kind of injury is four to six months. Doctors had to wait for the swelling to go down before doing surgery on October 22. The team leader was probably out for the season but he would not disappear.

"I know due to my nature and due to my personality that I'll find a way to contribute to this team whether I'm on the court or not." The decision to redshirt Johnson would not be made in the fall. The senior wanted to go out with his class and was on a pace to graduate with a degree in marketing. If he did redshirt, he would stay in Champaign and begin work on his MBA.

So just days before the start of practice, the start of the magical season, after *The Sporting News* had ranked Illinois No. 1 in the country, things had already begun to fall apart for Self. He knew that these things happen, that anyone can get injured at anytime. But why now in such a freak manner? And why did it have to happen to his team leader who means so much more to the team than points or rebounds? But like most coaches, Self had to look at the big picture and he immediately began to formulate a new lineup. He just had no idea where to begin.

On October 11, the day before the team met the press and unveiled themselves to their fans, Self hopped into a car with Sports Information Director Kent Brown and Promotions Director Dave Johnson and headed off to the Chancellor Hotel, where the Kiwanis Club was holding their weekly luncheon. On this day, the guest speaker was Self and the topic was Illinois basketball. On the way to the event, Self, Johnson, and Brown talked about the plan for Midnight Madness the following night and the schedule for Media Day the next afternoon, when Self and his players would face the press to talk about the upcoming season. A Media Day that is routine for most coaches and players would this year be unusual in two respects: the lofty ranking and the future of Frank Williams.

In discussions with Williams the previous season, it became clear to Self that this, his junior season, would be his last on the college level. Self and Williams had a good relationship, the coach seemingly one of the few to understand his star. On the court, he gave Williams the freedom to be creative, to take responsibility, to lead the team, and until he abused it, he would continue to give his star leeway. Williams had already passed up the NBA in the spring, and it would not surprise anyone to know that Williams would leave school early after this season. But it created a dilemma for the coach. Instead of allowing Williams and the team to face the questions from reporters all season long about his future, would it not be better to have Williams announce his intentions on Media Day? It may not seem like a major decision, but as a coach, Self understood the consequences. If Williams played poorly in a game this season, would he be accused of walking through his last year? Would it be a distraction for the other players to know he is leaving? Or would the distraction be avoided by announcing the decision now?

In a brief exchange with Brown, Self decided it would be best for Williams to announce his decision to the press on Friday, and he, Self, and the team would live with the consequences. The decision would become an issue months down the road.

As Self arrived at the Chancellor, the crowd was well into their lunch, and the coach grabbed some food off the buffet and headed to his seat on the dais. As he looked over the crowd, he saw more silver hair than black, more wrinkles than pom-poms. The Kiwanis Club is skewed toward the older crowd, but what they may lack in youth, they make up for in enthusiasm. After a generous introduction, Self began and soon had the crowd in the palm of his hand. He talked about the prospects for the Illini, the returning starters and how much they needed support from fans like those there at the luncheon. He then took questions from the floor and his answers got those in attendance rolling.

"Coach, don't you think officials are calling games unfairly?" an elderly man asked. "Well, just because the officials call fouls doesn't mean they are wrong—most of them are, but not all of them," the coach responded.

A middle-aged woman stood up, "Coach, what are your expectations for this year?" Without a pause, Self said "You know, it's funny. We went to the Elite Eight last year and no one comes up to me to say congratulations. They all want to know about this year."

Dressed in a black T-shirt with a tan jacket, the coach wooed the crowd, speaking for fifteen minutes. As the lunch concluded, he was swarmed by autograph-seekers as he made his way off of the dais. Bill Self is a good salesman, as most coaches are. He can get a crowd of 80-somethings excited about basketball as fast as a group of 14-year-old boys. He got back in the car with Brown and Johnson and headed back to the campus, just one mile away.

The next afternoon, it was kind of a weird scene. In the atrium lobby of the recently built Bielfeldt Athletic Administration Building, the press corps was eating lunch. That in itself is not odd, as the press and buffets go hand in hand. What was unusual about the lunch, which preceded Self's news conference on Media Day, was that the coach himself was there, eating alongside the scribes. An hour before his news conference, Self made his way to the lunch room, shook hands, walked from table to table, and took off his jacket and put it on the back of a chair. He headed to the buffet line and waited his turn for the beef grinds, corn, and cans of soda.

With the 40 or so members of the press, Self sat and had lunch, talked about basketball, summer vacations, golf, and reporters' families. Though there is a large media contingent that covers the Illini, the smallness of the Champaign-Urbana community and the constant presence of local beat writers allows Self to get to know many of them on a more personal level. Guys like Mark Tupper of the *Decatur Herald & Review*, John Supinie from Coppley News Service, and Brent Dawson from the *Champaign-Urbana News Gazette*, live Illini basketball, covering the team on a daily basis for more than half the year. Along the way, they get to know Self, and get a better understanding of what he is trying to do.

"Bill's personality is about as close to genuine as you can get," says Tupper. "He was barely on the job when my father passed away. He sent a handwritten note to the funeral home in Chicago along with flowers. Later when my mother was diagnosed with cancer, he called me in the press box of a fast-pitch softball tournament, expressing his support and asking if there was anything that he could do. It just shows you what kind of a guy he is." Supinie knew from his first meeting with Self that he was in for a treat. "It was like we were old high school buddies hanging out together," Supinie recalls, "and he has such a magnetic personality and is so smooth, that it is easy to be open with him."

So on this day, to an insider, it was not surprising that Self would role up his sleeves and break bread with the press. But to an outsider, it was shocking. How many coaches of Top 25 teams do you think not only enjoy the media, but would make the effort to sit and have lunch with all of them before a news conference? Sure, there may be ulterior motives—like ensuring positive coverage—but for a guy like Self, he didn't need to brown-nose; his coaching and demeanor speak for themselves.

As lunch ended, the horde adjourned to a media room next door, where television crews from Champaign to Chicago were lined up in the back. Writers took their seats in the auditorium-like setting, and the coach gave them what they wanted. "Coming into practice, I was saying that we are as healthy as we have been since I've been here. And then Lucas gets hurt, which is a real big blow to us, not just on the court but off as well. . . . We're in the game. We will be competitive with the top teams. . . . We will certainly play faster this year. We will have pressure defense. We need to set the tempo from the defensive side, rather than react to what the other team is doing."

Throughout the 45-minute "presser," as news conferences are often referred to by the media, Self answered honestly about his team's prospects, the play of Williams, and the Top Five ranking. He acknowledged the high expectations and agreed that they should be high. There were no confrontations with reporters, no glib answers by Self and everyone seemed to get what they wanted. Of course, Illinois had not lost a game yet.

An hour later, it was the players' turn, as the media met the team in the two-year-old Ubben Basketball Complex next door to the Bielfeldt building. The photographers snapped pictures, the players horsed around, and Williams was immediately swarmed by the press. As per instructions from Self, Williams announced that indeed, this would be his last season at Illinois. Reporters responded with probing questions as to his motives, and to the timing of the announcement. Williams was the star on this day. When pressed about his team's chances, the junior responded, "I think it is realistic for us to get to the Final Four." (Self believes that William's brutal honesty with the press throughout the season actually hurt his star player.)

Off to the side, many of the bench players, walk-ons, and freshmen sat in folded chairs, looking a bit jealous and a bit bored. Senior Cory Bradford leaned against a concrete wall as he talked on a cell phone with a radio host. When the media session ended, or more accurately, when the press had asked every last question, the team left the gym to go home. Self was in the adjoining women's gym filming a public service announcement on drugs with Illinois women's coach, Theresa Grentz.

Bill Self and his wife, Cindy, live approximately five miles from campus, in an upscale development in Champaign. The pool and backyard of their $1 million home was still under construction a few months after moving in. The house is just down the block from former Illinois coach Lon Kruger's mansion, who is now the head coach of the Atlanta Hawks. In the basement/entertainment room of their home, the team gathered, played pool, watched a baseball playoff game, and ate food, two hours before the Midnight Madness tip-off. Cindy likes to have the team over and the players like getting away from campus. Self's youngest child, Tyler, ran around the basement playing Nerf basketball with the guys and knocking into any stable object. His daughter, Lauren, was upstairs in her room, avoiding the crowd.

Close to 9:00 P.M., Self gathered the team together to set out the plans for the night. He split up the players into the Blue and White squads for the scrimmage later that night, told them to be quick with their dunks in the dunk contest, and reminded them to enjoy themselves after the game, but practice was at noon and 5:00 P.M. the following day. "Have fun out there tonight at Madness because it won't be like this again for a while," Self said turning serious. "Also, in the huddles last year our chant was 'Big Ten Champs.' I think this year the Big Ten champ has a real possibility of winning the national title. It takes small steps to get there, so should we stick with 'Big Ten Champs'?" The team members agreed. They stood up and held hands in a huddle, as Sean Harrington led the team in a quick prayer.

The players thanked Cindy for her hospitality and headed off to Ubben to get changed before heading over to Huff Hall. Before going to the office, Self changed into a blue Illinois basketball sweater vest, a pair of khakis and a brand new pair of Nike sneakers.

Self has a Rolodex in his head. He could teach a class on name association. From the sister of a recruit he failed to land five years past to the name of the woman who asked a question at a roundtable two years ago, he remembers. Of course, this gift provides assistance when you are a basketball coach, and meet close to 10,000 people every year. It's especially helpful when you can remember the name, school, scoring average, and "big" games that high school sophomores have played in.

As the Illinois basketball players got dressed downstairs in the locker room at the Ubben Basketball Complex, getting themselves psyched up for Midnight Madness, Self was directly above them as he entered the plush basketball office suite, doing what he did best. "Chris [recruit names have been changed], how are you doing?" Self asked a lanky 6' high school junior. Turning to the boy's mother and father, he greeted them by first names and inquired about the trip to Champaign. Chris was high on the wish lists of many schools, including Duke, Notre Dame, and North Carolina. He and his parents were at Illinois on an unofficial visit, allowed by the NCAA as long as the recruit pays his own way.

As Self and Chris' family walked through the basketball suite to Self's corner office, there was a crowd of ten waiting for the coach there. He immediately went into Rolodex mode and began to shake hands, give "prop hugs" to the players and handshakes to their coaches. He was right on with every name except for one boy who he had never met. After the brief pleasantries, Self sat down at his desk and did what he does best. (Gillispie, who has been with Self for eight years, marvels at the coach's ability with people. "Bill wants to know your name. The next time he sees you, whether you are the president of General Electric or if you have an eight-year-old who went to school five years ago with one of his sister's kinfolk, he is going to know the name.")

"Juan, are you keeping your grades up?" Self asked a shy sophomore slouching in a chair, complete with baggy jeans, a pager, and Tommy Hilfiger jacket. "Got to keep them up, you know."

Turning to another recruit, sitting upright and uptight directly across from the coach, "Sean, how is your jumper? You had that big game last December when you had 32 against St. Thomas, remember?" The teenager looked amazed and impressed that Self remembered that game and, more importantly, remembered how well he had played. "Make sure you keep bending the knees on the jumper."

This round of information gathering and exchanges goes on for close to 20 minutes. Self asked about players' sisters, mothers, high school teams, grades, summer plans, future visits to Illinois, expectations for Midnight Madness that night, and everything else that he could fit in. Administrative assistant Jeff Guin stopped by and said that the recruits better get going over to Huff Hall. Before they go, Self mockingly put his hand up on the desk, revealing a large, shiny Big Ten championship ring, one he had just received from the manufacturer. The kids' eyes stay on the ring as Self said, "It's nice, isn't it?" The coach rose from his chair and shook the hands of the young and old and told them he would see them after the festivities. You get the feeling that Self could run for political office and win in a landslide.

As the players and their families left his office, Self picked up the phone to make a few calls. One to his wife to arrange to meet and another to the parents of an Illinois player who had just arrived in town. As he talked on the phone, his eyes wandered around the office. Right next to his desk is a bookshelf, with items that reveal a lot about who Bill Self is. On the top shelf is a crystal figurine inscribed with "The John and Nellie Wooden Coach of the Year." Self had won the prestigious award in 2000, after leading his Tulsa Golden

Hurricanes to the Elite Eight. Above the award resting on the wall is a 2 × 3' family portrait of Self, Cindy, and their children, Tyler and Lauren. Below the award are his books.

The Holy Bible, My Life in Ministry by Oral Roberts, *Success Is a Choice* by Rick Pitino, *Values of the Game* by Bill Bradley, Richard Nixon's *In the Arena*, Harvey McKay's *Beware the Naked Man Who Offers You His Shirt*, and *College Sports, Inc.*, a critical review of big time college sports by Indiana professor Murray Sperber. There are many other basketball books by coaches, players, and media members, along with success and motivational books. Sitting next to the books on one shelf is perhaps Self's most prized possession: "The Best Daddy of the Year Award" given to Self by his kids. A look around the office and a visitor might be hard pressed to decipher that the occupant was from the prairies of Oklahoma.

The state of Oklahoma is known for cowboys, cattle, and Sooner football. Being a basketball star there is like being a world-class tennis player in Alaska. Bill Self grew up in Edmond, Oklahoma, 30 miles north of Oklahoma City. His parents were not rich, but were stalwarts in education. His mother was an English teacher, his father a basketball coach and teacher, eventually working for the Oklahoma Department of Education. As a youngster, Self found himself shooting hoops and developed a love of the game from his father.

In 1977, Self entered Edmond High School as a freshman, and began to get noticed for his prowess on the court. By 1981, his senior year, Self was selected the Oklahoma Big School Player of the Year, averaging 22 points, eight rebounds, and seven assists his final season. He was team captain that year and was selected a Converse All-American. Recruiting was a bit different back then, but many of the big schools in the Midwest wanted Self on their campus, including legendary Kansas, but only Oklahoma State offered him a scholarship.

At OSU, Self led the team in assists two seasons and was an All-Big Eight Freshman in 1982. Also a pretty good free throw shooter, he led the Cowboys in free throw percentage in 1983–1984 shooting over 75% from the line. In addition to his savvy on the court, Self worked hard in the classroom and graduated in 1985 with a degree in business. He had no illusions about playing in the NBA but he knew he wanted to coach; he knew he had the gifts—it was just a matter of where to start.

"When I was a junior in college, I knew I wanted to coach. I was the son of a coach and wanted to teach. I really loved the game." In 1986, Larry Brown offered Self a tremendous first coaching job, joining the staff at Kansas, and Self helped guide the Jayhawks to the Final Four that first year. After one season with Kansas, Self returned to Oklahoma State and learned the game from Leonard Hamilton and Eddie Sutton over the next six years as an assistant. It became clear to those in the basketball world that Self was a rising star, but without a head coaching job, he couldn't prove them right.

Many top assistants dream of their first head coaching job in the SEC or ACC, going up against the coaching greats and making big-time money. Self was not immune to those thoughts, but realized that *any* head coaching position was a good one. He certainly put that theory to the test. In 1993, Self was hired to take over the Oral Roberts University team, a NAIA school about to play its first season in Division I. Located in Tulsa, Oklahoma, Oral Roberts was familiar to Self and he certainly knew Oklahoma high school basketball. He slowly began to bring in top players and soon the Golden Eagles were no longer a "gimmie" game for the giants. His first season, Oral Roberts went 6-21, but by his last season in 1996–1997, the team went 21-7 and played in the NIT. His overall record at ORU was a deceiving 55-54, taking the team from 6-10 to 18-21 wins in his four seasons there. His striking success at Oral Roberts led to an offer from a cross-town school, the University of Tulsa.

It was at Tulsa that Self truly emerged onto the national scene. He led the Golden Hurricanes to two NCAA Tournaments in his three seasons, including a memorable Elite Eight run in 2000. Self was 74-27 at Tulsa, including the 32-5 season culminating in the Elite Eight appearance. He put Tulsa basketball back on the map and, in the process, had refined his coaching style and methods. He also garnered the attention of national media and athletic directors when he was named the Wooden Coach of the Year for 2000 and was a top candidate for many jobs. After a call from Illinois athletic director Ron Guenther, the sweepstakes seemed close to an end. But in fact, Self was so loyal to Tulsa and to his athletic director, that he refused to go to Champaign to meet with Guenther unless the Illinois job was his for the taking and that Guenther contacted the Tulsa athletic director as a courtesy, so Self would not be sneaking behind her back. The Illinois AD relented and Self was the new coach at Illinois in a matter of days.

"When I was at Tulsa, my goal was to win a national championship. So many coaches, at any job, as soon as you get a job you're already looking for the next one. At Tulsa, I didn't get the job at Illinois. My team got the job at Illinois," he says modestly. "A lot of coaching hirings are just being hot at the right time. I didn't interview for the Illinois job, I just got a phone call and an offer. A lot of moving up has to do with timing."

Mike DeCourcy from *The Sporting News* calls Self "a rising star in coaching, someone who's easygoing manner and bright personality lends itself to recruiting and coaching." The 39-year-old Self already has 18 years of coaching experience. The Oklahoma boy had come north and was at the upper echelons of college basketball. The only question: how long before his next step up?

A t ten after midnight in Huff Hall, Bill Self and his assistants came back onto the floor as the intrasquad scrimmage was set to begin. A look around the gym revealed students drabbed in orange and blue shirts, young children with paint on their faces and a large contingent of older-skewing fans. There were posters adorned in bright paints covering the second-tier railings. But they did not refer to Williams or Bradford or even have tame slogans like "We're No. 1!" Rather, the signs read "Welcome James Augustine No. 40. We Can't Wait to See You in the Hall," "The Krush Welcomes the Best Moms in the Nation: Barb Augustine, Jane Diogu, and Denise Smith," "Playing Ball in the Hall Like Ike," "If We Could Be Like Ike," and "Krush Wants Diogu." The signs were painted by the student group, "Orange Krush," to impress the three recruits and their families in town.

"Ike" is Ike Diogu, a 6'8", 240-lb. gentle giant from the town of Garland, Texas. Prior to the 2001–2002 season, his senior year at Garland High, most of the nation's scouts and recruiting magazines had him pegged as one of the top hundred prospects in his class. He is big and strong—a potential power forward—and, importantly, he's a fine student with a good head on his shoulders. As huge and menacing as Ike is on the court, he's small and quiet off it. The son of a PhD, Edward Diogu, and his wife, Jane, the brother of Eric, Eddie, and Love, Ike is a mama's boy in a man's body. Garland's Phil Sirois, in his twenty-first season as a high school basketball coach, considers Ike the best player he has ever coached. So it came as no surprise to Sirois that in the thick of the recruiting season the wolves were at Ike's door. Twenty points and 10 boards a game will have any recruiter licking his chops.

For more than two years, college coaches nationwide have been salivating at the thought of Ike suiting up in their school's jersey. As a freshman, he stood 6'3" and weighed in at 190 lbs. By the time Ike was a sophomore, Coach Sirois had been opening or tossing mail addressed to Ike for what already seemed ages and had fielded an endless stream of phone calls. Then, at the beginning of Ike's junior year—the year when NCAA rules permitted college coaches to contact prospects directly—a whole new ballgame began. On August 14, 2000, by the time the phenom had completed his first day of classes, his mother had signed for three or four FedEx packages at home; three days later 15 packages were on the dining room table; within a month what had seemed an innocent enough trickle had become a steady pour. And things were just beginning. The deluge continued throughout his junior year, and when the summer of 2001 rolled around and coaches could start calling, the Diogu phone never stopped ringing. Next came the recruiters themselves, in person, eager to convince Ike that he and their programs were the perfect fit. Most of them brought poster boards with graphics, some held up school jerseys decaled with Ike's name. Roy Williams hauled into the Diogu living room a box filled with 18 championship rings that he had won at various levels as a player and coach.

By the summer following his junior year, Ike had whittled his list of schools down to a large handful: Alabama, Arizona State, Baylor, Connecticut, Georgetown, Illinois, Miami, Seton Hall, and Oklahoma State. Along the way he had given the thumbs-down to several elite teams that had been in the hunt—Roy Williams' Jayhawks, Gary Williams' Terrapins, and Rick Barnes' Longhorns—so these nine were select company. Then in the fall of his senior year, Ike told Sirois he wished to make official visits to five universities, the maximum number of school-paid visits allowed by the NCAA. The final five were UConn, Arizona State, Illinois, Seton Hall, and Georgetown. As the dates of these "make-or-break" weekends approached, Sirois was confident that Ike would make a solid decision.

"He's played this like a poker game. He is talking to everybody to the end," said an obviously impressed Sirois. "I have spent a lot of time trying to explain to him that some people are going to tell him whatever he wants to hear. But he's done a great job of knowing who is messing with him and who is not."

Sirois has been in the coaching business a long time, and has helped Ike navigate the treacherous waters of college courtship. The coach told recruiters up front that he and his star player would be turned off by any unethical behavior or "negative recruiting"—coaches badmouthing other schools instead of talking up their own. It worked. For the most part, coaches had been up front with Ike, not promising him playing time or lying about the other student-athletes they were recruiting.

In early September, Ike began his tour. Way back when he'd toiled in obscurity for the Garland Owls' freshman squad, Arizona State and Rob Evans had shown the most interest in him and, like so many teens, he'd been intrigued. That first year, Sirois wanted Ike to play at the more competitive JV level, but Ike declined, preferring to play with his classmates on the freshman team. As more schools joined the hunt, Ike seemed to remain loyal to Arizona State, but how could he pass up a peek at the other schools?

The official visit is all about impressing the recruit, making sure he has a good time, and giving him time to get to know the players as well as the coaches, who are dressed to impress and fully prepared. Recruiting is all about information—at this stage it's information on the recruit's interests that coaches can use to impress him. Does he prefer Chinese food or Italian? Does he like to party or would he rather catch the latest blockbuster flick? Knowing the answers to these and other questions allows schools to create the perfect visiting experience. (See chapter 9.)

At Midnight Madness, Ike sat with the other recruits, Deron Williams from The Colony in Texas and James Augustine from New Lennox, Illinois, on a row of courtside bleachers as the Illinois team takes on itself. Self was on one bench, not doing much coaching, with Tyler and Lauren sitting on each side of him. The scrimmage was sloppy, run-and-gun with some alley-oops—what you would expect for a showcase like this? But in a matter of hours, the real work would begin.

Practice started with a double session on Saturday, October 13. Right from the get-go, Self introduced a rapid-fire touch drill that at first was comical and then frustrating for the Illinois players. It is a rather simple drill called "Pioneer," which Self had taken from a high school coach in Stillwater, Oklahoma, the home of the Pioneers. (Self learned early on from Larry Brown and Eddie Sutton that drills are often named, and credit given, for the schools from which the drill was taken.) The players form six short lines around the lane, four at each corner of the lane and two facing each other midway down the lane. A player starts with a ball in the top corner of the lane, and then quickly touches/passes it to a crossing player from the opposite middle position, who then touches it to the down position player, who then touches it back to the player opposite him, who then touches it to the middle player and finally passes it to the remaining line at the top corner. The process then continues. The ball never touches the ground—or shouldn't. The drill moves at lightning speed, and one mini-second of miscue or timing sends the rhythm into shambles.

At first, the team walked through the drill, as Self instructed them how to move. They then gradually sped up the pace, counting every touch out loud. With any new wrinkle, there are bound to be mishaps. From dropped balls to confusion about where to go to even a miscounting of touches, Self became a bit irritated. But after a few minutes the team got the hang of it, and before long, the drill became a staple in practices. It works on the players' coordination, touch on the ball and movement.

The drill itself is not as important as what it represents to coaches. Progress. From the introduction of a simple drill in October to the perfection of it in February, it means something to a coach. As the season moved on for Illinois, practices tended to be a bit shorter, less focused on conditioning and fundamental skills, and more focused on applications and sets. Self will often use a "shell drill" to work on defensive positioning as well as offensive sets. Shell drills are really just five players in position on the offensive or defensive side of the ball, forming a shell-type shape. With young players and a junior college player new to the fold, Self became frustrated at times in his early attempts to make them grasp the concepts, something that would continue throughout the year.

At one of Illinois' early practices, the team was turning the ball over, throwing it away more than usual. Self just smiled, turned to a manager, and asked, "Can you get us a new ball? The one that we are playing with is real defective, keeps bouncing away." Said sarcastically, the coach got his point across and livened up a difficult practice. The new ball wasn't any better.

Being a successful coach is knowing how to teach and when to teach, including times to use humor, praise, and criticism. "Very rarely will I applaud a guy for making a shot. I applaud a guy for running a lane so fast that the trailer got the shot. Once we get into practice, I like to let them play and then correct them when the possession is over. The last thing you want as a coach is a player looking at the bench when they play. And you have to put them through things in practice that are high pressure that prepare them for the game." Self admits that he is much calmer during games than in practice.

The players were wiped after the first two and a half hour practice and, after some encouraging words from Self, were sent on their way to rest up for the second session in just three hours. Self was not overly excited with the practice, but understood it was only the beginning. Over the next few days he introduced offensive and defensive sets and out-of-bounds plays and continued to be frustrated when the newcomers like Roger Powell and Luther Head did not catch on.

On Saturday, October 20, the Illini conducted a public scrimmage at the Ubben Complex and the balcony overlooking the court was standing-room only, three deep. Recruits, including 6'11" Keith Butler from Pennsylvania, Augustine, and top prospect Dee Brown were on hand. Sean Harrington had a bruised thigh, so Brett Melton started with the first string, joining Bradford, Archibald, Williams, and Krupalija. A week later the team scrimmaged again, this time in a full-blown game in the annual Blue/Orange Scrimmage.

In a period of just days in mid-October, Bill Self was a busy man, touching many aspects of a coach's life. He dealt with the media, recruits, injuries, families, egos, and practice. At a time when he should have been excited about *this* season's prospects at Midnight Madness, he was just as concerned about recruits for *next* season's outlook. As preseason practice got underway, his top ranked team faced some crucial questions: Will Frank Williams come to play and live up to the hype? Who will fill Lucas Johnson's shoes? How fast can the freshmen learn and contribute? With a nonconference slate of games against Gonzaga, Arizona, and Maryland early on, Self didn't have much time to find the answers.

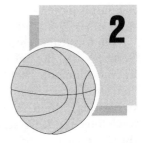

2

The Prodigy

EVERYTHING IS BLACK AND GOLD. EVERYTHING. THE CARPETS IN THE TEAM LOUNGE are a solid black with a golden *IOWA* at the center, matching the *IOWA* painted on the walls. In the bathroom, above the urinals, instead of staring at a white cinder block, visitors stare at the name *IOWA*. The locker room, players' lounge, and coaches' room are all new, thanks to the demands of the coach in his latest contract renegotiations in the summer of 2001. The renovations, costing close to $350,000, were arranged by Iowa athletic director Bob Bowlsby, paid for by a donor couple, and were completed just before the start of school in August.

Walking into the Iowa locker room in the bowels of Carver-Hawkeye Arena, the first thing you notice is the black and gold. From the floor to the ceiling, from east to west, from the chairs to the clock, everything is Hawkeye black and gold. Two feet into the locker room at the entrance is a picture of the current Hawkeye team, as well as the coaching staff. It serves as a reminder that Iowa basketball is about family. Next to the entrance sits a sign that simply reads: "Iowa Basketball: Work Hard, Work Smart, Have Fun." The atrium area is really a miniclassroom, with 16 black leather chairs arranged in a semicircle, auditorium-like seating facing the large white wipeboards mounted on the wall. To one side of the wipeboards rests a plaque: "Commitment to Excellence." Off to the side of the meeting area is an "Iowa Basketball Free Throw" chart, with consecutive free throw leaders written in black ink. Luke Recker is in the lead with 22.

On the opposite wall is another chart with categories deemed critical by the coach. "Charges Taken. Loose Balls. Five FTs Made. Rebounds. Putbacks." Underneath these various categories: "LITTLE THINGS LEAD TO BIG THINGS." There is also a team chart, with team goals for the upcoming game in such categories as field goal percentage defense, largest run, transition, and free throws. These charts will be furiously filled in with black and red pens by the Iowa managers at halftime and immediately following the games. It has to be clear to the team, and more importantly to the coach, what goals were achieved or what may have cost them the game. This room is where the teaching goes on. And the yelling. And the prayers.

The locker area itself is not as big as one might imagine, with 16 wooden lockers, seats, compartments, two cubbyholes fronted by a leather, folding Iowa chair—in black, of course. Above each locker is a glossy 8×10 color picture of the player, his name, and his hometown. Family. Class. Tradition. In the showers, the faucets are set to give tall men a dousing, with Iowa logos everywhere in the drying and bathroom area.

From the meeting area in the atrium to the players' lounge are three steps, giving a visitor, and a player, the chance to look at the large glass showcase covering the wall. Inside sits a 2001 Big Ten Basketball Tournament trophy, along with a ball from that memorable tournament. The rest of the enormous showcase sits empty. For now.

The players' lounge is typical of a lounge—except nicer. There are plush black leather chairs and sofas, pictures of current players on the walls, a large screen television and Sony PlayStation 2 (NASCAR, NCAA Football, Ready to Rumble Boxing, and NFL Game Day 2001 are the games of choice). There is a small kitchenette off to the side, with a soda machine, sink, and fridge. The players' lounge was designed with the intention of giving the team a place to chill between or after classes. Better to have them together and in the locker room than elsewhere in the town. On any given lunch hour, you will find four or five players watching television, playing PlayStation, or otherwise hanging out.

The adjacent coaches' room is most impressive, with two large televisions book ending a huge big screen, along with VCRs, telephones, and a lot of remote controls. On one wall is a large wipeboard, where practice plans and schedules are written two days in advance. It is an ideal place for coaches to break down tape. Like everywhere else, there are black and gold logos. The trashcans are black with gold bottom rims and a gold top.

It is hard to look anywhere in the team locker room, lounge, or offices and not be reminded of where you are. And it goes beyond the furniture, the walls, and the trashcans. From casual gray sweats with the university logo to turtlenecks with *IOWA* on the collar to even socks with the Hawkeye adorned, the coaches and players are a walking billboard for the university. It is just how the coach envisioned it when he first arrived in Iowa City three years ago. Build tradition from the ground up. Literally.

What amazes the casual or even fanatic basketball fan about this scenario is not the almost demagoguery of the school, the plastering of team logos or even the methodical approach to elevating the program. Nor is it the passionate Hawk's Nest full of students at every home game, *every* home game, or the 15,500 fans who showed up for an early November exhibition. What amazes the basketball fan is not the team's success or rabid following. Rather it is who the man is at the middle of it all. A high school legend, college All-American, Olympic gold medalist, NBA veteran, and award-winning coach, Steve Alford is supposed to be doing all of this—just not here.

I t was the second day of official practice and the net kept screaming "swoosh." It was in agony. Ball after ball was coming down hard on the intertwined strings attached to the metal rim at Carver-Hawkeye Arena. It was a shooting clinic. The boyish-looking shooter, dressed in Iowa sweats, nailed shot after shot from three-point range. Some of the players warming up just sort of shook their heads in amazement. Greg Lansing, one of the Iowa assistant coaches smirked, having seen it all before. The players gathered at midcourt to stretch as the shots kept falling.

Steve Alford still had his touch. Eleven years after playing in his last NBA game, and 15 years after tearing apart the Indiana record books, the man can still shoot. On some days before practice, like this one, the coach will shoot around with his players and continue solo while they stretch. He jokes with them as they try to match him shot for shot on some days. He is still the coach, teaching his pupils a lesson.

Practice this day would be close to a three-hour session. As usual, it took place on the floor of Carver-Hawkeye, the home of Iowa basketball. The new locker room is about 60 paces from the floor, right next door to a training room and weight room. The arena itself is sunken in the earth, meaning fans enter on the top level and proceed to walk down to their seats toward the court. On this Sunday afternoon in mid-October, the only sound is the squeaking of Nike sneakers and the bellowing of Alford's voice. Iowa practices are closed, and with the exception of a few friends of the coaching staff or local high school coaches, no one is allowed in. Alford is keenly aware of anyone coming or going, and the Iowa student managers hustle out onlookers.

Starting with some stretching, the players were put through some conditioning drills, various sprints up and down the court, jump roping, and agility drills across the width of the court. During a full-court dribbling drill, Alford hopped into a defensive stance and challenged senior Brody Boyd to beat him off the dribble. He couldn't. The coach then moved on to freshman Pierre Pierce, still adjusting to the fact that his coach still has "handles." Alford is known to "jaw a bit," give his players some trash talking on the court. In fact, he has established a tradition at Iowa, where incoming freshmen have to play the coaches in a game of three-on-three. The coaches usually win. He is a player like them, but is now a coach, the authority figure who can decide their fates. Alford's ability to demonstrate, get involved, and actively coach affects how Iowa practices go. He is intimately involved in every aspect, and when he lets the assistants run a drill, he is standing or squatting right off the court, contributing his thoughts every few seconds.

Like all other Iowa practices, this one was intense and physical, with bodies flying all over the place. Players battled for loose balls on the floor, threw elbows to chests when boxing out, and otherwise went so hard you might think there was an edict to kill. But Alford demands nothing less in his practices; no team *will* go harder than us. All-American Reggie Evans was a maniac on the boards in a rebounding drill, grabbing everything in sight, with his teammates trying in vain not to get killed. Boyd dived on the floor as the ball headed out-of-bounds and was toppled by Ryan Hogan going after the same prize. There were some bruises, and a little blood occasionally, but Alford would not have it any other way.

On the court, Alford took his team through various shooting drills, intense full-court passing drills followed by free throw shooting in triplets at the various baskets. The coach wanted his players shooting free throws when they were fatigued, a common occurrence late in games. Off to the side of the court, Steve's father, Sam, sat in a folding chair, legs crossed, holding the practice plan on an index card. As the Director of Basketball Operations (really an assistant), Sam is barred from coaching or interacting with the players during practice. He truly does adhere to the NCAA rules and stays off the court. Occasionally, when asked by his son, or through his own observations, he will let Steve know his thoughts on a drill, set play, or practice tempo. By the look in his eye, or the turn of his head, it is clear that there are times when Sam wants to jump onto the floor to correct something. Instead, he will quietly walk over to his son, both standing with their arms folded across their chests, and make a suggestion. At various times during practice, Steve Alford will be squatting observing a drill, and then say over his shoulder, without turning around, "Dad? Should we go to the 2 here?" His father will respond with a quick suggestion and then watch it be implemented into action.

It is rare at today's college and professional levels that a father and son coach together. The Meyers did at DePaul. The Knights at Indiana. But what about the father being an *assistant* to his son? Welcome to basketball, Alford style. After years of learning from his father, and knowing how invaluable his advice can be, Alford asked his dad to join him as an assistant coach at Southwest Missouri State in 1995. He did, and a unique relationship was made even more interesting. When the son made the move to Iowa in 1999, there was no doubt about Sam moving with him.

"I told my dad that I could either bring him along as an assistant or I start thinking about nursing homes," Alford said at his opening press conference in 1999. "As a head coach, you always want loyalty. If you can't get loyalty from your dad, you're probably not going to get it."

But make no mistake, this is not just a son repaying his father with a high-income, easy job. Steve makes his father do all of the work that an assistant would do, including tape breakdown, scouting, and writing hundreds of recruiting letters. For most family relationships, it would be hard to separate roles as a father and assistant, but not for the Alfords.

"I'm sure that once I walk out of the office I become dad again. We've always been good about keeping the two separate. I know when he first started playing for me as a freshman in high school, one of our first practices we had when we brought him up to varsity, he had a question and he said, 'Dad?' I said, 'No. Coach Alford. When we leave here, I will be dad, but here I am Coach Alford.'"

There are times when the younger Alford will come into his father's office next door to his, close the door, and ask his father for his opinion. If the older Alford sees something that he doesn't like, he in turn will walk next door and say "You may not agree with me, but I want you to hear me." It becomes clear on the practice floor or in the locker room at halftime of a game that their relationship is based on more than just basketball.

As this three-hour practice drew to a close, there was a different sound in Carver-Hawkeye Arena. It was the sound that kids make when they unsuccessfully try to whisper. At the far end of the court, Alford's wife, Tanya, had arrived with their three children: Kory (age 10), Bryce (8), and daughter Kayla (6). Tanya took a seat in a folding chair with Kayla hanging on to her leg as the boys ran to the far side of the court and then into the locker room. The coach and his players were not distracted by the family's presence. In fact, the young brood have become such a part of the Iowa program that they are *expected* to be at practice.

The next day at practice, Alford had his team doing a full-court, five-on-five transition drill. The pace was frantic, the concentration intense. As Alford bellowed out encouragement and criticisms from his position on the sidelines at midcourt, Kayla, dressed in a pink sweater and matching pants, approached her father. "Daddy, Daddy! Guess what? I got new socks today," the proud daughter showed her father. Instinctively, the hard-nose, no-nonsense warrior of a coach bent down, picked up his daughter, looked at her new purchase, praised her selection, and then turned back to the drill and shouted at a nice effort on a rebound by Reggie Evans. The drill continued for three more minutes with Kayla in her father's arms, the youngster more enamored of her new socks than of the transition drill. As the players went to their respective baskets for free throw work in threes, Alford walked to the side and gave his kids a hug and a cheek kiss to Tanya.

When practice ended, the ritual began. Bryce and Kory grabbed two balls and headed to a far basket with their dad. They shot for 20 minutes. They're pretty good shooters. The family then headed out to a local restaurant. Blending basketball with family. Something Alford learned from a very young age.

His childhood was not normal. He was a coach's son, in the Hoosier state, with an amazing passion for hoops. What at first was a child's fascination with his father and the more powerful pull of putting a ball through a hoop, soon grew into his current avocation. It's been a great ride for Alford, who has experienced way more than his "15 minutes of fame." He is a legend in Indiana. And "legend" is an understatement. He has a hotel named after him whose last four digits of its phone number are 1212—Alford's jersey number. His boyhood hometown of New Castle is a must-see for visitors. His name invokes passion in the eyes of Hoosier faithful, close to 15 years *after* he last played there.

Alford is who he is because of three things: his dad, his college coach, and his work ethic. His father, Sam, was a well-known high school coach throughout the state, guiding first Martinsville and South Knox and then leading New Castle's Chrysler High School to a school record in wins. Along the way, Steve was there at almost every practice and every game, chasing down balls for the players, sitting on the bench during timeouts, and talking basketball with his dad at dinner. When a 10-year-old was discussing the virtues of the matchup zone, the world should have taken notice. He was learning the game in a place where the game was God, and what he lacked in physical ability he would make up for in heart.

Every year, the Elks Club sponsored a shooting contest for kids throughout the state and the country and a young Alford took aim. "I can remember him in the five- and six-year-old bracket," his proud father reflects. "It was raining and he couldn't go out to practice. He would shoot Nerf balls at a basket in the house. He'd shoot ping-pong balls at Tinker Toy containers. He was just obsessed with shooting the ball at anything, baskets or not."

The intense drive was not limited to free throw shooting. "I'm very competitive and I have been from an early age. I can remember the neighborhood, whether it was a Wiffleball game or a game we would play in the garage," Alford says, smirking at both the memory and his excitement. "I took a lot of pride in that nobody came onto my driveway and beat me in one-on-one. That was the home turf."

Perfectionist might be too kind of word. As a teenager, in addition to battling the Indiana winters to work on his shooting, Alford fought himself. He would set goals for shooting free throws, and if he didn't achieve them, he would make himself do push ups or run sprints in the dead of winter as punishment. Some would say it was crazy, others that it was admirable. Regardless, it made him a better shooter and better player, and prepared him for what was to come. As a third grader, he won his age division in the Elks Club competition first in local and regional qualifying and then at the state level. His success took him and his family to Kansas City for the national competition, where Alford calmly took home fourth place. His exploits became known and soon everyone around the state knew of Steve Alford. But with that increased attention came increased scrutiny of his choices, both on and off the court.

By the time Alford showed up for his first high school practice at Chrysler High in 1980, there was no doubt about who the future star would be on that team. His freshman year he joined the varsity and averaged 1.7 points per game. By the time he completed his senior year, he had raised his scoring average to 37.7. And that was with double and triple teams from opponents who knew that to beat Chrysler you had to stop Alford. After games, he would be swarmed with autograph-seekers, young and old, and by flirtatious girls looking for a boyfriend. He was a bona fide star in perhaps the most hoops-crazed place on the planet.

He had been getting interest from college coaches as early as eighth grade, but in his heart, and in his state's, playing at Indiana University for Bobby Knight would be the ultimate dream. He knew the reputation of Knight, but also understood himself enough to know that he could flourish under the discipline and intensity of the coach. By the start of his junior year, his mind was made up. He would play for the Hoosiers. As the state exhaled, Alford continued to work on his game and was named the 1983 "Mr. Indiana Basketball" by leading Chrysler to the Elite Eight in the state tournament. He had become the most prolific high school player in the history of Indiana, and the expectations at the next level would be overwhelming for some—but not for Alford. Most fans wanted him to bring National Championships to Bloomington, though a few others cheered for his demise.

"I never told Steve this, but I got a long, type-written letter from a fan in Indiana right before he left for school. Steve mowed lawns in the summers to earn money and this fan knew that. The letter basically said that one week with Coach Knight after being babied by his father [me], that Steve would be back home in New Castle mowing lawns, and you could take that to the bank. I don't think people realized how tough Steve was."

Before Sam sent his son off to Indiana and Coach Knight, the father told him what to expect, that Knight would be a tough coach to play for. He left Steve with a typical fatherly thought, "If you need a shoulder to cry on or some advice, you've got our number." By the time Steve graduated in 1987, Sam Alford had never received that call.

After learning the game from his father, the young Alford would learn much more under Knight. His relationship with his college coach then, and now, was the subject of much speculation and rumors. It is said and written that they hated each other and that Knight was jealous of Alford. Knight never called to say congratulations on the Iowa job. That is why rumors are just that. Alford has a great appreciation for Knight, and the ultimate sign of respect is the fact that much of what Alford does as a coach in practice and in games is a direct reflection of Robert Montgomery Knight.

"Coach Knight is probably one of the more intelligent basketball coaches who has ever coached the game," says Sam Alford. "I think Steve did a very good job of keeping his eyes and ears open, picking up from Coach Knight more of how to play the game."

"I think Coach Knight was amazing with film breakdown," the younger Alford says. "I wish I still had more time with him to learn all of those things, because I was absolutely shocked in my first game that I played at Indiana. We did all of these walk-throughs, we did all of these film breakdowns and the game started and everything that we'd walked through was just taking place on stage. It was easy. I knew this guy was gonna cut from here to here and he did that. And we'd already walked through that. What amazed me most about Coach was his organization, preparation, and competitiveness."

At Indiana, Alford started 120 of 125 games, leading the team to a 92-35 mark over his four years. He was the team's MVP each year and led the Hoosiers to the 1987 NCAA Championship, when his teammate Keith Smart hit a jumper in the closing seconds to give Knight his third national title. Alford set a Final Four record when he shot 7 for 10 from three-point land to help Indiana defeat Syracuse that night. A two-time All-American and three-time Big Ten player, Alford rewrote the Indiana record books and made an imprint on the NCAA record logs. He finished his Indiana career as their all-time leading scorer with 2,438 points and his career free throw percentage of .897 ranks fourth best in NCAA history. He also led the nation in free throw percentage as a freshman. Must have been the Nerf balls. After his freshman year at Indiana, the star guard was selected to play on the 1984 Olympic team by Knight, a team that won the gold medal at the Los Angeles Games. His selection to the team had initially been controversial because he'd been picked by his college coach. His play at the 1984 Games clearly put that to rest. Alford averaged 10.3 points per game playing alongside guys like Michael Jordan and Patrick Ewing.

He had survived Bobby Knight and, in fact, flourished where others had failed. There were times, however, as in every relationship, when things were not perfect. In one instance, Alford had posed for a calendar in 1986, and although he received no payment for it, it was still an NCAA violation. Alford did not know his punishment, so he showed up at the Bloomington Airport to make the trip to Kentucky with the team. Knight told Alford he couldn't come on the trip and that he had to walk back to campus—six miles. After the team plane left, Alford flagged down the team bus that had brought them and got a ride home.

After graduating from Indiana in 1987 with a degree in business, Alford played four seasons in the NBA with Dallas (the 26th pick) and Golden State, retiring in 1991. He saw a different side to basketball, one in which business and selfish play ruled. It was an uneventful professional career, considering his successes at all other levels. It was at that point that Alford turned his life toward coaching, something he had been groomed for since birth.

Manchester College is a Division III school located in the farming towns of northwest Indiana. Better known for its English department than for its basketball teams, it was the perfect place for Alford to begin his coaching career. The team had been struggling, had little publicity, and was not the "big time" of college basketball. Alford could make his mistakes here, learn the game from a coaching standpoint and then look to move on. What Manchester got was a well-known figure but inexperienced coach, who could not only bring in better players, but put the program on the map. Not an easy thing to do.

Alford jumped in as coach eight games into the 1992 season, taking over a 0-8 team. He won only four games that first season, but began to build the tradition, like he would do at Iowa. The next year, his first full season at the helm, Manchester went 20-8—a remarkable turnaround, considering that in the last 100 years, Manchester had had only five winning seasons. In 1994–1995, they went 23-4 and, in his final year, they were 31-1 and advanced to the Division III National Championship game before losing to Wisconsin-Plattville. Among the accolades for the young coach: Indiana Collegiate Coach of the Year in 1993, 1994, and 1995. He had led his team to the NCAA Tournament three seasons and the conference title in each of those seasons. As a testament to Alford's achievements while at Manchester, he was inducted into their Hall of Fame in 2000. In just three and a half seasons, the "golden boy" had taken a small town, losing program to a new level. Even Indiana native John Wooden would have been proud. But it was time to move on.

Alford's success as a coach was starting to make waves around the country, but at tiny Manchester, "How hard could it be?" his critics wondered. He almost took a job at Indiana State, a logical next step for him, moving into Division I and doing it in his home state. But there was a catch. Alford knew that wherever his next job would be, he wanted to bring his father along as an assistant. When Indiana State officials refused to allow his dad to join his staff, Alford said "thanks, but no thanks" and looked elsewhere.

Alford would get a national platform at Southwest Missouri State when he was named coach before the 1995–1996 season. His first team went 16-12, then improved to 24-9 in 1996–1997, playing in the NIT. The crowning achievement was his Bears advancing to the Sweet Sixteen in the NCAA Tournament in 1999. They defeated Wisconsin and Tennessee before losing to Duke in the regional semifinals. He again had taken a program to unparalleled success, posting a 74-48 overall record in four seasons at Southwest Missouri and athletic directors around the country had taken notice.

After the 1996–1997 season when he led the Bears to the NIT, Alford began to get calls about coaching opportunities. In that postseason, it was Tennessee, Oregon, and Ohio State that showed interest, according to the coach. Alford pulled himself out of the mix at Tennessee, was never formally a candidate at Oregon, but wanted the Ohio State job. He met with athletic director Andy Geiger at the Final Four that year and ended up finishing second for the job behind current coach Jim O'Brien. He and Tanya had talked about where they would like to end up, and most observers thought Indiana was the place. But Alford never believed that Knight would step down or be fired, so he never realistically even considered coaching at Indiana. But soon, there would be a new suitor to catch his eye.

In April 1998, Iowa athletic director Bob Bowlsby had decided not to extend the contract of Head Coach Tom Davis, but allowed the coach to finish out his contract the following season. Davis had led the Hawkeyes to a 249-130 record, but the program seemed to be stalled. Bowlsby wanted new energy, new buzz and a young, successful coach. He set his sights on Steve Alford from day one, after deciding against extending Davis' deal. By December 1998, Bowlsby put out the feelers through intermediaries to Alford and other potential candidates, to see if the interest was mutual. He made it clear that Alford was the man they wanted and the only one on their wish list (though there might have been more). Bowlsby never called on SMS game days or even the day before games, as he did not want to bother the coach. By February 1999, as the seasons for Iowa and SMS began to draw to a close, Alford let Bowlsby know he was indeed interested. (Davis finished 20-10 in his last season at the helm.)

"We kind of had a gentlemen's agreement that Iowa was at the top of my list and Steve Alford was at the top of Iowa's list . . . and we let it rest," Alford says about the courtship.

The season would come to an end and soon they would make a deal. Though Bowlsby was already sold on Alford, he called coaches and athletic directors that he knew to inquire about the coach. He wanted to confirm his own beliefs. He called the former basketball coach at Northern Iowa, Eldon Miller, where Bowlsby had been AD before Iowa, and Miller gave Alford rave reviews. At the same time, Alford had done his own lobbying for the Iowa job, reconfirming his interest to Bowlsby. There are a few people in basketball who you would like to make a recommendation on your behalf if you are a coach. These include John Wooden, Mike Krzyzewski, Dean Smith, and C. M. Newton. Alford picked up the phone and called Wooden at his home in Encino, California, and asked him to call Bowlsby on his behalf. Wooden made the call. So did Krzyzewski and legendary coach and athletic director Newton. Not a bad trio of references. In fact, at one point, Bowlsby jokingly told Alford that he had enough references unless "Adolph Rupp [legendary Kentucky coach] comes back from the dead."

The deal itself was done on March 28, 1999. Alford received a five-year contract worth $600,000 annually with incentives that could raise it to $900,000. An Iowa private plane picked up Alford and Tanya in Springfield and flew them to Iowa City for a press conference at 12:30 P.M. on March 29. "Initially, I thought a guy that big must instantly bring a certain attitude to the program, but I wondered whether he could coach or not. He brought the sides but not the steak," thought Rick Brown, the Iowa beat reporter for *The Des Moines Register*.

At his opening press conference, Alford stated "I would like to be here for a long, long time. I have no aspirations of looking anywhere else, or moving on anywhere else." And then the Indiana questions began. And the Bobby Knight comparisons.

His relationship with Bobby Knight is a bit complicated, but the impact of their relationship is written all over Alford. He speaks of Knight as if he was still playing for him, referring to him as "Coach," talking about how Knight would do things, and ultimately, trying to prove himself still to his college coach. So much of how Alford runs his own program he learned from Knight. The discipline, the practices, the scouting, the demands he places on himself and his players are all derived from Knight. In fact, there are times when it seems Alford wished he was still playing, still suiting up for "The General." As he has developed into a man, a father, a husband, and a coach, Alford continues to be under the influence of Knight.

Author John Feinstein first encountered Alford when he was a junior at Indiana and Feinstein was researching what would become *A Season on the Brink*. Though the two are not close, Feinstein has watched Alford's ascent through the coaching ranks from afar. "Steve can be real successful, as he relates well to his players. He is an honest person who tries hard every day. It seems he took Knight's strengths and discarded the weaknesses. His competitiveness, however, can be a drawback."

Ask anyone who knows Alford to describe him, and you'll mostly hear the word "competitive." From his early childhood days in his neighborhood to his current days at Iowa, Alford loves competition. He lives for it. And it never wanes. At the Final Four in Indianapolis in 1997, the year that Arizona defeated Kentucky for the championship, Alford was in town with most coaches from around the country. At most Final Fours, CBS has a facility or gym where coaches and former players congregate to play ball and reminisce. That year, the gym was the National Institute of Fitness where the prestigious Nike summer camp is held every year. It was mostly pickup, and on this day, Alford was joined on his four-man squad by good friend, former UMass assistant and current Wright State head coach, Ed Schilling; best friend, former head of Nike college basketball and now agent Mike Barnett; and Erik Lautenbach a 6'7" former player and also a Nike employee at the time. All four were former college players and they had talent.

They beat all opposing teams, most of which consisted of former college or junior college players. During one of their games, Alford noticed that former Indiana University student-manager and assistant and close friend of Bobby Knight, Craig Hartman, had entered the gym. Hartman was dressed in IU gear from head to toe. It became clear to Alford and Hartman as the current game wound down that the two wanted to play each other. Alford had nothing personal against Hartman, but his association with Knight and Indiana made for an interesting matchup. He wanted to prove that he still "had it." Alford's team won the current game, and he walked off the court to get a drink. It was show time.

"Look, let me have this game," Alford pleaded with his teammates. "Don't set any picks and if I have to pass you the ball, give it right back to me," so the story goes.

The pickup games were "make it, take it" up to ten points, meaning the team that scores maintains possession. Alford's opponents never touched the ball. No one else shot besides Alford. There were no rebounds. Steve Alford made ten straight shots to win the game. As he shot the last one, Alford yelled "game" as he released it. Game over.

On Tuesday, October 16, Alford was frustrated. He had spent the last 35 minutes of practice on a variation of the triangle offense, and it was clear that some of the younger players had still not picked it up. Most coaches will tell you that the most important position on the floor is point guard. Each needs a savvy, experienced floor general who serves as an extension of himself—the coach—on the floor. The last two seasons, Alford was blessed with four-year starter Dean Oliver, now a guard with the Golden State Warriors. Filling Oliver's shoes would not be easy. There were guards from last season's team returning, notably Brody Boyd, a clutch shooter, but not a true point guard, and Ryan Hogan, another shooting guard, a transfer from Kentucky.

To remedy the gap created at the point, Alford had recruited two quick, athletic guards who he hoped could run the show. Pierre Pierce was from the public leagues of Chicago and was far from home in more ways than just miles. He was a shy kid, with sensational athleticism, but it would be a struggle for him to adjust to the college game and to college life. The other point guard recruit was junior college transfer Chauncey Leslie, from Indian Hills Community College. It became clear at this preseason practice that it could take a while for either newcomer to grasp the offense, and, ironically enough, neither was a vocal leader. Luckily for Alford, the burden of the upcoming season did not rest on the shoulders of the point guard, but squarely on the backs of Luke Recker and Reggie Evans. These two preseason All-Americans were poised to take the Iowa program to the "next level" and Alford eagerly anticipated the journey.

Luke Recker became a household name in college basketball largely because of what happened in his life off the court. A "Mr. Basketball" in the state of Indiana, Recker decided to attend Indiana and play for Bobby Knight. The Hoosier state was thrilled. Here was the schoolboy from a small town, a good-looking white male who bled Indiana basketball. His decision to stay at home and attend Indiana was front-page news. But not every story is a fairy tale. His freshman and sophomore seasons at Indiana were stellar on the court, as he started almost every game while leading the team in scoring. But Recker was not happy and did not enjoy playing for Knight. Ironically enough, Alford, who had befriended Recker when he was in high school and was close to his high school coach, Cliff Hawkins, helped convince the Indiana star to stick it out another year after his unhappy freshman season. During a round of golf together while Alford was the coach at Southwest Missouri, he told Recker, "We've all been there and you owe it to yourself to give it another shot." Recker stuck it out one more year but became depressed and knew that a change would be best for him. But he never could have calculated the risk.

Upon announcing his intention to transfer, Recker became Public Enemy No. 1 in Indiana. He was labeled a traitor, a liar, and a despicable human being. How could Indiana's pride and joy leave their university? Recker and his family received piles upon piles of hate mail and threats, and Recker became the target for fans, the media, and even his fellow students. One of his first calls was to Alford, who by now was at Iowa. In the spring of 1998, Recker said good-bye to Indiana and decided to attend the University of Arizona and play for Lute Olson. But he would never play a game for the Wildcats.

That summer, Recker, his steady girlfriend Kelly Craig, her brother Jason, and another friend, John Holberg, were riding in a car outside of Durango, Colorado, when they were hit by a drunk driver. In the devastating crash, Kelly was left paralyzed, her brother lay in a coma, and Recker barely survived, with internal injuries and massive wounds to his head and face. A nurse happened to be driving by the accident and applied medical aid to Recker, probably saving his life. Over the course of the next few months, Recker became healthy enough to enroll at Arizona in the fall and began to take classes. But his thoughts were in Indiana with Craig and her family. Eventually, the burden was too much to bear and Recker left Arizona to return home. Arizona coach Lute Olson was classy and compassionate, letting Recker go and offering his assistance in choosing another school. He knew he wanted to continue his college career and education, but where?

He found the answer in another Indiana Mr. Basketball. Steve Alford offered him a fresh start at Iowa. Recker's father lived in Iowa, and he thought it was close enough to family, friends, and Craig. But Iowa was a major rival of Indiana. Arizona was one thing, thousands of miles away in another conference, but Iowa was different. It was leaving your wife for your wife's sister, way too close to home. But Recker ultimately decided that Alford and Iowa were for him and made the move in 1999.

He had gained notoriety for the Indiana transfer and car crash, more so than for his shooting touch. Still, he was a high-caliber Big Ten player who had already proved his worth in his two seasons at Indiana. Recker sat out the 1999–2000 season and became eligible to play for the Hawkeyes in the fall of 2000, where his arrival was eagerly anticipated by the Iowa faithful. But just 13 games into his Iowa career, Recker injured his right knee playing against Indiana ironically enough. He sat out the remainder of the 2001 season, one in which Iowa went 23-12, including a dramatic four-game run to the conference tournament championship, earning them an automatic bid to the NCAA Tournament. For Recker, it was simply another crushing disappointment in a basketball career—and in life.

As the 2001–2002 season approached, Recker was again healthy, accustomed to the University of Iowa, and reaped preseason recognition and honors, including being a candidate for the Wooden Award. This would be his year to shine, to put his past behind him, to take Iowa and Alford "to the next level." Recker knew he had to have a good season to impress NBA scouts, and he also knew that he and Reggie Evans would be the targets for opposing teams.

Evans was returning after a shockingly productive junior year, one in which he was among the tops in the nation in rebounding and was a force inside in the Big Ten. From the projects of Pensacola, Florida, Evans never had the grades to make it to the Division I level out of high school, and instead headed to the farms of Coffeyville, Kansas, to play junior college ball at Coffeyville Junior College. It was there that Evans' reputation as a workhorse started to spread and top coaches from around the country began to pay visits to the small town. Ultimately, it was Alford and Iowa who were the lucky ones, and Evans did not disappoint in his first season in Iowa City, averaging 11.9 rebounds per game to lead the nation and earn Big Ten All-Conference honors. Like Recker, the 2001–2002 season would be an opportunity to shine for Evans and to improve his status in the draft. Evans had considered leaving Iowa after his sensational junior year to enter the draft, but Alford persuaded him that another year at Iowa would only make him more marketable. Of course, only if he had another good season.

There were other role players on the Iowa squad, including Jared Reiner, Sean Sonderleiter, Duez Henderson, Boyd, Hogan, and senior Rod Thompson, but none of the players came close to matching Recker's and Evans' abilities.

By the time of the Black and Gold Blowout on October 27, the annual intrasquad scrimmage, the team had begun to take shape. Alford was leaning toward Pierce at the point and he was praying that Recker's knee would hold out. The standing room only crowd of 15,500 saw an ugly scrimmage, but what did they expect? What the coach saw was "brutal defense." Alford went home that night and watched the tape of the scrimmage. He was not impressed by the defensive effort by anyone. He also had to decide whether or not to redshirt Marcellus Sommerville, Erek Hansen, and Cortney Scott.

The preseason polls had Iowa in the Top Ten, based mainly on the return of the two Wooden Award candidates. To some, the ranking seemed not high enough. To others, it was worthy of the chant, "Overrated!" Regardless, things were looking good in Iowa City during the first two weeks of practice. But looks can be deceiving, as Steve Alford would soon learn.

3

Hollywood

ONE OF THE MOST POPULAR TOURIST ATTRACTIONS IN THE LOS ANGELES AREA IS Universal Studios. A combination theme park and movie studio, it is a fixture for the millions that come to see Hollywood each year. The highlight of a trip to Universal is the studio tram tour—a mobile passenger carrier taking families "behind the scenes" of moviemaking. Along the way on the 45-minute tour, fans encounter a mechanical "Jaws" that rises out of nowhere to snatch at unsuspecting kids; an electric parting of the sea (a special effect from *The Ten Commandments*); and the Bates Motel and other famous landmarks—shocking tourists as to their smallness and facades. There are also the fake explosions, flash floods, and a mock gun battle along with demonstrations of how people in movies appear to fly, jump off 50-story buildings, and burn themselves up.

The Universal Studios tour is about entertainment and education. It is about appearance versus reality. What you *think* you may see on the movie or television screen is not reality. In a city all about image, about perception, about larger-than-life characters, what you see is often not what you get. Encounter Tom Cruise, Arnold Schwarzenegger, or Sylvester Stallone playing with their kids at a park in Brentwood or Beverly Hills, and most people's reaction is "Wow, he's much smaller in person!" You think you know Madonna, Brad Pitt, or Mick Jagger because you read about them in *People?*

Because today's sports stars, including their coaches, have become entertainment celebrities in their own right, the public comes to know these stars through the eyes and ears of the media. An article about a blowup between a coach and player; an editorial about how bad a job the coach is doing; rumors and misperceptions flying through the Internet by unidentified sources; accusations, innuendoes, and character assassinations by those in the *don't know*. Coaches are routinely portrayed in one-dimensional terms, put in simplistic boxes that make understanding them and reporting on them easier for the media and the public.

And then there is Steve Lavin. In a league of his own. A classic case of the picture-boy for misperception. Lavin may be one of the best examples to illustrate the difference between appearance and reality. As the coach at storied UCLA, in the media capital of the world, with an outward appearance that can fool even insiders, Steve Lavin is nothing like *they* say he is. And what do *they* say?

For starters, he was lucky and ill prepared to be anointed the head coach of UCLA at 32. He is not a very good coach and doesn't seem to run organized or disciplined practices. He is not a good recruiter and he doesn't develop his players. He is just a hotshot coach with slick hair. That's what *they* say. What does reality say?

Lavin's family background and early experiences prepared him for a life as an educator and coach. Lavin grew up in a middle-class family in Ross, California, a small town in Marin County, about a half hour north of San Francisco. His father, Cap, is a well-known Bay Area English teacher at local universities and high schools, and was an outstanding basketball player, suiting up for legendary Cal, San Francisco, and Michigan State coach Pete Newell as well as Phil Woolpert in the 1950s at the University of San Francisco. Newell would become a mentor and key advisor throughout Steve Lavin's career. As a student at Sir Francis Drake High School in San Anselmo, Steve Lavin played for coach Pete Hayward. In 1982, he played alongside current UCLA assistant coach Jim Saia and also covered sports for the Drake school newspaper. The two friends helped lead Drake to the CIF Division II championship in 1982 and a career record of 65-1 from 1980 to 1982. Lavin was not the star, but a gritty, hard-working, passionate player who did the "little things," like taking charges and making the extra pass, that helped win games.

He began his collegiate career at San Francisco State, winning the Scholar Athlete Award on a team that was NCAA Division II West Regional Champions. (It was on this team that he met Patrick Sandle, a current UCLA assistant.) After two seasons at SFSU, Lavin transferred to tiny Chapman College in Orange County, California, when his coach at SFSU, Kevin Wilson, was hired at Chapman. He spent his summers running the Lavin Basketball Camps with his father and sister, Rachel, in the Bay Area. Cap Lavin recalls first realizing that his youngest son had found his calling. "In the early days of the camp, Steve would be outside on the blacktop with 12 youngsters teaching them the game. His energy and enthusiasm were infectious and each summer the numbers would grow as word spread about the camp. He likes working with people and he has an enormous amount of energy and imagination that engages and motivates people." (In future years, the Lavin camps would grow to 2,000 strong in the summer heat.)

Cap and Steve Lavin have always enjoyed a remarkably close relationship, one typical of fathers and sons. They trade thoughts about teaching, basketball, and life. Steve admires his father, not only for his lifetime devoted to teaching and family, but also for his ethical approach to life. "Much of what I have accomplished in life," the son reflects, "I owe to my parents. It means so much that I can share my experiences with them." Through thick and thin, including the many frenzied and harrowing crises that come with coaching, Steve and Cap have a tacit understanding, often communicating with a simple word, phrase, or smile.

As his senior year of college was underway at Chapman, Lavin continued to pursue his goal: to learn all he could from the best minds in the game. To that end, he wrote six high-profile coaches he respected from a distance around the country, asking permission to observe their practices. He was persistent, but not a pest. Reading through his passionate letters, coaches could understand how eager and willing this young man from California was to learn the game. For some time, Lavin had been attending coaching clinics, gathering notes from some of the top coaches in the game. Two well-known coaches generously offered Lavin a chance to observe their practices over his six-week break between his final semesters at Chapman. His playing eligibility was exhausted by December 1987, but Lavin stayed at Chapman to finish his degree and work as a resident assistant.

Lavin hopped on a flight and traveled the 2,300 miles to his first stop, Bloomington, Indiana. He had seen and heard Bobby Knight at coaching clinics, and he was well aware of Knight's reputation and famous temper. Initially, the 22-year-old college senior was a bit intimidated, as one might expect. The first few days in Bloomington, he would sit in Assembly Hall and watch the legend orchestrate his practices, laced with hollering and colorful use of the English language. Before and after practice, Lavin would pick the brain of "The General" and his staff, assistants Ron Felling, Dan Dakich, Tates Locke, Joby Wright, and manager Craig Hartman, asking them about the motion offense, defensive stance drills, and leadership techniques. But on his third day at Indiana, Lavin may have worn out his welcome.

"I was in the stands watching practice and a coach from Colombia [the country] was also visiting. Before practice, I had taken notes on Knight's prepractice talk and was sharing those with the invited guest. He couldn't read my handwriting so I was helping him translate my notes. At one point, one of Knight's assistants, Ron Felling, came over and suggested we keep our talking to a minimum. Well, after practice, I followed Coach Knight off the court and asked if he was going to watch the video now. He ignored me. I kept following him and he finally just swung around and laid into me [use your imagination]. I was petrified. I remember thinking, 'I am getting out of here and heading to Purdue.'"

But Lavin persisted and did not give up simply because of the confrontation. In fact, the next night, there was Lavin on the Indiana bench during a critical conference game against rival Michigan. Imagine. A young college student, committed to the game, eager to watch and learn, getting the chance to sit on the team bench during a Big Ten game. It was beyond Lavin's expectations. The two weeks at Indiana were remarkable, as Lavin took a crash course on college basketball from one of the game's best teachers.

He then drove 80 miles to the north, to West Lafayette, Indiana, to spend two weeks at Purdue with coach Gene Keady, an encounter that would change Lavin's life. In Keady, Lavin found not only a great basketball coach, but also a man of his own heart, a man he admired and could emulate, and their meeting would lead to a long-term friendship. Lavin was attracted to Keady's personality, his humor, his humility, and his passion for the game. Over those four weeks in Big Ten country with Knight and Keady in January 1988, Lavin learned more about coaching the game than at any other time in his career. Inspired by the experience, Lavin was convinced a career in coaching was his destiny. Yet never in his wildest dreams did he imagine that nine years later he would be the head coach at UCLA.

A few years earlier, Lavin's father had a heart-to-heart talk with his son, reminding him of some of the limitations and pressures that are part of coaching today, especially at the most competitive level. Cap Lavin knew his son could excel at the profession, but wanted him to be fully aware of the drawbacks of coaching. His dad had seen the way the media and money had changed the coaching profession. Little did they both know at that time how challenging it *really* could be.

Lavin graduated in May 1988, and drove out to Indiana with longtime friend and teammate Jim Saia to work as coaches at the Indiana and Purdue summer camps. Toward the end of the summer, Lavin was about to accept his first full-time job coaching at

Fresno Pacific in the heart of California. But before Lavin could put on his Fresno coaching gear, he received a call that would change his life. Purdue assistant Kevin Stallings had left for an assistant's job at Kansas, and Gene Keady wanted to add Lavin to his staff as a graduate assistant. It was a no-brainer. He had the opportunity to coach in the Big Ten under a master teacher. So he packed up once again and headed to West Lafayette.

"Steve was dedicated, had a good sense of humor, good rapport with the players, and he really wanted to learn," the now 66-year-old Keady remembers. "He lived with a guy who was a friend of the program's, and Steve slept on his couch because we had no money to pay him."

Lavin's first year at Purdue was about sleeping on couches and floors, eating at Wendy's, using coupons that Keady had left on his desk. In fact, Keady would often give Lavin some money to drive Keady's wife into Chicago to shop or get her hair done, or to pick up visiting coaches, or to run errands. One problem—Lavin had no driver's license. Being the youngest of six kids, he never had to learn how to drive and he went through college without getting a license. Of course, he did not tell Keady about this oversight until years later at a roast for his former boss. Assistant coaches would pick Lavin up and drop him off that first year and Lavin worked with student manager Gary Harshlate at night to study and practice for the driver's license test. By his second year, Lavin managed to get an apartment and a car, but as a result, began to accumulate debt.

Even as an assistant at Purdue, Lavin continued to talk with other coaches, to receive and exchange ideas, to attend clinics, and to deepen his understanding of basketball. He has a remarkable appreciation for the history of the game and is well-versed in basketball theory.

Of course, Lavin was at Purdue, a close neighbor and conference foe of Bobby Knight's Indiana. It did seem a little awkward. Knight had opened up his practices, drills, and strategies to Lavin, who was now coaching for an archenemy. But as Keady made clear, there was nothing that Lavin could add that was going to help Purdue beat Indiana, not only since Purdue had been beating IU regularly for years, but also because the Purdue staff already knew everything about the Hoosiers. Lavin remained on Keady's staff for three seasons, performing a variety of duties as an assistant coach, including video exchange, scouting, monitoring study hall, teaching a coaching theory class to undergraduate students and wanna-be coaches and, of course, writing recruiting letters.

In 1991, USA Basketball conducted trials in Colorado and later practice sessions for the upcoming PanAm Games in West Lafayette. Lavin assisted Keady with the practices, and the young assistant quickly had a following. His intensity in leading defensive footwork drills caught the eye of many of the coaches on hand, provoking P. J. Carlesimo to say, "we should test him [Lavin] for drugs, not the players" and Jud Heathcoat to remark on the football-style intensity and footwork drills, "We may not play well, but we'll be ready to invade Kuwait." UCLA coach Jim Harrick was one of the coaches watching practices and he was intrigued at Lavin's energy and knowledge as he led the college all-stars in daily defensive drills. The young assistant knew of Harrick's own knowledge of the game and his ability to build a winning program through his friendship with UCLA assistant Mark Gottfried. Harrick was also at UCLA. When Harrick had an opening for a volunteer assistant in 1991, Lavin decided to leave Purdue and return to California.

For the next five seasons, Lavin would not only learn more about coaching, running practices, and recruiting, he would also see firsthand the immense toll that public scrutiny and media criticism can take on a head coach. First as a volunteer coach, then as a restricted-earnings coach, and then finally as a full-time assistant staff member, Lavin was the senior staff member by 1996 and had done every job imaginable for a coach. But no one could have expected what would happen next.

Harrick led UCLA to a national championship in the spring of 1995, and all signs indicated a return to the glory days of Bruin basketball. The following year was not as successful and as the 1996–1997 season got underway, rumors began to circulate of an investigation into Harrick's activities. Not only was the coach still taking heat for "Blazergate," when star player Baron Davis purchased Harrick's car, via one of Harrick's sons, but now attention turned to a recruiting dinner in the early fall of 1996. UCLA was investigating a recruiting dinner at Monty's Steakhouse in Westwood, when apparently Harrick broke NCAA rules by allowing an inappropriate number of UCLA players to eat. According to NCAA rules, the school can pay for a meal for only one player per recruit. There were three recruits but five UCLA players. What got Harrick in trouble was that he tried to cover up the discrepancy by saying that his wife and assistant coach Michael Holton's wife had eaten with them. UCLA professor and faculty representative Don Morrison and the PAC-10's David Price were chosen to lead the investigation. They concluded that Harrick had lied to UCLA administrators on more than one occasion. The Los Angeles media pounced on the story, fueling speculation with innuendoes and statements from anonymous sources.

On an early November afternoon in 1996, Lavin was out to lunch with Jim Saia, Pete Newell, and Jeff Felenzer, a hoops junkie and later organizer of the Pete Newell Challenge Tournament. They talked about the upcoming season, defensive strategies, and the coaching profession. Lavin and Saia got caught in traffic on their way back to UCLA and arrived only a few minutes before the 3:00 P.M. practice. But Harrick was not on the floor, and Lavin immediately knew something was amiss. Back in the coaches' locker room, Harrick told Lavin that the administrators wanted to see him at 6:00 P.M. and Lavin at 6:30. Harrick later left in the middle of practice and went to meet with his agent, Arn Tellem, while Lavin and the other assistants ran practice. Harrick returned with Tellem for the 6:00 P.M. meeting, but UCLA administrators did not allow Tellem into the meeting. Harrick was fired in a short meeting with athletic director Pete Dalis. He came back down to his office where his assistants were waiting, and Harrick sent Lavin up for his meeting, knowing that the next few minutes would change Lavin's life. The assistant walked upstairs to meet with Dalis, and he walked out moments later as the new interim head coach at UCLA.

"I think the only guy more surprised than me when he got the job was Steve himself," reflects Pete Newell.

UCLA assistant Lorenzo Romar would have been considered the front-runner for the opening, but he had left months earlier to take the head coaching job at Pepperdine. Mark Gottfried had left to coach at Murray State. Lavin was the natural interim choice because he was heavily involved in the current recruiting and continuity was critical and Lavin also had senior status on the staff, as assistants Jim Saia and Michael Holton were in their first years. Practice was well underway and Dalis had to make a quick transition. On November 7, 1996, he announced that 31-year-old assistant Steve Lavin would become interim head coach, and that a national search would be conducted for a permanent replacement.

From the moment of that announcement, Steve Lavin's world would never be the same. Lavin felt sorry for Harrick, the man who had given him a break in 1991, who had been his boss just hours earlier; yet turning down this opportunity wouldn't bring back his former boss. Lavin had a sense of purpose over this fateful chance to begin putting into practice all of the ideas and approaches he had learned. At the same time, he had seen first-hand what life as UCLA's head coach was like and he had no illusions about the extreme challenges inherent in the job. Lavin privately told his father about his concerns regarding the job, many of which were related to the transitory nature of the position since John Wooden's tenure (as evident by the short stints of Gene Bartow, Gary Cunningham, Larry Brown, Larry Farmer, and Walt Hazzard, the five coaches who succeeded Wooden before Harrick's eight-year tenure). His father was proud of his son's concern for Harrick and for his understanding of what was to come.

What troubled Lavin even more than public doubts about his qualifications was the innuendo that he somehow helped orchestrate Harrick's downfall. Nothing could be further from the truth, and in both the Morrison Report released by UCLA and in public statements to the press by Harrick, it was clear the Lavin had nothing to do with Harrick's dismissal. (In fact, in Morrison's investigation, UCLA players Cameron Dollar and Charles O'Bannon conceded that at practice the afternoon of the fateful dinner, Lavin had implored the players not hosting the recruits to not show up at Monty's for the dinner, a restaurant that routinely was a hangout for UCLA players and coaches. Lavin knew it would be a violation and was trying to keep his boss away from trouble.)

"When I first got the job, I was concerned about what the future might hold," says Lavin. "I assumed I wasn't going to be the permanent coach, so that part was clear. I was going to hold the fort down until they brought in Tubby Smith or brought Lorenzo [Romar] back. I figured I would be the assistant for a year with the new coach and then move on." Lavin's reading of the situation was very plausible, but destiny is often unpredictable.

"I never really wanted the UCLA job, but doors open and close; sometimes fate plays a hand in things. You go with your training and instincts. At the start of conference play that year, however, we lost to Stanford by 50 and it looked like I'd be fortunate to be a JV high school coach."

The mid-January loss to Stanford was actually by 48 and was followed by a huge win over California less than 36 hours later. As Lavin admits now, after the Stanford debacle, he was thinking that the odds were not good that he would keep the job. Before boarding the bus after the "Maples Massacre," as Lavin refers to it, his father pulled him aside and said three simple words: "You are you." The son understood. For years, Cap Lavin had reminded his son that no matter what happens in life, stay true to yourself and remember that who you are is about much more than a basketball game. Those three words were all that "Lav" had to hear. The Bruins came back, defeated Cal and, in early February, the Bruins beat Stanford by 19 and Lavin was given the job permanently a few days later. Criticism of Dalis' selection was instantaneous, with many alumni, journalists, and fans calling Lavin's readiness and experience into question. This wasn't just any coaching job. This wasn't Cleveland State in Ohio promoting an assistant with little fanfare and with little risk. This was the preeminent college basketball program in America, in the media hub of the world. The former third assistant had not only survived his first five months on the job, but he passed the test with flying colors. He wasn't nervous, he says, but rather had an "intense purpose" in games while trying to stay "loose and lucid."

Of course, good fortune and perfect timing created the opportunity for Steve Lavin. Yes, he was in the right place at the right time. But Lavin had been training for the job all of his life. He had worked the camps, played the game, traveled the nation, learned, searched, and absorbed. He had worked as an assistant coach, done the menial tasks, run practices, studied the game, the techniques, the greats. This is all Steve Lavin wanted to do with his life, and now he had the opportunity to do it—way ahead of schedule.

He's not a very good coach. If he was a good coach, we wouldn't lose to Ball State and Pepperdine. Perhaps, but top-ranked Duke wouldn't lose to Florida State, national runner-up Indiana wouldn't lose at home to Butler, North Carolina would not be embarrassed by Hampton and Davidson at the Dean Dome, Wright State would not beat No. 1 Michigan State, and Adolph Rupp's Kentucky would not have lost to Western Kentucky. Losses are expected—not anticipated, but expected—as part of a 35-game season. For Lavin, and other coaches, it's a marathon, not a sprint. It's about March, not November. But to many of those in the Los Angeles media, the same scribes that like to stir the pot to increase readership, victories at UCLA are not the result of good coaching, but rather raw talent or lucky breaks. "The other team played poorly; UCLA got some good calls; the Bruin players really stepped up; they were lucky to escape with a win."

Former Los Angeles sports radio host Arnie Spanier, notorious for his anti-Lavin rants, scornfully dismissed the coach's accomplishments in a 2001 article. "To hell with the record. Any loss at UCLA is unacceptable. Especially the loss to Cal State-Northridge [December 2000]; Lavin has disgraced the Bruin legacy." Spanier is not alone. To many "experts," any loss is a direct result of the inability of the coach, in this instance, Steve Lavin. But if losing is the criterion for judging coaching ability, then John Chaney, Bobby Knight, Mike Krzyzewski, Dean Smith, Roy Williams, Tom Izzo, and yes, even John Wooden, are not very good coaches, for they have all lost games they should have won.

"Steve has improved dramatically as a coach," his mentor and legendary coach Pete Newell says. "He has grown technically and has a lot of guts that most coaches do not have. Unfortunately, you are not allowed to learn from your mistakes at UCLA like at other places."

Again, the perception of Lavin's coaching ability runs counter to the reality. Yes, there have been games that UCLA could have, or should have, won, and the coach is quick to acknowledge that fact; but the many more victories in games they were not supposed to win clearly demonstrate the coaching ability of Lavin. What does reality say? Reality says that over his career at UCLA, Lavin boasts a career mark of 135-59 (69.6%). He has won a PAC-10 Championship, earned Coach of the Year honors, and taken his team to five Sweet Sixteens including one Elite Eight (1997), beating the likes of Duke, North Carolina, Kansas, Kentucky, Louisville, Arizona, Stanford, Syracuse, Michigan, and Cincinnati along the way. With five Sweet Sixteen appearances in the last six years, only the great Krzyzewski can boast the same claim among current coaches.

He does not run organized practices. As detailed later in this chapter, UCLA's practices are not "dodge ball, kick the can, capture the flag" affairs as Lavin so often jokes with the media. The perception is that since his teams lose some games, it must be the result of unorganized and lackadaisical practices. In fact, UCLA's practices, organized down to the minute with clear and specific coaching and player responsibilities spelled out, are very disciplined. With a light-hearted coach at the helm, the team has fun at times, but Lavin's practices are demanding and focused.

Former Bruin starter and current Seattle Supersonic Earl Watson came to appreciate the intense workouts once he got to the NBA. "The first year or so at UCLA, I didn't think I was going to make it through a practice, they were so difficult. But I kept at it and by the time I left, I could not have been more accustomed to hard work. At the NBA, the practices are nothing compared to UCLA, as other NBA guys struggled through the workouts."

Other former and current UCLA players are quick to differ strongly with critics who pounce on Lavin's practice techniques. Keep in mind that his practices have been molded by and reflect some of the best minds in the game. Lavin brought an intensity, particularly on the defensive side of the ball, to UCLA, and that enthusiasm coupled with discipline resonates in every Bruin practice.

He is not a good recruiter. The recruiting classes are consistently ranked in the Top Five nationally, and Lavin and his staff have signed seven McDonald's high school All-Americans in his years at the helm. In fact, in 1997, the Bruins had the No. 2 rated class in the nation, headed by National Player of the Year Baron Davis. A year later in 1998, UCLA had the No. 1 rated recruiting class, including All-Americans Dan Gadzuric, Ray Young, Jaron Rush, and Jerome Moiso. Lavin's 2001 class, Cedric Bozeman, Dijon Thompson, and Andre Patterson, was Top Five, and would have been No. 1 if recruit Michael Fey had qualified academically.

He can't "develop" players for the NBA. As the head coach, Lavin has seen nine of his former players go on to play in the NBA, with six of them still there—Baron Davis, Jelani McCoy, Jerome Moiso, Earl Watson, and rookies Dan Gadzuric and Matt Barnes (as of this publishing). Former players Toby Bailey, J. R. Henderson, and Charles O'Bannon have played at the NBA level and still play professionally. Watson and Barnes were not All-Americans coming out of high school. As for developing talent, almost every coach will tell you that a player who makes it to the NBA level has a drive that no coach can teach or develop.

He is a flashy, slick showman. Steve Lavin added the gel to his hair in 1993 and nothing has been the same since. Like movie stars critiqued for how they cut their hair, Lavin's thick black hair is the subject of much mindless chatter, even by the coach himself. The way he styles his hair and the fact that he does not wear a jacket when he coaches has created a false impression of Lavin. Those who don't know him, who don't know that he is anything but what his gelled hair may suggest, are quick to label him a smooth, L.A. guy. He wears well-tailored suits, drives a nice car, but then again, so do most coaches. It's the hair that calls attention to itself. Perception is often more flashy and entertaining than reality. True of many coaches around the country.

As you stroll into the UCLA office, the first thing you see is blue. Blue from floor to ceiling, from east to west, many-hued. The carpet is deep blue. Framed and exhibited on the south wall are like-colored jerseys—holy relics, to believers—once soaked with the sweat of a veritable Who's Who of NCAA basketball: Alcindor, Walton, O'Bannon. On the north wall of Lavin's corner office, crowding the bookshelves that flank a big-screen TV, is a collection of memorabilia from blue-sky, halcyon days—a basketball signed by the team that compiled "The Streak," a bronze plaque of John Wooden's "Pyramid of Success," and a color photo of the new guy coaching his first game.

The L-shaped desk is cluttered: books, snapshots, notepads, scraps of paper, information heaped in precipitous stacks. A copy of *Life's Little Lessons* tops one pile, a dog-eared book on leadership another. Nosing its way off the desk is an unframed certificate of appreciation from the City of Hope charity, expressing gratitude to the young coach for spending time with its sick children. Certificates like this one are everywhere, some on the wall, some in unpacked boxes on the floor.

In the cabinets behind his desk, there lie the treasures of Lavin's past. In one corner sit eight notebooks, each diligently labeled with a coach's name: "Knight. Krzyzewski. Newell. Grgurich. Johnson." In each notebook are hundreds of notes, diagrams, and drills of each coach's basketball knowledge. All of the years that Lavin was learning he was also retaining and refining. And the notebooks are not all. On the other end of the closed-door cabinet sits a pile of letters, probably 200 or so. Some are discolored by time, but all are priceless. Some are the responses to the letters that a young Lavin had sent out years ago. The return addresses are Bloomington, Durham, Chapel Hill, and Lexington. There are also congratulatory and encouragement letters he has received in recent years from coaches and mentors around the country. They include letters from Pete Newell, John Wooden, Phil Woolpert, Mike Krzyzewski, Bobby Knight, Jerry Tarkanian, Gene Keady, Bud Pressley, Terry Holland, and Tim Grgurich. Lavin treasures these kind words while others might discard them. His appreciation for the history of the game, for those who came before him, for those who helped him launch his career, and for those who taught him the game is never more evident than in those letters sitting behind him.

A conversation with Lavin is not for the fainthearted. For starters, there's his rapid delivery. Then there's his encyclopedic knowledge of college basketball. Add to that a penchant for free association, and before you know it, you're swept up in a heady current of names, dates, statistics, and philosophies, all pouring out from the coach behind the desk. When talking about the matchup zone defense that Lavin would employ later this year. . . . "Ray Mears really started it at Tennessee and he coached Bill Musselman. At Ashland College, Kevin Wilson played for Musselman and was an assistant to him at Minnesota coaching guys like Kevin McKale, Flip Saunders, and Dave Winfield. Wilson coached me at San Francisco State and Chapman College and I learned the matchup zone from him. Of course, when Flip Saunders coached the Timberwolves he employed parts of the same defense and now with zone allowed in the NBA, Minnesota is the best at it. . ."

In addition to the flowing torrent of basketball facts and insights, there are the incessant phone interruptions to endure. Like many college coaches, Lavin's lifeline is his cell phone; but Lavin's rings more frequently than others' because his "private" number is nowhere near private. Of course his players have it, as do his longtime girlfriend, Treena Camacho, his family, and his friends. Many members of the sports media have his number, plus hundreds of people he has met at UCLA gatherings or charity events, fund-raisers, and restaurants. He gives it out reflexively, the way Michael Jordan dashes off autographs.

Overriding all other impressions is the sense that there is no one in the world Lavin would rather be talking with than you, and nothing he would rather be discussing than the topic at hand. He has interested eyes. It is a gift. Some coaches have it; some ex-presidents are renowned for it. Lavin comes by it naturally and uses it expertly in recruiting players and dealing with the combative Los Angeles media.

Between the phone calls, the visitors stopping by to say hello and his own tangent digressions, Lavin shows himself capable of both brutal honesty and glowing pride when it comes to his team. Though less than 20 years older than his players, he is their coach, father, advisor, and—above all—friend. That's why they will sacrifice themselves for him, defend him to anyone who will listen, and trust their careers and lives to their young coach.

Six days after his team's first formal practice in October, Lavin's mantra is stability. "For the first time since we've been here, we have stability in the program. A good group of upperclassmen and freshmen, and a knowledge that we, as a staff, are secure." At least more secure than last year. Under the strain of a mini–losing streak in January 2001, UCLA athletic director Pete Dalis confessed to reporters that he had been in touch with Rick Pitino about the UCLA coaching job, confirming a report by Fox's Keith Olberman. Earlier that day Dalis had assured Lavin twice that there was nothing to the rumor and that he hadn't contacted Pitino. When Lavin and his staff heard the news—not from Dalis but from local reporters—they were stunned. Lavin told the press that he wouldn't comment until he heard the news directly from Dalis. The coach had already grown somewhat disillusioned with his AD for not publicly supporting him or any UCLA basketball coach in 19 years, and for frequently expressing a negative attitude. But he hadn't seen the Pitino business coming. Lavin received support from coaches around the country and even Dick Vitale went on-air and criticized Dalis. "I was hurt by the Pitino affair," the coach concedes more than a year later. "Once your boss lies to you it is difficult to reestablish the necessary trust to make a relationship work. I didn't know whether to quit. It was difficult, but I didn't want to let the players down. So I just went out each day and did my job."

Criticism by the press, some alumni and some UCLA fans has been incessant since the moment he was hired. That in itself would have brought an average man to his knees. But in the past two seasons, Lavin has also had to contend with alleged media leaks by members of the UCLA Athletic Department, as well as chilling extortion and death threats. In fact, just a day before the start of practice in October, the PAC-10 conference cleared Lavin of any wrongdoing with regard to false allegations made in the spring by "unidentified sources." What a great way to start off the year.

Lavin is in a unique situation in college basketball. He faces many of the same challenges as most other 320 head coaches, but then so much more. Being the head coach at UCLA, Duke, Kentucky, or Indiana is on a different level, and the media glare of Los Angeles puts the UCLA job atop them all. It is in that spectrum that Lavin coaches his team. Every day that he is on the job is one day longer than he, or the critics, thought he would be around.

The Preseason Wooden Award Banquet is always held just before the start of preseason practice at the Los Angeles Athletic Club, the host of the John Wooden Award. The luncheon attracts close to a dozen Southland coaches, mostly head coaches, but also some assistants sent by head coaches who were "on the road" or "meeting with administrators." Some of the head coaches at the 2001 banquet included Steve Aggers from Loyola Marymount, Steve Lavin from UCLA, Bobby Braswell from Cal State Northridge, and John Masi from UC Riverside. USC coach and UCLA alum Henry Bibby sent an assistant, as did a few other head coaches. In addition to the coaches, there were media people like *foxsports.com*'s Frank Burlison, as well as tournament and AAU organizer extraordinaire Dana Pump.

The cocktail reception before the banquet was not really one at all. Coaches exchanged pleasantries, media members picked up team information packets, and Pump held court.

Though Pump was the main attraction of the prelunch reception, there was one obvious absence. At 12:07 P.M., with the coaches seated on the dais and emcee and local television personality Darren Horton already into the introductions, Steve Lavin arrived, walked around the side wall of the room and up behind the dais to take his seat. (Lavin was meeting with his boss, UCLA athletic director Pete Dalis.) Dressed in a dark blue suit, white shirt, and blue tie, he took his seat between Riverside's Masi and Long Beach State coach Wayne Morgan. He sipped from a cup of coffee and winked off the dais to his many friends in the crowd.

Horton introduced each coach. Then, one by one, the coaches gave those in attendance a summary and prediction of the upcoming season. Using the typical "coach speak," they praised each other for their abilities, while downplaying their team's chances. Eight of the coaches made some reference or motion to Pump, seated at one of the front tables. As each coach spent seven or eight minutes fluffing feathers, Lavin wrote down some thoughts on a napkin. He had given hundreds of this type of speech, and it was second nature by now.

Lavin was introduced with high praise from Horton, noting the two Wooden Award nominees on his team, Jason Kapono and Dan Gadzuric, his stellar recruiting classes, and Lavin's success in the NCAA Tournament. Then Lavin stepped up to the microphone. "It's always an honor to be here. I think this is my eleventh year I've attended as an assistant or head coach. Obviously, it is an honor to be involved in anything Coach Wooden is associated with. (Getting the obligatory mention of the "Pope" in.) I have incredible respect for the people up here with me . . . partly because they have all beaten me."

The crowd and coaches roared in amusement at the slight exaggeration, but obvious reference to a previous upset loss to Northridge and a close call with Pepperdine. Lavin went on to talk about his team, his staff, and schedule, and wrapped up in under six minutes. The crowd applauded and Lavin took his seat. As the luncheon concluded, the coaches made their way off the dais and greeted friends and foes. But it was Lavin who was the main attraction. From media members to other coaches to 80-year-old members of the L.A. Athletic Club, they all wanted a handshake or a moment of his time. And he gave it to them. The room began to clear out, but Lavin remained, as waiters cleared the tables and a cleaning crew swept the floor.

Two weeks later, it was 3:45 P.M. on a Tuesday in mid-October and inside Pauley Pavilion, Lavin stood under one of the baskets, a rolled up practice schedule in his hands. He was dressed in a pair of blue UCLA gym shorts, with an Adidas windbreaker and, of course, Adidas socks and sneakers on his feet. His players were going full blast, running a drill called "Peer Pressure," a full-court, nonstop fast break drill. It may work on passing, catching, and transition for the Bruins, but it also gets them in shape. In Peer Pressure, three players pass and weave the length of the court and the one with the ball near the basket finishes with a layup or dunk. Each basket counts as a point, and the team must reach 15 in a row on this particular day for the drill to move on to the next stage. As a player scores, the team, in unison, chanted the number. "Three. Four. Five." They shouted out, drenched in sweat, their hands resting on their knees. On this day, Lavin was not in a very good mood, as the team had been looking for its focus to no avail.

As Lavin shouted encouragement from his post under one of the baskets, senior Ray Young came barreling toward him in the drill. Young took the ball, turned his back to the basket, and attempted to do an uncontested backhand slam. The only problem was that the ball didn't go in, clanked off of the rim, and slowly bounced back onto the court. The players stopped their count. Lavin stopped the drill.

"You know guys, it is pretty simple," he said in a booming voice to reach the players on the far side of the court. "Bust your ass down the court, make good passes, and finish with a layup. Is that too much to ask? You're shooting yourselves in the foot!"

Young shook his head, mumbled an apology to Matt Barnes and Dan Gadzuric standing next to him panting, and the drill continued, starting over at "One!" On his next trip back down to this same basket, Young drove the lane and slammed down a one-hander. Lavin shook his head, rolled his eyes, and let out a smile. "That's Ray being Ray, I guess. That's why we'll redshirt him!" The team finally reached 15 and the drill moved into its next phase as the 15-minute avalanche of sweat and sprints continued.

The Peer Pressure drill was just one of many that Lavin will put his troops through on this day, a practice that did not end until close to 6:45 P.M. Lavin has become notorious for running lengthy practices, but his troops are accustomed to the routine. If the quality of practice is not at a premium, Lavin may extend practice. The players refer to these as "Busters." Players realize they are simply running on SLST or "Steve Lavin Standard Time." Lavin learned from Keady, while at Purdue, that early in the season, there is always time to get in Busters.

Many UCLA practices this season start with a walk-through of OBs, or out-of-bounds plays, and offensive and defensive sets. The practice then moves into transition drills, shooting drills, and shifts again into "Post/Perimeter," where guards are at one end and big men at the other to work on specific parts of their games. There is time spent on free throws and almost always there is time for a short scrimmage, particularly as the season grows longer.

At most programs, the staff has planned out practice in the morning and has a schedule sheet to go by. You can usually find it rolled up in someone's hands, folded and tucked into shorts, or even on the floor. It is a timeline of the drills to be done in practice, an outline so coaches and the managers know what is next. But there are few practice plans as detailed as UCLA's. At the top of each plan, in addition to the requisite day and date, sits a headline of "Emphasis of the Day." On one particular practice day it reads "1) Attention to Details, 2) Information/Application." This will be the theme of the day, an effort by Lavin to ensure that his players know that it is just as important to be able to put information to work (application) as it is simply to listen. Another day, the emphasis may be on concentration or leadership.

On the left side of the Practice Plan sheet is the timetable of practice. Broken into five- or ten-minute segments, it details what drills will take place when. A sample Practice Plan for mid-October:

3:15	Stretch
3:25	Zone Out of Bounds
3:30	Flanker
3:35	Peer Pressure (15)
3:55	Water/FT's (1 & 1 for a 9'ER)
4:00	Post/Perimeter (Zone "O")
4:20	Introduce Regular
4:35	10 Man In the Paint
4:45	Possession Work (Regular vs. 2-3 Zone)
5:15	Press Period
5:45	Dummy Offense (Shallow, 3, High Post, Flat, Pacific, 5, Wide, Yankee Fist, Speed Game, 41, Wing Series, High Lead)
6:00	Water/FT's (1 & 1 for a 9'ER)
6:05	Possession Work (Sets)
6:15	Scrimmage
6:30	End Practice

In addition to the schedule, the plan has a list of coaching responsibilities, indicating the areas that each staff member covers in possession drills and what they are responsible for throughout practice. Also on the sheet is the assignment of players to the Blue and Yellow teams, with the "Blues" the first string.

Something unique to the UCLA basketball practice plan is the Progress Chart. In this box, areas of the game are broken down: Shooting, Free Throws, Zone Defense, and so on. How much time will be spent on them in the current practice is listed, as well as the total time spent on that aspect to date. For example, for work on the "Zone Out of

Bounds," the team will spend five minutes in practice on a certain day, bringing the total time spent on "Zone Out of Bounds" to one hour, 10 minutes on the season. The Progress Chart helps the players and, more importantly, the coaches, know what areas may need more time devoted to them. Of course, the times are not exact when drills run long and practices run even longer under Lavin. A final aspect to the Practice Plan is a box titled "Areas to Work On," listing up to 15 areas such as "Defense" or "Screening" or "Jump Stops."

At UCLA, the practice plan is detailed, printed in color, and done the afternoon before practice, after the staff has met as a group to plan the day's activities and emphasis. Most programs' practice plans are not as detailed and certainly not in color, and, in fact, simply list the drills to be done. The managers keep track of practice statistics at UCLA, from field goals attempted and made, to rebounds, steals, and blocks. These stats are then put into a table, and Player Points are determined, a formula involving rebounds, points scored, turnovers, and so on.

Practices at UCLA are now closed and, with very few exceptions, they remain closed. There are no media allowed in, no public visitations, and the UCLA managers ensure the privacy of the practices, often climbing into the stands to ask on-lookers to leave. Occasionally, a local high school or youth coach or team, a friend of a staff member or a scout will observe, but almost always there is no one but the team. For Lavin, closing practice is about limiting distractions, but it is a safety issue as well. When Lavin and his father received death threats in 2001, he decided it was time to shut it down.

A UCLA practice is about teaching, repetition, and time. The coaching staff stops drills occasionally to make a point and to demonstrate physically how to execute a specific move, noting a poor defensive stance or a pass that should have been made. There is enormous attention paid to detail, from where elbows are positioned on rebounds to how a skip pass needs to be a foot higher. This emphasis on detail makes the practices longer, but the extra time is well worth it in Lavin's mind. He wants to accomplish an objective in practice and he will patiently employ the methods, the repetition, and the time to achieve the desired goal. There is not a lot of yelling and screaming, temper-tantrums, or throwing of Gatorade buckets. There are some heated moments of instruction when Lavin will sternly encourage his kids to play harder, but there are also enough moments of light-hearted banter, when the coach will crack a smile or deliver an understated one-liner that will loosen the team up. The coach knows the seasons are long and teams can get tired mentally and physically, and tension can hold a team back. Although Lavin knows that the pressure is immense, he also understands that he cannot take himself or the game too seriously.

"I like it when he yells at you," says all-conference player Jason Kapono. "It lets you feel like you do have to step up your game, because he is pointing something out to you. He is such a good player's coach, because he makes you feel like you've got the green light. He is not one of those coaches that are going to beat you down. He's not going to yell at you where he makes you feel small."

The Sporting News' Mike DeCourcy contends that Lavin could be more successful if he, or a staff member, was "meaner." "There is no part of Lavin's character that is mean and he has a tough time tearing down his players. He needs a guy on his staff that his players will be fearful of. Of course," DeCourcy says jokingly, "we all know that California kids are not tough, so maybe that's part of the problem." None of Lavin's mentors were mean-spirited—all were disciplined teachers.

The longer the season draws out, Lavin cuts back on the length of practices; the more video the team watches; the more time devoted to scouting and walk-throughs. Lavin is consistent in the basic framework of practices, and though he relies on many fundamental drills such as Flanker and Peer Pressure, he always focuses on a different aspect of the drill on different days. The points of emphasis differ, but the drills do not.

As UCLA was underway with preseason practice, much of the attention was on Jason Kapono, the star on a team full of them, a roster that had the Bruins ranked in the Top Five of most national polls. They were led by the headband-wearing Kapono, a tall shooting forward notorious for drilling deep three's. The 6'8", 213-lb. junior from Artesia High School in Lakewood, California, had a stellar sophomore year averaging 17.2 points per game (ppg) in starting 31 of the Bruins' 32 games. As a freshman, he averaged 16.0 ppg starting every one of UCLA's games. In 2000–2001, Kapono was a Wooden Award finalist, All-PAC-10 selection and set a UCLA single-season mark of 84 threes—keep in mind, this is for a 6'8" *forward*. After each of his first two seasons in Westwood, Kapono tested the waters of the NBA draft, but in both springs, decided to return to UCLA.

Kapono continued to work on his game with personal trainers, shooting 1,000 shots a day. He spent the summer playing for the U.S. team in the World Championships, helping them earn a gold medal in Japan. Headed into the 2001–2002 season as a Wooden Award Nominee and preseason All-American, Kapono seemed poised to be the player everyone thought he could be.

Joining Kapono on the preseason All-American team and Wooden Award nominee list was center Dan Gadzuric, a 6'11", 240-lb. senior from Den Haag, Holland, who first picked up a basketball in high school. Gadzuric was part of the top recruiting class in the nation in 1998 joining former Bruin Jaron Rush and current senior Ray Young on the UCLA roster. Lightning quick for a big man, Gadzuric earned a reputation for running the floor and doing monstrous dunks, but also for getting in foul trouble and playing inconsistently. Like Kapono, he considered the NBA in the spring of 2001 but decided to finish out his college career. Nicknamed "Gadzilla," Gadzuric possessed a demeanor and personality that were contrary to the moniker. He is soft-spoken, polite and, in truth, does not understand the fuss over basketball players in America, since in his native land, soccer is king.

UCLA returned key players in senior guards Rico Hines, Billy Knight, T. J. Cummings, and power forward Matt Barnes. Hines had redshirted the 2000–2001 season after surgery on his right knee in November and was eager to get back on the court. He initially had been suspended by Lavin for the first two games of the 2001–2002 season for hitting Barnes over the head with a metal stool during an off-season pickup game in 2000, but after anger management counseling and community service during his red shirt year, the suspension was lifted. Knight started 18 games for the Bruins, averaging 7.9 ppg, and provided experience and leadership on the court and from the bench. Sophomore Cummings, the son of former NBA great Terry Cummings, exploded onto the Westwood scene as a freshman in 2000–2001 as a PAC-10 Freshman Team selection. In his first game in a Bruin uniform, Cummings scored 24 points in the season opener against Kansas in the Coaches vs. Cancer Classic in New York City.

Barnes' career had been a rocky one as he entered his senior year at UCLA. He had been frustrated for his first two years as a Bruin, contemplating transferring but deciding to stay. He had a breakthrough year as a junior in 2000–2001, averaging 11.6 ppg and 7.3 rebounds per game, selected honorable mention PAC-10. Barnes was in Lavin's doghouse for his first two years, but with a different attitude and maturity, he seemed to find his way out.

There was also senior Ray Young, a talented guard from Oakland, who struggled at times. Lavin wanted to stagger the leadership in each class, as he constantly managed the roster for the present and future, and suggested in a spring meeting with Young the possibility of redshirting for the upcoming season—the player was hesitant. Lavin felt that if Young redshirted, he could have a strong finish to his career the following season and have a chance to earn his degree. The issue would again resurface in the fall, with the arrival of a heralded trio of freshmen.

Cedric Bozeman, Dijon Thompson, and Andre Patterson arrived as a Top Five recruiting class for the 2001–2002 season, and arrived with the expectations of playing. If there was one gap in the Bruins' lineup, it was at point guard, a spot vacated by the graduation of four-year starter Earl Watson. It was apparent that Bozeman would be next in line, and Lavin put the reins in his hands from day one. Thompson and Patterson were Los Angeles natives and though not yet physically strong for inside play, they had the talent to contribute immediately. Thompson had strong ball-handling skills and could play the guard position while Patterson impressed the coaching staff with his shot-blocking and rebounding.

The three freshmen were not the only new faces in the Bruin camp. Lavin hired two new assistants to replace former assistant Michael Holton, who left to become head coach at the University of Portland, and Steve Spencer, who headed to Orange County Community College as head coach. Veteran top assistant Jim Saia remained, but Lavin had two spots to fill. He first hired former Bruin player Gerald Madkins, a 1992 UCLA graduate, who had played under Lavin when he was an assistant to Jim Harrick. That was followed by the hiring of Patrick Sandle, an acclaimed assistant to Ben Howland at Pittsburgh and Northern Arizona. A product of Crenshaw High School in Los Angeles, Sandle knew basketball and was a tremendous teacher.

So a new staff was in place as the Bruins looked to improve upon their 23-9 record in 2000–2001, which included a Sweet Sixteen appearance before losing to eventual champion Duke in Philadelphia at the East Regional. Lavin's squad had experience and scoring mixed with raw youthful talent; this would be the first time in three years that the Bruins did not lose any underclassman to the NBA. The challenge for the coach was to make it all blend, something that would prove to be much harder than he thought.

On an October evening inside Pauley Pavilion, as practice headed toward its conclusion, there was a visitor who was not asked to leave. In fact, he was treated like royalty as he slowly made his way to a seat right off the floor. The players noticed his arrival, as did the coaching staff, who took turns paying homage to the 91-year-old with silver hair and black-rimmed glasses. John Wooden had made the trip to Pauley to provide some preseason wisdom to the Bruins, speaking under 11 championship banners, 10 of which he helped raise.

Wooden watched the last 20 minutes or so of practice, joined by former Bruin player Andy Hill, a coauthor with the coach of *Be Quick But Don't Hurry*, life lessons Hill learned under Wooden. As the last drill finished up, the players and coaches settled into a side bleacher as Wooden sat in a chair facing them. Lavin and Saia had heard the "Wizard of Westwood" many times before, as had former player Madkins and the upperclassmen. They all listened intently, though the freshmen were more in amazement than guys like Kapono, Gadzuric, and Knight. Cedric Bozeman sat in the first row, his right leg shaking while Wooden spoke. Dijon Thompson and Andre Patterson leaned forward in their seats, their eyes fixated on Wooden. The older players sat silent and listened.

"I like what I have seen today," the coach began his remarks. "You have a great blend of old guys and new guys. And the intensity was great." Wooden went on to remind the players that time goes by quickly, to play hard in practice and in games, to understand their role on the team and relish in it, to have confidence in the coaches, particularly Lavin, who was more than competent. He concluded his 10-minute thoughts telling the players that though there may be championship banners hanging above them, they should forge their own legacy as a team in an attempt to raise their own banner at season's end. When he asked for questions, there were none. Wooden took the silence as an opportunity to question Ray Young's new-age Kobe Bryant sneakers, eliciting laughs and smirks from players and coaches. When Young responded that "UCLA gave these to me," there was an uproar of laughter and Lavin smiled sheepishly. Each player was handed an autographed copy of Wooden's famed "Pyramid of Success," a triangle of motivations and actions and a pathway to success in life. Though none of the players were even born when Wooden *stopped* coaching, they understood his place at UCLA. He posed for pictures with them graciously and talked with some individually.

Every season, Wooden comes out to a preseason practice, watches the team for a bit and then gives his sage advice. This year, Lavin had invited Wooden to join him and the assistants for a dinner at one of Lavin's favorite eateries, Mateo's Italian restaurant in Westwood, after practice. By the time Lavin and Wooden arrived, it was close to 8:15 P.M. But this was not an intimate dinner with just Lavin and his assistants. Staff members from UCLA joined them, including assistant Dana Martin, Director of Basketball Operations Jamie Angeli, and Administrative Assistant Doug Erickson. Also joining the group was Andy Hill, Jim Downs, an Internet columnist and friend of Lavin's, and Chad Kammerer, a volunteer administrative assistant for the Bruins. The group totaled 14 in all.

The selection of Mateo's was not random, as Lavin is a loyal customer. Never one to shy away from a good Italian meal or a glass of red wine, Lavin had become a frequent customer to the restaurant, popular enough to have a dish named after him: cheese tortellini. (It is somewhat odd to have dinner with someone who is listed on the menu.) In addition to eating at Mateo's, Lavin is a VIP at Carmine's in L.A. and Phil Traini's in Long Beach among other restaurants. He loves the cooking, the wine, the old black-and-whites of celebrities on the wall, the jazz music playing in the background and the atmosphere.

On this night, Lavin is seated next to "The Pope," as Wooden is affectionately called by the Bruin coaches. As conversation erupted around the circular table, Lavin and Wooden drifted into their own conversation for the next hour, interrupted only by the waiter and a question from a fellow diner. They talked about the upcoming season, about working with the trio of freshmen, and about the prospects for conference play. Lavin asked a question, and then listened intently as Wooden spoke, rarely turning his head toward Lavin, but talking straight ahead, arms crossed. When Wooden spoke to the group, there was silence as he told stories of some of his early championship teams. The discussion turned to the media and Wooden remarked that he left the game when the media became too intrusive. For his part, Lavin, who may have a future career in broadcasting, added that the media mostly is dry and grim to deal with on a daily basis.

It must be difficult, coaching at UCLA, under the intense spotlight of the media and the expectations, never winning enough games. Overshadowing the job is John Wooden, the larger-than-life figure who still towers over UCLA basketball 25 years after retiring. Fans and alumni wax about the Wooden years nostalgically, quick to bring up his record when discussing the current coach.

Lavin has come to understand the influence of Wooden and the enormity of the job at UCLA. The legendary coach does not call with advice, but will occasionally write Lavin an encouraging note. He shows up at every home game and sits two rows behind the Bruin bench. His name is on buildings at UCLA and on the covers of many books. There is no escaping the legacy of Wooden for Lavin, so he doesn't try. Rather, he embraces the lessons of basketball and life that Wooden can share and readily invites Wooden to be a part of the Bruin program, out of respect. A unique relationship has developed between the two, separated by 50 years and 10 championships. They have some things in common despite their age difference: Lavin's father and Wooden were both English teachers and both the mentor and his protégé coached at Purdue and UCLA.

It was close to 10:15 P.M. when Erickson left to drive Wooden home, with the rest of group slowly making their way to the exit. Lavin's Lexus-dealer car was pulled up by the valet and he got in, cell phone in hand, fingers ready to dial as he headed toward his home in Marina del Rey.

There were great expectations for this season's Bruin team, loaded with talent and poised to make a run at a national title. Lavin knew the expectations, but also knew just how hard it is to survive the marathon and go deep into March.

Steve Lavin has learned from his mistakes. Taking over UCLA with no prior head coaching experience, he expected to have setbacks and failures along the way. He has tried to learn from those challenges. Yet he remains an enigma to some vocal fans in the Los Angeles community. They simply do not like to admit, or understand, the reality. They enjoy more the perception. Just like the movies.

4

The Luck of the Irish

IT WAS A SCENE OUT OF A MOVIE, PART *HOOSIERS*, PART FOOTBALL CLASSIC *UNNECESSARY Roughness*. It was Wednesday night, October 17, and the Notre Dame basketball team was holding open tryouts for walk-ons for the upcoming season. The tryouts were being run by the three assistant coaches, associate head coach Sean Kearney, and assistants Anthony Solomon and Lewis Preston. Head coach Mike Brey was there but not really involved, preferring to stay off to the side, scanning the crowd. Dressed in a sweater, blue jeans, and a pair of brown hiking boots, the coach looked more like an archeology professor than a basketball coach.

At first the assistants had the players go through drills—layups and dribbling and shooting—and then they split them up into squads to scrimmage. It was the cast of characters that you might expect at an open tryout for a Division I basketball team. There were some decent players, guys who were high school standouts, but not good enough to play at the Division I level. There were some students whose concept of basketball was much different from the version being played on ESPN. Guys with socks hiked up to their crotch and headbands holding back flowing curly hair did their best to impress the coaches. (There was one player not required to tryout, senior Chuck Thomas, who had been a walk-on the past three seasons and who Brey would probably add again this year.) The staff did not expect to find anyone at the open tryout, but it was fun anyway, and hey, you never know. What they could have used was a big body for practices, to take the punishing blows from center Ryan Humphrey, but no one fit the bill.

At the end of the session, Brey gathered the auditioners at one end of the court and thanked them all for coming out. Telling them "we will be in touch if you fit any of our needs." It's the same speech he gives every year, one that he hates to give but knows that he has to. As the players get up to leave, one fellow comes over, with a backpack full of books and shakes Brey's hand. "Thanks, coach, for giving me the shot," the tired-looking graduate student says.

For many of the guys on the floor this night, they had no illusions about their abilities, or about making the squad, but they cherished the chance to live out a dream. And Mike Brey knows all about getting and giving chances.

Like so many other college coaches, Brey is the son of coaches and educators. His mother was an AAU swimmer, Olympian and educator in Rockville, Maryland; his father was a well-known physical education teacher and athletic director in the same town. His mother's brother, Jack, played on Duke's 1960 ACC basketball championship team. From a young age, Brey watched his family teach, coach, and play the game of basketball, and as early as the age of two, he was adorned in a Duke sweatshirt—an omen of what was to come.

Brey had a relatively uneventful childhood in Maryland, but knew by ninth grade that he wanted to play basketball. He had attended clinics and camps run by legendary coach Morgan Wootten, the coach of a Catholic school, DeMatha, in Hyattsville, Maryland, about 20 miles from Brey's home. The self-proclaimed "gym rat" was so enamored of the coach and of the success of DeMatha that he made the difficult decision to transfer out of the public school district that his parents both worked in to commute to DeMatha. He played on the junior varsity as a freshman and sophomore and played two seasons on the varsity under Wootten, helping the team to a 55-9 record. The coach nicknamed Brey the "Prudential Playmaker," because he always "gave everyone a piece of the rock."

He played his first three seasons of college ball at Northwestern Louisiana State, leading the team in assists and steals. He still ranks fifth all-time on the school's career assist list. After his coach was fired, Brey transferred to George Washington in D.C., to complete his degree at the school where his mother was the swim coach. With no real intention of playing, he got the bug again, and after sitting out the required year, the 1980–1981 season (a year in which he started dating his future wife, Tish), Brey averaged 5.0 points and 4.8 rebounds a game as a senior at GW and was named team MVP and captain in his only season at the school. He graduated in 1982 with a degree in physical education and looked to follow in his parents' footsteps as an educator and coach.

He got a job as an assistant varsity and head junior varsity coach at his alma mater, DeMatha, the preeminent high school basketball program in the nation. More legendary than the high school was Morgan Wootten. He was the John Wooden of high school basketball and joining his staff at any level would be a great opportunity. Wootten had won over 1,200 games, 31 conference titles, and five national titles in his 45 years as a high school coach. Brey stayed at DeMatha for five seasons, teaching history and helping coach the basketball team to numerous conference and state titles and a No. 1 national ranking in 1984. Then Mike Brey got the chance of a lifetime: Duke.

As Wootten's assistant at DeMatha, Brey was in charge of handling the recruiting process for the DeMatha players, and there were many who coaches came to watch. Coaches would come to scout players, meet with the coaches, and otherwise make themselves known. Along the way, Brey formed solid professional and personal relationships with many of the top level Division I coaches. One DeMatha player who ended up at Duke was All-American Danny Ferry, who joined the Blue Devils in 1983. Brey was the assistant varsity coach at DeMatha when Ferry signed with Duke. Three years later when an assistant position at Duke opened up, Brey was hired—not because Ferry played there, but because he'd already impressed Krzyzewski, who believed that Brey would stay at Duke for a long time, and Brey came with Wootten's and Ferry's strong recommendations. Brey's hiring was not without controversy, though. There was another DeMatha player, Jerrod Mustaf, who also attracted a great deal of college interest. Skeptics said that Krzyzewski hired Brey to sign Mustaf. As it turned out, Mustaf signed with ACC rival Maryland, and when he wanted to transfer later on, Duke again missed the boat.

When Brey joined Mike Krzyzewski's staff in 1986, Duke was about to enter into one of the greatest runs in college basketball history, and Brey was there for the ride. During Brey's eight seasons as an assistant at Duke, the team won two National Championships, went to six Final Fours, and the coach helped recruit and coach superstars like Ferry, Grant Hill, Bobby Hurley, and Christian Laettner. Most importantly for Brey, though, was the ongoing opportunities to watch a Hall of Fame coach do what he did best: coach. "Both Morgan [Wootten] and Mike [Krzyzewski] have influenced me. I've probably stolen from both of those guys and then put a system together and tweaked it to fit my personality and style. I really feel that with Morgan and Mike I've had like the Harvard Medical School of coaching."

As Duke became synonymous with success, Krzyzewski's phone began to ring with athletic directors looking for bright assistants to hire. At the time, current Michigan coach Tommy Amaker was an assistant with Brey. The calls would come from mid-majors and the biggies, looking for a big name assistant to take a program to "the next level." But Brey did not jump at the first, second, or even third opportunity, and as his career would prove, patience pays off. In the spring of 1994, Paul Houlihan, the Vanderbilt athletic director, called Krzyzewski and inquired about Brey. With a sound recommendation, Houlihan began to pursue Brey, along with five other candidates. Brey had passed on other opportunities, but he was intrigued by the Vandy job. Big conference, good salary, solid academics, it seemed like a good fit. It came down to Brey and Jan van Breda Kolff, and Brey was not the lucky one.

(As fate would have it, van Breda Kolff would leave Vanderbilt in 1999 for Pepperdine, and Todd Turner, the new AD at Vanderbilt, would pursue Brey, who by then was at Delaware. But Brey was not interested anymore and declined to meet with Turner at the Final Four in Tampa to discuss the opening again. Brey had called Krzyzewski and Kentucky legend C. M. Newton and asked, "Am I stupid for turning this down?" Both men responded no.)

In the spring of 1995, Brey sat in his room at the Queensville Marriott in Greensboro, during the ACC Tournament. The phone rang. It was C. M. "I have a good friend at the University of Delaware, David Roselle. He is a good man. Worked with him at Kentucky [where Roselle was the former president]. Would you be interested in coaching at Delaware?"

Brey was shocked and excited. He was from Delaware's neighbor, Maryland, and knew the area well. He could recruit those kids and knew that Delaware had a chance to be a great mid-major. He had also received some advice in previous years from older coaching colleagues who had told him to make sure he had the support of the guys hiring him and that he liked them. Brey trusted Newton who trusted Roselle. He told Newton that he was interested. Ensuing phone calls and meetings between Roselle, Delaware athletic director Edgar Johnson, and Brey took place in late April and in May 1995, Brey became the Delaware coach.

At Delaware, Brey's success was unparalleled. His overall record of 99-52, accumulated in five consecutive winning seasons, included two trips to the NCAA Tournament and a postseason NIT trip. He was the America East Coach of the Year for 1997–1998. His fourth season, 1998–1999, the team finished 25-6 and won the America East title.

The Blue Hens lost a thriller to Tennessee in the first round of the NCAAs, 62-52. In his last season at Delaware, the Hens went 24-8 and advanced to the NIT. Perhaps even more important to Brey's coaching resume, every player who completed their eligibility at Delaware had graduated. The former history teacher and high school coach had become one of the most sought after coaches in the country. Edgar Johnson knew it was a matter of time before Brey left. But the story of where Mike Brey *didn't* go is as compelling as the story of where he did.

John MacLeod resigned from Notre Dame after eight seasons and the Irish were looking for a new head coach as the 1999 NCAA Tournament got underway. With Delaware and Duke on his resume, and a solid reputation as a coach and educator, Brey became a front-runner for the Notre Dame job. But a crazy ten days in March 1999 ended up with Brey right back where he started.

Sunday, March 28. Brey took the Amtrak train from Wilmington, Delaware, to Penn Station in New York City, to meet with Notre Dame athletic director Mike Wadsworth and associate athletic director Bubba Cunningham. They met in the plush Waldorf Astoria hotel to discuss the job. After meeting for close to an hour, Brey headed back to Penn Station to catch the train. He was not as excited on the trip home as he had been going up. As he stepped off the train in Wilmington, he wasn't sure of his interest, but knew he was still one of five candidates.

In the meantime, Brey had also been talking with Georgia athletic director Vince Dooley, who was searching for a new coach. Dooley's assistant Dick Bestwick had gotten a call from his friend, Wyoming AD Lee Moon, who had offered Brey the Marshall job when Moon was the AD at Marshall. (Brey declined and the job went to a Rick Pitino assistant, Billy Donovan.) Moon recommended Brey to Bestwick who then told Dooley, and soon both Brey and Georgia were interested.

Monday, March 29. The day after Brey had taken the train to New York to meet with Notre Dame, he took a Delta flight from Philadelphia to Atlanta to talk with Georgia. He met with Dooley and Georgia President Dr. Michael Adams at the Delta Crown room in Atlanta. Brey was impressed with Dooley and certainly liked the large contract, but Georgia was balking at a six- or seven-year deal. Dooley and Brey agreed to meet in Tampa on Friday or Saturday during the Final Four weekend. Dooley was nervous because he knew Brey was in the running for Notre Dame and could be a candidate for other jobs. Brey got back on a flight to Philadelphia. Later that night, he heard from Bestwick, who told Brey that "he was their man."

Saturday, April 3. Brey convinced his wife, Tish, to go with him to the Final Four in Tampa, though she had been to so many already, because "these three days could change our lives." They met with Adams and others in Tampa on Saturday morning at a hotel far from the coaches' headquarters. Still in the running for the Georgia job was Tulsa's Buzz Peterson and Rhode Island former UCLA coach Jim Harrick. As Brey and his wife got back to the coaches' hotel, Brey sent Tish out to the lobby to scope the scene for coaches because Brey knew all too well how it worked—he would be swamped with coaches looking for assistant jobs now that his name was out there for Notre Dame and Georgia. At the second Final Four game Saturday night, Dooley sat two rows behind Brey, and in between games he told Brey that "you're our guy." They agreed to meet Sunday morning.

Sunday, April 4. Dooley and Adams met with the Breys on Sunday morning and offered the Georgia job to them. But something didn't sit well with Brey and, after letting Dooley and Adams know that he still wanted to meet with Notre Dame Sunday afternoon, it seemed that Adams cooled to Brey. He knew Dooley would be retiring soon, and without Adams' support, Brey wouldn't have "his guy" in there (remembering the advice from years past). Brey met with Notre Dame officials Sunday afternoon for what he described as a "general interest" meeting.

Monday, April 5. By the championship game, Brey had taken himself out of the running for Georgia, and he also was out with Notre Dame after he received a phone call from Bubba Cunningham. Brey didn't know who was getting the Irish job, but he knew it wasn't him. After the final game, he went to the Hyatt bar and sat with other Notre Dame candidates Dan Monson from Gonzaga and Skip Prosser from Xavier. They were teasing each other about losing out on Notre Dame. None of them knew who the next Irish coach would be and certainly had no idea Matt Doherty was in the picture. Brey called his boss, Edgar Johnson, who was also in town for the Final Four, and who probably was sweating out the weekend, to inform him that he would be staying at Delaware. He and Brey agreed that the coach would make it official the next night on his weekly radio show back home in Delaware.

Wednesday, April 7. While in his office on Wednesday morning, Brey received a call from his wife. Dick Bestwick from Georgia had called their home looking for him. "Uh-oh," Brey thought to himself. "They're calling to make sure I keep quiet about the Georgia search process and keep low on the PR radar." Jim Harrick was to be announced as their new coach and they didn't want other candidates' names out there. But when Brey returned the call, he discovered Bestwick's call had not been to keep him quiet.

"Mike, how would you like to be the next coach at the University of Georgia?" Brey realized that Harrick must have changed his mind; now it was an emergency. Dooley was on a hunting trip and couldn't be reached and President Adams needed a coach. "I'll give you an hour to think about it. Call me in the president's office then." Brey didn't need an hour to think about it. He was already committed to Delaware and didn't want the Georgia job anyway. He did call the president's office, but threatened to hang up if the secretary put him through. "Just tell him thank you, but I am not interested." It was a day later when Jim Harrick changed his mind, again, and became the Bulldog coach. Brey thought to himself, what if I had taken the job in the meantime?

A year later, in the spring of 2000, Brey's name was again mentioned for every coaching vacancy. He told Tish that his window of opportunity was getting smaller. Had he made the right choices by staying at Delaware? When is it best to jump ship from a mid-major? He did come to realize that he and his family had a good life in Delaware. He made more money than he ever imagined and lived in a great community close to his parents. He loved his job, had great support from the administration and had met with Delaware officials about the future. Life was pretty darn good. But was there another challenge?

In March 2000, Brey met with Georgia Tech officials in Philadelphia, at his home in Newark, Delaware, and again at the Final Four to discuss their coaching vacancy. However, in a week's time, new candidates had come to the forefront and Georgia Tech was off of his list. Miami coach Leonard Hamilton had decided to leave to take the Washington Wizards job and had called Brey asking him to at least talk to the Miami administrators, even though Brey knew from the outset that Miami was not a good fit for him. He met with the Miami officials in D.C., along with Hamilton. After the meeting, it was clear that Brey and Miami would not be happening. A few months later, though, things would be happening for Brey.

Rehoboth Beach, Delaware, is a vacation spot with which many on the eastern seaboard are familiar. A family beach, the sun, sand, and surf bring millions into the Delaware economy each year. Families from Pennsylvania, Maryland, and Delaware rent homes each summer on streets, "avenues," called Philadelphia, Atlantic, Chesapeake and, of course, First Street. In the middle of Philadelphia Avenue, about a block and a half from the sand, the Brey family has owned a home since 1998, which they visit for a few weeks every summer. It is a typical beach house, with three bedrooms upstairs, a den, a kitchen and bathrooms downstairs, and the obligatory front porch with chairs that have seen their prime.

The Breys would usually come to Rehoboth for the first few weeks of July, and Brey would come and go as he traveled the summer evaluation circuit to places like High Point, Indianapolis, Teaneck, and Las Vegas. Tish and the Brey children, Kyle and Callie, would stay behind, enjoying the warm weather and the many fine restaurants at the beach. Rehoboth was only an hour and a half drive south from Newark, the home of the University of Delaware and of Mike Brey's America East champions, but it was a getaway from the mayhem.

July 7, 2000, was a typical beach day, just like the ones he enjoyed when he was in town. The Breys would sit on the front porch in the morning, eat bagels, and read the papers: *The News Journal* for the Delaware tidbits, *USA Today* for the big time news. As he read through the sports section of *USA Today*, he came across an article regarding Kansas' coach Roy Williams' decision to decline North Carolina's offer to become their head coach. A light went on in Mike's head. "Tish," he said across the table from his seated position on the porch. "We may have to get ready for South Bend."

Like a great basketball mind, Brey always thinks two steps ahead. On this particular morning, he could see the pieces falling into place. Now that Williams had turned down the job, and after George Karl and Larry Brown had already said they were not interested in coaching the Tar Heels, Brey knew that UNC would go after Carolina alum Matt Doherty, who had taken the Notre Dame job just a year earlier, beating out Brey for the job. And as in 1999, when Brey did not get the Notre Dame job, he was anxiously looking forward to a potential move to South Bend.

July means evaluation and recruiting time for coaches, and they head out like cattle to scout the next crop of players. It was Saturday, July 8, and Brey was in Indianapolis watching players at the Nike camp at the morning session. He was approached by Perry Clark, a friend of new Notre Dame athletic director Kevin White, who had coached under White at Tulane. Clark asked Brey if he would be interested in the Irish job. Again. He told Brey what a great guy White was (remember the advice) and that Brey would be hearing from White. In between the morning and night sessions at Nike, Brey went to lunch at Palomino's in downtown Indianapolis. Who did he see upon entering the restaurant? Coach K. His mentor thought that Notre Dame was a perfect fit for Brey and it was time that he (Brey) got out of a comfort zone at Delaware. After the late lunch, Brey decided not to return to the evening session of Nike, for he knew he would be inundated with job requests as word spread. And he didn't even have the Notre Dame job yet.

Brey returned to Newark on Sunday and waited for a call from Kevin White. On Monday, he received a call from Notre Dame associate athletic director Missy Conboy, who had called Edgar Johnson seeking permission to talk with Brey. Conboy asked Brey if he was interested in the job and would he take it if offered. Brey again stated his interest and was told that White would be calling. He did call, the next day from Chicago's

O'Hare Airport, running to catch a flight to Rome to talk with P. J. Carlesimo about the Notre Dame job. White figured that Carlesimo was not interested, but he had to explore it. White told Brey that he would talk to him Thursday night in Washington, D.C., a meeting previously arranged by Conboy. It was during that initial phone conversation that Brey told White that he wouldn't get into a horse race for the Notre Dame job. "Delaware has been good to me and I won't have a public jockeying again." White assured Brey that he was one of "two and a half guys" up for the job. Brey, Carlesimo, and Oregon coach Ernie Kent—though White still refuses to acknowledge the candidates on the record.

On Thursday, July 13, Mike Brey had one of those days. The days that change your life. Most of the Notre Dame family (administrators, president, Board of Trustees) would be in D.C. for a ceremony honoring Rev. Theodore M. Hesburgh, C.S.C., the past president of Notre Dame who served 35 years in that role in addition to sitting on presidential committees and numerous boards. After the ceremony, Brey met with White, current President Rev. Edward A. Malloy, C.S.C., the vice-president and members of the Board for close to two hours. Kent was to be interviewed after Brey. While walking out of the meeting, White asked Brey where he could reach him that night. Brey was headed back to Newark and told White, "You know where you can reach me." As Brey got into his car for the hour and a half drive home, he had a good vibe about the Notre Dame job.

He called Tish and told her, "I think we will get this. If I don't and I am wrong, then I can't read people." He wasn't wrong. White called him at midnight and asked Brey if he was offered the job, would he take it? Without hesitation, Brey said yes. They hung up. A few minutes later, White called back and Brey was the new coach at the University of Notre Dame. He didn't even have a contract, but knew the numbers and terms would be in his ballpark. A Notre Dame private plane would pick him and Tish up at 9:00 A.M. Friday morning, the next day, just hours away, at the New Castle County Airport in Delaware. Brey wanted more time to tell his Delaware players, Johnson and Roselle. White said OK—the plane would be there at 10:00 A.M.

Early Friday morning, Brey called some of his Delaware players to tell them the news. The older ones had expected it, the younger ones were disappointed. Brey called Johnson and told him, and tried to see Roselle, but he was out of town. Notre Dame had called a press conference for 5:00 P.M. in South Bend. Brey and his wife headed for the airport to meet the plane at 10:00 A.M. On the tarmac, they were greeted by Mike Harkins, a major player in Delaware's political scene and, at the time, the head of the Delaware River & Bay Authority. Harkins was also a big-time contributor to the University of Delaware. "You sure you are going?" Harkins asked Brey. There were only two pilots on the plane, no Notre Dame officials. Harkins ducked his head inside the plane and told the pilots, "If there is no one there to meet him, you bring his ass right back here." Brey smiled, the pilots closed the door to the plane, and Mike Brey had finally said good-bye to Delaware.

Of course, upon landing in South Bend, Brey was whisked to his news conference and then had to face his new team. In a moment that tells you everything about Brey, he asked White for a few minutes to change before he met with his new team. He put on a short sleeve shirt, shorts, and sneakers and then went into the players' lounge to speak to his new players. "I knew from the first day he came in, he was going to be great," says junior Matt Carroll. It had been a long journey for Brey and his family, but they were finally where they were supposed to be.

Immediately after his hiring, Brey's first priority was recruiting. In particular, he had to solidify and reassure Indiana's Mr. Basketball Chris Thomas, a highly coveted recruit who chose Matt Doherty and Notre Dame when he was a high school junior. It was the summer recruiting period when Brey was hired, so he hopped a flight to Florida where Thomas' AAU team was playing in a tournament. For five days he watched the talented high school player dribble, pass, and shoot, all of which left college coaches salivating. A few days earlier, Thomas had turned on *SportsCenter* and was stunned to learn that Doherty was leaving South Bend for Chapel Hill. He was hurt and confused. Should he follow Doherty to Carolina or stick with Notre Dame? He couldn't decide.

"The whole recruiting process made me commit early," he says. "[As a junior] I wasn't in a position where coaches could call me yet, but I could take visits. I would get 10 to 15 FedExes a day, sometimes two or three from the same school.

"Sometimes I would read the labels or letters and they would be addressed to a different first name, but the last name Thomas. I thought, 'How many guys are they sending this to?' I sorted the mail out from the schools. Sometimes I would just throw it in a file. I had three wastebaskets filled three or four feet high. I started getting rid of them. They were all good schools, I just wasn't interested in them. When I would get 200 letters a day from one school, that would turn me off to them. Why would they do that just to convince me to come there?"

So when Doherty left, the last thing Thomas wanted to do was go through the recruiting process again. He was shocked and hurt by Doherty's departure. "At least he could have called me beforehand and let me know. To learn about the coaching change watching television wasn't fair." Doherty would contact Thomas shortly after the announcement, apologizing for the abrupt departure and offering Thomas the chance to follow him to North Carolina. "But I also understand if you stay at Notre Dame, because that is where you wanted to go," offered Doherty.

Thomas has no ill-will toward the man who recruited him and, in fact, is mature enough to understand that college basketball is a business. But as Thomas and his family got to know Brey, they came to the conclusion that perhaps Notre Dame still would be a good fit, and Brey would be a coach Thomas would want to play for. He reiterated his commitment to Brey and the coach had succeeded in solidifying the future of the Irish program.

In addition to securing Thomas, Brey also tracked down Jordan Cornette, another talented high school senior who could see playing time in the 2001–2002 season. It was a hectic summer for Brey, not only recruiting, but also putting together a staff while living in a hotel. Sean Kearney followed Brey to Notre Dame after being an assistant to him at Delaware, and Brey added former Clemson assistant Anthony Solomon to the fold. His final hire was former VMI big man and assistant coach at Coastal Carolina, Lewis Preston. The staff did not know each other, but would bond through the fire of the season. When the season finally rolled around, it was a relief just to be coaching. Of course, it helped that the cupboard wasn't bare upon their arrival.

Led by All-American Troy Murphy, the Irish went on to win 20 games in Brey's first season, including an 11-5 record in the Big East West Division, earning them a share of the Big East title. As Murphy averaged 21.8 ppg, junior Ryan Humphrey emerged as an inside threat scoring 14.1 ppg. On the perimeter, junior David Graves, sophomore Matt Carroll, and senior Martin Inglesby added a combined 34 ppg, with Inglesby running the show at point. The team lost in the second round of the NCAAs to Mississippi in the Midwest Regional. It was an amazing year for Notre Dame basketball and for their new head coach.

Most coaches will tell you that it is much harder to repeat and defend as champions than it is to win the first championship, a lesson the Irish would soon learn. There were new expectations and a new level of excitement in South Bend for the basketball team, surviving in the shadow of the storied football program. In the spring of 2001, after consultations with his coach, Murphy declared for the NBA draft, leaving a gaping hole for Notre Dame and suddenly lowering the expectations from the fans and media.

After Murphy decided to go pro, the day he announced his intentions at a press conference, Brey gathered the team at his house and popped in a tape of the Irish win over Georgetown the past season, a game that they finished without their star. Murphy had fouled out with the Irish down, but the team battled back in the final four minutes to win a crucial game en route to the Big East West title. The players watched themselves battle back and win on the road without Murphy. They could do it then, why not now? Particularly for the seniors, Graves, Humphrey, and Harold Swanagan, there was a chance to now enjoy the spotlight that previously shined on Murphy.

Even without Murphy, Notre Dame would still be a force in 2001–2002. Humphrey had transferred from Oklahoma in 1999, and sat out that season according to NCAA rules. In his first season with the Irish, the 6'8", 235-lb. junior from Tulsa averaged over 14 ppg and nine rebounds in starting every one of his team's 29 games. He was a third team all–Big East selection and scouts and media members took notice. Humphrey was an unabashed kid with a southern accent who seemed to flourish at Notre Dame, on and off the court. He was a conference academic All-Star with a high GPA. He was the workhorse for the team and would be the center of attention in 2002.

Joining Humphrey in the front court would be the 6'7", 247-lb. senior Swanagan from Hopkinsville, Kentucky. Swanagan's story is an uplifting one, a journey out of poverty to become the first member of his family to earn a college degree—at Notre Dame nonetheless. He is a likeable guy, funny, intelligent and everything that college basketball should be about. Coming off of the bench in 2000–2001, he looked to fill in for Murphy's absence in the Irish starting front court this year.

Swanagan's high school teammate at University Heights Academy in Lexington, Kentucky, was Irish senior captain David Graves. The son of a wealthy architect, and the neighbor of former Kentucky coach Rick Pitino, Graves had come to Notre Dame to build a tradition, to win, and to get a degree. There were times in his first three years when he questioned his choice of school, but ultimately came to the conclusion that it was the place for him, particularly playing for a guy like Brey. Though Graves was a scoring threat and experienced player, he was also a project for Brey. Graves at times became unraveled, upset at playing time, his contributions to the team, and his own ability. Brey knew he needed Graves big time this coming season and did everything he could to keep him happy.

Matt Carroll was from Horsham, Pennsylvania, and with deadly outside shooting, started as a sophomore, routinely scoring in double figures. Teamed up with Graves in the back court, he was half of an impressive shooting combo that would force defenders to hesitate when double-teaming Humphrey. Torrian Jones, Tom Timmermans, Chris Markwood, and junior Jere Macura were all in the mix and expected to get minutes. Added to this veteran group would be the freshmen Thomas and Cornette. Maryland transfer Dan Miller had to sit out the year, but would be instrumental in practices.

So as preseason practice got underway for Brey and his team, the coach had higher hopes than many in the media. He knew that his team could be solid even without Troy Murphy; he just didn't know how good. The afternoon after the open tryouts, Brey and his assistants sat in chairs in their meeting room. It's a miniconference room with a mahogany wood table, chairs, three television sets, and a small refrigerator. It was close to 2:00 P.M., the usual time for the staff to meet, to talk about practice, injuries, and recruiting for 20 minutes each afternoon. As they began, they talked about the health of their players, particularly Carroll, who had injured his groin the previous day in practice. Head trainer Skip Meyer popped in to give his input, and the coaches decided to have Carroll sit out practice that afternoon. They revised the practice teams and the numbers for drills to account for Carroll's absence.

"You know who is playing well is Jordan [Cornette]," Solomon noted, a statement greeted with support from Preston. The coaches threw out their opinions on who was playing well and who needed to step it up. They all seemed content with Thomas' progress so far and his level of maturity. Brey mentioned who the visitors would be at practice and reminded his assistants to make sure all visitors stayed above the lower seating in the arena during practice. As per schedule, the meeting broke around 2:25 and Brey headed back to his corner office to prepare for practice at 3:15 P.M. Brey has a great relationship with his assistants, and he allows them the freedom to contribute to discussions and planning, something that not all head coaches allow. "I don't think we have ever had a bad discussion," says Kearney, who has been with Brey for seven years. "We haven't always agreed on things, but he never makes you feel that you can't speak your mind."

The clock read 0:07 left in the game and the Irish were down by a point, 74-73. They had only one timeout left, but had a foul to give as their opponent inbounded the ball underneath their own basket. There was a sense of urgency and excitement on the Notre Dame faces and the coaches anxiously awaited the outcome. The ball was inbounded safely, and the player was immediately fouled by Chris Thomas, with only a second run off the clock. They inbound it again cleanly, and again, Thomas fouled the ball handler. He missed the front end of a one and one and the Irish raced the ball down court for a shot. Thomas spotted Matt Carroll open near the corner, threw the ball to him, and Carroll calmly sank a bucket from just inside the three-point line, giving the Irish a one-point victory. The crowd went nuts. All five of them.

This was not a heated Big East conference game on television, but rather a drill in one of October's practices. Every day, Brey has his team put into an end-of-game situation with time, fouls, score, and timeouts all playing a factor. He wants his players to face the urgency in practice, so come game time, it will all seem to move at regular speed.

Another thing unique to Brey's practices is the length. Sometimes the Irish will practice an hour, other days maybe an hour and a half, at the most two hours. Get in and get out. In fact, you get the sense that Brey wished there were fewer days and less time to practice. Game days could not come soon enough for him. His practices are nonstop, competitive drills, usually between the Whites and the Blues. The Whites are the starters with the rest of the team the Blues. Brey makes no bones about who his starters and key guys are. He doesn't keep the players guessing as some coaches might.

"These are my guys, and they need to know that. I don't play games with the kids' heads, keep them guessing about who is starting, making sure they all practice hard so I keep them wondering. No, they will practice hard anyway. And on the flip side, it even encourages the players on the Blues [nonstarters] to set a goal to be a White." As of late October, the Whites include Thomas, Carroll, Graves, Swanagan, and Humphrey.

In a typical Notre Dame practice, the Irish are on the floor of the Joyce Center, or their practice floor, "The Pit," by 3:15, shooting around. Strength and conditioning coach Tony Rolinski circles them up and stretches them out as a team, as Brey and the staff talk quietly off to the side. When the six minutes of stretching are over, the players scamper to their feet and run down to a baseline where they will slide across the floor in defensive stances until they hit the free throw line where Brey is standing. He will give them his prepractice thoughts. Of course, short and to the point.

Often the practices start with a "5-0" full-court drill. It is that simple. Brey, or one of his assistants, will take a free throw (hit or miss) as the Whites are positioned to rebound. Make or miss, the Whites are off and running to set their offense. The players hit their spots, make cuts, pick, screen, go backdoor, and pass until the shot is there. All of this is done with no defense. After the bucket, the players quickly hustle back on defense to defend a long pass. By the time the Whites have backed up to midcourt, the Blues are ready to go at the foul line, and the drill continues.

Also typical of an Irish practice, and in most coaches' practices, is the splitting of the team into "Bigs and Per" (UCLA's "Post/Perimeters"), referring to their height and position, not stature on the team. At Notre Dame, former Virginia guard and assistant coach Anthony Solomon takes the guards, and runs them through shooting and dribbling drills at one end of the floor. At the other end is associate head coach Sean Kearney and assistant coach Lewis Preston. They run the forwards and centers through drills as well, focusing on rebound positioning, inside offensive moves, and close-range shooting.

As practice continues, Brey brings everyone together and may run a three-man weave fast break drill. There may also be "shell" drill work or five-man defensive positioning, where the focus is not on the offense and the passes, but on the positioning of the defenders. This may include zone and man defenses, and may vary depending on the type of defense to be employed against an upcoming opponent. As usual, the Whites and Blues are the select teams.

Toward the end of most Irish practices, there is five-on-five full-court play. Brey is a big believer in letting the kids play and scrimmaging is the ultimate game-readiness drill. After 10 minutes or so of the five-on-five game, Brey will institute the game situation for that day. He will huddle the teams, inform them of the time left, score, timeouts, and fouls, and let them play. The score and time is also put on the game clock by the team managers. The team plays out the situation and may repeat it, to make sure they are comfortable.

At the end of practice the entire team lines up to take free throws and, as a group, they must hit 10 of 13 to avoid running. One by one, the players step to the line to the encouragement of their teammates as the coaching staff looks on. Occasionally, when the team has not hit the minimum, Brey will pick a player to shoot one-and-one and, if he makes both, the team is spared from running.

A typical Notre Dame practice schedule:

3:15–3:25	Stretch
3:25–3:30	No Walks-2 Man Pass-3 Man Pass
3:30–3:35	5-0 Full-Court Motion (Audibles) to 21
3:35–3:40	2 Baskets-Bigs 2 on 2 (switches, blockouts)
	Per 3 on 3 (switches)
3:40–3:45	4 on 4 (ballscreens, stagger, 5 trans)
3:45–4:05	5 on 5 (random, vs. zone, vs. pressure)
4:05–4:10	2 Baskets-White & Blue intro
	No. 2 and No. 3 set 5-0
4:10–4:15	5-0 Full-Court Motion No. 2 set end of clock
4:15–4:30	5 on 5 (sets, FT, sits)

4:30–4:35	3 in a row Break
4:35–4:50	5 on 5 (vs pressure)
4:50–4:55	Game Sit White 71 Blue 69, White 1 FT, 14 sec, both bonus, 2 TOs each, Blue possession arrow
	10–13

The environment at a Notre Dame practice is one of all business, perhaps inevitable when you only have 100 minutes to get so much done. There is the occasional joke or miraculous shot that causes a laugh, but in general, the practices are no bull, constant moving sessions. Brey instructs, but only in spurts, and only to make quick points. He relies on his assistants a great deal to run practice, often standing at midcourt swiveling between two drills at opposite ends. He remains calm, reflective of his personality, but there is the occasional outburst. Because Brey is not a big believer in intricate set plays, he does not have to devote a great deal of practice time to running them. Players who like to just play would like to play for Mike Brey.

The Notre Dame practices are efficient and organized and, at times, incredibly short. Brey believes that he can get more effort out of his players in 100 minutes than he could over two and a half hours of practice. The team does take a few breaks, but they do not leisurely walk from one drill to another. They know the routine. As the season goes on, the practices become even shorter in length, with an emphasis on five-on-five work.

Like the practices, the Notre Dame practice plans are short and to the point. They are often handwritten by Brey at some point during the day, and often hard to comprehend as his penmanship is not the greatest. But the plan serves its purpose, alerting managers and the coaching staff what the order of drills will be.

On Friday, October 19, practice in the Joyce Center had close to 25 onlookers. Why? Well, according to Brey, it's "the pilgrimage." Whenever Notre Dame has a home football game on Saturday, fans start arriving as early as Tuesday. By Friday, the campus is exploding with thousands of fans, and the Joyce Center and men's basketball office is not immune to the faithful. In fact, Brey and his assistants know the drill well, so on Fridays before football games they will arrive at the office as late as possible and make sure the door to the back offices is closed. It may seem comical, but the number of uninvited fans who just want to stop in and say hello is overwhelming. Brey doesn't have a problem with them at practice, as long as they stay quiet and sit away from the floor.

After the Friday practice, Brey and Tish, Solomon and his wife, Tracy, and Preston and his wife, Angela, all headed to athletic director Kevin White's house for a cocktail party. The night before all home football games, White hosts close to 400 coaches, staff members, alumni, and friends at his home on the outskirts of South Bend. Cars were parked all over the neighborhood, some five blocks away. Though they would probably prefer to be at home relaxing, the Breys are both personable people who know events like these are part of the job. So as Tish talked with Tracy and Angela, Brey gleefully answered alumni questions about the upcoming season, talked football with an athletic department staffer, and barely had a minute to grab an appetizer or take a drink of his beer. He and Tish stayed for almost an hour and a half, and then they headed home.

The Breys live in Granger, Indiana, just five miles away from campus, in a neighborhood that also is home to his assistant coaches and numerous Notre Dame football staff. The Breys home sits on a lake, complimented by a lakeside swimming pool, a large deck off the house and, of course, a basketball hoop. They entertain downstairs, where there is an entertainment center room, with a large screen television and black leather seats arranged movie theater-like. Everything from Brey's first-floor office to the family kitchen to the upstairs bedrooms was designed and decorated by Tish. The home is a far cry from the hotel and rented home the Breys lived in before building their home.

Absent from the soiree at White's home was Kearney. On this night, like on so many others, Kearney was at the office putting together a video highlight reel of the good and bad in practice over the past few days. Ten minutes of good, ten minutes of bad. Brey will show the tape to the team before the start of Saturday's practice, spending a great deal of time focusing on the starters, and pointing out many details to Chris Thomas. In the first few weeks of practice, Brey will spend a lot of time with his point guard, instructing him on when to make a pass, how to huddle the team after fouls, and when it is OK to shoot.

The first week of practice at Notre Dame coincided with midterm exams, so the excitement about the start of the season was tempered by late nights in the library. Preseason is the first part of a five-part season: preseason, nonconference, conference, Big East Tournament, and NCAA Tournament. Many coaches break up the season so players focus on short-term goals. Dating back to the first team meeting on September 1, Brey told his team that success depended on two things: trust and communication. Brey could trust this experienced team and the early practices showed it, with little instruction and a more relaxed atmosphere among the players.

The Irish had not escaped the first few weeks of practice unscathed. In fact, Thomas chipped a tooth and got a nasty cut under his chin in the first days of practice; Chris Markwood got a sore Achilles tendon, and Tom Timmermans had severe tendonitis in his right ankle. Not to mention Swanagan, who had a sore ankle.

Over the fall break, October 21–28, Brey did not take advantage of the extra time to run double sessions. Instead, the team lifted weights in the morning and then had the usual hour and a half practice session in the afternoon. "I think we are ready for an exhibition game. To dress in uniforms, have a crowd, game-type situations. It will be good for Chris [Thomas] and the team." As the exhibition season nears, the Irish practices were a bit more intense, a bit more testy, as the players and coaches were eager to play an opponent. As Brey looked back on October 31, he seemed pleased with the team's progress. "I think practice has been going well. We have probably had 13 of 15 great practices, one crappy and one mixed."

In addition to practice, Brey continued to work the phones and highways recruiting in October, and the Irish hosted some recruits on official and unofficial visits. He hosted a clinic with his mentor and former boss, Morgan Wootten, at the Joyce Center, which attracted some 120 high school coaches. A few days later on October 23, Brey headed off to New York City with Carroll, Graves, and Humphrey for Big East Media Day. They were there only one night, but the players were able to take in a Knicks game at Madison Square Garden—a venue they would see more than once during the season.

So as the team headed into their exhibition schedule and began their nonconference slate, Brey was optimistic. The Irish were picked to finish third in the Big East West, as voted on by media members, a slot Brey figured they would be. But he had coached long enough to know when his teams had talent, and privately, the coach knew that this team could surpass last year's success. Flying under the radar of the press or opponents was nothing new for Notre Dame basketball, or for Mike Brey.

Mike Brey is a high school history teacher and basketball coach. That's what he is. He just happens to be doing it at the highest level in collegiate sports. Instead of a messy, cramped office shared with other teachers, he has his own in the Joyce Center on campus. But like the office holder, his office is rather simple and plain. There are a few pictures on the wall, a framed empty bracket of the 2002 Tournament and a collage of Final Fours he went to as an assistant coach at Duke. On a bookshelf sits pictures of his children, Kyle and Callie. The office walls are cinder block, painted white, with new white carpet. The whole basketball suite was refurbished in the fall of 2001 by Tish, who added a classy, authentic touch to an otherwise sterile environment. There are mahogany furniture pieces, a deep blue rug with gold patterns, and freshly painted walls.

Instead of the office suites in South Bend, the man Dick Vitale says has "stardom all over him" could be just as happy with a desk inside the cramped gymnasium offices at DeMatha High School in Maryland. For Brey, it is not about the money, the lifestyle, the spotlight. It is about the kids. As author John Feinstein says about Brey, "He doesn't need to climb the mountain to bring him happiness."

Mike DeCourcy from *The Sporting News* says that "Brey is one of two successful coaches, along with Tom Izzo, who could be your next-door neighbors. In fact, they would be better and nicer than a neighbor. It is no surprise that he has had the success that he has had at Notre Dame."

Everything about Brey is as short as his name. His practices, halftime speeches, staff meetings, timeouts, you name it, he doesn't mince words and doesn't like the spotlight on him. Perhaps the only thing he took so much time on was his future.

For a man who espouses and lives by patience, so much so that he would wait five years at Delaware for the right job, Brey goes through everything just as fast as he can. He couldn't wait for the season to get underway. Enough of these practices.

5

Exhibitionists

I T WAS AN EARLY OCTOBER MORNING, AND LOYOLA MARYMOUNT COACH STEVE AGGERS was busy returning some phone calls from his Los Angeles office. The day was like the day before, phone calls, recruit letters, a newspaper interview, meetings with the academic counselor, and the usual putting out of fires. He had been in the coaching business for close to 30 years and knew the routine. There were days when he wished he could just be on the floor with a whistle and 12 hungry kids. The phone rang in his office and he let his secretary pick it up.

"Coach," she said, "It's Jimmy Kuhn." Aggers took the call.

Jimmy Kuhn had played for Aggers at a small NAIA school in Montana, The College of The Great Falls, in the early 1980s. He was not an outstanding basketball player, but he was the kid that every coach wants to coach. Disciplined, attentive, a good student with a great work ethic, who happily put the team before "I." Kuhn last played for Aggers in 1983, but since then, he would periodically call to say hello, to fill in his old coach on his personal and professional developments. The coach had last spoken to Kuhn immediately following the tragedies of September 11. Kuhn is a New Jersey firefighter. After news of the calamity reached L.A., Aggers picked up the phone to see if his former player was OK. To his relief, he was. When the call came through on that October morning, Aggers was excited to hear from his former player.

"Jimmy, how are you?" Aggers asked, talking in a tone reserved for a father talking to his long lost kid.

"Coach, it's been pretty tough," the normally stoic Kuhn responded in a low, slow voice. Kuhn went on to tell his coach the awfulness of the previous month. He is a fireman, at a time when it's both heroic and sad to be one. He described to Aggers his work at Ground Zero during the three weeks after the September 11 attacks. The digging for bodies, the massiveness of destruction, the stench, and the unending hours. He told a story that his old coach could hardly believe. A true story. A horrible story. But there was a silver lining for Aggers in the story.

"Coach," Kuhn said holding back emotion, "you know a lot of the things I learned from you and from athletics like 'winners try to find a way' and 'never giving up'? I thought about those things at Ground Zero. Thanks, Coach, it really helped me."

Aggers had to take a hard swallow and could barely get any words out. The conversation soon ended and Aggers hung up the phone. He hasn't minded the phone calls, the letter writing, and the demanding world of coaching college basketball since that day. He is doing something he loves. Something special where he can shape young men's lives. And sometimes all it takes is a phone call to remind him of that. The events of September 11, 2001, had shocked the world and certainly put college basketball into perspective for players and coaches.

Bill Self and his assistant Billy Gillispie were in Dallas the morning of September 11. They were there to do a home visit with recruit Ike Diogu and his family. After hearing the news on television, Self called the Diogus to see if they still wanted to do the visit. They did. So Self and Gillispie tried to sell Ike and his parents (his father was in a hospital bed in their home due to a hip replacement) on Illinois as the group watched news coverage of the attacks. The visit lasted about 90 minutes and with all airline travel suspended, the coaches rented a car and drove to Champaign. "I will never, ever forget that visit," Self reflects a year later. "It will be one of those moments that live with you forever. And certainly as far as home visits go, it would be hard to have one more memorable."

But the games must go on, and as Halloween came and went, coaches around the country galvanized their players for the start of the five-month journey. That journey begins with exhibition games. With the emphasis on making the NCAA Tournament in March, coaches and administrators are well aware of the impact that scheduling games can have on their chances of making the field. With RPI (Ratings Power Index) playing a prominent role along with a team's SOS (Strength of Schedule) in determining a team's resume for the Tournament, it becomes crucial for programs to play quality teams even as the season is in its infancy. A change from past years, when most coaches lined up cupcakes to play until conference play got underway in early January. But now the entire process has sped up, not only with tougher schedules, but also with preseason tournaments in Hawaii, Alaska, New York, St. Louis, and many other locales. The 2001–2002 season would open up with the Coaches vs. Cancer Classic at Madison Square Garden, showcasing Maryland, Florida, Arizona, and Temple. These are marquee matchups just days into November.

To prepare teams for these early season games, coaches often schedule two exhibition games for their teams in late October or early November. These games are always home games, but not always played against college teams. In the past decade, there has been an explosion of traveling professional teams, foreign tours, AAU organizations and quickly assembled scrimmage teams who, in exchange for guaranteed money, put themselves up against top-level Division I teams. The players on these exhibition teams earn a little money, $100 to $500 a game, travel the country, work on their game, and perhaps expose themselves to some scouts. In addition, the owners or operators of these teams can make six figures setting up whirlwind tours with games almost every night. These exhibition teams often have a sponsor or a commercial entity backing them up.

In the past few years, Dave and Dana Pump, summer camp and tournament organizers, have assembled six traveling teams made up of former college stars taking on any college who will play them. This year, their teams were sponsored by *EA Sports*, the guys that bring you hard-hitting sports video games for your PlayStation. These squads fly or bus from one city to the next in a period of three weeks in October and November playing games nightly. The *EA Sports* teams are in no way unique. They are joined by the Chicago All-Stars, Illinois All-Stars, Australian Select, German Stars, and hundreds more domestic and international teams, put together solely to play exhibition games. And it is big business. One of the Pumps' *EA Sports* teams, as well as other exhibition teams, can make between $3,000 to $4,000 a game, and with 14 games for six teams, you can see how profitable exhibition traveling teams can be. There is also the incentive for college coaches to make headway in recruiting—or so they think. Some AAU coaches of youth teams, which include the top high school players, often will also be owners/operators/coaches of these traveling teams. It can't hurt a college coach to schedule an exhibition game against a team that is run by someone who could be valuable in the recruiting of a prospect.

Most coaches just hope to get in and out of exhibition games without any injuries. The results are often lopsided in favor of the home team. (However, one exhibition team, one of the *EA Sports* squads, was formidable enough to beat North Carolina at home in the 2001 preseason.) Playing these early games allows players to get familiar with the crowds and game situations, and for freshmen, it offers a brief glimpse at what lies ahead. The games are often marred by sloppy play, run-and-gun basketball, and egos. (Exhibition coaches/ owners often will ask the college coach if there is anything in particular he would like to see. Zone defense? Full court press? Inside play? Keep in mind who is paying the bill.)

Iowa was the first to tip off the exhibition season with a game against the Chicago All-Stars on Thursday, November 1. Alford was eager to see his freshman point guard Pierre Pierce in action, but didn't expect much in this first warmup. The Hawkeyes held the "All-Stars" to just six points in the first seven minutes and rolled to a 57-31 halftime lead. As the second half progressed the lead grew, even as Alford subbed constantly, trying different combinations on the floor. The highlights of the night were an alley-oop dunk by Pierce, a rebound slam by Rod Thompson and a thunderous dunk to end the game by the athletic Pierce. Iowa shot 57% from the floor and was led by Reggie Evans' 22 points. The Chicago All-Stars shot 34% from the floor and committed 23 turnovers—due either to a great Iowa defense or fatigue.

Alford was pleased by the effort, but like most coaches, was able to find things to work on. Iowa still had too many turnovers for his liking and the passing was not crisp, though that could be expected for the first game. The coach then set his sights on the Hawkeyes second tune-up game, this one against the Harlem Globetrotters on ESPN2 in early November. But these were not your bucket-tossing, ball-under-shirt, play-with-the-crowd Globetrotters. Rather, they were a competitive team made up of college stars and former NBA players, including some that had been cut by NBA teams the previous day. Led by Aundre Branch, Oliver Miller, Chris Morris, and Donnie Boyce, the Globetrotters would not be pushovers.

Even in an early season exhibition, Alford approached the game as if his team was up against Duke. There were scouting reports on the wipeboard in the locker room, covered with three different colors of ink. On one side of the board were keys to the game for the Hawkeyes, including playing tough, limiting turnovers, and taking good shots. There was a new intensity in Alford's pregame speech. He had his game face on and wanted his players to wear theirs as well. He saw the "stocking" of the Globetrotter roster with NBA players as a challenge, and believed that his team would meet it. As the coach spoke to the team before the game, his assistants stood off to the side as the players sat in their leather seats. Luke Recker was on the floor, stretching his leg with towels wrapped around his knee. Pierce was visibly nervous, as his leg shook impatiently and his eyes showed fear. Alford was dressed in a black T-shirt with black pants and a beige jacket, a common color scheme for what one fan describes as a "hottie." Alford left the room, but returned within seconds to continue his thoughts.

"Let me remind you that we are ranked No. 8 in the nation," the coach pointed out as he underlined the fact on the wipeboard. "This is a nationally televised game and everyone around the country will be watching. Let's go out there tonight and prove that we deserve the hype. Prove that we are among the nation's best."

Iowa pastor Jim Goodrich led the team in prayer, and they said an additional one for a sick youngster the team had befriended. With that, the team headed onto the floor, energized by the 15,500-plus screaming Hawk fans adorned in black, white, and gold. The turnout for an exhibition game was phenomenal but expected. There were high expectations for this team, Alford was the hero of Iowa City, and the coach created a 2,000-seat student section called the "Hawk's Nest," encouraging a more rowdy atmosphere.

On Iowa's first possession, Pierce turned the ball over nine seconds into the game, not exactly the start Alford had hoped for. But things settled down and Iowa, with Evans and Recker combining for 14 of the Hawkeyes first 16 points, took a 16-9 lead just five minutes into the game. But then they hit a wall. They had underestimated the physicality of the Trotters, who seemed to be able to feed the ball down low at will. The Hawkeyes' opponents went on a 21-2 run to take a 30-18 lead midway through the first half. As Iowa turned the ball over again on a bad pass by Recker, Alford merely looked up into the sky, shook his head, and let out a deep breath. He was fuming on the Iowa bench and called a timeout to stop the run. He was incensed at the lack of defensive intensity by his team, particularly by his guards. He also was pissed off at the calls, and noncalls, by the officials, stomping his foot on the ground to get their attention. The game went back and forth as the half came to a close, and with a three-pointer at the halftime horn by Ryan Hogan, Iowa was down by only six, 47-41.

Once inside the locker room, there was vocal anger and frustration among the Iowa players. Recker was upset at the lack of effort by certain guys, Evans shook his head and talked about intensity, and Glen Worley's response to Recker's criticism ignited another round of shouting. When the coaches entered, the room turned silent. Alford began to lay into the team about the poor effort and a lack of defense. He stormed out of the room to the adjoining players' lounge. But he was back seconds later. "You guys are playing such selfish basketball!" the coach said in a threatening voice. "Do you think you have to impress people because you are on television? Who do you need to impress?"

After again pointing out the keys on the wipeboard, turnovers, toughness, and now, underlined, unselfish play, the coach calmed down and walked away. And then came back again. He challenged his players this time in a fatherly tone, wanting to know how they would respond in the second half. It all seemed hard to believe this was just an *exhibition* game.

Recker hit a three to start the half, one of five on the night for him, and the Hawkeyes fought every minute to stay close to the Globetrotters. The Trotters led until 3:53 remained when the Hawkeyes tied it at 68. With 54 seconds remaining, Donnie Bryce hit a three and the Globetrotters took a 78-73 lead. Pierce hit an awkward bank three-pointer with 11 seconds left, but a Globetrotter free throw made the final 79-76. Recker finished with 25 and Evans chipped in 20 points.

After the game, Alford told the media, "I want to thank the Globetrotters for giving us this game. We knew they were going to give us their best shot and this is what we needed heading into the season. It will help prepare us." The coach was not as gracious in the postgame locker room, and the silence now was even louder than at halftime when he walked in. He told the team the second half was better, but the effort was still poor. He did not yell, yet he failed to hide the anger and disappointment in his face. He talked for under one minute.

"We will practice tomorrow at 6:30 A.M. and then again at 3:30 P.M.," the coach announced, while writing the times on the board. "We will run hard at 6:30 and then practice at 3:30."

With that, the players put their heads down, not looking forward to the early run time. Recker laid on the floor, this time with ice on his right knee. With five minutes to go in the game, he felt a sharp pain and thought he heard a pop, putting a scare into Recker and Alford. After a short team prayer, the players hit the showers and the staff retreated to the coaches' room. Alford poured over the game statistics, shook his head, pointing out the weak spots to his assistants. His assistants did the same. His father, Sam, leaned over to his son and suggested that they not do the 6:30 A.M. practice. It wouldn't help them, wouldn't send a message they didn't already know, and Recker's knee would not enjoy it. Alford, the junior, relented and called in head manager Quin Collins. "I want everybody back in the locker room in a few minutes." When Collins responded that many of the players had left, Alford said "Get them on their cells and pagers."

And with that directive, Collins and the four assistant managers began frantically paging and calling the players, some of whom had left the arena to go home, eat with family, or share a bite with a girlfriend. Within 35 minutes, all but one of the players was back seated in a leather chair. "We are not going to practice at 6:30 A.M. tomorrow," the coach let his players know. "I shouldn't need to send a message by having the morning practice. At this level, you guys should be able to motivate yourself. So I am going to give you the benefit of the doubt this time that you understand." The coach continued, "And we are not the No. 8 team in the country."

He then motioned to the seniors and said that the team was playing selfishly and he expected them to right the ship, particularly during the game. The coach was finished, the players got up and left. Recker took his time, weighted down by the ice on his knee, holding anti-inflammatory pills in his right hand. He took a video copy of the game in his left hand, and escaped the media on his way out. As Recker hobbled out of the arena, he acknowledged they could have played better, but seemed frustrated that his coach was so disappointed. "I don't care what he says," Recker said with a stern look, "we are the No. 8 team in the country."

As Recker made his way home, the coaches were not happy. "He [Recker] refuses to wear his brace in practices or games like he should," Alford angrily noted to his assistants Greg Lansing and Rich Walker. "He's scared that an NBA team will think he is hurt." The coach gave a half smile, shook his head, and retreated again to the coaches' room. Alford's wife, Tanya, stopped in the locker room with the kids, and at close to 11:00 P.M., it was late for them. "What did you think?" Alford asked his wife as their daughter climbed onto her father's lap. "This team can play better, but it is early," Tanya responded. Alford and his family exchanged hugs and kisses and Tanya and the kids headed home.

Alford's night was not over. He is the ultracompetitor and wanted to get to work right away on breaking down the film of the game. And so it was, that the coach watched the game film *twice* that evening, grading player performances on every possession. It was close to 2:30 A.M. when Alford was finally able to go to bed. He did feel better after watching the game, especially about the play of Evans, but was still disheartened by the selfish play. And this was an *exhibition* game. But what took place during the game revealed a lot about what was to come—frustration by the coach, anger by the players, sloppy play, poor effort and cracks in the team chemistry.

On the same night that Iowa destroyed the Chicago All-Stars, Notre Dame similarly dismantled a SportIsWar.com All-Stars team, 108-75, in South Bend. The crowd was not as energetic nor as large as in Iowa City, but then again, it was still football season at Notre Dame. Notre Dame led 52-36 at half and six Irish players finished in double figures, led by Ryan Humphrey who had 21 points and 14 rebounds with five blocks. David Graves had 20 points, 10 rebounds, and seven assists while Matt Carroll had 21 points. Most important, freshman sensation Chris Thomas had 14 points and nine assists in just 29 minutes. The only downsides for the Irish were their horrendous 60% (18-30) performance from the foul line and the 16 turnovers they committed. Notre Dame showed some man-to-man and 2-3 zone defenses throughout the night.

Between their exhibition games, the Irish got some good news on signing day, Wednesday, November 8. They signed a Top 20 class headed by big man Torin Francis, who had verbally committed in August in a huge recruiting coup for Notre Dame. Forward Rick Cornett had committed weeks before Francis, and guard Chris Quinn came on board months earlier in May. But signing day made it official. Indicative of the changing times in college basketball, none of the three recruits took an official visit before committing.

The pregame speech is defined in our consciousness as the Knute Rockne, Vince Lombardi, Gene Hackman in *Hoosiers* rah-rah speech, motivating teams to play hard, play for honor, prestige, and victory. We have seen it in movies, read about it in books. The image is etched in our minds. The team sits quietly on benches, nervously chewing gum, waiting for the coach to solemnly enter. He appears as a larger-than-life figure, gathers the team, and talks about how "we" can do it. How we need to dig deep and listen to our hearts. How playing together is what it is all about.

Reality, unfortunately, is never as good as the story. Most pregame speeches given by coaches are scouting reports. There are no "win this one for so-and-so" speeches, and there are very few screams, dramatic entrances, or tears. To the ire of most coaches, in all honesty, pregame speeches have little impact on the outcome of the game. A coach may hope it does, but players say differently. Countless players can barely recall what is said, and those that do, find little motivation in the speech.

With a few exceptions, most coaches follow a similar pattern. The team arrives at the arena, changes in the locker room, heads out to the floor for a 30-minute warmup period while the coaches stay behind. When the team returns, the coaches go over the scouting report, remind the players of the keys to the game, and tell them to play hard. The team leaves again for the floor and returns 10 minutes later for a final talk. It is now when a coach may talk about the meaning of the game or give a brief reminder of an explosive player on the opposition. The team does a short prayer and chant and the game begins.

Inundated with statistics, messages, keys to the game, pressure reminders, and enough stimulus to override the senses, players often come out flat. It is apparent that when one or two players do not play well it may be an individual issue. But when a whole team takes the floor unready to play, the fault may be at the hands of the coach. "I guess you can say that," Bill Self concedes. "But in reality, coaches get too much credit and too much blame for everything. If a team is not ready to play, then yes, maybe it is the coach's responsibility. But at this level, you would expect the players to know what they need to do as individuals to get ready." Steve Alford agrees with Self, noting, "I shouldn't have to motivate players to play at this level."

Mike Brey enters the locker room in a fast-paced walk and starts talking immediately, opening with a line about toughness and playing hard like men. He then points to the board, where there are two offensive and two defensive keys written in green ink. He goes over them, starts to walk to the center of the room and stands over the ND logo on the carpet. As he takes his steps toward the middle, he claps his hands, signaling his players to gather for the prayer and chant. With very few exceptions, this is Brey's pattern, and it fits his personality. Get in, get out.

Though he keeps his pregame talks short, he has been laying the groundwork for days leading up to a game. Brey is a master at psychology. Perhaps more than any other of the hundreds of coaches in America, Brey keenly understands the importance of psychology. Maybe it is a brief phone call to a player the night before. Or a simple smile to a player in practice. Or even the creation of a little tension to refocus a player. His pregame routine is more like a week-long project, methodically getting his team where he wants it to go.

As much as Brey likes to keep to himself before games, he struggles to keep people out of the locker room. His first season at Notre Dame, he would be talking to the team and see "lots of people I didn't know in the back." That changed his second year, with very few visitors allowed in. Athletic director Kevin White occasionally stops in before a game, but it is hard for anyone to ask a boss to leave. It is clear that Brey wants to be left alone, but you can't always get what you wish for.

His Irish's second exhibition game was a bit closer than their first, taking on one of the traveling *EA Sports* teams run by the Pump brothers. This edition of *EA Sports* boasted mainly players from the Chicago and Detroit areas as well as from the Midwest. In the locker room before the game, Brey went over a very brief scouting report, short even by his standards. He then left with his assistants to the adjoining players' lounge, where he walked around and drank a bottle of water. Dressed in a maroon turtleneck and dark jacket, he has the isolated look on his face that he gets before tip-off. It's not disheartening, threatening, or arrogant, it's simply total focus. As the coaches waited and watched the game clock tick down on the wall, the players, led by Ryan Humphrey and David Graves, chatted amongst themselves. Chris Thomas was a bit nervous, and his legs could not stop shaking.

As if on a dime, the game clock hit 7:00 and Brey came flying into the locker room clapping his hands. He spent a moment reminding the team to play tough and to box out on rebounds and then left them with a thought. "No one comes in to our house and wins, let's start it now." Because this is Notre Dame, Brey gathered his team in the middle of the locker room, directly above the gold N and D sewn into the plush blue carpet, and the team said a brief prayer. Game time.

The *EA Sports* team turned out to be more physical than Brey or his players anticipated. There were hard fouls, intense boxing out under the basket, and a general roughness to the game. Thomas seemed rattled a bit by the physical play and turned the ball over too many times in the first half. With under six minutes to go in the half, Humphrey went up to dunk on a fast break, and was clobbered hard by John Mobley. Mobley hit Humphrey awkwardly and his body flipped over, head first. He came crashing down to the floor on his head, making a sound both scary and loud. The Joyce Center went silent. Humphrey lay still on the floor for 10 seconds as Brey, Graves, and trainer Skip Meyer rushed over to the fallen Irish. After two minutes on the floor, with no bleeding evident, Humphrey sat up and was taken back to the locker room. He was examined by Meyer and Irish team doctor James Moriarty. They looked over Humphrey and then took him down to "The Pit" to see his mobility. They cleared him to play, but were very cautious.

In the locker room at halftime, Brey was furious, though his team was up 50-36. Not so much for the silly turnovers and poor defense, but for an overall lack of toughness. "You guys are playing as pretty as your friggin' jerseys," the coach screamed, a reference to the players' pregame decision to wear the more flamboyant gold home jerseys. "You are playing to look good. Christ, Ryan gets taken down and you guys are still playing pretty basketball."

After a few more choice words for his team, Brey walked out of the locker room but stopped at the entrance. The priest assigned to this game for the Irish had been listening in, and to make sure he covered all of his bases, Brey stopped, put his arm gently on the elbow of the priest, and simply said, "Sorry for that one." The priest smiled back.

As the coaches met in the players' lounge, they looked over the first half statistics, noting that the team had not played that poorly. The saying goes that numbers don't lie, and for coaches entering a halftime locker room, they are the basis for hope or for despair. The casual fan may look at the halftime score or pretend they are really knowledgeable and talk about rebounds or leading scorers. But for the men who make a living from the game, those are just decorations for the media. They want to know more, and they look inside the numbers for answers.

Most coaches will, of course, notice the halftime score, the opposition's leading scorers and the rebounding margin. But then they go further. They look at field goal percentages on offense and defense, typically in the 40 to 50% range. Your team shooting above 50% from the floor is a great offensive showing while allowing that percentage on defense is inexcusable. They may also take a look at the three-point field goal percentage, but with a limited number of chances, usually between five and 10, the percentage is often misleading. Better to simply look at how many threes your team is attempting.

As for rebounds, it is not simply about which team cleaned the glass more. Rebounds are broken down into offensive and defensive rebounds, and any opponents' offensive rebounds are like salt on a coach's wound. They point to that stat as a lack of boxing out by their defenders. Coaches also look at turnovers and assists, and the ratio between them. Keeping turnovers to a minimum, around four a half, is a fairly accurate indicator of a team's overall performance. Assists indicate not only scoring, but also the passing of the ball—a team playing unselfishly and taking good shots. A good assist to turnover ratio for a guard, and for a team, should be about 3-1.

All of these numbers are provided on the official stat sheet, provided to media members and coaches at the media timeouts during the game and at halftime. As the first half comes to a close, a team manager will wait for the first half "finals," make copies for the coaches, and then rush into the locker room to provide the coaches with the fodder. But beyond these game statistics, many coaches have assistants or managers keep track of even more in-depth records.

The "red zone" is the hot phrase among coaches. The area extends eight feet from the center of the rim, where games are often won and lost. Many coaches have an assistant keep track of red zone points for each team. At UCLA, Steve Lavin reveals the current red zone tally at almost every timeout, to emphasize the importance of rebounding and scoring. In addition to red zone charting, coaches keep track of loose balls gained, charges taken, free throws shot, personal and team fouls, and even time of possession. Anything that can be taken from the numbers helps a coach figure out what to adjust. And that is typically what halftimes are all about—adjustments.

The main concern for the Notre Dame staff was the condition of Humphrey. The doctors suggested he sit out the second half, but Humphrey felt good enough to return to the lineup, if only for a few minutes. And there was a catch. Humphrey was ineligible for Notre Dame's first two regular season games for violating NCAA rules concerning participation in a summer league. With this in mind, Brey knew that Humphrey would get plenty of rest and accepted the plea of his big man to start the second half.

He didn't stay in for long. On the second *EA Sports* possession, Humphrey stuck an elbow into the jaw of Mobley, who had fouled him hard in the first half, though not conspicuously enough to get called for a foul. At the next stoppage, Humphrey immediately asked to be taken out and sat for the rest of the game, with Jere Macura taking his place. He had gotten his revenge. Notre Dame opened the second half on a 23-8 run to blow open the game and, led by Graves' 26 points and Thomas' 16, won 95-70, though they turned the ball over an inexcusable 20 times. Tom Timmermans made his first appearance in the second half getting some minutes as he made his way back from ankle tendonitis.

In the postgame locker room, the crowd had gotten bigger, with Notre Dame athletic director Kevin White listening in along with assistant athletic director Jim Phillips. Brey was impressed with the second half effort, he told the team, and promised them a light practice the following day. As the players began to undress, Brey made a point of going over to Thomas, Jordan Cornette, and Humphrey individually to give private words of encouragement. Particularly for the freshmen, the coach knew how important confidence is at the highest level.

Brey left the locker room, headed to the court to conduct his postgame radio interview and then met with reporters in a media room on the first floor of the Joyce Center. He answered their questions, speculated on the health of Humphrey, and as usual, cracked a few sarcastic comments. He left the room, made his way next door to the basketball suite, and spent the next 20 minutes with his assistants in the conference room, rehashing the game.

The staff would be back in the room at 9:00 A.M. the next morning, watching the first half and part of the second of the game the night before. Sean Kearney had stayed up late and made an 11-minute highlight tape, but Brey decided to show the team the entire first half—good and bad. So the coaches sat and watched the game with director of basketball operations Rod Balanis starting and stopping the video with the remote. Brey decided on a practice plan for the day and they broke to get to work.

Later that afternoon in practice, the team gathered in the players' lounge, complete with plush leather sofas and chairs, two computers, a stereo system, and large screen television. Brey showed them the first half of the *EA Sports* game, pointing out the tendencies and mistakes by individuals, though trying to remain positive throughout. After the video, the team did some light stretching and shooting in The Pit, followed by a workout in the weight room. As the team lifted, Brey rode an exercise bike, thinking about how good Chris Thomas would be his second year after putting some bulk on in the weight room.

At an old timers' game at the NBA All-Star Weekend years ago, legendary coach Red Holtzman was coaching one of the teams, in a meaningless game, and as he walked off the court at halftime, his team had just gone on a 15-0 run to take a big lead. A television reporter grabbed him and asked, "What happened there at the end, coach?" Holtzman responded, "You know, when I was coaching for a living I couldn't really answer that question honestly. But now I will tell you the truth: I don't know. Sometimes it works, sometimes it doesn't."

It may have taken Holtzman many years to answer the question candidly, but he spoke the truth. Coaches coach games and run practices with admirable goals, but "sometimes it works and sometimes it doesn't." Most coaches will tell you that they enjoy practice more than any other time in their day. It is a solace and escape from the daily grind, pressures, and responsibilities of being a coach. It is a time to teach, a time to assess, a time when a coach can use what he has learned to make his team better. But practices are ultimately just that—practice. Cincinnati coach Bob Huggins says, "I love practice, but you know, games are our test. How motivated would you be if every classroom never had a test? Would you be able to take a class where you never had to take a test?"

The classroom is the practice court and the games are the court of public opinion. Coaches organize and run practices reflective of their personalities and of their experiences. There is no other area of coaching where a coach's past meets the present so in tune. From the length of practices to individual drills, coaches often run their classrooms the way that their teachers did.

At Ohio University, Tim O'Shea runs his practices between two and two and a half hours, less as the season wears on. Often, the amount of time spent on fundamentals versus game situations depends on the team makeup. "If you have a veteran team with guys whose skills are refined, then you can spend more time on game preparation," the coach says. "But with a younger team, because they haven't mastered the fundamentals, that affects what you spend your time on." O'Shea draws up his practice plans in the morning, though the assistant coaches and players know what to expect. He is fairly constant with his practice routine and drills and doesn't like to shake it up too much.

At Iowa, Steve Alford has practice plans done two days before the actual practice, though tweaking may be necessary. Bill Self at Illinois may plan practice a half hour before practice starts. Some coaches use detailed practice plan sheets, while others simply make notes on an index card. A select few even make practice up as they go along. Some practices have water breaks, others do not. Some coaches have their team shoot many free throws, while others have the kids do it on their own time.

There are some coaches whose practices are more legendary than their victories, with Bobby Knight ahead of the pack. But there are others too. Temple coach John Chaney is often seen as a tough-minded, old school coach who punishes his kids by practicing at 5:30 A.M. every morning. Sounds like a punishment, but nothing could be further from the truth. As a player in the Eastern Pro League in the 1960s, Chaney had time to work during the day and took a job as a substitute teacher at Philadelphia's famed Overbrook High. He soon began to teach phys ed full time and was given the "cadet" team, or freshman team, to coach. The problem was, there was no time or space to practice. The small gym was taken up by the boys and girls varsity basketball teams as well as by other sports. Chaney couldn't take his team outside to practice, since winters in Philadelphia are not conducive to outdoor recreation. The answer? Practice at 6:00 A.M. in the gym when no one else was there.

When Chaney was hired at Gratz High School in Philadelphia, he continued the early practices with an added incentive: the smell of bacon. "There were so many kids absent from school that I organized a breakfast program. A lot of these kids were latch-key kids and the parents would go off to work and leave the kids at home, and the kids always came late to school. But then they started smelling the bacon and kids would come early." Chaney continued the early morning practices at the collegiate level at Cheney State and then at Temple University where he was hired in 1982. But there is an added benefit to the early practice time, from which all schools could benefit.

By practicing so early in the morning, the players are able to attend a variety of classes, which on college campuses are often scheduled throughout the day. At most schools, student-athletes need to choose classes that are over by 1:00 P.M. or do not start until after dinner, to avoid conflicting with their sport. This limits the classes they can choose from and ultimately, their choice of major. But at Temple, student-athletes can take afternoon classes and, with such a diverse curriculum, flexibility is a must. While other teams are lacing up their sneakers in the afternoon, Temple players are taking out their textbooks. There is a mandatory study hall from 4:00 to 6:00 P.M. everyday, where players do their work and receive tutoring. Especially with Prop 48 and academically at-risk kids, the daily study halls are essential to keeping them on track.

One more benefit. With the early practice times and long days of class work, players are wiped out by 10:00 P.M. and therefore cannot go out and get into trouble. As Chaney says, "I don't want them hanging around the streets at 11 or 12 at night."

Talk to most Temple players, and they will overwhelmingly choose the early morning practice time. It's not a punishment to them; it's a benefit. The Temple practice time is certainly not the norm, with the typical Division I program practicing late in the afternoon. Players that need to get taped, rehab, or even watch film will arrive at practice much earlier. If a practice is from 4:00 to 6:00, players and coaches do not simply show up at 4:00 and leave at 6:00. Many players arrive after lunch, get in personal shooting workouts, lift, ride a bike, talk to coaches, or simply hang with their teammates. After practice, players may stay to work on free throw shooting, post moves, or just have fun with halfcourt shots. The reality is that practice is really a five-hour commitment.

To prevent coaches from overworking players, and to ensure the "student" in student-athlete was being maintained, the NCAA imposed time limits on the number of hours that student-athletes could spend in practice. Players are limited to no more than 20 hours per week of practice and must have one mandatory day off a week. But how the NCAA defines practice is critical. According to Article 17.1.5 of the NCAA Manual, "a student-athlete's participation in countable athletically related activities shall be limited to a maximum of four hours per day and 20 hours per week." There are exceptions to the rule, and in preseason practice, there are no limitations. But what does the NCAA consider "countable athletically related activities"?

Practice is defined as "any meeting, activity, or instruction involving sports-related information and having an athletics purpose, held for one or more student-athletes at the direction of, or supervised by, any member of an institution's coaching staff. Practice is considered to have occurred if one or more coaches and one or more student-athletes engage in any of the following activities: floor activity (practice), setting up alignments, chalk talk, lectures, activities using a basketball, game film review, competition, and weight training" (Article 17.02.1).

So practice is not just stepping onto the court. Any team meetings, film breakdown, scouting reports, lifting, and so on, all count toward the NCAA limits. However, individuals can do all of the above on their own, without the activity counting against them. The bottom line: realistically, every program in America breaks the rules. In most programs, a student-athlete in basketball spends more than 20 hours per week in "practice" activities. In some programs, way more. For example, a team may practice at home in the morning, travel to another city, shoot around in the afternoon and review tape and scouting reports at night. Very few staffs keep accurate count of the total amount of "countable" hours, and very few coaches are going to give the team an extra day off simply to stay under the hour limit. Even the mandatory day off, really isn't, as players shoot, watch film or work out on their own. It's all in how you define it. So coaches practice to the max—and beyond it, particularly in the preseason.

Things were relatively quiet in Champaign in early November as the anticipation built for the season opener against Gonzaga on November 16. In the days leading up to their first exhibition game against the Illinois All-Stars, Bill Self was not pleased with his team's practice habits. In fact, the team went hard the afternoon before the game in practice, unusual in Self's typical routine. Before the game at Assembly Hall, the Big Ten championship banner was raised to the rafters. Self had let the team vote for the starters, selections based on the best defenders and who had been working hard in practice.

The Illini got off to a good start against the All-Stars, but began to play poor defense and selfish basketball. The bench contributed little and at times it appeared that the players were not listening to their coach. Though Illinois easily defeated the All-Stars, 104-81, there was something missing. Sean Harrington and Brian Cook scored 17 each and Frank Williams added 16. Harrington started for Lucas Johnson. Five days later when Illinois took on Division II Lincoln University, it was the same story. (Lincoln was coached by Bill Pope, who was the head equipment manager at Kansas the same year that Self was coaching there under Larry Brown.) Illinois ended up winning 111-60 with Cook leading the charge with 20. Williams finished with 13. The Illini were so dominant that at one point in the first half, they went on a 30-0 run. Williams did not start against Lincoln, but came off of the bench after four minutes. Self had punished his star for arriving late to a team meeting and for a general lack of effort and leadership in practice.

With their opener just days away, against a Zags team that had reached the Sweet Sixteen the previous year, Self was worried. "There is just something missing," the coach mused, "but I can't figure it out. Even all through preseason practice, there was something not right. I don't know if it is Lucas' injury or what, but we are not a top team in the country right now."

It was hard to believe that the coach was worried after two dominating exhibition performances. But Self understands the minimal value of the scrimmages. For him, there was a bigger picture, the practices, team demeanor, the little things on the court, and he was not convinced that this was a great team.

There was another problem. Self was not happy with Williams' practice effort and his weight and when the captain showed up late for a team meeting, he started with his star on the bench in the exhibition game against Lincoln. It would be a real test for Self to keep Williams focused this season, particularly now that the world knew where his heart lay— the NBA. But Williams is not a "born leader," a vocal guy who people naturally follow. He was thrust into a leadership role because he was the best player on a very good team.

There was more bad news to come. The early signing period in November rolled around, the time when recruits can sign National Letters of Intent with schools, a tense time for coaches around the country. Self had already received a verbal commitment from guard Deron Williams from Dallas, with whom Self had established a relationship when Williams was a ninth grader and the coach was at Tulsa. Also on board was phenom Dee Brown from Chicago who committed in June, as well as James Augustine and Kyle Wilson. Recruiting guru Bob Gibbons rated the class No. 4. Keith Butler ended up at Temple, however. But Self wanted a big strong man. A big man named Ike. Ike Diogu had made the official visit to Illinois weeks earlier during Midnight Madness, and came away from the weekend impressed, but was keeping his hand to himself.

His family and coach Phil Sirois knew that Arizona State and Illinois were the front-runners, with UConn a distant third. As the signing deadline approached, the pressure mounted to a terrific pitch. Recruiters wanted to know which way he was leaning; classmates buttonholed him in the hallways: "Come on, Ike, who's it gonna be?" But Ike was torn. He liked the basketball tradition at Illinois and UConn, but never fell in love with either school. There were not any major turnoffs for Ike at any of the three schools.

In Tempe, Rob Evans was nervous but confident. He believed that his personality clicked with Ike's, that the young man would be loyal to his first pursuers. Self was less hopeful of his own chances; he admitted he had "a feeling" the kid wouldn't end up fighting for the Illini. Two days before signing day, a Monday, Ike called Evans from his coach's school office.

"Are you going to become a Sun Devil?" the ASU coach nervously asked.

"OK," Ike responded.

"Uh-oh," Evans thought to himself. "What does 'OK' mean?" The call ended with the question unanswered.

The next 24 hours were nerve-wracking ones for the ASU coaching staff. At 6:30 Tuesday morning, Evans' assistant Tony Benford woke him with a phone call: "Rob, the kid's made his decision. He's announcing it this morning." Evans hung up, leaped out of bed and made a beeline for the campus. He arrived at 7:00, greeted his administrative assistant Jill Adams, dumped his belongings on the floor and headed for the restroom. When he returned to the office, his assistant was screaming jubilantly at Adams. "He's going to be a Sun Devil!" Benford screamed. After years of pursuit, thousands of phone calls, letters, FedExes, and official and unofficial visits, Rob Evans' ship had finally docked. And when the news arrived, he was in the bathroom.

Ironically enough, Evans and Self are very good friends. They served as assistant coaches under Eddie Sutton at Oklahoma State and regularly stayed in touch. But over the fall months of 2001, there was little contact. They both knew why and both understood. Conversations between two coaches battling over a recruit are awkward, with each coach afraid to spill any beans. After Diogu signed with ASU, the two resumed their telephone calls. Self had lost out on a major recruit, though it wasn't such a big surprise. "When you have been in this business long enough, you get a real sense of which way recruits are leaning. Sometimes it is a good feeling and sometimes it is bad. But it's part of the business. Not everyone you go after is going to sign."

Self had more immediate problems on his mind as he readied the team for Gonzaga. How could he wake this team up? Was there something different that he could do in practice? What was bugging these guys? He thought perhaps the team just wasn't having any fun. The previous season, Self had tried something different. On the last day of "boot camp," the early fall conditioning program for the team, the players lined up on the baseline to run the dreaded "suicides," or a series of sprints up and down the court, progressively getting longer. On this day, they were to do 30 suicides in 30 minutes. As they waited to start the run, they wondered aloud where Coach Self was. They soon had the answer.

There at the door stood the 6'3" Self, dressed head to toe in army fatigues with the word "WAR" written on his shirt. His face was painted with camouflage colors. He carried a box, which contained fatigue T-shirts for all of the players and assistants. "Yes, boys, we are going to war! Take those shirts off right now," he instructed his team. They were in battle, and in a battle together. The team put the shirts on, but still had to run the sprints, with a renewed energy level. As senior Lucas Johnson remembers, "He brought himself down to our level. He was one of the guys. He wasn't afraid to put the face paint on and just be like us. It allowed us to trust him a bit more." For Self, the fatigues were part psychology, part fun. He wanted to send a message to his players that he was in it with them, that they win and lose as a team.

Now in November 2001, should he try something along those lines? No, this team was too experienced for that. How about a change in the lineup? That really wasn't the answer either, as no one individual was playing poorly. He hoped that things would right themselves by Friday when Gonzaga came to Assembly Hall.

PAC-10 Media Day in 2001 was held in downtown Los Angeles at the home of the Lakers, Clippers, and 2002 PAC-10 Tournament, the Staples Center. On Halloween

Day, all 10 head coaches came to L.A. for a morning of meetings, interviews and more interviews. In addition to each head coach, some of the well-known players showed up, including UCLA's Jason Kapono, Arizona's Jason Gardner, Stanford's Casey Jacobsen, USC's Sam Clancy, and Oregon's Freddie Jones. It was on days like this when the most popular players and coaches give "great quotes" that attract the horde of media. Sitting apart in the stands at one end of the arena, the five players conducted interviews. Jacobsen, Kapono, Clancy, and the late-arriving Gardner were swarmed, while it took a while for Jones to get a bite. That's the nature of the business. A lesser-known star playing in a small media market, Jones was no longer a big fish when sitting in the same arena as the whales. (In hindsight, the media should have been talking to Jones.)

For coaches, Media Day is often a time to exchange summer stories, inquire about families, and any other topics that can possibly relieve the monotony of the interviews. On this day, there were clearly two stars: one, a white-haired gentleman of the game from Arizona; the other, the young, slicked-hair coach of UCLA. Olson commanded respect and attention based on his age, experience, and a 1997 National title. Lavin commanded the spotlight based on his charm, early successes, quick wit, good looks and, most importantly, simply being the coach at UCLA.

As each coach spoke to the general media from a podium assembled on the Staples floor, the other coaches were in the underground hallways, being shuffled between interviews with local affiliates, ESPN and Fox. Producers of the upcoming season's games come to media days and ask the coaches about the other conference teams and players, providing the producers with the soundbites that you see months later during a game. And so the coaches marched from room to room, directed by PAC-10 assistant media relations director Dave Hirsch. For many coaches, this is a time to talk about how strong your opponents are, how much respect you have for guys like Olson, and how your team is rebuilding and is not very good. The reporters and producers get bored by the conventional responses from the first three or four coaches. And then in walks Steve Lavin. They know he is the one who will give them lively quotes, humorous remarks about himself and other coaches, and otherwise charm the men and women holding the microphones. Lavin tries to bring some levity and lightheartedness to the mundane dealings of the same questions every year.

But before entering the rooms, Lavin was holding court in the sterile, cement-walled hallway, shaking hands with conference officials, reminiscing with coaching colleagues, and pausing to talk to each player. And not with just a handshake. Lavin gave Jacobsen, Clancy, and Gardner each a hug and asked about school while cracking jokes. UCLA Sports Information Associate Director Bill Bennett and Lavin have been good friends for years, and Bennett knows the coach well, though he still gets anxious, as trying to get Lavin from room to room is like getting Brittany Spears to her dressing room in the hallways of a junior high. It is a walk that normally would take close to eight seconds, but it becomes a 10-minute wait for Bennett. After Bennett gives Lavin hints, the coach quickly said his good-byes, gives a hug, and moves on. His SID told him where to go and who was waiting for him. That's all he needed to know.

It is rather remarkable really that Lavin can interact so affably with the media, considering what he has endured from some media members in his six years at UCLA. He has come to understand the nature of the beast and acknowledges that dealing with the press is part of his job description, especially in the media capital of the world. So Lavin answered all of the questions, talked about stability, a good mix of experience and rookies, and suggested that UCLA should battle for the conference title. He recited many of the same lines, jokes, and analogies to the various media outlets, a routine he had become accustomed to. He was in a very good mood this day.

In the next two weeks, his Bruins would defeat yet another *EA Sports* team at Pauley Pavilion, 102-77, and then a week later, beat Global Sports 86-60. But they were not at full strength. Freshman starting point guard Cedric Bozeman had injured his tailbone in the first minute of the second half of the *EA Sports* game and did not play in the second exhibition game. The real start of the season for UCLA would be the Maui Invitational. There, on the picturesque island, the Bruins would participate in the most prestigious of all of the preseason tournaments and join an impressive eight-team field that included No. 1 Duke and No. 3 Kansas. Lavin felt his team was practicing well, though he was a bit concerned with Bozeman's health.

Lavin wasn't concerned that his star freshman didn't know his teammates. He had played pickup ball with them every day throughout the summer at the famed UCLA Men's Gym, where current and former pros like Magic Johnson and Baron Davis hone their skills in the summer. Bozeman had also played on an elite AAU team and had played in the various national all-star games and summer camps. He was accustomed to the high caliber of play. But that didn't mean he could handle the pressure. As Maui approached, it seemed Lavin had settled on a lineup of Bozeman, Billy Knight, Jason Kapono, Matt Barnes, and Dan Gadzuric. They had size and experience.

Early on in practice, it became clear to Lavin that he might face a dilemma. He had superior skill and experience in his veterans, yet he had remarkable talent in his trio of freshmen: Bozeman, Dijon Thompson, and Andre Patterson. He had 10 guys who could start. Hopefully, Lavin thought privately, all would go well and all would play a role. But there was the concern that by relying too much on the veterans, he might dishearten and limit the development of the younger group. And then there was the issue of Ray Young.

Young had had an enigmatic career at UCLA, coming to the Bruins as an All-American player from St. Joseph's Notre Dame Prep in Oakland. Young struggled with his game and failed to find his place on the team. He never started more than 10 games in any one season and never averaged more than seven points per game. Heading into the 2001–2002 season, Young had played in more UCLA games than any other Bruin on the current roster, but never made a serious impact as a go-to player. With that in mind, and with the knowledge that the three incoming freshmen would see playing time, Lavin sat down with Young in the spring and proposed an idea—redshirt. If Young agreed, he could come back as a fifth-year senior captain, be one of the stars of the team, and finish out his career on a high note. Otherwise, he faced the prospect of shared playing time.

Young was hesitant. He had not had a rewarding career at UCLA, and routinely was bashed in the media for not developing (a criticism of his coach as well). Young simply wanted to get the whole thing over with, so delaying it another year was not in the cards. As the season approached, Lavin again met with all of his players individually, and anticipated the meeting with Young. The coach proposed the redshirt idea once again in October and Young again reiterated that he did not want to redshirt. But surprisingly, something changed over the next month and Young relented. Lavin was somewhat pleasantly surprised at the turnabout, and happy for the player's decision. He felt good for Young for making a decision that would benefit the young man in the long run. He implored Young to continue to practice hard, to stay positive, and to play a prominent role during games and in the locker room. In fact, as the season progressed, Young was seated at the coaches' end of the bench, yelling instructions, talking to players as they came off the floor, and doing exactly what his coach had hoped.

6

Turkey Time

URKEY DAY IN THE PAST MEANT PRO FOOTBALL, NOTABLY THE DALLAS COWBOYS AND Detroit Lions. Then the college football game crept into the picture, with many major rivalries taking place on Thanksgiving Day or the weekend immediately after. But in the last ten years, another player has emerged on the sports scene while families gather, give thanks, and get fat: college basketball. The most well-known of the Thanksgiving tournaments are the Maui Classic in Hawaii and the Great Alaskan Shootout in Anchorage. In recent years, many more have been added including the Guardians Classic, Las Vegas Invitational, Top of the World Classic, Hawaii Pacific Tournament, and an assortment of four-team minitourneys around the nation. All in all, almost three quarters of Division I teams play over the Thanksgiving break.

Most of these tournaments feature one dominant team, usually the host, and three lesser teams, meant as two easy wins for the home team. But the larger tournaments with greater exposure attract many of the top teams and are nationally televised. And so as the end of November rolls around, teams pack their bags and head to warmer—sometimes colder—climates.

Iowa would play in the inaugural Guardians Classic, a unique two-week tournament with 16 teams. The first two rounds of the tournament would be played at four sites, hosted by one of the entrants. On November 13, the Hawkeyes welcomed Maryland-Eastern Shore to Carver-Hawkeye Arena and abruptly disposed of them in an 89-59 rout. Reggie Evans and Luke Recker combined for 48 points. Iowa poured it on from the start, jumped out to a 14-3 lead and never looked back, paced by Evans' 18 points and 11 rebounds in the first 20 minutes. Alford was able to keep everyone happy by playing 10 of his 11 players. Pierre Pierce did not impress though, making just one free throw with two minutes left and turning the ball over three times. The team played well and things seemed to be OK in Iowa City. Next up for Iowa was Boston University, who defeated New Orleans 69-63 earlier in the night.

So the next night, just 20 hours after finishing off Maryland-Eastern Shore, the Hawkeyes suited up against BU. They were not as gracious a guest for this quarterfinal game in the Guardians Classic. The game had barely begun when Alford was off the bench calling a timeout. Just 90 seconds into the game, Iowa trailed BU, more specifically, trailed the Terrier's Matt Turner, 8-0. Turner hit two three-pointers and a long jumper to stake the early lead. Iowa eventually clawed back, and took their first lead of the game, 19-18. By halftime, they had extended the lead to six. This was not a game for the weak at heart. In the first half, physical play, fouls, and coaching protests dominated the storyline. Five technical fouls were called in the half. Boston had decided to use a zone defense to prevent Evans from scoring, but the constant double and triple teams down low made the game even more physical. Midway through the second half, Iowa turned it on, going on a 26-7 stretch and finishing with an 11-0 run to win, 90-61. The score was indicative of a blowout, but those who saw it knew better. The play of Chauncey Leslie off the bench was impressive, with 15 points, three steals, and four assists. A point guard controversy for Iowa?

After the game, when Alford faced the media, he seemed excited for a game the Hawkeyes should have won convincingly. "This was a tremendous game for us, especially the way we rallied. . . . We were unselfish on both ends of the floor and our bench was outstanding."

And then the coach said something surprising about Recker and Evans, two guys he had blamed for a lack of leadership in the Globetrotters loss. "We saw a lot in the last two days and to get two 30-point wins says a lot about the senior leadership."

Iowa would travel the following week to Kansas City, to play in the semifinals of the Guardians Classic against the No. 12-ranked Memphis Tigers. But before they could focus on John Calipari's team, they had to play a nonconference home game against Louisiana Tech, put on the schedule many months ago. The Hawkeyes played well, though they showed signs of fatigue, having played three games in five days, as they held on for a 75-67 win to go to 3-0 on the season. Leslie played well off the bench, taking over for Pierce—the point guard position still undecided. After the game, unlike after the BU game, Alford was not happy with his senior leadership and called them out in the locker room and in the press. They had to step it up.

In Kansas City on the night of November 20, the stage was set for the first real challenge for Iowa. Memphis featured rookie sensation Dajuan Wagner, Chris Massie, and shooter Anthony Rice, and looked to prove that they belonged with the big boys. The game was tight throughout, compounded by numerous turnovers by both teams. Iowa led 36-30 at halftime and held off four ferocious Memphis rallies in the second half, solidifying the win with clutch free throws at the end. Recker finished with 20 and Evans added 19. More important to Alford was the strong play on the defensive end. Iowa held Memphis to just 37% shooting and just 26% from three-point land.

The now No. 9 Iowa Hawkeyes had gotten the matchup that they wanted—a chance to take on No. 5 Missouri in the title game of the Guardians Classic. It's not that there was such bad blood between the two teams, though there certainly was no love lost between Alford and another hot young coach, Missouri's Quin Snyder. Last season, Missouri came into Carver-Hawkeye Arena and lost to Iowa in a thrilling double-overtime game.

Iowa again let their opponent stake a big early lead, this time falling behind 10-2 just four minutes into the game. The Hawkeyes battled back and led by four at halftime. The second half was a series of dramatic three-point shots, questionable calls, and an amazing finish. Iowa was up by 11 with 2:20 remaining, but couldn't hold the lead. With 42 seconds left, Iowa was still up by six, but Missouri battled to tie it at 77. Alford was incensed at noncalls on Missouri, including one when Recker appeared to have been tackled trying to maintain possession. The Tigers' Clarence Gilbert grabbed a rebound with six seconds remaining and the score tied at 77. He raced up the court and launched a shot from inside the three-point line, double clutching, drawing a foul on Glen Worley. With 0.8 seconds left on the clock, Gilbert sunk the second free throw, giving the Tigers a 78-77 win.

The loss was devastating for Iowa. They had been on a roll, 4-0 on the season, having defeated No. 12 Memphis the day before. They had been playing well, despite giving up the early leads, and Recker and Evans were on fire. In just five days time, the Hawkeyes were set to take on No. 1 Duke in Chicago, as part of the ACC/Big Ten Challenge on national television. What a great setup for the biggest game in Iowa history with a 5-0 record and wins over the No. 12- and No. 5-ranked teams. But it was not to be. Postgame, much of the Iowa emotions were focused on the officiating; the questionable calls down the stretch and the touch-foul on the Gilbert shot. But the officials did not blow an 11-point lead; Iowa did.

In the postgame locker room, Alford used the game as a teaching tool, about basketball and about life. "There is a life lesson to be learned here today," he told his downtrodden team. "You can try your best and do everything right in life, but sometimes it can still be taken away from you," an obvious reference to the officiating. "We are 10–15 points better than Missouri, I think you guys saw that tonight. We get them again in a few weeks." The coach instructed his players not to talk about the officiating to the media. Privately, Alford continued to fume about the officials, questioning why Missouri had two of the same refs on consecutive nights, something unusual in big-time college basketball.

The Hawkeyes flew back to Iowa City and gathered at the Alford's home for a team Thanksgiving dinner. Alford tries to get his players home for two or three days over either Thanksgiving or Christmas break, but the timing of the Guardians' Classic did not allow for Turkey Day to be that time. There was a subdued mood at the Alfords this Thanksgiving as the effects from the Missouri collapse still lingered.

Before playing Thanksgiving tournaments of their own, Illinois and Notre Dame had nonconference matchups. Illinois opened at home against Gonzaga, while the Irish took on New Hampshire and Cornell in South Bend. Both teams emerged unscathed. The Illinois-Gonzaga matchup did not turn out as competitive as many had speculated, with Brian Cook scoring 18 points to lead the way in a 76-58 Illini win. Robert Archibald scored 16, Cory Bradford had 17, and Frank Williams added 13. Gonzaga star Dan Dickau scored 19 to keep them relatively close, but the Bulldogs' 20 turnovers did them in. Illinois had a 30-8 advantage from the line. Gonzaga coach Mark Few was impressed: "If they keep listening to the staff and keep playing as unselfishly as they did tonight, that's the sign of a championship team. There must have been 10 or 11 times when all five players touched the ball."

Bill Self was pleased with the performance, though rebounding was still a concern, but he thought that maybe this team was back on track—that the "missing piece" had somehow made its way into the locker room. True, the injury to Lucas Johnson was devastating, but maybe they could learn to be a tougher team without their toughest player in the lineup. As for Williams' play, he did not lead the team in scoring, but that was fine with Self. "The fact is, if Frank is leading us in scoring in a game, then we must not be playing well as a team. It means that he had to take it upon himself. So if he scores 10, 11, or 12 points in a game, that's not necessarily a bad thing."

Of course, from a media standpoint, the reigning conference player of the year and now NBA-early draftee should be pouring in more than 12 a game. He looked a bit lethargic in the win over Gonzaga and a few reporters began to write about a supposed poor work ethic in practice. In fairness to Williams, many of the writers had not been at practice, but in fairness to the journalists, they were close to the mark. Williams had never been one to go all out in practice, to dive for loose balls, to put every effort into a mindless drill. But when the lights came on and it was showtime, Williams came to play—sometimes. Self would defend his star player, at least for now in the media, and pointed out that the Illini were just one game into the season.

Three days later, Illinois ripped Eastern Illinois at Assembly Hall 93-53 in the first round of the Las Vegas Invitational. It does seem odd that the *Las Vegas* Invitational was being played in *Champaign*, but like the Guardians Classic, early round games were at home sites around the country. This time, Williams scored 20, and the Illini got great contributions from their bench. Freshman Luther Head scored on an alley-oop toss from Williams, electrifying the crowd with his leaping ability. The freshman scored 14 points on seven of nine shooting.

Asked after the game if this was Head's coming out party, Self replied, "I thought he was pretty good, but I don't know about a coming out party. He's got to get to the point where he can make open shots," a reference to two wide-open misses.

The coach was content with the win, but still did not think his team had played aggressively enough. The Illini would head to Nevada to play Pennsylvania in the second round of the tournament.

For Notre Dame's Chris Thomas, it was much more than a "coming out party" in his team's opener against New Hampshire—he had a full-blown extravaganza. He set a school record with 11 steals and became the first Irish player *ever* to record a triple double. Thomas scored 24 points and added 11 assists to go along with the 11 swipes in the 95-53 win. The game was played after a Pep Rally in the Joyce Center for the football team, as they prepared to take on Navy at home the following day. Notre Dame played without Ryan Humphrey, who sat out the first game of his two-game NCAA suspension. Big man Tom Timmermans also did not play, due to a sprained medial collateral ligament in his right knee, an injury he suffered the day before in practice in a collision with Harold Swanagan. The Irish dressed just eight scholarship players for the game. To make matters worse, Swanagan injured his right knee just six minutes in and took a seat on the bench. The Irish went on a 21-1 run in the first half to blow the game open and kept it on cruise control until the buzzer. David Graves had 26 points as the Irish held New Hampshire to just 31.5% shooting from the field.

In their second game of the season, a 78-48 blowout of Cornell, Thomas had 22 points, including hitting six of seven from three-point range. Jere Macura, filling in for Humphrey, scored 16 points and Matt Carroll added 13. Swanagan did not start, feeling some "looseness" in his right knee, but did manage to play. Swanagan's knee problems would not get any better, but at least he appeared in his ninety-ninth consecutive game of his Notre Dame career. The Irish were sparked by a 16-0 run and their zone defense kept Cornell from attacking the basket. The Irish were 2-0, but faced five games in the next 10 days.

So Notre Dame packed their bags for Hawaii and Illinois was off to Las Vegas. In Sin City, the Illini faced off against Pennsylvania in the second round of the Tournament with the game being contested at Valley High School in Vegas, a little smaller than Assembly Hall. The Tournament had been moved from the Paris Hotel & Casino, because of the criticism over NCAA teams playing in a gambling facility. Illinois did not play well and trailed the reigning Ivy League champs by 11 at halftime, only kept in the game by reserve Nick Smith's nine first half points. But behind 71% shooting in the second half, Illinois came back and won 78-71.

After the game, Self told the media "We dodged a bullet. We were not a very good team in the first half. We were slow and got into foul trouble." Succinctly put, "we were flat." Self was not happy with Williams' play, especially in the first half, and was disappointed that freshman Roger Powell still did not seem to grasp the offensive and defensive sets.

Playing flat and practicing flat was the problem from October 13 and it seemed to carry over day after day. In a semifinal game against the ACC's Georgia Tech, Illinois was anything but flat, with five players scoring in double digits en route to a 105-66 rout to set up a championship game against Southern Illinois on Saturday night, November 24. Illinois scored 67 points in the first half, and led by 33 at the break. During a 27-3 Illinois run, Tech coach Paul Hewitt called three timeouts, but could not stop the onslaught. Before the game, Self had gotten on his team about their selfish play against Eastern Illinois and Penn, and the Illini got the message, dishing out 20 assists in the first half alone. Surprisingly, one of the five Illini in double-digits was not team scoring leader Frank Williams. In fact, Williams did not even make a field goal and finished with six points.

After the game, in response to a reporter's question about Williams' poor performance, Self defended his star, "Sure he didn't make shots, but he made sure their press didn't work and he pushed the ball up the court and found the open shooters." Just because Williams didn't score much didn't mean that he, or the team, played poorly in the eyes of the coach, who saw things that the media and fans did not.

In the championship game against the Salukis, Williams scored 19, but shot only seven of 21 from the floor in a 75-72 win for the No. 3-ranked team in the country. Southern Illinois made only one basket in the final 7:40 and Illinois hit nine free throws to end the game. It was a physical game and the Salukis did not back down. There were 51 personal fouls called, including a technical on each coach. Self earned his after protesting a call on Williams in a tie-up on the floor with Marcus Belcher. Assistant coach Billy Gillispie had to restrain Self from going after the officials on the court. Cory Bradford and Sean Harrington stepped up big for Illinois. Damir Krupalija played well enough throughout the tournament to be named tournament MVP. The Illini had escaped from Vegas with a tournament title, No. 3 ranking and an unblemished record, but they still were not playing with enthusiasm and were letting weaker teams remain in ball games. Things would not get any easier for Self's squad as they had a showdown with No. 5 Maryland in College Park on Tuesday, November 27.

The weather was a balmy 80 degrees in the desert town of Las Vegas, and it was much the same on the islands. The Marriott Hotel on Maui is ideally situated on beautiful beach front, with plush gardens, pools, and a genuine Hawaiian flavor. And on Saturday night, November 17, some really tall men invaded the scenery. The UCLA team hotel also housed South Carolina, another participant in the Maui Classic, the premier Thanksgiving tournament. This year's field was the strongest ever: No. 1 Duke, No. 3 Kansas, No. 4 UCLA, South Carolina, Seton Hall, Houston, Ball State, and host Chaminade—yes, the Cinderellas of Chaminade who shocked the basketball world with a stunning upset of No. 1 Virginia and Ralph Sampson back in 1982. UCLA was paired against Houston in their opener on Monday and would most likely face Kansas in the semifinals before a possible matchup with Duke in the championship game. The Bruins arrived in Maui on Saturday night, met in a banquet room downstairs, and had a quick dessert/snack—which meant pasta, salads, chicken, and ice cream. Steve Lavin wanted his players to enjoy the week and the beautiful scenery, but also implored them Saturday night to remember why they were there.

Sunday morning, Lavin joined the other seven head coaches for a brief coaches' meeting with tournament organizers followed by a press conference. The majority of reporters' questions were directed at Mike Krzyzewski, Roy Williams, and Lavin. In fact, Krzyzewski even took control of the news conference, calling on reporters and suggesting who should answer certain questions. All of the coaches spoke "coaches speak," playing up their opponents and praising the opposing coach. Not much news in this news conference. In the afternoon, Lavin spent an hour sitting poolside with his girlfriend, reading books, and enjoying the Hawaiian sun. The players, many of whom had never traveled this far, seemed to be enjoying themselves as well, sitting by the pool, taking pictures, watching the "honies" walk by.

Sunday night, the team headed over to the annual tip-off banquet, MC'd by ESPN's Bill Raftery. The Bruin players and assistants took their seats at a table in front of the dais while Lavin took his next to Ball State coach Tim Buckley on the dais. Raftery had the place in stitches, cracking jokes about Krzyzewski being a new grandfather, Williams' southern drawl, and Lavin's single status. Raftery pointed out that Lavin was the only single coach of the eight on the dais, a fact that made Lavin, and Treena Camacho, blush.

In his remarks, Lavin's self-depreciating humor came out as he jokingly said, "I checked into the hotel last night and the bellboy asked, 'Where would you like your bags, Mr. Pitino?'" (A reference to the Pitinogate fiasco of a season past.) When Krzyzewski got up to speak, he took some good-natured jabs at Lavin's single status, as well as the gel in his hair.

After the banquet, the team met back at their hotel in the banquet room for dessert and a brief scouting report on Houston. Assistant coach Gerald Madkins went over Houston's top players, with the Bruins following point-by-point on a handout provided to them by the coaches. The package detailed the strengths and weaknesses of each Houston player, the key strategies to stop them, and offensive and defensive team goals for UCLA.

Lavin then did something different, something to get the players excited. Jamie Angeli, director of basketball operations, had put together an entertaining highlight tape of great Bruin plays in the preseason and of some lighter moments in practice and the locker room. The highlight of the 10-minute video was a dance segment, filmed in preseason, when the players danced to club beats in the locker room after practice one day. The footage broke the players into tears. Lavin wanted to keep this group loose, particularly the freshmen.

On Monday, UCLA-Houston would be the last game of the day in the Lahaina Civic Center. The gym holds about 2,700 spectators, but it feels like 10,000 inside. There is a terrible heat inside the gym, and the humidity makes a Snowcone inedible. The team benches are just inches from the first row of fans, and there is not a bad seat in the house, with the top row only 12 rows from the floor. With media, NBA scouts, fans, and alumni packed in, there is no cozier atmosphere in which to watch college basketball. ESPN was in town with Dan Shulman, Raftery, and Jay Bilas on hand to broadcast.

As the Bruins relaxed back at the Marriott, huge things were happening at the Civic Center. Unheralded Ball State, coached by up-and-comer Tim Buckley, with talented junior college transfers, shocked the basketball world with a stunning 93-91 upset of Kansas. The small Cardinal cheering section went bonkers, and the Ball State players mobbed Patrick Jackson, who had hit the game winner with less than a second to play. Lavin and some of the players had been watching the game back at the hotel, seeing just another reminder of how anything can happen at anytime in college hoops. Their semifinal matchup with Kansas was now impossible, but if the Bruins could get by Houston, then Ball State would be an easier opponent than Kansas to get to Duke.

The Blue Devils meanwhile struggled mightily in getting by Seton Hall, 80-79, and got some help from some questionable officiating down the stretch. As the Duke game came to its conclusion, the Bruins arrived at the Civic Center and headed upstairs to a small atrium outside their assigned locker room. The facilities are poor by today's standards, and the locker rooms are on par with ones from high school days. Since Duke was assigned to the same one as UCLA, the Bruins could not enter until Duke had gone in and removed their belongings. So the Bruins talked quietly, stretched out, and got taped up on the floor just outside the locker room. There were screen windows looking down over the court, so the players and coaches stood and watched the end of the Duke game. Jason Kapono picked up a new white headband from manager Howie Keflezighi and almost every player and coach chewed mightily on gum.

After the final buzzer, the Duke players and coaches hustled upstairs into the locker room, with looks on their faces as if they had suffered a horrible loss. They indeed had won, but for Duke, it was way too close. Krzyzewski could be heard telling his team to get their stuff quickly, and on his way out, wished Lavin luck in the next game.

The locker rooms at the Lahaina Civic Center are nothing more than cement blocks, with a few benches, worn down lockers, and a bathroom. The walls do not reach the ceiling, so private team talks are not possible.

"Let's pop the cork on this new season," Lavin began his pregame talk. "We saw what happened to Kansas today. It is key to focus on competing and executing." He wrote "intensity, defense, and turnovers" on the board, after locating a pen, and reminded his players of their responsibilities. After the team chant of "Together. We Attack," Lavin pulled Cedric Bozeman and Dan Gadzuric aside and gave them last-minute instructions.

The first bucket of the regular season for UCLA was a Kapono three-pointer and the first foul was on Gadzuric, something not unfamiliar to the player or his coach. Gadzuric had always seemed to find foul trouble and often spent large portions of games on the bench. After that first foul, just three minutes into the game, Lavin benched Gadzuric. At the first media timeout, Lavin told his team the next two offensive plays and assistant Jim Saia talked about getting back on defense. Dijon Thompson nailed a three-pointer before the second media timeout and as he approached the bench, Lavin said, "Welcome to college basketball."

By halftime, the Bruins led 30-27 and up in the locker room, they remained calm. Lavin reassured them that the jitters were now gone, and the second half would be different, with better execution and fewer turnovers. He singled out Gadzuric for the stupid early foul, and reminded the big man how important it was for him to remain on the floor. Early in the second half, "Gadzilla" was back on the floor, but landed awkwardly on his left ankle. He would leave the game and not return. With 11:53 to go in the game, his team leading 56-42 but not playing particularly well, Lavin ripped into his troops during a timeout.

"Play some D," he screamed. "They are killing us in the paint! We know Houston is the worst shooting team in the nation, make them shoot outside," a directive the coach had been giving his players all game long. "No penetration, no dunks, and no layups!" Lavin shouted, slamming his clipboard to the ground.

The Bruins won the game 71-60, led by Kapono's 16 points and stellar play by Bozeman, who chipped in 13, at the point. Matt Barnes scored 11 of his 13 points in the second half. In the locker room, the players and coaches knew they could have played better, but for now their focus turned to Ball State. Lavin wrote the schedule on the board for the next day:

8:30	Breakfast
9:45	Leave for Shoot around
12:30	Meal
4:40	Game

"And lights out at 12:00 A.M. The coaches will be checking. No night owls."

The night passed, as the coaches stayed up late watching some film on the Houston game and also of the Ball State-Kansas game. They had already done some prescouting back in Los Angeles, but the speculation was that they would be facing Kansas, so the coaches quickly prepared for Ball State.

The next afternoon, Ray Young was dressed in street clothes, as he looked through the screen windows at the Civic Center down onto the court, watching Duke finish up its game against South Carolina. "It's hard to watch, man," referring to his being redshirted just weeks earlier.

In the locker room, Lavin gathered his troops, again, after waiting for the Blue Devils to exit. Once inside, Lavin asked Gadzuric if he wanted to start. His ankle had been iced and taped all through the night and day by UCLA trainer Mark Schoen, but this really was a game-time decision. Gadzuric did not answer right away and Lavin asked him again. The shy Gadzuric finally nodded yes, but Lavin and the team got a chuckle out of the big man's reluctance. "I am excited for this game," the coach told his troops. "Let's play hard, smart, and unselfish basketball today." With that, the team did their chant, the coaches did their own private chant—really, grunt—and then headed down the stairs onto the floor.

In the team huddle right before the opening tip, Lavin asked his players to be "first on the floor" for all loose balls and rebounds. Three minutes into the game, a noncall on a Ball State goaltending had both Lavin and Saia up screaming at the officials. This was only the beginning of their frustrations. As the first half wore on, it became clear to Lavin and the Bruins that this would be a struggle—that Ball State was for real. Ball State was able to easily beat the Bruins' press and take advantage of the slow feet of UCLA in their man-to-man defense. As the first half continued, the Bruins threw the ball away, gave up uncontested layups, and missed open looks. Upstairs, behind the screen windows, Krzyzewski watched the game, scouting his next opponent—whoever it might be.

By halftime, the Bruins trailed 44-40, but Lavin was not panicked in the locker room. "Guys, we need to get some cajones out there. We need to play tougher, better basketball." The coach continued, "We need games like this, we can learn from them. For as bad as we are playing, we are only down four at half. What we need to do is play some defense—we cannot win without it."

Ball State opened the second half with a 23-9 run to push the lead to 67-49. With 15:13 to go in the game, the Bruins were down by 13 when there was a media timeout. In the huddle, the coach was not mad, angry, or frustrated. Instead, he was calm and collected and told the guys how proud he was that they were sticking together despite the circumstances. "Let's get one stop at a time," he implored. "We've been down by 19 before and have come back to win, so there is no need to panic." With 7:32 to go, the lead was now 14 for Ball State, and the game looked over. Still, Lavin emphasized defense and told his players to hang in there.

You could see the look on Lavin's face, covered with sweat from the heat of the Lahaina Civic Center. His usual white shirt and blue tie would have been soaked right through, but he had a reprieve with a flowered-covered Hawaiian-flavored shirt and khaki pants. You could still see the huge sweat marks under his arms and below his neck on his shirt as he lost water by the minute. But it wasn't just the temperature that made him boil. With 2:37 left in the Maui Invitational semifinal, his No. 4-ranked UCLA Bruins trailed the relatively obscure Cardinal team by 14 points. He called timeout, if only to stop the bleeding. "Let's contest their shots. Keep them away from the basket. We need to play some defense," the coach said to the five players seated in front of him. From the look of their play, the players did not want to hear anything but the sound of the final horn. "Should we stay in Quicksand or go to man-to-man?" Lavin asked the players about the defensive alignment. With the subtle shaking of their heads, they agree to go with Quicksand, their matchup zone defense. Lavin learned from Pete Newell and Mike Krzyzewski that player input is critical to success.

In his pregame talk, and in *every* timeout during the game, Lavin had urged his players to concentrate on defense but to no avail. Lavin knew his team was a bit slow, so he focused on man-to-man defense throughout the preseason, hoping to stop penetration. Using a red zone chart, which displayed scoring inside the paint and defensive shooting statistics, Lavin still could not coax his Bruins into stopping Ball State. If one player didn't play "D" then that's usually the player's fault. If the whole team is like Swiss cheese, then all eyes look toward the coach.

The Bruin bench was silent as time ticked off and the Cardinal players began to celebrate their 91-73 upset. UCLA had turned the ball over 22 times and allowed Ball State to take 81 shots. We couldn't be that bad *could we?* Jason Kapono thought. How could this happen? Weren't they destined to meet top-ranked Duke in the Maui final the next day? We lost to *Ball State?* Kapono did his part, scoring 26 in the losing effort.

After the obligatory postgame handshakes, with Lavin telling Buckley "you've got a hell of a team," the Bruins ran up the stairs to the locker room and sat quietly until their coach came in. Barnes took off his shoes to have his ankle tape cut off, Kapono drank water from a blue water bottle, while super freshman Bozeman just shook his leg while awaiting the next word.

Remarkably calm and composed, Lavin began to write furiously on the board. On one wipeboard, to the right side of the players, he writes "Defense. Must get stops. Energy. Turnovers." On the left board he writes "What Now?" referring to both the immediate future (bus, food, hotel) and the season that lies ahead.

"We cannot cheat the game of basketball. We must play defense," the coach said. "We simply need to work on stopping somebody. And this is a simple game, take care of the ball, get good shots, and play defense," the coach said, referring to the 22 turnovers committed by his Bruins. "We have some great scorers in this room, but with no defense, we can't win." (In postgame interviews, Ball State frontline players stated that Kansas forwards were much tougher than UCLA's.)

The players sat restless, many with towels over their heads, their faces rested on their hands. The freshmen, Bozeman, Thompson, and Andre Patterson, sat upright, as if they were about to be punished. Because of the structure of the Lahaina facilities, and because of the magnitude of their win, the Ball State celebration began to fill the silence in the UCLA locker room. Lavin acknowledged the noise as he prepared to finish his four-minute talk. "Look guys, we got beat by Ball State. They were hungry and outcompeted us. The seniors in this room have been here before [upset loss]. Let's watch some tape, learn, and put this one behind us. We need the older guys to keep the young ones up. Where do we go from here? Now what?"

Billy Knight and Rico Hines shook their heads in agreement. Of course, as seniors, they *had* been down this road before. An early season loss to a lower level team automatically brought the calls for Lavin's firing; yet each time the team played well in March when it counted the most. But this year upsets were not supposed to happen. The early season losses were supposed to be a thing of the past. Lavin instructed his players to talk up Ball State to the media and to mention the Bruins' need to work on their defense.

That night back at the hotel, the team was much more subdued. Disappointed, angry, and generally upset about their play, they looked to refocus that night as the coaches prepared them for South Carolina in the third place game on Wednesday. Lavin reminded the team that you can never let one loss beat you twice—a team cannot be so down after a loss that it plays poorly in the next game leading to another loss—a mantra Lavin would bring out on more than one occasion during the season. The coaches and team spent two hours dissecting tape from the Ball State loss and watching some film on South Carolina. Back on the mainland, the Lavin-haters were out in full force, on talk radio, the Internet chat rooms, and in the local papers. Criticism of yet another early season loss to a lowly team was sure to be expected, and Lavin had been through it before.

The next day against South Carolina, a new Bruin team took the floor. These Bruins not only took care of the basketball, but shot an outstanding 72.9% on 35 of 48 shooting. Forward T. J. Cummings scored 25 points on 11 of 12 shooting. ("Every shot I put up I think is going in.")

UCLA led by as many as 21 in the first half and by 18 at halftime. It was a great performance by UCLA, though Bozeman did not play very well. More important for Lavin, the team was headed back home 2-1. "The three days here were a great experience for our team. We would have liked to have been 3-0, but only one team will. We learned a lot about ourselves and made it a positive experience." The team spent Thursday having Thanksgiving brunch in Maui before boarding a flight home.

UCLA had come to Maui to knock off Kansas and Duke, and instead beat Houston and South Carolina and lost to Ball State. There would be heat at home, and Lavin still had to get Bozeman confident. There was a "natural freshman learning curve" that would take time to establish. Gadzuric had to stay out of foul trouble and the seniors needed to step up leadership. They had to remedy all of this before facing Pepperdine the next week at home.

As UCLA was the leaving the fiftieth state, Notre Dame was just getting set to start their play on the main island. The Irish traveled 4,300 miles in 15 hours and arrived in Honolulu on Tuesday. It was the first flight for many of the Irish since September 11, but any apprehensions about flying were relieved when they were joined on their flight by the Air Force football team which was headed to the island for a game against Hawaii. Due to the terrorist attacks, the Air Force team traveled with six heavily armed federal marshals—the Irish felt safe. The team spent Wednesday morning touring the USS *Arizona* memorial at Pearl Harbor and then relaxed and swam at the home of a Notre Dame alum.

The Hawaii-Pacific Tournament was not prestigious, and the tournament field was not stellar either, with the host, Hawaii-Pacific, Notre Dame, Monmouth, Tennessee-Chattanooga, Akron, Vanderbilt, Liberty, and Hampton. Mike Brey knew the field was not strong, but also anticipated months ago when Notre Dame signed up that easy games early on could benefit his star freshman point guard, Chris Thomas. They would not be marquee matchups, but he could go home 5-0 on the season. Brey also thought that the trip to Hawaii would be a nice reward for his seniors, who had been through so much in their four years.

On Thursday, the team had Thanksgiving dinner at their hotel in Waikiki, the same hotel for the other seven tournament teams. They practiced earlier in the day and prepared Thursday night for Hawaii-Pacific. Playing at the 7,000-seat Blaisdell Center in downtown Honolulu, officials expected close to 1,000 fans for the opening games. They were wrong.

In his first game back after sitting out his two game suspension, Ryan Humphrey unloaded on the Sea Warriors, scoring at will, finishing with 31 points and grabbing 10 boards in front of a whopping *300* fans. David Graves added 17 and Matt Carroll had 15. More important, Thomas had 13 assists and *no* turnovers. As a team, the Irish had 28 assists and only nine turnovers. The Irish led by 16 at half and poured it on in the second, scoring 52 points to win the game, 98-58.

Their next opponent in Hawaii was Tennessee-Chattanooga, and the Irish had a harder time than with Hawaii-Pacific, but played well enough to win 97-84 to advance to the championship game against Monmouth. Humphrey and Carroll each scored 20 points, with Thomas and Harold Swanagan contributing 19 apiece. Carroll shot six for six from three-point land and the team shot 10-15 from beyond the arc. All five starters finished in double figures. Humphrey felt sick during the game, a condition he contributed to drinking too much Gatorade before tip-off to prevent cramping. The Irish were on a roll. The team was relatively healthy, Thomas was far exceeding expectations, and everyone was happy. For now.

In the championship game, Humphrey was again impressive, leading the way with 21 points and earning the tournament's MVP award as the Irish rolled 85-48. Notre Dame was up 36-23 at the half and had no problems attacking the matchup zone employed by Monmouth. Carroll and Graves joined Humphrey on the all-tournament team and Brey had gotten what he wanted. His team headed back to South Bend 5-0, their best start since 1979–1980, his team had a tournament championship, and perhaps most important for the coach, his team was confident. Nothing builds confidence like winning.

The calendar had not even turned to December, but already the pressure was mounting on three of the coaches. Steve Lavin's squad should not have lost to Ball State and would soon face an even bigger abyss. There was already talk of replacing Lavin in the print and electronic media, and UCLA fans were downtrodden again. Steve Alford's team blew a lead against Missouri, yet played relatively well over a five-game stretch in late November. There continued to be cracks on his team that would surface in a matter of weeks. They would face No. 1 Duke before the month's end. For Bill Self, his team kept winning, but they weren't having any fun. They struggled on defense, shooting, turnovers, rebounding, effort, and leadership, just to name a few areas of concern. There still was something missing. Could Self find it before the showdown with Maryland?

7

God at Power Forward

IT WAS NOVEMBER 27, 2001, AND THE IOWA HAWKEYES GATHERED IN THE DOWNSTAIRS conference room of the Hilton Hotel in downtown Chicago. The hotel is just minutes from the United Center, where in four hours, Iowa would take on the top-ranked Duke Blue Devils as part of the ACC/Big Ten Challenge. It was 4:00 P.M., and the team and coaches were in sweats, seated in chairs in four rows, listening to Jim Goodrich. A former college player and minister with Athletes In Action, Goodrich is a close friend of Steve Alford's and often traveled with the team to provide spiritual support and to lead pregame chapels. He was so integral to the program that he was pictured in the Iowa media guide under Staff. In every pregame service, in addition to the prominent Christian prayers and hymns, Goodrich tried to incorporate a religious message and secular story pertaining to the challenge at hand.

On this day, he spoke of the Apostle Paul overcoming adversity and taking his faith in hand as he took on challengers. He told the brief story of William Wallace, made famous by Mel Gibson's epic *Braveheart*, pointing out that he fought for his beliefs and fought with courage. "If you have strength," Goodrich told the team, "then believe in God and spread the word of Jesus Christ."

As he turned his attention to the game at hand, he reminded the players to find quiet time before the game, alone, to pour their hearts out to God. In his playing days, he revealed to his audience, he would go into a bathroom stall if only for a few minutes to let his heart speak to the Lord. "By playing hard," he reminded them, "you are speaking to God."

The pregame chapels are voluntary, though every player attends. It is against federal law to force students to attend a religious service at a public institution, so the voluntary services at Iowa are just that. In 2000, some members of the administration had been approached with concerns about the religious aspect of the program and summer camps, and they spoke with Alford and Goodrich, setting the ground rules for such exhibitions of religion. Their concerns were quelled when Alford promised that all religious activities would be strictly voluntary and no player would be punished for not attending. Goodrich knew that he must be careful and that others were watching.

These pregame chapel services are done on the road and at home. In hotel conference rooms, banquet halls, or back home in the team locker room, the team chapel usually takes place three to four hours before the game. It is often followed by the team meal and a review of the scouting report. The chapels at Iowa last about 20 minutes.

Alford is open about his beliefs and any potential recruit to Iowa knows all about the religious aspect to the program. It is a not a surprise when they first arrive on campus. However, though they may think they know what to expect, Alford's religious fervor is so great that it manifests itself in everything he does.

Alford does not drink, does not smoke, and is perhaps one of the most family oriented coaches in the country. His kids and wife are with him more than some of his assistants. In halftime talks, when he is fuming and his team is down by 10, it is rare that Alford will say any of the "ugly" words. He gets angry, but is always aware of his language. He does not want his players being exposed to sinful things, and among his many rules, no pictures of partial or full nudity are allowed anywhere on the team premises. So Alford does not just preach it, he lives it.

Alford is rooted in faith, family, and friends, but all three encircle the world of basketball. At the core of who Alford is as a coach, he is first and foremost a servant to God. It is a daily part of everything that he does, and he makes no secret of its importance to him, or what it should be to others. Recruits know it, the Iowa administration knows it, and so do those who work with him. If he ever needs a reminder, he finds it on his wrist, as he wears a bracelet that reads, "WWJD" or "What Would Jesus Do?"

"My relationship with Christ really began in the 11th grade," Alford proudly boasts, explaining that though basketball is his profession and love, it is not directly influenced by Christ. "The Bible becomes a little easier to me when I put basketball parallels to it. It's a playbook to be used on a daily basis," though he does not believe that God made all of his three-pointers go in—that was hard work. "You have to do it every day, not just Sunday. God is as interested in what you're implementing on Monday as to what you are saying Amen to on Sunday. . . . If we want to be better husbands, wives, better sons, better daughters, better at our careers, better at whatever we're doing, then we need to get better with Christ," Alford was quoted in a 1999 *Quad Cities Times* article.

Indeed, Alford's loyalty to his Lord is not just on Sundays. Each morning, he starts the day with Bible study at home or office, and every Tuesday, he has a Bible study for the entire staff at Iowa. Nancy Mills, his assistant at Southwest Missouri State, was quoted in an article saying, "I'd walk into the office and see my boss reading the Bible; it just gives you an awesome feeling." The Bible is, of course, his favorite book. Tanya Alford does Bible study daily and the Alford's three children are well versed in the way of the Lord through prayer and study nightly. Reading from the Scriptures is an important way for the Alfords to stay in touch with Christ and to implement Christian lessons into their lives.

One of Alford's closest friends, Ed Schilling, the 36-year-old coach at Wright State in Dayton, Ohio, is also a proud advocate of his religion. Like others in the profession, including Mike Davis and Tim Buckley, Schilling sees coaching as a platform for him to spread the word of God and to help others. But he keeps it as separate from his role as a coach as he can. "I want to have the biggest platform I can have. One, for the Lord and two, just to make a difference. You can go in and do some things that I'm involved with spiritually just because of my time in the NBA [as an assistant]. The whole platform is larger with the media." He knows what he stands for, the players know what he stands for, and if they want to follow, they can. "This is what I believe. This is what my staff believes. If you ever want to talk about it, it is my favorite subject. However, understand that I'm never going to twist your arm. I'm not going to try and jam it down your throat, because it doesn't work. None of my services are mandatory or required. It has absolutely no impact on playing time." Schilling, unlike Alford, does not attend the religious activities, including pregame services, so his players will feel no pressure about attending or not. Davis found his peace of mind through religion two years ago when "things started happening and I had no jealousy and no envy for anyone. I always pray and I've always had faith."

Perhaps the melding of religion and basketball is no clearer than before games. Many teams around the country join hands in a huddle to say a brief prayer before battle, asking God to keep them healthy and to play hard. At Notre Dame, where religion is an integral aspect of every activity, a pregame Mass is held, home or away.

Any Mass at the University of Notre Dame is special, particularly a pregame service with the basketball team. It is as much a part of the pregame ritual as stretching, or the team meal, or even pulling the Notre Dame jersey over one's head. And at Notre Dame, it has nothing to do with the coach. Mike Brey is not Catholic, but he is at a Catholic school, and no matter what the religious inclinations of the coach, this is Notre Dame. Players may not be Catholic, but they believe in those who are. It doesn't matter who is coaching or playing, the pregame Mass will be a part of all athletics for the Irish.

Most Division I teams have a student manager and team trainer who travel with them on the road. At Notre Dame, a priest travels with *every* athletic team (26 varsity sports) to *every* road game. It's a huge undertaking for the head of the priests, who must assign, coordinate, and confirm the various personnel and itineraries of the 40 or so who are assigned to teams. For a game against DePaul, just 90 miles away at the United Center in Chicago, Father Daniel Groody, C.S.C., was assigned to the Irish basketball team. The team arrived the night before the game, and after some brief free time, the team, coaches, trainers, and managers gathered in a second-floor banquet room at the Wyndam Hotel in downtown Chicago.

"Let us pray," Father Groody bowed his head and began the service. "We thank God for allowing us to arrive safely . . ." and so he continued, leading the team in a shortened 20-minute Mass. The players and coaches were seated in temporary chairs, common to banquet halls. They faced a window, covered by a white linen cloth, and a table with the sacraments and instruments of the Mass service. Father Groody was dressed in the traditional garb. (You might think you were in the Sistine Chapel or at least the main sanctuary on the campus of Notre Dame. But then you notice the television and VCR off to the side, to be used to watch a tape of DePaul later that evening.)

On this particular night before the service, Father Groody had asked junior Jere Macura to do the reading from the Scriptures, a task usually given to a player or coach. As Macura read his passage through his broken English, his fellow players sat at attention and listened. Toward the conclusion of every service, a traditional and unique ritual takes place. Each member at the service rises from his seat and begins to circle the room, exchanging "May God bless you" and other greetings with fellow players and coaches. These are heartfelt hugs and handshakes and no one misses anyone else. In that smaller room at the Wyndam Hotel, it became a little trickier, but movable chairs helped. As they completed these greetings, Father Groody led Communion, and one by one, the majority of players, managers, and coaches drank from the cup and swallowed a wafer. The service was complete. The Mass is repeated hundreds, if not thousands, of times by Notre Dame teams throughout the year. Each time it is a special reminder to them of the uniqueness of Notre Dame, and it serves as a reminder of basketball's place in their lives.

Bill Self is a devout Methodist who tries to attend church regularly. He believes that religion is the basis for family and life, and basketball is simply a part of his life. "We have a nondenominational prayer before every practice and every game here at Illinois. Of course, when I coached at Oral Roberts, we prayed all of the time, as many of those students wanted a career in ministry." On this Illinois team, Sean Harrington is the "spiritual leader," but anyone can lead the team in prayer on any given day.

As UCLA prepared to take the floor against Stanford on January 24, Steve Lavin went over the scouting report and gave his pregame talk. As he finished, the players rose and joined hands in a circle, coaches included. After a moment of silence, senior guard Billy Knight led the team in a prayer. With no references to a particular God, no mention of Jesus, the responsive prayer was nondenominational: "God our Father, hear our prayer. As we pause, to pray this day. Give us strength and courage too, to do the best, in all we do. Protect us, while we play, this we ask, in your name. Amen." They then huddled up and chanted "Together. We Attack!"

At the University of Mississippi, Rod Barnes has taken the program to a new level. With back-to-back NCAA Tournament appearances, a national ranking and a 20-win season, Barnes, at 36, is emerging onto the national coaching scene. He has already emerged on the pulpit. Barnes is a Southern Baptist who grew up in the church and whose brother is a pastor for a congregation in Mississippi. In an article by *cbssportsline*'s Dan Wetzel, Barnes says religion "is what really allows me from an integrity and honesty standpoint to balance myself. Because this business is so competitive, it is such a tough business, I need this." Each Sunday morning, Barnes and his family drive over an hour to the Duck Hill congregation, where Barnes teaches Sunday school and often gives a sermon. He never misses a Sunday. To him, his faith gives him strength, the ability to stand his ground, to do what is right, and to coach the young men in his grasp.

Former UCLA assistant Lorenzo Romar started a Bible study at UCLA in the early 1990s and carried the activity with him to the head coaching job at Pepperdine. "We caught some flak for it at UCLA, but we were not trying to develop a cult here and have everyone jump off of a bridge. This is something that these kids are looking for—answers—and this gives them an opportunity for answers." At St. Louis, his coaching stop after Pepperdine, the team had prayer at pregame dinners, but volunteer Bible study was not allowed. He is now at the University of Washington, but continues to believe that what is more important than a chapel or Bible study is the example he sets for his players. "I try to live it because it doesn't matter what you say if you don't live it. A lot of times I won't mention the word Bible or Lord, not because I am going to get into trouble, it's just that the same principles apply to the team. Painted on the locker room at Pepperdine was the saying 'Character is what you are when no one but God is watching.'"

In response to a postgame interview question about his great inside play in a just-completed game, often a college basketball player will respond with, "I just thank Jesus for giving me the ability to score." And when the going gets tough, sportsmen often look above for guidance: "I know we are in a hole, but I've been praying every night to the Lord to get us out of it." Sports and God have always been somehow linked, but never more so than now. Many college players and coaches find religion becoming increasingly paramount to all that they do. From the Midwest Baptist to the inner-city Protestant, they bring their faiths to school. Surprisingly, many schools bring faith to them.

Coaches with deep roots in their faith simply do not leave them at the arena door. They integrate faith into team prayers, program rules and, most importantly, how they go about doing their jobs. Religious men are religious coaches, for good or for bad. What may offend some, may also teach others morality, give credence to family, and strengthen the morals of the young. It is a powerful message when the coaching pulpit serves as a platform. And many of today's coaches are not shy about that fact.

I t was in this context that Jim Goodrich was in Chicago on a late November night presiding over the pregame chapel for Iowa as they prepared to meet top-ranked Duke. The ACC/Big Ten Challenge matched teams from the conferences against one another over two consecutive nights. Certainly for Steve Alford and his Hawkeyes, this was a "statement" game, one which could take their program to a whole new level. Evidenced by the number of media, the huge crowd, and a national television audience, this would be more than just any game.

The players arrived at the United Center 90 minutes before tipoff, listened to jams on their headphones, walking with a swagger but nervous in the eyes. As the team put down its bags and headed to the floor to shoot and stretch, Alford retreated to a side coaches' room with his father, Sam. His quiet time with his dad was interrupted by the pregame radio interview, and Alford participated in the Q and A with Iowa broadcaster Gary Dolphin. After the interview, Alford stepped out of the locker room to see what was going on in the hallway. Big mistake.

As soon as he emerged, *Chicago Sun Times* and *Sports Illustrated* columnist Rick Telander cornered the coach against the cement wall in the hallway. Telander proceeded to ask Alford about his coaching opponent Mike Krzyzewski, his former coach Bobby Knight, and the link between all three. Comparisons to Knight or Krzyzewski are not Alford's favorite subjects, especially just 30 minutes before playing the No. 1-ranked team in the country. He politely answered the questions and downplayed the significance and similarities of his matchup with another Knight protégé, Krzyzewski. As the interview concluded, Alford headed right back into the locker room.

While Alford answered the media inquiry, the team warmed up on the floor. First onto the court was Luke Recker, who drilled 3-point shots at both ends of the court. Reggie Evans took his time in the locker room, a set of very large headphones covering half of his face, before heading to the court. The team came back in as Alford finished writing on a makeshift board: three large pieces of poster paper taped to a wall by manager Quinn Collins. The players settled into seats in a semicircle around Alford and the room was silent. The coach began to go over each of the Duke players, their strengths, tendencies, and strategies to stop them. He had been over this before, earlier in the day and the previous night with the team, but you can never remind them enough. After breaking down the opponents, the coach focused on the Iowa keys to the game.

"Let's be patient on the offensive end of the floor. Crash the boards, get on the ground for every loose rebound. Do not rush the shots. On defense, boxing out will be a key. Somebody get a body on [Carlos] Boozer and watch their guards coming in for tap-ins."

While he talked to the team, he moved from point to point written on the poster sheets. There was hardly any blank space left. The information was almost overwhelming, almost too much. But Alford left nothing to chance, nothing unknown. His approach is to give the players everything, and he expects them to know it. He does, so should they.

The information he wrote on this day, and all other game days, could fill a textbook. Offensive sets, rebounding keys, defensive assignments, press breakers, diagrams, statistics, names, numbers. After completing the "review," he turned to his team and played to their hearts. "We must play tough. We must be willing to take the charges. Taking a charge from 280-lb. Carlos Boozer—now that is tough! Let's play hard-nosed basketball and have some fun."

With that, his Hawkeyes returned to the floor for their final warmup as Alford and his assistants watched the end of the Maryland/Illinois game on a television set in the locker room. The coach was focused but aware of the surroundings, and even cracked a smile when an assistant made a joke about another coach. Soon the team was back in front of him again, and this time, Alford put it in perspective.

"The Big Ten has not fared well this year [in the ACC/Big Ten Challenge]. We need to go out there and represent the Big Ten. To show that we belong with the big boys. We need to play hard and we need to have fun. Most of all, guys, think about the unique opportunity that you have tonight. Most guys never get the chance to play the No. 1 team in the country. But you have that chance tonight. On national television, you can do something very special for yourselves and for the Iowa program." They bowed their heads in prayer, huddled as a team, and ran out of the locker room for the "unique opportunity." As the pregame introductions were announced, the loudest roar from the 17,000-plus pro-Iowa fans was for Alford.

The first half began as it usually would for Iowa this season, with a turnover. Even after the pleas from Alford just moments earlier, the Hawkeyes threw the ball out-of-bounds. But then Recker hit some early jumpers and Duke's Jason Williams and Mike Dunleavy missed open looks. The play was physical, and Evans struggled down low against Boozer, an aggressive big man himself. The crowd was into every possession, and black and gold seemed to be on everyone. Duke coach Mike Krzyzewski was all over the referees in the first half, complaining about his players getting fouled going to the basket and noncalls on Evans. With 4:40 left in the first half, Iowa trailed by seven, 30-23. By halftime, the lead was nine.

The Blue Devils jogged, if not sprinted, from the court back to their locker room, passing by Iowa players walking quietly to theirs, across the hall from Duke's. As the Iowa players took their seats, Recker remarked that they are "still in this thing" and with "harder defense and toughness" they could play with Duke. Alford trailed the team into the locker room and it turned suddenly, almost eerily silent. It was clear who was in charge—whose words meant more than others. Whose presence commanded attention.

He is with his players at halftime, talking to them more often than not, and when he does leave, it is for only a moment. During some halftimes, Alford may leave the team three or four times, only to return with another thought seconds later. During home games, the coach simply walks back to the coaches' lounge, but on the road, like at Illinois, it can be tougher, where Alford physically has to leave the locker room, walk across a tunnel in the midst of fans to get to the coaches' room.

Alford relies on his father's words more than any other assistant's, and often he'll leave the team to have a moment with his father in a back room before returning. Alford becomes as enraged as perhaps most coaches, but almost unbelievably, he has an internal stoppage mechanism. When he raises his voice, frustrated at a lack of effort or too many turnovers, Alford will often stop himself midsentence. He cracks a brief sarcastic smile, and then continues with his points with a new, more calming voice. Parents are instructed to count to 10 before dealing with unruly children, to calm themselves down and to think before acting. It's like Alford does that routine in a half a second over and over again. Not only can he put the brakes on at times, he also refrains from most profanity in his tirades. They are not Christian-like words. His patience would be tested in the Iowa-Duke halftime locker room.

"Glen," turning to Glen Worley to confront him about a play at the end of the half against Duke, "you need to be aware of how much time is left. Why were you off Dunleavy so far? He's one of the best shooters in the nation," referring to Dunleavy's three at the buzzer to end the half.

"Well, the last play, I got beat on the backdoor lob so I wanted to shade and help out," the junior responded.

"You need to play defense on the man with the ball. He is the dangerous one!" Alford said clearly becoming more pissed off.

"Dunleavy didn't have the ball at that point when I was playing off of him." Maybe it was the frustration of a halftime deficit, or maybe because Alford cannot stand back talk, but it clearly incensed the coach.

"Anybody else got any more excuses?" he asked and, shaking his head, let out a sigh and walked to the adjoining coaches' office. He was not gone for long. Before the team had a chance to tell Worley to shut up, and before Worley could realize his mistake in talking back, Alford was back, this time talking strategy.

"We have to protect the ball. We need to play tougher, guys. We need to put them on their asses. We look tired out there. Duke has played five games in eight days and *we* are tired? You have 20 minutes left to prove yourselves."

Alford wrote on the impromptu poster paper boards some of the first half stats and in bold letters "TOUGHNESS" and circled the phrase. It would be a theme he would bring up to his team time and time again during the season. As perhaps the toughest player in Indiana history, he could not figure out why his team couldn't play that way.

Iowa remained close in the second half, but Evans could not get on track. The physical play heated up, and Krzyzewski magically avoided a technical after using some choice words in his protest of a charging call on Duke's Dantay Jones. After star guard Jason Williams threw the ball away on a Duke fast break, attempting to lob an alley-oop, Krzyzewski immediately called a timeout and screamed at Williams, as he walked off the court with his head down.

Iowa closed the lead to 73-61 with 3:47 to go in the game, but simply could not get any closer, eventually losing 80-62. Recker finished with 15 points while Chauncey Leslie (11) and Pierre Pierce (10) played well. Alford had decided to play them at the same time at points throughout the game, adding quickness to the Hawkeye lineup. But Evans was disappointing, managing only eight points while grabbing nine boards. As a team, Iowa shot just 39% from the floor and were outrebounded 36-30. They did not play well defensively, allowing Williams to score 25, Dunleavy 18, with Boozer hammering in 22 points down low. (Duez Henderson, who could have been a presence in the paint for Iowa, and who had played minimally against Missouri with bone spurs in his ankle, played just two minutes against Duke.)

"Where do we go from here," Steve Alford rhetorically asked his team in the locker room after the loss. "We have a goal of being better on January 1 and then even better by March 31. You should want the chance to play these guys again." Alford expressed his dismay at the team's discipline and focus, pointing out that players should be more punctual, more focused on the game rather than on family and friends. "When we need to be on the bus at 6:30, you better be there by 6:15. I want you in your hotel rooms until 6:00

and then get right on the bus. I don't want you hanging in the hotel lobby with friends, family, or girlfriends. We are also dressing sloppy, but that will change." To Alford, his team would do it the right way, and the classy way. They would not lose because of a lack of focus again.

Alford left for the press conference in the media room, as Recker sat alone in a chair, looking over the game stats. Shaking his head, Iowa's star just sat there slumped for close to 10 minutes. He had not been playing and shooting well, and seemed disappointed in himself. In response to a reporter's question after the media was allowed in the locker room, he simply said, "I need to find my shot and rhythm—I haven't had it all year."

The rest of the players jumped in the shower, answered reporters' questions, and otherwise remained silent. They got dressed in their Iowa warmups, put on the headphones, and walked to the team bus. Alford meanwhile walked into a throng of over 100 reporters in the media room, made no opening statement, and simply asked, "Any questions?"

He told the gathering that his team "is not starting and finishing well, the middle is OK, but we need work" and "we know we are very good, but we still have work to do." He left the media room and headed straight for the bus. It was a very quiet bus.

Moments before Iowa tipped off against Duke in Chicago, No. 5 Maryland and No. 2 Illinois were finishing up their battle in College Park, a place where Maryland had won 79 nonconference games in a row at Cole Field House. Off to its best start in six seasons, the Illini headed to Maryland looking to solidify its ranking and prove that it was capable of quality wins. The two teams had squared off in Hawaii in 2000, with the Illini winning 90-80. Maryland returned four starters led by superman Juan Dixon. After the Las Vegas Invitational, Illinois flew to Baltimore and arrived in the early hours of Sunday morning. They rested Sunday, practiced Monday, and prepared for the Tuesday night showdown.

In the first half, Illinois looked shaky, out of sync and tired, playing their fifth game in nine days and traveling across the country to play them. They were still able to go on an early 9-2 run and built a 17-10 lead midway through the first half, but then went cold from the floor, going six minutes without a bucket and playing poor defense along the way. They shot just 33% from the floor and turned the ball over seven times in the first half. Maryland led by 12 at halftime and started the second half with a 10-2 run to increase the lead to 20, 51-31. But Illinois never quit and battled back, aided by poor free throw shooting by the Terrapins. It became clear down the stretch that Illinois simply had no answer for Maryland big man Chris Wilcox, who scored 19 points and had six rebounds coming off of the bench.

With 2:56 left in the game, Illinois had closed the gap to 66-58 but a bucket and free throw by Wilcox gave Maryland a comfortable lead for good, as the Cole Field House crowd chanted "ACC! ACC!" Brian Cook fouled out with 5:11 left in the game and Damir Krupalija and Robert Archibald couldn't stop the Maryland front court. Of course, the Illinois guards couldn't stop Dixon either, allowing him to score 25 points. Little-used Blandon Ferguson scored 11 points for the Illini. After the game, Self was concerned about the foul trouble of Archibald and Cook, saying sarcastically, "They are spending too much time sitting next to me."

The team was disappointed in the postgame locker room, and began to wonder what their coach had been thinking all along—something was just not right. Fortunately for Illinois, they would head home to Champaign for an easy game against Texas A&M-Corpus Christi before another big game against Arizona in Tempe.

"We are not a very good team yet," Self told his players and then the media. "We were exposed. We don't trust each other very much." Self also hinted that some of his players, not singling anyone out, were interested in being selfish on national television and that it had hurt the team. Frank Williams and Cory Bradford were a combined seven of 30 for the game with just a handful of assists. It was clear who the coach was talking about. "I wish the leadership was spread more," Self lamented days after the loss, "but it's not. Frank is the guy." Williams had come into preseason out of shape, partly due to a chronically injured wrist, and his lack of effort and leadership needed to be addressed.

While Iowa and Illinois were losing to the top teams in America on Tuesday, November 27, Steve Lavin was one night away from losing to the lowly rated Pepperdine Waves at home. UCLA had returned from Maui 2-1, and the crescendo of the critics rose as they faced the team from Malibu. Former NBA head coach Paul Westphal had taken over the Waves' program, and some junior college transfers made them more than a pushover. Still, this was UCLA and it was at home. In the back of their minds, the veteran Bruins and their coach could not have forgotten two seasons earlier when they barely beat Pepperdine 68-66 at Pauley, saved when a last second Waves' shot was disallowed. The No. 10-ranked Bruins had a chance to go to 3-1 and put the loss to Ball State way behind them.

From the opening tip, Jason Kapono was on fire. The junior All-American was hitting from inside and out, including a stretch of four consecutive threes at the end of the half, helping to erase a four-point deficit to give the Bruins a three-point halftime lead. UCLA was still turning the ball over and doing nothing on the defensive side of the ball. Lavin was frustrated. In every timeout in the first half, the coach implored his players to focus on defense, reminding them that "we know we can score, but we need to defend." He couldn't find the answer. (By the end of the game, Lavin had used 10 players in his rotation in an attempt to find a tandem or trio who would play intense defense.)

UCLA had a two-point lead with just under seven minutes remaining, spurred on by a 17-6 Bruin run. That lead was erased, however, by a 17-8 Waves run and Pepperdine was on its way to its first win over UCLA in 56 years. Throughout the game, Lavin had utilized a full-court press in an attempt to throw Pepperdine off balance and force turnovers. But the Waves' guards had no problem breaking the press and, in fact, turned the tables on UCLA, forcing them into 15 turnovers.

Kapono finished with a career high 28 points, but admitted that the team faced a major issue. "Guys just don't want to play defense. The sad part is we know our problem and we can't solve it," as indicated by Pepperdine's shooting 59% in the second half.

"We were terrible," Lavin told the media after the game. "Obviously, that responsibility falls with me." Lavin is one to stand up and accept blame when he believes he is at fault, something he would do more than three times during the season. He believes that when he is wrong, he should admit it, not to get the press off his back, but to send a message to his players that he too will be held accountable. The media doesn't always accept his *mea culpas*, however. In fact, a *Los Angeles Times* columnist blasted Lavin later in the season for his approach to accepting blame in the media. Privately, the morning after the Pepperdine game, Lavin took blame for the ill-suited press. He thought he had put his team in a position to fail against Ball State and Pepperdine for insisting on the press. He had miscalculated the speed on the current roster.

In their losses to Ball State and now Pepperdine, UCLA was done in by a lack of defense. And there's really no defense for Lavin. But there was another issue for the coach. Freshman point guard Cedric Bozeman had left the Pepperdine game early, complaining of pain in his right knee, having played only 22 minutes. Tests the following day revealed a partial tear in the joint, an injury Bozeman apparently had suffered in Maui. The freshman had surgery the following Monday and would be out until at least Christmas. He hadn't been playing well, averaging 5.2 points per game and committing 15 turnovers to 13 assists.

These are the types of crises that coaches routinely face in the course of the season. Bill Self had lost Lucas Johnson just days before practice started and now Lavin had lost his starting point guard at a critical time for the freshman to learn the game. Not only would Bozeman fall behind in settling in, but his backup, Ryan Walcott, was a redshirt freshman. In meetings with his staff, Lavin thought he could have Kapono run the point, a tall forward who had excellent ball-handling skills. It would take some creative player management by Lavin, as well as some convincing of players that their new roles would be better for the team. Not an easy task.

The Bruins stood at 2-2 and the bandwagon was very light. The season before, UCLA had been shocked at home by Cal State Northridge, a loss that many UCLA fans deemed unimaginable. Yet even as the cries for Lavin's head mounted in Westwood, the coach had heard it all before and knew that his team was better than the two losses. Lavin's job had been in jeopardy the year before, but he felt fairly secure that he wasn't going anywhere this year, certainly not in the middle of the season. So as the circus winds swirled around him, the coach bunkered in to try to find a solution. He wasn't the only one.

On the last day of November, Iowa rebounded from their loss to Duke with a win over Alabama State in the Gazette Hawkeye Challenge in Iowa City. The emotions from the loss to Duke were still evident, however, as Alford's guys shot just 37% from the floor in the first half while allowing the SWAC defending champions to shoot 61%. Though Iowa started the game with a 5-0 lead, they quickly lost it on an ASU 9-2 run. As bad as Iowa played, they were only down by seven at half, 37-30. Alford fumed. There are two trademarks of an Alford team: toughness and defense. His players showed neither.

The locker room at halftime had an angry coach and players searching for answers. It's not that Recker, Evans, and their teammates disagreed with Alford; they knew that they were not playing defense, yet they couldn't find the answer. Toughness was the theme during the 15-minute break. Something that the coach said at halftime must have worked, as Iowa played its best basketball of the season in the second half. They shot 52% while holding Alabama State to just 33%, and two large runs by Iowa, led by Recker and Evans, allowed Iowa to pull away.

In the championship game of their own tournament on Saturday, December 1, Iowa cruised past Southern Methodist 86-69. The Hawkeyes easily penetrated the SMU zone throughout the night as senior Ryan Hogan scored 16 points while Evans had a double-double, scoring 17 and grabbing 12 rebounds. "He was tremendous," the coach said afterward about his super-sub Hogan. "We have been looking for a guy to step up. If anybody was going to ignite us, who better than Ryan?" Well, Recker and Evans for two, but on this night, it was the Kentucky transfer who took things under control. In response to a reporter's question about Iowa being back on the winning track, Alford responded, "Winning a championship like this definitely helps us and sets us up to get back in the right direction." Iowa was 6-2 on the year with losses to Missouri and Duke and still sat at No. 7 in the national polls.

Mike Brey's Irish continued in the right direction, easily beating Army at home, 86-49, before 10,200 fans to improve to 6-0 on the season. In the locker room before the game, Brey laid it out simply for his team. "Let's just continue what we have been doing, playing good basketball. Starting the season 6-0 would be great for us." He also pointed out that this would be Notre Dame's last home game for four weeks until a game against Colgate on December 30. The keys for this game for Notre Dame were limiting turnovers and offensive rebounds. For Brey, and probably for all of the Irish players, this was a gimme-game. Coaches often don't tell their players that before a game, instead, reminding them that "every game is big."

The Irish led 40-28 at half, but were not playing the physical basketball that Brey expected. He knew how rough the play can get in the Big East, and wanted his team to prepare for the challenge with these nonconference games. But he wasn't seeing it. His team continued to play "pretty," a theme he espoused from their opening exhibitions. "You guys are playing like country club kids," the coach screamed as he hurriedly made his way back into the locker room at halftime. "I'll let you guys figure this one out." And with that, Brey and his assistants left the room to look over the first half statistics.

In the locker room, David Graves and Ryan Humphrey took command, fathers preaching to their children. "He's right, guys," Graves shouted out, we need to get down on the floor and get every f—ing rebound!"

After what seemed like forever, but really was only five minutes, Brey returned to the locker room much more calm. He applauded Torrian Jones for his effort and encouraged his team to play harder. They did. Humphrey finished with 27 points, igniting a 19-0 Irish run in the second half. After the game, Brey was pleased with the second half effort, but reminded the players that they had a tough stretch ahead, including DePaul, Miami of Ohio, Indiana, and Alabama.

"We need to play like we are poor and there is no money in the bank," were his last words. They won their first six games by an amazing 33 ppg, but more pleasing to their coach, they were averaging 22 assists per game. But could they keep it up against superior opponents?

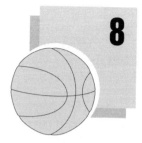

8

Family Man

THE NOTRE DAME COACHES GATHERED IN THE BASKETBALL CONFERENCE ROOM FOR their daily staff meeting on Thursday, November 29. The major topic of concern was preparing for DePaul, whom they would face on Saturday in Chicago at the inaugural Dell Classic 4 Kids. The coaches previewed a two-minute "hustle tape" of Irish players diving on the floor for loose balls against Army. Assistant Sean Kearney, who had watched tape of the DePaul-Syracuse game as part of his scouting preparations, briefed the staff on key DePaul players. Mike Brey had already been thinking for days about how to beat DePaul—the press. He pointed out to his assistants that in a teleconference with reporters earlier in the week, DePaul coach Pat Kennedy said, in a polite manner, that the Notre Dame guards were slow. Perhaps DePaul would press, Brey conjured up, and certainly would play David Graves and Matt Carroll tight. What better way to prove Kennedy wrong about his guards' speed than to press DePaul back?

The staff went over the itinerary for the Chicago trip, including team attire, departure, meal times, and ticket information. At the conclusion of the 25-minute meeting, Brey repeated his theme from the night before in the Army postgame locker room. "We are poor and there is no money in the bank."

At the start of practice, Brey showed the players the hustle tape and the team seemed to enjoy watching themselves and their teammates hit the floor. Practice this day was relatively light, as Ryan Humphrey took it easy on a sore ankle, as did Harold Swanagan with tendonitis in his right forearm. Brey introduced the team to the "32" defense, a full-court, trapping press that he thought they could use effectively against DePaul. The coach walked the players through the general concepts and player positioning in the press, and then had them scrimmage five-on-five, with both teams employing "32." After some shooting drills, broken up into bigs and perimeters, Brey put an end to practice, but instructed the players to hit the weight room. The coach joined them; not to bulk up, but to ride the exercise bike.

The team arrived at the Wyndham Plaza Hotel in downtown Chicago around 7:15 P.M. on Friday, November 30, and many of the players headed out to famed Michigan Avenue to walk around or shop, dressed in their Notre Dame sweats. Brey retreated to his hotel room to make some phone calls, while Anthony Solomon and Kearney watched the Arkansas-Oklahoma game in their room. Solomon made a few calls, including one to the high school coach of one of the Irish's big recruits coming in the following year.

The team met in a second-floor banquet room at 9:00 P.M. for Mass (see chapter 7) and adjourned next door for a late meal of sandwiches, ice cream, and sodas. As the meal concluded, Brey gathered the team in a huddle and asked them to get focused. On road trips, Brey has very few team rules, no curfews, and no problems. He treats his players like men and in return, they act like men. Maybe it is the type of young man who goes to Notre Dame or maybe it's the buildup of trust between coach and players.

On the road trips, the managers handle the per diem food money, game tickets for coaches and players, as well as the travel plans. The student-managers are the best of the best at Notre Dame, having gone through an intensive two-year Managers' Program. Managers must go through a mandatory two-year assignment with the football program, and then, if so inclined, they can apply to work for other teams. It is a highly structured and competitive program.

On game day, the team ate breakfast at 9:30 A.M., a meal of French toast, eggs, and bacon. Trainer Skip Meyer checked on the status of Humphrey's ankle and Swanagan's forearm off to the side in the breakfast room. They both seemed able to play, but would be watched closely throughout the game. The team gathered in the lobby of the Wyndam and got on the bus at 11:30 A.M. for the 20-minute ride to the United Center, the home of the Chicago Bulls and Chicago Blackhawks.

The visiting hockey team's locker room at the United Center doubled as a basketball locker room on this day and is typical of most new arenas. Pine lockers, close to three feet wide, surround the room, each with a small wooden seat and a place to hang clothes. One wall of the locker room has a large wipeboard, and a 19-inch television set is configured above the board. A red LCD game clock is mounted just above the television. An adjacent training room/bathroom area is large by visiting room standards, with three sinks, three urinals, three toilets, and a large shower area. And this is where Mike Brey stood just a few minutes before tip-off against DePaul.

Dressed in his typical maroon mock turtleneck with black pants, the coach had his arms crossed and stood in the shower area under the spigots. But there was no water. He had found the pregame solitude that he so craves, away from the media, assistant coaches, and his team. It was his time to think. As personable as Brey is at any given moment, he is untouchable before tip-off. The players dressed in the locker room, with the CD "Fabulous" blaring dirty lyrics throughout the room. The Notre Dame priest assigned to this road trip seemed not to notice. He was wrapped up in conversation with one of the old team doctors, a stately gentleman whose appearance only on game day was not lost on the players.

As the game clock from the opening game of the doubleheader, Texas and Stanford, counted down from 00:35, the music blasted as the players discussed among themselves intensity and hard work. David Graves watched the clock intensely, knowing that 00:00 meant game time. "I guess we'll know if it goes overtime if they reset the clock to 5:00," the senior captain noted, aware from the team managers that the opening game was tight as the end neared. The game buzzer sounded faintly in the locker room as the clock hit 00:00. Three seconds later it read 5:00.

So another delay and another dry shower for Brey. He had poked his head out from the bathroom area as the clock wound down, as if to prep himself for his entrance. But as the first game headed into overtime, he disappeared yet again. Finally, Texas completed its upset win over the ranked Cardinal, and the Irish players grabbed folding chairs, arranged them in a semicircle and awaited their coach. Brey had been isolated for more than 40 minutes, enough time to concoct a pregame speech worthy of Vince Lombardi to his 6-0 team.

"Let's play hard and methodical. Continue our good start and begin a tough three-game stretch well. Let's go." The coach clapped his hands three times and the players bolted out of their seats to form a human swarm with their arms raised together. They recited a two-line prayer (this is Notre Dame) followed by the team chant of "Together." The whole pregame speech, prayer, and chant took a whopping 27 seconds.

There are some coaches who live for the spotlight, and a few that shine that light on their players. Taking advantage of every moment to espouse encouragement or rehash information before games, some coaches talk incessantly. From the moment a team dresses for a game until the moment they leave the locker room for the floor, attention is commanded, and given, to the man in charge. Brey is not one of those guys.

"The longer I coach, the less I coach. I am afraid of overcoaching. I used to say there are guys in our business who coach every dribble. Like before the game, I like to stay away so they can talk amongst themselves until I come in and set the tone." The coach continues, "Look, a kid can only remember so much. I try to hit them with the highlights, as I like to say. One or two key things about the opponents and about our game plan. I don't want to inundate them with information before a game."

Having honed his coaching philosophy from his years with Morgan Wootten and Mike Krzyzewski, Brey developed his "hands-off" approach by his third year at Delaware. He came to realize that his teams responded better when they were given space, and the coach stepped out of the spotlight before games. Brey's approach is atypical in today's college game, but his successes at Delaware and Notre Dame have validated the approach.

The routine in Chicago was no different than during most Notre Dame pregames. Home or away, the players relax as they stretch and dress, listening to the latest hard-core rap on a CD player. The assistant coaches walk around the locker room, reminding individuals of the specifics of the man they will be guarding. As in Chicago, Brey is nowhere to be seen. At home games, he stays in the coaches' locker room, a long walk away from the team, spending time by himself, collecting his thoughts. It is only when the team comes off the floor 30 minutes before tip-off does Brey usually appear. He wants his players to talk with one another, encourage each other and motivate each other. With a veteran team but uptight seniors, Brey wants them to be as loose as possible before games. Graves will often throw out encouragement, punctuated by the deep bass voice of Humphrey, who will remind the team to have fun. There is certainly chatter in a Notre Dame locker room, exactly what Brey wants.

Notre Dame and DePaul had not faced off since 1994, and what was once a heated national rivalry, was not anymore. The Irish came into the game 6-0, but still unranked, while Pat Kennedy's team struggled to get back to an elite level. Thirty minutes before tip-off, Brey had given the team a two-minute scouting report on DePaul's top players. He reminded his team to play hard-nosed defense and methodical basketball.

Just five days after Iowa lost to Duke in the same building, Brey and his assistants followed their team onto the floor of the United Center. After the coach emerged from the tunnel, his daughter, Callie, screamed, "Dad! Dad!," as she leaned over the railing five rows up. Her father stopped and leaned over, gave her a kiss on the cheek, and continued to walk to the court.

Brey told his team to "set the tone early" immediately before the tip, and the game started off well for the Irish. Point guard Chris Thomas controlled the tempo running the offensive sets called out by his coach. On defense, the sets are 12 + 21, variations of zone and man-to-man. The Irish opened with the "32" press, used to slow down the offense, which DePaul was not expecting, and it forced the Blue Demons into early turnovers. By the time the first media timeout came at 15:45, Notre Dame was crushing DePaul, 14-4. "Sometimes it can be too easy," Brey warned his team in the timeout huddle. "You can see that we can pretty much do what we want tonight. Let's go out there and play methodically."

Since everything about Brey is short, including his timeouts, the team broke the huddle and then milled around on the floor by the bench, waiting for the horn. Out of the timeout, Notre Dame continued to play well, though Brey was not thrilled with some poor shot selections. Midway through the half, Graves missed a bad three and was quickly replaced by Carroll who was getting some rest on the bench. Thomas launched an awkward runner, earning him a seat on the bench, and was replaced by Chris Markwood. In a rather comical and sly move, Thomas originally took a seat in the middle of the bench, but at every available moment, made his way down closer to the coaches' end, one seat at a time, encouraging them to put him back in.

At halftime, with a comfortable 41-26 lead, Brey didn't have much to say. "I think we both know we should be up by 25, you know that. Just keep playing methodical basketball." He warned the squad to expect DePaul to come out hard in the second half.

DePaul did play more physical in the second stanza, but Notre Dame was simply too much, increasing the lead to 19 with just over 17 minutes remaining. Frustration set in for DePaul and the play turned from rough to cheap. On one play, with under seven minutes remaining, DePaul guard Imari Sawyer sucker-punched Graves in the groin, sending the Irish captain to the floor writhing in pain. Irish assistant Anthony Solomon leaped out of his chair and screamed at the officials, who apparently did not see the play. Graves got helped off of the court as Humphrey challenged a DePaul player, chest to chest.

In the ensuing timeout, Brey pleaded with his players to keep their composure. "Let's be men out there, don't go after anyone. DePaul is frustrated. And please, let me yell at the refs, not you. We need everyone for Indiana so don't be stupid."

The game was over well before the final horn, and in the last timeouts, Brey again reminded his players to keep cool in the closing minutes and in the postgame handshakes. They followed his wishes. The final score was 82-55, and Notre Dame was 7-0 for the first time since 1979. Humphrey scored 18 points and grabbed 16 boards, Swanagan added 16, and Graves had 14. Back in the locker room, as the team celebrated, Brey praised them for the constant effort and for keeping their cool. "Now we focus on Indiana," he told the team and, before letting them talk to the media, reminded the players to talk up DePaul in the press.

Things were good in Chicago for Notre Dame and Mike Brey, but not so good 90 miles to the south in Champaign. Returning from their cross-country trip, Illinois had only lost one game, to Maryland, but it seemed like they were in a crater. In practice they lacked enjoyment. Most days Bill Self thought they still practiced hard, and Self could not fault them for their effort, yet they hadn't gelled as a team, unable to play selfless, good basketball. The "missing" piece was still not there by early December (perhaps it was the injured Lucas Johnson) and Self was concerned. He was hoping for an easy win over Texas A&M-Corpus Christi, a program that was still a probationary Division I school. The big guys like Illinois schedule these games to get easy wins, pad their record and make money from the gate. The smaller sacrificial lamb schools often get guarantees to travel and play the big schools, usually in the range of $15,000 to $50,000. The smaller Division I schools need the money to support their basketball program and often their school's athletic budget as well.

Though it was a game against an opponent not many Illini fans had heard of, Assembly Hall was packed. The Orange Krush student section was filled with students with painted faces and vocal cords at full blare. The Pep Band played as the Illini players ran onto the court, preceded by a male cheerleader running in circles holding an enormous Illinois flag. The crowd got excited when Lucas Johnson suited up and participated gingerly in the warmup layup lines for the first time—a remarkable feat considering surgery was just six weeks prior. Self made his way to the court, dressed in a blue shirt and tie and tan pants.

In an attempt to shake things up, to find a pentagon of starters who produced with enthusiasm, Self started Frank Williams and Cory Bradford, replaced Sean Harrington with freshman Luther Head, and started Robert Archibald and Damir Krupalija down low. Harrington and Brian Cook started on the bench. The moves didn't work from the start, though the score would indicate otherwise, and Self put his regulars onto the court just five minutes into the game. Midway through the first half, Illinois led 20-8 over their obviously inferior opponents, but still did not play well. They turned the ball over, took unwarranted shots and played lethargically. With strong contributions off the bench by center Nick Smith and freshman Roger Powell, Illinois was able to take a 43-26 halftime lead.

As the players settled onto their stools in the locker room, the coaching staff huddled outside. Self thought about giving Powell the start in the second half and assistants Norm Roberts, Billy Gillispie, and Wayne McClain concurred. They headed inside and Self took off his jacket and prepared to address the team. "Guys, you know we can play better than this. It doesn't matter what the fans think, we know we are playing hard, we are just playing tired."

Then, turning to Archibald, who had missed wide-open midrange jumpers, "You must have a brainfart right now, Arch." The coach took the opportunity to call out each player, except for freshman Powell, for their uninspired play.

"Frank will hit his threes in the second half," Self said turning his head toward Williams, "and Frank you will hit your threes." The coach scribbled furiously on the wipeboard, spelling out for his players what they did wrong on both sides of the ball. His penmanship was not great, but the players got the message.

Eight minutes into the second half, Williams hit his first three and the game was never really in doubt. Self emptied his bench, using numerous combinations on the floor. Bradford finished with 23 points, including six threes, and Williams and Archibald each finished with 12. The final score was 80-56, but not everything was positive. Illinois had 21 turnovers in the game and shot just 41% from the field in the first half. Cook spent a large portion of the game on the bench and eventually fouled out. Head floundered in his first start, scoring zero points.

As the team made its way back to the locker room, there was not even a hint that they had just blown out a team. "We are missing that pop," the coach began his talk. "This wasn't pretty tonight. I don't know what it is, what is missing. We are just playing selfish basketball and not making the extra pass. It's hard to watch from the bench." After Self told the team practice would be at 12:00 the next day, Johnson raised his hand. "At least from the bench, it just looks like we are not having any fun out there. It seems like a business. Last year was fun."

And with that comment, the players opened up to the coaches and each other for the next 30 minutes, talking about attitude, practice work ethic, and suggestions for getting back on track. Ten minutes after the end of a game, Self is usually available to do his postgame radio interview followed by his press conference. After this game, however, the radio guys and Sports Information Director Kent Brown stood patiently outside the locker room. Inside, the discussion continued until 10:00 P.M., when the players finally hit the showers. Self walked into the adjacent training room, looked over the game stats, and watched the fourth quarter of the Colorado-Texas football game on a mounted television set. Brown came in and got the coach and they made their way up a flight of stairs to the press room, trailed by a security guard. Self took a seat at the podium, prepared to face the questions. Right from the start, he was asked about his team's sluggishness.

"We are not in a crisis, let me first say that," the coach began. "I knew two weeks into practice that something was off. I don't know what it is, but we will find it." After further prodding by the scribes, Self went on to indicate that "this [mood] usually doesn't happen this early for a team." When asked about his team's play, considering their No. 2 ranking, the coach responded, "I have said all along that we have done nothing this year to deserve the No. 2 ranking, but everyone expects us to play at our ranking." Self had a point. The preseason ranking was based on last year's Elite Eight run and on the number of veterans returning, having nothing to do with the first six weeks of this season, played without Johnson. Illinois sat at 6-1, but that didn't mean that they were one of the top two teams in America.

After the press conference, Self headed down to the coaches' locker room, across from the team training room in Assembly Hall. Everyone else was gone. There were a few game programs left on a counter, some gum packs, and bottles of water sitting unopened under a mirror. He grabbed a two-foot-high stool and sat down, holding the game stats in his hand. He looked tired, frustrated, and confused. Even the best coaches don't always have the answers. It was a picture etched in the coaching world—a coach, covered with sweat, drinking a Coke, sitting alone on a stool in a locker room. He was lonely not just in the tangible sense. He was a coach on an island trying to figure out his team. It was the side of coaching that the public rarely sees. The coach searched for answers, pouring over game statistics as if the solution would pop up from the numbers on the sheet.

"I can't figure it out. I don't know what to do. Maybe I will play Guns-N-Roses at practice tomorrow. Make sure the kids are having fun again."

And with that, Self headed back across the street to the basketball offices, spoke briefly with Gillispie, grabbed a videotape of the game, and headed home close to midnight. By now, his children, Tyler and Lauren, were asleep, as was his wife Cindy. His wife had gone to bed understanding that a long night was ahead for her husband. But understanding is part of a coaching marriage, when husbands and wives routinely sacrifice family time for the profession.

In most marriages, a man can only expect so many "I understands" from his devoted wife before she figures out that she is no longer a priority. For the wives of basketball coaches, understanding is part of the wedding vows, right alongside "in sickness and in health, till death do us part." The responsibilities of a college coach are time-intensive and the job is a never-ending one. Finding the balance between being a great coach, husband,

and father has never been harder. With outside interests such as media and fund-raising demanding a coach's time, in addition to the new recruiting calendar that keeps coaches out on the road, there is very little time left for a coach's family. But they understand.

Coaches' regrets do not lie in conference losses or turnovers, but in missing birthdays or holidays or just not being able to tuck their kids into bed at night. It is the nature of the profession, something that they and their wives learn quickly. Wives take over many of the jobs at home like paying the bills, disciplining the kids, and even coaching the kids' Little League teams. The saying that "behind every successful man is a successful woman" holds quite true in the coaching profession.

"Your wife has to be extremely strong and she has to be extremely understanding," notes Illinois assistant Norm Roberts, summing up the view of many of his colleagues. "Your wife can't just be normal . . . she's got to be special and really unselfish."

The wife is the rock of the family. For most coaches, their wives are their best friends. After a tough loss, they confide in their partners, not fellow coaches, often lying in bed just talking about the game. After a miraculous win, it is their wives they want to hug, not their athletic directors. Though most wives are emotionally supportive, some exhibit more vocal support than others, particularly at games. Tish Brey is known not only for her knowledge of the game, but also for her harsh words for referees, heard above the crowd at the Joyce Center. Tanya Alford can often be seen stomping her feet on the floor screaming encouragement during Iowa games. She too has lived the game her whole life and takes everything personally. Her seats are on the floor, directly across from the Iowa bench, and she is often the first one up protesting a call or cheering a great effort by a Hawkeye. She knows what she is talking about, having learned the game through the years.

Tanya and Steve grew up a quarter mile from each other in the small town of New Castle, Indiana, and became best friends in the fifth grade. Tanya was a huge basketball fan, so being friends with, and eventually dating, a basketball phenom did not bother her. "It was never difficult with him being in the spotlight—that's all I have ever known of him. I think it was good that we had a solid friendship before we started dating."

Tanya attended Indiana University with Alford for two years before transferring to physical therapy school in Evansville. She still never missed an IU home game and watched all of the away ones on television. Shortly after graduation, the pair married in July 1987.

As a coach's wife, there are some unique aspects to a marriage. On Valentine's Day in 2000, the Alfords spent a romantic evening—20,000 miles up. The coach had to fly to Coffeyville, Kansas, to watch junior college stand out Reggie Evans play a game. Tanya left the kids with her in-laws and the couple headed for Kansas. "Steve brought me flowers on the plane and he had a special meal catered for us," Tanya recalls with a smile. "It was fabulous fun. A lot of girls might think that's corny, but to me it was a blast." (Of course, Alford ended up signing Evans, who would become an All-Conference player.)

The family atmosphere at Iowa is something that Evans expected, but could not have imagined its impact on him. "He [Alford] is a good role model for me and his kids. I see him all the time with his wife and kids. My dad wasn't there for me and to see him balance his time with his family, I respect that a lot."

Alford includes his wife and his children in most work-related activities. His boys, Bryce and Kory, are ball boys for home games, and his daughter, Kayla, dresses in an Iowa cheerleading outfit. Tanya and the kids usually stop by the locker room before home games. In a poignant moment before taking on Indiana at home in mid-January, Alford had Kayla in his arms, whispering to her in a corner of the locker room, just moments before tip-off. Not all coaches include their wives and kids to the extent that Alford does, and rarely will you see a coach's wife in the locker room before or after a game. (Sometimes, Tanya will stop in the coaches' lounge after the players have left, to give her thoughts on the game to her husband.)

Most coaches' wives are not only devoted to their husbands and their jobs, but also open up their arms and homes to 15 additional children every year. They are surrogate mothers to the players, many of whom are far away from home.

"I remember sitting in an airport in December," Tish Brey recalls, "and four of the guys surrounded me and we were just talking life. One asked, 'How do you know when you have met the right girl?' Conversations like these bring us closer. I am kind of like their mom here."

The Breys often host the players at their house for team dinners or invite a few kids over just to hang out. Tish loves it and so do the players. "Coach Brey's wife is like a mom," says the loveable Harold Swanagan. "She is so nice. She talks with us, plays with us. Kind of a like a mom-sister. She thinks she can beat me in darts. Don't tell her I let her win."

Ohio University coach Tim O'Shea keeps both family and his profession in perspective, noting that those in "corporate America are under more pressure and stress." "Coaches have longer contracts, so if things don't go as planned, there is some security in providing for the family. As for the wife of a coach, she better know what she is getting into. We have a recruit in town today and we will have a cookout at our house for him and his family. A wife needs to understand that she is part of the job and part of the basketball family."

The relationship between father and child is often sacrificed and tested as well. On a snowy January day in Milwaukee, Marquette coach Tom Crean had given his team the day off. They had won the night before and the coach and his staff needed time off as much as their players did. A day off for a basketball coach is not one when he relaxes at home, runs some errands, and goes out with his buddies. A day off simply means no practice, it doesn't mean no work. But without practice, a coach does have a few extra hours to spend on recruiting, scouting, media—or his family.

"Before I came into work today, I took one of my boys to McDonald's for a bite to eat and then we went to this bookstore where we played with things," the proud father of two says. "I bought him a book on trains. You know, that was the best hour and a half that I have had in a long time. It is times like that when you remind yourself to do it more often."

Though children of coaches sacrifice time with their fathers, they are able to reap the rewards of his profession. Not only do they get great tickets to basketball games and concerts and get to meet famous people, but perhaps more importantly, they get the experience of being around the players. "Kyle and Callie hang around the players," says Mike Brey. "Especially Kyle, and he gets to see what David Graves and Matt Carroll go through. They are class guys who work hard in school and in basketball, and as competitive young athletes, they are great role models for Kyle."

The negative, of course, is getting lost in the fray as the child of the coach. Trying to be your own man or woman is tough enough. Kyle Brey likes the fact that on his youth basketball team, there are no names on the back of the jerseys; he can simply play and not worry about who is watching. People may expect more of you, as an athlete and as a person. Teachers may even treat children of coaches differently, with mixed results. It is definitely harder on a son than a daughter, especially a son who plays sports. "Sometimes I think my son wishes he could just be Kyle Brey and not the coach's son," the father remarks. "Whether it is at school, on the floor, or just with his friends, there are times when it gets to him." Brey's daughter, Callie, seems to relish the status of her father, though at 10 years old, things could change, as they do with most teenagers.

Brey's top assistant, Sean Kearney, worries a bit that the great experiences his children have may get them a little too spoiled. "I fully expect one of the kids to come to me as we are going to the airport or getting on a plane, and say 'You know, Dad, Harry and I have been talking. We don't really like this commercial stuff. We kind of like the charters.'"

The first year at Notre Dame, Brey felt guilty about not spending enough time with his kids, but now with his success and security, he can make it a priority. (For the 2002–2003 season, all Sunday individual workouts will be done from 2:00 to 5:00 P.M., and he insists that he and his assistants will be home every Sunday night for a family dinner.) Like many coaches, Brey often sprints from a practice to catch a son's basketball game or daughter's volleyball match. Bill Self will often run from a practice to see his daughter Lauren's violin recital or attend son Tyler's Cub Scout meeting. There's also gymnastics, basketball, and school functions to attend, and the coach tries his best. It is easier when your team has its own basketball court, like Illinois does in Ubben, so Self can schedule practices around major family events. Alford will miss the first half hour or so of his weekly radio show (with an assistant filling in) so he can watch one of his son's basketball games.

Alabama coach Mark Gottfried has five children at home, as well as a very understanding wife. He wants to spend equal time with all five, and that often means shutting it down when he is at home. "I could watch *SportsCenter* or make calls, but you have to shut everything off to spend that time with your kids. No success in your professional life, no matter what you do, can overcome failure at home."

At Yale, James Jones has come up with a different approach, though most coaches would be too weary-eyed to follow it. "Sometimes I will go home, spend time with my wife and daughter and then go to bed for a few hours. Get up and between two and five A.M. watch tape. I get to spend time with my family as well as keep up with work."

Though Washington's Lorenzo Romar attempts to make time for his family, he knows that they understand the demands of his job. "In fact, if we have lost two or three in a row, the kids will tease me and ask, 'What are you doing home?' You need to be out there getting players!"

Sometimes, coaches must pay the ultimate price for a coaching career, losing a wife through divorce or alienating their children for never being around. Pat Flannery at Bucknell suffered a divorce when he moved for a coaching opportunity, but now remarried and the father of a five- and seven-year-old, he understands the consequences of neglecting family. They are now his priority. Many coaches learn that lesson the hard way.

So as coaches play out their lives in the public arena, their families are often the ones who sacrifice the most. The missed birthdays, late dinners, and the daily little things that a coach gives up in pursuit of wins. With any demanding profession, families and marriages are sure to struggle and for coaches, finding the balance between work and home seems to come with age. So as Bill Self headed home that lonely night after the Texas A&M-Corpus Christi game, he faced uncertainty about his team, and had a family fast asleep.

One coach who never had a problem balancing his family with his work was John Wooden, a coach who has won more national championships than any other in college basketball history. Though he has not coached a game since 1975, he is still regarded as the preeminent spokesman on the game of college basketball.

Wooden lives in the same two-bedroom condominium that he shared with his wife, Nellie, before her passing in 1985. His condo is in a nondescript neighborhood in Encino, California, just eight miles from Westwood. He spends most of his time when he is at home in a den which, for most visitors, is a sports museum. There are books everywhere, from the latest on politics to an epic on Abraham Lincoln, one of his two favorite figures, alongside Mother Theresa. There are pictures covering every space on the wall, of Wooden with players, coaches, politicians, and family members. His phone is constantly ringing with former players and friends wanting to talk to the legend, or arrange a visit.

Wooden gets to most UCLA home games, where he takes his regular seat just two rows behind the UCLA bench. He is greeted like the Pope by adoring fans, who want pictures, autographs, or simply a word of wisdom. For a 92-year-old man, John Wooden is remarkably agile and articulate. He knows names, faces, dates, teams, players, and most of all, every game that he coached. It has been a generation since the Wizard last paced the sidelines in Westwood, but his love for the game has not waned.

"I think I would love to coach today," he says in a deep but hushed voice, "but I think some of my methods and ideas wouldn't work today. The game has changed and so has society. I was pretty old-fashioned. You have to give in to the youngsters more today. They are more individual and demanding. I guess I could make changes to my methods. I would always enjoy teaching, today, tomorrow, yesterday. But no one has offered me a job."

"Most things in life improve with time. There is no progress without change, I like to say. Maybe team play has improved, but not nearly in relation to individual play. The athleticism is outstanding so most coaches let them go on their own. That can certainly hurt team play."

As the players have changed in the game, so have the coaches. "I wouldn't be critical of today's coaches. If players are better today, and they are, shouldn't coaches be better too? And I think they are. I believe there is too much catering to the players today by coaches. I think you can be firm without being stubborn. How many coaches insist that when we leave the dressing room that there should be no orange peels left? I didn't want towels anywhere or gum wrappers. How many coaches insist on that today? I think it all has to do with giving in. If you give your children at home a piece of candy, and then another piece, and another piece and ask them to be quiet, they'll continue to ask for more. We give in."

The role of the coach has changed since 1975. Coaches are in demand for media appearances, fund-raising, charity events, and certainly recruiting. But Wooden had demands too; he just simply said no. "When I was coaching, 80% of my time was preparation and teaching and studying. Now could I have done other things? I refused to do it at times. I refused to go to cocktail parties. During the season I wanted two to two and a half hours every day uninterrupted when I'm planning my practice schedule for the afternoon. If my boss or my family called, that would be all right. When basketball season was over, I would devote myself to studying the game. Rebounding, next year's zone attack, this and that."

As for the explosion in the college game's popularity: "Television is the worst thing that's happened to intercollegiate basketball. It's made actors out of players, coaches, officials, and to some degree, even fans. But there are always two sides, and we must remember that. It's been the savior of nonrevenue-producing sports. We couldn't be doing what we are doing for women's athletics if it wasn't for the TV income in many cases."

"And money has changed the game for coaches. Everyone thinks it's the position to be in. So many coaches get involved in other things outside of their job to make money. Two different shoe companies offered me $50,000 to have the team wear a certain shoe. I turned them down. I did change shoes once, but not because of money, because the shoe fit better. In retrospect, I should have accepted the money for scholarships for the school."

Wooden also has some ideas on how to improve the college game. "Abolish the dunk. Too much showmanship, we don't need it. And move back the three-point line, it is too close. And I don't know exactly what to do about it, but recruiting is a mess."

Wooden has always been silent when it comes to UCLA coaches and their successes and failures. They all coach and live under his shadow, yet he refrains from making judgments. He has a fond friendship with Steve Lavin and respects his abilities and resiliency. Wooden makes it clear that coaching at UCLA is not any harder than it was when he patrolled the sidelines. It has been 26 years since he retired and he doubts that he still has an impact.

"It [coaching at UCLA] isn't a hard thing. It's the easiest place in the world. There's more material here, they have the best place to play on, and good coaching. It was hard when I came here. I had to sweep the floor every day. We had no private dressing rooms. We had no private showers. Just one big shower that everybody used. We had tin lockers. There was wrestling at one end of the gym, gymnastics at another, and at times, a trampoline on the side. Don't tell me it is difficult [to coach] at UCLA. It's one of the best places in the country.

"I try to be available for anything Steve [Lavin] or the coaches ask. I never keep them waiting. If they come to me, I'll give them an opinion, not advice. They [coaches at UCLA] don't need my blessing. They have it, whoever it is."

Another "old timer" disagrees with Wooden when it comes to coaching at UCLA, perhaps because he sees it from the outside. "It is a very difficult job at UCLA," Pete Newell insists. "You are not allowed to learn from your mistakes at UCLA like you could at other places. No one can change the atmosphere there. I think you will always be fighting the shadows. As for Steve, I think he has done a tremendous job. He has learned from his mistakes, but the media is so quick to react. He might be better off if he left UCLA."

Has Newell seen a change in the game in terms of coaching? "One major change has been the exposure of coaches. In the past, it was only the football coach on the hot seat. There were no talk shows about college basketball, no betting on the games, and coaches didn't get paid much. I made $12,000 at Cal in the 1950s. Coaching today is so much tougher. Kids all think they are going to the NBA and they have a lot of voices telling them different things. It is hard to project four years in a program now."

"Also, coaches get used to a certain lifestyle, but they can go from the penthouse to the outhouse overnight. There are so many pitfalls. The media is one of them. There is a certain element in the media who make a reputation by knocking or bad mouthing coaches and teams. So many fans are influenced by first impressions which are scripted by the media."

"Would I want to coach today? No. I would rather coach when I did and make less money. It was more enjoyable."

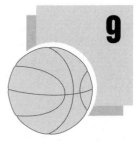

9

Skinning the Cat

A CHEF IS ONLY AS GOOD AS THE INGREDIENTS IN HIS FRIDGE. THE BRILLIANT conductor saddled with a mediocre symphony will never win acclaim. In today's college game, a coach's success—and his team's skill—is rooted only partially in his coaching ability. Without talented players to win the big ones, there's no getting to the big ones. So it's no coincidence that the best coaches in today's game are also the best recruiters.

For John Wooden, the college game's most hallowed figure and the man at the helm for the most astounding championship run in NCAA hoops history—10 national titles in 15 years, and an incredible four 30-0 seasons—things were different. In the 1960s and 1970s, if you were an All-American anywhere in America, *you recruited UCLA*. Every kid in every high school gym in the country dreamed of playing for the Wizard of Westwood. The Bruins no more had to put out feelers for recruits than the Nobel Prize Committee has to advertise for applicants.

The game has changed dramatically since 1975, and so have the rules. Today's recruiting battles for the nation's top prospects are as fiercely contested as a Final Four game; only the madness isn't confined to a single month. An assistant coach spends an average of three or four hours a day on recruiting activities, 365 days a year; in a week's time he may write 10 to 200 handwritten letters. Assistants are now hired on the basis of their recruiting touch, and head coaches are axed if they can't land the top players. It's just about impossible to be a successful coach in today's game without being a solid recruiter.

To safeguard prospects' personal and scholastic lives, and to rein in the recruiters' more rabid instincts, the NCAA has developed complex guidelines dictating when a prospect may be courted. Here are some of the highlights, in chronological order:

Pre–High School: A coach may evaluate a player and send a standard questionnaire, but cannot have any contact with the student. Coaches can, however, speak with the youth's coach about the prospect. (Some coaches do not believe NCAA rules apply to students before ninth grade.)

Freshman Year: Players are now considered "student-athletes" and recruits in the eyes of the NCAA. Coaches can watch players in the high school gym and at AAU tourneys. There are no in-person, off-campus contacts, telephone calls, and correspondence with the recruit or his parents, but coaches can contact high school or youth coaches. Students can make unofficial visits, those paid for by the student, at anytime and coaches and recruits can have contact on the university campus. Recruits can call coaches at anytime as long as they pay for the call.

Sophomore Year: The same rules apply from freshman year. After the completion of the sophomore year, coaches may begin to write individual correspondences to recruits and coaches may also receive calls. Recruits can use toll-free numbers or call coaches collect at anytime following their sophomore years. Under no circumstances may a coach initiate contact, either by phone or in person.

Junior Year: After January 1, official visits are allowed, those paid in full by the school. In April of the junior year, coaches may make one phone call to a recruit and can visit with him one day in April. From June 21 to June 30, coaches also can make one call to a recruit. After July 1, coaches can call recruits no more than one time per week.

Senior Year: Outside the dead periods (no contact whatsoever) and quiet periods (no off-campus contact), coaches can evaluate players, call them once a week, write them often, and make a home visit. Once a player signs with a school, as early as the National Letter of Intent day in early November, the limitations on contact are lifted.

What makes the rulebook less a book than a tome are the strictures concerning *how* coaches may recruit. What size pictures may be mailed out? How many separate visits to campus is a prospect permitted? What week of the year is any contact with a recruit strictly verboten? Few coaches know every letter of the law; and even fewer follow them to the T. The NCAA manual is close to 450 pages. But don't blame the guys at the NCAA.

"The rules in the NCAA manual are created by the schools themselves," says NCAA Vice-President Wally Renfro, a reference to the fact that the NCAA is an organization made up of the colleges who create the rules. "Many of the rules are supported by the have-nots. That is why you see a limit on the number of color mailings a coach can send out a week. The smaller and less wealthy schools put those rules in to try to even the playing field." Regardless of who makes the rules, and who complains about them, it is incredible the lengths that coaches will go to follow the rules, or to circumvent them.

When it comes to recruiting, coaches follow two mantras. First, "Don't do anything to hurt yourself" such as forgetting to call a recruit, saying something stupid in a home visit, or misspelling his name. Second, remember the idea that "There's more than one way to skin a cat," as coaches use a variety of methods and tactics to convince a player to sign. These two axioms dictate how coaches go about convincing kids to come to their schools. Recruiting is a battle, and in battle, there are casualties. Perhaps there is no other part of college basketball that comes under closer scrutiny, or stigmatizes the game with a brighter negative light.

More than 550,000 American boys play high school basketball, and a Coach K or a Roy Williams will end up signing three or four of them. So how does a coach go from a half a million kids to only three? On the wall of Steve Lavin's UCLA office is the Recruiting Board. It is a blueprint, a map, a lifeline. The dry-erase board is divided into five columns, each marked with a year. In each column are listed the names of 12 to 15 players, their year in school (or eligibility year), and the number of scholarships Lavin projects will be available that year. With each program permitted 13 scholarships a year, coaches must be tight-fisted in doling them out. Only players considered the cream of the crop will receive a scholarship offer; all other hopefuls may try out as walk-ons and, if they're lucky, eventually earn a free ride. But there are no guarantees.

Look closely at the Recruiting Board and (after a couple of double-takes) you'll realize that Lavin and his staff have mapped out potential rosters and scholarships through the 2004–2005 season. Making assumptions about what recruits they will land (and, from there, which players will forgo the NBA riches for a junior or senior year), the Bruin staff has a feel for how many scholarships will be available in any given year. Incredibly, they have projected high school *freshmen* into their rosters. To succeed, they always keep an eye on tomorrow and try to keep one step ahead of the competition.

How do coaches even draw up a wish list in the first place? The odds that a high school hoopster will ever play for a Division I program are roughly one in a thousand. Given these odds, there are approximately 500 Division I recruits to be evaluated. It is impossible for a staff of four to observe and weigh the merits of every player. So to begin with, they consult the hundreds of publications that style themselves as the Bibles of basketball recruiting, such as *Prep West Hoops* and *All-Star Report*, which rank up-and-coming players as young as 12 and 13. These publications draw on leads provided by "professional" scouts at 12-and-under tournament games, at junior high scrimmages, and at summer camps for kids.

Of course, to cover their bets coaches also go straight to the source: the recruiting and scouting services themselves, which identify, evaluate, and rank prospects according to their skills. Such services, with names like *World Basketball*, number in the hundreds, and most programs subscribe to five or more. While their value on the whole is undisputed— every player in the last five years who has gone on to college or professional stardom has appeared on some scout's radar—the quality of the individual service ultimately depends on the ability of the scouts each service trusts to be their eyes and ears. But it's all about perception. If a scout happens to catch a freshman on a night when the kid plays the game of his life, that player may skyrocket overnight to a top ten ranking in his class, in turn attracting recruiters like flies. Two years later, when it becomes clear that the performance was a freak mountain on a low-lying plain, the "next big one" may be off the radar entirely.

Dana Pump and his brother David are known to every coach in the land as "The Pump Brothers." The 36-year-old twin redheads know everything and everyone in the basketball universe. From their offices in Chatsworth, California, they operate Double Pump Basketball, running camps and a recruiting service and sponsoring traveling teams—as well as coordinating the nation's greatest showcase of high school talent, the Las Vegas Adidas Big Time Tournament. The Pumps also run a minitournament for junior college players and for lesser-known college talent, exposing them to possible scholarship offers. The Vegas tourney and the Best of the Summer Classic, routinely draw over 300 coaches from around the nation, take place every July and are seen as the last chance for high school ballers to make an impression, and for impressionable coaches to drool over that year's crop of teenage phenoms.

The walls of Dana Pump's living room and office are covered with framed photographs featuring Dana or David (or both) posing with the greatest legends of the game:

Dean Smith, John Wooden, Rick Pitino, Mike Krzyzewski, Roy Williams, Bobby Knight, Michael Jordan, Larry Bird, Karl Malone. To call men like the Pumps the heart of the college basketball world is no overstatement. But the brothers routinely come under fire from critics who claim they exploit youngsters to make a buck; that their methods corrupt the sport. Among other things, they've been accused of funneling players to schools at the behest of sneaker companies or boosters, and of exercising an unhealthy degree of influence over coaches' hirings and firings. The Pumps see it differently.

"We did not create the summer tourneys, the recruiting services, or even the rules," David says, relaxing on a plush couch in his brother's house. "We simply made a business model and followed it, bringing it all under one roof. Those that say we have ruined the game or take advantage of kids or coaches are simply jealous."

He has a point. The Pumps didn't set the guidelines; they simply spotted a demand and they do their best to satisfy it. One thing is beyond dispute: They can make a relatively unknown teenager a hot commodity overnight, because when they speak, coaches listen. (For all of the criticism the Pumps attract, there are the good deeds that go unnoticed: the nonrevenue-producing exhibitions for lesser-known talents and junior college kids so they can get scholarships; the hundreds of thousands of dollars they raise each year and contribute to cancer research.)

The various summer AAU camps and tournaments, such as those that the Pumps run, are college recruiters' meccas. For 20 days every July, they make pilgrimages to such hot spots as Las Vegas, Indianapolis, and Teaneck, to watch the best of the best hoop it up. At the tournaments, talent-loaded AAU teams from across the country compete in two or three games daily in full view of a horde of coaches. The games start at 7:00 A.M. and last until midnight, and the wise recruiter squeezes as much as he can out of every minute. "If a kid you are recruiting is playing at 8:00 A.M., then you'd better be there at 7:30 standing under the basket watching him warm up," declares Illinois assistant Norm Roberts. "You can't talk to him, but you'd better have your school sweatshirt on so he knows you are there."

Coaching staffs will often split up around the country to ensure that they cover all of their bases. Some assistant coaches may even be assigned one or two highly coveted players to "follow" that summer. That is, where the recruit goes, so does the coach. It's a huge risk, but many coaches are willing to take it if it means the possibility of signing a top prize. At the summer tournaments, hundreds of family members and fans, watch alongside some of the top coaches in the game. Lute Olson may be watching a game along with Eddie Sutton and Quin Snyder. Except for the most recognizable faces, every coach wears an article of clothing identifying his school. They move from one gym to another, following a schedule (complete with information on the players) sold by tournament organizers for as much as $200 a piece. When the games finish for the day, many coaches take the opportunity to hit a local night spot or socialize with fellow coaches.

In recent years the sneaker company camps, Nike and Adidas, have witnessed a dilution of talent according to critics. Why? In the late 1990s, AAU coaches began demanding that, along with their star players, the shoe company reps accept one or two other lackluster kids from the same team. What has resulted from these package deals are ballgames showcasing very good players mixed in with mediocre talent playing run-and-gun. When sloppy play predominates, it muddies the waters of the fishbowl; it's not easy to identify a master of the set offense when his teammates are trying to be like Mike—or just dunk like Mike. Hardly the ideal circumstances in which to size up talent. But AAU games are still by far the best venues for evaluating prospects, because they afford recruiters the opportunity to see the best players at one fell swoop.

"Of all the players who will sign with schools in November, I guarantee the colleges have never seen 30 to 40% of them play in their high school uniforms," vows Frank Burlison from *foxsports.com*. "They are signing players based on seeing them a couple of weeks at camp, which is contrary to the way basketball is played. By doing that, you are putting more value on the summer period, which in turn leads to poor evaluations."

In addition to recruiting services, summer camps, and tournaments, recruiters also rely on word of mouth—primarily through a network of university alums, high school coaches and friends. Every day, someone will excitedly call to tell a coach about "the next Michael Jordan." While the recruiter's first impulse may be to smirk and laugh off the comparison, the caller can't be taken too lightly—especially if he's a respected source, such as a former player who spots a potential star at his local playground, or a high school coach whose players have succeeded in the college ranks. If and when the next Michael Jordan does materialize, the coach will kick himself for not having followed up on the tip.

Every year coaches nationwide receive piles of letters from kids and their parents, begging them to come watch them play, ticking off their statistics and honors, and insisting they're the perfect fit for the school's offensive or defensive scheme, or both. These letters are filed away and a questionnaire is usually mailed out to the would-be prospect. If a player is good enough to compete at the Division I level, chances are the coaches will find them.

And then there are the "drop-ins"—students and families, who while touring the campus, make a point of dropping in to see the coach. Though coaches would never admit it publicly, they dread these unannounced visits that soak up precious time; and all for a kid who may not even be a fit for junior college ball. However, most coaches will tap someone on the staff to provide the kid with a brief tour of the facilities and field his questions because, well, you never know. Even if the visitor himself isn't the next Jordan, he may be the next Jordan's high school teammate, and you want him to go home raving about the lush campus, the banners in the cavernous gym, and the friendly coaching staff. You never know who might be listening.

By the start of a given class' junior year, most of the top programs have whittled their wish list down to a hundred or so players; by the end of the school year the list is down to 20. Some coaches prefer to concentrate the full glare of their attention on six or seven kids, hoping that four or five of them will sign. Other coaches will recruit several players at each position to cover their bets, hoping that at least one player at each slot will sign. By the time a recruit's senior year gets underway, coaches are usually clear about which kids they want and which ones are interested in them. In recent years the timetable has been bumped up, with prospects committing during their junior year, in turn accelerating the entire process. Hence, the reason coaches begin pursuing high school freshmen, and the demand for 12-and-under camps.

But in the hunt for skilled players, recruiters simply don't handcuff themselves to the high school bleachers. They also fish the junior college (juco) waters, which are stocked with mature players ready to step in and contribute. Many of these programs field top-flight talents who either couldn't qualify for Division I academically or who left a big school for personal reasons and dreaded the thought of sitting out a transfer year. The move from the big-name school to the no-name juco gives these players a different outlook on life.

Illinois assistant and former junior college coach Billy Gillispie, appointed the head coach of UTEP in October 2002, points out, "The juco guys have a different hunger, their window of opportunity is closing a bit."

Juco players, like minor league baseballers, are denied the perks of the big leagues: they routinely take vans to games and eat dinners at McDonald's. Their hunger to play Division

I ball and their experiences make them especially prized by the coaches of mid-major schools who, lacking the clout of the Top Twenty teams, have trouble signing the high school stars. But they have a good chance of landing a juco kid, who can often play immediately. The stumbling block? Many top colleges frown on accepting a junior college player, insisting that a basketball-first mentality runs contrary to the university mission.

So just how do coaches pursue their coveted recruits, particularly those in high school? It all starts with the United States Postal Service. Schools may mail recruits standard questionnaires about their program as early as the sixth grade. Schools can begin to write individual correspondences at the end of the sophomore year. Some coaching staffs, such as USC's and Iowa State's, are notorious for the "more is more" philosophy: they inundate recruits with wave after wave of mail, sometimes as many as 200 letters daily! (Although perhaps now that USC assistant Dave Miller is no longer on Henry Bibby's staff, the letter writing will diminish.) Other coaches insist that less is more, sending out one letter a week.

Cedric Bozeman will never forget the day he received 250 letters from Bibby's USC; he opened only six. Each letter was simply a short note like "Come to USC" or "It's a $130,000 education." (USC head coach Henry Bibby declined to be interviewed.) For schools like USC, it's a means of reassuring the prospect that he's still on the top of their mind, but what at first is flattering can ultimately turn a kid off. It's a fine line between pleasantly feeling worshipped and unpleasantly feeling smothered with affection. Bozeman ended up in a UCLA jersey.

September 1 had been the red-letter day for FedEx offices nationwide. Now, it is the week when school lets out in June. It's the first time the NCAA permits programs to woo rising high school juniors through individual correspondence and coaches waste no time, using delivery services. They don't hesitate to send a prospect three or more packages overnight. Ideally the package arrives on a Saturday morning, when the entire family is likely to be home. Coaches know all the tricks. They want the recruit or his family to be handed the package, not just come home on a weeknight to find it sitting there.

While the envelopes may be the same, the substance of the packages vary depending on the personalities of both the school and coach. Some are typed-out form letters, others, like Bozeman's from USC, are a few simple words on university letterhead. Many coaches get a kick out of dreaming up creative ways to grab the player's attention. Illinois has enclosed a *Sports Illustrated* photo of history's Top 50 NBA players, reproduced with the smiling faces of its staff superimposed on the bodies of Bird, Magic, Wilt, and Oscar. At Notre Dame, assistant Anthony Solomon will paste into an article about the top guard tandems in history a coveted recruit's name, fabulous statistics and all. (But the low-key Brey tries to limit this "gimmickry.") Other letters will include drawings of a coach reeling in a "big fish"—the kid himself, thrilled to land in such expert hands—or *Sports Illustrated* covers of the player in school colors, cutting down the nets.

Phone conversations are absolutely critical to the recruiting process. They allow the coach to get a feel for a player's personality, to get to know his family a bit and to glean whatever information he can about his life. For example, a coach may overhear a recruit's stereo in the background and infer he's a Tupac or Green Day fan based on what he hears. Or maybe a recruit's sister answers the phone and a coach spends 20 minutes talking to her before asking for the player. When the rules are further relaxed, permitting high school juniors and his family to phone coaches on the schools' bills, they may call collect or call a toll-free number as often as they like. However, it's still a one-way street: The NCAA restricts only the number of calls a school can place to a recruit, not the number of calls the recruit can make. (Of course, some coaches break the rules by making additional, untraceable calls from unlisted cell phone numbers.)

Recruiters are always on the lookout for new avenues of communication, so it's no surprise that with the explosion of the Internet, they're quick to exploit the opportunity e-mail offers to convey information at unprecedented low cost. The NCAA is attempting to clarify whether e-mails and instant messages are on a footing with mailed letters, phone calls, or both. Until those parameters are settled on, recruiters will continue to forward articles and exchange e-mails with their prospects, often more than once daily.

In the rarefied air of Top Twenty basketball, a buzzer-beating Christian Laettner jumper or a fluky Chris Webber timeout is often all that separates two elite programs with perennial championship hopes. When a player has his pick of several schools with a crack at winning it all, it's the intangibles that sway him: the coach's personality; his chances of starting; close friends attending the same school; the weather; the girls; the number of television appearances; the season schedule; the campus' comforting proximity to Mom and Dad, or its liberating distance from them.

Hyperaware of this, recruiters continuously maintain archives on their most coveted prospects. These files cover every aspect of the recruit's life, from the important to the apparently trivial: his birthday (as well as his family's and girlfriend's), social security number, childhood memories, best friends, former coaches, sleeping patterns, best and worst academic subjects, and favorite food, TV show, movie, NBA star, song, and so on, ad nauseam. Does the shot-blocking menace from Peoria like Domino's or DiGiorno's? Will the partying point guard from Detroit bristle at the mention of Chaney's pre-dawn workouts? Is the soft-spoken Texas forward better motivated to pick up his game by a coach's screams or a teammate's nudge? The files have the answer.

How do recruiters dredge up all this information? By drawing on every resource they can: the player himself, of course, as well as his family, friends, girlfriend, coaches, and teachers. The aim of a recruiter in the information-gathering stage is to identify and make friends with the prospect's closest confidantes. Along the way he has to weed out the hangers-on, the guys down at the playground who profess to know what's going on, but really have no clue. The sooner a coach can determine the main characters in the player's life, the faster he can get a foot in the inner circle.

By the time recruits make their maximum allowable number of five official campus visits, those trips paid for by the schools, they know the recruiters and the programs reasonably well, as do their families and high school coaches. The formalities are out of the way. The file, now packed with information, is exploited to its fullest potential. For example, the recruit may have dinner with the head coach on Friday night at the Panda Garden and not at a fancy steakhouse. Saturday night will be spent partying hard at the hottest spot in town with the team's shooting guard, not catching a late showing of *Pearl Harbor*. Sunday afternoon he'll get to sleep 'till 10, not be roused at nine for a tour of the library by an assistant coach. The official visit is planned down to the minute, with nothing left to chance. With the margin between elite schools so thin, it had better be.

At UCLA, Lavin and the coaching staff have a fairly set schedule for official visits. The recruit arrives and is driven to his hotel, the Park Hyatt in Century City near Beverly Hills, and is greeted by five-foot high posters of the recruit in a UCLA jersey on the cover of a mock *Sports Illustrated*. Preferably, the official visit takes place early in the fall on a football weekend, so recruits can take in the atmosphere of the football game played at the Rose Bowl. Over the course of the weekend, recruits will meet many of the players, former UCLA athletes, a professor or two, and for some highly coveted recruits, a meeting with the chancellor or vice-chancellor. Lavin will often have the recruit and possibly his family over to his house in Marina del Rey to hang out, play pool, or swim. Many of the official visit activities revolve around food, so there are trips to Gladstone's restaurant on the beach in Malibu, R. J.'s steakhouse in Beverly Hills, the Cheesecake Factory, and other assorted Los Angeles eateries.

Like on an official visit to UCLA, Illinois recruits are treated to a variety of hearty meals and entertainment, all tailored according to the likes and dislikes of the recruit. The recruit and his family will stay at the Hawthorn Suites, just blocks from campus, where they are greeted with posters, jerseys, or other creative enticements. The recruit will often go to Silvercreek for brunch or Aunt Sonya's for breakfast, and local places such as Kennedy's or Juniors for dinners. The Selfs will also host the player and his parents at their home for a BBQ or late lunch. A player may have a meeting with the chancellor, but as Self points out, "the parents are often more impressed than the recruit." There are also meetings arranged with professors, academic advisors, and deans, according to the fields of interest expressed by the recruit.

"It's important for me that the team hangs out together on an official visit and the recruits meet everybody," Self says. "I want feedback from the players and I want everyone to be comfortable with someone who could be in our family."

The official visit to Notre Dame is quite similar to most other major college programs, except that Mike Brey has the lure of Notre Dame football to help sell the school. Official visits, 12 allowed to each school a year, are scheduled on home football weekends in South Bend, when school pride is at its peak.

Recruits stay at the Varsity Clubs of America just two miles from campus, where they are greeted by creative posters or *USA Today* banner headlines, jerseys with their names on them, and perhaps a videotape in the VCR showing highlights of Notre Dame basketball. (A locker will be set up with an Irish jersey with the recruit's name sewn in, in the Irish locker room.) On Friday, recruits spend most of the day as regular students with their hosts—going to class, eating in the dining halls, playing pickup games with players. They will also have meetings with academic advisor Pat Holmes, possibly a dean in an academic area of interest, time with strength coach Tony Rolinski, and for some recruits, a meeting with school president Edward Malloy, a former Notre Dame basketball player himself. Friday night is the emotional Pep Rally for the football team which is followed by a meal for the recruit with his hosts, while Brey and his assistants entertain the parents at establishments like Houlihan's, Famous Dave's, or Outback Steakhouse.

Saturday morning is a pickup game, if there was no time on Friday, and a tailgate lunch 40 yards from the football stadium, so recruits get the feel of the legions of Irish fans and get to see firsthand the well-wishers and autograph-seekers approach the players and staff. The recruit sits in the student section for the game. Saturday night is dinner at the home of the Breys followed by a night out for the high schooler. If the player is Catholic or has an interest, Sunday Mass at the Basilica on campus is worth the time. Brey almost always drives the recruit to the South Bend Regional Airport, to get a sense of the recruit's thinking as he leaves the state.

Steve Alford's recruits get a strong sense of family on their three-day visit to Iowa City, spending a great deal of time with the entire team and the coaching staff. The coach sees the visit as a chance for him to evaluate the recruit as much as the recruit evaluates the school. "We want to be sold on a recruit, to know that he will fit into our family here at Iowa. We have a family atmosphere and it is important that he fit in well." To that end, Alford makes sure that every player and every coach spends time with the recruit and immediately after the official visit ends, the coach will call six or seven players to get their feelings on the recruit. He wants to know how the recruit acted socially, if he got along with the guys and what their overall impressions were. Like the other coaches, Alford will always have the recruit and his family over to his house for dinner, and the player-host will take the recruit to various restaurants on the mall in downtown Iowa City.

In addition to the official visits, the coach's home visit can be equally important. The coach, usually with one assistant, travels to the home of the recruit and spends one to three hours talking about the program and the future. In many instances, the coach has a packed crowd, including immediate family, uncles, cousins, friends, neighbors, and so on, whoever might be close to a recruit. Lavin brings three binders with him, covering the academic, athletic, and social benefits of UCLA. He sees the home visit as a conversation more than a presentation, and spends a great deal of time answering questions about himself and the Bruins. With so much misinformation out there about him, he must first gain the confidence of the recruit and his family, before doing what coaches do best—sell.

Self will spend no more than an hour or an hour and a half in a recruit's home, and tries to limit the props. He will bring a poster board listing reasons why that recruit should choose Illinois and he will often bring along a videotape of highlights from basketball and scenes from campus, particularly if a recruit has never visited Champaign.

"I think the home visit has become less of a factor," says Brey, "because kids are getting on campus for unofficial visits their junior years. They and their parents have met the staff, toured the campus, met some of the players." In fact, in his two years at Notre Dame, Brey has only gone on two home visits and had only one planned for the fall of 2002. His 60- to 90-minute visits with the lead assistant recruiter and the recruit's family are all about enthusiasm. Brey sits on the end of the chair or sofa, talks about his plans for the future and how the recruit fits into those plans. He may bring along pictures of the campus, a video of games or of South Bend, as well as an academic plan and folder prepared individually for the recruit. During one home visit when he was the head coach at Delaware, Brey even dribbled a basketball between his legs as the point guard recruit did the same, leaving the high schooler impressed.

Alford tries to keep his home visits to 45 to 60 minutes, the maximum he thinks he can hold the attention of the player and his family. He comes in organized and is clear in his message. "We cover the four main areas of the Iowa program: Spiritual, Social, Academic, and Athletic. The player knows exactly what to expect." The coach might also bring along a video tour of Iowa City for recruits who have not visited the campus.

With so much time and effort expended on a kid who can attend only one school at a time, recruiters quickly learn about heartache. If they go after 20 kids hard, they may sign one or two; many others have turned them down. Coaches may get accustomed to rejection, it's part of the game, but it still hurts. Many of them develop strong relationships with the recruits and their families, so it's tough on all parties when the recruit decides to pack his bags for another school. But if there were no possibility of that happening, there would be no recruiting wars at all.

Some in the NCAA wish there weren't. No other aspect of college basketball triggers as much controversy, malevolence, and slanderous rhetoric as recruiting. Coaches are under enormous pressure to win, and winning is usually the result of signing great recruits. With such a small pool of talent available, and such a miniscule margin for error, the competition for kids often turns ugly as coaches claw, scrape, and bite each other in the fight to sign a prospect. The boundaries of black and white are blurred, and coaches' means and methods have created a gray moral universe.

When there are rules, coaches find ways to break them. During periods when coaches cannot talk with parents, they "accidentally" bump into them at AAU or high school games, say hello, and move on. They've accomplished their mission—the parents and player will know he was there.

On the first day of an evaluation period in 2001, Florida coach Billy Donovan allegedly flew from Gainesville to Raleigh, North Carolina, rented a car, and drove to Broughton High School, home to power forward Shavlik Randolph. Donovan sat in the parking lot, waited for Randolph to pull in, and . . . waved. He then got back in his car, returned to the rental agency in Raleigh, and flew home. Many coaches routinely "bump" into recruits or their parents at games, on planes, or at hotels. The NCAA has attempted to crack down on these "bump" encounters.

Are Donovan and his coaching colleagues crazy, unethical, or just workaholics? It depends on who you ask. Technically, they do not break NCAA rules that ban contact during certain periods, but in bending the rules, did they violate the spirit of the law? The NCAA is so busy investigating the rule-breakers it doesn't always have time to reprimand the rule-benders.

So how do coaches cheat? Besides making illegal phone calls to recruits and violating evaluation rules, coaches may offer money directly to a prospect for signing a letter of intent, or they may arrange for an unscrupulous third party—an AAU or high school coach, or an advisor the recruit trusts—to "deliver" the player to them for an agreed-upon sum. A direct payment cannot be made lest a scandal ensues (like the one a Kentucky assistant triggered in 1988 when he sent the father of forward Chris Mills $1,000 cash in an Emery Worldwide envelope.) So coaches get creative. They arrange for a booster to make a donation to a nonprofit foundation that—surprise—is run by the AAU coach or employs him; or perhaps the booster sponsors the AAU team outright. The going rate for delivering an elite recruit is in the $10,000 to $20,000 range. The practice isn't much talked about, but it's there.

"Trust me," confides UCLA assistant Gerald Madkins, "if a dollar amount is placed out there, you can very easily get an AAU coach to come on your side."

Dan Wetzel, reporter for *cbssportsline.com* and author of *Sole Influence*, an exposé of corruption on the recruiting circuit, knows the payments are there; it's obvious when AAU coaches actively seek to sell their players. "Ninety percent of summer coaches are great guys and are in it for healthy reasons. But 10% of summer coaches control about 50% of the top talent. They literally make a living coaching these summer teams. They don't have jobs, they get money from sponsors, agents, or schools, and they are profiting off these kids. When that happens, your motives change. You make decisions that are in your best interests, not the kid's."

AAU coaches and teams are often at the whirlwind eye of controversy and scandal. Among the most notorious was Kansas City's Myron Piggie, a convicted crack dealer who sold his AAU phenoms to the highest bidders—all the while on Nike's payroll.

David Pump admits that payments are a part of the recruiting game. "There are some AAU coaches who try to sell their players to the highest bidder. There can be a lot of NCAA rules, but the reality is that coaches push those rules to the limits."

It's not unusual for sneaker companies to forge a bond with AAU coaches—it's a good way to establish a foothold (so to speak) with tomorrow's superstar sponsors. But guys like Piggie give AAU coaches a bad name. According to many college coaches, there are only a few bad apples in the AAU ranks. Blame must also fall on high school coaches and parents, some of whom actively seek the highest bids. Coaches at Top Twenty programs may receive a mysterious call from a third party, declaring that such and such a school offered $15,000—would they care to outbid?

"There is certainly stuff going on at the summer camps and tournaments," says *The Sporting News'* Mike DeCourcy. "There probably is some illegal recruiting, but it certainly is not as bad as it was 10 or 15 years ago."

But how much of the recruiting process is tainted? "Word does get out," UCLA assistant Jim Saia notes. "You have to understand that a lot of it is rumors too. They could be saying things about your program and your head coach which aren't true."

Illinois' Gillespie, who lives to recruit, claims that it's "very competitive to get players, and if guys don't get the best players, then there are not too many guys that will say, 'Well, they just beat us.' There has to be a reason. There is always an excuse."

"We're all supposed to be following the rules," Mike Brey acknowledges, "but not everybody is following the rules like they should be. Fewer are breaking the rules than the public thinks. If you get into a recruiting battle over someone, you'd better know going in that you have a shot and what it might take to sign him. If you are not comfortable with that, then you walk away."

But some rumors are more than rumors, and what is public knowledge is probably only the tip of the iceberg. In fact, some head coaches may be unaware when their staffs are cheating—the signings get done, and they don't inquire into the details. Some coaches despair about the state of affairs. "Why is there nothing done?" Notre Dame's Anthony Solomon laments. "Who's going to do something about it? College coaches? The NCAA? It's just like the law—innocent until proven guilty. And if you are guilty, who is going to do something then? If we know others are cheating, how come we as coaches don't report it?"

There is also the package deal to contend with, in which the parent or coach of a hot prospect is offered a place on the staff of a college if the kid signs. More than a dozen current Division I coaches rode into the college ranks on a recruit's coattails. The most high-profile "packaging" in recent years took place in 1985, when high school phenom Danny Manning enrolled at Kansas for Larry Brown—and his truck-driving father was tapped as assistant coach. Manning Sr. certainly knew the game and had been a coach before entering the trucking field. Former NBA star Milt Wagner became Memphis' director of basketball operations under John Calipari, a year before his son Dajuan signed with the Tigers. USC's director of basketball operations is Tim Farmer, the older brother of sophomore player and highly coveted recruit Desmond Farmer.

The trend is not a new one, as researcher Mike Douchant points out. In 1973, high school coach Duncan Reid followed forward Norm Cook to Kansas and joined Ted Owens' staff. Four years later, Owens hired high school coach Lafayette Norwood just as Norwood's star guard, Darnell Valentine, signed with the Jayhawks. In 1977, high school coach Kevin Mackey landed a spot on Tom Davis' staff at Boston College the same year as his center, Joe Beaulieu; both were joined a year later by Beaulieu's high school teammate, Dwan Chandler.

The list goes on and on: In 1996 NC State's Herb Sendek signed Damon Thornton; coach Mark Phelps came along for the ride, hauling in tow (a year later) Thornton's old teammate Kenny Inge. In 1998, Tennessee's Jerry Green signed Vincent Yarborough; coach Ray Grant tagged along. In 1996 Villanova's Steve Lappas signed Tim Thomas and coach Jimmy Salmon in one fell swoop. The practice has become so routine that only in extraordinary circumstances does it raise eyebrows. So what do coaches have to say about it? Those who have taken advantage of these opportunities will defend their hirings to the death, rattling off their qualifications for the job until they're hoarse. Of course, no coach will admit that his signing was tied up with a recruit's, although the evidence to the contrary is overwhelming.

Then there's the practice of a school helping to relocate a recruit's family—complete with a guaranteed job for Mom or Dad—to ensure his signing. The job, which usually pays well, may be with a local business or high school, or even at the university itself. But even if the circumstances are suspicious, little can be done unless proof surfaces that a deal was explicitly prearranged.

Far more prevalent and dismaying to coaches than outright cheating is the practice of negative recruiting—of painting other schools in a bad light in a bid to snag prized prospects. Hypothetically, a coach, in a recruiting battle with two conference rivals may tell a player, "You know, Coach A is probably going to end up somewhere else and Coach B is getting old—planning retirement in fact." Accurate or not, this constitutes negative recruiting.

When UNLV was being investigated for alleged violations, coaches recruited against them continually, warning hot prospects of the impending doom in Vegas. At Marquette, Tom Crean has to go the extra mile to convince recruits that he is staying put, no matter what other coaches had told them. Bill Self faces the same task when it comes to rumors of his imminent departure for the NBA. In a now notorious case during the 2002 season, a Cincinnati assistant faxed a letter to a recruit implying that John Chaney's age at Temple was a problem, and that the old master was losing his grip on the game.

Where negative recruiting is most virulent, nothing escapes its taint. Shrewd recruiters will plant seeds of doubt in a kid's head about another coach's ability to develop players, to groom them for the NBA, to lead them to a national title. Coaches routinely point out to recruits the other players that other schools are recruiting, leaving a recruit doubtful if he'd ever start. Coaches may criticize another school's academics, its party scene, its frigid or torrid weather, and so on. If it means swaying the prospective player one inch in your direction, anything goes.

But none of it is against the rules. Nowhere in the NCAA Bylaws is negative recruiting explicitly forbidden. Of course, every coach denies that he uses such tactics, and some don't. But many do, and even more cry foul when it comes to their own schools being badmouthed. Precisely where the truth lies is uncertain. There is a large gray area when it comes to negative recruiting. If a coach from School A tells a recruit that the coach at School B has never coached an NBA player, is that simply a fact or negative recruiting? Or both? How about a coach from School A telling a recruit that School B has already signed two other players at his position? Is that fair? Where most coaches think it steps over the line are rumors, innuendoes, assumptions, or blatant lies to gain an advantage.

A given school's approach to recruiting—its methods and ethical standards—are dictated by the head coach: he gives the orders and his assistants do most of the legwork. But the coach's philosophy itself is influenced by a number of factors: the school's size and location, its academic stringency or laxity, the budget it accords the athletic department. A smart coach at a mid-major school adjusts to his parameters; if he goes about recruiting like Coach K or Mike Davis, he'll be gone before the morning shootaround.

Farleigh Dickinson's Tom Green: "I think it's probably easier at the bigger-level schools [to recruit]. Everybody can tell who the five-star player is. But it's that three, three-plus player that we are going after and predicting how good they might be as a sophomore in college. I think it is much more difficult at our level to project how players are going to be."

Rick Boyages at William & Mary, Dave Faucher at Dartmouth, and James Jones at Yale are all in a sense straitjacketed by their schools' severe academic requirements. It's hard enough trying to find a high school senior with a 3.8 GPA, let alone one who's 7', 260 lbs., with a soft jumper and a bruising inside game. "I'm going after kids who care about the next 40 years, not the next four," Jones declares. "It is harder to recruit kids at this level, taking into consideration the academic mission."

Other coaches, given more elbow-room academically, are hampered by their schools' smaller name. Tim Carter at the University of Texas-San Antonio has what he sees as an uphill battle. "I spend a lot of time recruiting on the phone, trying to convince kids to come to us over an ACC school. I don't have a private plane for recruiting trips, so much of my work is done on the phone, driving in a car for hours to see a kid." Smaller schools generally have a more limited recruiting budget, which translates into fewer flights to see recruits and more modest recruiting mail-outs.

Jeff Jones at American University sees a tradeoff. "At the higher levels, you can get in almost any door and can string kids along and then at the last minute come in and beat somebody out for a kid. The stakes are not higher at our level but different. If you lose a recruit [at a Top Twenty school], the 300,000 people that log onto the universityX.com for the chat room know you lost him. Here, other than a few people in the department, no one will know we may have lost a recruit."

As Jones points out, because the chances of trumping a Kentucky or Arizona in a recruiting battle are so slim, mid- and low-majors have to fish a bigger lake. And even then, the perennial powerhouses can reach in anytime and steal the recruit away. They have the means not only to grab the Parade All-American, but the mid-major's All-Conference sophomore center too.

How much clout does a coach exercise in getting his school to admit the "at-risk" kid who dribble-penetrates like Iverson, but struggles with the SAT? The backing of the coach often goes a long way; just how far depends on the institution. Maybe it's one "at-risk" player a year at an academically rigorous school like Notre Dame, William & Mary, or Dartmouth. But no coach, no matter how powerful, is granted carte blanche. Admissions staffs always have the final word. To help avert any improprieties, policies are often instituted that limit communication between coaching staffs and admissions officers—though it would be naïve to assume that the latter are oblivious to the team's needs.

The Patriot League, to which Pat Flannery's Bucknell belongs, uses a formula incorporating a student's GPA, SAT score and high school class rank to create a number index. Flannery knows at a glance whether or not a potential recruit meets the minimum academic requirements. He also has a feel for which borderline recruits the admissions staff will deem equal (or unequal) to the school's challenging curriculum. "I can't go up to the Admissions Office and cry and beg for a kid—we want kids who we know can succeed here. If there's a kid who falls below what the standard is at Bucknell, all I want is for the admissions office to give him an interview, to see what he is all about." Flannery's relationship with admissions is a two-way street: "They use us as much as we use them," he asserts, alluding to the exposure the basketball program gives the school.

Remember Illinois recruit Ike Diogu who eventually signed with Arizona State? Five months after committing to Rob Evans, Ike sits back and relaxes in front of the TV—and his coach Phil Sirois can get back to the basics of coaching, at least until his next hot prospect comes along. After flirting with Ike and Coach Sirois for so long, the recruiters on the losing end are now suddenly out of their lives. "It's all just a business," the coach says. "You make some good relationships and then it all ends. But you never know, somewhere down the line we could speak again."

Ike himself is clearly relieved. The incessant phone calls and the flood of FedExes started to get to him, as had the constant questions from his family, friends, and classmates. "I would still do it all over again," the 17-year-old says. "It was fun but hectic. I can live a normal life now."

The Sun Devil coaches have already put him on an intense workout regimen, to prepare his body for the bruising college game; they're also keeping an eye on his grades, making sure he continues hitting the books. March Madness is on the tube, a promising career at ASU is on the horizon. Ike has a feeling that someday the two will cross paths.

Tuesday, December 4, was "Terrible Tuesday" for three of the teams. Illinois was in Phoenix to play Top Ten Arizona, the first game of a doubleheader followed by Utah and Arizona State. The matchup was a big one for Illinois, who played poorly in a loss the previous week against Maryland and in the win at home against Texas A&M-Corpus Christi. His players were pumped, but uptight. The coach was not.

At the noon shootaround, Bill Self, dressed in blue jeans, a T-shirt, and a blue windbreaker, watched as his players shot jumpers and free throws at both ends of the court in America West Arena. After 30 minutes of shooting, the starters and two main subs took a seat on the bench as Billy Gillispie proceeded to walk through the Arizona scouting report, which was placed firmly in his hand. He had been assigned Arizona earlier in the season, meaning he was the assistant responsible for watching tape, preparing a scouting report, and walking Illinois through their opponent's set plays. Using his players as Arizona stand-ins, Gillispie showed the team offensive sets and out-of-bounds plays, moving the Illinois players around the court, showing the moves that the Wildcats will make.

"The key," he told the team, "is to play tight defense on Gardner [Jason] and double-team Walton [Luke] when he gets the ball in the post."

Gillispie hurried through the last plays, as Utah players began to walk toward the court for their 1:00 P.M. shootaround. As Illinois exited, Self ran into Utah coach Rick Majerus. They exchanged hellos and wished each other the best of luck in their games that night.

Five hours later, as his team warmed up on the floor, Self was not compelled to remain behind in the locker room. Instead, he wandered from the bowels of America West Arena and stood 10 feet from the court between two sets of stands, observing the atmosphere. Noticing the chill in the arena, he turned to some teenage Arizona fans sitting by the tunnel and talked about . . . the weather. "Boy, it is chilly in here. Kind of cold outside, but you would think it would be better inside here," he leaned over and said to the two fans.

Almost in awe that the Illinois' coach had engaged them in conversation, especially while wearing Arizona apparel, the young adolescents quickly agreed with Self's assessment of the conditions. The coach exchanged a few more words with them and continued to scan the crowd and watch the teams warm up. He then retreated to the locker room to await his team's arrival and began writing on a poster board easel.

His concern this night was not so much on the physical play, but on the attitude of his players. Some games the mind wins over matter. He knew that if they had fun and enjoyed the game, good things would come. Before the team assembled in a semicircle in chairs, facing Self in front of the easel, the coach made a bathroom visit. He had had terrible stomach pains for the past 10 hours and contemplated going to a Phoenix hospital, but decided it would pass.

In a matter of moments, he had gone over the 30 or so terms on the board. Rebound. Press. Guard Play. The players knew what they meant, so Self only briefly elaborated. He finally reached the end of the list, and there, in different colored markers were three words. *Family. Fun. Focus.* "These words say it all. We have got to start having fun out here. We did last year. It's still just a game, guys, let's have fun. If you are not having fun I am going to take you out," he threatened his team, who saw no humor in his threat. "Remember we are a family. We win together and we lose together. No matter what, we stay as a family. And finally, keep yourselves focused on the game and what you can be doing, whether you are on the floor, or on the bench."

Self put the cap back on the marker, and put the marker on the easel board. He turned back around to his team and with a more serious tone and look he reminded them of a game 10 months earlier, when Arizona knocked Illinois out of the NCAA Tournament in the Elite Eight, 87-81, ending the Illini season. In fact, the teams' meeting in the Tournament was their third of that season. They met in Maui in November in the championship game, a Wildcat win. They played again a week later at the United Center, as part of a home and home series, and in a physical and rough game, Illinois prevailed. Before their meeting in the NCAAs, Lute Olson talked often in the press about the rough play of the Illini, causing a minicontroversy.

"Let's not forget last year and how they made us feel," Self said that night in December. "We owe them not one, but several, but we must get one before we get several." And with that, his troops were ready, clapping and hollering as they sprinted onto the floor.

Self reminded his team going into the Arizona game that they "owed them one," but the pregame reminder didn't work. Illinois led early, 13-7, before Arizona caught fire with a 10-0 run as Illinois looked very tentative on offense. Cory Bradford picked up two quick fouls and Self was all over the officiating crew, coming dangerously close to a technical. Illinois' shooting woes continued, hitting just 28% from the field in the first half as Frank Williams was nonexistent. Illinois scored exactly zero baskets in the last seven minutes of the first half. The Illini trailed by 16 at the break, 47-31. As the team walked into their expansive locker room, Self stopped outside the door and talked to his staff for a moment. They discussed the poor play of Brian Cook and the turnover-plagued performance of Luther Head.

The assistants headed in followed by Self, who asked for a chair. He wanted to talk with his team on their level, and wanted to sit eye to eye with them and have a frank discussion. Self is a fairly even-keeled fellow, and though he does have his moments, on and off the court, he speaks in a constant tone and in a familiar level to his players. He didn't use this halftime to draw diagrams on the easel, or to even pour over a coach's best friend—stats. Instead, he sat in that chair and talked.

"Cookie [Brian Cook], you are not playing very well. Are you nervous? You probably think the pro scouts are out there looking at you. The way you were challenging shots I thought you had two fouls on you, but you only had one? You can do better."

Turning his attention to the athletic, but often out of control, freshman Luther Head, who had three turnovers in 10 minutes and got the start despite his poor play against Texas A&M-Corpus Christi, Self challenged the youngster. "You didn't play like this on the playgrounds in Chicago, did you?" Next on his list was Bradford, a three-point specialist who was shooting nothing special on this day. "Cory, I don't know what's in your head, man, but boy do we need you. The shots will eventually fall, but you have to play good defense and play smart."

Turning to Williams, "And Frankie, the pro scouts are looking at you too, but they are not seeing much out of you today. In fact, we don't have any pros in this room," Self remarked, a comment intended to hit Williams and Cook the hardest.

Self was very direct with his comments, but not with his eye contact. While addressing a player, he rarely looked at him. Rather, Self looked at another player, into space, or at the floor.

"Look, guys, everyone goes through the tough times, but we must grind through it. Let's be men out there. I want you to be proud to wear the Illinois uniform. This is a defining moment for this team. How we go out and respond in the second half will tell us a lot about our season."

Before letting his team go, he told them he wanted the lead down to 12 by the first media timeout at the 16:00-minute mark. Then to eight by the 12:00 stoppage. He knew his team could play better, and knew that dividing the half into four-minute stretches made the deficit look a lot smaller. They didn't have to get it back all at once.

In the second half, his team did play much better, cutting the lead to four on one occasion, after trailing by 19. But they couldn't catch the Wildcats. Bradford ended up shooting 0-8 from three-point land, Cook played better but not well enough. It was the All-American and reigning Big Ten Conference Player of the Year Frank Williams who led the Illini comeback late in the game, taking Illinois on a 20-6 run. But as one of the pro scouts in attendance remarked, "It was a little too late. Where was he in the first half?" (Williams finished with 30 points, scoring 16 in the final 4:19.) As the game wound down, Self turned to his bench to put Head back in to finish the game. Head refused.

In the America West locker room after the loss, Self again pulled up a seat in front of his players to talk with them. "The second half was a defining moment for this basketball team. We didn't fold and played hard to the end. I am proud of the way you played in the second half. It's not often that Cory shoots so poorly, and they will go in for him. To be honest with you, yes, the officiating was horseshit, but we still got beat."

Turning his attention and frustration to Head, "Luther, I am disappointed in you. When you didn't want to go into the game at the end, that is really disappointing for a coach. You dribbled off of your foot a couple times, you must be nervous. But that's my fault. Maybe I shouldn't have expected you to be ready." Head was scoreless in the game.

Before breaking as a team, they huddled in the center of the locker room and Self instructed them to talk up Arizona to the media in the postgame interviews. The team chanted "family," and Cook apologized to his teammates for his poor play, promising them that it would never happen again. Self left the locker room to do a press conference as the effects of the loss took hold. Senior Robert Archibald put his arm around the dejected Head, encouraging him to keep his head up. Then, it was injured Lucas Johnson's turn, who sat with Head on a counter in the back of the locker room. Cook sat in front of his locker, burying his face into his hands.

In his press conference, Self refused to comment on the officiating, but did say it "was interesting how the fouls evened up when Arizona was ahead by 19."

Outside of the locker room, the Illinois beat writers talked with Williams and Self, both of whom did not look, or sound, good. The assistant coaches were inside the locker room, seated in folding chairs, going over the game stats. Self joined them a few minutes later. They attempted to find the answer—again. Self considered benching Cook, but would give it a few days to see how he reacted in practice. Arizona was a top team so the loss could have been worse. They could have lost to Northern Iowa.

The Iowa Hawkeyes were paying a visit to their smaller in-state foe, as part of a forced home and home series. The Iowa legislature mandates that all four Division I teams in Iowa play each other yearly, and the schools rotate the site. Iowa entered the game 6-2, having lost only to Duke and Missouri, but was not playing to its potential. UNI was 4-2 but had played a much weaker schedule. And so the two Iowa teams met on the first Tuesday in December and, as they say, anything can happen in basketball.

Alford was worried in the pregame locker room that his team would not take the in-state rivals seriously, that they would see the name on the uniform and assume it would be a win. "This is their game of the season," he told his troops, "they point to this game all year long and will play like it."

By midway through the first half, Iowa led 23-14 after Chauncey Leslie nailed a three. But Northern Iowa's Robbie Sieverding got hot along with David Gruber, and Northern Iowa took a 34-33 lead into halftime.

"This is what you get when you don't prepare properly," Alford fumed at halftime, well aware that his team had not practiced or prepared well for UNI. "Now we have a real dog-fight for the next 20 minutes." The coach tried to figure out a way for Iowa to stop Gruber and Sieverding and implored his players to get aggressive defensively. The game was back and forth in the second half, with Luke Recker keeping Iowa in it and Reggie Evans work-ing his way to yet another double-double. In the second half, UNI shot 54% from the field and made 64% of their three-pointers. Iowa hit just one three. With nine seconds left in the game, UNI's Andy Wooley stole the ball and Sieverding hit two free throws with six seconds left and Northern Iowa was on its way to a shocking 78-76 upset of the Hawkeyes.

For most of the second half, Alford and his assistants simply sat on the bench and did not go out of their way to instruct or manage the team. Alford felt the players were not listening to the coaching staff, paying no attention to what they said in timeouts and at halftime. In the postgame locker room, the coach was frustrated, as one might expect, as Iowa had lost to a team they should have beaten. He believed that his players did not appreciate what putting on an Iowa uniform meant, and the responsibility that came with it. There should be no difference between playing Northern Iowa or Illinois. What's on "our jerseys is what matters." The coach was so frustrated that as the team boarded the bus, and pizza was delivered for the ride home, Alford intercepted the pies and gave the pizza away to astonished UNI students. His players didn't deserve the treat.

In a game played 310 miles away in Bloomington, Indiana, Mike Brey's undefeated Irish took on in-state rival Indiana. Notre Dame had not won in Bloomington since 1973–1974, losing 12 straight to the Hoosiers. Ten minutes into the game, Notre Dame was already down 10, and had to fight back the remaining 30 minutes. At halftime, Brey told his players to slow things down offensively, that they could work themselves back into the game. He implored his guards to get the big guys touches down low.

Late in the game, the Irish went on a tenacious 10-4 run to close the gap to 72-70 with 54.9 seconds to go. Over a frantic one minute, Indiana held on. Tom Coverdale hit two free throws with 30.6 seconds left and Chris Thomas hit a three-pointer with just under 23 sec-onds remaining. Coverdale then hit two more free throws followed by a bucket by Ryan Humphrey, and the score was 76-75 with 2.4 seconds left. After Notre Dame fouled IU's Donald Perry, Perry missed the front end of a one-and-one and Humphrey threw one last prayer that ricocheted off the shot clock. Game over. Jared Jeffries scored a career-high 28 points and Coverdale came off the bench to add 11 for Indiana. Brey had tried to stop Jeffries by employing a triangle-and-two defense, with Matt Carroll all over the Indiana for-ward, but it didn't work. Thomas led Notre Dame with 24 points and Humphrey had 23 points and 12 rebounds. Two telling statistics: Notre Dame had only three assists in the dreadful first half and the Indiana bench outscored the Irish bench 22-3.

Notre Dame did themselves in with a poor start, a proclivity that would hurt them in future games as well. They had their chance, on the road, to go to 8-0 and earn some much needed national respect. "One thing that I am happy for," Brey reflected the next morning, "is that the kids know there are no more moral victories with this program. Our success last year and the team we have now should not be content with any moral victories. I am glad the kids were disappointed."

UCLA meanwhile played its first game without Cedric Bozeman at the point and found a way to win an ugly 65-50 game over the University of California at Riverside. Rico Hines started for Bozeman and Lavin moved Jason Kapono to the point. UCLA was favored by 29 points and played before a lethargic crowd of 6,700 at Pauley. The Bruins had dropped to No. 20 in the polls after their loss to Pepperdine, and played like an unranked team. Kapono scored 18 points, a high number considering he spent a great deal of the game at point guard. To compensate for the loss of a true point, Lavin used a three-guard lineup at times, with Hines and Billy Knight joining Kapono. UCLA did not make a field goal in the first five minutes and trailed the 0-4 Highlanders 16-12 to start the game, but pulled even at 28 by halftime. Midway through the second half, UCLA pulled away, despite committing 18 turnovers.

"It wasn't a pretty effort," Lavin said after the game. "We're searching for combinations of lineups and defenses that will allow us to get stops." Perhaps Kapono summed up the Bruins' attitude by saying "it was just good to get a win."

Lavin and his staff were still searching for the answers. To find the right lineup, to find a point guard. Should he go with the veterans, trusting their experience, or should he give the youngsters a try to see if they are ready? It was the answer that took Lavin too long to find.

Self continued to search for answers after the disappointing Texas A&M-Corpus Christi and Arizona games, wondering what he could do to liven up his team? Perhaps with so much talent and such high expectations, his players were afraid to have fun, afraid to fail. And Steve Alford's team suffered a humiliating loss to Northern Iowa, proving that maybe the coach was right in the preseason, that Iowa didn't deserve to be ranked in the Top Ten. As his team prepared to take on yet another in-state rival, Iowa State, there was little time to get things figured out.

10

Ambassadors

A S THE COACHES SEARCHED FOR ANSWERS ON THE COURT, THEY STILL HAD TO FULFILL their job responsibilities off the court, many of which had nothing to do with watching film or planning practice. Coaches have become ambassadors of their schools, as one of the most visible and recognized figures on the university campus, and in some cases, around the nation. With that recognition comes a responsibility to the school and community, to be the face of the university and to represent it to the world. Everyone wants a piece of the coach. Alumni want him to speak at gatherings; the development officers want him to have dinner with a potential big donor; civic groups want the coach to "just do this one" engagement; professors request his presence in classes to talk about leadership. And these requests are on top of the media interviews, recruiting visits, and personal player issues that coaches deal with every day.

As the coach of UCLA, Steve Lavin is asked to do hundreds, if not thousands, of speaking engagements and appearances each year. There is at least one Bruin booster function every week, sometimes more, such as the San Fernando Bruins and the L.A. Bruins, and there are numerous invitations to speak or make appearances at golf outings, grammar schools, and community groups. Then there are the appearances at the Adidas clinics and the speeches, as well as favors he does for friends. He devotes a portion of his time to charitable work, particularly with cancer foundations and the City of Hope's children's hospital, and he sits on the Board of Governors of his alma mater, Chapman College. With the intense interest in UCLA basketball, the coach is always in high demand, speaking at alumni gatherings for breakfast and big donor dinners at night. Coaches at major universities are really politicians, going to their constituencies and keeping supporters satisfied. Almost all coaches have friends among the alumni and donors—who can come in handy at crunch time.

Mike Brey looks at his job at Notre Dame as an ambassadorship for the university. Like it or not, the high-profile nature of his job puts him front and center in the public's image of Notre Dame. Fortunately for Brey, it is a role he both cherishes and does well. "I don't mind being the ambassador, and in fact, it is part of what they pay me for. I talk up the program and the university and it works because it is something that comes naturally to me—speaking and connecting with people."

Brey is required by his contract to make five speeches every year to Notre Dame Alumni Clubs throughout the country. Usually scheduled for May and June, the 2002 slate had Brey speaking to groups in Fort Lauderdale, Florida, Minneapolis, Minnesota, Dallas, Texas, Hartford, Connecticut, and Washington, D.C. But these would certainly not be Brey's only public appearances. Throughout the year, the coach is asked to speak to various groups in the South Bend community and within Notre Dame itself, many of which have nothing to do with basketball. On a football weekend in 2001, Brey was asked to speak to the Board of the Notre Dame Law School. He talked up his program not to seek financial support explicitly, but to enhance the university and his own image. "Much of what I do has nothing to do with raising money for basketball. But you never know. Maybe the guy that hears me speak will be the same guy who may donate $20 million for a new facility down the road."

In his first year at Notre Dame, Brey rarely turned down invitations to speak at the Kiwanis Club, alumni groups, or school functions, as he wanted to get his name and face out there. In his second season, however, he cut back on the number of engagements, instead sending one of his assistants for some appearances.

At Villanova, Jay Wright does the prerequisite alumni and community events as well, and his timetable is not limited to the offseason. When the team travels to South Florida to play Miami, he speaks to the Villanova alumni club there; in Boston to face Boston College, it is the same thing; in New York City against St. John's, still yet another group wants him to speak. Wright also meets with donors, but by the time those meetings, golf outings, dinners, and so on, are arranged, the potential donor is a die-hard Wildcat supporter and Wright simply closes the deal.

Bruiser Flint saw a difference in his role as university spokesman moving from Massachusetts to Drexel—the money. At UMass, he often had five to six speaking engagements a month, many of them two hours away in Boston. He also had his television show, which he calls "really an infomercial for the school." When he took the job at Drexel, the demand for him is a bit less, but he continues to speak at alumni functions and attempts to raise money for the program anyway he can. The difference is that he doesn't get compensated for those appearances at Drexel as he did at UMass. There are also the spring and early fall golf outings and meetings with big donors.

The name of the game for many coaches now is golf. Alumni and donors want to play a round, charities want you to make an appearance in their tournament, the university fund-raising events often include golf. "I could be the next Tiger Woods if I said yes to all of the invitations," notes Alabama coach Mark Gottfried. "People expect the coach to be accessible, have dinners with donors and such. Which I will do sometimes, but you can't do them all."

Coaches are often asked to go beyond the call of duty, to represent more than their basketball program. In December 2001, it became public that the Laurie family, heirs to the Wal-Mart fortune, had donated $25 million to the University of Missouri to build a new basketball arena. The gift was not made without condition, however, including the use of skyboxes, tickets, naming rights, and approval over major changes to the arena. The family stipulated that none of the facilities could be named after a former player or coach—a clear reference to the exclusion of 32-year-veteran former coach Norm Stewart, who apparently did not have a great relationship with the Lauries—major donors to the university. Bill Laurie went out of his way to praise Missouri coach Quin Snyder in a newspaper article for his efforts in securing the funding from the state for the sale of $35 million in state bonds. "I felt our new coach had a lot to do with the success that we had," [in getting the state legislature and Governor on board for the project]. Not every coach has to lobby state politicians, but many find themselves in the political arena.

(In late April 2002, politicians again played a role in college basketball, but this time in the "public's best interest." Western Kentucky and Louisville were scheduled to play in the 2002–2003 season, but Louisville coach Rick Pitino backed out, costing the school $25,000. Western Kentucky fans were in an uproar and the Kentucky legislature took up the issue. The legislature was in special session trying to hammer out a budget deal when Senator Richie Sanders added an addendum requiring the two schools to play one another. The budget bill with the addition passed the Senate but was rejected by the House. But the point had been made and Louisville agreed to reopen talks with Western Kentucky.)

At the lower levels of Division I, the duties can be even more time consuming, but in a different way. Instead of meeting or playing golf with big time donors, a coach at a smaller school may be organizing food sales for home games. "I oversee the booster club totally. I have no other help," says Farleigh-Dickinson's Tom Green. Like Green, many lower level Division I coaches must be actively involved in fund-raising for their program—they need it to survive. At Texas-San Antonio, Tim Carter gives between 15 and 20 speeches a year to local groups. He has no radio and TV show, no "weekly luncheon with the boosters." Four times a year he may be asked by the school to go out and raise money, but his public appearances are few compared to what the big-time schools ask from their coaches.

For Lorenzo Romar, formerly the coach at St. Louis and now at the University of Washington, the word is "accessible." "I know the university and athletic department appreciate if you have an antennae up for a potential donor and you give your time when needed. Whatever I can do to help promote the university I am going to do, not just the basketball program."

James Jones at Yale talks to alumni as well, often before tip-off. "Sometimes I will be preparing for the game and then have to talk to three or four alumni who drop in to say hello. It's part of the job here. I speak to alumni groups, high schools, and go to golf outings. We need to raise money for our athletic association. Ninety percent of my time is devoted to nonbasketball related events and issues."

Pat Flannery at Bucknell organizes tailgates, biweekly luncheons, and alumni gatherings (as an alum himself). "Many of the events and golf tournaments that I go to I enjoy, because many of the people there are my friends, or people that I know through playing and coaching at Bucknell," the 44-year-old notes. "I am an ambassador for the university and fund-raiser, helping to raise the necessary funds each year."

It seems that the smaller the community, the higher the profile of the program, the more civic events coaches are asked to do. For example, in Athens, Ohio, Ohio coach Tim O'Shea hits them all. "March of Dimes, Rotary, Lions Club, Chamber of Commerce, every civic organization under the sun I've been to. About 50 events or so a year. Then there are the golf tournaments, alumni functions, and such. I don't need to be contractually obligated to speak to these groups, I just know it is what I am supposed to do—it is part of the job."

Author John Feinstein recalls a conversation he had with the late Jim Valvano, near the end of the former N.C. State coach's career. "Jim told me that the only thing he liked about being a coach was the 40 minutes during the game. He hated the fund-rais-ing, the recruiting, as most coaches do." Valvano may have had his own reasons for dis-liking that part of the job, but other coaches seem to genuinely enjoy it or accept it as par for the course.

The John Wooden Classic is a four-team, single-day doubleheader, traditionally held at the Arrowhead Pond of Anaheim, a 40-minute drive south of Los Angeles. The Classic honors the legendary coach while providing support for the Southern California Special Olympics. It has showcased Wooden's old team five out of the six years the tour-nament has been played. The 2001 edition in the first week of December had two intrigu-ing matchups: Arizona versus Purdue and UCLA taking on No. 22-ranked Alabama. It was experience and longevity in one game, with Lute Olson going up against Gene Keady. It was the past and the present colliding in the other, with Steve Lavin paired up against his old friend and staff colleague, Mark Gottfried.

At the Friday morning press conference, it was clear that Lavin was not in a great mood. Not joking around with the 20 or so media members; not displaying his usual quick wit. He was under some stress, after his team sat at 2-2, losing to unheralded Ball State in Maui and to Pepperdine at home. Some of the media and fans were already calling for his head just four games into the season. *You don't lose to Pepperdine at home! That's cause for fir-ing. Yea, UCLA beat Houston, but only by 12!* From the expressions and demeanor that Lavin exhibited, it seemed clear that perhaps it was getting to him.

After the press conference, Lavin joined his players on the floor to conduct a shootaround with Special Olympians adorned in Wooden Classic T-shirts with smiles as big as the basketballs they held. A smile came back to Lavin's face as he taught one youngster how to bend his knees, played mock defense on a teenage girl at midcourt, and watched senior Rico Hines lead his team and the Olympians in hustle drills. Lavin's smile and laugh were as big as the kids' and he seemed to have found solace in those 30 min-utes. He gathered with his team, the Classic organizers, and the Special Olympians to lis-ten to Wooden give a message. Lavin had heard it before, but he always looked for another nugget of gold.

The shootaround was over and now it was back to reality. Lavin rarely has an open practice, and very few people, especially members of the media, have ever seen him in action. The arena emptied out quickly; the stragglers were asked to leave by UCLA managers and Pond security. Lavin was in lockdown mode and in no mood to be accommodating.

At storied UCLA, a crisis comes about every fourth day. With intense fan and media expectations, any loss is picked apart and registers with the magnitude of a 6.5 earthquake. But Lavin and his team had become accustomed to the hysteria by now. Lavin's approach has been refined by six years of crisis management. Bunker down. We only have each other. There is no need to panic. In the days leading up to Alabama, however, Lavin ripped into his team for playing selfish basketball and not focus-ing their work efforts.

Lavin finished writing on the wipeboard in the locker room at the Arrowhead Pond on Saturday, December 8, and slowly made his way over to the center of the room where his assistants watched the Arizona-Purdue game on TV. There was an eerie silence in the pregame locker room, and if there were such thing as a "game silence," like a "game face," this would be it. As the coaches watched the closing minutes of the first game on TV, the UCLA players stretched on the floor of the locker room. Sophomore T. J. Cummings did leg stretches on his butt, all the while reading passages from a red-covered

Bible resting next to him on the floor. Jason Kapono worked on stretching out his back while trainer Mark Schoen taped up Matt Barnes. The Arizona-Purdue game was over; it was time.

The players gathered in folding chairs in a semicircle, facing their coach and the wipeboard. "We must compete on every possession! We must work our asses off. (He repeated the phrase three times.) We must have active hands and feet, have good vision, and talk to one another," Lavin said, going down the list written in blue ink on the board. "Let's play hard and compete for 40 minutes." The team huddled, said a quick prayer, and did their usual chant. Lavin yelled "Together" and the team responded with "We Attack." The players shuffled out of the locker room and the assistant coaches and trainers joined Lavin in a pregame tradition.

As Lavin headed onto the floor, he knew that this was a big game. Most coaches will lie and say, "every game is a big game," but they all know that some are bigger than others, and this was a big one for Lavin. A nationally televised game against a ranked opponent, playing in the tournament named for a predecessor and legend—with two very bad losses already on the ledger, Lavin was more anxious than usual.

The game got off to a good start for the Bruins, with Kapono and Barnes converting some good looks. UCLA had the lead going into the first media timeout, and the players were obviously pumped. "That's the way to play hard," the coach shouted above the sound of the UCLA pep band. "We are doing a good job in the red zone so far," he said, looking over a red zone chart handed him by an assistant. That is where the game is won or lost. UCLA had been badly outplayed in the red zone in their losses to Ball State in Maui and to Pepperdine at home, partly because Lavin had opened the floor by staying with the press.

The Bruins continued to dominate in the first half against Alabama, as Lavin assumed his usual position: squatting on his legs, three quarters of the way down the bench, shouting instructions. He did not take a seat the entire game, nothing unusual for the tireless coach. Assistants Jim Saia and Gerald Madkins sat at one end of the bench, along with redshirt senior Ray Young and director of basketball operations Jamie Angeli. In between players further down the bench sat first-year assistant Patrick Sandle, who pointed things out to the youngsters around him.

As the half came to a close, Lavin jumped off of his feet to protest a referee's call. "How can you call that walk against us down there, but not call anything down here?" he pleaded to no avail to the ref. Lavin has a temper, but up by double digits in this big game, he'll let this one go.

At halftime, UCLA was up 40-25 on a pathetic-looking Alabama team. Lavin did a television interview on his way into the locker room where Saia had already begun to talk to the team, praising them for their effort. Lavin came flying in. "That is good basketball, fellas. We worked our asses off and competed every play," his voice somewhat hoarse from the first half. "Basketball is a simple game. You can draw up 1,000 plays, but it comes down to working hard." He paused, caught his breath, and continued. "But I know Mark Gottfried, I was an assistant with him for five years, and I know he is in there right now firing his team up. He will bring out his 'A' game to get them back in this, so we have to be ready." Lavin certainly knew Gottfried well.

Under Jim Harrick, the two were almost inseparable as assistant coaches, talking about the game, planning their futures, and sharing late-night pizzas on the road. In the spring of 1996, Gottfried accepted the head coaching job at Murray State, leaving the Bruins one year after they had won the national championship. In a matter of months after Gottfried's departure, Harrick would be fired for rule violations and a coverup, and

Lavin would be the new head coach of UCLA. Gottfried was fiercely loyal to Harrick and the relationship with Lavin quickly cooled, with Gottfried suspecting Lavin's involvement in Harrick's dismissal, despite later pronouncements by Harrick that his assistant had nothing to do with the firing. The two friends quickly grew apart, but seated together on an airplane flight in 2000 en route to an AAU Tournament, the two attempted to "clear the air" and began to make amends. It progressed to the point that Lavin and his girl-friend, Treena Camacho, went to Alabama over Labor Day in 2001 to watch the UCLA-Alabama football game and spend the weekend with Gottfried's family.

Alabama did come out inspired in the second half, but could do nothing against the aggressive matchup zone defense of UCLA, which the Bruins displayed for the first time in the young season. Lavin used freshman Ryan Walcott at point guard, a tiny but skilled dribbler who seemed to be up to the challenge. The second half started with a 10-point UCLA run and by the 12:00-minute media timeout, the Bruins smelled blood. As the players came over to the bench, Lavin high-fived them, pumped with excitement. "Let's put a dagger into their hearts," the sweat-soaked coach exclaimed, pounding his fist against his heart five times. "Let's go for the kill." He wanted the game finished.

They did, eventually coming away with a 79-57 victory. Lavin and his boys had done it again. Kapono finished with 22 points, five assists, and no turnovers, playing a good deal of the game at point guard. Walcott came off of the bench to play 11 minutes at point, going two for two with three assists.

In the postgame locker room, the coach gathered his players one last time in a hud-dle. "We are not dead yet. There are those that may jump off the wagon, but what mat-ters most are the people in this locker room." The coach continued, "And our player of the week and player of the game is Ryan Walcott, who stepped up while dealing with the adversity of his grandfather's passing this week."

With that, the Bruins began to celebrate the win. As Bill Bennett prepared to let the media onslaught into the locker room, Lavin reminded his players to study on the Sunday and Monday off days, and "to be careful tonight. Let's not do anything tonight that will stop us from making progress."

The win over Alabama in early December did not make or break the Bruin season, but it was critical *at the time*. Lavin's teams had a reputation for winning the ones they shouldn't win, for coming back after a bitter loss, and for making fools out of Lavin-haters. Lavin thrives under adversity. He loves to teach and learn from his setbacks. As a result, by March, when it counts, his teams are tough. They have learned from mistakes. Lavin has fierce loyalty from his players, so the chances of their abandoning their captain are slim.

But UCLA's gutty performance against ranked Alabama looked like an aberration after the Bruins played University of California-Irvine at home on December 15. The week between Alabama and Irvine was finals week at UCLA, so Lavin decided to hold practice at 6:00 A.M. every morning. In practice the day before the game, Barnes stepped awkwardly on Dan Gadzuric's foot, spraining his own ankle. X-rays were negative, but he would sit out the Irvine game. Freshman Dijon Thompson would start at point guard, joined by Hines, Knight, Kapono, and Gadzuric in the starting lineup. The Bruins played uninspired basketball throughout, despite pleas for a better effort from Lavin in timeouts in the first half. At halftime, Irvine led 29-27 as the coaches gathered in the small coaches' locker room down the hall from the players', and debated what offense to run.

"We need all five MFs on the boards," Lavin said to his team, returning to their locker room. "We will get back in this, let's just play hard and smart." For a coach losing at home, again, Lavin remained remarkably calm.

The second half was a better story for the Bruins, and with some fortunate bounces and calls, they escaped with a 75-74 win. Thompson was the hero, playing 38 minutes, scoring 14 points, grabbing seven rebounds, dishing out four assists, with two steals. Most important, he only turned the ball over twice. Postgame, Lavin invoked the words of his legendary predecessor. "Coach Wooden used to say he'd rather be lucky than unlucky, rather be ahead than behind, and rather win than lose. He also said other stuff but you get the idea." Then the coach reiterated a mantra he had been telling the team all along, "The season is a marathon, not a sprint." He noted to the team that in games without Cedric Bozeman or Matt Barnes in the lineup, the team was 5-2 and ranked No. 19. But conference play was right around the corner.

An Illinois practice is quite intense, with Bill Self the purveyor of all of the happenings. In many practices, assistants Norm Roberts, Wayne McClain, and Billy Gillispie will take a group or station, and work with the players on individual skills, as Self walks from group to group, lending encouragement or noting a mistake. Occasionally, he will stop all the drills to illustrate a point to the entire team. "Look guys, on defensive positioning, you need to be aware of where the line of the ball is and where the basket is," the coach demonstrates in a defensive stance. "The ball and the basket and get your hands up!"

The shooting drills at Illinois practices are fun to watch. With three-point specialists Cory Bradford, Sean Harrington, and Frank Williams, joined by an impressive shooting touch from big man Brian Cook, the nets get a workout. In one shooting drill, the team is divided into the guards and the big men, each group at one end of the court, with five minutes on the clock. With players working in tandems, one shooting, one rebounding, the teams attempt to make as many baskets as possible in the five-minute span. The guards take mostly 14 to 17-footers while the big men shoot from a shorter distance. A manager or assistant coach will keep count, with the teams usually coming in with a score around 150. It puts a competitive nature and some fun into an otherwise routine shooting drill.

Self organizes his practices around quick, intense drills, not spending a great deal of time in any one area, a different approach than some coaches, who tend to keep players in a drill until the coach is satisfied. Of course, Self spends more time on offensive and defensive sets and OBs than on a passing drill. A brief look at a typical Illinois practice schedule:

1 min	Pioneer
1 min	2 on 1 Passing
2 min	2 on 1 Passing with Traps
2 min	GdBall Screens
12 min	Shell (Everything)
5 min	5 min Shooting
10 min	BigLittle
	(3) Post Moves w/Dummies(6) Shots
	(2) Flash High (4) 3 on 3 Live
	(2) Trap on Post
	(3) 2 on 2 Live
5 min	Red 10 Shell
30 min	Zone Offense vs. Red 10

10 min	Press Offense vs. 30/40 Red Both Ways
10 min	Trap Post
5 min	Trap Ball Screens & Post
10 min	Scramble Both Ways (6 men)
10 min	Box Out & Break
10 min	3-Game vs. 1–2–2-Court Trap
10 min	Dummy Offense
5 min	Dummy O.B.
5 min	O.B. Live
	Free Throws

Self is flexible enough that he is willing to adjust his practice plan when needed, and observant enough to know when that is necessary. The practices are rapid, though not everyone is intense (as most coaches would like), and at times, players lose their concentration, or can't remember simple plays, which frustrates Self more than anything.

As his team practiced on Thursday, December 6, having suffered the defeat to Arizona in Phoenix, Self's assistant coaches were concerned with the players' attitudes as they prepared to meet Arkansas in Chicago on Saturday. They had played well in the second half of the Arizona game to prove something to the coach and to themselves, but how could they put it together for an entire game? As the team practiced, Self was not there. The stomachaches that he had in Phoenix had not gotten any better, and he checked himself into the hospital Wednesday morning and his assistants ran practice. Doctors believed Self suffered from diverticulitis, an inflammation of the pouch in the intestinal wall in the colon.

With a big game against Arkansas at the United Center on Saturday, Self was "released" from the hospital to attend practice on Friday and the game on Saturday. From the moment he left the hospital at 2:00 P.M. on Friday, the coach was accompanied by his personal physician, Dr. Jeff Kyrouac. Self oversaw practice on Friday and then headed with the team to Chicago. Throughout the afternoon and night, including a 3:00 A.M. wakeup, Kyrouac administered medicines and IVs to Self. He was not well as the Illini prepared to take the floor against the Razorbacks.

Illinois was 13-6 at the United Center since 1994–1995 and the game would be played in front of a very partisan 18,600 fans. The Razorbacks were the not "40 minutes of hell" 1994 champions, but still posed a good matchup for Illinois. Self decided to start Blandon Ferguson, who had been playing well in practice, in place of Sean Harrington.

Arkansas came out with pressure defense, and distracted Illinois' offense enough that they couldn't get open looks. The Arkansas press forced Illinois into 17 first half turnovers. The saving grace? The intense pressure defense resulted in many Razorback fouls and the Illini hit their free throws (Illinois finished with a 37-13 advantage at the free throw line). The halftime score was 38-36, Arkansas. Arkansas led by as many as 12 in the second stanza, spurred by a 10-0 run to start the half, but Illinois rallied and hung on with key free throws down the stretch to win 94-91. A questionable charging call on the Razorbacks' Brandon Dean by official Ted Hillary sealed the game for Illinois with 5.5 seconds to go. In the second half, the Illini turned the ball over five times. Frank Williams scored 25 points and was involved in almost every Illinois possession. "Frank had the ball the majority of the time," his coach said afterward. "I wish he would have had it more."

It was a strong game for Williams, who many in the media attacked as he struggled. He was shooting 36% from the field and 27% from three-point range on the season, and his coach had asked him to step up his leadership, both in private meetings and in the media. The All-American was finding a way to get it done—from the line, as an assist man or simply through will.

After the game, the team headed back to Champaign. The bus dropped the team off at the Ubben Complex and then took Self and Kyrouac immediately back to the hospital, where Self would stay Saturday and Sunday nights before officially being released on Monday. His team had eight days off for exams before playing Western Illinois at home.

In their next two games, No. 10 Illinois easily defeated Western Illinois and Illinois State at Assembly Hall, two of six in-state schools the Illini would face in 2001–2002. Williams scored 17 points against Western Illinois, even though he was suffering from the stomach flu, and spent part of the game in the men's room. Luther Head came off of the bench and hit three of five three-pointers in scoring 14 points while classmate Roger Powell finally got on track with 12. Illinois led 13-0 before Western Illinois first scored with 10:42 left in the first half. Against Illinois State, Robert Archibald and Cook found foul trouble again and combined for just six minutes of playing time in the first half. Williams poured in 29 points, despite still playing sick; so sick in fact that he started the second half throwing up in the locker room. The wins helped propel Illinois to No. 9 in the polls as they headed into a showdown against Missouri in St. Louis the following week.

Two days before their game against Miami of Ohio, Notre Dame's Ryan Humphrey injured his lower left leg in practice and Brey declared that it was "time to shut him down." Humphrey had first felt pain in the leg after the Hawaii trip, and didn't practice before the DePaul and Indiana games to rest. But after the Hoosier loss, the pain was too much and doctors were concerned about a stress fracture. Upon review of an MRI on December 7, team physician Fred Ferlic cleared Humphrey to play against Miami. The Irish had two weeks off for exams following the Miami game so Humphrey would have time to rest then.

Notre Dame got back on track with a stirring comeback in a 70-69 victory in Oxford, Ohio, over Miami of Ohio. Humphrey played 40 minutes and led a late 18-4 run and the Irish moved to 8-1 on the year. Notre Dame again had to play catch up, falling behind by double digits and then working their way back into the game, trailing 41-35 at halftime. Brey employed man-to-man and zone defenses to try to slow down Miami, neither too effective, but clutch shooting by Humphrey and Chris Thomas gave Notre Dame the huge road win. Torrian Jones blocked a Miami shot at the buzzer to preserve the win.

It was final exam time in South Bend, with no games scheduled for two weeks, so the Irish minds turned to Physics and the Classics.

In Ames, Iowa, on December 8, Steve Alford's postgame comments said it all: "That's the way this team can guard. That's the way this team can punish someone."

His team had just beaten Iowa State 78-53 on the road, holding Iowa State to 34.7% shooting from the field and outrebounding the Cyclones 47-24. The star of the game for Iowa was Reggie Evans, who scored 24 points and had 17 rebounds. It was the continuation of the Jekyll and Hyde season for Alford's team, playing great one night, losing inexplicably the next.

The Hawkeyes continued their solid play back home on Wednesday, pounding Drake 101-59. They led 45-19 in the first half and 55-30 at halftime, and shot the ball well (58%), while playing great defense (36%). Luke Recker had a great shooting night, scoring 24 points as Evans continued his torrid play with 19 points and 10 rebounds.

Alford had watched game clips from the previous season's Drake game and noticed that Recker had an easy time scoring when he took one dribble before pulling up. He called his senior the night before the game to give him the suggestion—it must have worked. Pierre Pierce and Chauncey Leslie got their same amount of minutes, and at times played together on the floor, with Pierce finishing with 12 points. Next up for the Hawkeyes was a much-anticipated rematch with the Missouri Tigers in Columbia. Could they continue their hot play on the road in a hostile environment? Would the memories of the late collapse against Missouri just weeks earlier creep back into their thoughts? Was the poor play behind them?

They found their answers on Saturday, December 15, when the Hawkeyes blew their hosts out of their building. Missouri came into the game ranked No. 3 in the nation, while Iowa had slipped to No. 15. The first few minutes of the game were ugly. Both teams shot air balls, threw the ball away, and looked like scoring was furthest from their minds. But then Recker caught fire. He shot 10 of 17 for a career high 31 points and Evans added another double-double. Freshman Pierce seemed to have settled into his role at point, scoring 17 points and dishing out assists like candy. The final was 83-65. The Iowa defense was superb, shutting down the Tigers' Kareem Rush and Clarence Gilbert. Alford's club now stood at 9-3, with losses to Duke, Missouri, and Northern Iowa, and with a break for final exams on the horizon, he was pleased. Things seemed to be back on track.

11

Oh, and Don't Forget to Study

NOTRE DAME HAD JUST COMPLETED THEIR DAY BEFORE SHOOTAROUND AT THE Canisius gymnasium in Buffalo, and Mike Brey decided to get in a little sightseeing, so the team headed to Niagara Falls on the bus. It was a cold, snowy day, typical weather of the Northeast in late December, but the Notre Dame basketball team was red hot. Going into the nonconference game, the Irish were 8-1 on the season, and the players were upbeat and well rested on the bus, as they joked around and peered out the windows. Freshman Jordan Cornette's cell phone rang and he answered. A moment passed before Cornette broke out into a huge smile.

On the other end of the phone was Pat Holmes, the academic advisor for the Notre Dame basketball team, calling from his office in South Bend. He informed Cornette that he had received a 3.0 GPA for the fall semester. Holmes had promised the players that as soon as he found out their semester grades he would call them. The players at Notre Dame are students, and their GPAs mean as much as their scoring averages. For the fall 2001 semester, seven of the 13 players had a 3.0 GPA or higher and the overall team average GPA was also above a 3.0.

Holmes did not have all of the players' grades at the time of his first call to Cornette, but he did have big man Tom Timmermans'. He told Cornette that Timmermans had a 2.97, and after Cornette had passed the info on, Holmes could hear a deep laugh and scream over the phone. Timmermans had worked hard all fall on his academics trying to reach a 3.0. At Notre Dame, per rules set by the Big East, the school can spend up to $150 per player on academic rewards such as watches, jackets, or school supplies. Notre Dame had decided on nice winter parkas and Timmermans wanted one badly.

"What? A 2.97. But I want the jacket!" Timmermans was heard screaming and laughing from the back of the bus. He had come so close, yet was so far from the parka.

The next day, the Irish defeated Canisius 84-73 behind a gutsy performance by Ryan Humphrey, who continued to be hobbled by a bad ankle. Notre Dame hit 35 of 44 free throws to clinch the win, though they trailed at the half. During the game, Canisius students chanted "O'Leary! O'Leary!," a reference to the football coach "scandal" taking place in South Bend, when George O'Leary was forced to resign after a week following discrepancies on his resume. (In fact, during the coaching search, Brey became frustrated at the press' probing for his comments on the football program, not on his successful basketball program.)

After the win over Canisius, the Irish were waiting in the Buffalo airport for their flight home, when David Graves' cell phone rang. It was Holmes, who had more news. Graves had also earned a 2.97, just missing the jacket. The senior passed the phone to freshman Chris Thomas who had received a 3.33. Additional phone calls to Harold Swanagan, who passed the phone to Torrian Jones, informed them of their 3.0 plus GPAs just as they waited to board the plane. Academic counselors at most schools would have waited until the team returned to campus. Most would only call the coach if a player was bordering on ineligibility. But this was Notre Dame, where things are done a bit differently.

The role of academics in college basketball has taken on a much more serious tone in recent years as schools and coaches strive to satisfy critics. Basketball players are technically "student-athletes," but how little student and how much athlete? Iowa athletic director Bob Bowlsby, a member of the NCAA Management Council, knows well the ills of college basketball. "Shop around the country and you could come up with a list of 25 schools that never graduate anybody, have kids on the police rolls all of the time, and basically are running basketball mills."

Perhaps more than 25, perhaps fewer, but the reality is that some college players just do not care about their education. They care about their playing minutes and their performance on the court. But blame cannot be placed solely on the teenagers attending the universities, as schools also must take responsibility for their declining emphasis on education and the loosening of their admissions policies for athletes.

What is a coach's role in the academic progress of his players? How much accountability should be placed on the coaching staff for making sure players go to class? Should coaches be responsible for players graduating? Coaches and administrators have divergent views on these issues. Most coaches would like to see their players graduate, but believe that they are not empowered by the schools to make that happen. Many administrators believe that part of a coach's job is to fulfill the university's academic mission by placing a premium on academics. Perhaps they are both right.

The headline focused on one simple number. Zero. By itself, the number is certainly positive for a coach, if it refers to turnovers or losses. It is an evil number if it relates to wins, rebounds, or made free throws. But zero took on enormous significance in 1999, when an article in the *Cincinnati Examiner* reported that the University of Cincinnati and its head coach Bob Huggins graduated exactly zero players for a 0% graduation rate over his tenure. The national media ran with the story, isolating the Bearcats as the paradigm for the ills of college basketball. But was it true? And if so, how could the University and Huggins have allowed this to happen? Before taking a look at the specifics of Cincinnati, it is imperative to understand the term of the day in college basketball: graduation rate. How it is defined and how it is applied are controversial topics for all parties involved, from the federal government to the NCAA to the coaches who are held responsible.

A graduation rate is a complicated formula. In basic terms, it tracks the number of individuals who earned degrees within six years after first entering their original university or college of choice. Athletes who leave school to transfer, to jump to the NBA, are injured, or just quit playing count *against* the graduation rate. The graduation rate percentage is the percent of those individuals who complete their degree within a six-year period after entering school, and it is best looked at as a four-year aggregate. For example, the four-year graduation rate at Kentucky for 2002, which included the 2001 graduates, would be reflective of the freshman classes who entered the school between 1992 and 1995. That is, if 10 players entered Kentucky during that time, two transferred and one left early for the NBA, their graduation rate is already down to 70% (assuming the remaining seven players stayed and graduated within six years). But here is the kicker. If a student leaves Kentucky after one year, transfers to UCLA, and plays there for three years and graduates, he counts *against* Kentucky, but not *for* UCLA. The reverse is true as well. If a player goes to UCLA for three years then finishes up at Kentucky, it counts *against* the original school, in this case, UCLA. Keep in mind that these rates are only for scholarship athletes. Walk-ons and other nonscholarship athletes, who may have great GPAs, major in engineering and graduate in four years, do not count under the NCAA formula.

Using the criteria set out by the NCAA, who point the finger at the federal government for the misleading statistic, as part of the Federal Student Right-to-Know and Campus Security Act, it is easy to see why coaches complain about the graduation rate. Their teams' graduation rates are hurt by players going elsewhere and graduating, yet they get no credit for a student who transfers in and graduates after spending three years at their school. There are two ways that the NCAA and colleges look at graduation rates: four-year spans, providing a more accurate picture, and one-year snapshots for a single freshman class.

The most recent data from the NCAA, published in September 2002, reflects the graduation rates for students who entered schools in the 1995–1996 year and graduated by 2001, at the end of their six-year grace period. Again, it is imperative to keep in mind that the four-year aggregate statistics are only representative of four freshman classes, which could be as small as 10 recruits. If just two left school after their freshman year, the graduation rate would, at best, be 80%.

The overall graduation rate was 43% for male basketball players, up from 40% in 2000–2001. This 43% is compared to an overall student body graduation rate of 57% for the same time period. Broken down by race, 35% of black players graduated compared to 53% of white players, a gap that continues to widen. A more telling statistic is the graduation rate of basketball players compared to the rate of the overall student body. At over a fourth of schools, the rate for basketball players was greater than 20 percentage points *lower* than the student body rate.

According to the NCAA data, Stanford University, Bucknell University, and Centenary College of Louisiana were the only schools to have graduated all of their basketball players. Four schools, Elon, Hofstra, LaSalle, and Santa Clara, graduated all of their white basketball players. The report shows that for students entering their universities between 1992 and 1995, the following schools did not graduate a single player, white or black: Cal State Sacramento, Jackson State, Louisiana/Lafayette, Memphis, UNLV, Oklahoma, VCU, and Houston. Among the 17 schools that did not graduate any black players are Florida State, Georgia Tech, Cincinnati, Louisville, Arkansas, Texas Tech, and Kent State.

To rectify the poor academic showing of basketball players, the Knight Commission on Intercollegiate Athletics proposed a postseason ban on schools that do not graduate at least 50% of their players. If the rule had been in effect for the 2002 NCAA

Tournament, over half of the teams would have been prohibited from playing. Only nine of the 65 teams had graduation rates higher than their student body average. Some numbers from 2002 NCAA and NIT Tournament teams, a four-year graduation rate aggregate: Stanford (100%), Notre Dame (75%), Duke (73%), Kansas (70%), Iowa (55%), Illinois (43%), UCLA (36%), Indiana (25%), Cincinnati (17%), Maryland (14%), and Oklahoma (0%).

With these numbers, it becomes clear why coaches do not like the way the NCAA tabulates graduation rates. Programs that accept junior college transfers will traditionally have low graduation rates, as will teams that lose players early to the NBA. Calculating individual year statistics based on just one entering freshman class is misleading, because the number of individuals in any one entering year can be very small. But no matter how the NCAA calculates the graduation rate, it is clear that many college basketball players are at schools to play basketball, and little else. Yes, there are some players who play basketball simply to get the scholarships so they can get an education, but at many of the top programs today, they are the minority.

Backed by an understanding of the graduation rate formula, let us revisit the 0% graduation rate at the University of Cincinnati in 1999. According to the NCAA formula, it is true that no Cincinnati player graduated in the six-year span. In actuality, Bob Huggins will tell you that 15 of the 31 players who he had brought into UC have graduated. Some may have earned a degree from another school and some may have completed their coursework long after their playing days were over for Cincinnati and their six-year grace period exhausted. He lost some players to the NBA. Huggins sees the 0% as an inaccurate number, one which the media seized upon to sell papers.

"I say to people who sit there and try to tell me I don't care about education, I'll put my transcript next to theirs anytime and they would be embarrassed, it's a joke," Huggins responds to his critics. "I hear that we don't want to embarrass these institutes of higher learning [with poor graduation rates]. Well, why can't institutes of higher learning police themselves? They talk about all of these high-risk kids we have. Well, then throw them out. If that is the mission of your school, don't let them in. Why are you letting them in?"

Instead of focusing on why kids don't end up graduating, perhaps schools should be looking at who they are admitting. If they are admitting "at-risk" students, or student-athletes who may not be able to make it in college, it is only likely that some will not make it. It is no coincidence that many of these risky admits play for the basketball team. The perception across the country is that coaches walk into the admission offices and tell them which high school senior basketball stars to admit. But the reality is that now many schools have strict procedures and policies to eliminate any relationship between the athletic department and the admissions staff to avoid inappropriate contact. Schools such as Cincinnati have a department policy. A faculty representative and an athletic director must approve the recruitment of a student-athlete before an official visit is scheduled to ensure that standards are maintained.

"I don't have a relationship with the admissions staff," admits Huggins. "I couldn't tell you who our Registrar is. I couldn't tell you anybody that works in the admissions office. Before I bring a kid in [on an official visit] I have to take his transcripts, grade scores, and stuff like that to be evaluated by our academic support staff. That staff then forwards it to our Assistant Athletic Director who then forwards it to the AD for approval."

Regardless of the admission policies in place at institutions, the degree of emphasis on academics in a basketball program ultimately comes down to the philosophy of the head coach. If he views graduating his players as a priority, then he will only recruit those who have the best chance to graduate, and will do everything he can to see that they do. The problem is that often the best players who can win games for you and get you into the Tournament are not always the ones who have the best shot at graduating. So coaches face a dilemma between what is best for them and their teams and what the university perceives as best for the student-athlete. In the ever-changing environment of college basketball where wins, not degrees, decide a coach's fate, it is hard to ignore the temptation of a quick fix. Regardless, is it a coach's job to make sure a player graduates?

"It's not a coach's job," Huggins emphasizes. "Why is it a coach's job? You have academic counselors; we have five. What is their job? Why is it that coaches are accountable for everything? Why? I can't bring a kid to my house to study. I'm not really allowed to sit down with a kid and tutor him. I can't go see a professor to see how a student is doing. Academic support staff can do all of those things. The problem is that we have all of the accountability, but none of the resources. We have associate ADs for academics and faculty representatives who sign off on everything. What is their charge? Not that I don't bear some of the responsibility, but what about the faculty and the academic support staff?"

His views on the role of the coach in academics may seem a bit brash, but they are not out of balance with his colleagues. Many coaches agree that they are being unfairly held responsible for their players' education, though most would not go as far as Huggins in articulating their frustrations. Perhaps this is because they have not encountered the avalanche of criticism that Huggins has seen.

Gene Keady has seen it all in his years coaching basketball at Purdue. He knows how the game and the players have changed and he knows what impact a coach can really have. "You know why a kid graduates? Because he wants to. I don't know if we [coaches] do any good or not. If we didn't have motivational talks about academics, it might not change. No one had to motivate me, but that was a different era. Now everyone thinks they are going to the NBA and they don't think they need an education. I think our job as coaches is to educate our players on the chances of making the next level, which is about 1% to the NBA and 3% playing somewhere professionally, and to make sure that they are on pace to graduate."

Former Arkansas coach Nolan Richardson pointed out in an interview with ESPN in 2002 that Vince Carter and Michael Jordan returned to school to get their degrees for themselves, not for anyone else. "You think it was because of Dean Smith or Mike Krzyzewski. I don't think so."

Pepperdine coach Paul Westphal has a unique and honest approach to graduation and education. What's important to him is not the diploma, but what happens while a student is on campus. "We are accountable to help the young person to be better off when they leave here than when they came. Everybody can't graduate from college. Everybody doesn't belong in college, but the system is such that this is virtually the only place a lot of these guys have, the only level to pursue their dreams when they are a certain age. I think it is up to us to give them the opportunity to graduate. Regardless, it's up to us to have them be more educated and better ready to pursue their dreams when they leave than when they came. If that means graduation, that's great, but honestly, it doesn't always mean graduation."

How much has the environment changed? Class checkers and student managers now routinely show up in classes to make sure players are in attendance at many universities. When Anthony Solomon arrived at Notre Dame in 2000 as an assistant, he asked academic counselor Pat Holmes if he needed to walk the players to class. "We don't walk kids to class here, Slo [Solomon]," Holmes responded. Halfway through the semester, Solomon told Holmes that he woke up in the middle of the night worrying about the kids. "I've got some time," Solomon pleaded. "I can follow the kids to class."

If a kid is not going to class at a small, academic-intensive university like Notre Dame, the counselors and coaches will know about it. Yale coach James Jones walked kids to class and checked in on them while an assistant at Ohio University, but he doesn't have to do that at his current school.

At Illinois, Bill Self is realistic about his role in graduating players while acknowledging that he can make some difference. "You can have an impact on them going to class, getting together with tutors and going to study hall. I do think that with the climate of college athletics and the academic side of it, coaches have less to do with it than they did 15 years ago, without question. We have class checkers who try to do that. I really think the ultimate responsibility is on the players. All we can do is help them carry out their game plans. And they need us to help carry out those game plans."

How important has the academic progress and graduation rate of players become for coaches? When Steve Alford renegotiated his contract with Iowa in the summer of 2001, he had a graduation clause added that gave him a bonus for graduating 70% of his players. The bonus goes up for winning 60% of his games and graduating 70% of his players and grows even larger if he wins 80% of his games and graduates 60%. The Iowa athletic director, Bob Bowlsby, who gave Alford the incentives insists that he doesn't have any incentives in his contract, nor should he—"it's my job."

Alford is not alone. Many coaches now have incentives for graduating players, even the ones like Keady, who grew up not needing one. "I get a bonus for some of my kids graduating, but it is very small," says the 66-year-old coach. "If I didn't have a bonus, it wouldn't change my philosophy, as I expect my kids to graduate. I have mixed emotions about it. I don't need incentive. I don't think they are good clauses, but I'm not going to turn it down."

Believe it or not, Bob Huggins has no incentives for graduating players. "I don't want to get paid if a guy graduates."

When Self was hired away from Tulsa in 2000, he asked Illinois athletic director Ron Guenther about a graduation bonus. "Bill," his new boss responded, "I thought it was your job to graduate kids." Self has no graduation rate bonus. Guenther shares the same philosophy as John Wooden, who believes that education is "part of a coach's job, and it may be his first job."

"In my view, there isn't any other segment on campus that is more tied to the academics of students than coaches," Notre Dame athletic director Kevin White says. "They enjoy a high degree of accountability, and their community is not held to the same degree of accountability. Holding them to that kind of accountability in my sense is a high-risk, high-reward game."

White's right-hand man at Notre Dame, associate athletic director Jim Phillips, perhaps put it best. "Whose job is it to help these kids graduate? I think it is everyone's. The coaches, players, administrators, ADs, school presidents. Everybody."

Some coaches believe that the best motivational tool for encouraging academic progress and responsibility is the bench. When players do not work hard in practice, come late to a team meeting, or mouth off to a coach, they end up on the bench. A coach can use that same motivation for academics. If a student does not show up for class or does not complete assignments, then the coach can send a powerful message by sitting that player. Not for failing to get a 3.5 GPA, but for not putting in the required effort. But there is a catch with this approach. As a coach, you are paid to win games and your job depends on winning. Sitting a star player because he didn't go to class is a fundamental risk.

In addition to getting benched, any athlete who has played a competitive sport knows another punishment for messing up: sprints. Coaches employ the sprint as a motivational tool for academic failings as well. Many staffs have an assistant coach who oversees sprints at 6:00 A.M. every morning for players who missed class or blew off assignments. No one likes to get up that early to run, so it may be a motivational tool that works.

Coaches must rely on the academic staff at their institution to keep them updated on their players' academic standings, because most schools have rules that prohibit contact between a professor and coach. Many schools send evaluation forms to professors three or four times a semester, inquiring about the attendance, attitude, and grade performance of student-athletes. Since the response rate from professors is generally about 30%, much additional work must be done on the part of the academic staff to follow up.

"If they [players] are 10 days late on a paper and you have not heard from that professor," said Self, "there are very few student-athletes that are going to come up to you personally and say, 'Coach, I screwed up today. I'm late on a paper.' Of course, they are going to try and sneak by. And why would a faculty member want to bend over backward to help an athlete who doesn't present himself well in class? We can make them sit in the first three rows, prohibit headphones, and work on their seating posture, but we can't force them to participate in group discussions."

One of Self's most outspoken players, senior Lucas Johnson, makes no bones about the role of academics in big-time college basketball. "There are definitely kids in the program that aren't here to get a degree. There are kids who are here to play the game. There are definitely guys who come, who use college strictly for basketball." Johnson adds, "Across the country, there are coaches that, if you are eligible, you're okay." He admits that it doesn't have to be that way and puts the responsibility squarely on the player. "I think that there are so many aids here that there really doesn't need to be a choice between basketball and school. There are so many different things that colleges provide to student-athletes for them to do well in class, there doesn't need to be a choice. If that choice is made, it's by the student, not a choice forced by others."

Notre Dame All-American Ryan Humphrey takes the other side to the trend of poor academic showings by basketball players. "It's sad. They [schools] just kind of use kids to play basketball. There is more to life than basketball."

With the increasing pressure on coaches to win and to keep kids eligible, there are times when efforts are more than simply help. In an ongoing case, former Minnesota coach Clem Haskins was fired for alleged academic fraud throughout his program. Some of the charges? In 1999, a former office manager in academic affairs admitted to completing at least 400 assignments for over 20 players over the years and a former student secretary said she wrote 50 papers and typed 200 more in exchange for money and gifts from Haskins. An investigation revealed the cheating had been going on as early as 1986 when Haskins first arrived. Minnesota is not the only school to be exposed for academic fraud, nor will it be the last. The fact is that with the pressure to win, the pressure to make sure you have the players to win, coaches will sometimes break the rules.

One coach who knows all too well the perilous relationship between academics and basketball is Temple's John Chaney. He is a man who has won over 675 games, taught the game of basketball to thousands, and truly cares about his players and their futures. He is also known for being a hard-nosed, old school disciplinarian who runs daily practice at 5:30 A.M. Inducted into the College Basketball Hall of Fame in 2001, Chaney is an outspoken critic of the NCAA and its "discriminatory policies" when it comes to race and academics. He takes pride in working at Temple, a school whose mission allows for at-risk students to be welcomed, including "Prop 48" kids, players who do not meet the initial eligibility requirements set by the NCAA. "I've had a number of Prop 48 kids come into the program and eight of them have graduated so far, on time. One that I have now will graduate on time and start work on his Masters," boasts the coach.

Chaney's program is unique in that he and his school admit at-risk students who otherwise would not be offered admissions. Many schools have banned "partial qualifiers," students who don't meet the university-wide and NCAA requirements for entrance, but are allowed to enroll conditionally. Chaney welcomes those kids to Temple, seeing an opportunity to improve their lives.

He has become legendary for his early practices. But the early time is not a punishment (as explained in chapter 5). Rather, it allows for a mandatory two hours of tutoring and study hall every afternoon. As much as Chaney provides the opportunity and resources for academic success and graduation, he understands that his role is actually quite limited. "We don't teach classes. How the hell can you be responsible for a kid graduating if you don't teach classes? The responsibility is with the school. If you tell me don't bring in kids who are risk factors, you're telling me I need to go get another job, because most basketball players are coming from disadvantaged backgrounds."

Chaney believes that coaches can use the bench to punish players for skipping class or falling behind academically, but ultimately, getting a degree is up to the player. And for schools and athletic directors to talk about the importance of graduation rates for coaches, but then turn around and fire even those with a strong graduation rate, it doesn't make sense. "How about all of this crap that we've heard for years about guys standing up and talking about graduation rates?" Chaney demands. "'I graduated 100%'. Well, shit. His ass is fired too! He wasn't fired because he didn't graduate anybody, he was fired because he didn't win games."

As you might expect, Chaney takes issue with the formula for calculating graduation rates and the fact that some schools and coaches publicize it. "What about the at-risk kid who busts his ass to get an education but falls just short?" And it's not just the NCAA or schools who spark the ire of John Chaney. "I know what happened when Digger Phelps left Notre Dame. He was at Notre Dame, a prestigious school, and then was fired and all of a sudden was singing a different tune about academics. They [coaches] sang the nice songs that were needed in the higher education schools and left to go to schools that took risk players and everything changed. 'We can't be charged with graduation rates, that's the schools.'"

The Chronicle of Higher Education printed the following comments from Oklahoma's Kelvin Sampson, a man at a school with a very low graduation rate: "Raising admissions standards and academic standards are good, but so many kids come to these universities to play basketball. Their goal is to get a college education, a college experience, to play basketball, and at some point go on and play basketball professionally. . . . In four years a (nonbasketball player) student goes in and gets a degree, and then goes and gets a job. These kids though are basketball players, and they are getting jobs in basketball. Then they're getting degrees later."

The problem with Sampson's approach is that most college players are not getting jobs in basketball and never play professionally. The odds are against them that they will ever earn a living playing hoops, so why not ensure they get that degree to help them get *any* job?

At the opposite end of the argument sits Northwestern's athletic director Rick Taylor, who, in a letter to *The NCAA News*, argued that things have got to change: "There is a very simple solution to low graduation rates; take better students initially who desire a true college education. . . . Let's stop the hypocrisy of majoring in eligibility or special classes that amount to nothing more than a pre-NBA curriculum. . . . Let's stop running off recruits. . . . Let's pretend this isn't happening across the spectrum of Division I basketball."

Where you sit is where you stand. As Chaney pointed out, often the coaches screaming about the importance of academics are the ones at schools where they get the top students and lose out on recruits with academic problems, while coaches at institutions that may have lower standards are as vocal contesting stringent standards as their contemporaries. In 1996, the NCAA raised the minimum entrance standards to a 2.5 GPA and an 820 SAT test score, on a sliding scale, requiring a higher GPA for a lower test score, but neither below the minimums. In October 2002, the leadership of the NCAA lowered the standardized test qualifying score, under pressure from organizations who claim that the tests are biased against minorities and the poor.

If there are academic standards for college athletes, as there are for nonathletes in the student body, then why do so many below-average basketball players get accepted? In a unique research study conducted by two members of the Mellon Foundation, James Shulman and William Bowen, data revealed that being an athlete gave applicants a 48% advantage in admissions over nonathletes, compared to a 24% advantage for legacies, and 18% for minority applicants. The message? If you can hoop it up regardless of your academic ability, you will probably get in.

How do academics affect the product on the court and how coaches go about coaching? At the elite level, stringent academic schools like Stanford, Penn, and Notre Dame find ways to admit great students and great athletes. But the educational mission of the school affects more than simply who is admitted. At Notre Dame, teams often charter back after late games, not to spoil teenagers in luxury, but to get them back to campus for homework and class. There are no study halls for the Irish. There are no class checkers and no curfews. The educational aspect also affects how a team might play. "With the type of student-athlete at Notre Dame," Mike Brey says, "I am able to treat them like men and let them run their own things on the court. We have kids with good minds and I would like to think I have taught them to think for themselves."

At Dartmouth, coach Dave Foucher makes even more accommodations for academics. He routinely excuses players from practice for classes, labs, and study groups, even though it makes it difficult to work on team sets. Furthermore, the team tries to travel on game days, by bus, so as not to miss much class time by leaving the day before.

The role of athletics in a university setting is a controversial issue with merits on both sides. It has become clear, however, that a paradoxical justification system exists to satisfy all relevant parties. Here is how it works: College presidents are under constant pressure from professors and some alumni to rein in intercollegiate sports and the associated spending it takes from a school's budget. To calm down these critics, university officials insist on a minimum academic performance by their student-athletes, including graduation. Though many basketball players can barely make the minimum, it gives the officials and the athletic department administrators and coaches room to breathe, "See, we do care about academics," they proclaim.

At the same time, those with athletic interests understand the magnitude of signing a particular player and keeping him eligible, particularly with so much on the line for the coach, and for the school. Coaches need to justify why they need a player and the school needs to justify letting him in. All the while, the bottom line is money. College presidents understand this, which is why they allow for below-standard student-athletes to play at their schools, and when criticized for that practice, they can claim they are doing something about it. Whether or not coaches should be held accountable may be up for debate. Most student-athletes will tell you that balancing a sport and a course load is beyond the scope of many of their peers. And that balance is never more tested than during exams.

The period in mid-December is always a difficult one for players, as they attempt to balance final semester exams with practices and games. Luckily, some schools refuse to schedule games during exam week, which explains why Mike Brey's Irish had two weeks off. They still practiced, but the minds of the players were on their classes. Iowa had a week off for exams, and then got back into action on December 22 against Kansas State, a member of the Big 12. At 9-3 and the winners of three in a row, including the win over Missouri, the Hawkeyes had climbed back to 12th in the polls, and played like it for most of the game against Kansas State. Luke Recker continued his hot streak, scoring 29 points, 20 in the first half, and Iowa held off a second half KSU rally to win 89-70. Iowa sophomore Glen Worley stepped up for Reggie Evans, who was saddled with foul trouble most of the game. Worley scored 11 points and grabbed 12 boards, but he was not the only bench player to make a contribution, with Chauncey Leslie, Ryan Hogan, and Sean Sonderleiter all doing their part. Alford challenged his bench at halftime, asking them to step it up in the second half. They got the message. The first half the bench scored four points; the second half they scored 17 straight.

There was a special visitor at the Iowa-Kansas State game. World champion boxer Roy Jones, Jr. came to town to watch Iowa. Alford was a huge boxing fan and Jones was a huge basketball fan. In addition, Jones and Evans were friendly, playing pickup basketball in the summers in their hometown of Pensacola. Jones sat right behind the Iowa bench and cheered vociferously for the Hawks. After the game, he spoke briefly to the team, encouraging them to keep up the fight.

The team had a few days off for the Christmas break and many of the players headed home for a night or two. From December 15 to January 23, all the players had to do was focus on basketball. But their coach sensed something over the break. The focus and mental sharpness waned. Players did not show up to work at the gym on their own game. They didn't hang out as a team and do things together, as they had in previous years, led by guys like Dean Oliver and Jason Smith. Alford faulted the lack of senior leadership by Recker and Evans.

A week later at home against Mercer, the bench also was instrumental, particularly Hogan, who scored 18 points, including four three-pointers. For the first time in their four-game winning streak, Recker and Evans did not play well, scoring five and 12 points, respectively. (Recker's wrist was bothering him but X-rays were negative.) Iowa's defense stepped up, holding Mercer scoreless nine minutes into the game. Turnovers (17) still plagued Iowa, but Alford was happy that they were on a roll headed into conference play. "To get 11 wins in the nonconference schedule was big. We have a lot of momentum heading into the new year. 2001 has been very good to us and we look forward to 2002."

The year 2001 had been a good one for Mike Brey, as his Irish were 9-1 heading to New Orleans to play Alabama in the Sugar Bowl Classic. They had split as a team after the Canisius win in Buffalo so the players could return home to their families for a short Christmas visit. They would reunite in New Orleans on Christmas night. Harold Swanagan and Tom Timmermans stayed in South Bend and spent Christmas with the Breys. In New Orleans, the players enjoyed the festive atmosphere surrounding the Sugar Bowl, including some time on Bourbon Street.

Against the No. 21-ranked Tide, Notre Dame started out the way it had been accustomed to—in a deep hole. Yet again, the Irish staked their opponents a large lead and spent the rest of the game trying to get it back. Alabama played stingy man-to-man defense that seemed to fluster the Irish, forcing them to shoot just 28% (9-32) in the first half and endure a six-minute scoring drought. By halftime, Alabama was up 18 points. As you might expect, Brey was not a happy camper in the locker room. He was steamed and let his team know it.

The second half was different, as it seemed to be for the Irish in 2001, and Notre Dame stormed back to take a 62-61 lead on a Chris Thomas jumper with just 6:22 left in the game, even though they had trailed by as many as 21 in the second half. Their intense zone defense got them back in the game. Five minutes later, the game was still tight, with Alabama holding a 77-76 edge. The Tide's Rod Grizzard hit two clutch free throws with 12 seconds remaining to give Alabama a 79-76 lead. Notre Dame brought the ball down court and Thomas launched a three-pointer. The ball caromed off of the rim and headed for the sidelines, as Ryan Humphrey sprinted to track it down. With under a second to go, the big man hurled a desperation three from the corner, which had a chance—but didn't go in. David Graves scored 21, Humphrey finished with 16, and Thomas had 14. Swanagan was not in at the finish, because he had sprained his left ankle midway through the second half when he stepped off the temporary flooring at an awkward angle.

So now Notre Dame had been brought back down to earth, done in again by a poor start, the kind they'd had against Indiana just weeks earlier. After the Alabama game, the team was disappointed. "There are no more moral victories for this club," Brey said afterward, and he was proud to say it. As Brey thought about it, the problem wasn't the Irish defense, it was their offense. "We are such an offensive team that can score. But when our shots don't fall early on, we get flustered and we end up focusing too much on scoring and not enough on defense."

The Irish closed out the calendar year back at the Joyce Center in South Bend against Colgate, an easy 92-61 win over the Raiders. Swanagan sat out with his bum ankle, snapping his consecutive game streak at 108, and watched as the Irish poured it on after leading by only six at the half with a 10-0 run to the start the second. Thomas was again outstanding, scoring 28 points. At one point in the second half, Brey was concerned that Thomas was not looking to score, but rather looking to make extra passes. He lashed out at the young point guard (fatherly love) and Thomas exploded hitting seven of his next eight shot attempts. Notre Dame sat at 10-2, with losses against ranked Indiana and Alabama, yet they still received no respect in the national polls. "That's OK," Brey said, "we're happy to be flying under the radar."

In a unique quirk in the schedule, UCLA opened PAC-10 play at Washington in mid-December. With the conference up to 10 teams and with the postseason conference tournament making a return after a 12-year absence, the schedule had to be moved up to accommodate the limited weeks of play. So on Thursday, December 20, the 5-2 Bruins took on Washington in Seattle. But things would not be easy. UCLA had lost four straight to the Huskies on the road, their last win coming in 1997. The four losses were by one,

10, one, and two points. The Bruins caught a break, however, when Washington's leading scorer, Doug Wrenn, was benched for the first six minutes for violating team rules.

The Bruins, however, could not take advantage of Wrenn's absence and trailed by seven at the break, 37-30. At halftime, Lavin was concerned about his players' nerves and poise, something he worried about with the freshmen, but not his upperclassmen. Strategically, the coach wanted his guards to feed the ball down low to Dan Gadzuric who had size and skill over the Washington big men. They listened. Playing smart, controlled basketball in the second half, UCLA rode Gadzuric to an 85-79 win. The big man scored 23 points and grabbed 13 rebounds, and Jason Kapono scored 14 of his 19 points in the second half. The Bruins were undefeated in PAC-10 play at 1-0. They had been picked to win the conference in the preseason media polls and were on their way. Andre Patterson did not play, though he suited up, and already Lavin could tell he would have to keep the freshman focused and "on board."

Games in the PAC-10 are Thursday–Saturday pairings, so UCLA traveled to Pullman to take on Washington State on Saturday, December 22. Like their game at Washington, the first half was a struggle for the Bruins. They played with little enthusiasm and found themselves trailing 37-29 at halftime. Like two days earlier, Lavin wanted the ball to go inside and wanted his players to play with more energy. Like Thursday, they did, and the second half was dominated by UCLA, though the outcome was still in doubt in the last minute. UCLA hung on to win 79-74. It was the eighteenth consecutive win for UCLA over Washington State, but it took more sweat than it should have. Lavin had used a point guard by committee since Cedric Bozeman's absence, giving Kapono, Dijon Thompson, Rico Hines, Ryan Walcott, and even Matt Barnes a chance at running the offense. Bozeman was recovering faster than expected and the coach could not wait to get him back on the court. After the Washington State game, the Bruins drove to Spokane, spent the night, then flew back to L.A. for a short Christmas break. Hines flew back east to his North Carolina home while the other Bruins stayed in California.

Usually, Christmas is a time for presents and good cheer, but the Bruin coaching staff was dealt a blow when prized recruit Michael Fey did not get a passing score on the SATs. He had enrolled at Harbor College after being declared academically ineligible after signing his National Letter of Intent with UCLA in November 2000. The Bruins could have used another big body to back up Gadzuric, but it was not to be. Fey would not join the Bruins in December and after the winter quarter began in early January, it was clear that he would not be able to help anytime this season. (Fey would get a qualifying score on the ACTs in mid-January.)

Returning home for a nonconference game against Columbia on Thursday, December 27, the Bruins sat at 7-2 and were ranked No. 19 though they were not playing like many expected. Bozeman had been cleared by the doctors to play before the Columbia game, but Lavin did not want to rush him back without enough practice time. UCLA had not played an Ivy League opponent since being upset by Princeton in the 1996 NCAA Tournament and the Lions were in the midst of a 15-day road trip. The game was a clear mismatch.

For UCLA, it was the same old story. Play poor, uninspired basketball in the first half, come back with clutch shooting and solid defense in the second. This time their formula almost didn't work. Midway through the second half, with a comfortable 22-point lead, Lavin sat down his regulars and gave some bench players some playing time. But they couldn't hold the large lead, as Columbia went on a 24-7 run and closed to 59-55 with 1:42 remaining. Clutch free throw shooting by Kapono down the stretch allowed

UCLA to escape with a 64-55 victory. With Kapono playing point, he managed only two shots in the first half against Columbia, a number way too low for an All-American shooter. In the second half he got more looks, with Thompson and Walcott running the offense. Kapono hit a three-pointer in the second half to raise his career total to 198, breaking Tracy Murray's school record set from 1990 to 1992.

UCLA had now won six in a row, but were inconsistent and fortunate in the streak. They barely escaped the Washington schools, and now Columbia at home, and they still had not settled on a lineup.

A few days later, with his penchant for history and for drama, Steve Lavin talked about the Big East versus PAC-10 rivalry in the locker room before the Bruins' home game against No. 19 Georgetown on Saturday, December 29. The Big East was supposed to be the "rough and tumble" conference and the PAC-10 was said to be "soft." In reality, Lavin told his No. 15 team, "the PAC-10 has won more championships in the 1990s than the Big East." He talked about the PAC-10 success in football, and how "the other major sport" had brought the conference a reputation for toughness. "We need to rebound today and keep our turnovers low," he said as he underlined those points on the board. "On defense, we need to stop [Drew] Hall and [Kevin] Braswell and we can't give them penetration."

As his team warmed up on the floor, Lavin watched the Missouri-DePaul game on a television set in the locker room, anxiously scribbling notes on the board in the process. When the team returned, assistant Patrick Sandle went over the Georgetown scouting report. Before the team prayer and chant, Lavin left them with this thought: "This will be a grind it out, physical Big East [type] game today. The score may not be high, but we need to stay focused and play tough."

Lavin was wrong on both fronts. The game was not as physical as promised and it was not low scoring—for the Bruins. UCLA jumped out to a 16-6 lead with stingy defense, allowing the Hoyas only two points in the red zone in the first five minutes, a fact that Lavin pointed out to his team in the first media timeout. "We need to keep playing good defense in the red zone and we need to score inside," he said, while assistant Jim Saia screamed over the pep band music something about defense. UCLA was easily able to break Georgetown's press for easy buckets.

By the second media timeout at under 12 minutes, the lead was up to 24-8. "We've got a smaller lineup in there," Lavin reminded his team. "Who is going to take the ball out on the press?" he asked. "I'll do it," Matt Barnes replied. Turning to forward T. J. Cummings, Lavin asked him to play more physical with the Hoya big men, to play "like you're a tight end in football."

It was a remarkable first half for UCLA, a turn from the disappointing openings over the last month. Going into the halftime locker room they led Georgetown 55-35. The game was nationally televised by CBS, so it came as no surprise that Lavin's team was playing so well. They always seemed to play well in the spotlight. In the locker room, Lavin praised his team for their strong defense and sound shooting, but warned them of the pressure of history on Georgetown. "I tell you what. Right now, the Georgetown coaches are all over their team. How they are letting down the history of Georgetown. Patrick Ewing and John Thompson being disappointed. The mothers of players, nieces, all of D.C. They [the Georgetown coaches] are challenging their manhood right now."

It is understood at UCLA that you coach and play under 11 national championship banners, and history is a part of the atmosphere, so you don't need to be reminded who you may be letting down.

Saia pointed out to the team that the fouls were 11-4 in favor of the home team, so he warned them to expect the officials to even it out in the second half. Georgetown coach Craig Esherick had been protesting calls throughout the first half to the officiating crew of Ted Valentine, Ed Corbett, and Donnee Gray, Big East officials. Typically in big nonconference games, officials from the visiting conference referee the game. The Big East crew was used to physical play and let a lot of the inside roughness continue without calls. Sandle, who had given the Bruins the pregame scouting reports, reminded the team to contain super senior Braswell, who was sure to try and win the game on his own in the second half.

Halftimes for UCLA are part lecture, part team teaching, and part collective reflection. Often, Lavin will ask the team what defensive schemes are working best or who they should double-team on the opposition. Barnes and Hines often speak on behalf of the team. The players know best because they are the ones out there, and Lavin uses this method of active participation to engage his players and to get the most out of them.

The second half did not start very well for UCLA, as Georgetown hit their open looks. "Get your heads out of your asses," Lavin screamed in a timeout huddle. "Every time we get a 20-point lead we lose our heads! Stay poised and settle down out there." As the second half continued and the Hoyas chipped away at the lead, Lavin turned his attention to the officials, who were making up some of those calls—just as Saia predicted. Lavin wasn't screaming, but was rather polite when questioning calls. He was so low-key in fact, that going into a timeout, Teddy Valentine, one of the officials, walked over and joked that "you [Lavin] don't know how to argue. Obviously, Keady didn't teach you too well."

UCLA let Georgetown get back into the game with poor defense and an outside shooting barrage by Braswell. With 7:40 remaining, the Bruin lead was down to eight, 71-63, but Lavin did not panic. "We need this," he told his team in the under 8:00 media timeout, "it will make us better." The Bruins had let a 22-point lead evaporate to single digits for the second consecutive game, but they did not let this one slip away. Despite heroics from Braswell, who dribbled down the court and hit three on numerous late possessions, the Bruins shot well from the line late in the game and came away with a 98-91 win. (Later that night, Lavin admitted privately that he should have put in a zone press toward the end of the game to force Braswell and the Hoya guards to go side to side, chewing up the clock, not just allowing them to dribble up the court for quick pull ups. Lavin, who was still learning as a coach and about this team, put this lesson in his bank.) Billy Knight finished with 20 points, Barnes had 19, and Cummings and Gadzuric each had 18.

"We won two good games the last three days," Lavin began his postgame talk. "Thursday, we beat Columbia from the Ivy League, which plays a slow, methodical basketball game. Today against the Big East and Georgetown, we played up tempo." Always thinking of March, Lavin added, "this was like a Sweet Sixteen game with the play and atmosphere—it is good preparation." He told the team that with all of the injuries and adjustments they had had to make, to be 9-2 overall and 7-0 in December was a proud accomplishment.

Headed into their showdown against No. 9 Missouri at the Savvis Center in St. Louis in late December, Bill Self described his team as a MASH unit. In the days leading up to the game, here was an injury status report on the Illini: Archibald (back), Krupalija (ankle), Head (ankle), Harrington (flu), Cook (knee), Williams (stomach flu). The Illini did an easy walk-through on Thursday before heading to Missouri and a relatively light practice Friday in St. Louis.

Missouri came into the game having lost to Iowa at home, 83-65. All-American Kareem Rush was not up for the challenge of Illinois. He shot just 6-15 in front of the 22,000 at the Savvis Center, as the teams traded baskets and leads in the first half. Illinois led by two at halftime, but turned it on in the second, shooting 50% from the field. All No. 8 Illinois really needed was Frank Williams. The All-American finally had the game everyone expected, scoring 22 points on jump shots, layups, baseline jumpers, three-pointers, and every other way imaginable. Missouri simply could not stop him. "I felt like Superman tonight," Williams said after the game, "I got this feeling. I got in the groove and I kept getting the ball from my teammates."

As for his star's performance, Self said, "Frank is so confident, sometimes you just hold your breath when he shoots. Tonight, he elevated his game." Williams was on a tear, averaging 24 points in the Illini's last five games, shooting close to 50% over that span. With solid defense and contributions from Brian Cook, the Illini headed into Christmas 10-2.

"This means a lot to me," Self joked with the media after the game, "My wife said I can now eat (at) Christmas."

After Self filled his stomach at Christmas, Williams continued his hot hand with a win at home over Loyola of Chicago, 87-72. Williams scored 25 points to carry Illinois, which did not play as well as they had against Missouri. The real hero of the game for Self, however, was redshirt center Nick Smith, who started and played 30 minutes, scoring a career high 17 points. Smith was inserted into the lineup because of the sprained left foot of Krupalija and a sore back for Archibald. Illinois played with 10 healthy guys including football player walk-on Clayton Thomas. (Meanwhile, Lucas Johnson continued to make impressive progress with his rehabilitation, and was fighting to get back playing before the Tournament. He had no interest in redshirting for the season, as this was his last run.) Though Illinois pulled away in the second half and won without its big men against Loyola, Self was still not happy with the team's play. He criticized the team for playing selfish again, as they committed 17 turnovers to just 15 assists.

It was now conference time, time for the real Illinois to show up. Would they live up to their No. 2 preseason ranking? As the team prepared for its conference opener at home against Minnesota, Self rested many of his players in practice including Krupalija and Archibald. When questioned by a reporter about sitting his big guys out of practice, Self responded, "If our goal was to win the Minnesota game, then they would practice . . . but it is a long season, and that's not our goal. Our goal is to be as good as you can be over a period of time." My, how times have changed. It's all about March.

Bill Self with wife Cindy and
children Lauren and Tyler

Self with coaching legend John Wooden and assistant Billy Gillispie

A postgame interview with ESPN's Jay Bilas after a win over Arizona in 2000

Celebrating the second consecutive Big Ten title in the visitors locker room at Minnesota, March 3, 2002. From left to right: head trainer Rod Cardinal, Wayne McClain, administrative assistant Jeff Guin, Norm Roberts, Bill Self, student assistant Nate Mast and Billy Gillispie

Self draws up a play before an NCAA Tournament game

All-American Frank Williams
gets some mid-game instructions

Steve Alford and wife Tanya at 1999 press conference introducing him at Iowa

Getting the Hawkeye fans ready
during Game Night celebration

Alford with wife Tanya, daughter Kayla, and sons, Bryce (left) and Kory

During a timeout with assistant coach, and father, Sam Alford

A postgame interview with CBS' Billy Packer in 2001

Reggie Evans confers with Coach
Alford

Steve Lavin at age 5 looking toward his future in basketball

Lavin giving instructions during a game

Lavin speaking at the annual basketball banquet

Lavin with his mentors (From left to right: Gene Keady, Pete Newell, Lavin, Cap Lavin and John Wooden)

Senior captain Rico Hines gets some advice from Lavin

Lavin visits with a patient at the
City of Hope Children's Hospital
in California

Mike Brey coaching in his standard mock-turtleneck at the Joyce Center

The Brey family: Mike, Tish, Callie, and Kyle

Mike and Tish Brey at the annual golf outing in August

On the set of *Inside Irish Basketball with Mike Brey* hosted by Jack Nolan

Getting a point across in a timeout huddle to David Graves, Chris Thomas, Matt Carroll and Jere Mecura (left to right)

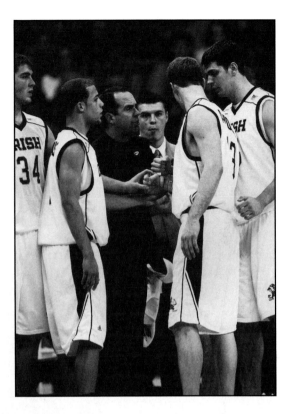

Brey and Mike Krzyzewski share a private moment before their second-round game in the 2002 NCAA Tournament in Greenville, South Carolina

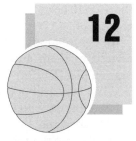

On the Block

ET IN AND GET OUT. THE MIKE BREY PHILOSOPHY HOLDS TRUE TO PREPARATION AS well. Though assistants Anthony Solomon, Sean Kearney, and Lewis Preston may have spent hours watching tape and preparing a scouting report, the information actually gets to the team is quite minimal. The day before the game, the team will gather in their locker room, or in a hotel banquet room, and the assistant responsible for preparing for the game will quickly go over a highlight or two of the opponent's top 10 players, with Brey interjecting a comment of his own, explaining how an opponent's tendency could effect how the Irish play them. The scouting report takes no more than 10 minutes, with the team writing down the information in their own notebooks. (Studies have shown that subjects are more likely to recall information if they have written it down as opposed to simply listening to it.)

After the scouting report concludes, the team adjourns next door to the players' lounge, where Brey takes them through some tape on the opponent, broken down into possessions on offense and defense. Brey does not believe in overcoaching or over use of film, so these tape sessions are short. Even on the court, the Irish do not spend a lot of time walking through an opponent's sets or plays. To Brey, it's not about what others do but what *we* do. So this was how Brey was preparing his men for a game against Villanova to open Big East play. The staff was all business, knowing how important an early conference game can be down the road. It was a Saturday morning over Christmas break, so the players had nothing but basketball on their minds. When they showed up at the Joyce Center for practice there was a sense of excitement, that they were part of something special and unexpected.

The next day in the pregame locker room, the team was chatty; in the players' lounge, Brey's mind was fast at work. The clock hit 7:00 and in he flew. Instead of walking to the board, he walked over to Harold Swanagan in the far corner of the locker room and asked him to stand. He then shook his hand, looked him in the eye, and said, loud enough for the team to hear, "Let's be men today." He then moved on to David Graves, Matt Carroll, and the other players. Brey went from one to another, shaking their hands, looking them in the eye, reminding them that they were men. As he completed the unusual process, he relayed to them an article he had read in the morning paper, identifying them as "Defending Big East Champs."

"We may be, but it starts over right now. We need to play with a purpose. They are all gunning for us, with a target on our backs. Let's play like men."

He knew that Swanagan was a man; that he played like one and acted like one off the court. You grow up fast when you grow up like Harold Swanagan, and he didn't need a degree or an NBA career to be considered a success. And that's why Brey couldn't understand when one of his seniors, his go-to guy, his paradigm of success, was so upset after Notre Dame had just beaten Miami of Ohio in December, saved by a tenacious defensive block by Torrian Jones. The team and coaching staff were jubilant, but Swanagan was not. Always on the lookout for the emotional signs of despair, Brey walked over to his captain and inquired as to the mood.

"I'll talk to you later," was all Swanagan could muster. So the next morning came, and Swanagan took a seat in a chair in his coach's office. It was only a matter of minutes before the 6'7", 247-lb. giant was sobbing.

Swanagan had beaten the odds. From the deprived area of Kentucky where Hopkinsville sits, Swanagan never dreamed that he would play basketball at, and eventually graduate from, the University of Notre Dame. "It's been the chance of a lifetime to come through here and get your degree. Nothing against where I am from. It's just there is nothing but trouble there. I was one of the lucky ones to get out of there and succeed at doing something I am good at." He ignored the critics, even those in the previous Irish administration, who "told me that I wouldn't be able to do the work. So far, I've done it."

And what he is good at is basketball, academics, and people. He would graduate in May 2002 and looked forward to continuing his playing career—somewhere. But if basketball was not in the cards for Swanagan, he still would have made it. He already had. And much of that success can be attributed to Mike and Tish Brey.

"It's an eight-hour drive [home] and I can only fly home every now and then," says the senior. "I don't have that kind of money. So the Breys had me over for Christmas dinner because I couldn't go home. It's the little stuff like that. Every opportunity he gets he invites us over to his house for dinner and to interact with his family. A lot of coaches would never do that. You get to see what kind of values his family has and what kind of people they are. In some cases, it rubs off on you. He invites everybody into his home and treats them like they're his kid."

And it was in that role of father that Brey found himself that morning in December when Swanagan was crying. Swanagan's older brother had been in jail and had been released, but was not able to make it home for some reason. He was struggling on the outside and his younger brother was scared he would end up back in prison. Swanagan had been trying to reach him, but his calls were not returned.

"I think Harold had some guilt with the situation," says Brey. "He couldn't really help him and he felt helpless." All of the guilt, anger, and frustrations came out that December morning, as Brey listened as a friend and father, not as a coach. Though there was little Brey could do, he offered to talk to the brother to at least establish a line of communication. His call was not returned. With some support from his coach, Swanagan managed to get through that tough time before Christmas, and reestablish his usual jovial mood.

As the season wore on, he and his brother did manage to get back in touch, and Brey—the friend and father—periodically checked in with Swanagan on the status of things.

"It's just part of the job," quips Brey, "change the hats."

The hat that Brey was wearing Sunday afternoon, January 6, was the coaching one. The one that lets the whole nation see your strengths and weaknesses over 30 times a year. Brey had challenged his guys to be men before the game against Villanova, because Brey knew that winning the Big East was about being men. He knew that the mental aspect of the game was as important as a shooting touch, and the coach constantly worked on the psyche of his players. The night before the Villanova game, after a team Mass in the players' lounge and a team dinner in the Monogram Room in the Joyce Center, a second-floor reception room, Brey sat down in the conference room in the basketball office and watched some Big East games on three television sets. As he headed for home around 8:30 P.M., he picked up the phone and called some of his players. He called senior captain David Graves and talked about leadership; he called Chris Thomas to make sure he was not nervous before his first Big East game. The coach didn't call every player, just those that he thought could use one. By Sunday morning when the team had breakfast at the Residence Inn in South Bend, Thomas was still nervous, but that was to be expected.

As the team warmed up on the floor near game-time, Notre Dame athletic director Kevin White and associate athletic director Jim Phillips made their way into the locker room. Brey was sitting in the locker area on a stool, focusing on the game by himself, of course. White and Phillips came in and wished Brey good luck and then proceeded to ask about the day's opponents. Brey was courteous and talked about Villanova's good shooting but prone-to-turnovers team, and after four or five minutes, his bosses left.

The Irish had lost eight straight to Villanova and had never beaten them in Big East play, and with a raucous Joyce Center crowd, today might be the day to end that streak. The game was not pretty, particularly in the opening minutes, and by the 15:46 timeout, the visiting team had a 7-6 lead. The Irish had made only one of their first eight shots. Swanagan had been cleared to play but Jordan Cornette got the start; however, he was not able to matchup with the physical Wildcats inside. "We need to fill the holes on defense," Brey said in the timeout, seated in a chair facing his five starters seated on the bench in front of him. "And watch for Ricky Wright."

The first half continued back and forth and with under 12 minutes to go, Villanova still led 19-14. In a timeout, Brey decided to switch from the "12" defense to "32," the three-quarters-court zone press he first used against DePaul. The "32" knocked the Wildcats off their game, as point guard Derrick Snowden turned the ball over on successive possessions. Notre Dame was not shooting well from the floor, but was stepping it up on the defensive end to keep the game close.

"You guys are playing like crap," Brey screamed at his players before they even had a chance to take their seats in the locker room at halftime, trailing 40-36 at home. With an impressive use of the English language, Brey got and maintained the attention of his players for close to two minutes. Turning to big man Tom Timmermans, Brey yelled, "Tom, you can't get a friggin' rebound!" His sights now on Thomas, Brey went after him for complaining to the refs at the end of the half instead of concentrating on running a play. The coach stormed out of the locker room followed by his assistants.

"He's right," Graves said soaked in sweat, "we go through this every game." He followed that up with a plea to get tough, stay focused, and play for pride at home. Humphrey chimed in with his deep, baritone voice, "It's not that hard, fellas, play like men."

Next door, the coaching staff was into their scanning of the halftime stats, but there was little to be positive about. Brey decided to start Swanagan, who continued to be hampered by the sore ankle, in the second half, and the coach asked his assistants for suggestions on the defensive alignment the Irish should open up with. Returning to the locker room, the coach was still heated but much more calm, and made the necessary adjustments to the lineup and defense. He ended his brief talk on a positive, encouraging the team, "Let's get 'em, it is a long game."

The second half did not start well for Notre Dame as Villanova got hot and took a 14-point lead with 8:17 remaining. Brey's frustrations were evident as he yelled at his players and the officials. But he never lost sight of his duties as a coach, and with the need for points quickly, he switched to a full-court press. Villanova crumbled under the pressure, throwing balls into the first rows of seats. Notre Dame went on a 23-8 run and took a 72-71 lead after Graves hit two free throws. With 26 seconds remaining, Wildcat guard Derrick Snowden made a lay up to put his team back on top, 73-72.

On the next possession, Thomas rushed down the court, beat Snowden off the dribble, but put up a poor shot with just under three seconds to play. Reggie Bryant grabbed the rebound and was immediately fouled, making one of two free throws to give Villanova a 74-72 lead. Humphrey launched a half-court prayer as time expired, and the Irish were 0-1 in the Big East. Graves finished with 22 points and Humphrey and Thomas added 18, the freshman shooting just 5 of 18. (Forward Jere Macura did not play, as he hadn't in four of the Irish's last five games, and Brey knew he needed to talk to him to keep Macura's head focused. They would meet the following morning for an hour and the coach would impress upon the forward to "get meaner" and play tougher.)

The loss was a difficult one for Brey and his team. They had been on a roll; had won these types of games last year; and now had lost on national television and *at home*. The coach and players were frustrated by their poor play and heads hung in the postgame locker room. Brey did not scream; in fact he was rather collected and encouraging. He knew that he couldn't let the effects of this loss carry over into the Big East season.

As Brey talked to his team, Wildcat coach Jay Wright faced the media, talking about the gutsy performance of his team and their need to cut down on turnovers. Wright was in his first year at Villanova, a young 40-year-old who had already earned a reputation as a good coach and excellent recruiter. Like Brey, he had been patient waiting for his first big job, and how he ended up at Villanova reveals much about the business side of coaching.

In the America East conference, the season-ending conference tournament is a bit different than most others. Teams play quarter and semifinal games on the higher seed's home court, and then the two finalists take a week off before playing the championship game at a predetermined site. Instead of an action-packed four days, like the ACC, Big Ten, Big East, and other major conference tournaments, the America East takes some time off to build up to the climatic finish. For this conference, like many mid-majors, the only shot at making the NCAA Tournament for a team is winning the conference tournament, so winning that final game means everything.

The week between the semis and finals for Jay Wright in 2001 should have been a time to prepare his Hofstra University team to meet Delaware in the conference championship on March 10. Wright was in his seventh year at Hofstra and was looking to win his second America East crown and second birth in the Big Dance. But in addition to looking at tapes of Delaware, who the Flying Dutchmen had already faced twice during the season, Wright spent time deflecting speculation about his future. He was on the coaching "hot list" for big-time programs, and schools wasted little time going after him. He had fielded some overtures the previous year at season's end, but he wasn't ready to leave and the opportunities did not seem right for him.

In fairness to himself, his athletic director and, most importantly, his players, Wright made it clear to all interested parties that he would not discuss his future until Hofstra ended its season. That could come on Saturday with a loss in the conference final to Delaware, or perhaps a week later after an early exit from the NCAA. Whatever the timing of his team's exit, Wright had no idea where the journey might take him. He was happy coaching at Hofstra, had a great relationship with the administration, and had great success in the America East. But like most professionals, he sought a bigger challenge, and for Wright and most basketball coaches, that meant moving up into the major conferences.

On March 10, 2001, Hofstra defeated Delaware 68-54, to advance to the NCAA Tournament. The following day they learned their first round fate, a date with storied UCLA in the East Regional. Hofstra was seeded No. 12 and gave the No. 4-seeded Bruins all they could handle, but simply did not have the manpower to win. The Flying Dutchmen's season was over with the 61-48 loss to UCLA in Greensboro—but things were just starting for Wright.

Before the UCLA game, Wright had sat down with his athletic director, Harry Royle, and Hofstra president Stuart Rabinowitz. They all knew what was going to happen when the season ended, and they all wanted to be "on the same page." They agreed to communicate with each other about developments. It was like a father giving his only daughter permission to date—you don't want to, but you know you have to. The day after the UCLA loss, the calls started coming again. The initial list of interested schools were all East Coast, major conference schools: Rhode Island, Massachusetts, Rutgers, and LaSalle, all expressing interest in that order. Wright was from the Philadelphia area, his wife was a graduate of Villanova, and he was an assistant under Rollie Massimino at Villanova—he knew the East Coast very well. Any of those schools would be a good fit and certainly would be a step up in pay and prestige.

Bob Mulcahy was the athletic director at Rutgers, a Villanova alum, and a good friend of Wright's, and when Rutgers' coach Kevin Bannon was let go at the end of the season, Mulcahy's friend was at the top of his list. The coach had already been in preliminary talks with UMass about their opening, and when Rutgers opened, Wright asked for some time from UMass officials to explore the Scarlet Knight's opening. The Massachusetts administration agreed, since they were looking at other candidates as well.

"I had a feeling that both Rutgers and UMass wanted me to be their coach. It was just a gut feeling that I had and it was up to me to make a decision," Wright said, thinking back on that week. Little did he know how complicated the picture would become. "During that week, I couldn't go anywhere without being hounded by the media. The Boston reporters about the UMass job. The New York and New Jersey folks coming at me about the Rutgers job, and then the Philly media interested in me as a local guy. All of this was happening so fast, in a period of three days."

The phone rang in Wright's Long Island house on Wednesday, March 21, and a man on the other line spoke with a deep southern twang. "Mr. Wright, this is Joe Dean, former athletic director at LSU." The accent was so dead on and the call so random, Wright thought it had to be one of his friends playing a joke on him. "I am representing an SEC school," Dean continued, "and they would like to know if you would be interested in coaching in the SEC?"

Wright nervously said yes and the conversation soon turned into more. They talked about Wright's coaching, his family, and his future, and after a few moments, it became clear that this was no joke. His interest solidified, Wright wanted to know the school, and asked Dean the question.

"Tennessee."

Now another school was in the Jay Wright hunt, and this was a really big one. Coaching in the SEC against the likes of Kentucky and Florida would be incredible, and the money in coaching contracts in that conference was exorbitant. It was all happening so fast, pulling Wright in so many directions. Dean asked if the school's AD, Doug Dickey, could call Wright, and sure enough, five minutes later, the phone rang in Long Island and the two men spoke, with Wright sitting on the sofa in his basement—his home and "war room" for the duration of the process. They arranged for Wright to meet with Tennessee officials and Joe Dean in New York City the following Tuesday, March 27.

At this point in the process, Rhode Island and LaSalle had gone in different directions, leaving Wright in the hunt for Tennessee, UMass, Rutgers, and the possibility of staying at Hofstra. The same men who had given him room to explore other options, were also trying to persuade him to stay, inquiring what it would take to keep the young coach where he was. As Wednesday, March 21 continued, he had somewhat ruled out returning to Hofstra, so UMass, Rutgers, and Tennessee were still on the plate.

He woke up Thursday morning and called down to Philadelphia to speak with his friend, Villanova coach Steve Lappas. He had been an assistant with Lappas at Villanova before Lappas went to Manhattan and later returned as the head coach of the Wildcats.

"Rutgers would be a great job, Jay. But UMass could be special as well. In fact, UMass might even be the better fit for you in the Atlantic Ten."

Wright decided to talk with Tennessee and Rutgers, and meet with UMass officials on Tuesday, the same day he had originally planned to meet Dean in New York City . He would meet with Bob Mulcahy from Rutgers on Sunday. Surely, it would all be settled by Tuesday night.

On Friday morning, March 23, Wright's "agent," a close friend of Villanova legend Rollie Massimino, called the Massachusetts AD to tell him that Wright was seriously interested in the UMass job, but wanted more time to explore the Rutgers and Tennessee jobs. The AD called Wright and told him it was fine to take time to explore. At 3:00 P.M. on Friday afternoon, a Philadelphia reporter who Wright had befriended in his days at Villanova called with some startling news. "Did you hear that Lappas resigned and was taking the UMass job?" Wright responded, "That can't be, I just talked to him yesterday. He said nothing about it. It's not true."

It couldn't be true, could it? Had Wright not just spoke at length with Lappas just hours earlier? Had Lappas not told his protégé that UMass would be a great job for him [Wright]? The irony was dripping from the sudden change of fortune.

A few hours later, one of Wright's Hofstra assistants called to tell him the news about Lappas. Perhaps it was true, Wright thought to himself. What better way to find out the truth than to go directly to the source? "Steve, it's Jay," Wright began the conversation. "Did you really resign and are you going to UMass?" he asked.

"Yeah, I had to do it," replied Lappas. "It was a great opportunity for the family and me. I don't want you to think that I took your job," Lappas responded.

"Not at all," Wright shockingly said. "I was going to tell UMass I wasn't interested anyway. No wonder they seemed so happy when I was talking with them this morning, asking for more time."

Harriett Lappas, Steve's wife and close friend of Jay's, got on the phone.

"If they offer you the job here [Villanova], you better take it. It is a much better job than Rutgers."

Steve interrupted, "I don't know, it's pretty tough here, Jay. Think about Rutgers."

So UMass was out, as Lappas incredibly took the job himself, Tennessee was still a possibility, Rutgers was still his for the taking and perhaps Villanova might come calling. On Friday night, Wright did what every college basketball coach would do under such pressure and chaos. He went to see the clowns. Wright took his son to the circus to spend some time with him and to get away from the craziness for a while. While watching the tigers and elephants run around the ring, his cell phone rang.

"Jay? It's Dick Vitale. Did you take the Villanova job? No. Shit. I better get back on the air for a retraction. Would you be interested? Yes, well, when they call you, please call me." The whole conversation was surreal, but somehow the words "circus" and "Vitale" seemed to go together.

On Saturday morning, Vince Nicastro, the Villanova athletic director, called Wright and asked if he would be interested in the job. Wright asked Nicastro if the job was being offered. He said "yes."

"I'll take it right now if you offer it to me," Wright responded.

A few minutes later, Father Edmund Dobbin, the president of Villanova, called to talk about the job. It was clear to Wright that the job was his, even though they hadn't even talked about a contract. With no interview, no campus visit, and no contract, it still seemed like the saga was over. Not yet.

So impressed with the professionalism and classy way in which all of the interested schools' administrators had dealt with him, Wright made it a point to call each of them to tell them about Villanova on Saturday. Doug Dickey at Tennessee was happy for Wright, but left the door open, implying that if a contract could not be worked out, that Wright should get back in touch and they could still meet on Tuesday. He then called Mulcahy at Rutgers.

"Have you signed anything yet?," the AD asked.

"Not really," the coach replied.

"Great then, we will meet tomorrow as planned."

Wright's representative met with Villanova officials late Saturday night to hammer out a contract. All parties agreed to meet Sunday morning at a tiny diner in Cherry Hill, New Jersey, where Wright's wife is a native, to go over the contract. All Wright really wanted was a long-term deal for security.

So on Sunday morning, March 25, Wright drove to the diner in Cherry Hill, finalized the deal, but did not sign anything. At that point, Wright tried to reach Mulcahy on his cell phone, but couldn't get through. He wanted to tell him that he had accepted the Villanova job. Wanting to handle things right, Wright got back into his car and drove one and a half hours up to the Rutgers campus in New Brunswick, New Jersey, to track down Mulcahy. The AD had been at a luncheon and wanted Wright to sit down first with Rutgers football coach Greg Schiano.

"Bob, I need to talk with you first," Wright pleaded with his friend.

"Talk with Greg and then we'll meet," responded Mulcahy.

So Wright sat down with a stranger to talk about a school where Wright would not be the coach. Instead of the B.S., he told Schiano about the Villanova job. They spent the rest of their time talking about their wives and kids. After meeting with Schiano, Wright was finally able to tell Mulcahy about his new job.

On Tuesday morning, March 27, Villanova scheduled a press conference to announce the hiring of Jay Wright. In the president's office, just 10 minutes before being introduced as the next coach, Wright affixed his signature on a five-year contract. He then went to meet the media where he was surprised by former players and coaches who had come to express their support. Wright became emotional at the outpouring. Or perhaps he was just glad the whole thing was over.

At the same time that Wright was pondering his choices and Lappas was on his way to UMass, former Minuteman coach Bruiser Flint was out in the cold. But not really. He had been fired from UMass, a move he anticipated all season long. "After last year [end of 2000], I met with the ADs and administrators after going to the NIT and it became clear that I had to get to the Tournament the next season or I was done. It actually took some pressure off that season."

Flint never felt he was on the same page as the Massachusetts people. As an assistant to John Calipari there, Flint had seen the highs and lows and came to understand that UMass wanted basketball to provide for all of the other sports, which meant winning deep into the NCAAs. The problem: he was not given the resources to get it done. (A common complaint among fired coaches.) But for Flint, because he knew that his release was coming, he was able to plan ahead. "I knew that I could coach and that I would be able to get another job," Flint now reflects. "I had people contact me through feelers as to whether or not I would be interested in certain opportunities."

As fate would have it, Flint flirted with a number of positions, including Duquesne, but all along, Drexel had stayed in touch, imploring Flint not to accept another job. A product of the streets of Philadelphia, Flint was intrigued about returning to his roots. It was exactly 21 days after being released by UMass that Flint became the new head coach at Drexel University in Philadelphia. For Flint, the process may have been slower, but the results were worth the wait.

At first, the hiring of Jay Wright at Villanova may seem complex, crazy, incredible, and yes, comical. But like the hiring of Mike Brey at Notre Dame (discussed in chapter 4), that's the way this business goes. For all of the talk about pursuit of victory, graduation rates, and the drama of the NCAA Tournament, coaching college basketball is, at its very core, still a business. The best and brightest are in the highest demand and can command the largest contracts. The market is highly competitive and the stakes are high.

The courting of Wright by the various schools, the negotiations, and the actual hiring took place within a matter of 96 hours. That can be long by today's standards, especially when compared to Flint's timetable. The process of hiring a coach at the Division I level has become an exercise in preparation, relationships, and time constraints.

Preparation. The motto of the Boys Scouts is "Be Prepared," and the majority of athletic directors and presidents must have been Eagle Scouts. Though some will not admit it on record, they are always prepared to hire a new coach. In today's environment, when coaches are hired and fired at an alarming rate, switch schools for more lucrative deals, or hop to the NBA, athletic directors never know when they might lose their coach. Instead of starting from scratch, they are prepared, if and when, they need to conduct a search.

At Illinois, athletic director Ron Guenther thought he was secure with Lon Kruger as his coach and was shocked when Kruger decided to bolt to the Atlanta Hawks. He may have been shocked, but he wasn't unprepared. "I had a list of guys that I was following, tracking, and you can do that quite discreetly while they are employed someplace else. When Lon did decide to go, obviously, Bill Self was the hot guy at the time, but we had already put together a short list."

Guenther is not alone in assuming the best while preparing for the worst. Most athletic directors have assembled a list of head coaches and assistant coaches who they would consider as candidates at their respective schools. They do it discreetly and even the candidates on the list may have no idea they are being considered.

Relationships. If there are "six degrees of separation" in the world, then in the athletic realm, there are only three degrees. It is very hard to find a current head coach, or assistant coach for that matter, who has not worked with, or does not know, an athletic director or prominent coach. It is a small world indeed, which makes putting together a candidate list easier than you might think.

"About six days prior to Matt Doherty actually leaving, I had a sense that he would go, so we were already working on the next coach," explains current Notre Dame athletic director Kevin White. "I made probably 50 phone calls initially to people who I trusted, to get some names and thoughts on candidates. I called coaches, commissioners, television people." Starting with a rough list of about 15, he quickly got it down to about seven, before deciding to interview three: P. J. Carlesimo, Ernie Kent, and Mike Brey (though White refuses to publicly confirm the three finalists).

Many athletic directors call only a handful of coaches, with Mike Krzyzewski at the top of their list. They want their programs to emulate Duke's success as much as possible, so one way to do that is to look at coaches with a pedigree, i.e., ones who worked under a Krzyzewski or a Rick Pitino or a Dean Smith. They are getting a known quantity, in that they know that their new hire has been trained by the best. Quin Snyder and Tommy Amaker were once Krzyzewski assistants, along with Brey and former Washington coach Bob Bender. It becomes apparent why ADs call Krzyzewski. But then often, as expected, candidates that he may suggest are part of his "family," which is why so many Duke assistants are mentioned for vacancies. In addition to Krzyzewski, other people whom ADs call include C. M. Newton, Rick Pitino, Lute Olson, and, yes, Dick Vitale.

In March 2002, former Duke guard Jeff Capel, III was hired to be the head coach at Virginia Commonwealth, becoming the youngest Division I head coach at the ripe old age of 27. Capel had been an assistant for only two years when he got the job. VCU athletic director Richard Sander had called Krzyzewski to get his thoughts on candidates, and the Duke coach gave Capel his blessing. The hiring of Capel infuriated many coaches around the country, particularly assistant coaches, many of whom thought that they were much more qualified for the job. Capel's hiring showed the power and influence of Krzyzewski, and perhaps the overreliance by ADs on trying to create a "Duke" at their places. Hiring a former player or coach from Duke or Kentucky or Kansas does not make another program similar. But as Dick Vitale points out, ADs are not going to hire a coach based on one coach's recommendation—even though the recommender is Mike Krzyzewski.

In addition then to preparation, there are the relationships which facilitate a coaching search. ADs must also be ready to move quickly if needed and often speed is critical.

Timing. Many coaching changes occur during or after the NCAA Tournament, which coincides with an allowable recruiting and evaluation period for coaches starting the day after the Final Four. Not having a head coach in place during this time means critical days lost building a recruiting class. Early April is not the only critical time. Some moves are made over the summer months, with July the heart of recruiting. In exceptional circumstances, such as the firing of Bobby Knight at Indiana, immediately before the beginning of practice in October, the timing could not have been worse. UCLA coach Jim Harrick was fired a few weeks into practice in 1996. One can only wonder if Mike Davis at Indiana (interim coach following Bobby Knight's firing) and Steve Lavin would be where they are if their respective ADs had had time to conduct a thorough national search before appointing them interim? (This is not an indictment of Davis or Lavin, but merely speculation about timing. Of course, both hirings proved to be great ones with Davis taking Indiana to the title game in 2002 and Lavin guiding UCLA to five Sweet Sixteens in six years.)

In addition to the impact on recruiting, administrators are often vying for the same "hot list" of coaches. If an AD takes his time conducting a national search, some of the better coaches who may be looking to move may commit elsewhere. Everyone knows who the top guys are, and it is rare that a name comes out of the blue. Competition for their services benefits the coaches, but not the schools trying to hire them.

These three factors, preparation, relationships, and timing, create an environment where stories like Jay Wright's and Mike Brey's can happen. Regardless of how they got hired, *why* did they get hired? What are administrators looking for when hiring a coach?

"This market of coaches has become a pretty restrictive market," Notre Dame's White says. The former AD at Arizona State, Tulane, and Maine has seen it from a variety of perches. "If you've got somebody pretty good, you are going to protect your investment from a contractual standpoint. Far different from five or 10 years ago. The mobility of choice has really changed the mechanism. When you make a whole bunch of early inning phone calls, you get a pretty good sense of people's levels. First of all, whether or not they're a performer. What their mobility might be like, financial considerations. Whether they're an institutional fit. What kind of characteristics they're going to bring."

"Fit," "match," "representative" are words that athletic directors use to describe their coaching hires. It's not simply about who is the best coach, but who is the best fit for the university. Determining a coach's ability as a coach is very subjective and sometimes their records may be indicative of success. But there may be an excellent coach at a school with limited resources or at a school with little exposure. In addition, records can be deceiving. A coach at a low mid-major might have to play four guarantee games a season, almost ensuring automatic losses to power schools in exchange for income to help support the athletic department. It goes without saying, however, that any coach being considered to coach at a high level is expected to be able to coach Xs and Os.

A coach's ability to recruit is now a key factor in hirings across the country. "He got Player A to come to that school" or "Bob Smith is a great recruiter." Perhaps, but it is much more complicated than that. (See chapter 9 on recruiting.) Rarely is it just one assistant coach who builds a recruiting class, but rather a culmination of a staff's work. Players may attend a school for a variety of reasons *besides* the coaching staff, but coaches will take credit for any signee. ADs are also cognizant of regions in the nation where a coach has recruited before. It may not make sense to hire a guy who has coached and recruited in Texas to expect him to make inroads signing kids from the streets of New York City. That does not mean he cannot be successful, it just makes it harder.

Flexibility in a coach's current situation also plays a role. If a coach is in a complex, long-range deal, which can be costly to terminate, that may eliminate a prospective coach for an opening. Some coaches have "noncompete" clauses in their contracts, prohibiting them from coaching at another conference school or nearby university. Often, this flexibility is determined through intermediaries or "feelers" who are knowledgeable of the coach's current situation.

Then there is the issue of money. Can a university afford to hire a big name coach and pay him the current market rate? Some schools have a philosophical practice of limiting what they will pay a coach, while others will open the checkbooks for any amount to get the coach they want. The financial considerations depend on the conference and the financial contributions of the school's basketball and football teams to the overall athletic budget.

Finally, and most importantly, is a coach a good fit with the institution? Does he share the same values as the college community? Does he place an emphasis on academics as the school may require? Does his personality fit with the local community? A coach who may be a great fit for UNLV may not work at a small Midwest school. ADs are well aware of perceptions of certain coaches and, right or wrong, those perceptions become a huge determining factor in hirings. If a coach is said to be loud, slick, or a "party guy," he may not fit at a more conservative place, where fans may want an old-school, conservative coach, who would rather wear a sweater than a $1,000 Armani suit. Many of these "fit" determinations are based on personal recommendations, referrals, and brief meetings between candidates and ADs. It is not surprising then, that not every great coach is a good fit at every school.

ESPN basketball analyst Jay Bilas, a former player and coach at Duke said, "You don't always have knowledgeable basketball people making decisions about hiring. A lot of programs don't really understand it internalizes who they are." Bilas continues, "There are a lot of terrific coaches out there that are not going to make you a stunning press conference and get you patted on the back for two weeks after you make the hiring, but are going to do a hell of a job with your program. I think too many people hire based upon the short-term jolt they're going to get out of hiring a sexy coach, a hot name, or someone who's going to make them a really good press conference for a good *SportsCenter* bite."

Of course, in hindsight, both administrators and coaches second-guess themselves in the decision-making process. Jim Harrick took the Georgia job twice, after changing his mind. Bobby Cremins was headed to South Carolina—and then not. And in a strange turn of events, Bowling Green head coach Dan Dakich was hired to coach at West Virginia—only to go back to Bowling Green a week later after he found out about possible violations committed at WVU.

New Mexico AD Rudy Davalos offered the head job to Arizona State's Rob Evans, who then turned it down. But in remarks the following days, Davalos denied ever offering Evans the job, even after Evans had told his staff and bosses at ASU about the offer. There was a war of words in the papers the ensuing days, with Evans accusing Davalos of "trying to slander my integrity." Sometimes things are just not meant to be.

Just as administrators are preparing for their next move, so are many coaches. Head coaches at Division II or III schools are sometimes looking to make the big jump; head coaches at smaller Division I schools are seeking a better job in a bigger conference; assistants at all levels wants to move 18 inches to sit in the head coach's seat. So underneath the public displays of loyalty and allegiances to schools, do not be deceived—a coach is also an individual and a businessman, often looking out for his own interests.

The Sporting News' Mike DeCourcy has noticed the "careerism" trend develop over the last five years. "For some reason, a career track has developed among coaches. They feel if they are at a lower level they have to move up. It's the nature of the business. Not only do coaches want to coach at the top levels, they want security. They know that one bad season and they're fired. They would rather be making $750,000 to $1,000,000 when they are fired than $75,000 to $150,000. It's not unanimous; some guys like where they are and stay there, but for most coaches, there's now a distinct career path for success."

As assistants together at Duke, Mike Brey and Tommy Amaker were often the subjects of coaching rumors, and Krzyzewski was inundated with inquiries about the two. When one of them was "in play" and was a candidate for a job, they said they were "on the block." Each was a "hot" coach for a specific job but could very easily be taken "off the block" if an opportunity disappeared.

UCLA assistant Jim Saia is considered by some a "hot" assistant, since he is the top assistant at perennial power UCLA. Bringing in solid recruits and being part of a winning program has its advantages. "We've always happened to win at the right time. But when you're at UCLA and things are well, it's like the stock market. I'm Steve's top assistant. You might have a real successful season. Go to the Final Four. Patience is great at that point because now your stock goes way up. If we happened to go .500 and get released, I'm still the same coach. I'm as good of a coach as if we went to the Final Four as I am if we go .500. It's who's hot, who's not. You have to ride the wave."

Saia has been around long enough to understand how the business side of the game works. Like many assistants, he wants to be a head coach, and is certainly aware of potential openings around the country. He was a finalist for the Fresno State opening in April 2002, but lost out to Oklahoma assistant Ray Lopes, who helped guide the Sooners to the Final Four. Norm Roberts at Illinois and Anthony Solomon at Notre Dame are ready to run their own programs, but Solomon believes that doing the best where you are is enough to get you that next job. "I'm aware of the openings because I am a junkie for the profession. If you take care of business where you are, doors will open for you elsewhere."

Since there are 321 Division I staffs with an average of three assistants, there are close to 1,000 assistants looking for their big break. They know it, and their bosses know it. As Purdue assistant Jay Price remarked about his boss, Gene Keady, "He doesn't want coaches that don't want to be head coaches." But assistants are competing against each other, against head coaches at mid-majors, and even against former players with little coaching experience. It is the precious few who can crack into the big time, without first being a head coach at a mid-major. Quin Snyder and Tommy Amaker were the exceptions, but it is not surprising, considering who recommended them for the jobs.

Assistants and their bosses seem to know when junior staffers are ready, but being ready doesn't mean it is going to happen. As in most things in life, timing is everything. Being on the staff of a Final Four team gives you more exposure, like Lopes at Oklahoma or Marquette's Tom Crean, who served as an assistant at Michigan State during their Final Four runs. But you also need people pulling for you. You need "your guy" in the inner circle making things happen. Maybe it is a big name coach, or an AD or Sonny Vacarro, even a Dickie V. But without someone whispering in the right ears, opportunities to move may not be as abundant as one might think.

Crean at Marquette had Tom Izzo pulling for him. Ed Schilling at Wright State had John Calipari. Billy Donovan had Rick Pitino. The list is continuous, and often, comes full circle. It is clear that to be a "hot" candidate you need to: 1) be in a high-profile situation, either because of the school's popularity or a winning team; 2) have someone working the jobs on your behalf; 3) have solid recruiting classes that you can take credit for; and 4) be able to sell yourself and the school.

"There are a lot of good assistants and a lot of good head coaches," Bilas believes. "Everybody's looking for the one that's going to be great. There aren't that many great people in any job. We probably throw the term 'great' around too much. There are different ways to make it."

Bill Self was a hot commodity after leading Tulsa to the Elite Eight in 2000, and Illinois snatched him. He has his own theories on the pedigrees of coaches: "I think sometimes we get so hung up on where they [coaches] come from that we don't look as much at the qualities that make a coach successful. But if a coach is a Duke assistant, how could he not be a part of your consideration?"

In addition to assistants moving up to take head jobs, there are also head coaches of mid-majors or low Division I schools looking to make a move to the big time. As a former assistant at a big-time school, Manhattan coach Bobby Gonzalez has seen both sides. ("My cell phone bill at Virginia cost more than the house I grew up in.") Having finished his third season at Manhattan, he too, looks for the big-time job. "I think guys at mid-majors, when they get a chance to jump, they don't look back. I think if you have been successful at this level then you can get it done anywhere."

Crean learned to stop looking for the next job while an assistant to Izzo at Michigan State. "When I stopped looking to get ahead as an assistant, that's when things started clicking and people came my way. You just need to do the best you can at wherever you are."

Tom Green at Farleigh-Dickinson finished the 2001–2002 near the bottom of the RPI rankings—it was not a very good season. "I'm not sure if it is ever OK to have a bad season. I think all coaches are very sensitive about their won-lost record. There are a lot of sleepless nights after the season we just had. I don't think there is ever anybody that is totally secure in coaching. That's for sure. I don't know how to get another job, but I do know how not to lose the one I do have."

Michael Holton was hired in 2001 to turn the University of Portland program around. On the day of the press conference introducing him as the new coach, Holton met with the team at 1:00 P.M. to introduce himself and to get started on the right note. "I told them about playing hard, playing defense, and being unselfish. I also told them I had an open-door policy and I want them to feel free to come to me to speak about anything." About 15 minutes after the team meeting, a mere 45 minutes before the press conference, Holton sat in his new office organizing his desk, when he noticed a player outside the office. He invited him in. "I'm thinking to myself that, 'Wow, I gave a great speech, a player is already here to talk.'" In reality, the player walked in and quit. He said he was transferring and that he had made the decision before Holton arrived. "It was a bit humbling for me. I hadn't even been introduced in my press conference and I already had a player quit. It said a lot to me about being a head coach, that you are not able to control everything." Not everything is rosy after, or even before, the press conference.

At the start of the 2001–2002 season, there were 47 new head coaches at the Division I level. Out of 321 positions (a turnover rate of 15%) close to one in seven coaches would not be returning to their respective schools. (At the start of the 2002-2003 season, 45 new head coaches were in place.) Some of these positions are high profile, such as Louisville's hiring of Rick Pitino and Texas Tech's hiring of Bobby Knight, and the search process is very public.

In the spring of 2002, University of Wisconsin-Green Bay did something very unusual in the hiring process. The five finalists for the head coaching job appeared at a public forum where they answered questions from the public and the media, and then gave closing statements. It was just like a presidential debate, candidates looking to make the best impression. The winner of the horse race? Green Bay native and Marquette assistant Tod Kowalczyk.

When a coaching position opens, that means someone is no longer there. He may have left for a better job or was fired. The term "fired" is used frequently, because it is an easy term. Placing it on every coach's situation is a bit of a stretch, however. The irony in a vacancy is this: coaches are competitive, and in some cases may not even like each other, but when one of their brethren is forced out, they all feel sympathetic, even if they are going after the guy's old job.

"You see a guy and you're kind of pulling for him because you don't want anyone in the profession to lose his job; there is nothing worse than seeing a guy lose his job," Wright State head coach Ed Schilling remarked. "But watch out, because the vultures will be out there circling."

Administrators or coaches will hardly ever admit to the real reasons a coach was fired. Some situations may be more complex than just a coach's won-lost record. There may be an NCAA investigation, personal misconduct, or the new hiring of an athletic director who wants to make a change to put his own stamp on the athletic program. The bottom line in today's college basketball: win or get out.

Legendary coach John Wooden feels strongly that the trend is upsetting. "Personal misconduct and not showing proper respect to the administration and showing a disregard for graduations, and the academic progress of players, I think are all reasons [for dismissals]. But just winning percentage? No, you shouldn't be fired because of that."

An incredible thing happens after a coach is fired. He never seems to knows why he was let go. Speaking to many coaches around the country who have been let go, they seem to not fully understand it. "I still have no idea" or "I didn't do anything" or the best one "If I only had some more time." But time is not a luxury in big-time basketball anymore. Fans, media, and administrators want winning teams now, not later. The whole process is accelerated.

Just like in any profession, one does not put "terminated" on his resume, but in such a public profession, there is no escaping one's past. Many good coaches are let go from one job, and then need to rebuild their reputation by taking an assistant's job or by coaching at a lower level. It is the nature of the beast.

"Professionally, it is hard to get another head coaching job," notes Dick Vitale. "Unless you have a godfather of sorts looking out for you. In this high media world, everyone knows when you get fired. ADs are afraid to hire a guy who has been fired, even if they like him."

B illy Bayno. The name just exudes fun and excitement. His is a cautionary tale for the younger generation about the perils of fame, especially in a city with lots of temptations. But Bayno's quick rise and rapid descent may be more about losing than about sex, alcohol and Sin City. Bayno was fired from UNLV on December 12, 2000, in the heart of his nonconference schedule. It did not come as a complete shock to him, or to the UNLV faithful, as his downfall was a long, tedious one. Amid an NCAA investigation and disturbing stories about his personal life, Bayno was finished at UNLV. To the administrators at UNLV, he was the root of all evil. To Bayno, he was a scapegoat caught up in a PR dilemma.

At the age of 32, Bayno took over the Runnin' Rebels program, after being an assistant at UMass to John Calipari. He was a brash, well-dressed, sometimes cocky young man, who had a lot of Vegas in him. He had well-placed friends in the business, including John Calipari, Rick Pitino, and Mike Krzyzewski, and he knew the game of basketball. He also loved living the coach's life.

His teams fared well after his initial 10-16 season at the helm, going 22-10 and 20-12 (WAC champions) in consecutive years, and playing in the NIT and NCAA Tournaments, respectively. In his last full season, 1999–2000, his team won the Mountain West Conference and Bayno was named Co-Coach of the Year, though he watched his team lose to No. 7-seeded Tulsa in the South Regional in the Tournament. He brought in some solid recruits, but UNLV was not the draw that it was under Jerry Tarkanian in the early 1990s. As Bayno would later say, "They had Kentucky expectations but not Kentucky resources." Perhaps it was the pressure to win, or simply some ill-advised associations, but things started to go badly for Bayno in 1999. The NCAA began an investigation into alleged improprieties in the UNLV program, including payments to recruits and current players.

Much of the ignition for the NCAA investigation came from the Rebels' recruitment of high school player Lamar Odom, now an NBA star. A troubled figure off the court, Odom did not have the grades to make it, and he was dogged by a sexual assault allegation. UNLV was one of the schools that was still interested. According to the NCAA, Bayno's close friend and UNLV booster, dentist David Chapman of Las Vegas, gave Odom $5,600 in 1997 in an attempt to entice him to enroll at UNLV. Bayno acknowledges his friendship with Chapman, but denies knowing of any payments. Odom was not admitted to UNLV. But the damage done to the program would not go away.

The investigation continued, and an announcement of the "official inquiry" was made in March 2000. As a result, Bayno came under increasing pressure from fans, the media, and his own administration. He denied any wrongdoing, but it didn't seem to be enough. Then the juicy gossip about his lifestyle began to appear in local reports, and soon even the NCAA troubles looked tame.

"I was having a good time, going out and partying, but never during the season," Bayno admits. "Buddies would come into town so we would go out. I don't deny wanting to have a good time. But some of the stories were blown out of proportion and were out and out lies."

In 2000, the federal government brought racketeering charges against Steve Kaplan, the flamboyant owner of Atlanta's famous Gold Club strip bar. In documents related to his federal case, the government contended that Kaplan had been supplying athletes with strippers for sex. Among the names mentioned in the court papers was Billy Bayno. According to the documents, Kaplan had arranged and paid for two Las Vegas strippers to have sex with Bayno in the Mirage Hotel in 1998. The incident gained national headlines when *Sports Illustrated* made note of it in a 2000 article.

"I'm not saying that I haven't had sex with girls at the Mirage, but if it was arranged by Steve Kaplan, it was unbeknownst to me. I just went to a buddy's pool party, met some girls, and you know, things happen," Bayno admitted.

The ongoing NCAA investigation, coupled with the latest allegations, made coaching at UNLV extremely tough for Bayno. It seemed like it was only a matter of time, and that time would come in December 2000. The NCAA released its report to UNLV confirming violations within the Rebel program, and it eventually imposed sanctions, including a ban on postseason play for a year and the loss of two scholarships for two years. The President of UNLV, Carol Harter, released Bayno from his coaching duties immediately. (Assistant coach Max Good took over for the rest of the year, and after pursuing the high-profile Rick Pitino, UNLV eventually hired 61-year-old Charlie Spoonhour to take control of the program.) Bayno was in a no-win situation in his eyes. "My dilemma was that I didn't know if I could trust the administration. In the end I was exonerated. I was deemed not the problem and the NCAA placed the blame on the administration for not having policies and procedures in place."

"Because it was a severe sanction, the president, in my opinion, felt that if she didn't fire me, she would have to fire the AD, Charles Cavagnaro, and that was her guy. They [the NCAA] came in with a fine-tooth comb and went through my program from head to toe and came up with no violations. Yet, the national perception is that I was fired because of NCAA violations."

Reflecting on the tumultuous period at the end of his tenure at UNLV, Bayno shakes his head and can't believe that he actually made it as far as he did. "When it happened, I was just relieved because I was starting to get burned out. The stress and pressure, the expectations and my feelings and frustration with the administration . . . you just feel like you are out there by yourself. It had been going on for two and a half years and I was just relieved."

Bayno has not coached in college since, but certainly has learned his lessons. He stopped drinking midway through his tenure at UNLV, which allowed him to focus solely on basketball. He admits making mistakes in the basketball program and in his personal life, but he understands. "I'm better prepared for the next job. I've learned from it and I've grown from it." He blames much of his troubles on his young age and on the media. He lived in Scottsdale, Arizona, just outside of Phoenix, and coached the new ABA franchise in town for a month before heading to the Philippines to coach in a professional league. He would like to coach in the NBA someday soon, but as for a return to the collegiate ranks, he is not sure. "For me to get to where I want to be in college, I would have to go become an assistant at a big-time program with a coach that is going to help me repair my image, like a Pitino or Krzyzewski."

Image is everything. Bayno had it all at a young age, but his past mistakes may prove too costly for his future. Bayno was fired. There is little argument over that fact. Why he was fired depends on who you ask. If UNLV was a national power, selling out the Thomas & Mack Center, would Bayno have had more rope? Compared to the controversial stint of Jerry Tarkanian at UNLV, you might think so.

Jeff Jones has a similar tale, a young, successful coach, brought down by a losing record and untimely rumors. Unlike Billy Bayno, Jones has resurfaced as a head coach at the Division I level, making a comeback to the ranks of the big time. "JJ," as his friends call him, was a player at the University of Virginia in the heydays of Ralph Sampson. He was a good-looking, popular player who, upon graduation, had many offers for jobs in the "real world." He had not planned on coaching, and didn't know what to do with his life, he sheepishly admitted. His former coach, Terry Holland, offered him a job as a graduate assistant at his alma mater. He would rise up the assistant coaching ranks at UVA, and when Holland announced his resignation in 1990, Jones became the youngest head coach in ACC history at the age of 29.

He led the Cavaliers to five NCAA appearances, one NIT showing, and a regular season ACC Championship. That 1995 championship season, Jones took Virginia to the Elite Eight. He accumulated 100 wins faster than all but four other coaches in ACC history. His first three seasons he led the Cavaliers to 20-plus wins. Even more impressive was that Jones had the early success with kids that he had recruited as an assistant coach under Holland. Jones was on a roll and so was UVA. But things began to slow down in the season after the Elite Eight run, when Virginia finished below .500 in 1996 and 1998. As Jones would soon find out, losing brings out all kinds of problems.

Jones had married his college girlfriend, Lisa, his senior year at Virginia. They remained in Charlottesville and raised three children in the very public eye of such a small community. In late 1995, talk around Charlottesville centered on the head coach and his relationship with a Virginia coed. As the rumors became louder, Jones did, indeed, move out of his family house into a townhouse a few miles away.

Despite his early successes, his teams struggled to below par performances, and along with his personal life in crisis mode, his players' personal conduct also came into question as well. Over the span of two years, Virginia had five players arrested for crimes, including shoplifting and assault. It was not an image new AD Terry Holland wanted for "The University." But things really hit the fan in 1998. The NCAA began investigating secondary violations and the pressure on the coach mounted. The investigation was known only to those involved and, to this day, seems to have played little part in Jones' firing, according to insiders. It was the losing record and what he, and his team, had "apparently" done to the UVA image.

In the spring of 1998, Jones was called into a meeting with his former coach, and then boss. At that meeting, Jones was asked to resign. The Cavaliers had just posted their worst record in 35 years, 11-19, and with the player arrests and personal turmoil, Holland wanted a change. Virginia gave Jones a $600,000 buyout and that was it. His almost 20-year association with his alma mater was over. "When I left Virginia, I would say that I was confident, not certain, that I would get another job," the now 41-year-old Jones reflects. "I would hope that athletic directors would do a little better research than simply looking at the headlines."

He received some interest from other schools, including Western Kentucky, but as buzz of the NCAA investigation emerged, they backed off. The violations were secondary in nature, the ones that almost every school commits on a daily basis. But the headlines of the NCAA investigation tainted Jones and he decided that he needed some time away from the game to put his life in order. He did not coach for the next six months and instead, spent time with his children, girlfriend and later wife Danielle, and most interestingly, relearned the game of basketball. In what he calls a "sabbatical," Jones spent time with various coaches around the country, including Dave Odom at Wake Forest and Rick Majerus at Utah, learning new plays and watching other coaches work. He knew he wanted to coach again and was preparing himself for that day.

In the fall of 1999, Jones was hired to be the associate head coach at Rhode Island, a school where he had applied for the head coaching position, which went to his new boss, Jerry DeGregorio. After one very difficult year, Jones was hired as the new coach at American University in D.C., returning to the Virginia region. It was not the ACC, but he was a head coach again at the Division I level. He seemed to be on a roll. By 2002, American University won the regular season conference title and Jones was closer to returning to the big time. His team lost in the Patriot League Championship game, just missing a chance at the NCAA Tournament. His comeback is almost complete, and in fact, may be complete. Being able to be a head coach at a Division I school after being fired at another one is more difficult than one might think.

Not all coaches who are fired suffer from the multitude of factors that led to the ousters of Bayno and Jones. Simply a poor record is enough justification for an athletic director. Coaches are not retained for a variety of reasons, often never known to the public. Sometimes, it can be a personal clash with an administrator, but announced as a "new direction by mutual agreement" by the parties. Some are forced out by pressure applied by prominent boosters who may not get along with the coach. While still others insist they never knew the reason for their dismissals.

LaSalle head coach Billy Hahn has seen a lot in his years of coaching, most recently as Gary Williams' top assistant at Maryland for 10 years. Before heading to College Park, Hahn was an assistant to Danny Nee for six years at Ohio University, before taking over for Nee for three seasons. In his three years at the helm, he compiled a 42-45 record. In March 1989, Hahn was fired after his team went 12-17, finishing in last place in the MAC, after preseason predictions of a MAC title. He had been under fire from the fans and the media during a six-game losing streak, which was compounded by internal problems within the team. "I was called into the AD's office after the season. I figured it was the usual end of season review. But in a 10-minute conversation, he told me he was letting me go and wanted to go in a new direction. After the years I had given to that university, it was over in a matter of minutes. They never gave me a reason. My record was 42-45 after three years, right around .500. I was never given a reason like 'you're not winning' or 'you're not graduating kids,' because I was."

Furious and perplexed, Hahn stormed out of the office. His first thoughts were of his family. He called his wife, hopped into his car, still in disbelief, and went to his son's elementary school to pick him up. He knew how small the Ohio community was and didn't want his son to hear about it from a classmate, teacher, or parent. He was no longer the head coach at Ohio. In fact, he was no longer a coach anywhere. But he was only 35. "I was dumb because I moved up pretty quickly in the business and became a head coach at a very young age. I thought I knew everything and I didn't know anything. I was in too much of a hurry. I didn't appreciate and enjoy the moment."

But the anger, frustration, and hurt cannot overshadow the fact that fired coaches need new jobs, and Hahn went right to it. For three months he sat in Athens, Ohio, making calls, talking to anyone who would listen. During that time, Hahn realized what so many other fired coaches learn, and only they can learn. "You find out how valuable your job is and how you should cherish it, instead of taking it for granted and trying to see where you are going to be next. Before Gary Williams hired me, I told myself that if I ever got a job again, I was going to enjoy where I was and quit worrying about where I was going to be next."

Hahn, along with other fired coaches, learned another valuable lesson—he works in a cold, cold business. Guys who are your friends turn out to be nothing more than competition. As Hahn puts it, you become a "forgotten man" in this business when you are let go, and people who initially call you to offer their sympathy and to offer help, somehow seem to be too busy to return your calls a few weeks later. The lesson stuck with Hahn now that he is at LaSalle. "If I personally know anybody who gets fired, I stay in touch with them for long periods of time until they have found another job."

Dick Vitale remembers getting fired from the Detroit Pistons and realizing that many people he considered friends would not take his calls. "You are like damaged goods when you get fired. You only have your mother, father, and family and maybe a few very close friends."

It is true that most coaches still get paid for the remainder of their contract after being let go, but that is only good for the short term. The damage to their careers can be insurmountable, and the emotional toll on the coach and his family can be immeasurable.

Not every coach who leaves a school is fired. Many leave on their own terms, to take a better job, to move on to the NBA or to simply retire from coaching. The domino effect comes into play often when there are coaching moves, best illustrated by the North Carolina search three years ago, when Bill Guthridge announced he would step down. After Carolina "family members" Larry Brown, George Karl, and Roy Williams declined the job, Notre Dame's Matt Doherty signed on. Notre Dame then hired Mike Brey from Delaware who was eventually replaced by David Henderson, a Duke assistant, at Delaware. His spot on the Duke staff was taken by former player Chris Collins. The domino effect occurs at almost every turn—the three degrees of separation.

In a way, the coaching profession is much like the mob, except without the murders, threats, and "made men." Most coaches are part of a coaching family, descendants of one of the original greats of the game, or in this new era, "relatives" to a successful coach. Many of the current or former Division I head coaches have some relation to Dean Smith, Eddie

Sutton, and Bobby Knight. In fact, Coach K is part of Knight's family tree, playing for Knight at Army. Everybody seems to know everybody in and outside of the families. Many coaches remain close friends with those in the family, and often recommend each other for jobs. A look at just some of the family trees and a few of the offspring (only current or former head coaches included and some, like Steve Lavin and Bill Self, could be placed in more than one "family"):

Dean Smith: Eddie Fogler, Larry Brown, Roy Williams, Bill Guthridge, John Calipari, Ed Schilling, Kevin Stallings, Jerry Green, Steve Robinson, Matt Doherty, Neil Dougherty

Lefty Driesell: George Raveling, Oliver Purnell, Terry Holland, Shannon Dillard, Chuck Driesell, Paul Hewitt, Charlie Parker, Jeff Jones, Dave Odom, Ricky Stokes

Eddie Sutton: Bill Self, Bob Cleveland, Leonard Hamilton, Pat Foster, Bob Gottlieb, Tim Jankovich, Paul Graham, Gene Keady, Fred Trenkle, Tom Aple, James Dickey

Jim Boeheim: Scott Hicks, Louis Orr, Tim Welsh, Ralph Willard, Wayne Morgan, Rick Pitino, Billy Donovan, Herb Sendek, Tubby Smith, John Phelphrey, Shawn Finney

Bobby Knight: Mike Davis, Dave Bliss, Steve Alford, Mike Krzyzewski, Bob Bender, Mike Brey, Tommy Amaker, Quin Snyder, David Henderson, Pat Harris, Jeff Capel III, Tim O'Toole, Mike Dement

Jim Harrick: Mark Gottfried, Brad Holland, Greg White, Larry Farmer, Paul Landreaux, Lorenzo Romar, Tony Fuller, Steve Lavin

There are so many other smaller pods in basketball families. Tom Davis, Jud Heathcote, and Rollie Massimino all have a growing number of offspring in the coaching ranks. All coaches in some way are tied to a select few former coaching legends, which is why it is so difficult for a new coach to come out of the blue.

Many of today's top young coaches take a more expedient route to their head coaching jobs. Almost all are former players, who served as assistants at big-time programs, and then got their first head coaching jobs. Billy Donovan went from a Kentucky assistant to head coach at Marshall to the coach of the Florida Gators. Tommy Amaker went from an assistant at Duke to head coach at Seton Hall to the current head coach at Michigan. It wasn't always this way.

Current UNLV head coach Charlie Spoonhour has been in the profession for 37 years as a coach. His path?

1961–1963:	Head Coach, Rocky Comfort High School
1963–1967:	Co-Coach, Bloomfield High School
1967–1968:	Head Coach, Salem High School
1968–1972:	Assistant Coach, Southwest Missouri State
1972–1974:	Head Coach, Moberly Junior College
1974–1975:	Assistant Coach, University of Oklahoma
1975–1981:	Head Coach, Southeastern Community College
1981–1983:	Assistant Coach, University of Nebraska
1983–1992:	Head Coach, Southwest Missouri State
1992–1999:	Head Coach, St. Louis University
2001–Present:	Head Coach, UNLV

Many of the older coaches followed similar paths, starting out at the high school level, serving as an assistant or head coach at the junior college level, then moving on to the bigger Division I schools. Lute Olson was a high school coach. So was John Chaney. And John Wooden. But then there are Mike Krzyzewski and Bobby Knight, who never coached at the high school or JC levels, and neither have many of today's current coaches. That is not their fault. ADs are looking at more than a resume and experience when they are making hiring decisions. It's not necessarily about the years you have been in it, but rather where you have spent that time. Perhaps in 1968 if Spoonhour was an assistant at UCLA instead of Southwest Missouri State, he would have been a head coach at the Division I level much sooner than 1983.

Almost as gossipy as Hollywood producers, college coaches are, by nature and profession, information guys. Whether it is details about a recruit, an opponent's strategies or game statistics, they survive on the flow of information. Potential hirings and firings spread like wildfire in the coaching ranks. At the start of the 2001–2002 campaign, it was widely known and discussed that Herb Sendek at N.C. State might be fighting for his job. The vultures were out and rumors ran rampant throughout the coaching circles as to who might be discretely contacting Wolfpack AD Lee Fowler, making sure their names were in play. Of course, Sendek kept his job leading N.C. State to a remarkable season, finishing at 23-11, including a second round showing in the NCAAs.

At the same time coaches feel empathy toward a guy like Sendek on the hot seat, they are strategizing how to get his job. One coach that garners almost universal sympathy is Steve Lavin. All across the country, coaches express their concern for him, how he is treated by the fans, media, and his own administration. "I don't know how he puts up with that shit," remarked one coach, and most coaches feel similarly. They read the papers, listen to the radio, and watch *SportsCenter* like everyone else and feel for Lavin in his predicament. But make no mistake. Many of these same guys would give their right arm to be the coach at such a storied school as UCLA. They all think they could do a better job at any school than the current coach—it's just part of their nature.

The trend in hirings and firings in the future may be surprising. Many athletic directors believe at some point soon, they, as a group, will step back from the rapid hiring and firing process and take time to make better decisions. The era of the "press conference" coach may be gone soon, and administrators may look toward the older generations for stability, teaching, and an emphasis on education. But it won't happen unilaterally. College presidents and administrators must reevaluate why they are firing coaches and what criteria they are using to hire them.

One final point. Remember those most affected by changes—players and families. For the juniors and seniors at Notre Dame, there were three coaches in three years. Coaches routinely shift schools without penalty. Players must sit out a year as punishment for moving schools. Coaches' wives often have to pack up and move their families numerous times, while children are taken out of schools and put into new environments. Often, it is the wife who must stay behind, sell the house, take care of the kids, and then pack up and move into a new city where they know no one.

It is the nature of the beast, something that young coaches frequently ignore, thinking that a good thing can last forever. But if a coach is at a school now for five or six years, it is considered a very long tenure. In reality then, almost every day, at every level, almost every coach is "on the block."

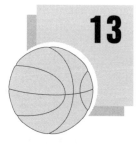

13

Show Me The Money

"IZZO GETS $6 MILLION DEAL!" SCREAMED THE HEADLINES IN EARLY DECEMBER 2001 when it became public that Michigan State had upped the ante. What appeared to be an outrageous sum of money for a college basketball coach was not a renegotiated compensation package, but rather incentive for Tom Izzo. With contributions from major Spartan donors, the school had established a private fund to grow over the next five years with interest. The money is not Izzo's now, but can be in five years. It's a longevity deal. If Izzo is still the coach at Michigan State in 2006, he will receive a $3.4 million bonus, plus five yearly payments of $300,000, plus investment earnings. He already has a compensation package worth $1.3 million. He is a coach who has flirted with the NBA and other Division I schools, and Michigan State wants to make sure he goes nowhere.

Though the headlines may be a bit deceiving, and most coaches do not make anywhere near the money that Izzo does, the reality is that coaches make much more than the average fan and, in many cases, a lot more than their bosses. In a survey of 2000–2001 head coaching salaries, a head coach made on average $115,586 in salary, which does not include many of the "extras" such as endorsements, camps, television fees, bonuses, and apparel contracts, which can double or triple the base salary. The top coaches in big markets and basketball-crazy states traditionally receive the bigger compensation packages, since there are more opportunities to sell themselves and their program.

For every "million-dollar coach" like Florida's Billy Donovan, there sits former Long Beach State's Wayne Morgan, who earned a base salary of $115,000 with minimal endorsement and apparel money or Ed Schilling at Wright State who renegotiated his contract with *no* raise at $110,000. The head coaches at the Top 50 schools can make large sums of money, but the majority of coaches are compensated on a much smaller scale. Coaching contracts are based on market demand and the priority that schools place on athletics and individual coaches. What is a Rick Pitino worth to Louisville? What does Bobby Knight mean to Texas Tech basketball and the university as a whole? It is often hard to measure the true economic impact of a hiring, and there are so many subjective flaws in negotiations that relying on a formula is futile.

As college basketball has grown, so too have the escalating salaries to the ire of many, including Hall of Famer John Wooden. "I don't think a coach should ever be making more money than the president of a university."

Of course, the Wizard of Westwood coached in a different era. Coaches' contracts are really complex compensation packages divided into the following: base salary, endorsements and apparel deals, media fees, summer camps, bonuses, perks and speaking fees. Not every head coach gets something from all of these areas, but the majority of contracts include income in some form from these areas.

Base Salary. In most professions, particularly those where the negotiation of contracts is permissible, the base salary is the "chunk of change" in an employee's deal. That salary is guaranteed, paid regardless of performance, and is the basic figure that an individual can expect to earn. Except in a few careers, bonuses, performance incentives, and endorsements are not part of the picture. For college basketball coaches, they make up most of the picture. In fact, many coaches have compensation deals where the salary is dwarfed by other means of income.

When Bobby Knight was fired at Indiana University in the fall of 2000, he had a base salary of $163,118. Doesn't seem like much for a Hall of Fame coach with three national championships, but that figure is simply his salary, not total compensation, which included huge deals for endorsements, camps, and Nike apparel.

Endorsements. In many circumstances, coaches and athletic directors, or other school representatives, know what external opportunities may be available to a head coach. From car dealerships to local food chains to Mom and Pop home stores, coaches can earn significant money simply by appearing in an ad on television or radio or making a public appearance at a store. Coaches and/or their agents know the market potential, and many schools have endorsement deals already in place with a former coach, into which a new coach would fit. The endorsement compensation depends on the market size, visibility of the program, and most importantly, on the individual coach. Manhattan's Bobby Gonzalez's outgoing, flashy personality may lend itself to more commercial opportunities than a low-keyed Jim O'Brien at Ohio State.

Apparel. The big one. Nike and North Carolina concluded a $28-million apparel deal, which included equipment, uniforms, academic donations, and compensation for Carolina coaches. Basketball coach Matt Doherty is given $500,000 a year from Nike. Maryland coach Gary Williams is reported to make $250,000 from the same company. Though the "shoe money" has been drying up in recent years, as the major shoe companies are not handing out the huge amounts of cash to coaches anymore, most coaches are receiving some form of payment to wear a brand, to dress their players in certain clothes and shoes, and to speak on behalf of a company.

Media Deals. When a game is over and the coach does an interview with the hometown play-by-play radio host, it's not just because the coach wants to, or even that he is required to do so. It's what he gets paid to do. Many coaches have payments in their compensation deals for television and radio appearances, such as postgame interviews, call-in radio shows and weekly television shows. These are interviews with the "friendly" media.

Summer Camps. Summer basketball camps can attract hundreds of kids each summer, willing to pay to be taught by coaches and, for the older kids, to be exposed to college coaches. Many head coaches are tied to the camps, and in fact, attach their names to them.

Most coaches are allowed by their contracts to run camps in university facilities and promote them on the college's dime. The larger camps, which are often staffed by noncollege coaches, can bring in thousands of dollars for a coach and his staff. Because of recruiting schedules, many head coaches make only a quick one- or two-hour appearance at their own camps.

Bonuses. A new trend has developed in coaching contracts giving coaches incentive to win and graduate players. Some bonuses are based on winning percentage, while others offer a flat amount, such as $200,000 for winning a national championship or other on-court achievement. Because "graduation rate" has become a hot term, many coaches are asking for, and receiving, bonuses for making sure their players graduate, though education incentives often depend on the school's president and athletic director's philosophies. There are even a few attendance bonuses for coaches, where the more fans that come to watch, the more the coach makes.

Perks. Country club memberships, cars, airplane rides, tickets, home improvements, even meals are typical benefits included as part of coaches' contracts. The value of these are often totaled into the overall compensation package. These perks can make or break a deal, or allow schools the ability to further compensate a coach when they simply cannot afford to offer additional money.

Speaking Fees. In addition to representing the university at fund-raisers, booster events, and other university-related programs, and in addition to endorsement deals, some coaches can make money speaking throughout the country. These coaches can earn up to $25,000 a speech, but only a select few can command such exorbitant speaking fees, and often, these outside appearances are not included in a contract.

O f course, all contracts, like coaches, are unique, and some coaches demand more than others in certain areas. One coach may place a priority on the bonuses if he wants those performance incentives while another coach may want additional perks for his family. College basketball is a multibillion-dollar business and coaches can demand lucrative contracts. However, much of what is negotiated in these deals is often based on perception, not reality, on implied threats, not real ones, and on what someone else offered, not on what a coach has accomplished.

Mike Barnett is well-known in basketball circles, particularly by coaches, as a former category director of Nike's college basketball division. It was Barnett who negotiated deals on behalf of Nike with coaches around the country, who decided which coaches got what amount of compensation, and who might be the next hot coaching prospect. In 2000, Barnett left the company and began to represent coaches, including Steve Alford, in contract and endorsement negotiations. He is in a unique position, with his background and current profession, to assess the changes in coaching contracts.

"The truth be told, the market is driven by what NBA teams have done. They paid Rick Pitino a lot of money to coach the Boston Celtics. Then, obviously, colleges are going to have to pay more to keep coaches at the schools."

In the spring of 2001, with Alford completing his second year at Iowa and with the potential of the Indiana job open for his client, Barnett went into lengthy discussions with Iowa AD Bob Bowlsby about renegotiating Alford's contract. But he did not come unprepared. "I spent a lot of time researching what the market would bear for a guy like Steve Alford. Through public records, contacts, ADs, and so on, I could find out what other coaches were being paid and what was in their contracts. Larry Eustachy at Iowa State, Dan Monson at Minnesota, Bill Self at Illinois. We didn't grab Tom Izzo's contract. He had won a national championship. We wanted to compare apples to apples."

Barnett understood the complexity of coaching contracts and often what you don't see is more important than what you do. Money is hidden and shuffled around. Income from camps and appearances and perks like cars and memberships all play a role. So do the priorities of the coach. In Alford's case, he wanted to be compensated at the same level as other coaches in the Big Ten at his age and with his experience. He also insisted that Iowa make a commitment to the basketball program, not just to Alford, which included assistant salaries, locker room renovations, and academic centers.

Overshadowing the Barnett-Bowlsby negotiations was the media frenzy around Alford's potential return to Indiana. Though it was never acknowledged, simply the unspoken threat of Alford's departure may have played into the hands of Barnett, who knew that Bowlsby could not afford to lose Alford to Indiana. "I can tell you, that it was never, ever mentioned between Bob and me. It never came up. However, it was there. We never used it as leverage and Bob never feared it."

For his part, Bowlsby entered the negotiations with an open mind and a willingness to be competitive. "I would not draw a line in the sand. I think in a secondary market like we're in, we don't have the advantage that an Illinois has with 20 million people and some major media markets. An awful lot of the money, fully half of what Alford's contract pays him, comes from camps, shoe contracts, radio, and television. Those things are worth a lot more at a UCLA or Notre Dame. We have to be innovative and creative to compete."

So over the course of a month, Barnett and Bowlsby talked on the phone, trying to hammer out the details of Alford's new contract, both men knowing the desired outcome—keeping the coach at Iowa. What they agreed upon and what Alford signed on March 29, 2001, was a new, eight-year deal which, with a total compensation package of close to a million dollars a year, is almost double Alford's original deal worth $585,000.

The new yearly base salary is comprised of money from the University and from the Iowa Foundation. In addition to the base salary, there was guaranteed money from camps and endorsements, from Nike and from radio and television deals. Alford was given cars for his family use, a family membership to an athletic club, and 12 tickets to every home game.

A big part of Alford's new contract was incentives and bonuses. First, there is a longevity clause which rewards Alford for staying put at Iowa. He will receive a six-figure payment in 2004 if he is still the coach of the Hawkeyes. He will receive additional payments in 2006 and 2008 if he remains at the school. And then there are the bonuses for a National Championship, a Final Four, a Big Ten regular season championship, a Big Ten Tournament championship and for any NCAA appearance.

There are incentives for the coach to make sure that his players graduate (as discussed in chapter 11). However, unlike the NCAA formula, Alford will not have players who leave school early for the NBA count against his graduation rate, as long as they are in good academic standing when they leave Iowa.

The contract can be renegotiated annually after the 2002 season and if Alford is terminated without cause, he will be compensated for each year left on the contract. He has no restrictions in his contract for leaving for another school, but he must notify Bowlsby before discussing other opportunities. In addition to the changes to Alford's contract, Bowlsby agreed to some physical plant changes that Alford deemed necessary to compete at the highest level. Included in these renovations were a $350,000 state-of-the-art locker room (funded by an Iowa donor), players' lounge, coaches' lounge, refurbished basketball offices, and new computers for an academic center.

Bowlsby had gotten what he wanted—he kept Steve Alford at Iowa. Using outside income and creative financing, he was able to present Barnett with a competitive package to keep his coach. Alford and Barnett got what they wanted—a new, lucrative contract and improvements to the Iowa facilities. All seemed well for both parties, though the future remained uncertain.

"I've never distrusted Steve's commitment to us," remarks Bowlsby. "When I hired him the first time, I told him that I couldn't have him leave for Indiana or any other Big Ten school. He gave me his word that he wouldn't. I've never gone back and questioned that word." Barnett insists that neither he, nor Alford, ever made that promise to the Iowa athletic director. However, regardless of who you believe, it is clear that Alford, while he is in Iowa City, will be paid very well to be there.

When Bill Self left Tulsa for Illinois in 2000, the negotiations between him and Illini AD Ron Guenther were simple. Guenther asked Self how much it would take to entice the hot coach to come to Champaign. Self gave a number, Guenther agreed. Done.

A look at some of the compensation levels and incentives in coaching deals around the country reveal mostly six-figure salaries and some creative incentives and perks. Remember the $163,118 Bobby Knight made in his last year at Indiana? He also had $300,000 worth of endorsements and outside income, two scholarships to Indiana for his sons, a car, and the use of an official aircraft. Things are not always what they seem. Now at Texas Tech, Knight has a base salary of $250,000 with additional compensation and incentives bringing the total close to $900,000 a year. And he can command large speaking fees around the country.

Tom Izzo is currently under a five-year deal, which includes the longevity fund. He also has many bonuses, such as the $400,000 he got for winning the National Championship in 2000 ($200,000 from Reebok from which he gave $110,000 to charity). Like Alford, Izzo has a graduation rate incentive built in, with the coach earning 10% of his base salary, about $19,500 for any year his graduation rate is over 66%.

Larry Eustachy at Iowa State was another hot coaching candidate and the Cyclone administration wanted to do everything they could to keep him there. He signed a new 10-year deal, which will pay him over a $1 million a year. Included in his contract is a base salary of $220,000 and guaranteed outside income brings the total to $880,000. He got a signing bonus of $120,000, a car, a country club membership, and season tickets for football and basketball. Like Alford, Eustachy has bonuses for achievements and a $2.5 million buyout clause up to 2006, at which point it drops $300,000 each year. One caveat to the Iowa State deal: Eustachy is prohibited from taking another job in Iowa or within the Big 12 conference and he must pay the school $400,000 if he leaves before 2006 to take another coaching job.

Mike Davis at Indiana now makes a base salary of $225,000 with a total compensation package that could be worth close to $800,000 guaranteed for the first three years and $900,000 in the final three of the six-year deal. Like Izzo, Davis now has a longevity incentive that will pay him $100,000 in the fourth, fifth, and sixth years of his deal if he is still the coach at Indiana. Billy Donovan makes close to $1.2 million a year at Florida; Tommy Amaker at Michigan signed a five-year deal worth $3 million; Pete Gillen at Virginia has a 10-year, $9-million deal.

We know Matt Doherty makes $500,000 from the Nike deal but he also has a base salary of $145,000, which could rise to $181,250 a year, in addition to $185,000 from television and radio. Another hot young coach, Quin Snyder at Missouri, has a five-year deal guaranteeing him at least $800,000 a year with bonuses that could bring that figure up to $1.27 million. His base salary is only $185,000.

Public universities must release salary information and contracts upon request but private colleges are a lot more reluctant to release contract details. Here is a look at what some other coaches around the country are earning:

Coach	School	Approximate Annual Total Compensation
Bill Self	Illinois	$825,000
Stan Joplin	Toledo	$115,000 rising to $127,000
Paul Hewitt	Georgia Tech	$500,000
Mark Gottfried	Alabama	$650,000
Tim Welsh	Boston College	$550,000–$700,000
Tubby Smith	Kentucky	$1.5 million
Charlie Spoonhour	UNLV	$425,000
Jim Harrick	Georgia	$700,000
Dave Odom	South Carolina	$750,000
Rod Barnes	Mississippi	$650,000
Bo Ryan	Wisconsin	$437,000
Jim Baron	Rhode Island	$350,000
Jeff Ruland	Iona	$250,000
James Jones	Yale	$200,000
Gary Williams	Maryland	$1.1 million
Keith Richard	Louisiana Tech	$130,000

Coaches want security and schools want commitment. The problem is that schools or coaches can walk away at anytime. The trend in longevity clauses and bonuses is to try to entice coaches from jumping ship. But are they effective? Coaches who receive a bonus for staying a certain length of time could be bought out by another school who agrees to match that bonus. Ten years ago, five-year deals were not the norm, but now 10-year deals? Million-dollar bonuses simply for staying put?

Some of the "sneaker money" has dried up in recent years. The trend in the early 1990s was for Adidas and Nike to give top coaches and rising young assistants lucrative deals to wear, endorse, and otherwise promote their products. Some of the larger contracts for guys like Lute Olson and other top names may also include speaking engagements and commercial endorsements. Of course, the level of compensation depends on who you are. Many mid-major coaches only get up to $50,000 or less, but their teams are provided with apparel. With the economy slowing down, the sneaker companies offer less money, there are fewer deals with coaches, but more deals for equipment and apparel. Then there are the schoolwide deals, such as North Carolina, where a deal for the basketball coach is built into the overall school package. Though the endorsement deals may be lavish, only a small percentage of Division I coaches actually have them. At smaller schools with little recognition, coaches get *nada*.

Nike dominates the sneaker business in college basketball as evidenced by the fact that Nike has been worn by seven of the last eight Final Four participants. In 1985, 1997, and 2002—all four teams were awash in the Swoosh. Of the 65 teams in the 2002 Tournament field, 49 were Nike schools, nine Adidas, four for Reebok, and three for And 1.

In addition to the cash and apparel, coaches are treated to lavish company retreats in exotic places in the world to build relationships and to offer their input on company products. For example, at a Nike retreat in Mexico, the company may present a fashion show with upcoming clothes and sneaker lines to get the coaches' input.

Finally, there is the notion that a contract is not really a binding document, but a temporary fix to negotiations. Almost all contracts can, and are, renegotiated at any time, with extensions from one to seven years commonplace. Billy Donovan has had his contract restructured four times in the last five years. Bobby Lutz at Charlotte signed an extension in February 2002, giving him a gross of close to $425,000 and extending the length of the contract to 2008. His comment on the new deal: "This contract provides a commitment that enables me to remain at Charlotte for a very long time."

Was Charlotte not committed to him before? Of course, Lutz is one of many coaches who can use on-court success as leverage to get better deals out of their schools. Win 20 games or even a conference championship? Well, then the school is going to have to pay. Particularly for coaches who do well in the postseason, just the threat or possibility of leaving for another school provides them with great leverage to renegotiate a deal. Ben Howland at Pittsburgh had an incredible year in 2002, winning the National Coach of the Year honors. He was sought after by schools with openings, as he continued to negotiate with Panther officials. Having signed an extension last year through the 2006 season, Howland was able to secure a longer deal giving him a raise in compensation from $300,000 to close to $800,000. Mike Davis got a hefty raise after leading Indiana to the national title game in April 2002. After leading Wisconsin to a share of the Big Ten title in his first year, Bo Ryan got a $100,000 raise, bringing his package up to $437,150. A month earlier, he was given a contract extension through 2008–2009.

What about assistant coaches salaries? In many major conferences such as the SEC and Big Ten, assistants make over $100,000, a portion of which is from summer camps. At the lowest levels of Division I, assistants may make only $15,000. At Texas-San Antonio, Tim Carter's third assistant makes a whopping $18,500 a year, but when compared to his coach's total of $85,000, it doesn't seem as small. At Illinois, Self's top assistants make a base of under $100,000 but with camp income, that figure crosses over into six digits, comparable to the income of the Iowa assistants. Most assistants at a Top 25 school make no less than $50,000 a year and, obviously, veteran assistants make more.

Coaches get paid well to do a job they love, but the job is not an easy one. It comes with a personal and professional price. After each heartbreaking loss, coaches cannot shake it off just because they make a decent living.

Notre Dame rebounded from their home loss to Villanova with a shockingly close three-point win in Morgantown on Wednesday, January 9. Chris Thomas nailed three free throws in the final 19 seconds as the Irish came back again from a large deficit, this one a 15-point halftime hole. They came out and hit six three-pointers in the first five minutes of the second half to pull even at 41-41. After trading buckets for most of the second half, Notre Dame's Torrian Jones hit a jumper with 43 seconds left to tie the score at 64. Thomas followed with two free throws with 19 seconds remaining, and after the Mountaineers' Jonathan Hargett missed a three, Thomas grabbed the rebound, was fouled, and hit one more.

Ryan Humphrey led Notre Dame with 18, with Thomas (15) and Matt Carroll (14) aiding in the effort. Again for the Irish, it was a tale of two halves. In the first, they let West Virginia shoot 51.5% and shot only 28% themselves. In the second, they held WVU to 22.7% shooting and they got hot, hitting 54%.

In Iowa City, the Hawkeyes and the town were pumped as Iowa opened up conference play at home against Wisconsin. Iowa was riding a five-game winning streak and, more importantly, the team and coach seemed to be getting along. Winning does that. So as the Badgers came to Carver-Hawkeye Arena, which was sure to be rowdy with a capacity crowd, Iowa was confident. Luke Recker came out on fire, hitting driving layups and three-point buckets as Iowa built an early lead, 26–19. Wisconsin relied on reigning Big Ten Player of the Week Kirk Penney to lead the way, and he single-handedly kept Wisconsin in the game. Of the Badgers first 18 points, Penney had 14 of them. As the half came to a close, Iowa went on an 8-2 run to lead 36-27 at halftime. In the second half, it was more Recker and Reggie Evans as Iowa played well enough to keep the lead around 10, eventually winning, 69-57.

Three days later, on January 5, Alford led his troops to Columbus, Ohio, to take on the Buckeyes, who were a surprising 9-2 on the season. Iowa went back to its old ways, giving up an early lead—a huge one, 20-2 just eight minutes into the game. It was embarrassing and ugly. But Iowa did not give up, going on a 14-2 run and by halftime, they trailed by just six. Evans was the *only* Hawkeye to score more than three points in the first half. Iowa stayed close for most of the second half, getting to within two, but Ohio State was simply too strong, winning 72-62, snapping Iowa's win streak and evening their conference record at 1-1. The Hawkeyes would rebound days later at home against Northwestern, shooting 60% (though committing 22 turnovers), winning 70-60. They now turned their attention to their next opponent, the Indiana Hoosiers, who were coming to Iowa City on Sunday, January 13.

On top of their struggles on the court, Alford waged a war of words in a local newspaper with one of his former players in early January. Cortney Scott, a redshirt sophomore, had not returned to school after the Christmas break. He had not called the coaches to let them know of his intentions to transfer. In an early January edition of the *Iowa City Gazette*, reporter Pat Hardy wrote about Scott's departure, citing interviews with Scott and his father. According to the player, Alford had "forced him to redshirt," lied to him and his family, played favorites in practice, used reserves as "punching bags" for players like Evans, and ultimately could not be trusted. Stinging indictments of a popular coach.

Alford initially refused to comment on the matter, but in his weekly teleconference the following day, he spoke his mind. "You guys want to write stories you think will be Pulitzer Prize-winning stories," he said about reporters, and began to refute Scott's allegations, some directly, others more obtusely.

Scott had come to Alford asking to be redshirted, Alford insisted, when he realized that his playing time would be limited with Iowa's current roster. Alford denied giving favorable treatment to players in practice, but acknowledged that his practices are demanding and physical, and some players do get hurt. Alford's comments appeared in a story the following day, and with Scott not returning to school, it seemed a dead issue. But out in public were incendiary comments about Alford and his program.

Illinois opened up conference play with a home game against Minnesota, then hit the road for games at Wisconsin and Purdue. No place is easy to win on the road in the Big Ten, so it was imperative for Illinois, and their conference mates, to hold their home courts. Illinois was short-handed, playing another game without Damir Krupalija, who was still nursing a foot injury. Before the game, Bill Self had reminded his guys to take care of the basketball and to make the extra pass. With a lack of big men available to play, his guards would have to control the play and the team "should be ready to zone it if we need to." Frank Williams had an abscessed tooth, but was ready to play.

Minnesota's coach Dan Monson is one of the nation's hottest young coaches. The former coach at Gonzaga had earned his spot in a major conference with his extraordinary postseason runs with the Zags, and the Golden Gophers were the winner of the Monson Sweepstakes. He took over a Minnesota program still reeling from the Clem Haskins academic scandal and knew his job would be difficult with sustained repercussions. Still, Minnesota was 7-4 heading into Assembly Hall to take on No. 7 Illinois. Before tip-off, it was clear that Monson was concerned about getting calls from the officials. His team was playing on the road in the Big Ten and he figured he was going to get calls against him, so he might as well protest before one was even called.

"Just because we are at Illinois doesn't mean it's a one-way street," Monson responded to an official after his bench players were asked to sit down by the ref before the tip. Later on in the first half, Monson would reiterate his theme after official Tom O'Neil did not call what Monson thought was an obvious walk on the Illini's Frank Williams, saying "Just because he wears an Illinois shirt doesn't mean it's not a walk." Monson continued to protest calls throughout the game, mocking the officials, and finally with under four minutes remaining, O'Neil ran over to the coach to tell him to shut up. "And you're lucky that I didn't hear what you said!"

Monson's effort to get some favorable calls from the officials did not help Minnesota win the game. Illinois started slowly, making just one shot in the first 4:30 of the game and they trailed 12-6 before switching to a zone to pressure the Gopher ballhandlers. Led by two threes by Williams, Illinois regrouped and went on a 24-7 run and took a nine-point lead into halftime. Perhaps because of the Minnesota size down low, the Illinois team shot more threes than jumpers in the first half.

In a timeout midway through the first half, Self asked his team, "What are we doing down here [on offense]? Geez, we are taking some poor shots." In most of the timeouts on this night, Self used all of his time, calming down his freshman Luther Head, imploring Brian Cook to be a presence down low, and encouraging the Illini defense.

Head had been playing brilliantly yet immaturely over the last five games, and Self loved the athleticism that he brought to the floor. It was the stupid turnovers, the silly shots, and his inability to grasp simple concepts that frustrated the coach. At one point, Head threw the ball behind Williams, and Self immediately pulled him from the game. As Head walked over toward the bench, he was greeted by his coach who reminded him that taking care of the basketball is one of his biggest concerns of the player, and that sometimes "you just don't think." The scoring for Illinois on this night came not from Williams, who finished with eight points, but from Cook who had 16. Robert Archibald returned to the lineup and scored 14. The final score was 76-53 and Illinois looked good enough in the second half to be impressive.

"It was good team effort," Self told the team after the game, "especially with our injuries to Damir and Lucas. I was disappointed with us not jumping on long rebounds and some of the silly shots and turnovers, but all in all, it was a good effort." Turning to their next opponent, Self reminded the team how difficult it was to play on the road at Wisconsin, and they would need another big effort Saturday night.

They did play with effort at the Kohl Center, a place where Self had never coached, but it wasn't necessarily a good effort. In a game that ended with Badger fans storming the court at the buzzer, No. 7 Illinois was upset, 72-66. The turning point in the game was a technical foul called on Cook early in the second half, with Illinois leading 37-29. After he slammed a dunk, Cook either pushed Badger player Charlie Wills in the back or patted him on his behind, earning the ire and whistle of official Rick Hartzell, who tagged Cook with a technical for taunting, giving Cook his fourth personal foul. Moments later, Self earned himself a "T" as he continued to protest the call on Cook. Afterward, Self acknowledged to the press that Cook "needs to be smarter than that," but also indicated that in his two seasons coaching Cook, he knew his big man was not one to taunt or talk trash. For his part, Cook said it "was an accident." Regardless, the two technicals swung momentum and Wisconsin, which played just seven players in the game, pulled to within three. Trading baskets and free throws down the stretch, Illinois could not maintain the lead before the fans rushed the court.

Afterward, Williams put it best: "I don't know what it is about this place, I'm just glad it's my last time playing here." Cory Bradford scored 13 for Illinois and Williams added 12. Wisconsin scored 23 points from the line while Illinois went 13 of 16. Illinois continued its foul problems, with Cook, Nick Smith, and Archibald spending key minutes on the bench straddled with fouls. Illinois fell to 12-3, 1-1, and lost for the first time since the Arizona game in early December.

There was some good news for Self. Johnson continued his speedy recovery and on January 7 was fitted for a knee brace. He was scheduled to return to practice on January 10 after the Purdue game, and looked to work his way back into the lineup in two weeks. Illinois could have used him sooner. Krupalija meanwhile had an MRI on his foot, which revealed the early stages of a stress fracture. He was fitted with an immobilizing boot, and with rest and ultrasound treatment, hoped to be back in a week.

In West Lafayette, the Illini shockingly didn't play any better before 12,876 at Mackey Arena. Though 10-point favorites, Illinois had a one-point halftime lead, 41-40, which they couldn't hold on to and trailed by double-digits in the second half, eventually losing, 84-75. Williams had 23 points. Purdue was 35 of 46 from the line while Illinois was just 16 of 23. Cook and Archibald continued their foul trouble, spending key minutes on the bench. Late in the game, the Boilermaker fans began chanting "Overrated!" They may have been right.

The familiar mantra of Self early in the season returned. "We are not a very good team right now." The highly ranked Illini had now lost two on the road to two teams that did not come into the season with high expectations. In fact, Purdue was 8-8 and 0-2 in conference play heading into the game. Self was worried that his team had not found its identity yet and he searched to make changes. He declared publicly that he would shake things up before Michigan on January 12, but what shake-ups were undetermined.

As for UCLA, the Bruins played host to the Washington schools the first week of January, facing them just two weeks after the Bruins' trip to the Northwest. UCLA won both games at Pauley Pavilion to extend their winning streak to nine, but they were not dominant. In fact, the visitors came closer than they had in years at beating UCLA on the road. A bright spot for Lavin was Cedric Bozeman's return for the first time since surgery in early December. The Bruins beat the Huskies 74-62 and Washington State 81-62. Billy Knight scored 32 points against Washington State. The sweep of the Washington schools sent UCLA to its ninth straight win and a 4-0 conference record to set up the highly anticipated rivalry game against 4-0 USC on January 10. In fact, as the second half wound down against Washington State, the Pauley students began chanting, "Beat SC! Beat SC!"

The next day, Lavin and his Bruins made their annual visit to the City of Hope Children's Hospital in the City of Duarte, about 20 miles from Los Angeles. The players and coaches visited with the terminally ill children, took photos, and cheered up the youngsters. Lavin enjoyed his visit and seemed to take pleasure in bringing some temporary relief to the kids. The look on his face was the same as when he played one-on-one with the Special Olympians at the Wooden Classic in December. Beating SC was not on his mind this day.

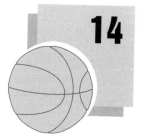

14

Heart Surgery

STEVE LAVIN IS A STUDENT OF THE GAME—THE GAME'S HISTORY AND THE HISTORY OF UCLA basketball. He can tell you what his team's shooting percentage was in a 1997 game at Oregon as fast as he can rattle off the biggest victories and defeats in his tenure as coach, or the name of the coach of Alabama in 1968. While realizing that each game is just a piece of a larger puzzle, improvement is what he looks for, and if winning is a part of it, then great. Lavin always looks at the big picture, and that picture is all about March. He understands that winning in the NCAAs is a by-product of doing things the right way over the course of the season.

At the start of PAC-10 play in late December, he began talking to his team about individual and team improvement. "A 5% improvement individually and collectively will take us where we need to be come March." He reiterated this theme in pregame talks, reminding the Bruins that every game was an opportunity to get better. Their first big PAC-10 test to get better was against cross-town rival USC in early January.

It is hard to fully appreciate the bitterness between the schools unless you attended one of them. Even the hardcore sports fans in blasé L.A. don't really get it. But the alumni and players do. Oh, and so do the coaches. In the Trojan home team locker room that night sat their coach, Henry Bibby, a former All-American at UCLA with a 1-10 record as a coach against his alma mater. He had revived the USC basketball program and with an Elite Eight run in 2001 and his team was now a force to be reckoned with. Both teams entered the January showdown undefeated in conference play, having swept the Washington schools.

Lavin had tough, physical practices in the days leading up to USC for he knew that the game itself would be the most physical the Bruins would play. Practice was so intense that team leader Rico Hines suffered a cut above his left eye and a mild concussion diving for a loose ball in practice on Tuesday, January 8.

"This will be a rough, physical game," Lavin told his team again in the visiting locker room at the famous Forum, home for two weeks for USC as the U.S. Figure Skating Trials took over the Sports Arena in downtown Los Angeles. "They are still salty about last year when they thought Earl and Dan had hard fouls early in the game," the coach continued, referring to the week's newspaper quotes where Bibby had been talking about the "cheap shots" from last year's game and predicted another physical one.

Before Lavin had a chance to speak to his team, PAC-10 coordinator of officials and former California coach Lou Campanelli had come to the locker rooms and had spoken with the coaches. He warned them that the game would be called tight, that the players needed to avoid flagrant fouls, and that the coaches should pass the message onto their respective teams. Lavin did, and made it a point to remind his players to keep their cool.

The visitors' locker room at the Forum is old and small, yet brings a sense of nostalgia to the occupants. The same room where the Celtics and Sixers suited up; the same boards that Red Auerbach and other coaching legends drew up plays; the same room that was the scene of disappointment and despair by Lakers' opponents.

After quickly going over the typical keys to the game—defense, boxing out, red zone play, intensity—Lavin returned to the bigger picture. First, in black ink on the wipeboard in the locker room, there was a four-team bracket, complete with team names and lines, similar to the NCAA Tournament office pool sheets. On the bottom half of the bracket was No. 1-ranked Kansas advancing past Nebraska to do their part in setting up a Saturday showdown two days later against the Bruins at Pauley Pavilion. The top half of the bracket pitted UCLA against USC, with an open line for the winner. "This is like a mini NCAA Tournament. Same Thursday–Saturday format and turnaround. Taking care of business in one round to get to the next game. Kansas did their part so now we need to do the same," said Lavin.

Underneath the bracket on the wipeboard was the phrase "5–8% Improvement," referring to the individual and collective goals Lavin had set for the team. On this night, there was an unusual amount of writing on the board for a Lavin pregame, but true to form, much of it was not USC-game specific, but rather about the bigger picture. Some coaches take a more focused approached, not talking about the next games, looking ahead or thinking about March. But Lavin has a plan for this team, as he has had for previous ones as well. Improve throughout the season, work on various parts of the total package, and good things will happen come March. Two years earlier his team was 4-8 in PAC-10 play at one point, written off by fans and the media, but they won eight straight and peaked come Tournament time to advance to the Sweet Sixteen.

"The season is a marathon, not a sprint," he told his team on more than one occasion during the season. "It's about getting better every day in practice and in games."

Lavin was loose before the USC game, reminiscing with his assistants and talking about the USC game the previous year. UCLA had won 13 of the previous 14 meetings between the schools, and with first place in the PAC-10 on the line, the game was sure to be intense.

The first half was dominated by the Trojans, as UCLA seemed unable, or unwilling, to keep USC off the boards. Followup dunks and offensive rebounds by USC star Sam Clancy and David Bluthenthal made Lavin none too pleased. "We are getting killed on the boards," he screamed at the 10:44 timeout. "USC has nine offensive rebounds so far. What did we talk about before the game?" The Bruins had started the game in a matchup zone, something they had relied on in their winning streak, but USC seemed to be getting to the basket at will. "Should we go to man-to-man?" Lavin asked his players, looking directly at Jason Kapono. With a nod of his head followed by a barely audible "yea," the Bruins' leader agreed to man defense. Lavin quickly went over the matchups and sent his team back on the floor. The switch on defense didn't help, as USC continued to dominate inside. Dan Gadzuric and T. J. Cummings could not stop the Trojan big men. Matt Barnes was playing solidly for UCLA, but was more content playing on the perimeter than on the inside.

At halftime, USC led by eight as the Bruins walked back into the Forum tunnel headed for the locker room. Once there, Lavin unleashed a fury. "They are kicking our asses all over the place," he screamed, covered in sweat and loosening his tie. "This is a street brawl. It's the New York Knicks versus the Pistons. We need to play tougher and go hard." The coach got fired up, bent over, and put his hands on his knees as he stared ferociously at his team. "We've got 20 minutes to play our asses off. We are only down by eight, that's just three possessions." Assistant Jim Saia chimed in with a few choice words, turning red in the process.

The second half was better for UCLA, as they climbed back into the game. With 11:51 to go, the Bruins were down by only 52-50. Nine minutes later, Hines hit a jumper to pull the game even at 64 before USC super-freshman Errick Craven took over, scoring seven in a row for the Trojans as they went ahead, 71-66. UCLA was not out of it, as Barnes, Kapono, and Billy Knight hit some incredible three-pointers. The Bruins, however, played sloppy basketball down the stretch, with turnovers and fouls ruining their chances for a win. The Trojans hit their free throws in the closing seconds, with point guard Brandon Granville hitting three of four, and USC beat No. 11-ranked UCLA, 81-77. Barnes finished with a career high 34 points, including seven three-pointers. Clancy led USC with 19 and Granville added 18. The Trojan faithful mobbed the court and the USC players. This was not just another PAC-10 win. This one was huge.

Back in the locker room, Lavin went immediately to the wipeboard. He headlined a chart "Good" and "Bad" and began to make a list for the team. "The Bad is that we lacked poise, we missed rebounds, we didn't play hard, we didn't execute in the first half. The good is that Matt [Barnes] and Ryan [Walcott] played well." Filling in for Bozeman during December, Walcott had gotten valuable minutes at point and proved himself with his decision making in tight games. Bozeman only saw seven minutes of action in the UCLA loss.

Lavin continued, "You can't let a loss beat you twice. You need to keep your heads up and have the confidence that you can turn it around. This was one game, yes it was a big one, but it is just one game. We have Kansas at 12:00 on Saturday on national television, and we need to learn a lot in practice tomorrow."

As the team undressed and showered, and as the media was let into the locker room, Lavin made his way over to where Bozeman was taking off his sneakers. In a two-minute conversation, the coach encouraged the freshman to keep his head up, that although he didn't play much this night, they would need him against Kansas. Even in the midst of defeat, Lavin was setting the stage for the future. Bozeman continued to look depressed, but at least his coach was in his corner.

That night, as his team grabbed some shut-eye, Lavin laid in his bed in Marina del Rey and watched tape of the USC game until 2:30 A.M. He saw some good things as he replayed possessions, something most coaches find when they have time to watch a game unfold on tape. He was angry at himself for not playing the youngsters enough. "I probably cost us the game for not using the bench enough," he told reporters afterward. Bozeman and Andre Patterson did not play in the second half and Dijon Thompson played only two minutes. He would not make that mistake again.

He got to the office on Friday, January 11, around noon, having already returned dozens of phone calls, given interviews to the press over the phone, and read the local papers while working from his home office. He knew that once he hit his UCLA office, he would have no time, as the interruptions were nonstop. Once at his desk, assistant Jim Saia stopped in and the two immediately began to talk about the game.

"I think I should have gotten some of the freshmen and younger guys more minutes against USC," Lavin told his six-year assistant. "It's better to have them learn trial by fire now to have them ready for March." The coaches decided to let Hines start against Kansas, but insisted that Bozeman would play 25 minutes and the other freshmen, Patterson and Thompson, would also see significant minutes. It was a defining moment for Lavin and the team, and it occurred in a brief conversation hidden from the team and the public. At that moment, Lavin decided that playing his youngsters, despite their inexperience, would prove more fruitful in two months, rather than exclusively sticking with his experienced starters. Though he was loyal to his seniors, Lavin believed that it would be the younger guys, Bozeman, Patterson, Cummings, Thompson, and Walcott, who could take them deep into March.

Before practice that afternoon, the team and Lavin met the media in a divided-off section on the floor of Pauley Pavilion. The team was generous as they answered questions about the crushing loss to USC and the matchup against the top-ranked Jayhawks. As usual, the biggest crowd was around the coach and, as usual, Lavin answered all of their questions. He then let most of the beat writers get some one-on-one time with him. As the coach spoke to the media, the players assembled on the floor where they warmed up, stretched, and shot. Saia had pulled off five guys for the scout team, John Hoffart, Ray Young, Gene Barnes, Jon Crispin, and Janou Rubin, and was walking them through Kansas' offensive plays. As practice began, the team headed to the locker room (except for the scout team who remained on the floor with Saia) as Lavin prepared to show them some tape. "We don't usually watch film on a game from the last night, but we need to see what we did wrong against SC," the coach said as the lights went dim.

The team watched the spliced "low-light" tape of poor defensive positioning and sets by the Bruins from the night before. Lavin had seen it many times over lying in bed, but his team had not. The coach stayed remarkably positive throughout, pointing out mistakes, but in an encouraging manner. After the team watched the tape, Saia came in and went over the Kansas scouting report, using the wipeboard to demonstrate Kansas sets. They hit the floor for some drills and Saia walked the scout team through the Jayhawk plays for the benefit of the rest of the team.

Just two days after the loss to USC, ruining the minibracket on the board, the Bruins hosted the No. 1-ranked Jayhawks in a nationally televised CBS game. Tip-off was at high noon in front of a packed crowd and 50 members of the media including ESPN's Andy Katz and Grant Wuhl from *Sports Illustrated*. The local hometown paper, *The Los Angeles Times*, sent four reporters and columnists, as if it were a Final Four. Lavin, as usual, had arrived around 9:00 A.M. to the office, drank a cup of coffee, and read the sports pages alone. Thirty minutes prior to tip-off, he had some company. In addition to the players, coaches, trainers, and managers, UCLA chancellor, and big Lavin supporter, Albert Carnesale and his then-fiancée, Robin Gerber, were standing in the back listening to the coach's pregame words. Lavin again noted history in his talk.

"This is the fourth No. 1-ranked opponent we have played in the last four years. We beat Stanford at Maples Pavilion the last two and lost to them here. So we are 2-1 against No. 1-ranked teams. Most players never even get the opportunity to play the No. 1 team once in their careers, let alone four times. But this is why you came to UCLA: to play in games like these. This is a great opportunity for you. You will remember this game for years to come. We need to stay poised and together."

The team hit the floor for more warmups, while Lavin relaxed in the locker room, watching the final seconds of the South Carolina-Kentucky game on TV. He has a remarkable ability to appear calm, relaxed, and "in the moment" before games. But talk to him after a game, and he has trouble remembering the details before tip-off. Joking with managers, watching the TV, and getting up out of his seat a few times to write on the board, he chewed his gum like it was a red-eye steak.

As the team returned to the locker room, Lavin stopped Hines on the way in and asked the senior how the teamed looked. "Relaxed, not too jacked up." As they got their water and new Adidas headbands and assembled in their seats, Lavin had a different message for them before tip-off. "Let's just have some fun and play some ball. You are prepared." That's it. No more history lessons, no more scouting reports, just "have fun and play some ball." Earlier in the morning, the coach had a good feeling about the game, telling Treena that UCLA would win and echoing that thought privately to the assistant coaches.

Pauley Pavilion was louder than it was for most games, a sense of excitement brought back into the hallowed arena. It was clear after tip-off that this was a pumped up and intense Bruin squad, a team vastly different from the one that had shown up in the losses to Ball State, Pepperdine, and USC. From the early moments, UCLA crashed the boards, played physical down low, and dove on the floor for loose balls. Their defensive intensity forced Kansas to commit 16 turnovers in the first half and shoot an unimpressive 34%. Kansas was not playing like the top-ranked team in the nation but UCLA was playing like one. Midway through the first half though, the Jayhawks led 20-19. In a time-out, Lavin praised his kids for the early effort and encouraged the extra passes on offense. Lavin got contributions from his bench, from his freshmen, from his guards and big men, and from the crowd at Pauley, who never stopped cheering as the Bruins pulled ahead and took a 46-35 lead into halftime.

Lavin kept it simple. "We need another 20 minutes of solid basketball. Everybody is playing great and we are getting contributions from everybody. Each one of you should know your role on this team and your role in the game."

Watching the game from a seat in the upper sections was former UCLA head coach Gene Bartow who was now a scout for the Memphis Grizzlies. He had not stepped foot in Pauley Pavilion since coaching his last game in 1977. It had been 15 years since any Bruin team had defeated a No. 1 team at home and Bartow could be a witness to history.

The second half was all UCLA, as they staked a 15-point lead with 14:04 to go. Kansas' stars got into foul trouble and guards Kirk Hinrich and Aaron Miles found themselves on the bench along with center Nick Collison. However, there was a reason the Jayhawks were No. 1, and their shooting got them back in the game. They hit a barrage of shots to cut the lead to four with 7:38 left. UCLA countered with big buckets from Kapono and Barnes down the stretch, but Kansas still managed to get it to 78-74 with 1:57 remaining. The rest of the game was spent at the free throw line for UCLA as Kansas missed its field goals and quickly fouled. When the final buzzer sounded, the fans rushed the court with the 87-77 UCLA victory. The players were mobbed and it took close to eight minutes before the coaching staff and players all made it back to the locker room.

They were joined there by a room full of people. UCLA administrators, recruits and their families, and former Bruin players. It was a mob scene.

"This is one game, yes, it's a big one, but still just another game," an ironic statement from Lavin who had given the team the same line two days earlier after the loss to USC. "This win will help us down the road with seeding for the Tournament. Today, we improved 5 to 8% and it proves that you can bounce back in anything that you do in life." The coach continued, "Years from now when you are in business and have a bad day, you need to be able to adjust and come back and be successful."

The coach always looks for the bigger lessons for the season and for life, and tonight he continued to look ahead to March, as he had been doing all year. It was more than a big win for Lavin and UCLA, and it went a long way in boosting the confidence of the team and fans. But to some, that still wasn't enough.

For critics of Lavin, they didn't play well enough; Kansas just played poorly; UCLA got lucky. It could not possibly have anything to do with the coaching. *Maybe they beat Kansas, but they still lost to Ball State and Pepperdine.* For many coaches, particularly for Lavin at UCLA, nothing is ever good enough. Jim Harrick won a national championship in 1995 with UCLA, but was still criticized and hounded before being forced out in 1996. As an assistant to Harrick for five years, and as the head coach for six, Lavin had not become immune to the fans' ire, but certainly he'd come to understand it and, at times, could even laugh it off.

The 38-year-old had not only defeated Kansas, but a Kansas team led by one of the premier coaches in America. Roy Williams was roundly respected for his success at Kansas, though he had yet to win a national championship. A disciple of Dean Smith, Williams had flirted with the North Carolina vacancy before deciding to stay in Lawrence in 2000, and Jayhawk fans couldn't have been happier. But somehow overnight the 51-year-old Williams had gone from being a hot, young coaching prospect to one of the older deans of coaching. Not surprisingly, he defends experience over age.

"If you were to have heart surgery—would you rather have an older surgeon who has performed heart surgery 100 times or an eager young doctor who has never performed one? I think most of us would choose the one who had done 100 surgeries. I think ADs are looking for the quick fix now. They see the young, eager, and maybe personable young coach, but seem to overlook what experience brings to the table."

It is an age-old question—pun intended. Are young coaches better because they can "relate" more? Because they bring energy and enthusiasm and because they understand the complex job duties? Or are older coaches the ones who should be hired because they bring experience and knowledge but maybe not flash? There is a perception that the game of college basketball is getting younger, that the coaches are mere pups now. But what is the truth?

The misperception surrounding age is perhaps the biggest miscalculation. Why? Look at some of the higher profile hirings of the past years. Many are young guys in their thirties and when they get a job, we all hear about it. But they are such a small fraction of the coaches in America. We tend to think that coaches in general are getting younger, but that is the case only because we see the young ones on television more.

So let's go to the numbers. Taking a look at the coaches' ages when coaching at schools in the seven big conferences (ACC, Big East, Big Ten, Big Twelve, Conference USA, PAC-10, and SEC), there is a revealing trend regarding the supposed "babying" of today's college coaches. Using the 2002 ages of the head coaches at the end of the 2001–2002 season, regardless of their actual birthdates in the year, the numbers reveal that the average age of the coaches in these top seven conferences in 2002 was 48.0. Probably seems a little high, considering the emergence of young coaching stars, but in reality, most professionals, regardless of careers, do not peak until their mid- to late forties.

If today's coach is, on average, 48 years old, how does this compare to yesteryear?

Going back 22 years to 1980, when college basketball was not the behemoth it is today, the average age of coaches from the major conferences was 44.4, almost four years *younger* than it is today. In 1980, a 33-year-old former Army coach was leading the Duke Blue Devils against North Carolina State's 34-year-old Jim Valvano. In the Big East, Jim Boeheim was a meager 36 facing 39-year-old Digger Phelps of Notre Dame. Other well-known coaches and their ages in 1980: Bobby Knight, John Thompson, and Larry Brown, 39, Eddie Sutton and Gene Keady, 44, and Lute Olson was a boyish 46. Those that rose to national stardom were the young guns of two decades ago.

As college basketball grew in popularity through the 1980s, the age of the men leading the game rose slightly. By 1990, the average age was up from 44.4 in 1980 to 47.3. The young coaching stars in 1990? Kelvin Sampson, Lon Kruger, and 29-year-old Virginia coach Jeff Jones. Five years later in 1995, the average age of coaches had risen by a year to 48.7, before dipping to the current average age of 48.0 in 2002. So, even in the past five years, the myth that college coaches are getting younger, may not be true if you believe the numbers.

There are a few caveats to this analysis. The seven conferences profiled are only the most prolific and well-known, excluding the likes of the Atlantic 10 among others. Especially at lower to mid-major Division I schools, there may seem to be younger coaches, since they are the proving grounds for many of today's major college coaches. However, many great coaches stay at smaller schools for personal and professional reasons, leaving older coaches at the lower levels of Division I. (Davey Whitney has been at Alcorn State for 26 years; Mike Ving at Louisiana-Monroe for 20; Tom Brennan at Vermont for 16 years.) The statistics, therefore, reflect only the coaches at the big-time schools in college basketball, not every coach at every school. It is fair to look at the big seven conferences, since they are the ones grabbing the proportionate amount of media coverage, money, and NCAA Tournament titles.

Looking at a breakdown of the average ages of the seven conferences in 2002, the "oldest" conference is the Big Twelve at 50.2 led by Eddie Sutton and Bob Knight. This is the only conference with an average age for coaches above the half-century mark. Of course, with the arrival of the brash, good-looking, 36-year-old Snyder at Missouri, it may seem the young onslaught is underway. Following the Big Twelve is the PAC-10, with an average age of 49.6.

So even with the arrival of the baby-faced crop of coaches, the age of coaches has remained fairly constant. With more jobs available, a changing role in the responsibilities of coaches and an ever-present media, younger coaches are getting their shots without a great deal of assistant experience. But let's not forget that Knight and Krzyzewski were in their twenties when they first became head coaches (Army) and Dean Smith was in his early thirties when the future Hall of Famer took over for Frank McGuire at North Carolina.

Another surprising revelation is that head coaches at all Division I schools have, on average, 9.6 years of Division I head coaching experience. Again, the perception may be that, especially with the younger coaches, they have less experience. That may be true, particularly for those who are assistants at top programs and then get their first head coaching job at another. But it is important to remember that the majority of coaches do not jump from one or two years of being an assistant to running their own program.

Many coaches put in years as assistants, followed by head coaching stints at lower level schools. A small few make the leap to the big-time programs, but most remain as head coaches at the smaller schools, accounting for the many years of experience.

As for longevity and tenure, the only coaches from the major conferences that were coaching in 1980 and are still coaching today: Krzyzewski, Boeheim, Knight, Sutton, Olson, and Keady.

"The young coaches view the world differently than the coaches that I first worked with when I was in the business," reflects Iowa's Bob Bowlsby. "Most of those coaches came out of the classroom. They were teaching coaching theory class. They were maybe even on the health and physical education faculty. Of course, many years ago at Iowa we had Dr. Eddie Anderson when he coached Iowa's 1939 football team. He did surgery in the morning and coached football in the afternoon. He used to do press conferences with blood speckled on his lab coat."

Certainly, times have changed and, hopefully, basketball coaches will not be asked to perform surgery anytime soon. If we go by the axiom that "where you stand depends on where you sit," it is clear which side coaches fall on when asked if being a younger coach is better in today's game. We hear phrases like "he can relate better," or "he's more in tune with the kids today," or "he knows what they are listening to." The thinking is that perhaps a younger coach, closer to the age of his players, can relate better, and, therefore, can be a better coach. The old guard will tell you that it is B.S., that age has nothing to do with being a great coach. In fact, older coaches have irreplaceable experience over a young coach.

Lute Olson has been coaching for many decades and is considered one of the deans of college coaching. At 68, Olson should be outdated, out of touch, and not effective as a coach. But he isn't. In fact, he took a very young Arizona team to the NCAA Tournament in 2002 and garnered many votes for National Coach of the Year. Pretty good for an old guy. "I think kids still want structure and discipline. I don't think they are looking for a coach that's going to jive with them," Olson sarcastically states.

One of Olson's contemporaries, Gene Keady, doesn't see "old" age as an issue and, in fact, thinks that being young can be harmful for a coach. "A lot of the younger coaches are ill-prepared, especially toward the media. They have worked with good coaches, so they have the recruiting scenario down pat, but a lot of them don't understand how to work with the media."

Older coaches may be jealous, envious of the rapid ascent to the top of the profession by some of the younger coaches, but not jealous of their salaries. To them, it's about paying dues. "I don't think they can appreciate what they have," believes Keady, "because they haven't worked their way up the ranks. The step process to a coaching job is not to be a grad assistant, be an assistant coach, coach junior college, and at 45 get your head coaching job. Now you can get your head job in your twenties. There is no way they can appreciate it, but I don't know if they need to appreciate it—they need to win."

Keady concedes that younger coaches "know what they are doing" and doesn't characterize them as unprepared. He does, however, believe that the younger coaches do not give back to the game enough, a sentiment echoed by many older coaches.

Mike Brey at Notre Dame thinks he is a perfect fit. He's not old enough to be considered the "old guard," but he is old enough to be a father-figure to some of the younger coaches. "One of the reasons I think I am respected in this business is that I've paid my dues. Guys in the business look around and say, 'Son of a bitch, he started in high school. After that he went to Duke, but you know what? He didn't go to Tennessee from Duke. He went to Delaware. And he stayed there.' What helps me in our fraternity is credibility." At 43, Brey is certainly not old, and according to the numbers, is still five years *younger* than the average head coach.

Bill Self is just 39 but takes the middle ground in the young versus old debate. "The biggest misperception is that older coaches can't relate to today's players. B.S. You don't think Mike Krzyzewski relates to his players? People just assume that is the case. How about Larry Brown and Allen Iverson in the NBA? Or Eddie Sutton at Oklahoma State? They get along great with their players." In fact, a look at the top teams in the country late in the season in 2002 reveals that older coaches must be doing something right. Guys like Krzyzewski, Sutton, Knight, Williams, Olson, Jim Calhoun, Gary Williams, and Jim Harrick all had their teams in the Top 25.

According to Self, age and experience can be a *benefit* not a hindrance. "Dean Smith, Lute Olson, these guys have earned their credibility through time. In fact, that is a better recruiting tool than any other skill. A guy like Dean Smith can get more out of one conversation with a recruit than a Bill Self can in a week."

But getting on in age might make a coach less patient with all of the new demands. For instance, guys like Dean Smith, who many believe would still be coaching if it weren't for all of the other responsibilities demanded of coaches today. Many of the older coaches are simply not having as much fun as in earlier years. As Self notes, "recruiting, media commitments, alumni dinners, NCAA rules, and the pressures" force many coaches to retire. Even Sam Alford, Steve's father, sees the game turning toward younger coaches, as he believes they have the energy to fulfill the duties.

Steve Alford, a standard bearer for the new generation, recognizes that it is the stuff off the court that may make younger coaches better suited for today's game. "There are an awful lot of coaches in their fifties and sixties that have a lot more experience, a lot more games and teaching under their belt. But are those same guys willing to do the same things as us young guys are doing? I do 20 Hawkeye Club events every spring. There aren't a lot of guys wanting to do that. You have to do a lot more to promote your program and it requires a lot more energy out of you."

For a time, Ed Schilling was the second youngest Division I head coach in college basketball and the youngest assistant in the NBA under John Calipari with the New Jersey Nets. He took a head coaching job at a high school when he was just 22, the youngest coach in his high school conference by at least 20 years. Schilling knows the criticism and knows that many see his age as a detriment to his coaching, but you can't let that affect how you coach. "You've got to look professional. You've got to carry yourself with more maturity. Some things that maybe you could get away with when you're older, you don't try. For many years when I was a high school coach, refs would come in and ask, 'Where's the coach?' You can't get offended easily."

Having success at a young age can lead to false expectations. By the time he was 32, Schilling had already coached in a Final Four, coached against Michael Jordan, coached in the Tokyo Dome, and had seen a glimpse of the big time. Taking a job at Wright State was not easy. "You come in and expect everything to happen quickly. But it doesn't. The players and program have a great foundation and heart, but that doesn't equate into success right away. Doing it the right way takes time."

Wayne McClain, a 45-year-old assistant at Illinois, acknowledges that sometimes the younger coaches have a better grip on things. "I'm sure if you talked with every older coach in America they'd tell you that they got that 'feel.' I don't know. It could just be perception, but I think that as a coach, you got to understand what they are thinking, talking, doing. I think the closer you are to that, the better you understand it." (During

Midnight Madness celebrations in Iowa City, Iowa star Reggie Evans caught Alford singing the lyrics to a Nelly song playing over Carver-Hawkeye Arena's sound system. It cracked him up.)

The dynamics of the coach-player relationship have changed as well. Instead of an older father figure, the relationship has become "brother-brother or "friend-brother" as Notre Dame associate athletic director Jim Phillips puts it. It seems only natural that those closest in age will view each other as contemporaries and as friends, as opposed to something more paternal. But sometimes younger coaches have a hard time finding and maintaining the balance between coach and friend, something that UCLA assistant Gerald Madkins acknowledges. "You can be friends. Like parents, you want to be cool with the kids. You want the kids to be able to come to you, but they also have to understand that you're the parent—the same thing with coaches. You can be cool with your players, but then again, they have to understand that what you say goes and that's it."

Mike Davis at Indiana thinks it is all about the individual. Coaches who want to relate can, and make the effort. There are others who are content, both in their job security and financially, that they don't need to relate. Drexel's Bruiser Flint agrees. "Some guys get into a routine and make just minor adjustments to it through the years. You know, for a lot of the older guys, there was no money when they got into coaching. Now there are big bucks, beat reporters, the Internet, and all other sorts of demands." As for relating to players, Flint likes to spend time with them away from basketball, so they understand that he cares about them as young men, not just as ball players.

Jeff Jones was only 29 when he took over at his alma mater, Virginia. "I wasn't prepared for the emotional toll that the job takes. As for on the court stuff, dealing with the media, alumni, I was comfortable with all that. But the emotional toll. This truly is a job as a coach, particularly when you are under intense scrutiny 24 hours a day. I did not sleep particularly well." Has anything changed now that he is ten years older? "Not much. I still get every bit knotted up now as I did then before games. The worst part is still waiting for tip-off."

Bucknell's Pat Flannery interviewed for his first head coaching job at the Division I level and was told he was too young at age 30 to be considered. Things have changed since then, but there is still a perception that younger coaches may not be able to lead a program and certainly not win at the highest level.

Are the young guys winning? Well, yes and no. Only eight coaches under 40 have ever won a National Championship, with the last being the late Jim Valvano at N.C. State back in 1983 when he was 37 years old. At the Final Four in 2002, the coaches' ages were 57 [Gary Williams], 51 [Roy Williams], 46 [Kelvin Sampson], and 41 [Mike Davis].

Occasionally, there will be a young, hotshot coach who leads his team to a conference championship or a great run in the postseason, but that is the rarity. Steve Lavin at UCLA has done it, as has Quin Snyder, Bill Self, and Stan Heath, among others.

"Age should not be a factor," says Dick Vitale. "Talent and the ability to inspire should be. Some coaches are fortunate that they don't have to pay the price of going through the high school, juco, low, mid, and then high Division I. You can't hold it against a Quin Snyder or Tommy Amaker for not going through that process. But they still have to prove themselves as a coach."

Again we turn for philosophical help from Bob Huggins, who, when asked if being a younger coach can be an advantage, said the following: "There are indeed a lot of old guys who are incompetent. But there are a lot of young guys who are incompetent. There are a lot of guys my age [47] who are incompetent. It doesn't necessarily mean that age has anything to do with it."

"Middle-aged" coaches Mike Brey and Pittsburgh's Ben Howland faced off in a game at Pitt on January 12. Pittsburgh entered the game ranked No. 23 and came in as the nation's top defensive team, the winner of 10 straight. But Notre Dame played well and scored the final eight points of a see-saw battle to beat the Panthers on the road, 56-53, ending Pittsburgh's winning streak and giving Notre Dame a victory in their last game in Fitzgerald Fieldhouse, which was to be replaced next season. Notre Dame trailed by five in the second half, but battled back, and with a David Graves' three-pointer with 54 seconds left had the lead for good, though they had to survive two misses by Pitt in the closing seconds. The key to the game for the Irish was their use of the diamond and one zone and man-to-man defenses intended to stop Pittsburgh's Brandon Knight, who finished with just 13. The Irish stood at 12-3, 2-1 in Big East play and headed to New York to play No. 8 Syracuse.

Things did not work out as well for Notre Dame in New York. The Irish had lost the last three to Syracuse and five of the last six, and knew they had to solve the Orangemen's 2-3 matchup zone to have a chance. But the Irish shot poorly from deep, just five of 24 three-pointers and could not overcome another deficit on the road, dropping their second Big East game, 56-51. The 51 points were the third lowest Big East point total since the Irish joined the conference. Ryan Humphrey did his part, scoring 28 points before 20,008 in the Carrier Dome. The other four starters for Brey shot a combined nine of 42 from the floor. The game was not pretty on either end for either team. Notre Dame left disappointed because they had had their chances. After the game, Brey waxed philosophically about the road trip. His Irish played three consecutive road games in the Big East, two of them against ranked opponents, and came away 2-1, much better than skeptics would have predicted. They stood at 2-2 in conference play with their first four conference games decided by only 3.2 points.

15

The Colors of the Game

IT IS HARD TO PUT THE INDIANA-IOWA RIVALRY INTO PERSPECTIVE—IT'S ONE OF THOSE battles you have to witness firsthand. Throw in the fact that both teams in 2001–2002 expected big things and had gotten off to solid starts and the frenzy only intensifies. Add the fact that "Mr. Indiana" Steve Alford would be coaching against his alma mater, the school at which some believe he should be coaching. Add in Luke Recker, who bolted Indiana and ended up at Iowa, earning the ire of the Indiana faithful. It was no wonder that Carver-Hawkeye Arena was at a fevered pitch on Sunday, January 13, when the Hoosiers paid a visit to Iowa City. This was the fourth meeting between Alford and Indiana, with the Iowa coach 2-1 in the first three games. Last year against Indiana at home, Iowa trailed 43-26 at halftime, but buoyed by Recker's amazing second half, they won the game. This year's game was to be nationally televised by CBS and the crowd looked ready for its appearance. There were no more than 20 Indiana fans dressed in red in the entire building; it was a sea of black and gold.

Inside the Hawkeye locker room hung articles about Indiana and quotes from Hoosier players, all posted by the Iowa managers, on the order of Alford, earlier in the week. Downloaded from the Internet, the articles covered the walls and doors, specific quotes and statistics highlighted in yellow. The wipeboard on this Sunday was covered with red and blue ink, Indiana's personnel written on one side and keys to the game on the other.

"We must play our toughest game yet," Alford told his troops, as Recker, on the floor, warmed an injured hip and sore knee with wrapped towels. "We must play physical but we need to play smart." Alford emphasized toughness over and over, citing his team's extremely physical "Rodman Drill" in practice earlier that week, an intense and rough rebounding drill. With 20 minutes until tip-off, the Iowa team hit the floor to a roar from the crowd. Back in the locker room, Alford was still making some late additions to the board. He was writing furiously, but neatly, when Tanya and daughter Kayla entered the locker room. As Tanya spoke with her father-in-law, assistant coach Sam Alford, Kayla ran to her father and leaped into his arms. Father and daughter walked over to a corner of the locker room and shared a private moment. It was a telling scene. Here was the ultimate warrior, just minutes before battle with his nemesis, whispering to his young daughter and stroking her red hair. After a kiss from his wife, Alford returned to the task at hand. Upon returning to the locker room, the players found these words written in large letters on the board: "Physical, Pressure, Punk." The coach didn't have to say much more.

It would be a battle and Iowa was not at full strength. Recker continued to nurse a hip flexer and had sat out practice on Friday. Iowa's other star, Reggie Evans, was battling a head cold and also took it easy in practice. Their health was not a topic before the game, nor did the media know about the ailments lest Indiana find out.

Just 38 seconds into the game, Recker lobbed a back-door alley-oop to Pierre Pierce who slammed home a thunderous dunk, exciting the crowd and evening the score at two. The teams traded buckets and turnovers, and with stellar outside shooting and strong inside play, Indiana looked tough. They had great guard play in Dane Fife, Kyle Hornsby, and Tom Coverdale and excellent big men in Jared Jeffries and Jeff Newton. Indiana never led by more than four points and when Iowa's Ryan Hogan hit two free throws with 7:03 left in the first half, Iowa pulled ahead, 22-21. But the tide soon shifted. The Hoosiers exploded on a 13-0 run over the next two and a half minutes and led 34-22 at the four-minute media timeout. Coverdale and Hornsby had hit threes to spark the run and Alford was not happy.

"You guys need to play physical," the coach demanded during the timeout, slamming his clipboard to the ground. "Cover your guy and grab some rebounds!" Though he might not admit it publicly, this game meant more to Alford than any other. It was Indiana, after all.

Halftime came with the Hoosiers up 40-29. They shot eight of 13 from three-point range and 54% from the field. A year earlier, in the same building, a similar scenario occurred with Indiana jumping to a first-half lead before an impressive second-half comeback by the Hawkeyes.

Like many other coaches, Alford breaks the halves into five, four-minute periods, with the opening and closing periods critical indicators of a team's success. Returning to the locker room, he pointed out that Iowa had lost four of the five. "In the last period, we were outscored 15-2! Heck, Coverdale and Jeffries have 24 and Luke and Reggie have two. I think that tells you all you need to know." Alford made a point of singling out his two senior stars, for he knew that they needed to produce for Iowa to have a shot. In the biggest game of the year, Alford wondered, how could these two disappear? Challenging them might be the only way to entice a better performance.

"I am not going to stand up here and go crazy," Alford calmly told the team. "We have no senior leadership today. And stop looking over at me on the bench. Just run your own things, because you are playing so selfish. I haven't even brought up the fact that we're on national TV and playing for a ranking."

Having studied hours of tape on Indiana with his staff, Alford knew that Iowa had to stop Indiana's three-point assault. He figured before the game that if the Hoosiers hit 10 or more threes, it would be very difficult to beat them. He pointed out to his team at the end of halftime that Indiana already had eight.

In the first 1:35 of the second half, Recker responded to the challenge of his coach. He hit back-to-back three-pointers to cut the lead to five. Indiana responded by going down low to Jeffries, for whom Iowa had no answer, and the future conference player of the year led Indiana on a 13-2 run, giving them a 16-point lead with 13:13 left in the game. Encouraged by Tanya Alford's loud cheers—directly across the court from her husband—Iowa tried desperately to get back in the game, but only managed to cut the lead to eight. Indiana hit 17 of 22 free throws in the second half, maintaining the margin. With an anticlimactic ending, Indiana cruised to the 77-66 win. Ryan Hogan led the Hawkeyes with 15 points while Recker and Evans combined for just 19. Evans hit only one of his seven free throws.

"I will take this one," the coach told his players after the game in a sedated and silent locker room. "It's my fault for playing Luke and Reggie [when they had sat out practice] and starting them, so I will take this one. But it all stops here. I will take control of this thing now. I will play guys who want to bust their butts in practice and in games."

He was clearly talking to his two senior leaders and stars. They had a horrible game against Indiana, not scoring, missing free throws, and generally showing a lack of effort. What Alford thought would help the team, resting his stars in practice, may have ended up hurting the team more, as other players watched Alford rest his stars. What message did that send to the other players? "Fife is diving three rows into the stands for a loose ball when they are up 11 with seconds to go," an envious Alford fumed. Alford was that type of player; he would have dove for that ball.

"Some of you complained when we had two-a-days. We shot around for 30 minutes and then practiced for an hour and twenty. That is not a two-a-day," a reference to a practice days earlier, when Iowa students were still on Christmas break, and the team practiced twice in one day.

When Alford finished, the team sat quietly in their leather seats; some slowly made a move to the shower. Recker was disgusted and laid still on the floor with his groin, hip, and knee wrapped in towels and ice. The coach left the locker room and headed across the hall to the media room to face the 40 or so reporters gathered there. He repeated what he had said to his team, and took blame for the loss while giving Indiana credit. He mentioned the health issues of Recker and Evans, but made a point that their injuries were not excuses for poor play.

After finishing with the press conference and a one-on-one radio interview, Alford sought the seclusion of the coaches' lounge. But awaiting him there was a recruit and his parents. So the coach dutifully put on a smile, joked with the player, asked about their visit to Iowa City, and made the obligatory small talk. It was a difficult job. Any coach or athlete who has just finished a game, especially on the losing end, is challenged to put on a smile and turn on the charm. But coaches know that these short interactions can make or break a recruit's impression of a coach or school.

Losing to Indiana was a blow to Alford, more so than losing to, say, Ohio State. He had come close to coaching at his alma mater and may perhaps end up there one day, but on this night, it was Indiana's Mike Davis who could boast proudly of a hard-working, tough team. In his first full season as the permanent head coach at Indiana, Davis had led the team to an 11-5 overall record and 4-0 in Big Ten play by mid-January. He had his share of critics, and in a basketball-crazed state like Indiana, they can often number in the thousands. But Davis fought off criticism not only for his perceived lack of coaching experience and skill, but also horrendously—for his color.

According to the most recent data, the Black Coaches Association reports that of the 321 Division I programs, fewer than 30% are headed by a minority coach. In a sport where African American players make up close to 70% of the student-athletes, the discrepancy raises the angst of many. Basketball is certainly not the only sport where race is an issue, and sports is hardly the only area of life where race is a factor. But as the visibility of the game has increased in recent decades, so have the voices of activists who demand more opportunities for black coaches. One of those coaches who got an opportunity was Mike Davis.

The details of Bobby Knight's demise at Indiana are well documented. Suffice it to say, four weeks before the start of the 2000–2001 season, Knight was fired from Indiana University and his assistant, Mike Davis, was named the interim coach. Taking over for a legend such as Knight would, no doubt, be one of the most difficult situations in college basketball for any coach. Being a black man in traditionally white Indiana made it tougher.

Davis grew up dirt poor in Fayetteville, Alabama, so ashamed of his family's home that he had his friends dropped him off far from his own block so he wouldn't be embarrassed. He grew tall and grew to love basketball. In 1979, he was named Alabama's High School Player of the Year and was a high school All-American. He stayed close to home and played four seasons at the University of Alabama, participating in two NITs and two NCAA Tournaments. Drafted in the second round by the Milwaukee Bucks in 1983, he played two seasons with the Bucks before heading overseas to play two seasons in professional leagues in Switzerland and Italy and, in 1988, returned to America to play for the Topeka Sizzlers of the CBA.

When his playing days were over, Davis turned his attention to coaching. First he was an assistant at Miles College in Alabama, then headed to Venezuela, where he coached in the professional leagues and with the national team. In 1990, he returned again to the United States and coached in the CBA for the next five seasons, including one year as a player/coach. He served as an assistant at Alabama under David Hobbs in his first Division I coaching job, before moving to the Indiana staff, with the help of Knight's son and assistant, Pat.

In September 2000, Davis was sitting on a gold mine. He was now the head coach, albeit interim head coach, of one of history's most famous college basketball programs. He had risen from the back streets of Fayetteville, overcome a severe speech-impediment, and worked his way through professional basketball. But none of that mattered to the Indiana faithful—they just wanted to win. There was an immediate backlash to his appointment with fans criticizing his lack of college coaching experience. Though most would never openly point to his color as a reason for the criticism, it surely played a role.

"This state does not have a lot to be proud of when it comes to integration," remarks *Bloomington Herald Times* sports editor Stan Sutton. "I don't think the racists are going to be brave enough to come out and say anything, but in the barbershops they might say it."

So in addition to fighting off the Knight loyalists, the critical media and the fans, Davis was faced with the fact that being black made his job harder. "There are certain things you can say about a black person that people automatically believe," the 41-year-old Davis says. "He can't develop players. He can't coach. He can't communicate. There are certain things that people say that people will automatically believe."

In a tumultuous week in September 2000, Davis was conflicted. His loyalty to Knight weighed heavily on him, but so did the opportunity of a lifetime. He had interviewed for some mid-major head coaching jobs that summer, but did not get them. He was content to spend another year working as an assistant at Indiana. "Everything happened so quickly," reflects Davis. "I had no time to prepare. I got a call from the AD and vice-president the night before the announcement. They invited me over to the vice-president's house and offered me the job. So here I am, September 13, and I'm a head coach. It was going 1,000 miles per hour."

Davis was confident that he was ready to do the job, but wished he had more time to prepare. In addition to planning practices and strategies, he was suddenly in demand by the media and for speaking engagements. Fans vocally criticized his selection and some players refused to play for him, expressing their loyalty to Knight, and stating so publicly. Even a few of the student managers did not want to work for Davis. On top of that, there were rumors that Knight was trying to convince players to transfer out and that he had offered Davis money not to take the job.

As for the rumor that Knight offered to pay him not to coach at Indiana, Davis denies it. He still respects his former boss. Sort of. "Coach Knight was a great coach and he allowed me to coach. Do I still have a relationship with Coach Knight? No. Is that sad? No."

In his first year at Indiana, Davis led the Hoosiers to 21 wins and an NCAA Tournament berth, but it was not easy. The Hoosiers endured a three-game losing streak and several times blew seemingly insurmountable leads in Big Ten games. But Indiana played great defense and it carried them. In fact, they held opponents to just 38% shooting from the floor in conference play, setting a Big Ten record. "Race matters," Davis says. "Here I am in my first year and we set the all-time Big Ten field goal percentage in history and it's hardly ever mentioned. Had I been one of these young coaches, these other [white] coaches, I'd be selling tapes on defense. People would be calling me and saying, 'What's your secret?'"

When he was an assistant coach at Indiana and interviewing for jobs, Davis felt that his color was used against him. "At Delaware, at Tulane, a lot of those jobs I was trying to get, but I couldn't get a sniff." Why is that? "They don't respect black coaches a lot of the time." (As it happened, Delaware did in fact hire a black coach in 2000, Duke assistant David Henderson.)

As a black assistant, Davis was fortunate to coach under Knight, who trusted him to scout and prepare game plans. "If you have a guy prepare a game for you, you trust him," says Davis. "If you don't have him prepare a game for you, you don't trust him as a coach."

In March 2001, Indiana was playing in the Big Ten Tournament and faced off, ironically enough, against Steve Alford's Iowa team. Iowa won the game, adding fuel to the fire that Davis would not be retained at the end of the season and that Alford would be the Hoosiers' new head coach. The intense media frenzy caused havoc for Davis and Alford as they led their teams into the NCAAs. Alford denied wanting the Indiana job and was adamant that he was staying at Iowa. In late March, Indiana removed the interim tag from Mike Davis' title and he became the Hoosiers' permanent coach. But there is more to the story.

The committee in charge of hiring a permanent coach at Indiana first had to decide whether to retain Davis before even considering other candidates. It was reported that a deal was in the works to return Alford to his alma mater, though no direct talks had taken place between the Iowa coach and Indiana officials.

A member of the committee, Cara Smith-Breckenridge, an IU grad, and a member of the National Board of the NAACP, pushed for Davis to be retained, giving him a chance as an African American. "Race always plays a part," Breckenridge states. "Mike Davis could become the first African American coach in any sport at IU. His race was discussed and it was an overriding factor for the committee." Breckenridge acknowledges that committee members understood that there might be protests if Davis were not hired, and certainly those threats may have overshadowed the discussions.

But university vice-president Terry Clapacs, a member of the committee and negotiator on behalf of Indiana, denies that race was ever discussed. "Race played no factor whatsoever. After Mike was hired, I was told that he was the first African American head coach at Indiana. I didn't know that. The only thing[s] that counted in regards to Mike Davis was how well he did during his interim year and the fact that he was a very inexperienced head coach."

Al Hamnik, a reporter for the *Hammond Times* newspaper in Indiana, reported on a possible Alford deal weeks after Davis was given the job permanently, stirring controversy throughout the state. Had Indiana administrators lied to the media and public about their dealings with the Iowa coach? Why was Alford not hired? What role may race have played in Davis' hiring?

"It seemed clear that the Board of Trustees were split," Hamnik says. "Some knew about the discussions about Alford, while others did not. There were two or three power people with knowledge of the Alford possibility. When wind of their dealings got to parts of the state and to other Board members, there clearly was a divided camp. In fact, the Board was probably naïve about mouthing off." Much of the speculation was wrong about Alford's return. Of course, Alford had to deny any interest in another coaching position, so as to not damage recruiting efforts or his team's performance. The irony is that race played a part in the unfair criticism of Davis, but it also may have saved his job.

(Of course, in his first full year as the permanent coach, Davis took the Hoosiers to the National Championship game, silencing many of his critics and proving to Breckenridge and other committee members that they had done the right thing. "All he needed was a chance," Breckenridge proudly boasts. "That's all we need to do is remove barriers and give people a chance.")

There is the old guard of college basketball, and the old guard of African American coaches. People like John Chaney, Nolan Richardson, Rob Evans, and John Thompson. Even as they have grown older and solidified their reputations, they, too, feel that race continues to play a role in their careers. In a tumultuous late-February week in Fayetteville, Arkansas, Richardson raised eyebrows with his comments about stepping down as coach and about racism at Arkansas. The Razorbacks were 13-13 at the time and headed for the NIT, at best. The local criticism of Richardson was increasing. "When I look at all of you people in this room," the coach remarked at a press conference on Monday, February 25, 2002, referring to the white reporters in attendance, "I see no one look like me, talk like me, or act like me. Now why don't you recruit? Why don't the editors recruit like I'm recruiting?" Richardson continued, implying that editors failed to hire any black reporters.

"My great-great-grandfather came over on the ship, not Nolan Richardson. I didn't come over on that ship so I expect to be treated a little bit different." And then, in his sharpest criticism yet of his school: "I know for a fact that I do not play on the same level as the other coaches around this school play on. I know that, you know that. And people of my color know that. And that angers me."

Perhaps Richardson was frustrated, fed up, and overemotional, but perhaps he spoke the truth. Black coaches may be held to higher standards by the media and their schools, especially in traditionally white communities. Richardson's friend, Kentucky's Tubby Smith, responded to the situation a few days later. "He's my mentor and has been for a number of years. Being black and being in a place where they expect you to win every game, I probably understand his frustration better than anybody. If you don't win every game, there has to be a reason."

In response to Davis' belief that his race plays a large factor in his treatment, Arizona State coach Rob Evans explains that Davis' circumstance and young age are the more critical issues. "I think Mike is a bit young. I think the way he got the job at Indiana probably made him put up his antennae a little bit. I feel very comfortable in the coaching fraternity," Evans concluded. He added, "Most of the young African American coaches call me every other day asking me questions and asking me different things."

Former Long Beach State coach and current Iowa State assistant Wayne Morgan believes that race did not play a factor in any of his coaching moves. However, he fully understands the impact of being black. Morgan related a story from his college days, an encounter with a professor. "We were in a bathroom, and he said to me that being black can be a tremendous psychological disadvantage. At that point, I took it almost as a racist statement and I said, 'What do you mean?' He gave the example of the two of us, me being black and he being white, walking down a street. 'Let's say we both knew a guy standing on a corner. You walk by and say hi but he doesn't say a word to you. You say hi again and he still doesn't say a word. You start thinking, is it because I'm black? Because his friends don't want to see him talking to a black person? All kinds of thoughts go through your mind. I walk by and say 'How are you doing?' and he doesn't say anything to me. I think, did he just lose his girlfriend? Did he lose his best friend?' The professor told me that being black can be very bad psychological damage. I never forgot that lesson."

With John Thompson retired from Georgetown, Temple's John Chaney is the dean of current black coaches. In his 30 years of coaching and a lifetime of facing the challenges of being a black man in America, he has seen it all. He has seen black players transfer to play for white coaches and white players transfer to play for black coaches. He sees no pattern of black players only wanting to play for black coaches and he doesn't think that race plays a large factor in who gets a job. At one stage in his life, however, he may have. "We won a National Championship at Cheney State in 1978. I was there for 10 years and really had to fight. I was not even offered a job after winning the national championship until Temple offered me the job. I was 50 years old when I got this job. Many times today we find people trying to seek out talented black coaches for whatever reasons. I think right now we have reached a stage where the kind of measurement that's used in sports today is truly unfair."

Illinois assistant Wayne McClain suggests that black players are more willing to trust a black coach, simply because of familiarity. "Just like anything, I think there is a trust factor. I think if an African American saw you and me standing here, naturally, he's going to put a little bit more trust in me than you because we are both from the same ideology. Do I think it is a necessity to have an African American coach on a staff? No."

Drexel's Bruiser Flint believes that African American coaches can relate better to African American players. "I can talk to my players about the projects; about growing up poor; about walking into a store and having people follow you. I have lived it and they understand it. They believe in me because I know what they are talking about."

Flint also points out that black coaches are not only expected to meet a higher standard, but when they get fired, they face particularly difficult challenges in getting another job. "I was really lucky because after UMass I had some opportunities. But many black coaches do not get recycled."

As for black coaches getting fired more quickly than white ones, CBS' Clark Kellogg believes there is some truth to it. "I don't know if they're overtly judged differently, but sometimes you get the feeling when you compare records, there's always a sense that there has to be a little more. I can't document it, but it is a feeling." University of Texas-San Antonio's Tim Carter is a firm believer that black coaches are held to a higher standard, and receive less compensation than their white counterparts. "You don't find African American coaches in programs that lose longer than two years. If you look around the country right now, one thing you'll notice is that African American coaches are winning. If you're not [winning], then you're gone a lot quicker."

Washington's Lorenzo Romar agrees with Carter. "I think there are some guys out there doing a lot of crazy things behind closed doors, but are still able to maintain jobs. Whereas if you know the same thing about some African Americans, they get eliminated quicker."

When it comes to getting hired, Andy Katz from *espn.com* clearly thinks that race plays a part. "There is absolutely no question. There are very few staffs that are all white. In fact, they are absolutely petrified to do that, but at the same time it makes sense to have a staff that reflects in some degree your team. It wouldn't make sense to have an all black team with an all white staff. That just wouldn't make sense."

"You rarely see an all black staff and a token white," notes Kellogg. "I always want to see more African American coaches get a chance. I think it is happening. Is it happening enough and as fast as I would like to see it? Maybe not."

Notre Dame assistant Lewis Preston takes issue with coaches hiring an African American symbolically for their staffs. "If there is ever a situation, and there probably are throughout the country, where there are certain coaches that just hire an African American coach just for the sake of having an African American on staff and really do not challenge him to his fullest potential, I think that is one of the biggest tragedies that you could do as a coach."

"Race plays a factor in everything," notes Yale's James Jones. "There are bigots in every area."

In addition to the idea that race plays a role in who gets hired and who gets fired, the color of a coach's skin can come into play on the court as well. Mike Davis has been critical of referees, accusing them indirectly of racism in their refereeing, then retracting and saying he didn't accuse them of racism, but rather felt that officials held his inexperience and youth against him. But Tim Carter has no confusion about the issue. "I have definitely seen where it [the impact of race] comes to officiating and how my teams are treated. I think every minority coach who has ever had three white officials do their game, the natural tendency is to think that you might not get a fair shake."

Race is never an easy issue to talk about, and some coaches interviewed for this book refused to talk on the record about their own experiences. Officials, coaches, and athletic directors are human, and humans are influenced by a variety of emotions—some good, some bad. Perhaps more black coaches will get opportunities in the future. Perhaps college basketball will lead the way in diversifying the coaching ranks. Perhaps.

Bill Self was dressed in a pair of blue jeans, a white turtleneck and a Nike Illinois windbreaker. He sat on a folding chair underneath a basket in Assembly Hall in Champaign, drinking a cup of water. He leaned back in the chair, scratched his head and surveyed the action on the court. Self is a white southerner, along with his close friend and assistant Billy Gillispie. Joining them on the Illini staff are two African Americans, Wayne McClain and Norm Roberts. The players on Illinois' roster were about as even as you can get on a college basketball team today: seven African Americans and six whites. They existed in harmony, for the most part. They bonded not by race, but by class in school and common interests, and it seemed that the colors of the game at Illinois were simply orange and blue.

There were five players on the court as Self sat under the basket: Jerrance Howard, Nick Huge, Roger Powell, Lucas Johnson, and Blandon Ferguson. The rest of the team was sitting on the home bench watching. Coordinating the movements was Gillispie, dressed in a pair of blue Nike sweats with a gray Illinois basketball shirt. He was holding a packet of stapled papers, motioning with his hands, as if directing a movie scene.

"Lucas, you are Recker. Rog, you're Evans. Now in thumbs down, Recker will do a UCLA cut as Evans pops out of the block," Gillispie illustrated by moving, sometimes grabbing a player and directing him to a spot. The players on the floor, the "scout team" for the moment, were walking through Iowa's offensive sets the day before the Illini's showdown with the Hawkeyes.

Illinois had beaten Michigan at home three days earlier, 94-70, led by Brian Cook's 20 points. Self did follow through on his plan to shake things up after the losses to Wisconsin and Purdue. He decided to start Blandon Ferguson for Sean Harrington. But when Frank Williams showed up five minutes late for the Michigan game, he found himself starting the game on the bench, and Ferguson started alongside Harrington. Williams was off the bench four minutes into the game and finished with 14 points. After the game, neither the player nor his coach made a big deal out of the benching, pointing out that Williams' tardiness was a rare mistake. Illinois played again without Damir Krupalija, still nursing a bad ankle, and without Lucas Johnson, who did, however, practice before the game for the first time this season. The Illini cruised to the win, shooting 68% from the floor and holding Michigan to just 38.1%, extending their home-unbeaten streak to 26.

Illinois had already practiced for close to an hour and a half on their home floor ("sloppily" according to Self) before Gillispie's scouting report on the Hawkeyes. Gillispie walked the five players on the floor through close to 25 different offensive plays and out-of-bounds plays run by Iowa. The squad on the bench watched the walk-through, trying hard to pay attention, but it was clear they might have been lost after the first few sets. It was hard to remember where players were moving on the first set, let alone another 24. But on it went for almost 30 minutes, with Gillispie the director, positioning his actors.

After finishing the floor exercises, the team retreated to the Illinois locker room for the actual scouting report. On the left side of the large wipeboard in the locker room was a personnel report on the Hawkeyes, written in blue. Under each Iowa player was his jersey number, key stats, and tendencies like "goes left on drives" or "pump-fake before shot." Every Hawkeye player had some scouting tendencies listed, even the ones who only got a few minutes a game.

On the right side of the wipeboard were 20 diagrams of offensive plays, each a half-court drawing with five numbers, arrows, and a name. For "42," there is an arrow indicating a "1" move to another position on the floor, while additional arrows indicate other player movements. The diagrams on the board are the print versions of what Gillispie just finished walking the players through. He rapidly went through each play, noting the key Iowa player in each set.

At the conclusion of the diagram diagnostic, Gillispie, with input from Self, talked about the keys to winning the game. Summed up, it came down to containing Recker, trapping Evans, watching the deep Ryan Hogan threes and being prepared for Pierre Pierce to drive to the hoop. The coach turned on a VCR and television in the locker room, and the team and coaches watched various Iowa possessions from their previous games.

After the team clips, there were shorter individual film clips of Iowa players and their tendencies. The film session lasted just under 10 minutes.

In that practice alone, the Illinois coaching staff spent close to an hour and a half telling their team about Iowa. Gillispie, the assistant assigned to scout the Hawkeyes, spent many times simply preparing the report and diagrams. He sat and watched seven Iowa games on film, slowing down the tape to diagram plays, noting tendencies, and picking out possessions to put on a "possession tape." It was a very thorough scouting job. But would it work? "I don't know how much our kids really take in," Self admits. "But if you repeat things a bunch of times, some of it will eventually sink in."

To Self, the goal of scouting and preparation is not to make his players memorize names, stats, and diagrams, but to make them familiar with an opponent. In a game situation the next night against Iowa, Self wanted his players to be able to recognize who can do what on Iowa's team and to be able to react quickly to directions from the bench. Often, an assistant coach will shout out what offensive set an opponent is running and quickly remind players where their opponent may go.

After Illinois concluded practice, Iowa was to take the floor at Assembly Hall at 6:00 P.M. to shoot. On his way out of the arena, Self ran into Steve Alford as he and his team made their way from the bus onto the floor. It was a brief and cordial conversation between the two, as they genuinely respected each other, despite the rivalry between the schools. They asked about one another's team injuries, and got the usual coach-speak answers, and then went on their way. It's always somewhat awkward that close to a game.

"They don't like us and we don't like them," Self was quoted the day before the game. The coaches like each other but the fans do not. Much of the animosity stems from an incident in the late 1980s between the coaching staffs. Both schools were recruiting Deon Thomas out of Chicago, and the battle turned ugly. Bruce Pearl, then an assistant at Iowa, taped a phone conversation between himself and Thomas, in which the recruit allegedly admitted that he had been offered money and a car (a charge he later denied by Illinois). Pearl turned the tape into the NCAA and after an 18-month investigation, the NCAA concluded there was no proof of improprieties. However, the NCAA did find a "lack of institutional control" at Illinois and banned it from the postseason for one year and limited the Illini to offering just two scholarships to recruits for a period of two years. Illinois fans have never forgotten.

In a very light shootaround for 45 minutes, Iowa players took turns shooting jumpers and free throws at either end of the court to get accustomed to the rims and atmosphere. Alford, dressed in black slacks and an Iowa sweatshirt, joked with his players and coaches. Assistants Rich Walker and Brian Jones pulled aside some of the Hawkeye players to remind them of their defensive assignments.

Before leaving Iowa City earlier in the day, No. 17 Iowa had gone over the scouting report and conducted a light workout at Carver-Hawkeye Arena. That night at the Hawthorne Suites in Champaign, Alford would again go over the scouting report, as his players sat with their notebooks open. For Iowa, the keys would be hitting the offensive and defensive boards, sticking to Frank Williams and Cory Bradford, playing physical underneath the basket and limiting their own turnovers. Getting to the foul line and converting would also be critical.

After his team's practice, and after returning some calls in his office, Self headed over to the Theta sorority house on the Illinois campus for his weekly radio show. Throughout the season, his Monday night show was broadcast from a variety of residences around campus, from fraternity row to freshmen dorms. The goal was to liven up the show and increase the student interest in Illini basketball. Self sat in a plush chair, surrounded by students sitting on the floor, dressed in orange and blue, answering their questions and some from callers.

The next day, Self got into the office around 11:30 A.M., returned some calls, watched some more tape, and met the team at Assembly Hall for shootaround at 3:00 P.M. The players joked with one another, as did the coaches, and assistant Norm Roberts even jumped into a shooting game with the guards. No. 11 Illinois split into bigs and smalls and ran shooting drills at both ends in five-minute periods, then shot free throws. Gillispie went over again most of the Iowa offensive sets and the out-of-bounds plays. Earlier in the day at 11:00 A.M., the Hawkeyes had practiced, doing shooting drills, taking free throws, and running offensive sets. Their coaching staff would remind the team of their keys to the game, the ones already ingrained in the players' heads from the various scouting reports.

Later that day, moments before their showdown on Tuesday, January 15, the Iowa Hawkeyes sat quietly in a cramped visitor's locker room in Assembly Hall. Alford pleaded with the team to stay focused and to think about their assignments as he headed out the door. At Assembly Hall, the visiting coaches' room is across a 20-foot hallway from the visitors' locker room, and coaches must make their way through security, ushers, fans, and players to get there. Alford would make the walk eight times that night.

"It's pretty simple, guys," Alford said, returning to the locker room. "We need to help each other out there on the floor tonight. We need to get to the line and make them. If we take 30 or more free throws and convert 80% of them, we will win this game. And our bench needs to be great too. I think our bench is better than theirs, so let's use it to our advantage." Alford, as though he knew what lay ahead, concluded by saying, "watch for the lobs—they love to lob."

Steve Alford wants, in fact expects, his players to want it as bad as he does and to be capable of doing what he did. It is reflective of Alford's competitiveness, of his desire for perfection. He does trust his players' fundamentals, but doesn't seem to trust their ability to understand and to desire. The amount of information that Alford provides his players is overwhelming and he expects them to remember it all—because he can. After all, he learned the game from Bobby Knight, who prepared his team so well his teams knew what was coming.

Across the hallway and around the corner, a mere 25 feet from Iowa's locker room, Self prepared his troops for battle as well. Reminding them to contain Recker and double-team Evans down low, Self was calm on the outside but excited on the inside. "The atmosphere will be great tonight," he pointed out. "Let's not get too caught up in all that."

Indeed, Assembly Hall would be loud. Illinois fans saw Iowa as a real hated enemy. At Illinois, opposing teams are seated just feet from the rowdy student section known as the "Orange Krush." Legendary for hurling insults and jeers at opposing players and coaches, they were in top form this night. Just minutes into the game, as Alford was out of his seat protesting a call, the chants of "Sit down, Bobby!" and "Baby Bobby!" began, a reference to Alford's mentor, Bobby Knight.

Illinois retained possession from the tip and their first play of the game was a lob—exactly what Alford had predicted. As Brian Cook slammed it home, the look on Alford's face said it all. The first half was a battle, and literally turned into one with 8:14 remaining. Iowa's Sean Sonderleiter was called for a hard intentional foul when he grabbed the waist of Illinois' Robert Archibald who was headed to the hoop on a fast break. Tempers flared and Archibald got in Sonderleiter's face; their teammates moved in and the crowd rose to their feet. "It was a hard foul," Self told the media after the game, "but I don't think it was anything close to punching or throwing."

Perhaps incited by the confrontation, Illinois went on a 10-3 run en route to a 15-point lead as Cook hit his second three of the game. Recker, who had not scored a point 13 minutes into the game, suddenly came alive and scored Iowa's next seven to trim the lead to eight. With 3:16 left in the half, Illinois led 33-22. In a matchup of major accomplishment versus major potential, Illinois' Williams and Iowa's Pierre Pierce got into a jawing match minutes before halftime. Williams had been known to talk a little trash on the court, and Pierce was not intimidated by the All-American. But Pierce was not smart enough to know that getting Williams angry is not a good thing. Iowa's Reggie Evans quickly got between Williams and Pierce and then got in Pierce's face in an attempt to calm him down, telling him to shutup. By halftime, the lead for Illinois had shrunk to five and Iowa was back in it, thanks to Pierce's scoring the final five points of the half, including a desperation three at the buzzer.

"The first 10 minutes was all Illinois but the second 10 was all Iowa," Alford began his halftime talk. As his players got retaped, grabbed water, and pumped each other up, Alford made the walk across the hall to the coaches' room, where his assistants joined him. The coach returned to the team moments later. "It is going to come down to who wants this more. How bad do you want it?" he rhetorically asked his team. From the look on their faces, they wanted it, but how much was unclear.

In his locker room, Self talked to his team about poise, about playing smart basketball and about making sure they were on their defensive assignments. He praised them for the good start, but got after them about the lazy finish to the half. "This is our game to win," he told his guys.

The second half was all Frank Williams. He made unbelievable passes in the game, including one, a behind-the-back-over-the-shoulder-no-look-while-flying-out-of-bounds pass. He wowed the sellout crowd with a no-look, behind-the-back pass on an Illinois breakaway. He scored at will, pulling up and driving to the basket. He finished the game close to a triple-double, scoring 16 points, dishing out nine assists, grabbing seven rebounds, and making four steals. "He was awesome," Self said after the game. "I don't think there are very many people in America who can dominate the game without shooting the basketball. And that's what he does." When a reporter asked Williams after the game about one of his incredible passes, the star replied, "Which pass are you talking about?"

Williams' heroics, Cook's 21 points, Iowa's poor shooting from the field, and the Hawkeyes' horrible free throw shooting gave Illinois the 77-66 win. The Illini's strategy of limiting Recker and Evans worked, as Recker scored just 16 points and Evans added 12, both well below their averages. Illinois went on a 23-8 run in the second half to pull away as they hit nine three-pointers. Damir Krupalija was expected to make his return, but did not play.

"That was awesome," Self said excitedly in the locker room afterward, the most animated he had been all season. "That is how you play basketball." He continued, "They could not play with us tonight, but let's not forget they are a very good basketball team." (Because of the unbalanced Big Ten schedule, Illinois would not have to face Iowa again, unless they met in the Big Ten Tournament.) "We are on our way," Self concluded, and before the team huddled for its chant, Self added, "Let's say Big Ten champs like we really mean it." It was the loudest chant of the season.

For Iowa, it was their second straight loss; they were outplayed and out toughed. In the stuffy locker room, Alford questioned the team's heart and willingness to do the things necessary to win. After the Iowa players showered and Alford faced the media upstairs in the media room, the players began to stream out of the locker room to talk with friends and family loitering outside. Upon his return from the pressroom, the coach wanted to talk to the team again, so the managers and assistants hustled the players back into the locker room. In a defining 10-minute monologue, Alford talked about the season, about playing with grit and selflessness, about how he would make changes to the lineup and practices until he got five guys putting in effort. The team made its way to the bus, heads down, in silence.

In the ensuing days, Alford again promised changes and pointed to Christmas break as a turning point when the fundamentals seemed to collapse. His players tried to find the answers publicly, with Glen Worley saying that there were "too many outside influences" affecting the team. The coach criticized Recker for being out of shape and playing poor defense and Evans for a lack of concentration and a shoddy work ethic in games. Recker accepted blame, but Evans seemingly was at a loss. With Pierce and Chauncey Leslie getting the guard minutes, the rumor mill had Brody Boyd transferring to Valparaiso, a rumor he denied.

It is hard to pinpoint exactly when things started to crumble. Maybe it was the home loss to Indiana 77-66 on a Sunday afternoon, with the nation watching on CBS as Alford faced his past. The poor performance at Illinois did nothing to help the cause, as the Hawkeyes lost by 11 with their two stars, Evans and Recker, combining for just 15 points in the first half. Maybe things began to crumble back in November after the Globetrotter loss or the upset at Northern Iowa or the late game debacle against Missouri. There were signs. As Iowa prepared for Northwestern, it was clear to the coach and to his players that they were on shaky ground and in crisis mode. But nothing could prepare them for the catastrophic collapse that awaited them in Evanston.

After the loss at Illinois, Alford decided his team was playing selfishly and changes needed to be made. Those who worked hard in practice would be rewarded with playing time, he promised his team. The team returned to Iowa City and began to focus on Northwestern, just days away. By tip-off on Saturday in Evanston, the lineup in fact did not change, nor did the poor effort and lack of Hawkeye spirit.

The 63-50 loss to Northwestern was "embarrassing," according to Alford, but the score and Iowa's performance on the court was nothing compared to the internal combustion off the court. Iowa had missed 17 free throws, shot only 30.8% on 16 for 52 shooting from the field and threw the ball away 17 times. They played with little effort and even less heart, two things an Alford-coached team must never do. The Hawkeyes lost their third game in a row and had hit rock bottom.

With just over a minute to go in the game, Alford motioned for starting freshman point guard Pierre Pierce to come off the bench and sub for Brody Boyd. The game was already in the loss column for Iowa and Alford wanted Pierce to get the extra minute or so of action. Pierce grudgingly got up out of his seat with his head down, and began to walk slowly toward the scorer's table to check in. Maybe it was Pierce's body language, or maybe the stress of the third consecutive loss had finally gotten to Alford. Before Pierce could get past the bench, Alford stuck his arm out and stopped Pierce's progress. "You sit down!" the coach screamed, almost shoving Pierce back to his seat. He called a time-out. (Later, Alford pointed to that moment when he first thought that the poor attitude of the upperclassmen had rubbed off on the younger guys.)

A player in any sport hates to be in the coach's doghouse, especially at the end of a loss. Pierce made the mistake of making it worse for himself and for his coach. As the players sat disgusted on the bench, waiting for Alford's words, their coach was heard shouting about their poor effort and lack of toughness to his assistants. These were not quiet comments between coaches, and perhaps were intended to send a message. In his mind, Steve Alford, the player, could never imagine not being willing to go into a game, no matter the score or time remaining. And as a player for Bobby Knight, it wasn't even an option.

The game concluded and the team headed to the locker room, listened to their incensed coach talk about pride, unselfish play, and heart. He told the team that he thought that he had compromised too much, gave them too much freedom. He pointed to a leadership void and a lack of team chemistry. What more could be wrong? Alford then faced the media.

"We wanted to make it a new season," Alford began, "but we did that tonight in about the worst way we could do it. Now our backs are against the wall in a lot of different ways." The coach continued, "For the first time, I've realized the chant of 'overrated' does make sense. I've got to get my team back."

In his talk with reporters, Alford pointed to his players' unwillingness to work hard over the Christmas break or to listen to the coaching staff. He ended his remarks with a promise. "We will not play like this, with this kind of effort and this kind of [lack of] paying attention to what we want to do offensively and defensively again. I've got to get that point to the team. I'll do that tonight on the way home on the bus."

But Alford would not do that, because he never rode the bus back to Iowa. The team had taken a bus from Iowa City to Chicago for the game, a four-hour ride, supposedly to bond. Before boarding after the game, Alford decided not to ride back with the team. His anger and fury would only exacerbate the problems, so he decided to hop on a private plane with a team booster. So as the players and assistant coaches settled in for a long trip, Alford, his mother, and son Bryce were on their way to Iowa in less than 50 minutes. Assistant coach Greg Lansing took them to the airport—Lansing would be spending the next day on the road recruiting—and they discussed what would come next.

The team bus was quiet, with some players dozing off, others listening to Jay-Z on their headphones, and others talking about the game. Recker was the team's vocal and emotional leader and, as a former player for Knight, he knew what was coming. "He will be there waiting for us," Recker told the younger guys, predicting that Alford would be sitting in Carver-Hawkeye Arena waiting for the team to arrive. "I played for Coach Knight and I guarantee that he will meet us and we will practice." The younger players disagreed, noting that it would be close to 2:30 A.M. when they returned, and their coach would surely be sleeping at home or watching game tape in his living room.

Upon his return to Iowa City, Alford was still fuming and searching for answers. There were the physical mistakes, the turnovers, missed free throws, and poor shooting. But what ate at him more was the poor effort and lack of heart his team had displayed. He knew that he could not lose his team now. No matter how pissed off he was, he knew that the Big Ten season was a long one, and he needed to get them refocused. Some of the players were unhappy with their lack of playing time. Others questioned the playing of Recker and Evans when they hadn't practiced. Still others wondered to themselves and to teammates if Iowa was really the place for them. Recker was angry with Alford at times, believing that he was being singled out by his coach and Alford was frustrated with Recker for a lack of leadership and selfish play.

Alford put on a T-shirt, grabbed a ball, and headed to the court in Carver-Hawkeye. He had called the managers in, those who did not travel to Chicago, to rebound balls for him and to help him devise a plan. This was after midnight. Alford stepped to the free throw line and did what he does best—shoot. He took 200 free throws in a cold, empty arena and made 193 of them, "without trying," he would say later. He wondered to himself how his team could miss so many free throws in a game (17) when he could make 193 out of 200 (97%) in the middle of the night. And that was where the crisis revealed itself. Alford wanted his team to want it as much as he did. He wanted them to dig deep like he did. He wanted them to make 97% of their free throws.

After shooting at the line, the coach retreated to the locker room with the managers who had come in to help. They were pissed off, too. Not for having been called in at such a late hour, but for the poor play of their fellow students. They knew that this team was better than the three consecutive losses, and they themselves questioned how much the players really wanted it. In many programs, coaches don't know managers' names, let alone allow for their input. But perhaps because there was no one else around, or perhaps because he knew of their loyalty, Alford asked for suggestions. How could he send a message to the team? What should he do to turn this around? Hesitant at first, the managers became engaged, empowered as part of the decision-making process.

The result of the group brainstorm turned the Iowa locker room area into something very different. One of the managers went into a back room and emerged with a roll of construction tape. If the players didn't want it that much, then perhaps they didn't deserve their state-of-the-art players' lounge with phones, large screen TV, beverages, plush leather couches and, most importantly, video game console. Tape was put across the entranceway from the locker room area to the players lounge, affixed with a sign reading, "Coaches Only. No Players Allowed." They had taken away the players' privileges, and now they would take away their identities.

Turning their attention to the locker area, Alford and the managers took down the players' pictures of themselves and of their girlfriends, families, etc. They covered up the nameplates with tape and took out many personal items from the lockers. The locker room was now truly a team locker room, stripping each of the players of their individuality, similar to what Mike Krzyzewski had done weeks earlier after Duke's loss to lowly Florida State.

The emotional message would be sent, but what about those free throws? Alford devised a plan: he would have each player shoot five free throws, with the number of misses resulting in that number of team step sprints or court runs. Using his managers as willing participants, the coach determined how long it might take his players to run the steps of the arena and to do full court sprints.

It was 2:15 A.M., he was getting tired, and his team was still on the road. The coach was given updates on the bus' proximity as the managers with him were relaying messages from the on-board manager. "Mile marker 254, 15 minutes from arrival," they would report to their commander. As Alford relaxed on a couch in the coaches' lounge, he realized this was hardly a time for sleep, though exhaustion had set in. The bus finally approached and he took his position.

The bus pulled up to the back runway of the arena where trucks and teams unload. The players anxiously got off the bus and collected their bags, scanning the area for Alford. As they walked down the tunnel into the arena, they could see down the long hallway that the court lights were on. "This can't be? He really isn't there, is he?" they asked one another. As they proceeded down the hallway, they saw Alford, arms crossed, sitting on the team bench. A manager put it simply: "Coach wants everyone on the floor in five minutes."

Five minutes later, Alford talked to his team about the loss and where they would go from there. It would start now, here, with free throws—and collective punishments. Alford put his plan into action. Each player shot five free throws, and the misses turned into team sprints. One after another, the players stepped to the line and the team did more sprints. By the time the "practice" was over, it was 3:45 A.M. in Iowa City. Fortunately, Iowa University was still on winter break so the players did not have homework or classes to worry about.

By the next afternoon, Sunday, January 20, when the team practiced "for real," they had gotten the message—sort of. In front of hundreds of kids, ironically observing the practice as part of a youth league community day that Alford himself had organized, the Hawkeyes practiced hard. The changes that Alford had promised were realized. All-American and team leader Recker was now on the Gold team, or second string, in scrimmages. This sent a clear message to whomever was watching. But Recker and his fellow Gold teammates did not respond with the expected effort and were dominated by the new starting five Blacks. Alford decided that the next day of practice would determine the starters for the home game against Michigan State on Tuesday.

In the meantime, the bandwagon was getting lighter. There was grumbling among the Iowa faithful about the losing streak and about Alford's ability to pull Iowa out of it. The "illegitimate media," the Internet crowd, attacked "Stevie Wonder," as Alford had been nicknamed by them, criticizing his lack of compatibility with Iowa and accusing him of not being fully committed to the Hawkeyes.

Hawk1324 posted: "Is it me or does it seem Alford doesn't want to be coaching here? The losses mount, yet he doesn't make changes like he promised. I think he is as over-rated as his team."

Alford was not in a good mood, and sometimes an unhappy coach finds the little things to criticize. Before the Michigan State game, Alford was quoted in the *Iowa City Gazette* pointing out the complacency and aloofness of his team. "We had guys before the Northwestern game who ended up not liking the pregame meal. We're talking about a $15 to $18 meal probably that a lot of people end up killing for. We've gotten so picky, our pregame meals aren't right." Things are pretty bad when the pregame food is a topic of concern.

By Tuesday afternoon, Alford decided to start Evans, Jared Reiner, Glen Worley, Ryan Hogan, and Pierce. (Pierce had come into the office on Sunday before practice and apologized to Alford for the Northwestern incident at the end of the game.) But as the MSU game time approached, all of the players had not arrived for the pregame rituals. Pierce was missing. Alford immediately went to the tunnel entrance, where his star freshman would arrive, and waited for him. Pierce arrived 15 minutes late, got an earful from his coach, and lost his starting position.

In his pregame speech, Alford talked about intensity, selflessness, and solid defending. What more could he say? No more rah-rah speeches could be made. It was now or never. The game would be nationally televised on ESPN and the Hawkeyes faced a Spartan team that had beaten them six straight times. There was a lot riding on this game.

In the end, the late-night practice, soul searching, and construction tape paid off, as Iowa won a tight game 75-71 to end the losing slide. They made 23 of 31 free throws (74%) and hit six of seven in the last 1:30 of the game to win it. It was Recker, who started the game on the bench, and Pierce, who joined Recker on the bench, who won it for Iowa at the line in the final minutes. The team played with passion, diving for loose balls and mounting a stellar defense, but most importantly, it stayed focused.

The game was not perfect, and Recker and Alford did exchange words late in the game. Alford yelled at Recker because he believed the player had not tried hard enough to get around a screen and then had talked back to his coach. That quickly earned him a spot on the bench and a stern threat from Alford, but the All-American would be back in the game in a matter of minutes.

The postgame comments from Recker said it all. "It's not a monkey, it seemed like we had a gorilla on our back. He jumped off tonight, thank goodness." He continued, "We needed a big win like this. We couldn't afford to lose another one on our home court. We dug it out at the end and that's what's important." As for his benching, "My sister called me today and said, 'It's not who starts the game, it's who finishes the game.' Obviously, I'd like to start, but whatever is best for the team, I'll do."

Alford was beaming with pride, like a father of a kid who hit the homerun. "I'm very proud of our basketball team. We've been through a lot the last ten days. I told the team, 'You can easily start thinking about your failures. But you didn't do that. You focused on what you came here to do.'"

Alford learned about crisis management from Bobby Knight, and, obviously, his methods are not universally accepted. To some, a 2:30 A.M. practice may seem a bit unfair, even cruel. But to Alford and his team, it was what they needed. Alford had taken the approach that a slump, a losing streak, and internal strife could be sweated away with hard work. He did it himself as a child, and he learned from the best. "You have got to stay constant with who you are," the coach was quoted as saying before the season started. "You got to like who you are, and then, because of liking and believing in who you are, then your team is probably going to like you and believe in who you are." Perhaps he and his team would show their true colors.

16

The Men in Black—and White

UCLA PLAYED PHENOMENALLY IN ITS GAME AGAINST TOP-RANKED KANSAS AND THEY looked to continue their solid play on the road against Arizona State and Arizona. In Tempe, the Bruins simply looked awful, barely escaping with an 82-79 victory, sealed only by a missed buzzer-shot by the Sun Devils' Curtis Millage. Dijon Thompson sat out with a sprained ankle, and Rico Hines was saddled with lingering effects from his concussion, though he had played against Kansas. Cedric Bozeman returned to the starting lineup, but did not score in 23 minutes of action. Steve Lavin summed up many of the Bruin deficiencies in a postgame remark. "We've got a lot of areas to improve on— time and score, late-game situations, too many open three-point shooters. We didn't use enough clock. They missed some crucial free throws. That can add up to a loss somewhere down the road."

That loss wasn't "somewhere" down the road, but just 48 hours later and 120 miles down the road in Tucson, as the Bruins faced Arizona. The Wildcats had gotten off to a surprising start to the season, with victories over Florida and Kentucky. Lute Olson returned only one starter after three of his key players left early for the NBA and one graduated. It was an incredible start for the Wildcats and perhaps Olson's best coaching job of his career. Against first place USC on Thursday night, the Wildcats crushed the visitors by 17 points. UCLA had climbed to No. 9 in the polls and was 13-3, 5-1 in PAC-10 play. They had lost three straight to No. 15 Arizona at the McKale Center and the Bruin seniors had never won a game there.

The game started off well enough for Lavin's troops, with Matt Barnes scoring on a layup just five seconds into the game. UCLA's first eight made shots included six threes, which gave them a 23-9 lead and they appeared to be playing their best basketball of the season. By halftime, they had increased their lead to 15, 58-43, relying on record-setting three-point shooting, hitting 11 of 17 three-point shots.

"In the first half," Lavin said after the game, "we played as well as we have all season."

The torrid shooting continued as the second half got underway, as UCLA hit five of their first six shots, including three trifectas, to increase their lead to 20, 73-53 with 13:37 left in the game. This was a defining game for Lavin's team and defeating a ranked Arizona team on the road for first place in the PAC-10 would be sweet. But then came a collapse of record-breaking proportions. In a span of just under four minutes, the Wildcats erased the deficit, sparked by a 27-2 run, and took a 80-75 lead with seven minutes to play. It would be the most remarkable four minutes in the college basketball season. Lavin called timeout during the amazing run trying to calm his team, reassuring them that with good defense, they were still going to win it. But the psychological damage in losing that big of lead in such a short period of time may have been too much to overcome. Jason Kapono and Barnes did hit threes, to cut the lead to one with 4:56 to go, but unbelievably, UCLA did not score another point, missing their last eight shots. The Bruins had scored 58 points in the first half, but managed only 28 in the second. The final score was 96-86.

"We lost our heads," Kapono said after the game, clearly understating the calamity that had just occurred. "This is the most disappointed I have been all season. For us to not win here all my career, then be up by 20 and lose by 10, is really heartbreaking."

He had done his part, scoring 25 points and tying a school record with seven three-pointers. As a team, the Bruins set a school record for threes with 17. What do you say to your team after such a crushing loss? Lavin maintained his composure as he addressed his team in the locker room after the game. "I am disappointed that we couldn't get a win down here for our seniors," Lavin began. "We played well in the first half, probably our best half of basketball at Arizona since I have been here. This hurts, I know, but we need to work on the things to help us in March." There was another fact that did not bode well for UCLA. In the three years that UCLA had beaten the Wildcats at Arizona since Lavin came to UCLA, 1992, 1995, and 1997, the Bruins had gone on to win the PAC-10 title. Maybe it was not meant to be.

The cafeterias on the campus of the University of Notre Dame resemble most colleges' libraries. With ornate hand-carved wooden walls, chandeliers, and the atmosphere of an Ivy League library or gothic church, it seems almost sacrilegious to eat macaroni, green Jell-O, and drink soda at the tables. The South Dining Hall holds close to a thousand and at 6:30 P.M., things were at a fevered pitch as underclassmen threw their meals down. On Thursday night, January 17, students were just returning for classes after the Christmas break and the Notre Dame athletic department arranged a pep rally for Mike Brey and his players during dinner. It seemed like a good idea; a built-in audience at a time when most were not sleeping. Brey and his players were going to try to pump up support for their Saturday home game against Kentucky on national television. It was important for the team, but also for potential recruits, that the Joyce Center be packed and loud. The promotions staff had arranged for thousands of green shirts to be handed out at the Pep Rally and at the game to make an impressive display on CBS.

As the students ate their meals, Brey arrived and immediately got a standing ovation from the front part of the crowd. He walked over to some of the tables and gave students high-fives and handshakes. He was given a microphone, stepped onto a chair, and began to address the crowd. "We need you at our games," he began, and educated them on why a great crowd on Saturday was so important. He went on to explain RPI to the students listening (the ones in the back seemed to have no clue what was going on). Brey still captured the attention of hundreds and methodically explained how a win over a team like Kentucky could help them come Tournament time.

"And we also need you for Georgetown on Monday," Brey concluded. "I talked to Dr. Hatch [the Provost] and Monk [the President] and you don't need to crack your books until Tuesday," to which the cafeteria crowd responded with a loud roar and applause.

Playing against Kentucky at home was a highlight of the Irish schedule and a chance for them to prove that they belonged in basketball's elite. Kentucky was one of the game's most storied programs, along with UCLA, Kansas, and North Carolina, and a win on national television would let the country know that the Irish were for real. Brey was a little tense in the days leading up to the game and practice that Thursday was indicative of just how important the game was. After the tough three-game road swing, on which the Irish went 2-1, the coach gave the players Tuesday and Wednesday off to rest. But as the Irish slugged through practice on Thursday, Brey was not happy with the effort and the lack of concentration by his players, particularly his seniors. Around 4:30 P.M., the coach had enough and asked the managers to clear out any spectators watching practice in the Joyce Center, which included former Irish coach and South Bend resident Digger Phelps.

Brey was pissed. He began to rip into the team for their shoddy work ethic, lack of effort, and for not playing tough in practice and in games. His voice grew louder and the coach became uncomfortable with the potential listening ears in the arena, so he reconvened the team in The Pit and continued his assault. It was rare that Brey lost his cool, and even rarer that his team practiced with little effort and heart. His guys got the message. After a frustrating practice, Brey headed over to the dining hall for the Pep Rally.

The team and coaches had a better attitude with a light practice on Friday afternoon, and after the team Mass and dinner, it seemed that the Thursday episode had been forgotten. The atmosphere on Saturday for the noon tip-off was unlike any the Irish fans had seen in years. A sold-out game, with students camped out the night before to get good seats in the student section. Brey made his way into the office around 9:30 A.M. His assistants were already there, making phone calls and talking with recruits who were in town for the game. The promotions staff and Brey had gotten what they wanted inside the arena, a sea of green shirts and a rowdy student section. Fans, including the "wine and cheese" crowd, as Brey referred to the older alumni and donors, were greeted by green T-shirts on their seats upon arrival. Encouraged by the student body, almost all of them put the shirt on over their nice Saturday dress. It made for an impressive sight on CBS.

Ironically, Brey was more relaxed than usual in the locker room before the game, joking with his team and assistants. He told his players earlier in the week that the athletic department would add some spotlights, music, and drama to pregame introductions for the big game. But by game time, the arrangements could not be made and after breaking the news to his guys in the locker room, Brey told them, "I know I promised you the spotlights, but I will stand behind you and shine a flashlight on your head. How about that?" The players cracked up. Before letting them onto the floor, he talked about resiliency after losses (having lost to Syracuse five days earlier) and reminded them to have fun.

Kentucky was the third straight ranked opponent for Notre Dame, who had already faced Pittsburgh and Syracuse the previous week. The game was particularly poignant for Notre Dame senior David Graves. Graves hailed from Lexington, Kentucky, where UK basketball is a religion and way of life. He grew up watching Wildcat games and in his junior high and high school years, lived next door to Rick Pitino and his family, and still considered the former UK coach and now Louisville coach as a godfather. Graves' career at Notre Dame had not been easy and, like fellow senior Harold Swanagan, he had played under three coaches in four years in South Bend.

In his junior season at Notre Dame in 2000–2001, Graves had not been playing well going into a road game versus Virginia Tech, one in which the Irish could clinch the Big East West title for the first time ever. He played poorly again in the game, yet the team won, securing their postseason berth. Graves was not happy and did not understand his role. That night in a Blacksburg hotel, he knocked on his coach's hotel room door at 11:00 P.M. For the next four hours, he would pour his heart and tears out to his coach, in a search for answers. On a night when Brey should have been receiving congratulatory calls and relaxing, he was sitting on a bed talking to one of his star players until 3:00 A.M.

"That talk meant so much to me," Graves remembers. "It was a bad time for me. I didn't start the Tech game and thought I wasn't a part of this team. Coach Brey talked to me for hours about what I bring to the table and it helped me keep my head on straight. I will always remember that talk."

It would be great to think that Brey's only motivation was to keep Graves happy. But there was a reason behind everything. Brey knew that an unhappy Graves could mean trouble for a team on a roll. If he became disillusioned and practiced poorly, it could affect other guys and Brey wanted no part of that. So on the bed that night he listened, talked, and listened some more. "That night, I think I became more of a friend than a coach," Brey says. "But I guess being a friend is part of coaching."

Despite the tension at times between the two, the senior has the utmost respect for his coach. "You go and admire somebody who puts themselves in a position to be just bombarded with hatred and negativity," Graves reflects. "You look at him [Brey] and the way he handles it and the way he conducts himself under the toughest conditions. You want to play hard and you want to give it your all so you don't let him down."

Brey is a master of psychology. He knows that the game is 90% mental and therefore as a coach, spends a great deal of time preparing his players to win the mental battle. Having sit-downs with players like Graves, calling a freshman the night before a big game, or knowing when a player had a bad day in class, are all part of coaching to Brey. His emotions translate messages to his players, which is why you will rarely find Brey panicking or outwardly fretting a loss. He leads by example, and knows that his players are watching.

With this in mind, Brey went out of his way to talk with his captain in the days leading up to the Kentucky game and in the moments before tip-off. He knew that Graves would be emotional and try to do too much. Usually in these instances, players either have huge career nights or they fall flat. Brey hoped for the former. As usual, Graves had shot for an hour at midnight the night before the game and was in the Joyce Center shooting three hours before tip-off.

Both teams played well in the first half, but the visitors played better. With 7:45 to go in the half, the teams were tied at 20, and in his timeout huddle Brey switched to the "32" defense, hoping Notre Dame could pressure Kentucky into rushed shots. "We are playing well so let's keep it up," were his last words to his players as they retook the floor.

After a back and forth opening 16 minutes, Notre Dame's Jordan Cornette scored on an offensive rebound and was fouled to pull Notre Dame to 34-33, but Cornette could not convert the free throw. Kentucky's Cliff Hawkins scored on the next possession and stole the ball from the Irish's Chris Markwood and scored again, opening up a five-point lead for Kentucky en route to a 41-35 halftime lead.

"We played very efficient basketball and they played really well," Brey began his halftime talk, not raising his voice or chastising his players. "Let's be real careful about taking quick shots." Brey left the players alone for a few minutes and when he returned, he continued his caring tone. "If we play like that in the second half, efficiently, we have a chance to win this thing," he told his team. Graves sat and listened, though a frustrating opening 20 minutes did not leave him much to raise his head about.

At halftime of the game, new Irish football coach Tyrone Willingham was introduced to the crowd and was given a standing ovation, perhaps more out of relief than expectations. Brey had spent a few minutes with Willingham the previous week and came away thinking, "impressive." The football coach at Notre Dame is the king, so having a king you like is good. Brey thought that having an African American football coach could only help in recruiting African American basketball players.

The second half opened with Kentucky's Keith Bogans, a graduate of DeMatha High School, where Brey had played and coached, hitting a three to increase the lead to nine, but a 7-0 Irish run cut the lead down to two and excited the Joyce Center crowd. The experienced Wildcats did not wilt, however, and turned up the defense, prohibiting Notre Dame from scoring for the next five minutes to put the game out of reach. The final score was 72-65. Notre Dame had let Bogans score 23 points, including five for eight shooting from beyond the arc. Matt Carroll led the Irish with 18 and Ryan Humphrey had 14, despite numerous double-teams. Chris Thomas struggled on four for 15 shooting and Graves finished the game with 12 points, six from three-pointers.

The loss dropped the Irish to 1-4 on national television for the season, but they would have another chance to get a win on Monday night when Big East foe Georgetown came to town.

"We played well, we just came up short," Brey told his team in the postgame locker room. "We don't have time to pout guys, we've got Georgetown on Monday in 48 hours and need to regroup."

In the Kentucky game, Swanagan had not played well and, in fact, was limited to just 23 minutes. His bad ankle had gotten worse, despite efforts by trainer Skip Meyer, and Brey had to make a decision. Immediately after the Kentucky game, it became clear to the coach what he had to do: sit Swanny. He did not want to battle a very rough Georgetown team without his toughest player, but Brey looked at the bigger picture and knew that by resting Swanagan now, he might have him down the season's stretch. He broke the news to Swanagan the next day before practice and the senior captain took it well.

The team met Sunday afternoon for a film session and light walk-through. In the players' lounge, the team and coaches gathered to watch parts of the Kentucky game. Brey started and stopped the tape with the remote, pointing out mainly positives. He knew he had to remain positive to set a tone for his players, because if he didn't panic, then perhaps they wouldn't. After watching tape for twenty minutes, the team walked into the adjoining locker room where the Georgetown scouting report was already written on the board. Assistant coach Anthony Solomon quickly went over the personnel and Brey chimed in with his thoughts.

On the board, Brey had listed the current Big East standings, with Notre Dame at 2-2. "We are still in this thing," he told his team; the team believed him. Just four games into the conference season, Brey and his team were already thinking about positioning for March. That's the way college basketball is these days. Coaches are always looking ahead. They log onto the Internet every day to see the results of other games, to check Web sites like *collegerpi.com*, which calculates the ever-important RPI. They play out scenarios in their heads and on paper. Earlier in the day, Brey asked Sean Kearney to do a bit of research, to find the RPIs and records of the at-large teams from the 2001 Tournament, to see what it might take for the Irish to get in.

After the film session, scouting report, and the peek ahead to March, the team hit the floor and played a hard 20 minutes of the 5-on-5. Brey went over the defensive schemes and quickly walked through two of Georgetown's offensive sets. The coach had never been a big believer in overscouting, and did not usually walk through opposition plays with his team. His film sessions are short, his scouting reports even shorter, and he doesn't seem too interested in what the other team is doing when it comes to preparing his team. It's a practice he developed after years on Krzyzewski's staff at Duke, where the head man would have his assistants up all hours of the night watching and breaking down film and preparing detailed scouting reports. Brey thought to himself back then that when he became a head coach, he would keep meetings, scouting, and film review to a minimum, so his staff and players would not get burned out.

On game days, Brey usually arrives at the office late, depending on commitments on campus, and often will go home around 4:30 P.M. to change and grab a quick moment before returning for the chaos. At 3:00 P.M. on game day against Georgetown, Brey hopped into his SUV and drove from his office across campus to one of the all-boys dorms, where the team would gather for Mass. This day, Mass was held in a first-floor chapel, which seats about 100, and the players and coaches spread out in the various rows. The service felt more religious, being conducted in the chapel, as opposed to a hotel banquet room, with the adornments of Jesus on the walls, the stained glass windows, and the piano. On this day, leading the service was Deacon Samuel Peters, a Jon Gruden look-alike. Kearney did the reading from the Gospel of Mark, and Peters began a two-minute sermon. As a basketball player himself, he fully understood the game and the emotions that came with playing it.

The passage read by Kearney was about stringent rules placed on followers, who spend so much time trying to adhere to rules that they cannot flourish as people. "It is like placing an old piece of cloth on a new jacket," Peters told the team. "Sometimes, it can be a restraint."

"Does anyone know what they used to do after every basket in college basketball?" he asked the players. "They would do a jump ball. How about Notre Dame games long ago when there was no shot clock? They would run 4 corners for 10 minutes. Today's athlete is different, with more ability and athleticism. You need to be able to reach that potential and not be shackled by rules." The players nod in agreement, understanding the Scriptures more with a basketball analogy. The service concluded with the greetings and Communion.

The team headed to the nearby on-campus restaurant/café and in a private room, sat down for the pregame meal of chicken, pasta, salad, and fruit. As per custom, the seniors got their food first, followed by the juniors, and so on. The coaching staff usually waits until the players are seated. Brey was calm, but had that look in his eyes, the one that says you can talk to me, but don't bother me. He decided to start Jordan Cornette for Swanagan, a big move and one for which Brey hoped Cornette would be ready.

Dressed in a black turtleneck and black pants, he seemed uptight before the Georgetown tip-off. He took the team down to The Pit a half an hour before the game to walk through the two Georgetown sets that he had gone over the day before in practice. "We need to play tough and efficient," he told the team, knowing that the former would be hard without Swanagan. Having already lost two in a row, the Irish really couldn't afford another Big East defeat, particularly at home.

As the game got underway, Brey's worst fears were realized, as the Hoyas took advantage of size and strength and went down low with the ball from the start. Mike Sweetney grabbed every rebound (11) and scored 11 points in the opening 12 minutes of the game. Down 22-12 at a timeout at 11:51, Brey remained remarkably calm. "We're not playing well right now," he told his team, something they already knew. "Grab a rebound and hold on to the ball. And box somebody out."

As the first half continued, the play continued to be physical and, at one point, the officials stopped the game so Irish trainer Skip Meyer could wipe someone's blood off the court. Notre Dame's Jere Macura got into a jawing match with Georgetown's Harvey Thomas to highlight the rough play. Georgetown increased its lead to 33-18. Notre Dame shots were not falling, particularly from deep, and they had no answer for Sweetney or guard Kevin Braswell. Even the Hoyas' Courtland Freeman got into the act, scoring 11 points in the game and finishing with seven rebounds.

"This ain't a game for no choir boys," Brey blasted into the locker room, his team trailing by 11 at the half. He was furious at the pretty play once again from his team, and did not allow them to use the loss of Swanny as an excuse. "Somebody get some man in them and play like you are not scared of these guys," his calmness from the first half seemingly disappeared.

Settling down a bit with his assistants, he talked with them about changing the defensive schemes as the coaches met in the players' lounge. In a much more hushed tone, Brey talked about getting Torrian Jones more involved and "boy, how they really missed Swanny." After a few minutes, manager Greg Weber entered and gave a copy of the stats to each coach, who then took 40 seconds of quiet time to pour over them. "I think we have to go with Torrian," Solomon remarked. "David is just not getting it done."

Graves remained in a shooting slump and it was affecting his play on the defensive side of the ball as well. Brey and the assistants decided to let Graves start, but to get Jones a lot of time in the second half. (Graves went 1-9 with five points against the Hoyas and sat on the bench for the last 11:33 of the game.) They all agreed that Georgetown was the best team they had faced all year. The Irish had shot the ball fairly well and their defense wasn't atrocious; they were simply getting outplayed and outmuscled. As the game clock in the player's lounge hit 7:00, Brey got up and walked into the locker room.

"First of all, let's play tougher," Brey said. "It is rough out there. Let us talk to the officials, you guys keep your mouths shut. No extracurricular stuff, no B.S. either. Just play like men. This is a 20-minute battle, now let's go."

Notre Dame came out inspired in the second half, behind solid play from Humphrey down low, and the Irish were able to cut the Hoya lead to 11 with five minutes to go in the game. At the conclusion of a 20-9 run on a Matt Carroll three, the lead was still seven. With 1:15 left, Brey had had enough of his team, and the officials. Georgetown's Gerard Riley was fouled and missed the front end of a one-and-one, but Sweetney grabbed the rebound over the shoulder of Carroll.

From the early minutes of the game, Brey had been out of his seat protesting calls to official John Cloughtery. (By the end of the game, the fouls were 19-18, not out of the normal range of a typical game.) Sometimes though, losing brings out a more critical eye from coaches, as they look for someone to blame, someone to take out their frustrations on, someone like a ref.

As the second half wound down, there were hard fouls committed by both teams, but it was clear that Notre Dame was being manhandled. The referee crew that day was a diverse one. Cloughtery was an older, shorter gentleman with silver hair who had been around for years—maybe too long according to some coaches. Also on the crew was Teddy

Valentine, a well-respected veteran ref who kept the calm in many games. Curtis Shaw was the third member of the Big East crew, a relative newcomer compared to his crewmates.

Carroll had gone up for the rebound, and was apparently pushed from behind by the Hoyas' 6'10", 310-lb. Sweetney. There was no call on the play and with the offensive rebound, the game was basically over. But as the Hoyas got set again in their offense, there was an extra person on the court.

Upset at the no-call on Sweetney, Brey not only walked onto the court, he proceeded to walk all of the way to the center of court, standing on the Notre Dame logo. At first, the players and refs did not know how to react. And then Clougherty called a technical on Brey. As the coach walked off the court back to the bench, he used his last few steps to get in the ear of Clougherty, arguing his case to no avail. Valentine came over and told Brey "I'm not going to throw you out, Mike." The final minute wound down and the Hoyas came away with a 10-point victory.

What was surprising about Brey's technical was not that he had walked onto the court in the middle of a play. Nor was it that he got it at a critical time in the game. What was so shocking was that he got a technical at all. In his seven years as a head coach at Delaware and Notre Dame, Brey had received only *four* technicals, all of them in his years at Delaware. He did not have a reputation as a hothead and was not into the theatrics of many coaches. But on this day, in this game, he knew it was time for his fifth. "I knew exactly what I was doing. It was more for our players and our fans that someone would at least make a stand before the game was over," Brey would comment later.

After the game, he would look at the game tape and see that in fact, Sweetney had not fouled Carroll. It didn't matter. He had made his point for that game. In fact, as soon as he returned to the bench, Brey was as calm as a sunset. Even ESPN broadcaster Bill Raftery commented that the technical seemed "orchestrated."

Brey was not the first coach, of course, to plan out a technical. Some coaches use it to inspire their teams. Others use it to send a message to a particular referee who they might see again in the season. Still others, unfortunately, play to the television cameras and the fans and seek a confrontation for little other than the purpose of show. But the technical is a rarity in most games. In fact, over the course of a year, coaches average fewer than two technicals a season each. A technical foul on a coach is usually the culmination of many smaller outbursts or conversations between coach and referee. It is the last straw. The dynamics of the relationship between coach and ref is about negotiation, about pushing the envelope, and about the consequences for doing so.

Hank Nichols was the NCAA Officials Coordinator of Men's Basketball, having spent over 20 years on the floor as a man in stripes. He's got plenty of stories about memorable games he's reffed and even better ones about some of the coaches he has listened to over the years. Of all of the coaches that have been in his ear, he points to the late N.C. State coach Jim Valvano as the most entertaining.

"I was doing a game at N.C. State and Valvano became upset at some of the calls early in the game. He started yelling at me and I just walked down the court. The next time down, he is still yelling. I said 'Easy it does it, Jim.' About the third or fourth time down the floor, he is really hollering, and I say 'Jim, you've got to stop it or I have to give you a technical.' So he calls a timeout. Gives me a finger motioning for me to come over, so I do. I said, 'What's up, coach?' He says, 'Can you give me a technical for what I am thinking?' I said 'Of course not.' He says, 'Well, I think you stink.' I laughed so hard I couldn't even think about giving him a T."

Valvano was not the first, nor last, coach to crack jokes at the expense of the men in stripes. Many of the game's great personalities have had their share of encounters with refs, some funny, some heated, some resulting in ejections. One thing has changed, however, over the years, and that is the relationship between coach and ref.

"Up until the last 15 years, you could have fun with the coaches," reflects Nichols, who along with his brother, has reffed thousands of games. "You had to be on your toes because coaches had some zingers. But it's not like that anymore."

Perhaps the officials, the most objective in the game, the ones immune to the growing pressures in college basketball, have changed along with the game. As coaches are under greater pressure to win, with every call seeming to mean the difference between winning and losing, the pressure on referees has increased as well. Most games are not won or lost on one foul call, however, and, if they are, it is usually a correct call. Though the pressures have changed for both coaches and officials, their relationship is still unique.

Nichols has seen it all in his years in the refereeing business, and what used to be very friendly, humorous conversations on and off the court between coaches and refs, has turned into a me versus them attitude. But he doesn't blame coaches, he blames the system. "I think that coaches will be quicker to get upset because they know if they don't get into the NCAA Tournament, they don't win 20 games, that they are going to lose their job quicker than they used to. There's no fun left between coaches and refs anymore because of the pressure. Everybody is just so uptight because of the pressure."

Manhattan coach Bobby Gonzalez responds, "The Ws and Ls don't go on their record. The refs and coaches will always be on opposite sides of the fence. No matter how good you may be with refs, I don't think it is a winning situation."

We know about Bobby Knight throwing the chair. We have heard the stories of John Thompson towering over a ref. And we know what fans have to say about the refs, especially the hometown ones. But for good or bad, they are part of the game, and part of a coach's life.

Many coaches feel that the deck is stacked against them, that particular referees are out to get them, and that for the most part, they get shafted on calls. The reality is that calls usually even up over the course of a game and over a season. There are particular refs who certain coaches dread having assigned to their games. Perhaps they had a run-in at a previous game or perhaps the coach simply thinks the ref stinks. Whatever the situation, coaches often take a look at referee assignments on game day or even a week before, already thinking they might get screwed.

"When we played DePaul, I didn't recognize one of the ref's names," recalls Brey. "I say to myself, 'Is he a Conference USA ref? Does Pat [Kennedy] know him better than me? How many games has Pat had him on?' I guess coaches are a little paranoid."

"Pure math says that the breaks even out," conjures Pepperdine coach Paul Westphal. "Over a long period of time the breaks even out. Every coach understands that, but there's not one coach who believes it. I think what bothers coaches and players the most about referees is when they'll never admit they made a mistake. I just want them to acknowledge that maybe they missed one once in a while. Then I'll sit down and let them work."

Phil Martelli at St. Joseph's looks at a refereeing assignment and looks to see who is in charge. If there is an "A" guy on the crew, a respected veteran ref, it doesn't bother him. "When you're in an outside environment, on the road or in the Tournament, you find out right away who is in charge and then you have to trust that guy will not let it become the world of the bizarre." According to Martelli, refs do not decide the outcome of games, but they sure have an impact on the tone of the game. "It could be what they are calling or what they are not calling. To say that they don't have an impact on the game is foolish."

Veteran Loyola Marymount coach Steve Aggers takes a peek at the refereeing assignments, as "one man's junk is another man's treasure." The level and nature of the competition creates a feeling that certain officials are better than others, but Aggers is somewhat sympathetic. "They have a hard, hard job to do and they earn every penny for it."

Coaches will look to have any advantage with a referee. Before the tip-off of Indiana's game with Butler, Hoosier coach Mike Davis approached the officiating crew and asked them to watch Butler players grabbing onto jerseys, a tactic Davis had seen on tape in some of their previous games. Butler upset Indiana that night and Davis blasted the officiating after the game, going so far as to state that the refs may have held that pregame comment against Davis and his team.

Nichols admits that referees are human and do make mistakes, and they understand when games are more high profile. They read the papers, watch *SportsCenter*, they know when a lot is on the line in a game, but the good referees are not affected. And how about refs who are calling a game with a Krzyzewski or Williams or Olson? Can't that be a little intimidating? "Maybe some of the younger guys the first time in big games or with big time coaches are a little affected by it, but I don't think that is an issue."

As in many professions, the newer, less experienced referees start out at the lower levels where the spotlight is not as bright, much to the ire of mid-major coaches. The pressure is just as great for them and the consequences just as damning, but almost universally, they agree that the refereeing is not as good. "Let's face it, the refs at this level are trying to get to the next level but they are here for a reason," explains a mid-major coach. "If they were really good, they wouldn't be reffing at this level."

Farleigh-Dickinson coach Tom Green has been at the school for 19 years, and has outlasted four school presidents, six athletic directors, and numerous referees. "I've been around so long that I know a lot of these guys reffing our games. Of course, the better ones get plucked by the bigger conferences and are then on television."

Referees are human and, at times, their own emotions come out on the court in comments to players and coaches. Official Tim Higgins was accused of using profanity toward Boston College player Ryan Sydney during the Eagles matchup with Duke. "Shut the f— up and run down the court," Sydney claims Higgins screamed at him, aware that the player was unhappy with a noncall. Big East commissioner Mike Tranghese investigated the claim, but the results of his probe were not released. After a conference loss to Air Force early in the season, New Mexico coach Fran Fraschilla complained in the press that the referees were giving Air Force the benefit of the doubt and not calling fouls on them because of the September 11 tragedies. It was a far stretch for the coach—but was there any truth to it? And Portland coach Michael Holton recalls one game this past season when a referee gave him some unwanted and unwarranted advice. "I was asking about a call and he responded 'Get better players.' I said, 'We're working on that, but in the meantime it is still a foul.'"

Current American University coach and former Virginia coach Jeff Jones remembers a time early in his career, when referees would give him advice, though he didn't heed it. "There was a time when [referee] Fred Barakat told me that I may need to yell a little more. My whole point is that they are supposed to do a good job whether I yell or not. I don't want to accept that I have to yell to get somebody to do what they are supposed to do."

In a game in the early 1990s, Atlantic Ten head of officiating Mickey Crowley was refereeing a Temple game in which the Owls were up by close to 25 with just five minutes to go in the game. Chaney was trying to get his bench into the game at the scorer's table, but there wasn't a stoppage of play to sub them and Chaney didn't have any timeouts left to stop the clock. The opposing coach wouldn't call a timeout to get the guys in and there continued to be no dead balls.

"Coach, you want these guys in?" Crowley asked Chaney who replied in the affirmative.

So on the next Temple possession, Crowley called a travel on one of the Temple guards who was simply dribbling the ball. The player was incensed but Chaney was grateful to the ref and simply said, "Thanks."

With Iowa leading Michigan 74-54 at home on Senior Day, February 24, with just over 90 seconds to play, referee Steve Welmer called a "phantom" 30-second timeout to stop the clock and allow the Iowa seniors a chance to leave to an ovation. Alford knew that the ref was doing a classy thing by calling an officials' timeout. Referees are indeed human, and sometimes that makes the best ones better.

What makes an official great? John Chaney has his theories. "The great officials are not threatened at all by circumstances happening around them. They will gladly come over and talk to you, calm you down, and admit if they missed a call. A great official knows how to take the teeth out of a lion's mouth." A good official has a feel for the game, is not bigger than the game, and understands that he makes mistakes.

For Bill Self, the best officials are ones "that you don't know are there. I want them to be consistent. They are going to make mistakes but overall, just be consistent. They have a very hard job to do, but if I am doing my job well, then I shouldn't worry about the refs." Self admits to peeking ahead at refereeing assignments a week ahead of game day, but only for select games when officiating may play a key role, like in a game against a well-known physical opponent. But on some days, Self doesn't know who is reffing until he takes a seat on the bench.

ESPN's Andy Katz believes that refs are "too caught up themselves" and that there is too much "power control going on between refs and coaches." He points out that the rule limiting coaches to the coaching box is rarely enforced, as "some of these coaches could get called for three seconds."

Katz' media colleague, Clark Kellogg from CBS, also notices the rift between coaches and refs. "As much as they would like to discard that, I think sometimes little things come into play and create a chasm and friction that exist. Most coaches and refs try to be professionals about it."

In an article on *espn.com*, Katz wrote a story about the often overworked referees in college basketball, pointing out that some of the top refs would officiate about 90 games in the 2001–2002 season, including Welmer, who, at 51, flies from city to city each night to ref a game.

The top concern for many coaches is that referees do too many games, have too little time to review their work, and therefore do not get better. Former Virginia coach Terry Holland agrees. "The worst thing I think is that they call too many games and they go from last night's game to the next night's making the same mistakes they made the previous night. Coaches get fired for that and players lose their positions for that."

Coastal Carolina's Pete Strickland understands that his conference, the Big South, will get a big name ref for a Monday night game who was in the area doing an ACC game the previous night. Make a little extra and then hit the road. "Sometimes we get a top guy who does a great job, but often these guys don't want to be there, just get their money and get back home, especially after doing a big ACC game the night before."

"I think the money is tremendous for officiating right now," notes West Virginia's John Beilein. "They are under a lot of pressure to perform."

Referees are independent contractors, paid per game by leagues. Most refs usually officiate games near their geographical residence, and therefore become known as PAC-10 or ACC officials, though they have no contractual obligation to the league. Referees earn between $400 to 800 per game, depending on the conference and their level of experience. Pretty good money for a few hours of work, but for what they put up with, it is money well-earned. Refs also get travel money and per diem for meals, valued from $100 to $150 a day.

Some referees have no other jobs and simply earn a living off the game. Some run summer camps for players or for want-to-be refs. Some, like veteran ref Mark Reischling, are your typical high school English teachers by day and college referees by night. Reischling has been doing Division I games since 1976, primarily doing games in the WAC, WCC, PAC-10, and Big 12. He also reffed in the 2001 Final Four. "Officiating is all about seasoning. The more you do it, the better you often will get. For the largest percentage of officials in Division I, it [refereeing] is an avocation. For a few that are overexposed, it has become their vocation."

Reischling, like other referees, understands the immense pressure put on coaches to win, which therefore increases the pressures on the men reffing the games. "What other situation in life are you in such a volatile environment where people's jobs are on the line and there is a reasonable accounting of a play, which can be verified by videotape? How many times does that happen in a CEO's office when they say 'Let's go back to what happened in yesterday's meeting?'" Officials are cognizant of the magnitude of games, yet find a way to keep it in perspective and to drown out the atmosphere. "Officials want to have the opportunity to be in big games. But after those games, you want to be able to walk out of the building feeling that you took care of business and you didn't put your head down. As for the crowd, you don't really hear it, it is just a wall of sound. Now, in early season nonconference games with small crowds, you hear things—some of them are pretty funny."

For Reischling, those big games have included numerous NCAA Tournament games and a Final Four semifinal between Duke and Maryland in 2001. It was a culmination of years of hard work, a moment he could share with his family—and his students. But one of his most memorable games was not a Tournament game, but rather a regular season matchup between Fresno State and UTEP. Sounds crazy, but the coaches in that game were two Hall of Famers, Jerry Tarkanian and Don Haskins. "I don't even remember who won and who lost but just the fact that I was on the court that night was so meaningful to me."

As for dealing with coaches, the veteran referee says that it is all in how you handle them and communicate with them. Sometimes a simple smile or a nod is all it takes. "But you can't just ignore them, you have to say something. They just want to know that you are willing to listen. But they can't be a distraction."

Like Reischling, now retired official Tom Rucker was also an educator—for 35 years before retiring from teaching in 1997. He got into officiating by accident, telling the story to Terry Hutchens of the *Indianapolis Star*. Rucker and a friend were watching an intramural game at Wayne State University when the refs did not show up. Rucker was asked to fill in and he has been reffing ever since, from CYO games to high school to college. "I tell the young guys that every time you go out and work, you'll never know who's up in the stands watching the game." In a statement that says a lot about Rucker, and the relationship between coaches and referees, the former ref simply says, "It's all about the players, not the coaches."

USC was leading Arizona on February 16, 31-23, when Trojan Sam Clancy raced back the length of the court and apparently blocked Arizona's Rick Anderson's breakaway dunk attempt with less than five minutes to go in the first half. But referee Mark Ayotte called a foul on Clancy. Anderson stepped to the line to take his free throws when the whistle blew again. This time, a technical foul was called on USC coach Henry Bibby by Ayotte. In the days after the game, Bibby was quoted taking issue with the technical in the *Orange County Register*. "The technical foul was [B.S.]. I was talking about a foul and he said, 'Easy, easy, easy.' I told him, 'I don't have to take it easy, this is for first place in the PAC-10.' Is that deserving of a technical foul?"

Bibby was not just perturbed at the foul call on Clancy, but was irate at the technical called on him. "If I am annoying him that much, walk away from me. Tell me, 'Henry, I don't want to hear it' and walk away. You don't give a technical foul at that point in the game. Doesn't happen. And again, would big-name coaches get a technical foul on that? I don't think so."

While Bibby is never one to hold back, he brings up three good questions: 1) Why don't referees just walk away from confrontations? 2) Is there ever a *good* time to call a technical on a coach? 3) Is there truth to the perception that well-known coaches are not "T'd" up as often as others?

As for question No. 1, in most instances, the public never knows what is said in those heated confrontations between coach and referee, and if they are privy to the conversation, it is usually from the coach's side as referees are not available to the media after games. There are times when coaches clearly cross the line, but referees are not immune to sticking around for a good fight. The NCAA has tried to avoid these confrontations by having the "calling ref" or reporting ref, the one who called the foul, quickly move to a position on the far side of the court. A referee uninvolved in the foul call or dispute with the coach takes the position in front of the coach's bench. This is no accident. "It has always been part of the system," Nichols explains, "even when there were two men. The guy that reports the foul goes across the court. Stay out of the emotion and stay out of the confrontations when you can. That way it gives the coach a chance to settle."

It is a legitimate policy meant to avoid confrontations like the one between Bibby and Ayotte. Some refs may have reached the end of their tolerance level and a little utterance by a coach can get him a technical. Other refs may have a very high threshold for calling a "T," and are more likely to avoid confrontations, or know how to calm a coach down without giving him a technical.

As part of the three-man referee system, one of the referees is often positioned right next to a bench, getting an earful. In most cases, that ref is not the one drawing the ire of the coach, so the two men can have a conversation and the ref can attempt to settle the coach down. Take a look at an irate coach, and he is usually scowling at one particular ref, not just anyone in pinstripes.

In response to question No. 2, Bibby's statement that you don't give a technical "at that point in the game" is based on reality, not the rules. Bibby's observation is based on the actual practice, not the rulebook. Bibby has been around the game enough to know that most refs are cognizant of the game situation when deciding to give a coach a technical.

If referees were not aware of their environment, and called games strictly by the book, then we would see a lot more technicals called. The reason? Referees know game situations and know when a technical can influence the game. You will very rarely see a technical called on a coach in the last few minutes of a tight game, but often will see one against the losing coach in a blowout. Why? The consequences of giving a coach a technical when the outcome is decided are minimal versus assessing one in a two-point game. Refs also know that coaches use technical fouls as motivational tools, for setting the stage for a future game, and for venting frustrations. In those instances, experienced refs know how to handle the coach without assessing a technical.

As to the final question, do well-known and "big-name" coaches get a break when it comes to technicals? Referees will adamantly say no, as will "big-name" coaches, but many other coaches will acknowledge that refs are a lot slower and more lenient in assessing technicals on certain coaches. Maybe some big-name coaches don't act up as much as others and therefore are less deserving of a technical. Maybe they do cross the line but their celebrity keeps them out of trouble—something officials deny. It is indisputable that many of the well-known coaches have been around the game a long time and therefore have long-established relationships with many referees. Those relationships may help calm a coach down or prevent a ref from assessing a technical. Just as every referee has a different threshold for giving a tech, every coach has a different way of earning one.

Which brings us to the story of former Richmond coach John Beilein, now at West Virginia, who received one of the more improbable technicals in 2001. His Spiders were trailing William & Mary on the road and Beilein had been all over the referees in the first half. As the half came to a close, the teams and officials headed to their respective locker rooms, which at William & Mary are located down a flight of steps in the arena. The Richmond players entered their locker room as the coaching staff waited outside to discuss adjustments, as most staffs do. But located across the hall was the officials' locker room, and for some reason, the refs had trouble getting in. And that was trouble for Beilein.

"We were just talking as a staff but it wasn't good that the refs were locked out. I started in again about the officiating and things got a little heated. The next thing I know, referee Vinnie Evans pulled out his whistle, blew it, and gave me a technical. Right there in the hallway."

The scene was somewhat comedic, as you think about the ref blowing the whistle and giving the "T" sign in a downstairs hallway below the court. The Richmond players heard the whistle and stuck their heads out of the locker room to see what was going on. As the teams took the floor at the start of the second half, William & Mary made the technical free throw and scored on the ensuing possession. Those points would prove to be the difference in the game.

Dartmouth coach Dave Foucher made light of the reffing in a game in late February 2002. A ball went out-of-bounds and two refs looked at one another for the proper call. They couldn't decide, so there was a jump ball. Three minutes later, the same situation occurred, and the same scenario developed. At the next timeout, Foucher called the refs over. "Hey, you guys sure do have that call down. You practice that one pretty well." When the game was over, Foucher poked his head into the officials' locker room and jokingly asked, "Hey, did you see it? I didn't see it. How about you?"

At Coastal Carolina, coach Pete Strickland accidentally had six guys on the floor near the end of the game and was assessed a technical. He said to the ref sarcastically, "Mike, I thought they changed the rules. When you are down by 10 under five minutes, you can add a sixth player." At first the ref thought he was serious, then understood the sarcasm.

Terry Holland has seen hundreds of officials in his decades in basketball, and has come up with a very good question: Who would want to ref? "I think officials, by and large, do as good a job as they can. You've got to remember, you have created a set of parameters that make absolutely no sense. So, if you ask yourself why would someone want to be an official, you've eliminated a huge part of the population. It's almost like who would want to be president? Why should we wonder why these people who are president do crazy things?"

Mike Brey certainly wouldn't vote for the three guys he had against Georgetown that cold Monday in January. After he got the technical protesting the noncall on Mike Sweetney, the coach settled down as his Irish tried unsuccessfully to get back in the game in the last minute. Back in the locker room, there was a deafening silence. This loss was a tough one for the players and coaches.

"This is what Big East basketball is all about," Brey reminded them. "We can't wait on our heels before we start playing. We spotted them eight points at the start. I was talking to the assistants at halftime and Georgetown is the best team that we have faced this year. I think you realize that we can't play pretty anymore. No more pretty shots, holding your pose, like they have in the media guide," as the coach demonstrated a one-handed jump shot, freezing his position. "We got outplayed and outmuscled. It's one game and now we have to sneak one back somewhere. There were some positives so let's not hang our heads."

Brey walked over and put a hand on the shoulder of his star freshman point guard, Chris Thomas. With a brief smile, pat on the back, and encouraging words, the coach made sure his floor general was not too despondent over the loss. (At the conclusion of the season, Brey will reflect that the home loss to Georgetown was one of three memorable games and a defining point in the season for the Irish.)

In the conference room after the game, the coaches ate pizza and dissected the loss, much of which centered on the poor play of Graves. Against his home state team, Kentucky, Graves struggled mightily, scoring just 12 points. He played poorly again two days later against Georgetown, playing just 23 minutes. Even though he was averaging a career high 14.2 ppg, he was eight for 30 in the last three games.

Earlier in the day before the Georgetown game, Graves had gone to Brey's office and they had a heart-to-heart like they had a year earlier in a hotel room. Again pouring his emotions out to his coach, Graves needed Brey to help keep him focused. But talk can only do so much. After the poor performance against Georgetown, the staff agreed that a change needed to be made. Perhaps Torrian Jones could fill Graves spot in the lineup? As for more talks, the doctor was no longer in. "No more talks with Graves," Brey said the following day. "We are all talked out. It's about playing like a man now."

17

Command Is Lonely

F OR A PLAYER WHO GREW UP IN THE SPOTLIGHT, WHO DID INTERVIEWS WHEN HE WAS 10, who learned long ago not to listen to what others thought, who proved his nay-sayers wrong with hard work, who doesn't care what people think, this much is true: Steve Alford cares what Bobby Knight thinks.

In January 2002, as his team struggled through a horrendous losing streak culminating in the loss to Northwestern, and as Alford searched for answers, he decided to make the call. He dialed the 806 area code number for Texas Tech basketball and asked to speak with Coach Knight. It had been three years since the two men had spoken, with Knight even throwing barbs in 1999 when Alford returned with Iowa to Bloomington. It was not surprising that Alford chose this day, at this point in the season, to reach out to Knight. He was directionless but, more importantly, wanted a relationship with his college coach, perhaps the only validation that would mean anything. So he placed that call to Texas and got what he needed.

It was the first conversation between the two since March 1999. Knight congratulated his protégé on his coaching job last season and on his good start this year. The conversation then turned to what Alford could do to stop the bleeding now.

In fact, that call in January led to another, and soon developed into regular conversations between the two men. In one of the first talks between them, Knight pointed out to Alford how tough it is to win with the mixture of seniors on his team. Of the five playing for Alford, two had been recruited by previous coach Tom Davis and the other three were transfers. No one had been with Alford throughout, able to understand him and his methods. Knight told Alford to stick to his principles, that they were more important than any wins and losses. As the weeks went by after the initial conversations, Sam Alford noticed a change in his son, and Steve did as well.

"I let my guard down this year and did too much compromising. Since the phone calls, the team is playing better," the younger Alford remarked. "We're not getting the wins, but I don't have the same empty feeling after losing. Before when we lost, the things I did weren't right." Both men have been open about their conversations, and, in fact, looked forward to a visit to Texas by Alford in the summer. It had been a difficult season for him, a crisis situation, but one of the men he admired most had come to the rescue.

When is a crisis really not a crisis? Is Kansas losing to Ball State in their opening game of the season a crisis for the Jayhawks? How about Matt Doherty's North Carolina squad losing *at home* to Hampton and Davidson? Does the midseason Butler home loss to Wright State qualify as a crisis? What may seem like a crisis to fans may really be nothing more than a bad loss or two to a coach. Or what may seem like an innocent loss may be masking a real crisis in the locker room. Regardless of how one defines a crisis, or to which situation coaches may apply it, it is clear that coaches manage minicrises every day and some must face the larger abyss every season.

In reaction to his No. 1-ranked Blue Devils' road loss to lowly Florida State, Mike Krzyzewski had the players' locker room in Cameron Indoor Stadium cleansed of name plates, pictures and other identifying items, to make a point to his players that there was no "I" in team. Going into the early January game against the Seminoles, Duke was on a roll, having won all of its games by an average of 20 points. For Duke to lose to Florida State is, well, unacceptable. To some, it was a crisis for the Blue Devils, but to others, just an expected bump in the road. But their coach treated it like a crisis to get the point across to his team that a change was needed. Weeks later, Gonzaga coach Mark Few would take down pictures of previous Gonzaga NCAA Tournament teams from the Zags' locker room when his team played poorly in February. It was about playing in the moment, not relying on the past.

Mike Brey at Notre Dame has a unique take on adversity, one that is reflective of his personality. Brey is a cool customer, maintaining an even keel through low levels of despair and high levels of exaltation. To him, there never really is a crisis. There are bumps in the road and issues with which to deal, but none could ever reach the panic stage. At the same time Iowa was falling apart, the Irish were losing three in a row. Expectations for this year's squad were high, as the Notre Dame faithful had tasted the NCAA Tournament the previous year and wanted more.

As the losses mounted, Brey did not have midnight practices, but neither did he ignore the problems. Instead, he worked on the psychological component of coaching, creating an environment in which his players believed that they *could* win while continuing to praise the positives. He had a veteran team; they knew they should be playing better and, yes, perhaps a tweak in playing time or a sit-down with a key player might be necessary. But Brey believed that if he remained calm, it would lead to a calm team. If he did not panic and talk about "rock bottom" and crisis, then the team will not believe that things are out of control. "Some coaches love the crisis. They love to make every loss a catastrophe. Some do it as a motivation, while others do it because they love crisis. But hey, keep things in perspective and keep basketball in its place."

John Beilein takes a similar approach, noting that the term "crisis" is probably "too strong of a term." By keeping an even keel, not getting too excited or too down, Beilein keeps a balance. Even more intriguing to Beilein is the result that can come from the low points. "Sometimes the worst losses can turn your season around. You've got to find the positives, find another way to win. It is not a sprint, it is a marathon. You've got to just keep on going."

Many coaches around the country agree that there is some sadistic part of every coach that wants a crisis. They love hunkering down and dealing with problems. They love the challenge of bringing a team back. They love proving the critics and media wrong.

As Portland coach Michael Holton suffered through a 10-game losing streak in 2001–2002, he saw the opportunity for coaches and players to learn. "I probably operate best in adversity because I think of others. I didn't say, 'You guys are embarrassing me.' I looked at it from the standpoint of what can I do to keep them moving forward and to keep them together. In a sense, I just operated outside of myself from a feelings standpoint."

Star player Brandon Hunter of Ohio University had an awful game against Akron, frustrated by poor officiating, and Hunter took the loss too hard and too far, criticizing his teammates and turning over a ball rack in the locker room after the game. Head coach Tim O'Shea suspended Hunter for one game, and the team defeated Marshall without their star. What could have turned into a major crisis for a team was really simply a learning experience. Hunter learned that he had to control his emotions while the team learned that they could win without him. "We deal with minicrises all of the time," says O'Shea. "They have a way of working themselves out. It is important as coaches that we have solid emotions, not overreact to the ups and downs. We could have a crisis every day with academics, basketball, life, and player behavior."

Particularly in crisis situations, but ultimately every day, command is lonely. There it is. Simple, yet sad. From the POTUS to a high school principal to a head coach, leading is often very, very lonely. Perhaps it is the nature of the job, the many hours put in every day. Perhaps it is the celebrity, which comes from being in a highly visible profession. Or perhaps it is an internal mechanism in coaches that reminds them not to trust anyone. Whatever the cause, many coaches are lonely. Their wives are not only their best friends and partners, but their "buddies" as well.

Most coaches admit that they have very few close friends, and of those close friends, not many are in basketball. Coaches have a paradoxical relationship with each other. They hate to see bad things happen to each other, but they are all guilty of contributing to the losses that may have cost a coach his job. There is a certain amount of respect between most coaches, but you can't expect 321 men to be close. Coaches are bonded by past experiences together, by family trees, by mutual friends and, ultimately, by similar interests. But with competition and the pressure being at such a high level, the relationship between coaches has changed dramatically.

In yesteryear, teams would come into a town the night before a game and, after saying goodnight to his team, the opposing coach would go meet his counterpart for a late dinner to talk hoops and schmooze. This doesn't happen anymore. Not only have coaches drifted apart, but with scouting, film review, and preparation the night before, there simply is no time.

"On a night before a game, you are generally busy with your team," says Lute Olson. "When we are on the road, we have tape sessions at 9:30 every night before the game, so it is the last thing they do before they go to bed. Before, you would have a bit more flexibility to do what you wanted. Also, I think there is just a whole lot more pressure to win and a coach knows that if he is not spending the time at it, eventually he's not going to win." Today, Olson is friendly with most PAC-10 coaches, and points to Stanford coach Mike Montgomery as his best friend in the conference, mainly because Montgomery's wife and Olson's late wife became friendly.

The night before a meeting between Kansas and Indiana in 1994, which Kansas would win at the buzzer, Kansas coach Roy Williams went over to Indiana's hotel to give Bobby Knight some brownies that Roy's wife had made. Knight took the brownies and said, "Where is the mother f—ing ice cream?" Perhaps that is Knight being Knight, or perhaps that's as good as it gets between old friends now.

The demands of the job, the time-consuming nature of recruiting, and the competition for recruits do not allow coaches time, or motivation, for socialization. "I'm not buddies with very many coaches," Bill Self explains. "Some coaches have a clique with whom they talk everyday and there is nothing wrong with that. I'm not like that. In this business it is hard. It's hard to be buddy-buddy with guys that you're recruiting against and competing against."

"In recruiting you don't have much time to socialize, you have time for business," Self acknowledges. "I don't have time to pick up the phone and chat for an hour and I don't think other coaches do as well." In fact, as the recruiting battle for Ike Diogu heated up between Arizona State and Illinois, Self and Rob Evans did not speak, even though they are close friends. They both just kind of knew. When it was all over, Self picked up the phone, said congratulations and, "You know why we haven't been talking."

Underlying the issue of friendships between coaches is a sense of paranoia and mistrust. Does he really want to be my friend? What kind of information is he looking for? It seems childish or something out of a spy novel, but many coaches are not very trustful of others because they all are good salesmen. As Self noted, "I think coaches like to pick people for information so you have to take something for what it is worth."

For Rick Boyages at William & Mary, "I always hit it off better with people who have their own business and their own life." At Dartmouth, Dave Foucher doesn't pick up the phone often, or write letters to coaching friends. "If we see each other once a year or once every two years, it doesn't change. We're still friends."

Many coaches are tight with former colleagues, coaches they worked under or assistants with whom they worked. As their respective careers take them down different paths, they rely on each other for support, suggestions, and career advice. Bruiser Flint served under John Calipari at UMass and still talks to "Cal" two or three times a week. Flint speaks frequently with former Cal assistants, as well as Al Skinner, Mike Jarvis, and Phil Martelli. Bobby Gonzalez at Manhattan is tight with former bosses Rick Pitino and Pete Gillen, as well as Providence's Tim Welsh and Holy Cross' Ralph Willard.

And then, of course, there are those coaches who move up the ladder and forget about their friends or who view them with a different eye. "You know some friends of mine that have been at bigger programs for a long period of time," reflects Tom Green, "I think they look at the low- to mid-majors that way, like their job is more important."

Mike Brey and Tommy Amaker were close friends. They spent long nights together watching film, planning their futures, and joking with Coach K when they were assistants at Duke together. When Brey moved to Delaware and Amaker to Seton Hall, they continued their friendship, talking many times a week, sharing ideas and emotions. But then Brey got the job at Notre Dame and suddenly the two friends were competing against each other in the same conference and for the same recruits. They don't talk very often.

"Last year [2000–2001], we were winning the Big East West and Seton Hall was struggling. I called Tommy the night before our game and asked how he was doing. I mean, this is the night before a big game on CBS! We had won like nine in a row and they had lost like 10 in a row. Damn if they didn't beat us. First thing he says to me after the game is 'Hey, I really appreciated that call last night.' Sometimes we forget what we're all going through." Of course, Amaker left Seton Hall at the end of the summer to go to Michigan and he and Brey decided they could get back to where their friendship had been. "Unless we join the Big Ten, of course," Brey jokes.

But as Brey serves as a friend and mentor to Amaker, and to former Duke assistant and current Missouri coach Quin Snyder, Brey himself has a mentor—Mike Krzyzewski. "I talk to Mike maybe once a month, every six weeks when the season is underway. During the summer, when there is more time, he usually organizes our group going out, with Tommy and Quin." Though Brey remains close to his former boss, he clearly has become "his own man" and, in fact, at times seems a little annoyed when people ask him about Krzyzewski. He certainly still respects him and learned much from him and Morgan Wootten, but at age 43 with a Big East Championship, Brey is out of the Duke shadow.

You really know who your friends are when the going gets tough. Which coaches call you when you have lost five in a row or when you are about to get fired? When Nolan Richardson was on the hot seat for five days at Arkansas after his controversial remarks, the coach received calls from over 40 coaches, both friends and strangers, lending their support. When Steve Alford was down as his team struggled to finish the season, he relied heavily on his conversations with his college coach, Bobby Knight, as well as with many others. John Calipari called, so did Buzz Peterson at Tennessee, Steve Lavin at UCLA, and, ironically, Bill Self at Illinois. Though their schools are heated rivals, Self and Alford have a strong mutual respect for each other and Self picked up the phone in late February and gave Alford a call. "It was just a gesture from one coach to another," says Self. "It was not awkward at all—at least on my part. I think Steve is a good coach and was struggling. Just because our schools may hate each other doesn't mean we have to."

Tim Buckley gained a lot of respect around the nation after defeating Kansas and UCLA at the Maui Invitational. He may have gained respect from fellow coaches, but he is aware he didn't gain many friends. "I think that I respect what people have to say when they throw roses at you. But at the same time you have to understand that even though they say good things about you, they're also trying to figure out ways to beat you behind closed doors."

For Mike Davis at Indiana, being friends with other head coaches is not something he even wants to do. To him, the coaching circle is full of B.S. "I don't want to be in the coaching fraternity—they are always trying to get you," Davis exclaims. "They say bad things about you and it's a fake thing. It's not real. So I don't want to be a part of that. I respect a lot of coaches. I mean, I admire a lot of coaches. But I don't want to be a part of when you walk up to a coach, shake his hand and say 'blah, blah, blah' and then go bad mouth him to a kid."

For Davis, the friends he does have in the profession are assistant coaches. That's who he talked with before he became the Hoosier head coach so why would he make new friends now? In fact, when he was an assistant, "a lot of head coaches wouldn't even speak to you." He notes that coaches are often jealous of another's success, and inherently question whether a coach deserves a particular job, which clearly gets in the way of developing lasting friendships.

Sometimes as assistants, it is easier to develop friendships with other assistant coaches, since you may see them more on the road, have similar goals and still do not understand the loneliness of command. Jay Price, an assistant at Purdue, recounts the absurdity of avoiding the competition. "When Pat Knight was at Indiana, he was a friend, and when we would go watch a game together or recruit a kid, we would sit together and talk. People would come up to us and ask, 'Why are you sitting together?' We are not mortal enemies here. We all understand what everybody's going through and we understand how much it takes."

Paul Hewitt was a well-respected assistant coach and head coach at Siena before he was hired in 2000 to take over for Bobby Cremins at Georgia Tech. He has solid relationships with most coaches, perhaps reflective of his kind nature and warm personality. But he did not think for a minute that fellow ACC coaches would be calling. "No one called to say welcome or to congratulate me. Maybe it's because they were busy, but it's just the business. Bill Guthridge did come up to me at a summer game to say congratulations."

Billy Hahn at LaSalle is certainly not camera or people shy, but even an outgoing coach like Hahn admits to having very few friends whom he can trust. "I don't think in our business you can be out and about with a lot of people. Actual acquaintances where you are really tight with people in the business? There's not very many because we're all so competitive. There are only 300 coaches or so in the country, we all know of each other, but we're not good friends."

Another Philadelphia coach, St. Joseph's Phil Martelli, thinks the reason for so few solid friendships in the game is simple: ego. "It is a very egotistical job. I don't know that many people would admit that, but egotistically we are sitting here preparing for Gonzaga. I believe that the game plan that we come up with will be better than the one Mark Few at Gonzaga comes up with. That doesn't mean I think less of him. I want to think that what we do is at the highest level." As for being lonely, Martelli says, "There are only 300 guys who know exactly how you feel. The day after a loss, the day you don't get a recruit. You get a feeling of loneliness."

And that is the paradox of the coaching fraternity. There are so few men in the world who can truly understand what you go through on a daily basis, but those same men are the ones that cause you the heartache.

Martelli ended up developing great friendships with basketball coaches—*women's* basketball coaches. People like Geno Auriemma at Connecticut, Jim Foster at Vanderbilt, and Pat Knapp at Georgetown. They are coaches at the highest level so they can empathize with you, but he is not competing against them. Maybe that's the answer to coaches' isolation. Go to the women's Final Four and make new friends.

"There are a lot of jobs besides coaching which are lonely," notes Alabama's Mark Gottfried. "Being a pastor, a company CEO, those are lonely jobs, too." When Gottfried was a graduate assistant coach at UCLA in 1988, he sat next to his boss, Jim Harrick, on the bus headed to a shootaround at California. He asked his mentor what the biggest difference was between being an assistant and being a head coach. "Being a head coach is often lonely."

It's not just that loneliness comes from being in the public eye, being removed from the "commoners," but the necessity of the job is lonely as well. Coaches spend many days and nights on the road, in hotels, eating meals by themselves. Don't pity them, but understand how it can be isolating work.

A unique relationship developed in the late 1980s between a young kid from California and an older Midwestern throwback. Steve Lavin had come to Purdue first as an observer of Gene Keady and then as an assistant coach. He was only on Keady's staff for three years before heading to UCLA, but even in that small time frame, the odd couple developed a great respect and camaraderie for each other. "Socially he is like a brother, coaching he is like a son," reflects the 66-year-old Keady. "It's a relationship that is pretty unusual, there is a big age gap, but it's like there isn't one."

In 1997, Keady took his Purdue team out to Los Angeles to play Villanova in the John Wooden Classic. Purdue lost and Keady was embarrassed with their performance in front of Wooden. The team had planned to go to Disneyland after the game, but Keady was so furious with their play, he gave them each $12 for food and locked them in the hotel. Lavin and his girlfriend came up to Keady and his wife's hotel room and talked for five or six hours and then headed out to eat. "My wife is my best friend and my best judgment and Lavin is kind of like a son who tells his dad what to do. He was there for me when I needed him then."

History is what brings men together, says Pepperdine's Paul Westphal. Coaches who have a history together as coaches or players remain lifelong friends, but the demands of the job prevent new relationships from developing.

Westphal's neighbor in L.A., Steve Aggers at Loyola Marymount, is one of the classy, older generation coaches who understands the competitiveness, but doesn't view it as a battle between enemies. "It's based on mutual respect. There is nothing worse than having to compete against your friends. There are a lot of coaches who look at it as a battle against an enemy, whereas a lot of the older coaches look at it as competition against a respected opponent."

A grizzly veteran, Temple's John Chaney has a lot of good friends in the coaching fraternity, including Nolan Richardson, George Raveling, John Thompson, and Speedy Morris, yet most of his friends are not in the basketball world. "I don't break bread with a lot of coaches; you see them at conventions and stuff. I do talk to Lute Olson frequently and Vivian Stringer, the women's coach at Rutgers, almost nightly. I talk to Bob Knight once in a while."

Olson is a friend to many and a mentor to even more. He has earned the friendship of many older coaches and the respect of the young ones. Lavin talks openly about his admiration for Olson, going so far as to tell a television reporter at PAC-10 Media Day in October that he wanted to dress up as Olson for Halloween. Another fan of Olson is Marquette's Tom Crean, who remembers fondly time spent with the Arizona coach. "At the Nike retreat last summer, we were having dinner and it started to get dark. Some people went swimming, others took a walk. Lute and I stayed at the table and talked about a full-court press for hours. He was scribbling notes and diagrams on a piece of paper and a napkin. I still have the paper. Lute just loves the game and is willing to share his knowledge with many. It says a lot about the man." Crean also fondly recalls sitting in summer gyms late at night during recruiting season, when he was a young assistant to Tom Izzo at Michigan State, talking with Olson for hours when hardly anyone was left in the stands.

Another unique friendship of which Crean was a part came out of his current situation. He had always been a huge Marquette fan and his earliest memory of college basketball was watching Al McGuire win the national title in 1977 and then break down in tears. Little did he know that over 30 years later, he would be by McGuire's side as the legend was dying of cancer. "Coaching here at Marquette, he is Marquette basketball and has been such a great friend and mentor to me. Even up to his last days on this earth, he would always call me before games to see how I was doing and to lend advice if asked. It meant so much to me." Crean last saw his friend at his bedside three days before McGuire died in 2001. There was no one else in the room and he sat and talked basketball and life with the coach. It is a memory Crean will always cherish.

With the pressure and stakes so high, it is only natural for competition to spill over, sometimes in public, sometimes behind closed doors. There are some coaches who simply do not like each other. Maybe their personalities clash or maybe one thinks the other is a cheater. Perhaps an acquaintance turns into a heated rival by rough play in a game or by a pregame quote in the paper.

Coaching feuds have been going on since the invention of the game, and even the "nice" coaches have been known to mix it up. Dean Smith, the winningest coach of all time, had heated relationships with many coaches at one time or another, including conference foes Lefty Driesell, Terry Holland, Norm Sloan, and, yes, Mike Krzyzewski. One particular and well-publicized feud began in the 1995 ACC Tournament, as Smith's Tar Heels faced off against Rick Barnes' Clemson Tigers. The game was heated and Smith took offense at what he thought were hard and cheap fouls by Clemson players. At one point during the second half, Smith pulled a Clemson player aside and gave him a warning and talked to him about his play, infuriating Barnes. The emotions carried over into the postgame comments and things would never be the same between the two. In fact, a year later, Smith again talked to a Clemson player during a game, adding more fuel to the fire.

A legendary feud of the 1980s took place between Indiana's Bobby Knight and LSU coach Dale Brown, with accusations and barbs traded for years. At one point, Brown simply suggested, "They should put us naked in a room and have us wrestle."

Perhaps the most public, and extreme, coaching clash took place in 1997 during the Atlantic Ten Tournament, when John Chaney burst into Massachusetts' coach John Calipari's postgame press conference and threatened to kill him; the Temple coach was infuriated with physical play in the just-ended UMass victory. Caught on tape and replayed thousands of times, the incident became as well-known as the parties involved.

Roy Williams made accusations against Quin Snyder in 2000, alleging that Missouri was breaking rules in recruiting. The rumors spread quickly and, ultimately, Snyder picked up the phone to confront Williams and put the rumors to rest. Former South Carolina coach Eddie Fogler ripped into Florida's Billy Donovan's recruiting tactics a few years ago causing an uproar in the SEC.

Mike Brey is a "solid" guy, as coaches around the country will attest, and rarely does he take offense at another coach. To him, it's more than about being a nice guy. "I don't think you have time for grudges. You know, we all got a pretty good life. We all got a good gig now. It beats a real job. I don't have the time or energy to get into a grudge match with a guy or get into a pissing contest."

The most respected coaches in the game have been in intense rivalries that occasionally spill over into personal attacks. But they are the rare moments when competition grabs hold of common sense. For most coaches, they may not have to have too many friends, but they cannot have too many enemies.

Having all the friends in the world doesn't help you win ballgames, but it certainly makes coaches a bit more stable. Having rebounded from the three-game slide with a win over Michigan State at home, Iowa hit the road for a game against Purdue, who, despite the win over Illinois, was still struggling in the Big Ten. In a surprise to the Hawkeyes and to their coach, the Boilermakers shot the ball exceptionally well in the first half to take a 42-35 halftime lead. The lead would grow to as many as 17 in the second half, but Iowa continued to battle, cutting the lead to 71-65 with 46 seconds left. Late shooting heroics by Luke Recker were not enough as the Hawkeyes lost 73-68. Recker finished with 20 points, but Reggie Evans could only manage nine on just four shots. The Hawkeyes turned the ball over 22 times and fell to 3-5 in Big Ten play, 14-8 overall.

The chemistry issue on the Iowa team appeared to be between coaches and the team and between veterans and the rookies. The coaches were pissed that the players were not listening to them; the players felt disrespected by the coaching staff; the older guys felt threatened by the younger ones; and even the team's two leaders, Evans and Recker, were not getting along.

As Iowa continued to struggle, Illinois and Bill Self seemed to be OK. They had a convincing win at home against Wisconsin, 80-48, and not only did Self get a big win, but he witnessed the return of Damir Krupalija and Lucas Johnson to the lineup, earning a roar from the Assembly Hall crowd. Johnson had not played a minute all season, and it was emotional for him, and his coach, to see him make it back on the floor, three months to the day after surgery. Johnson scored five points in his return. Unbelievably, in that same rout against the Badgers, Frank Williams scored only two points and took only four shots. As Self reiterated after the game, sometimes when Williams doesn't score, his team plays better. Nick Smith started for Brian Cook who had arrived late for a pregame meeting.

At Indiana, Williams scored 11 points, all in the first half, in a dismal defensive effort by the Illini. The final score was 88-57, but it wasn't even that close. Indiana set a school record with 17 three-pointers, handing Illinois their worst loss in over 10 years. For its part, Illinois made only two threes, both in the closing seconds of the blowout. The Hoosier crowd chanted "Overrated!" for much of the second half and it was hard to argue the way No. 9 Illinois played. Despite being bigger and deeper, they were outrebounded 42-34. "They dominated us," Self said after the game. End of story. Illinois was 15-5 overall and 4-3 in the Big Ten, tied for third place. They were 0-3 on the road in conference play.

Things were better against Ohio State on the road on January 29, but the result was the same. Brent Darby scored 22 points and lifted No. 25 Ohio State to a 78-67 win over then No. 12 Illinois at Value City Arena. Illinois trailed by as many as 19 in the first half, spurred on by a 17-2 Ohio State run. The Illini fought back the rest of the way and pulled to within seven with 1:09 left in the game, but couldn't catch up. The loss dropped Illinois to 4-4 in Big Ten play, three games behind Indiana and Ohio State, who improved to 7-1. Robert Archibald and Williams each had 16 points to lead Illinois, who had now lost more conference games in January than the entire season last year. Indicative of the Illini problems was the stunning first half statistic that Ohio State had 11 assists and Illinois had but one.

After the game, Self and his players seemed shocked. They had lost again, even with the return of their big men, and were healthy for the first time all season. Why weren't they playing well now? "We need to get better every day. Forget about the league race and March. Each day we need to get better as a basketball team," Self demanded. In response to a reporter's question about whether Self was concerned, he replied, "Hell yeah, I'm concerned." The flight home to Champaign was a quiet one.

On Wednesday, January 30, Brian Cook headed home to Lincoln, Illinois, to spend time with his mom and his friends and to clear his mind. He was struggling on the court and was searching for answers. He returned on January 31 and met with Self, and the two had a heart-to-heart about basketball and life. Self was pleased with what he perceived to be Cook's changed attitude. Only time would tell.

Stanford's Mike Montgomery's nemesis in recent years has been Steve Lavin, who has taken his team into Maples Pavilion and beaten the No. 1-ranked Stanford Cardinal two years in a row on their home court. For his part, Montgomery has taken his team into Pauley and won four straight years. As the battle heated up in the newspapers, Stanford's Casey Jacobsen, a Southern California product, was quoted as saying, playing at Pauley "is like a home court" for Stanford, drawing the anger of Lavin. Bruin players accused

Jacobsen of guaranteeing a victory before last year's game at Pauley. Words from both sides appeared in print and the war of words was on by the time Stanford came down to play UCLA on January 24. UCLA was ranked No. 13 and Stanford was No. 17, entering the game with a 4-2 PAC-10 record.

"You are prepared now at this point in the season," Lavin told the team before tip-off, "now it's just a matter of execution. Watch [Casey] Jacobsen and [Julius] Barnes, make sure you guard them tight. And we must win in the red zone today." And then the coach strayed from the game at hand and revealed his inner thoughts to his team. "I feel better about this team right now and for the future than I have felt about any team in my six years here at UCLA," a comment both surprising and encouraging to his players. Lavin had some good teams, with guys like NBAers Baron Davis and Jelani McCoy. He turned back to his pal Montgomery. "As usual, Stanford and their coach have said some things in the paper this week, not to mention that they have won four in a row here. Let's take it to them."

Rico Hines had been having headaches before tip-off, likely an aftereffect of the concussion, so Bozeman started in his place. With a deep three-pointer by Jason Kapono, UCLA opened up an 18-10 lead midway through the first half, but then the hot shooting of the Cardinal took over. They outscored the Bruins 28-15 over the next eight minutes, including a 10-0 run, to take a 38-33 lead with just over four minutes left in the half. Even more devastating for the Bruins was Dan Gadzuric's picking up his third foul of the game with 2:06 left. Without the big man in the lineup, the Bruins had no answer for 7' Chris Borchardt.

In the locker room, the Bruins were soaked with sweat and were trailing by two, but not due to a lack of effort. "They are getting too many rebounds," Lavin pointed out. "This is our house, our paint, our living room. Don't let them come into our living room and steal rebounds from us."

After emphasizing the need for transition defense, boxing out, and containing penetration, the coach left his team with this thought: "In conference games you must play hard and this is one of them. It is a one possession game right now."

The first 10 minutes of the second half went back and forth, with neither team able to pull away. With 9:25 left in the game, the score was tied at 57. Gadzuric had already picked up his fourth foul minutes earlier and was sitting on the bench. Stanford went on an 18-7 run and never looked back. Jacobsen hit two three-pointers in the run and the sizable Stanford fan contingent went crazy. The Bruins fell apart toward the end, frustration resulting in a lack of concentration, a hanging of heads, and a failure to do the simple things like huddle before a free throw. The final was 86-76, with Jacobsen finishing with 20 and Barnes with 23—the two guys Lavin had told the team before the game they had to stop. The loss was the Bruins' second in a row, the first time they had lost back-to-back all season. Matt Barnes had 20 for UCLA and Gadzuric had 19, despite seeing plenty of time on the bench with foul trouble. The Stanford streak at Pauley continued. The Bruin youngsters, Bozeman, Andre Patterson, Dijon Thompson, and Ryan Walcott combined for only three points.

After this loss, the UCLA locker room was coaches and players only—no visitors. They met for 20 minutes, keeping the press and families waiting. "The good thing is we don't have to worry about the bandwagon now," Lavin said sarcastically but realistically. "They will all jump off, saying that we can't win another game, that we stink, that I can't coach."

He was well aware of what a home conference loss did to the bandwagon and to the media, fans, and critics, who no doubt would raise their voices in calling for Lavin's head. On the board in blue ink, Lavin wrote "Lose Game, Can't Lose Lesson," a theme he had preached throughout his career.

"We are 5-3 in PAC-10 play and we got beat in every possible way tonight. They were the better team. What I am more disappointed about is that we didn't stick together toward the end. We hung our heads, didn't huddle before free throws and showed no senior leadership. We need that out of Jason [Kapono], Gadz [Gadzuric], and Matt [Barnes]. It's tough without Rico in there." The coach knew that even though they lost, in a month they would be a team to be reckoned with, with a healthy lineup and experienced freshmen. After the team broke, Lavin spent a few private moments with Bozeman and Thompson, again reassuring the freshmen that the world had not ended and that they would have many more games to play.

"I'll just say this," Jacobson said after what would be his last trip to Pauley, "no matter what kind of quote they put on the board, I just want to let my play do the talking. I do enjoy coming to play here and who wouldn't? But I don't disrespect the program. I like all the players a lot and we're going to have to play them again."

His coach was a bit more direct, asking, "Why would you have to manufacture intensity?" a jab at Lavin's references to Stanford in pregame quotes. "We've won the conference the last three years. Shouldn't that be enough?"

After the tough loss to Stanford, John Wooden picked up some stationery and wrote a short letter to Lavin, encouraging him to keep his head up and to persevere despite the challenges.

Two days later, the Bruins faced another tough PAC-10 team, as Ben Braun brought the Cal Bears to Pauley with a 5-2 conference record. Lavin was frustrated with the two losses, the collapse against Arizona and the home loss to Stanford. He decided that his team, and his coaches, needed to keep things simple and upbeat. That new line of thinking was evident in his pregame talk before Cal. "You know what we need to do and you have heard this all before. Every game for the rest of the year is a big one," he continued. "Let's win and set up a first-place showdown with Oregon on Thursday." He kept it simple and short.

Gadzuric managed to keep himself out of foul trouble early on and the Bruins played inspired at times, including a 12-0 run midway through the first half. With under four minutes to go, Lavin emphasized defense in the timeout huddle. "On the ball, play tough defense. Off of the ball, play help defense." Kapono and Bozeman hit three-pointers in the closing minutes to put the Bruins ahead at half, 32-30.

"This is a grind it out game like we told you," Lavin began halftime. "You know what the biggest stat of the first half is?" he rhetorically asked his team. "Turnovers? Nope. Dan Gadzuric has zero fouls"—the team clapped and let out a laugh. Turning to the big man, Lavin said, "Now you can play wild and hard, don't go crazy but be aggressive."

Assistant coach Gerald Madkins, who scouted Cal, went up to the board and diagramed two plays that the Cal offense had been running in the first half, freeing them to get open looks because of a high pick. "How do you want to defend the pick?" he asked the team. Kapono, Barnes, and the dressed-in-street-clothes Ray Young all gave suggestions.

The second half was interesting as the introduction of the three-point shot to college basketball has always made the final 20 minutes fun. The Bruins maintained their lead but twice Cal got to within a point, the last with 10 minutes to go. Both times, UCLA got help from its freshmen, with Barnes scoring on a layup from a Bozeman assist and Thompson scoring off of a steal moments later. With 8:54 left, Bozeman hit a layup to give UCLA a 50-45 lead but Cal would not back down. Jamal Sampson and Joe Shipp hit free throws and Gadzuric and Bozeman missed on the front end of one-and-ones. Leading by three, UCLA finally broke free on a 14-10 run behind Billy Knight's consecutive baskets. Kapono hit a shot and followed that up with two free throws to give UCLA an eight-point lead with 22 seconds remaining. The final was 64-57. Cal could not repeat its heroics from two nights earlier when it beat USC in overtime on a deep three by Shantay Leggins at the buzzer. Hines returned to the Bruin lineup and played five minutes. The win snapped UCLA's two-game slide, moved them into a tie for second in the PAC-10 at 6-3 and more importantly, reminded the players that indeed, they were a solid basketball team.

"There are many positives from this game," Lavin began. "Great rebounding, solid defense, Rico's back, Dan's two fouls. The only negative was the turnovers. We played as a team, as on almost every possession except for two or three, we passed the ball and helped each other out. And now we have our showdown with Oregon."

As the team headed to the showers, Lavin reminded them of the dinner at the chancellor's that night, an annual affair with Grant-in-Aid donors, or GIAs, mingling with the team. "These are the real fans who have invested in your future."

The morning after the Stanford loss, John Wooden sat down and penned this letter to Lavin:

1/25/02
Dear Steve,

I was severely criticized when I permitted Notre Dame to score the last twelve points and break our eighty-eight game winning streak, permitting North Carolina State to overcome our eleven point lead in the second half and seven point lead in the first overtime in the Final Four in 1974 and told if a humming bird had my brains in his tail end, it would still fly backwards.

Others could not understand why it took me fifteen years to have a national championship team and why I did or did not do many things that all knowledgeable basketball fans knew.

Best of luck against California tomorrow and for the rest of the season. Those who know you, love and are with you and as Pearl Mesta said, "Those that mind don't matter and those who matter don't mind."

Keep it up.

Sincerely,

John

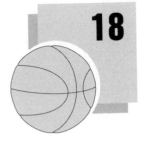

18

The Fourth Estate

IF THERE IS ONE RELIEF FOR A TEAM ON A LOSING STREAK, IT'S THE CHANCE TO RETURN home. For Bill Self, home was more than just a slight advantage. He had not lost in Assembly Hall since he took over at Illinois and the program was 27-0 over the past two seasons. Their opponent on February 3 was Michigan State, not the dominant force it had been in previous years. Self was quite friendly with the Spartans' Tom Izzo, and they shared a mutual respect as men, and as coaches.

Heading into the game against MSU, Illinois had lost two in a row to Indiana and Ohio State, and had fallen to 4-4 in the conference, well behind co-leaders Ohio State and Indiana. The crowd at Assembly Hall was loud as usual, but many wore a concerned look on their faces. Their team, a preseason No. 1 or No. 2, was now struggling to stay in the conference race, let alone the one for the national title. To loosen things up a bit in the locker room, Self showed up wearing a bright orange, 1970s sports coat, which he wore during the game. He thought it might bring some luck.

The home rims would not be friendly on this day, however, as Illinois struggled from the start to get their offense going. The only player for the Illini who made a contribution in the first half was Brian Cook, who scored 20 of Illinois' 33 points, including three three-pointers. (His trip home to Lincoln and the talk with his coach must have helped.) The other four starters combined for eight, as Michigan State led by three at the half. Early in the first half, Damir Krupalija landed awkwardly on his already injured left ankle and did not return after being taken for X-rays.

The Spartans made adjustments at halftime and Cook could not get on track in the second half, scoring only two points. MSU's Marcus Taylor, who had spearheaded their first half assault, left the game with a concussion early in the second half after a collision with Lucas Johnson, but Adam Ballinger picked up the slack. Despite a two-point Illinois lead with 4:37 left in the game, spurred by 11 straight points by Frank Williams, Michigan State fought back with clutch shooting and free throws. Illinois missed its last eight shots and their home winning streak was over. The final was 67-61, Michigan State, and the Illini had now lost three in a row and dropped to 4-5 in the Big Ten.

In the game against Michigan State, which was nationally televised by CBS, analyst Billy Packer criticized Williams for his lethargic play, saying at one point he was "sleep-walking" and at another, "he is playing like a dog." The criticism was mounting. A week earlier, before the Ohio State game, Williams and Self talked for almost two hours about the captain's attitude and future. The coach determined that Williams' mind was not on the NBA and the future, something he had feared. It was a matter of getting Williams motivated every night from the tip.

Self had tried various motivational tools throughout the season with his team, from singling out players, to encouraging more fun practices to having a team *mea culpa*. Nothing seemed to work. When the Illini did win, it didn't seem to be the result of a team effort. If he couldn't get the team going, maybe someone else could. Not another coach, but a brain doctor.

Motivational speaker Jim Cremins paid a visit to the team the day after the Michigan State loss. He had worked with Self's teams at Tulsa, and had been successful with other teams around the country. Former Tulsa coach Tubby Smith had brought him in to Kentucky and Self wanted the team to hear a different perspective. Cremins talked about how the brain worked, how to stay positive, and how to get things done regardless of who got credit, for close to 90 minutes. The coaches learned as much as the players. "It wasn't so much what he said," Self reflected, "but it came from a different source shedding some new light on things we may have already talked about." The next day in practice, Self noticed a changed attitude from his team.

M ike Brey didn't bring in a psychologist, but he probably could have used one after the Georgetown loss. The Irish had two games against Seton Hall sandwiched around a home game against Pitt, who had steadily been climbing in the national polls. Notre Dame had lost three in a row and it was now or never for the team. Harold Swanagan would sit out another game because his ankle had not healed. The Irish had four focused days of practice and their concentration was good, Brey noticed. The game plan for Notre Dame was simple—contain Seton Hall guard Andre Barrett, double team him in the back court, and take away the penetration of Darius Lane. To do that, Brey planned to use the "32" jam, the pressure defense put in originally to contain DePaul's quick guard Imari Sawyer, but intended in the long term for Big East guards like Barrett.

Behind 16 points and 12 boards from Ryan Humphrey, the Irish took care of Step One at home, beating the Pirates 60-51 on January 26. Graves came off of the bench to score 11 points and grab four rebounds in 30 minutes of play, more than he would have gotten if he had started. The first half was not pretty, as the teams shot 17 of 55 from the floor and a combined one of 19 from three-point land. (Brey would point to the Seton Hall win as his best coaching job of the season.)

Four days later, the Irish, 3-3 in the Big East, welcomed No. 21 Pittsburgh who were 6-2 in conference play. Matt Carroll had come down with a flu the day before the game and was hooked up to IVs before and after. Swanagan returned to the lineup as the Irish shot the lights out against the Panthers, hitting 67% of their shots en route to an 89-76 win. Chris Thomas scored 19, Graves came off of the bench to hit for 19 and Humphrey added 17 as Notre Dame scored 32 more points than Pitt had averaged giving up. The physicality and toughness that Brey had been searching for appeared in the game, with

64 fouls called and with a near brawl almost erupting at halfcourt after Pitt's Ontario Lett and Humphrey got into it with 9:30 remaining. Step Two.

The rematch against Seton Hall at Continental Airlines Arena just a week later was nothing like the first one, and one of four games Notre Dame would play in a professional arena during the season. In the first seven minutes, the Pirates jumped out to a 15-2 lead, and Notre Dame did not get its first basket until Swanagan scored nine minutes into the game. But then the Irish got their confidence back and went on a 28-11 run, to take a 33-26 lead into halftime. The second half went back and forth until a frantic closing minute. There had been seven ties and six lead changes in the second half alone, and it appeared the game would be decided on the final possession. Seton Hall had the ball with the scored tied at 61 with 39.1 seconds left in the game and 28 seconds left on the shot clock.

Seton Hall coach Louis Orr decided to run down the shot clock to leave Notre Dame with as little time as possible to get a last shot in. But the Seton Hall offense wasted too much time and Barrett launched an awkward shot off a drive that bounced off of the rim. Humphrey grabbed the rebound, threw it to Thomas, who made a layup with just under six seconds remaining. In the ensuing six ticks of the clock, Seton Hall called two time-outs in setting up its final shot, a clean three-point look by the Pirates' Charles Manga. The ball managed not to go in, and the Irish won their third in a row. Graves continued his stellar play off the bench and led the Irish with 20 points. Perhaps his benching sent a message, and the senior was responding in a big way.

Iowa meanwhile sat at 3-5 in the Big Ten, 15-8 overall as it faced Penn State in Iowa City on Saturday, February 2. With the Hawkeye bench outscoring the Nittany Lion bench 34-4, Iowa rolled to an 81-64 win, led by Ryan Hogan's 15 points, on three of five three-pointers, in just 16 minutes of action. Iowa found itself down 8-2 in the first three minutes of the game, and Alford watched as his team struggled from the outset yet again. But the Hawkeyes responded behind Luke Recker and went on a 15-0 run to lead by as many as 17 in the first half, taking a 35-24 lead into the break.

"I don't think teams have beaten us because of effort," Alford told the press after the game. "We just need to get a flow. There hasn't been the enthusiasm to go out and play the game. A lot of that is pressure and we have to get used to that." The coach continued, "All we have to do is take care of ourselves and the rest will fall in line."

Alford's relationship with the media had never been warm, perhaps fueled by the coach's experiences from a young age with an intrusive and often critical media. He had survived under the spotlight playing at Indiana, but the lights didn't shine too brightly at Manchester and Southwest Missouri State. Now he was in the Big Ten with a great deal more interest and attention, and the media commitments were a daily occurrence in his job, but not one that he enjoyed. The chilly relationship between coach and scribes came to a head a year earlier, born out of frustration.

The NCAA has a strict procedure for media at NCAA Tournament sites. The day before their games, coaches appear at a press conference to talk about their upcoming matchups and give the reporters the typical "they're a very good team" praise for their opponents. But as Iowa coach Steve Alford took the podium in Uniondale, New York, before his team's first-round game against Creighton in the 2001 NCAA Tournament, Alford was already boiling. Before the start of that season, Alford's college coach, Bobby Knight, had been fired from Indiana for personal conduct and was replaced on an interim basis by assistant Mike Davis. In September, as Indiana began its search, Alford was quoted as saying, "I wish them the very best in their search, but I don't want that search to include me. I don't want to be hounded for the next nine months. Other coaches have used the Indiana situation against me."

Indiana did well that year, finishing at 24-10. But Davis still had the *interim* in front of his title. If Indiana was to hire a new coach, it made sense to many that it would be Alford. The Indiana legend comes home to guide his alma mater to greatness. But with his Iowa team preparing to play an NCAA game, and having already denied his interest in the Indiana job, Alford was in no mood to talk about it anymore. At the press conference, the NCAA media rep called on *Iowa City Gazette* columnist Mike Hlas.

"Steve, national newspapers and radio shows have continued talking about you and linking you to the Indiana job. Should those stories die?" Alford grew intensely red, gave Hlas the stare of death and asked, "You're from freaking Iowa. Why are you asking that?"

The soundbite would be played for days to come on *SportsCenter* and local news stations around the country. Alford had blown up under the intense scrutiny and began to defend himself and attack others. During the press conference, Alford denied again his interest in the Indiana job. (Days earlier, during the Big Ten championship telecast, CBS' Billy Packer said that the final three minutes of the Iowa-Indiana title game would determine the future of Indiana basketball and Steve Alford, implying that if Alford won, he would be the next Indiana coach. In the postgame interview, Jim Nantz asked Alford about the Indiana job, infuriating the coach as it took away from what his team had just accomplished, winning four games in four days to advance to the Tournament.) The coach noted to the media members that he told Southwest Missouri athletic director Bill Rowe a few years earlier, before Alford left for Iowa, he'd wanted the next move he made to be his last. It was not Alford's greatest moment and the media and fans took note.

Melissa Isaacson, in the *Chicago Tribune* the following week, under a headline that read "Alford Steps Up As True Heir to Knight's Crown," wrote the following: "Iowa reporters last week were met with even more than Alford's usual dose of arrogance and contempt when they dared inquire about his future and, more specifically, his level of interest in the Indiana coaching opening."

"I think I have always tried to be up front and honest with the media and give them what they are trying to get," says Alford. "The media to me, the print guys, the TV guys, college shows—that's not media. Those are armchair quarterbacks. Most of them have no clue. They have no idea the environment you're in, the decisions you have to make. Anytime somebody is talking about you, you want to know what it is. That's just human nature. But when I stopped doing that [reading and listening to the criticism], I was a lot better off."

Alford sums up the opinion of so many coaches who work in a world dominated by media, twenty-four-hour cable sports, talk radio sports shows, Internet chat rooms and, of course, beat writers. There is no escaping the eyes of the lens, the head of a microphone, or the ink of the pen. But coaches use the media as much as the media use them. There is a curious level of respect between many coaches and reporters, a mutual understanding of the jobs that they do. But in most cases, the same engine that has brought college basketball to the forefront of sports in America is also the nemesis of coaches. The value of the NCAA Tournament has turned college basketball into a money-making machine, and with it, comes the intense scrutiny, impure motives, and hangers-on looking for a piece of the pie.

This is a media time with a premium on media-savvy coaches. Many of the high-profile hirings of young coaches include good-looking, camera-friendly, well-spoken young men. Quin Snyder, Billy Donovan, Bill Self, and Steve Alford among others. The media is great when you win, a necessity for recruiting, a boost to the ego and to the contract demands of a coach. In most cases, coaches will tell you that the media can do much more harm than good for them and their teams. Especially since the goal of the media is to sell and to make money. And in 2002, what sells is scandal, negativity, crisis. Perhaps the increased pressure to win on coaches is a partial result of fans, boosters, and administrators seeing other schools celebrating on Selection Sunday. But negativity is not new in the world of journalism.

"I think in sports the media is always looking for angles," says John Wooden, "and the angles that appear generally are the angles that are negative. The positive, you don't hear too much about." There has been speculation that a reason for Wooden's retirement in 1975 was due to the opening of the locker rooms to the press. Though he denies that was a reason for stepping out of the game, he was greatly concerned that the press was allowed too much access, especially in the hallowed ground of a team locker room. Wooden was not perceived by the press as particularly media-friendly. "To imply that I was uncooperative, that hurt me. Did that [media] force me to retire? No. Did it have an effect on the way I felt? Yes. In fact, at the Final Four, I think I was as cooperative as any other coach that I know. I never missed a meeting where I was supposed to be. I never failed to attend those meetings."

How coaches look at the media is often dictated by circumstance. Some coaches tend to see the media as decent, hard-working guys (and they are still mostly guys) who have a job to do. Then there are those who see reporters as blood-sucking leeches who should be put out to pasture and shot. Somewhere in between is this balanced view of Cincinnati coach Bob Huggins, who has had his share of bad press, particularly when it comes to graduation rates and player behavior. "I think there are some really good ones [reporters]. I think there are some really bad ones. I think there are some lazy, lazy guys in the media. I think there are some other guys who really research things and are well-informed and ask intelligent questions. They are actually quite delightful to be around."

Huggins is right. There are good and bad members of every profession, and certainly in the media, there are lazy ones. The majority of reporters covering any given game are hometown newspaper beat writers, who cover the team on a regular basis. They have established relationships with the coaches and players and often submit an article a day.

There are also the benefits. The press are often provided with food, drink, and gifts at games or tournaments, travel with the teams on charters (paid by the media companies), and get free passes to the best college basketball games in the nation. But there are also long hours, days away from home and deadlines to meet, and writing is not easy. What irks most coaches is that very few journalists are former players and coaches. They are "armchair quarterbacks" who "have no clue."

"I think the press has too much rein," says former UNLV coach Bill Bayno. "They are not held accountable. You've got a lot of good guys in the media that are fair, but you have so many more who are unfair. I think the media in the last 20 years has been given way too much freedom and I think they have abused it. They've used it to create the news that they want to create, to pick and choose what they want to report on." Bayno probably would have a negative view of the press, in light of his two main experiences with the media. As an assistant at Massachusetts under John Calipari, he witnessed first-hand the power of the media. *The Boston Globe* ran an extensive investigative series of articles that detailed allegations, violations, and unruly behavior within the UMass basketball program.

"The *Boston Globe* broke every rule of journalism to attack our players and painted an untrue picture of our team." If Bayno thought that the *Globe* was vicious, he had yet to experience the personal attacks of coaching in Sin City. "I think that *Sports Illustrated* article was an attack," Bayno says referring to a 2000 article, which revealed court documents in a federal racketeering case indicated that Bayno was provided with two strippers to have sex with at a Las Vegas hotel. He acknowledges his mistakes (see chapter 12), but it is clear that he sees the adversarial media as partly to blame for his undoing.

Many of the older coaches grew up and coached in a time when reporters and coaches helped each other out. The reporter would write positive stories about the team and, more importantly, keep indiscretions out of the newspaper. In return, a coach would give reporters access to them and their teams, in many cases spending personal time with them. Gene Keady has been around and seen it all develop. "I'm a little bit like the media should be helping us, but that has all changed, that has changed more than anything. A local sportswriter would never write anything controversial about the program like if a kid got a gal pregnant or drugs or got caught shoplifting. Now the drugs and shoplifting are what they are looking for. They don't protect you. Sportswriters used to protect coaches when I started. I'm not sure that was right, but they did it."

Times have certainly changed since those good old days when writers and broadcast-ers were "homers." Now many local beat writers are looking for the negative angle and the "big story." *Los Angeles Daily News* reporter Billy Witz has written about alleged violations, improprieties, and other Steve Lavin "mistakes." The coach has been cleared by the PAC-10 and NCAA on most of the allegations. Witz responds that, "I have never written any-thing without confirmation." The reporter, who has covered UCLA basketball for three seasons, says his job is "not to protect the coach, it should be to tell readers as much about the program in a fair and balanced way and let them decide."

Other coaches have their own takes on the media. Ball State coach Tim Buckley says "the media has a job to do. I think that the more entertaining the coverage is, and that usually happens at the higher levels, the more the fan base and the more excite-ment is created."

Rob Evans at Arizona State thinks his relationship with the media is determined by his own attitude. "The negativity of the press has grown. I can deal with that because I am pretty blunt." Illinois assistant Norm Roberts concurs with Evans. "You understand that the press has a job to do, so you talk to them. Dealing with the press is part of your job. I mean, in your job description, dealing with the press is part of it. And you don't have to be fake."

Coaches are not alone in their criticism of the press. Players, often the focus of many stories and profiles, are amazed at the inaccuracies of the media. They too, understand the press has a job to do, but as younger adults, they seem dumbfounded at the irre-sponsible journalism.

Luke Recker's tragic yet uplifting story has been told, shown, and talked about thou-sands of times. "I think the media has overblown a lot of things," the mature 24-year-old remarks. "It's a story they like to tell, the transfers, the car accident. If people think I sit around and I'm depressed all of the time, I'm not. I'm happy with what's going on in my life. Yeah, I've been through some tough times, but I think it has made me a stronger per-son." He continues, "I don't think anybody in the media knows me. I don't believe they try to get to know you and really try to display a 'personal' knowledge on a 10-minute clip on ESPN. I think that's tough to do."

Recker's conference mate, Lucas Johnson at Illinois, is intelligent, calm, and very mature about the game and its place in education. When it comes to the media, he has his moments. "I wish there was a good sportswriter who actually played the game and then would go and write about it because the stories would be much different. You get a different perspective when you're in the trenches and you're fighting the battles instead of just sitting on the sidelines pointing fingers."

John Feinstein has long been a print journalist and, at his core, is a reporter. He is dismayed at the increasing restrictions put on the print media by coaches, limiting their access not only to locker rooms, but also to only a select group of players. "As a reporter, you can really get a sense for what is going on talking to the walk-ons, the guys at the end of the bench, even the managers. But now, locker rooms are closed and only the big stars are brought out to press conferences where nothing new is ever said."

Feinstein believes that coaches are public figures and, as such, the media have an obligation to report on what is going on inside the programs. There is a lot of negativity in the media, he acknowledges, and he also understands that there is no such thing as objectivity—"we are all bias in some way, objectivity is B.S."

So what recourse do coaches and players have in dealing with the media? In most cases, coaches simply shake their heads, laugh it off, or otherwise keep their emotions in check. Every so often, you will see a coach go off at a reporter's questions, as a certain coach at Texas Tech has been known to do. Though Alford did succumb at the Uniondale, New York, press conference, he takes a different approach when dealing with certain reporters. "There is good and bad written, but I never respond to that. Now, if it's a writer or newscaster that said something I thought was particularly wrong, I pick up the phone. I ask, 'what were you trying to get at? Why is the slant you have that way?' I think there's a point where you're selling papers and there's a point where you've got to be selling what's really out there."

One area of the media that gets a tremendous amount of attention from coaches, fans, and the press itself is rankings and polls. Those subjective lists of who the best teams in the country are in any given week. They are the subject of outcry and ridicule, the voters either "intelligent observers" or "blind biased hacks," according to where a fan's team is ranked.

At Notre Dame, Mike Brey's Irish started off the season 9-1, the best start in the history of Notre Dame basketball. With their only loss to a ranked Indiana team, one might be surprised that they hadn't even cracked the Top 25. Teams ahead of them included Butler, Marquette, and Ball State. Before their game against DePaul, Brey made a point of telling his team where they stood in practice the day before. "Hey, if we are under the radar, so be it. We just keep taking care of our business and things will take care of themselves." He reiterated that theme three days later before the loss to Indiana. And with wins over Miami (Ohio) and Canisius, the Irish headed into a showdown against No. 22-ranked Alabama, still not ranked. "I think it is kind of surprising," said the normally down-playing Brey. "I guess because we lost Troy Murphy people think we are no good. But hey, it's about respect. If they don't want to respect us, then we will just slip under the radar."

Rankings, like the men and women who vote them, are imperfect. It is not just basketball. *Sports Illustrated* anointed Oregon State the best football team in the country before the start of the 2001–2002 season, only to see the Beavers end up 4-6. There are numerous examples of false predictions and poor rankings made by magazines, the AP and *USA Today/ESPN* polls. At the start of the 2001–2002 season, it was clear that the only solid position in the polls was No. 1, and that belonged to Duke. So how do these "experts" even come up with the rankings?

The *USA Today/ESPN* coaches poll is made up of 31 Division I head coaches around the country, who vote every Sunday on their top teams. In reality, it should be a fairly accurate poll with those who know basketball best voting in the rankings. Two problems with that theory though. First, coaches are human and they let emotions dictate decisions like everyone else. A voting coach may believe that a conference foe is worthy of a Top Ten ranking, but would hate to see them there, so he votes them low in his poll. Or perhaps a coach had a falling out with another coach years ago and punishes that coach's team by voting them low. Second, many of the 31 coaches who are eligible to vote in the *USA Today* poll may not even vote. The last thing a coach wants to worry about, especially on a Sunday after a big game, is calling in to the 800-number to vote. In many instances, it is the Sports Information staff member or an assistant coach who calls it in.

There was a "scandal" in January 2002 in the Coaches Poll, when it was revealed that Utah coach Rick Majerus had been letting one of his assistants do the voting. How did the organizers of the poll find out? They became suspicious when one voter continued to vote Temple in the Top 25, even though the Owls had a 3-7 record. They tracked the votes and it brought them back to Majerus, who admitted the fraudulent vote, claiming that personal reasons, including his mother's battle with cancer, precluded him from voting. He is not the only coach in the "Coaches" Poll to pass on the duty.

For the 2001–2002 season, the coaches in the Coaches Poll included Dan Hipsher (Akron), Davey Whitney (Alcorn State), Joe Mihalich (Niagra), and Tom Green (Farleigh-Dickinson). More well-known coaches voting in the poll included Gene Keady, Dave Odom, Jim Boeheim, Bob Huggins, and Gary Williams.

How accurate is the *USA Today/ESPN* coaches' poll? A look at Week 1 rankings, November 5, versus Week 8 rankings, December 24, and the final poll released April 1, reveals mixed results. Of the Top 25 teams in the first poll, 18 are still ranked by late December. By the end of the season, the number of original schools had dropped to 10. Of the original Top Ten in November, eight teams remained there in late December but only three by the end of the season. The biggest miscalculation? St. Joseph's, Temple, and North Carolina, none of whom remained ranked by late December, and all of whom struggled throughout the season. Teams that made a run in the Tournament were in the final poll, such as Kent State, Southern Illinois, and Xavier.

The AP poll may appear to be a bit more fair, with 72 journalists around the country voting each Sunday. Representative of media types, the AP polls are often considered more seriously, as objective journalists surely would not let bias into their rankings. Again taking a look at Week 1 versus Week 8 rankings versus the final poll: the AP poll had 19 of its original 25 still ranked by Week 8, and like the Coaches Poll, it overestimated St. Joe's, Memphis, Temple, North Carolina, Indiana, and USC. Eight of the Week 1 Top Tens remained there. Of course, by the end of January 2002, there were still some major inconsistencies: Virginia was fifth in the ACC but still in the AP Top Ten. By the end of the season in the final AP poll, only 10 of the preseason Top 25 remained in the poll, with just three of the original Top Ten. (It is important to note that the "final" polls are released before the start of the NCAA Tournament, which is why eventual title game competitor Indiana is not even in the AP Top 25 at the end of the season and only comes in at No. 22 in the Coaches' Poll.)

The three key letters in college basketball are R-P-I: Ratings Power Index. It is a statistical analysis of a team's schedule and how it does against that schedule. It does not take into account margin of victory or where the game is played. The formula is 25% team winning percentage, 50% opponents' average winning percentage, and 25% opponents' average winning percentage. It is a number to which the NCAA Tournament selection committee pays close attention. Evidence of the human nature of the polls, when compared to the statistical objectivity of the RPI, is clear as early as the Week 8 rankings. (It must be noted that with so few games played before the end of December, it is expected that a team's RPI may not be reflective of their strength.) Most of the Top Ten are the same, but further down the RPI list come surprises. Michigan State was ranked

No. 13 in the AP and No. 12 in the USA Today/ESPN poll in the December 24 poll, but was only No. 40 in the RPI rankings. They were followed by Missouri at No. 41, ranked as high as No. 10 in both polls. The biggest discrepancy? Boston College was at a No. 11 and No. 13 ranking in the polls, but was ranked No. 50 in RPI. Georgetown, with a record of 8-3 and the 133rd toughest schedule in the land, came in at No. 70 on the RPI list, but the Hoyas were ranked No. 20 and No. 18 in the two polls. On the flip side of the debate were the relatively unknown schools South Florida and Bowling Green. In Week 8, they had RPIs of No. 18 and 19, respectively, but were nowhere near the poll rankings. Same for Utah State at No. 22 in RPI and No. 25 Texas Tech.

By the end of the regular season, the rankings were more in tune with the computer-based RPI. Duke was No. 1 in both final polls, though their RPI was rated No. 4. Mississippi State had the eighth-best RPI but was ranked low at No. 17 and 18 in the polls. On the flip side, Oregon was ranked No. 34 according to RPI but was ranked No. 11 in both final polls. Gonzaga was ranked No. 6 in both polls but only had an RPI ranking of 21. The argument over how reflective RPI is of a team's strength can go on for days, but it is a critical component for getting into the Tournament and that alone makes RPI a true reflector of a team's potential Tournament success.

It is clear to many coaches who the top teams are, but after the top ten or so, it is really just mix and match. Who could have predicted in October that storied North Carolina wouldn't even be ranked, and have home losses to Davidson and Hampton by December? Or that Arizona, despite the loss of four starters to the NBA, would start off the season 8-2 with wins over Florida, Maryland, and Illinois? Anything can happen on any given night, particularly with a more level playing field. For many coaches, rankings are simply entertainment for fans and indicators of just how good, or bad, their teams and their coaching abilities are.

"It is a lot different now than 10 or 15 years ago," Alabama's Mark Gottfried says. "We beat Kentucky and Georgia and had the highest ranking in 28 years at Alabama [No. 5]. Everybody thinks what a great coach I am. We lose to Kent State in the NCAAs and all of a sudden people think I don't know the difference between a bounce pass and a chest pass."

The debate over rankings is just one of the topics appearing on the Internet, the latest forum for fans to vent frustrations. It has created a new kind of "media," and with it, a new type of journalist. Many are vocal fans who post columns, analyses and "inside" information on a daily basis. The Internet has not changed the way coaches coach, but it certainly has made them more conscious of who is watching.

"The melding of talk radio, the Internet, and supposedly traditional print media have created a new form of entertainment journalism," Lavin laments. "The lines have blurred. It's really hard for me to differentiate between a beat writer, a talk radio host and a guy that creates a Web site."

One of Lavin's former assistants, now Portland head coach Michael Holton, credits Lavin for teaching him about the media. "I learned a lot from Steve. He taught me a lot about media relations because he is probably one of the best in the country at dealing with the media. He stays a step ahead."

As the UCLA Bruins packed up their belongings at the Lahaina Civic Center after their loss to Ball State and headed back to their hotel, 2,000 miles away in Westwood, California, the hot seat machine was just getting started. Any loss is picked apart by the Los Angeles media, some UCLA fans, and any other interested party, and surely this early season upset loss would just be the beginning. A look at *bruinzone.com*, one of numerous

Internet chat rooms devoted to UCLA basketball, reveals the anger and angst of the Bruin faithful:

> Rudy: I think Lavin has no clue how to run a program. Do you think we could get Billy Donovan or Steve Alford who are fiery and have a vision—things that Lavin lacks?

> Rfeder: Personally, I think Steve Lavin has some sort of psychological need to be on the hot seat. If he is self-destructive or has psychological problems, he should work them out with a shrink, not on the job.

Firestevelavin.com (name-explanatory Web site) had been relatively quiet over the summer, but now postings were at a high pitch. The explosion of the Internet or "Information Superhighway" has also become "*Mis*Information Superhighway." Almost in real time, facts, figures, rumors, incidents, plays, scouting reports, you name it, appear on computer screens. Added to the list of false reports are Internet chat rooms, where garrulous fans can vent their frustrations, point others to damning information, and otherwise say what they want. True or not. Fair or not.

Lavin is not the only coach to be affected at the hands of the Internet. At Illinois, Self has closed many practices and kept play design in check because he fears they will be posted on the Internet within hours. Though he does open some of his practices to select media and high school coaches, he and his staff know who everyone is in the facility; they are fearful of "dirty laundry" being posted. "I don't want my team's stuff on the streets. Guys come and watch pickup games and then post that I chewed some kid out. That's not fair to the kid or to me. I don't want my business on the streets." Self continued, "There are times when I can't coach them the same if people are in there. I don't want to coach and have to watch what I say."

At Notre Dame, Brey is well aware when foreign eyes are watching. Though he opens many practices, it is mainly high school coaches and Irish alumni who observe, but even still, he can sense a difference in his approach. "Absolutely, I know when people are in the gym. You learn as a coach to have that sense and sure, I probably don't say some things that I might say to the team in private. But you know what? Most coaches are the same. There was only one coach who didn't give a hoot who was watching and he was fired."

True, Bobby Knight did not care much about who was watching, but then again, very few were watching his practices. Knight was notorious for having a strict closed practice policy. In fact, there are some reporters who never saw an Indiana practice after covering the team for *years*. Stan Sutton, former reporter for the *Louisville Courier-Journal*, and now sports editor at the *Bloomington Herald-Times*, has been covering Indiana basketball for over 20 years, and he thinks it is a relief that Knight is no longer there. "You could ask Knight a question, and it could be a very good one, but if he didn't like you, he simply ignored it and asked, 'Does anybody have a good and intelligent question?' But then there were also times when he'd invite you to practice and talk to you afterward for hours."

Sutton and his colleagues now deal with the opposite end of the spectrum, new Indiana coach Mike Davis. "Mike is outstanding with the media," Sutton says. "Very open, very accessible. The only place that Davis really messed up last year [2000–2001] is that he was really too candid. After the Kentucky game when Indiana lost a real heartbreaker and played poorly, Davis went into the press room and said, 'I don't think I can coach this team, they better find someone else.' It wasn't 'coaches speak.'"

Talk to the beat writers, the guys who are there day after day, and you will get a good picture of a coach and his relationship with the media. As a basketball writer for the *South Bend Tribune*, Tom Noie has seen up close Matt Doherty and Mike Brey—two very different media types. "I thought Matt would be very removed from the media, having dealt with it at Carolina and Kansas. But when I worked with him day-to-day, I would basically be called into the principal's office on some things I had written that he just didn't understand. It surprised me."

Many coaches will deny ever listening to radio stations, reading postings on Internet chat rooms, and picking up the morning paper. But in reality, they are human, and they want to know what others are saying about them. "I get five to 10 e-mails a day, some of them criticizing me," Self chuckles. "Once, when it got personal, I wrote back—that was a mistake." Self does admit going onto *illiniboard.com* every so often to read the postings, but he has learned not to reply. Not all coaches go into Internet chat rooms to see what the "fans" are writing, but almost all read the sports pages, watch the television, and even listen to talk radio.

Mark Gottfried reads the sports pages each morning, and acknowledges that most coaches who deny taking a look are lying. For him, and many coaches, they understand that media relations is part of their job, though the only opinions that truly matter are from the AD, president, and Board of Trustees.

Jay Wright reads *The Philadelphia Daily News* and *The Philadelphia Inquirer*, and sometimes listens to talk radio and reads the Internet. "But for everything positive that is said or written about you or your program with zeal, they will cover the negative with the same enthusiasms."

Many coaches are accustomed to the criticism, so it is more entertaining than hurtful to them. However, when attacks turn personal, they take a keen interest. "The media is not my friend," remarks Jeff Jones. "There are members of the media that I consider friends, but just because someone writes a nice article about you doesn't mean they are your friend. It's just a business. But I do have a problem when things cross the line and someone has a vendetta against you."

Of course, for all of the negative comments about the press from coaches, and the developing "gotcha game" between them, there are also the benefits that coaches reap from the media. From an economic standpoint, coaches can make thousands of dollars by agreeing to do weekly interviews or a coach's show. Many Division I coaches have a weekly radio and television "Coach's Show," where they go over highlights of that week's games, look ahead to the upcoming opponents, and answer soft questions from the team's play-by-play man. The shows are often filmed on Friday or Sunday mornings at a local television station. The radio shows are done on a weeknight, and frequently are done on location at a local bar or restaurant. The personalities of the coaches come across in these one-on-one sessions, and coaches get a chance to put positive spins on their handiwork. Surprisingly, Lavin does not have a weekly show in the media capital of the world. Go figure.

Phil Martelli at St. Joseph's in Philadelphia does, and it is like no other. Martelli became a favorite of the media during the Hawks run in the 1997 NCAA Tournament. A colorful character, straight out of Philly, Martelli has fun with the game and the press. His personality lends itself to television, and his weekly coach's show became appointment television for regional viewers. You get the feeling that even if he wasn't compensated for the show, he would broadcast it out of his basement.

Many coaches at smaller schools do not have deals for a coach's show or pregame and postgame radio. The market simply doesn't demand it, like at Bucknell, where Pat Flannery has no television or radio deal but does the shows anyway because it is part of his job. At Coastal Carolina, Pete Strickland only has one beat writer following his team and the reporter doesn't even go on the road with them. "In March, I probably had one media interview. You, for this book," the coach says with a laugh. "I am not in high demand."

Most coaches at the lower levels of Division I do not have to devote a great deal of time to the media, certainly not when compared to the big boys. But they have other duties that a Roy Williams or Mike Jarvis at St. John's may not have to deal with such as travel, game day operations, and even the driving of a team van.

There is another benefit beyond compensation that the media can provide to coaches, who now see it as integral to their coaching. Coaches talk to their players and send messages through the press. Every coach of every sport does it, but college basketball coaches have made an art form of it. A star player doesn't get the message from you to work harder? Make a reference to it in the teleconference. Some seniors are disinterested and not playing well? Call them out in a postgame interview. It is almost a game between coach and player, with the media all too willing to play along.

As Iowa's season was crumbling in January, Alford and his senior stars, Luke Recker and Reggie Evans, battled through the media. In a locker room setting, a player cannot challenge the coach but in the media, well, somebody asked the question, right? "We would rather try a no-look pass to get on *College Hoops 2Night* instead of making a simple play and getting two points," Alford said sarcastically referring to a bad pass by Recker in a loss. "It was not the no-look passes, they were just passes that weren't completed," Recker responded.

A few losses later, Alford took the blame for a home loss to Indiana, saying "I've let it go. Seniors are taking possessions and practices off. That's my fault." A clear reference to Recker and Evans.

Alford is not alone in using the media as a motivational tool. Bill Self had been battling to get Frank Williams to play hard for an entire game to no avail. As early as December 1, 2001, Self talked about Williams' lack of intensity and his being out of shape in the media, perhaps in an effort to kick-start the guard. With Illinois struggling two months later, Self, along with the media, really turned up the heat on Williams in the press accusing him of dogging it, playing when he wants to, and not having the talent to play at the NBA level. For Self, it wasn't about sending a message, as much as it was about creating a bond. "The media got on him, and I did too in the press. Frank knew that I was there for him, that no matter what people said, only he and I knew what was going on."

At Notre Dame, Mike Brey talked through the media to his star senior David Graves during a slump, hinting that it was time for "seniors to play defense."

Coaches can send a message to their team and the community when they step up and take blame for losses or poor coaching decisions. On December 9, 2001, in *The L.A. Times*, Lavin took blame for early season struggles. "I put the team in a position to fail by pressing earlier. I got a failing grade for the month of November for the fifth year in a row." In late January and again in early February after losses, Lavin took the blame for not switching defenses, for not calling a critical timeout or for not substituting better. To some, it is a breath of fresh air, listening to a coach admit to mistakes and taking blame. To others, it is clear evidence that he should be fired for such incompetence. Lavin views taking responsibility publicly as a model of accountability and leadership to his players.

Players also use the media to talk back to their coaches. It works both ways. New Mexico's Marlon Palmer, who had been clashing with coach Fran Fraschilla and his teammates, was quoted in a newspaper after his team's loss to Utah as saying Utah was "better coached and had a better team." Fraschilla was clearly not happy and things escalated to the point that Palmer quit the team, before being kicked off. In later interviews, he accused Fraschilla of verbal abuse and of threatening to sabotage his NBA career.

Of course, many coaches use "poster board material" to try to motivate their clubs. Often, an opponent's comment about a team or player will be cut out, blown up, and posted in every player's locker. Coaches may deny doing it, but they do.

The late legendary Alabama football coach Bear Bryant had a saying, "If you want a lot of trouble on Saturday, just run your mouth on Friday," referring to media days on the Fridays before big college football games. The point? Don't say anything to piss an opponent off.

It's not just coaches and players using the media to get a point across. UCLA guard Jason Kapono's dad outwardly questioned the UCLA coaching staff's ability in the local media, wondering aloud why his son was not getting more shots. When North Carolina's Adam Boone announced his intentions to transfer, his father caused a stir when he told reporters his son was leaving because of a lack of respect in the program under Doherty.

Dick Vitale. He is the face and voice of college basketball, for better or for worse. He burst onto the scene in the 1980s and became synonymous with the college game, creating a new vocabulary along the way using terms like "diaper dandy" and "PTPer." No one argues whether or not Vitale is good for the game of college basketball. He is the undisputed king of promotion for the sport, and for himself, and he brings excitement to an arena just by showing up. "I was told early on that the best broadcasters entertain and educate," the former coach says, "you need to talk to the audience as if you are talking to your buddies at home."

Vitale believes that he has more than a responsibility to break down the game for the fans as a color analyst. He has a "unique voice" in the game, contributing to *SportsCenter*, *ESPNRadio*, the Internet sites, and much more. These diverse roles force him to be more than just a game analyst, which is why you often will hear Vitale talking about larger issues in the game, top assistant coaches, and his All-American teams.

But what do coaches think of Vitale? Almost universally, they praise his promotion of the college game and his support for its coaches. But they are not without criticism. A complaint by coaches of Vitale is his insistence on compiling and broadcasting his list of "top assistants" or great coaches who should have jobs. Inevitably, Vitale leaves out many, if not hundreds, of great coaches who may not have strong pedigrees and who may not come to Vitale's attention through Mike Krzyzewski or Rick Pitino. A familiar refrain from coaches, echoed by Bill Self: "Just because Dick Vitale says their name on television doesn't mean they are a good coach." Vitale's response: "I understand how some coaches feel but I have a job to do just like they do. I give my opinion of who I believe would be excellent coaches. I don't have the power to place a coach."

Make no mistake, Vitale is a powerful man in college basketball and in college sports. Unbelievably, major Division I athletic directors now call Vitale when they are looking for a coach. And not just basketball coaches. He has been involved in *football* coaching searches at some major schools. The broadcaster regularly receives calls from ADs looking to get his feelings on four or five potential candidates, and Vitale gives them his thoughts. But he also thinks we all are disrespecting ADs if we believe they are hiring a guy simply because he or Krzyzewski says good things about him. "Ultimately, the guy must be able to coach and that reflects on the AD."

Another criticism of Vitale from a few coaches (not to be identified) is his approach to games. He does so many games around the country in any given week, that it appears that he has little time to prepare. Whereas some broadcasters watch practice the day before games or even sit down with the coaches well before tip-off, Vitale has taken a unique approach. Often, he will go into the locker room during warmups to talk with the coach about the game, his players, and his assistants. The last thing a coach wants to be doing an hour before game time is talking to Vitale in the locker room. In these conversations, Vitale gets the tidbits of information he uses during the game.

After talking with coaches, Vitale will often take to the arena floor, slapping hands, and taking pictures with fans. But he continues his research. He will pull aside players during warmups to talk with them about the game and their futures. Some coaches are infuriated with the interruption, but very few complain—they know the power that Vitale has with the microphone.

Vitale, however, sees the pregame visits as the culmination of hours of preparation, reading, talking, and living basketball. "I pride myself on being prepared. In fact, many people that I work with would say that I overprepare. You don't survive 23 years in this business, get choice assignments, if you are not prepared." With a schedule of games that takes Vitale to many different cities on consecutive nights, he doesn't have time to come into town days earlier to talk with coaches and players and watch practice.

Every morning, one of Vitale's daughters puts a packet of information, articles, and news clippings on his desk for her father to dissect or e-mails them to him on the road. With his responsibilities to *SportsCenter*, radio, and the Internet, as well as writing columns for weeklies, he must be up to date on everything in college basketball.

"Dick is an ambassador for the sport," says John Feinstein. "He talks about where he had dinner last night, who the top assistants are. He is a promoter, not real concerned with breaking down the game." Vitale is a promoter of the game, and perhaps the staunchest supporter of coaches. As a former coach, he knows what they go through on a daily basis, and cringes when he hears of a coach being fired or vilified for things he can't control. Vitale has a close relationship with many coaches, and is not afraid to give advice to those he doesn't know as well.

After Indiana fell to 7-5 losing at home to Butler, Indiana coach Mike Davis criticized the officials and was fined $10,000. Vitale did not have a friendship with Davis, but was concerned enough to pick up the phone to call the coach. "I said, 'Mike, you can hang up on me, but I am just calling you as somebody who cares, to pass on some advice.'" Vitale proceeded to tell Davis that he was not going about things the right way. He was acting as if he "had a chip on his shoulder."

"Think before you speak," was the older coach's advice. "Going after the officials after a loss makes you look like a crybaby." Vitale then implored the 41-year-old Davis to stop moaning about the Bobby Knight supporters and how difficult they make things. Reminding Davis that many coaches would "give their right arm to coach at Indiana," Vitale advised Davis to embrace the job, to understand that it was a golden opportunity for him.

Davis couldn't thank him enough. Vitale sent some follow-up notes to him throughout the season and at the Final Four in Atlanta, Davis again reiterated his appreciation to Vitale in the lobby of the Marriott.

After the season, Vitale received notes from the likes of Mike Krzyzewski and Matt Doherty, thanking him for being such a strong supporter of coaches and a fan of the game. It is a blurry line between journalist and friend, but somehow Vitale walks it confidently.

Would he want to coach today? "No, I would be dead. There is not a job in America that I would take right now. When I coached, I had a bleeding ulcer, giving myself to the game—I don't know any other way. If I was coaching, I would not have made 50. I truly believe that." So for now, Vitale looks forward to spending time with his eight-month-old granddaughter, doing speaking engagements around the country, and continuing to promote the game that he loves.

There are many other faces of college basketball including former coach Bill Raftery, Billy Packer, and rising star Jay Bilas. Andy Katz, a former writer for the *Fresno Bee* has become a central player in the media, now writing for *espn.com* and appearing regularly on ESPN. Katz is the information man. He reports on which coaches may be headed where, which players may transfer out, and what issues affect the game, such as the story in early 2002 on overworked referees. Katz's power comes not only from respect, but also from a national audience. When he posts his *Daily Word* column everyday, millions of fans, and coaches, read it, giving credence to what otherwise may simply have been rumors.

There exists a paradox in the world of coaching, one that has turned their profession into a lucrative one. The advent of ESPN and the explosion of television in the 1980s and 1990s made coaches into stars and celebrities and added to their coffers. Many profit from the fact that there is such intense media coverage, not only from television and radio deals, but from any media entity. Though talk radio and Internet sites may, in some instances, make their jobs more difficult, it is that interest that allows them to command the salaries that they do and keeps them in the spotlight—ingredients for ego-driven men.

The game was a complete disaster from the opening tip, and falling behind at Mac Court in Eugene, Oregon, was not the suggested route to victory. UCLA had lost to USC, beaten Kansas, beaten ASU, lost to Arizona and Stanford, beaten Cal and now, according to their recent history, they were due for a loss at Oregon—but no one could have predicted the debacle that lay ahead. Behind Freddie Jones' 28 points, Oregon outplayed, outshot, and outscored the Bruins 91-62, giving the Ducks their biggest win over UCLA ever. The win put Oregon at 8-2 and in first place atop the PAC-10; the loss dropped UCLA to 6-4. UCLA shot 1 of 14 from deep and no one played well. *It was one thing to drop a conference road game every now and then, but to get blown out by 29 points to Oregon? This just can't happen at UCLA.* The pressure mounted on Lavin and the loss gave his critics more fodder. Lavin and the team stayed up until 1:00 A.M. after the loss, watching tape of the game. Lose the game, don't lose the lesson.

But as they had on so many occasions already in the season, the Bruins bounced back in an impressive 70-48 rout of Oregon State at Corvallis. They used a mix of man-to-man and matchup zone to shut down the hosts. Jason Kapono and Dan Gadzuric combined for 37 points, and though UCLA did not play pretty in the first half, they turned it on in the second to pull away. UCLA used a zone defense that Oregon State could not figure out, and at times, played a slow, methodical game that seemed to work better than an uptempo, run-and-gun approach that they had used against Oregon.

The Bruins finished the first swing through the PAC-10 at 7-4, having finished the season series with the Washington schools. Up next on the schedule—a highly anticipated rematch with USC at Pauley Pavilion, with more than just bragging rights on the line.

19

Center Stage

WELL BEFORE IOWA GATHERED IN A BANQUET ROOM AT THE COURTYARD MARRIOTT
hotel in Bloomington, Indiana, for a scouting report the night before their showdown with Indiana, the players knew all about the Hoosiers. Not only had they
faced them a few weeks earlier, but they had been given the scouting report back in Iowa
City, complete with notebooks, film breakdown, and personnel reports and the players
had their notebooks with them on the road to study in their hotel rooms. So at 9:00 P.M.
that night, there was little new information.

Steve Alford took the team through some additional tape breakdowns, things Indiana
liked to do on offense and individual tendencies of their key players including Jared
Jeffries and Dane Fife. Using a remote control to start and stop the tape and a red laser
pointer to identify parts of plays, the coach took the players through the various film clips,
reminding them of their defensive responsibilities along the way. At the conclusion of the
film review, the lights were turned on, and Alford went over the scouting report, again,
point-by-point, as the players read along in their notebooks.

"We must play tough, have more assists than turnovers, and get to the free throw line
30 or more times," Alford told his team. "And let's get them on their heels. Davis
[Indiana's coach] gets upset when things don't go well, so let's try to rattle them."

The players were tired. They had already traveled four hours from Iowa City, had a
shootaround at Assembly Hall, and had eaten a hearty meal at the Colorado Steakhouse
before settling in for the scouting report. (At the Steakhouse, as the team walked through
the restaurant to their tables in the back, Luke Recker ran into former teammate and friend,
Dane Fife, who was dining with a friend. The two gave each other hugs and spent a few
minutes catching up. But like coaches talking before games, this encounter was awkward.)

There should have been no doubt in the Iowa players' minds as to their responsibilities against Indiana. No team in America should have been more prepared to play.
But being prepared does not always translate into victory. Alford brought his struggling

Iowa team into Bloomington to face the Hoosiers, who were 9-2 in Big Ten play, just a game behind Ohio State. Alford had lost by three at Assembly Hall two years earlier, facing off against his old coach Bobby Knight. The two teams did not meet in Bloomington in 2000–2001. This year was different. Not only did his team need a huge win but Recker, the former Indiana standout, was making his return to Bloomington and expected a rude reception. Alford had another chance to prove to the Indiana faithful, and to himself, that he could coach. He would return home and be triumphant—as if he needed to prove anything.

The morning of the game, Alford sat in the lobby of the Courtyard Marriott, relaxing and joking around with his players. He was still relaxed at the shootaround later that day, standing in familiar surroundings. Indiana athletic department personnel stuck their heads in the gym to get a glimpse of Alford, and some long-time employees came in and got hugs from the former Indiana star. Alford seemed at peace in Bloomington, but his home was in Iowa City.

Back at the Marriott, the players took naps, watched television, and tried to take a dip in the hotel's whirlpool, but it was closed for maintenance. Alford put on a jacket and took a walk with friend and agent Mike Barnett around Bloomington. It was a time for the coach to breathe the fresh air, collect his thoughts, and put the game in perspective. It would be hard to believe that any member of the Iowa contingent felt more pressure than Alford on this day, but in fact it was Recker who took the cake. From the moment he signed with Iowa two years ago, he knew that he would have to return to Bloomington as the hated villain. The buildup for this game started earlier in the week, as the talk from Hoosier fans was nothing but passioned poison. Everyone it seemed was talking about Recker's return and how Indiana fans would treat him. They soon got their answer.

From the moment that Recker walked on the court for warmups, the boos and insults started. The student section was packed with students carrying signs that read "Recker Sucks," "Recker = Traitor," and a sign that had a picture of Recker next to one of Osama bin Laden. He had expected a tough atmosphere and the Hoosier faithful did not disappoint. The day before in Iowa City, Alford pulled Recker aside for a talk, reminding him not to try extra hard against Indiana and to keep his composure. It would be difficult, he told Recker, but Recker's maturity and life experiences had prepared him for challenges such as this.

The visiting locker room at Assembly Hall on this night was the women's basketball locker room. As the arena filled to capacity, 60 minutes before tip-off, Alford wrote on the board in the cramped quarters. "We need to play with passion and play like men," the coach began, underlining the words *passion* and *men* on the board. The coach set up the first Iowa offensive play, a backdoor screen and pick for an easy Recker layup. Turning to the obvious undertone of the game, the coach suggested, "don't worry about what goes on outside the lines, things that we can't control. They [the fans] don't control the game. We are 1-0 in the month of February, so let's keep it going."

The team seemed fired up, but Recker was a bit hesitant. There was a look in his eyes of bewilderment, of experiencing something out of body. He was facing 15,000 people who truly wished the worst for him, and it would not be easy, even for the calm and mature Recker. His mother and family w ho lived in Indiana did not attend, nor did his fiancée, Megan. They knew better.

In the first play of the game, Pierre Pierce got the ball to Recker off the pick and screen, and just as Alford had drawn up in the locker room, the senior went in for an uncontested layup. Jarrad Odle hit a jumper for Indiana to tie the game at two to start the Hoosier scoring. Just three minutes into the game, Iowa didn't know what had hit them, falling behind 11-2. With eight minutes to go, the lead was 21-11, and spurred by a Hoosier 17-7 run late in the first half, the Hawkeyes found themselves down 40-21 at half. Recker was playing horribly, missing jump shots and getting beaten on defense. During the Indiana run, Alford called timeout to try to refocus his troops. At a timeout with 4:48 remaining, the coach went ballistic. He turned a bright shade of red and ripped into his team in the timeout huddle, challenging them to play like men. He became so infuriated at one point that he snapped his clipboard over his knee, breaking it in two.

Alford walked into the halftime locker room, and was at a loss for words. What more could he say to this team? He had done everything to try to pull them out of their slump, used every motivational tool, but now what could he say? He really didn't say much. "I don't know what to say," was his response to his team, and the coach walked out to a small adjoining coaches' room.

His assistant Rich Walker went on a rampage, screaming at the players to play like mature men and to "do what we tell you to do." Assistant Greg Lansing was calmer, imploring the team to follow the staff's instructions. Alford returned to the locker room and simply walked around, collecting his thoughts. With a few minutes remaining in half-time, the coach drew some diagrams on the wipeboard, and in a calmed, hushed tone, explained to the team how they would start the second half. "Let's play smart and get back in this thing. Let's run 32 and 2-down on offense and work our way back in this." It was the least Alford had talked during any halftime, probably in his career.

But except for a mini-run early in the second half by Iowa's bench, the second half was a disaster. It was clear that this night belonged to Indiana. They led by 32 with three and a half minutes to go and the Hoosier fans were loving it. They wanted blood, and they wanted Recker's blood. As the Iowa guard sat on the bench late in the game, the crowd chanted "We Want Recker!" begging Alford to put him in for more abuse. One woman, in her late forties, seated 10 rows from the floor by the Iowa bench, harangued Recker throughout the game. When asked why she felt such venom for the former Indiana player, her answer was both surprising and sad. "It wasn't because he left Indiana or that he is playing for Iowa," she responded, "it's that he left Kelly, his girlfriend, paralyzed and just moved on." There was no sense of compassion or understanding from this crowd.

The game was a nightmare for Recker, who scored only eight points, took poor shots, and allowed the Indiana guards to score from all over the floor. As the final buzzer sounded and the teams shook hands, Alford and Recker gave congratulations to the Indiana players, and Recker even got a few hugs from his former teammates. Somehow as players, they understood what Recker had had to endure, though no one could fully comprehend the emotional toll.

After the loss, Alford returned to the locker room, asked, "Who has a prayer?" and then bowed his head as Rod Thompson led the team in a prayer. As the team huddled and joined hands to chant "Hawks," Alford walked out of the room. In his postgame com-ments to reporters, he heaped praise on the Indiana players and coach Mike Davis. Things could not get much worse. Or could they?

(Four days later at home against Minnesota, the aftereffects of the Indiana loss seemed to have been present. The Golden Gophers trailed by nine at the half, but Iowa wilted in the second half as Minnesota won 86-78 in Iowa City. Recker rebounded from his poor performance at Indiana to score 25 points, and Iowa was in the game until the closing minutes. The loss dropped Iowa to 4-7 in the Big Ten and they had now lost three of their last four games. Afterward, Alford again promised changes to the lineup for a road game at Penn State on Wednesday, February 13.)

It seems a bit harsh that a young man such as Luke Recker must endure such a discouraging and hostile life event, simply because he wore the jersey of a rival school. In big-time college basketball, players are no longer anonymous and, like professional athletes, are fair game for fans, media, and critics.

In today's college game, many coaches have become stars as well, a far cry from just two decades ago. With the explosion of televised games and highlight shows, coaches have become recognizable faces on their own campuses and around the country. The impact of the media coverage has made them celebrities, heroes, and scapegoats. Indeed, being well-known is not all glamour, as coaches and their families face the challenges of fame.

The death threats were sent via e-mails to Steve Lavin and athletic director Peter Dalis at their UCLA addresses. The author of the e-mails wanted Lavin fired in the next few days, threatening that he and his father would be killed. The coach had received threats against himself before, and after watching Jim Harrick go through so many, he could shake them off with relative ease. But this one was too personal, going after his father.

Everyone who knew Steve knew Cap Lavin, and knew how tight the father-son bond was. Steve could live with the public criticism, and even grew to accept what he calls "typical death threats" as part of the UCLA head coaching job. But a threat to his father's life was an entirely different ballgame. "At first, the threats came through e-mails and it was a threat on myself. You're really not alarmed because it is UCLA. I'd already been through the bomb threats against Harrick and the bomb squad coming into our offices. Someone had sent him some type of feces in a box," after a first round loss to Princeton in the 1996 NCAA Tournament.

When Lavin received the threat against his father, Cap Lavin was actually visiting Los Angeles and read the e-mail himself. His reaction? "I guess this is one case where the apple didn't fall far enough from the tree." In fact, it was not Cap or Steve who pushed to get the authorities involved, but Mary Lavin who expressed great concern. In the ensuing investigation, including subsequent threats by the same man, the local district attorney brought charges against Eric Weli Lin, who plead guilty to one misdemeanor count of making threatening and annoying phone calls and was sentenced to 10 days in jail and three years' probation. He was ordered to stay away from Lavin and the coach was given a picture of Lin to alert local security if he neared.

A few months later, in the spring of 2001, the wackos were out again, but this time it was a well-executed extortion plan. On March 6, 2001, Arn Tellem, Lavin's agent and well-known agent to stars like Kobe Bryant, received an anonymous letter containing numerous accusations against Lavin, threatening to send the details to UCLA administrators, local newspaper writers, and the PAC-10 commissioner if Lavin did not resign or be fired by April 2. The letter charged that Lavin had, among other things, participated in improper conduct in recruiting, knew of cash payments to former star Baron Davis, arranged automobiles for Bruin players, and provided benefits to trainers for their help with players. Tellem showed Lavin and Dalis the letter.

On March 26, the extortion letter was sent again, this time via e-mail to Dalis. The March 26 e-mail to Dalis was sent by a "Dave Gibson." Additional e-mails and threats were sent to Dalis and UCLA informed the PAC-10 about the allegations. From April 3 to April 19, a series of articles appeared in both major newspapers in Los Angeles concerning the allegations including quotes from "eyewitnesses" to the wrongdoings. At the same time, local *Daily News* beat writer Billy Witz wrote an article about Jason Kapono's workouts with a trainer the previous summer and questioned who had paid for them. An e-mail to Dalis citing Witz's article was sent by an "Earl Jones," a fan who runs an anti-Lavin Web site. Elliott spoke with Dalis to "clear the air" after saying that previous Dalis' remarks about him [Elliott] "opened me up to injury."

The PAC-10 and UCLA eventually cleared Lavin of any wrongdoing, but nonetheless, damage had been done. National media outlets had picked up on the story and the local newspapers' coverage painted an unglamorous picture of Lavin and the Bruin program. As with most media stories, there was little room in the pages for reversals or follow-ups.

"Those were probably the toughest 12 months of my career and for the first time I seriously wondered whether this particular coaching job was worth it all. I considered coaching elsewhere.

Of course, not many coaches get violent threats against them, and certainly not against their families, but then again, nowhere is a coach more of a target than at UCLA. Dealing with fame and being in the public eye is now a part of the job description of a college coach. No longer are they former athletes with whistles around their necks, residing in a gym office all day. With the intense media coverage, coaches become celebrities, for better or for worse.

For Mike Brey, his postseason success has taken his status to a new level in South Bend and across the country. He has become a household name and face in Indiana and is recognized wherever he goes. In fact, his fame is at such a level now that he and his family prefer to eat at home, because the interruptions and requests when eating out make it not worth it. He and his family receive some complimentary meals, but since they don't eat out much anymore, there is little benefit to them. In addition, he points out, there may be the expectation of something in return. Perhaps a restaurant owner may start calling for tickets or asking the coach to make an appearance.

It's not simply the interruptions during meals. Sometimes Brey just wants to be a husband and dad. His teenage son Kyle plays for a local AAU team in South Bend, and when he can find the time, Brey just likes to go and watch. "Hell, I can't even watch my own son play without the autograph requests. You don't want to be mean about it so you honor all of the requests, but then you miss a lot of the action. Those are the times when I just want to be Mike Brey, the father."

Like Brey, Alabama's Mark Gottfried has taken to eating in a lot more. "The public believes that coaches are everybody's property," says Gottfried. "The best is when people come up to your table at dinner and say, 'I don't mean to interrupt but . . .' When you hear but, you know a request is coming."

Bill Self recalls being on Larry Brown's staff at Kansas, and going out to eat with the staff after games at local restaurants. "Soon, everyone knew we were there and our 'staff' dinner now had many other people." But it didn't stop Brown from going out after games. "You have to be responsible for your own actions when you are out in public," Self says. "When I walk into a restaurant here in Champaign, people know who you are. But, of course, they also keep some places open for you late at night after games."

Most coaches are very wary of their fame, and take all necessary precautions. On their anniversary this past year, Self took his wife Cindy out to a local restaurant and bar, and while waiting for a table, Self ordered a drink at the bar. But he thought twice. What would people say if they saw him drink a beer? How might people misinterpret such an innocent act of an adult man? Many coaches have an internal gauge that reminds them of where they are and who is watching. Do you stop in the parking lot of a shopping mall to talk to an enthusiastic fan, who happens to be a 25-year-old beauty? What would people say?

There are also the "spoils" that come with fame including the many beautiful women who want to be with a famous and rich man, particularly a young, good-looking coach. There are always temptations. But there are also rumors, like the kind that swirl around rock stars, actors, and politicians. There are stories about alleged affairs, kinky sex, and other indiscretions by coaches.

In addition to the rumors and falsities that can harm a coach and his family, there are also the taunts, confrontations, and dirty looks that many coaches face on a daily basis. Especially during a losing season, coaches often face difficult situations with the public and endure nasty comments about themselves and, occasionally, their families. "You need to draw the line and say something when it concerns your kids," says Tanya Alford. "I think my faith allows me to be able to bite my tongue and allows me to not retaliate or say something unless it is directed at my children or said in front of them." Though not as serious as the death threats against Lavin, the verbal assaults lobbed against coaches during and after games must certainly raise one's blood pressure night after night.

The perks of fame, however, are bountiful and help to make the downside of celebrity less painful. In addition to the compensation packages from their employers, coaches are able to cash in on their celebrity status through endorsements and appearances. Showing up at a convention, speaking at a company's annual meeting, or even being the grand marshal of a local parade are just a few of the opportunities for coaches to earn money and further their celebrity. There are coaches representing car dealerships, local McDonald's restaurants, and Mom & Pop diners. Of course, at the higher levels of Division I, those opportunities can be even more vast and coaches can pick and choose. At smaller schools, though they may be local celebrities, coaches may not earn much additional money from outside sources.

Aside from the opportunities for earning additional income, coaches have access to major discounts or free services and products. Want an addition built onto your home? A local contractor or builder will build it for you at cost. Take a friend out to a local TGI Friday's? Just sign the receipt and it will be taken care of. Need tickets to a Brittany Spears concert for you and your teenage daughters? What day and what row? It's not that many coaches ask for special treatment, or even expect it (except for a few), but why not take advantage of the perks of celebrity? People want to associate themselves with famous people, actors, politicians, athletes, and coaches, and therefore offer services or benefits that the average man would not receive.

"We don't take advantage of a lot of the stuff, premieres and shows, we get invited to or could ask for," Lavin says. "Treena [Camacho] and I would much rather stay at home and rent a movie than to do the social thing on the town." In Los Angeles, the social thing can mean unlimited parties, celebrity award shows, movie premieres, the Playboy Mansion, and other temptations. (Lavin prefers to stay home in his Marina del Rey home with a Jacuzzi, swimming pool, and game room, but not a lot of furniture. Lavin is gracious with out-of-town visitors and routinely offers up a spare bedroom for a friend, coach, or family member.) When he does go out, Lavin does not use his status to get to the front of the line, but if offered, he doesn't turn it down. Most coaches admit the same. They don't see anything wrong with taking advantage of something that is offered.

Brey takes occasional advantage of the ticket perks of his status, getting Chicago theater tickets, Cub seats, Bulls tickets, or Indy 500 passes for himself and his children. He tries not to use his status to request too much, but let's face it, it comes in handy. Brey, Self and Alford have all sung the famed "Take Me Out to the Ballgame" at Wrigley Field and Alford appeared on ESPN's *2-Minute Drill* last summer. Gottfried points out another perk of being a local celebrity: getting out of speeding tickets. "We probably get a lot more warnings than tickets."

Manhattan's Bobby Gonzalez has earned a reputation as a fast-talker and fast player on New York's night scene. Frequenting chic clubs, bars, and restaurants, with friends or girlfriends, Gonzalez lives up the part of being a coach in a big city. "I guess I'm kind of like a celebrity now, everybody knows me," the 37-year-old gushes. "Wherever I go, not to sound like a movie star, but wherever I go, I do get recognized. People read the *Daily News* and *Newsday* and see us play on MSG [Madison Square Garden Network]. But I think the celebrity can be good and bad. I try to look at it as a positive."

A coach's celebrity status often depends on his own personality and where he coaches. A low-key guy in a small Midwest town may not attract the attention that a brash, outgoing coach in a large metropolitan area might. Alford is a celebrity in Indiana, of course (with a hotel named after him), but his fame is not due to his coaching; it's due mostly to his days as a player. He is the exception. Most well-known coaches are famous for what they do after their playing days are over. Bill Self is certainly a celebrity in Champaign, Illinois, but might not be recognized in Los Angeles. Bob Huggins may rule Cincinnati, but may hardly get noticed in Miami.

"I do get recognized," says Villanova's Jay Wright, "but it is not out of hand. There are six Division I schools in Philadelphia, each with its own supporters. And then there are the professional teams, so there are a lot of sports going on here."

Jeff Jones paid the price of celebrity in Charlottesville at the University of Virginia (see chapter 12), but now he's practically anonymous in Washington, D.C., coaching at American. "I still get recognized. But most of it is, 'Didn't you used to coach at Virginia?' When you are in a bigger area, it is easier to blend in." Especially in cities with other collegiate teams and professional sports, it may be easier for a coach to live a normal life.

Besides the perks and benefits of food, services, and home construction, there are the bonuses of free travel to exotic locations around the globe. For those under contract with Nike or Adidas, there are all-expenses paid retreats at locations such as Cancun, Mexico or the Bahamas. These coaches are wined and dined by company staffs, engage in discussions about issues in the game, and the apparel company, and otherwise are encouraged to swim, run, and talk hoops. Wives and children are included on these trips so coaches get their family vacations, too. (Again, not all coaches have endorsement deals and a lesser-known coach at a smaller school may be busting his butt just to take his family to Disney World.) Some coaches receive free trips in exchange for a speaking engagement or appearance. Of course, almost all schools pay for their coach and his wife to go to the Final Four for a week of games, meetings, and networking.

The Alfords, the Selfs, and the Breys, like all coaching families, must learn to deal with the perks and perils of fame rather quickly, and how they react says a great deal about who they are as people. Coaches have become stars, a far cry from decades ago when the coach was a forgotten man and very few people outside of his program knew who he was. ESPN's Dick Vitale believes that his employer had a lot to do with changing the coaching profession. With the advent of ESPN in 1979 and the explosion of televised games in the 1980s and 1990s, coaches have become stars. "The positive is that many are making millions and the negative is that there is such intense scrutiny and critique on these coaches—unbelievable pressure," says Vitale.

But no one forces coaches into the profession and though coaches at times complain about the pressures and the unfair criticism, they cherish the lifestyle their work has afforded them. Is it worth it? Legendary coach Pete Newell, who earned $12,000 a year coaching at Cal in the late 1950s, believes the issues and problems coaches face today are not worth the price. "There are so many pitfalls in coaching today, from kids leaving to the NBA to a focus not on education but performance. The exposure of coaches has made them known, but also encouraged second-guessing. A coach knows that he can go from the penthouse to the outhouse in a moment's time."

Steve Lavin is recognized on the streets in Los Angeles, particularly during the season when his face is on television nightly. And there is no event that brings out more cameras in L.A. (besides a movie premiere) than the UCLA-USC game. As usual with these games, there is a great deal of pregame hype and media coverage in the local papers. USC came in ranked No. 25 and sat at 8-3 in the PAC-10 while the Bruins were No. 15 and 7-4 in conference play. USC had not swept the Bruins in a season since 1991–1992, and Lavin was going to do all that he could to keep that streak alive. Before the game in the locker room, the coach was more relaxed than usual, joking with Gerald Madkins and watching the Missouri-Iowa State game on television. His players returned after warming up and the coach immediately focused on the keys to the game.

"We need to rebound tonight, not like we did at the Forum," a reference to the manhandling of the Bruins by USC in their early season loss to the Trojans. "We need to play physical. Watch [David] Bluthenthal on the boards and let's limit [Sam] Clancy's touches on the ball. We need to play 40 minutes of solid basketball and 35 seconds of defense on every possession!"

The inspirational words of their coach did not inspire an impressive performance by the Bruins in the first half, however, as they allowed USC to crash the boards and get easy inside buckets. The UCLA guards missed their jump shots and the slower pace of the game kept the scoring low. By halftime, USC led 39-33 and a different side of Lavin emerged in the locker room, after his team was outmuscled and outplayed. "You guys are not playing your asses off," he screamed covered in sweat. "They pushed you around at the Forum and they are doing it to you now on your own court!" Infuriated at his team's lack of passion and failure to execute the game plan, Lavin ripped into his players. "You are playing like you are scared," he screamed.

His rhetoric was echoed by assistant Jim Saia, who singled out Jason Kapono for playing his own game and for not following instructions. "If you guys do what we tell you to do and we lose, then that is our fault," Saia said. "But you need to execute the game plan. Do what we worked on all week in practice. We do it for a reason." Lavin jumped back in, reminding his players that they only trailed by two possessions. "We couldn't possibly play any worse and we are still in it, so let's get it done." The Bruin staff decided to switch offenses to run a 4-out, 1-in motion against USC in the second half, which hopefully would allow them to get better looks at the basket against the Trojans' multiple defenses.

Perhaps it was the halftime speeches or the offensive adjustments, or maybe the team just decided to kick it into high gear on their own, but the Bruins played inspired basketball in a memorable second half. After trailing at the break, UCLA pulled even at 40 as the Bruins went on a 7-1 run to start the half. USC had a four-minute scoring drought six minutes into the half, and UCLA took a 47-42 lead. Led by Kapono, UCLA went on another impressive run to go ahead by 11, 61-50. After the teams traded baskets and the Trojans hit some outside shots, USC went on their own 7-2 run, behind a Bluthenthal three-pointer to close the gap to 64-63 with just 1:38 left in the game. USC's Brandon Granville was fouled with 33 seconds left and hit both free throws to put the visitors ahead by one; impressive considering they had trailed by 11 just five minutes earlier.

Down by one, Lavin called a timeout and set up a last possession, diagramming a play for Kapono or Matt Barnes to get the last shot. But things didn't quite work out that way. As Cedric Bozeman ran down the clock with the ball, he had to rush a shot and with less than four seconds to play, Gadzuric grabbed the rebound and put up a shot, but he missed. He got his own rebound, but was trapped under the basket by the end line and USC defenders. The big man spotted Billy Knight alone at the three-point line in front of the Bruin bench and threw the ball to the senior. Knight calmly caught and shot, nailing a three to send the Pauley crowd into hysterics. Knight was mobbed by his teammates as fans flooded the floor, and a euphoric and relieved Lavin made his way to USC's Henry Bibby for a postgame handshake. Another big win for UCLA.

In the weeks that UCLA and USC face off, there is only one conference game for each, and while USC chooses to leave the date open after the UCLA game, the Bruins typically schedule a difficult nonconference game. This season they headed across the country to Philadelphia to take on the Villanova Wildcats. The game came down to the final two minutes. With his team up by one and 75 seconds on the game clock, Lavin had Kapono at the scorer's table to check back in but chose not to use a timeout to get his star in the game. Instead, with Knight and Barnes still in there, Lavin thought they could afford to wait for a stoppage of play. They finally got the stoppage but only with three seconds left on the shot clock, and the ensuing out-of-bounds play failed. The next time UCLA touched the ball they trailed by one and hurried for a last shot. The hero of the USC game, Knight, could not convert two open three-point looks as time expired. Lavin did not call a timeout to set up a final possession. UCLA fell on the wrong side of the clock this time, losing 58-57. The crowd at The Pavilion ran onto the court, all 6,500 of them, and the Bruins were caught up in another crowd frenzy—but this time they were the victims.

After the game, Lavin was criticized in the Los Angeles media for poor game management and a failure to take a timeout during the last possession. UCLA had won two in a row before Villanova, but again had lost a game they should have won—the story of their season. They were 16-7, 8-4 in conference play, tied for second with USC, California and Stanford, all with four losses apiece.

On the same afternoon that the Bruins lost to a Big East opponent, Notre Dame and Georgetown played what would be the most memorable game of the college basketball season. It was an epic so great that it was replayed on *ESPN Classic* just days later. Notre Dame had beaten Rutgers 89-72 earlier in the week and traveled to the nation's capital looking for its fifth straight win. Against Rutgers, Chris Thomas scored 32 points and dished out 11 of his team's 24 assists. David Graves had back spasms the night before and spent the night in the infirmary, but was able to play and scored 18 points for the Irish. They improved to 6-3 in the Big East, after starting out 2-3, making a remarkable turnaround from their early slump.

Earlier in the week, Brey had sat down the team and explained to them about their chances in the Big East and NCAA Tournament, including an update on the team's RPI and where Brey thought they might finish. He was up front with the team the last month and a half of the season, telling them exactly what he thought they needed to do to get back to the NCAAs. Last season the Irish had gone on an eight-game winning streak in January and February and over the past two seasons, had gone 14-5 from mid-January on. A win on the road against Georgetown would help.

The classic battle between the schools can best be summed up by the statistics: four overtimes and 227 combined points. Chris Thomas was the only player for either team to play all 60 minutes and finished with 22 points and 12 assists. Matt Carroll led the Irish with 30 points and Ryan Humphrey added 23. For the Hoyas, Mike Sweetney scored 35 and had 20 rebounds while his teammate Wesley Wilson helped out with 26. Near the end of regulation, with the score tied at 84-84, the Hoyas' Kevin Braswell's shot at the buzzer was blocked by Tom Timmermans, sending the game into overtime. At the end of each of the first three extra periods, Georgetown had the last chance to win it, but could not convert, including a basket by Braswell that was waved off at the end of the third overtime. In the fourth overtime, Carroll scored seven points on a three-pointer and four free throws as Notre Dame pulled away and won 116-111. There was absolute exhaustion on the faces of the Irish players, and Brey seemed emotionally spent as well. These are the games that will age a coach five years, especially as Notre Dame had to fend off four different potential game-winning shots.

In the postgame locker room, Brey was in disbelief. He had never been in a game like this one as a player or coach. At times, it was almost comical. At the end of the second overtime, Ryan Humphrey walked off the court and he and Brey exchanged looks and smiles that simply said, "Can you believe this?" Immediately following the game, Brey did postgame television interviews and by the time he got back to the locker room, he was wiped. He and his staff stood off to the side with assistant athletic director Jim Phillips and, while looking over the stat sheets, couldn't believe what they had just witnessed.

"You are my Road Dawgs," Brey said to the team, a play on the team's recent moniker, "Road Warriors." "You came here and took care of business. I was just telling Jim and the coaches that I had never been in a game like this," Brey told the team in the locker room with a look of relief and exasperation on his face. "It's hard to put this one in context."

The game did not come close to the seven-overtime thriller between Bradley and Cincinnati in 1981, but it led the lineup on all of the major sports shows that night. It gave Thomas some national exposure and gave the Irish some well-deserved respect around the country. More importantly, it was a big conference road win and a big RPI victory for Notre Dame as the postseason approached.

After he had brought in the motivational speaker to talk to his team following the Michigan State loss at home, Self noticed that his boys seemed to have an awakening. Things were not perfect and there still was work to do, but the ensuing three games showed promise. On the road at Michigan, the game was crucial for Illinois. After trailing by 13 in the first half, Illinois played inspired and aggressive ball behind an impressive effort by Lucas Johnson, who had now returned to the lineup fulltime. Johnson scored seven straight points in a five-minute stretch and Illinois went on to beat the Wolverines 68-60 behind Brian Cook's 19 points. (Self was concerned about Cook because an intimate article concerning his estranged father was printed in *Sports Illustrated* two days prior to the Michigan game and the coach didn't know how Cook was going to take it. For his part, the player said it was a "relief" to have it all come out.) Down the stretch, the Illini went on an 11-3 run to put the game away. After the season was complete, Self instinctively pointed to the first half Michigan comeback as the defining moment in the Illini's season.

The only negative for Self after the Michigan win was the seemingly disinterested play of Frank Williams. He finished with 10 points, but didn't score at all in the first half. Despite the big road win, the postgame questions were all about Frank. "I really don't care what people say about me," the junior told reporters after the game, when asked about his poor play. "I know what I do out there and my players know what I do out there." In defense of his player, Self added, "no player in the country gives 100% effort in every game." Privately, Self was concerned about Williams and acknowledged that the star guard was not playing hard all 40 minutes.

Two days later at home against Purdue, Illinois fell behind by 18 in the first half, but used a 17-0 run and a pressing defense and survived a Purdue attempt at the buzzer, to win 69-67. Robert Archibald started on the bench with a sprained ankle and Damir Krupalija sat out with his injured ankle. Illinois looked horrendous in the first half, falling behind 24-7. Self switched to a zone defense, which seemed to stumble Purdue. For eight minutes in the second half, Illinois did not let Purdue score and led by Williams' eight points during the run, took the lead for good. Though they escaped with a victory, no one seemed happy with Williams for the second game in a row. He managed only one shot in the first half and scored only one point with two turnovers. He finished with 13 points and sparked the second half Illini comeback, but his disinterested play continued to draw criticism.

After the game, Williams refused to speak with reporters, but his coach did and now was unabashed about going after his star. "I am not pleased at all. He's [Williams] trying to do the right thing, but the right thing is for him to play like he played those six or seven minutes in the second half. Once again, he was not a factor in the first half at all."

Self was now on the offensive in the media, frustrated at his failed attempts to get Williams going. Perhaps the junior would respond to his coach's criticism, perhaps not. Did Williams' preseason declaration for the NBA draft open him up for the intense criticism? Did he really not care about the Illinois season?

The Frank Williams that NBA scouts loved showed up in East Lansing on Tuesday, February 12, as the Illini got revenge for their home loss to Michigan State. In a hostile environment where the Spartan fans chanted "Lucas is trash!" at Johnson and "CBA! CBA!" while Williams was on the foul line, the star guard scored 22 points, including five in the last 75 seconds. In the final timeout with 10 seconds remaining, Self drew up a play for Williams. The coach noticed the focus on his players' faces. "Win this basketball game," Self told them. "These final 10 seconds can change our season." Williams walked away focused and Self knew the game was his. He hit the game-winner as Illinois won their third in a row, 63-61. The star guard not only turned it up offensively, but on the defensive end as well, shutting down the Spartans' Marcus Taylor, who shot just four of 15. It was MSU's second loss at home in 58 games and the first loss to Illinois at home since 1997.

After the game, Self admitted that the victory was "the biggest win since I've been here, outside of the postseason" and the Illini were back on track.

20

More than a Coach

THEY SEEMED LIKE TWO GUYS WHO COULDN'T BE MUCH FURTHER APART IN LIFE. STEVE Lavin was a white, 30-something coach from California, making a great deal of money coaching basketball in sunny California. Earl Watson was a black teenager from the poor neighborhoods of Kansas City, who played the game of basketball. As fate would have it, Watson ended up playing basketball thousands of miles from his home and family, all because of his new friend.

"Coach Lav was so nice to me during the recruiting process," says the now Memphis Grizzlie guard Watson, "even when I wasn't at the top of UCLA's list. I just felt comfortable with him." Watson came to Los Angeles as Lavin was about to enter his first year as head coach. The two had established a relationship when Lavin was still an assistant to Jim Harrick, recruiting in the Midwest. But now that "nice" and "comfortable" relationship would be put to the test. And it passed with flying colors.

Watson would go on to start at guard for Lavin for four years, emulating and being influenced by his coach and friend. "What people don't realize when they gave me any praise for great leadership, toughness, and stuff is that I was simply an extension of Coach Lav on the court. We saw things the same way, and when we didn't, we could openly disagree about things."

Perhaps there is no greater staunch supporter of Lavin than his former player. On Lavin's perception as a slick guy: "So he dresses well, has slick hair, and lives in a nice house. What does that have to do with winning games? It has nothing to do with it at all." On Lavin's ability as a coach: "From my first year until I graduated, I saw him grow as a coach, as he kept getting better. He hasn't even peaked yet as a coach." On the idea that Lavin's practices are disorganized and laid back: "Crazy. His practices were so hard, there were times when you didn't think you could make it through—they tested you physically. But now I am in the NBA and practices are nothing, because of what Lav prepared me for physically and mentally in practice."

As Watson watched Lavin deal with the public, the media, and the pressure through the years, he developed an admiration for his coach, beyond that of role model. He respected Lavin as a man, watching him deal with the world around him. "You know, whenever Lavin would meet someone, a kid or an older person, he never just said, 'Call the office.' Lav would get their names and addresses and send out a packet of UCLA goodies. He is just a nice guy. He also does a lot for charity that people don't see. He has an amazing character and is caring."

The unique bond between player and coach was cemented in late January 2001, when the Peter Dalis–Rick Pitino episode occurred. "It was all over the news, everyone was talking about it. But every day he came down to practice with a smile, just like he had signed a 20-year extension. He would even joke about it with us in practice. But he showed a lot of strength. He was the coach until they fired him or kicked him out. But I sensed that he was down about it."

Watson picked up the phone and called his coach on his cell, returning a favor done so many times over the years. "Coach, it's Earl. I know what's up. You can't leave me here. You can't quit. Let's talk."

It was difficult for Watson to watch as the media put Lavin through hell, and even worse that the coach would not lash out at the administration, media, or Pitino. Enough was enough and his "extension" took it upon himself. Watson began to defend Lavin in the media and go after the UCLA administration, by name or by implication.

Watson learned about resiliency from his coach, and those lessons still carry with him. "He is such a role model, a big brother. I took so much of what he taught me and I use it every day in the NBA, where the competitiveness can be overwhelming."

After Watson graduated, the relationship grew even stronger. In the predraft camp in Phoenix in the spring of 2001, Watson needed a good showing to impress the scouts. The PAC-10 coaches' meetings happened to be going on in Phoenix the same week, making it easy for coaches to come watch their players perform. Lavin came and watched Watson play in every game, and then took him out to dinner afterward to talk about his performance and life. "There were other PAC-10 guys playing in the games and I couldn't believe their coaches didn't come out to watch. But Coach Lav was there for every game. It meant so much to me that he came."

When Earl Watson first arrived at UCLA, he had dinner with Lavin and his girlfriend, Treena. After the meal, Watson pulled his coach aside and said, "By the time I graduate, you better marry her." Camacho stuck by Lavin's side through everything, and though the couple was serious, they had yet to tie the knot by the time Watson left UCLA. "That's OK, I guess he needs to find the time. He is just so devoted to his job, he is a workaholic."

But Watson still does have the words "Lavin" and "wedding" in mind. "Whenever I get married, I want Coach Lavin to be in my wedding, to be a part of it. That's how much he means to me."

Lavin and Watson's relationship is built upon the many moments when a coach is no longer a coach, but a father, brother, and friend. They are surrogate family members for players away from home or for players who never really had a home in the first place. The most important, but often overlooked, role for coaches today is the one that has the real impact on the players down the road. Despite what the public believes, most coaches do truly care for their players as people, not just as scoring machines. The moments when the compassion comes out are not during the heated battles on the floor, or even in practice. They are moments in private.

"I think the kids now are very different from when I first started," says the 68-year-old Lute Olson. "I think there are a lot of reasons for that, but I think the single biggest one is the lack of family environment that there was when I first started. It seemed like everyone had a mom and dad and they had a schedule and everyone got together for dinner. Now it seems there are an awful lot of kids who have one-parent homes. . . . It's made my job more difficult. I make a point of telling the parents that I have probably 13 kids that I have to be concerned about. As soon as the parents have the same concern for the other 12 that they have for their own son, then let's discuss it."

Olson's point about the change in the home environment over the years has seriously altered the job of coaches. No longer do most players come to them with a strong support system, no financial need, and carrying little emotional baggage. It is all part of the job now. A coach must not only be the teacher and advisor, but fill many of the traditional family roles of the father and brother.

In response to criticism about his poor graduation rate at Arkansas in an ESPN interview, former coach Nolan Richardson responded, "Do you realize that 80% of my kids that come here to play basketball come from a single parent? Did you realize that?" Perhaps that is an excuse, and perhaps family structure and academics should not be inherently tied together. However, like Olson, Richardson acknowledges that the change in family structure and home life has had a profound impact on his job.

Bill Self approaches his role as a coach, as his father did for him, as a combination of parent and friend. Upset at a missed curfew or a silly turnover in a game, but calm and supportive when it comes to the important things in life. "I want my players to be able to come to me, or another coach, and let them know what is going on in their family and personal life," Self says proudly. "In fact, as a coach, I want to be able to read my players and know if something is wrong."

At Illinois, every player is required to come by the basketball office before practice everyday, to talk with a coach about life, school, or basketball—something. It creates a stronger bond between the players and coaches. Self gives his guys a great deal of freedom, and until they abuse it, he will continue to do so. That freedom builds up trust, which furthers the coach-player relationship. "Coaches need to allow players to feel good about themselves as people and players. I want them all to live up to their potential."

Experienced coaches such as Self also know that you don't need to treat all players the same, but you do need to treat them all fairly. One kid may need more advice and guidance in academics, while another needs support for family problems at home. No matter the circumstances, coaches and players can have a bond that is lifelong. Former players still call Self to congratulate him on big wins and give suggestions when the Illini don't play well. As Self says, borrowing a phrase from Roy Williams: "They are players when they are here and family when they leave."

Like Lavin, Self had a unique bond with a point guard, a walk-on, at Oral Roberts. "He was an extension of me," the coach says about Earl McClellan. "He was a guy that took responsibility, that sacrificed. We stay in touch and always will."

All Mike Brey needed was a touch on the shoulder from Ryan Humphrey. For road games, Brey was always the last one off the bus, waiting for the team and assistants to shuffle out. The senior captain sat in the last row and before stepping off the bus, would always put a simple squeeze on Brey's shoulder as he walked off. They never made eye contact. "The first few times he squeezed my shoulder, I got chills," the coach says. "It was very settling for me as a coach." They just kind of understood each other.

Iowa's Reggie Evans admires Steve Alford's ability to be a father and a coach and found him to be a role model to emulate. "I kind of look at him as a father-figure. I like him as a coach. I like him as a friend. I like him off the court."

For Villanova coach Jay Wright, establishing that bond takes time. It is during the recruiting process that coaches first encounter players and their families. If a coach goes after a recruit when he is a junior, and that player stays in school for four years, then a coach would have spent six years with the player and his family. "Between the ages of 16 and 22, there are a lot of experiences for kids that age. I don't try to take on the extra role of a parent, but I am an extension of the parent. The parents have gotten them that far and now I must look after them. The kids that don't have parents or come from broken homes require a greater parental role on my part."

(The parental role is one that is "day-to-day" according to Ohio coach Tim O'Shea, and one "that a coach can be proactive on," recognizing when something is not right with a player.)

In late April 2002, weeks after UCLA's season had ended, Lavin sat in his office in the J. D. Morgan Center writing some letters when senior Rico Hines walked in. He had not seen Lavin for a week or so, but had talked to him about getting a job. Hines and Lavin sat down and went over Hines' resume, with Lavin, the son of an English teacher, bringing it to a new level. The pair then talked about what Hines wanted to do and how Lavin could help. For Lavin, coaching is about a long-term plan, about teaching lessons and forming relationships that will last a lifetime. Helping a player find a job is just one part of the process.

Notre Dame was on a five-game conference-winning streak in the first weeks of February, but they needed a few more wins to solidify their spot in the Tournament. They had defeated Georgetown in an epic four-overtime thriller in Washington, D.C., and had five days off before facing Rutgers on the road, a team they had beaten easily just two weeks prior. Upon returning to South Bend on Saturday night, February 9, assistant Anthony Solomon was pleased with the team's performance. They were on a roll. But as the team took a few days off to rest, Solomon took no breather. The game against Rutgers on Thursday could mean so much for the Irish, and Rutgers was "his" team. He had been assigned the Scarlet Knights earlier in the season, and had already prepared one scouting report just weeks earlier. But this was now a different Notre Dame team and a different Rutgers team. So he settled in after putting his daughters to bed on Sunday night, and popped in some tape.

It is really hard to imagine what life was like for coaches before the emergence of the VCR and videotape. Coaches rely on film more than they rely on themselves. A tape of a game doesn't lie. Film can show missed block outs, poor defense, and times when charges could have been taken. But film can also teach a team about an opponent—about what players like to do what, when, and where on the court.

Every coach in America must have a VCR in his home, and the majority have one in their offices, or at least in the basketball suite. On most nights, after putting the kids to bed and spending a few minutes with their wives, coaches settle on their favorite sofa or Lazy Boy and begin to watch tape until well after midnight. This ritual is performed around America all through the season.

Lute Olson has been involved in basketball at various levels since the 1960s. He has seen the advent of the shot clock, the three-pointer, and cornrows on top of players' heads. He has witnessed the explosion of media coverage, changes in recruiting rules, and an evolution of the men patrolling the sidelines. But if you ask Olson what one thing changed the way he coaches, what revolutionized the game and created a new form of basketball, his answer is surprising: the VCR. Yes, that same machine on which a family can watch *Bambi* or *Terminator* changed the way coaches coach. Its impact is immeasurable, to the delight of coaches, but perhaps to the ire of a coach's family.

The reliance on film has changed the way that coaches scout and prepare their teams for opponents. Assistant coaches still have the primary responsibilities for scouting, but with tape, it is easier for head coaches to weigh in, because they now can see the opponent play as well. With the ever-increasing demands on a coach's time, preparing for opponents and for practices has unfortunately taking a back seat.

"I spent 80% of my time as a coach preparing and studying," notes John Wooden. To him, a coach's role is to prepare himself and his team for what lies ahead. He obviously could prepare fairly well. Another coach whose preparation may be unparalleled is Bobby Knight's; known for hours of film work, Knight could script a game for his players.

As in recruiting, coaching, and practicing, coaches have different philosophies on how best to prepare a team for an opponent. Preparation and scouting include personnel reports, walk-throughs, film breakdown, and other things that a coach can use to prepare his team for battle. Some coaches watch hours and hours of tape, while others watch very little. Some coaches prepare detailed notebooks for players with opponent statistics, tendencies, and set plays of an opponent, while other coaches simply let their team know who likes to "go inside" on the opposition. Some coaches like to practice hard the day before a game while others would prefer to play HORSE. Whatever gets it done.

Some coaches love to look back and go over things that their team did wrong. After an *exhibition* loss to the Harlem Globetrotters in November, Steve Alford replayed the game twice until 2:00 A.M., grading his players along the way. But Alford does not grade players with an A or B, but rather with a complex point system he recently adopted, originally created by Dean Smith. Other schools have similar grading scales and place similar emphasis on the "little things" that win games: charges, rebounds, box outs, defensive stances. Watching tape of your own team usually occurs right after the game, at home late at night, or as a staff in the office munching on pizza. Watch it and move on.

When coaches are not watching tape of their own team, picking it apart, looking at the negatives (and sometimes positives), coaches are watching upcoming opponents play. They don't simply go to the local Blockbuster for the game tapes, but rather to the team managers or video coordinators, who tape game after game on a daily basis. On one Saturday, the head manager at Notre Dame may tape up to 15 games through the Dish TV system, a necessity for all coaching staffs. These tapes are labeled, catalogued, and placed on a shelf, ready for the coaches.

In most programs, assistant coaches are assigned a particular team to scout long before game day approaches. Some staffs even assign the games before preseason practice. The assignments are given out for specific reasons. Perhaps one assistant is more familiar with a certain team or another had coached in an opponent's conference. Maybe an assistant is a defensive specialist and an opponent requires complex defensive schemes. Whatever the reason, coaches know whose "game" it is and prepare accordingly. It is then their job to watch film, break down tape, prepare a scouting sheet, and come up with some ideas on how to play the opponent. All of which is then run by the head coach who makes the ultimate decisions.

This process of watching tape may begin a week before the actual game date. Head coaches focus on the game at hand while most assistants are focusing two or three games ahead. At Illinois, all three assistants are assigned games to scout; same at Notre Dame and UCLA. At Iowa, mainly assistants Brian Jones and Greg Lansing scout teams, although Alford spends a lot of time watching opponent tape as well.

At Illinois, the assistant responsible for scouting an opponent will watch six or seven games that the opponent has played, and prepare detailed tendencies, stats, and diagrams of offensive and out-of-bounds plays. He will then take the information and tape, along with some suggestions as to how other teams have played the opponent, and sit down with Self. Self himself will watch one or two opponent games and a "possession tape," a highlight reel of different offensive and defensive sets prepared for the head coach. He will then decide how to play the opponent, with input from all of the assistants.

The UCLA locker room was small, old, and not conducive to watching tape. But there sat the Bruins, the day before their home game against Arizona, sitting in folding chairs looking up at the screen pulled down from the ceiling. They were watching Wildcat possessions, from earlier games and from the first half of the UCLA/Arizona game a few weeks earlier. The coaches did not show any parts of the second half of that game, the one in which the Bruins let a 20-point second half lead go in a remarkable collapse. They ran the tape of the first half for about 20 minutes, long enough for the Bruin players' attention to start to wane.

Before they watched the tape, assistant Patrick Sandle had gone over the scouting report, typed up by Basketball Operations man Jamie Angeli. The packet was neatly organized with scouting reports on each player, keys on the offensive and defensive side of the ball, statistics of the Arizona team, and a box score of the last meeting between the two schools. Sandle went over the report, player by player, with Lavin injecting a comment or two.

As they concluded the scouting report, the players headed off to the showers. On the court, they had already walked through the Arizona sets with Sandle using the scout team as stand-ins. On some days, Lavin will have the team watch tape first, and then hit the court for the scout team walk-through.

One interesting tactic that the UCLA staff employs takes place at halftime at home games. After the team has left the locker room for the second half, UCLA managers bring in a large corkboard and begin to post. They put up statistics, player biographies, box scores, and conference record of the Bruins' *next* opponent. By the time the team returns to the locker room at the conclusion of the current game, the focus is already on who is next—win or lose. The staff wants the team to focus on the next challenge ahead, not celebrate or dwell on the outcome of the game.

But the task at hand for the Bruins was Arizona, a team that continued to surprise the nation, rising to No. 9 in the polls and 10-3 in the PAC-10. Dan Gadzuric led the early charge in the first half with eight points in the first six minutes and with contributions from Jason Kapono, Dijon Thomspon, Matt Barnes, and Billy Knight, the Bruins went into halftime leading 40-34. In the second half, Arizona roared back and led by as many as eight before UCLA caught up in the closing minutes. With 19 seconds left, and UCLA trailing by two, Barnes found Kapono alone at the arc and the junior nailed the three, giving the Bruins a one-point lead. Arizona's Channing Frye missed a shot to win it with three seconds left and the fight for the rebound ran out the clock. Erasing the memory of the disastrous second half collapse in Tucson, the Bruins had jumped right back into the PAC-10 race with only four losses, joining Arizona, Oregon, Cal, Stanford, and USC. Gadzuric came up huge with 22 points and 16 rebounds and Kapono had 20, including three trifectas in the closing three minutes to pace UCLA. Cedric Bozeman played terribly but Ryan Walcott did not, and when Bozeman checked back in the game with just over seven minutes left in the game, he was booed by the Pauley fans.

The Jekyll and Hyde team of 2002 did not stray from its past performances, following up a good win with a bad loss. After upsetting Arizona, the Bruins lost at home, 69-68, to Arizona State when the Sun Devils' Curtis Millage hit a three-pointer with 13.8 seconds remaining to give ASU the upset. It was their first win over UCLA at Pauley in 15 years. Critical turnovers and missed free throws down the stretch, in addition to a lack of effort on the defensive end, doomed UCLA. The Bruins were up 66-63 with 3:35 left but couldn't hold the lead. Coaching decisions again played a role in the final minute as they had against Villanova a week earlier. Lavin decided to use his final timeout with 2.3 seconds left to try to "ice" the Sun Devils' Kyle Dodd who was at the line shooting a one-and-one, up by one. He missed, Billy Knight grabbed the rebound, but without a timeout, looked confused, dribbled into traffic, and was called for traveling to end the game.

It was another bad loss for the Bruins, in a season filled with them. They had lost to teams that they should have beaten: Ball State, Pepperdine, Villanova, Arizona State. And they had looked terrible in narrow victories over UC-Irvine, Oregon State, and Washington State. But they had beaten teams like Kansas, USC, Arizona, and Cal when no one gave them a shot.

For Notre Dame, the prep work done by Anthony Solomon did not help against Rutgers in Piscataway, New Jersey. Clutch free throw shooting by the Scarlet Knights down the stretch proved the difference as Rutgers won 65-62. Notre Dame had opened strong, leading 16-6 just minutes into the game, but their lead soon evaporated and they led by only three at the half. In the victory over Rutgers a week earlier, Chris Thomas had scored a career high 32 points, but in the rematch, he would score only six points, going 0 for 9 from three-point land and 0 for 14 overall in the game. Thomas had a chance to tie the game at the buzzer, but his three-point attempt bounced off the rim as time expired. The Irish fell to 7-4 in the Big East, and Brey was already looking ahead to the remaining games to figure out if his team still had a shot in the conference race. The top two teams in each division of the Big East got first round byes in the Big East Tournament, and Notre Dame and Syracuse were battling for the second spot in the Big East West. At 17-8 overall, Brey still thought the Irish needed some quality wins over the likes of Miami and Syracuse to help solidify their resume for the Tournament. Only once has a Big East team won 20 regular season games and not made the NCAAs, Connecticut in 1980. The Irish had a good strength of schedule and an RPI in the thirties.

At home against Syracuse, Notre Dame led by as many as seven points in the second half, but could not hold on, losing 68-65. Tom Timmermans played 21 minutes, playing in front of his family, who had flown in from The Netherlands for the first time. David Graves missed a three-pointer with two seconds left that would have tied the game, and amazingly, the Irish went 5:17 without a field goal in the half. Thomas continued his woeful shooting, scoring eight points on 3 of 11 shooting, including just one point in the second half.

The freshman was struggling and his confidence was shaken. All season long, Brey had made it his priority to stay close with Thomas, both physically and mentally. In fact, before every game, home or away, the guard and coach met to review a highlight tape, talk about the game and otherwise for Brey, to make sure his star guard was ready. They also talked often by cell phone every day as Thomas had "a special line direct to me."

Notre Dame now needed a big road win over Miami to have a shot at a bye in the rapidly approaching Big East Tournament. More importantly, a win over a good Miami team would bolster their RPI and enhance their NCAA resume.

I owa had lost to Indiana and Minnesota and Steve Alford did make a change to the lineup as promised, bringing Reggie Evans off the bench against Penn State in State College. He responded with 23 points and 13 rebounds, but Iowa lost 71-65 to fall to 15-11, 4-8 in the conference. After the game, the coach made public that Evans had been skipping class. Three weeks into the semester, grade and class check reports were issued and it was then that Alford learned of the problem. Jared Reiner was out injured and Alford was forced to play Evans, despite his plan not to. "In the old way," the coach said, "Reggie wouldn't have played." The coach had compromised.

For the Ohio State home game, the Iowa Sports Information Office decided to tout Luke Recker and Evans for postseason awards, a rather unfortunate bit of timing. Evans did not play due to his academic problems and Recker had only three points. Iowa did lead by as many as 11 in the first half but each Iowa lead was cut by a Buckeye run. The game was tied at 60 with less than four minutes to play, but it was the Buckeyes who were able to play poised in the closing minutes and hit their free throws in winning 72-66.

Alford had continued to tinker with the lineup, trying to find a combination that worked, composed of guys he thought had been busting their butt. In his conversations with Bobby Knight, his mentor had pointed out to Alford that the seniors had to give it their all or the coach had to look toward the future. To Alford, his seniors meant his two stars, Recker and Evans. If they were not getting it done, then perhaps he had to look for alternatives. Against Ohio State, Alford started Brody Boyd, Ryan Hogan, Chauncey Leslie, Sean Sonderleiter, and Rod Thompson. The five had started a total of nine games in the season, a rather inexperienced group.

Surely against Wisconsin, the Hawkeyes could break into the win column, but playing in Madison would not be easy. The Hawkeyes turned the ball over too many times and could not convert enough of their free throws. At halftime, Alford talked about the "NIT or NCAA" in the locker room. Which one did the Hawkeyes want to play for? It was all on the line, "Our backs are against the wall." Behind good shooting and good defense, Wisconsin beat Iowa 64-56. The Hawkeyes fell to 15-13 and 4-10 in the Big Ten. They had lost five in a row and nine of 11. Forget about the NCAAs; Iowa would be lucky to get a berth in the NIT at this point. They had two regular season games remaining and then the Big Ten Tournament.

M eanwhile, in a rare late season nonconference game, No. 18 Illinois beat Seton Hall on the road, 75-65, to win their fourth in a row. Like all coaches around the country, Bill Self was glad to see his team peaking in late February, when wins matter most. Perhaps the Illini had put the losing streak and the missed expectations behind them. Maybe it was their destiny to be winning now and perhaps losing earlier only made them stronger. Whatever the case, they headed into their last four games against Penn State, Northwestern, Indiana, and Minnesota on a roll, with an outside shot at the Big Ten title.

21

Playing for Keeps

UCLA WAS STRUGGLING AS THE REGULAR SEASON CAME TO A CLOSE. THEY WERE 6-6 in their last 12 games heading into a late February swing to California and Stanford. In a show of unity before the Cal game, UCLA players all donned white headbands, à la Jason Kapono, before the start of the game. By halftime, with Cal leading 33-18, many had taken them off, indicative of the disunity on the court. The Bruins looked awful, eventually getting blown out, 69-51. Not only did they play poorly, but senior Matt Barnes hit Cal guard Shantay Leggins and was ejected, with the possibility of being suspended for the Stanford game just 36 hours later. It could have been a time for panic: a late season collapse, suspended starter, the criticism mounting. But it was all about resiliency and an opportunity to learn to Lavin.

"In past years, I have had more reasons to be discouraged than this year, believe it or not. There have been no off-the-court distractions, allegations, threats, ADs talking to other coaches [the Pitino episode] and frankly, we have a good team. We have a freshman point guard who needed time to adjust. I have always believed that we will be good in the long run," Lavin said the day after the Cal loss.

The next day, 24 hours before the showdown at Stanford, a place where the Bruins had won the past two seasons, Lavin took a different approach to practice—an upbeat one. He did the usual walk-through by the scout team, but mostly he had the players do competitive shooting games and scrimmage. Lavin wanted the players to enjoy playing the game, not worry about having to win at Maples Pavilion. In another change, Lavin decided the Bruins would employ a motion offense against Stanford, a move that the coach would later say was critical to the team's run. Replacing the structured 1-4 offense with 4 around 1 motion, which they had used in the second half against USC, would allow for better spacing on the floor. The Bruins often did a "60 point" game in practice, a drill focusing on backdoor cuts, passing, catching, spacing, and reading the defense.

The new offense must have worked as the Bruins dominated the Cardinal for most of the game and held on to win, 95-92, playing without Barnes who was suspended for his actions against Cal. Rebounding from yet another bad loss, the Bruins beat Stanford at Maples for the third time in three years and Cap and Mary Lavin were on hand for their son's win. The victory took UCLA to 18-9 and 10-6 in the conference, tied for fifth, with two games remaining at home against Oregon and Oregon State.

No one is really sure when the change occurred, but it was a titanic shift for all coaches. Maybe it was due to the increased exposure, the billions at stake, the Dick Vitales of the world. It became clear by the early 1990s that success meant winning in the postseason. Not just conference tournaments, but "The Big Dance." Failure to reach the Tournament is a black mark on a coach's record, a sign that perhaps his world is falling apart. It has become a benchmark for most coaches, one that they know they must reach in order to keep their jobs. And they must reach the Tournament now with ever-increasing speed.

With the growing importance of postseason play, there have been many changes in how coaches go about their job and how schools go about winning. Regular season matchups are no longer compelling, unless they can be a "good RPI win." Coaches look at the big picture at schools like UCLA, Duke, Arizona, and Kentucky. They know they are going to the Tournament so everything they do during the regular season is geared toward peaking in March. It is a marathon, not a sprint. With the increased pressure on coaches to win, and to win now, it means the door is open for coaches to use any means necessary to get there. Coaches, particularly young ones, will often break rules to get the players who will get them to the Tournament, who will get them exposure, which will lead to a better, higher profile and higher paying job. It's all about the Tournament.

It affects who teams play. In 2001, Alabama was left out of the NCAA Tournament, partly because of its weak nonconference schedule. They quickly remedied that, facing a much more difficult slate the following season. Wins over Division II schools or very weak Division I schools are no longer the best route to the Tournament. Schools need to play the big boys, which results in the major programs playing hellish schedules in nonconference, all in an effort to boost their standing and seeding for the NCAA Tournament. Before Arizona even played a game in the PAC-10 Conference, they had faced Florida, Illinois, Maryland, Texas, Kansas, Purdue, and Michigan State. These games were in addition to their conference slate that included playing Arizona, Oregon, USC, UCLA, Stanford, and Cal, all of them twice.

For smaller schools, like a Winthrop, UNC-Wilmington, Sienna, or McNeese State, just getting to the Tournament is the goal. The exposure and the financial rewards can put a program on the map, and make a relatively unknown coach the next "hot" candidate. But for the elite programs, just showing up for the Dance is not enough—you need to advance and dance late into the night. The bottom line is that coaches of low- to mid-majors know what a Tournament appearance can mean for them and their program, while the big-time school coaches know what *not* making the Tournament can mean.

Just imagine our vocabulary without terms like "bubble teams," "RPI, "March Madness," "strength of schedule," or "bracketology." The analysts start earlier and earlier every year, predicting who is in and who is out, which wins are critical, and who could be potential high seeds. It makes the game and the season more fun for fans as they follow their teams.

Notre Dame had been under the radar screen the entire season. They went about their business in the Big East, beating West Virginia at home 89-76 and upsetting No. 17 Miami on the road, 90-77 for a good RPI win. Chris Thomas scored a career high 32 in the Miami win, picking up the slack for Matt Carroll who had suffered an ankle sprain against West Virginia. David Rivers, a former Notre Dame All-American, watched the game at Miami Arena and gave the players a brief pep talk before tip-off. It was a big win for Notre Dame and especially satisfying for Mike Brey who beat his old high school assistant coach, Perry Clark. In a period of a month, the Irish went from being an NIT team to a bubble team to a lock to back to a bubble team. As March approached, Brey, like all other coaches, was calculating, formulating, and predicting his postseason lot.

"I don't go out there and campaign publicly for a spot in the Tournament," Brey said days before the Big East Tournament. "I don't think it helps and I just think that your play and record should speak for themselves." Brey had been critical of Michigan State's Tom Izzo for a media-lobbying barrage on behalf of his team. Izzo talked about their early season injuries, the strong conference schedule, and their tough nonconference slate. He wasn't just talking to the Spartan fans; he was attempting to talk to the Men's Selection Committee. This is what irked Brey. Izzo is not alone in the frenzied campaign for a coveted Tournament spot. With so much on the line for programs and coaches, why not shed some light on your credentials? Well, for one, no one is listening.

Former University of Virginia coach and athletic director Terry Holland served on the Selection Committee for five years, including 1996–1997 when he chaired the committee. "I don't think I was paying any attention to that at all. There is so much written at that time of year," Holland says with a laugh.

The Selection Committee works on the Tournament field all season long. The 10 Committee members are assigned particular conferences to watch throughout the season, to become experts on them, and to share their thoughts with the other members. Some Committee members watch four to six games during the season. As the Tournament draws near, voluminous packets are put together on every potential candidate including schedules, rosters, injuries to note, RPI and NCAA history; information put together by the NCAA Championship staff in Indianapolis. Schools also send materials to the Committee touting their season achievements.

There are 65 spots in the NCAA field, with 31 spots taken for automatic qualifiers, the conference winners. The remaining 34 spots are considered at-large, and it is up to the Committee to decide who gets in. Every year there are controversial picks, and nonpicks, and the Committee makes the difficult decisions up to the last minutes on Selection Sunday, though most of the at-large spots and seedings are done in advance of the deadline.

The rewards of postseason glory are a boon to any coach. Over the past decade, many coaches have used postseason successes to get more money, build new facilities, and get better jobs. For the coach of a top program, advancing deep in the tournament can mean hundreds of thousands of dollars. For a mid-major coach, taking his team to the tournament is the key to the big-time job kingdom. They know it and so do ADs. In the 2002 Tournament, Mike Davis took Indiana to the Final Four and got a large increase in pay. Kent State's Stan Heath positioned himself to become the next big thing.

Bruiser Flint believes that coaches are viewed in a different light if they get a team to the Tournament and then win a game or two. "We got to the Dance at UMass and it told people that I could get it done. We, and I, became a household name in a matter of three weeks."

Terry Holland views the whole process as the bathing suit competition in the "Miss America" pageant, with the year's "hot" coaches getting the interest because their teams made a run. Whether or not they cash in is another matter. "You get in the Tournament for a few years, maybe win a game or two with a program that probably can't continue to do it, and certainly are not going to compete for a national championship, and you may have the chance to move on to one of the bigger leagues. But some don't for whatever reason. The timing just wasn't right."

Getting into the Tournament can mean everything. For a coach like Tim Carter at Texas-San Antonio, making an appearance in 1999 meant more exposure for his program and for himself. "It increased the level of expectations. Even though they didn't give me any additional resources, they increased their level of expectations. As for me personally, any time you reach that level, what it does is give you the opportunity to maybe have a chance to move up in the profession."

The best example of the "Dance Enhance," or upward professional, or economic mobility for coaches as a result of Tournament success, was Kent State's Stan Heath in 2002. A former assistant to Tom Izzo at Michigan State, Heath took Kent State to the Elite Eight in his *first* year there. His well-publicized success made Heath a top coaching candidate and within 10 days, he was the new coach at the University of Arkansas, replacing Nolan Richardson. His salary went from $120,000 a year to close to $800,000 overnight. It never would have happened for Heath in 2002 if Kent State stayed home from the Tournament.

In the 2001 Tournament, Heath's predecessor, Gary Waters, took Kent State to an opening round NCAA win over storied Indiana—his prize? A bigger paycheck and respect in the Big East at Rutgers. Skip Prosser went from Xavier to Wake Forest after an NCAA appearance. Dan Monson went from Gonzaga to Minnesota. Buzz Peterson from Tulsa to Tennessee.

Ohio coach Tim O'Shea was an assistant for 17 years and was working under Al Skinner at Boston College when he interviewed for the Sienna and Delaware jobs. "I had a great AD at Boston College, and schools began to contact me. I interviewed at those schools and was a finalist, but didn't get them. We went from an RPI of 146 to five the next year, won our league, and were a No. 3 seed in the NCAA Tournament, and now I had a better standing."

After taking his team to the National Championship game, Mike Davis was asked by a reporter the day before the game what he hoped that Indiana's incredible run had done for him.

"I hope I get a raise." Said in jest, Davis spoke the truth—and he did get a huge raise. Coaches expect to be rewarded for impressive postseason showings.

And then there is Don Holst at the University of Montana, who was fired despite taking Montana to the NCAA Tournament in 2002. His team went 16-15 and 7-7 in conference, but only got to the Tournament by winning the conference tournament. Officials wanted to "breathe new life into this program." Sometimes just getting there is simply not enough. (Holst would be replaced by former DePaul and Florida State coach Pat Kennedy.)

"A crap shoot" is how West Virginia coach John Beilein describes the postseason, particularly the season-ending conference tournaments, where for mid-majors, it may be their only way into the big Tournament. "You have a great year, win 18 games but then you've got a three-day crap shoot. It has very little to do with your coaching ability. It's the bounce of the ball. I've coached in four Championship games and we could have won all four or lost all four." Beilein continues, "It's important for a big-major coach to get there and he's got numerous opportunities to get there because his strength of schedule improves as the year goes on. Of course, he's also paid well to get there."

For Rick Boyages at William & Mary, getting to the Tournament, as it is for most coaches, is almost a must. But much of the pressure depends on who your bosses are. "Here at W&M, I have a great AD who played in the NBA, knows basketball, knows the academics of what we do here, so he knows what is reasonable to expect. But there are a lot of ADs who I don't think necessarily understand." As Boyages goes on to point out, as well as many other mid-major coaches, the bottom line is dollars and winning. Making it to the Tournament means an economic windfall for the school and the conference. A mid-major school advancing a few rounds in the Tournament can mean millions for the conference, money that goes to support other sports as well. Some schools, especially those without major college football, depend on basketball revenue for athletic existence. With that kind of pressure, it is no wonder that coaches are given little time to make the Tournament. For the 40 or so top schools in college basketball, making the NCAA Tournament field is just the start. They have to advance to have a successful season. For the smaller schools, just getting there is success enough.

Flint takes an even broader approach to the meaning of making the Tournament. To him, the exposure, prestige, and media coverage can have an incalculable impact on the institutions overall. "Athletics is the front porch of the University. Get them there and then maybe they knock on the door." Potential students from around the country may suddenly be interested in a school because they followed them in the Tournament.

With the importance of making the postseason and advancing once there, the end of the regular season takes on greater meaning. For Iowa, it was a matter of pride, knowing that the NCAAs were out of reach. They took on Michigan at home and played the way their fans had hoped for all season. The first half was a seesaw battle with both teams going on impressive runs, with neither able to pull away. A stingy Iowa defense in the second half, indicative of seven charges taken, allowed Iowa to control the tempo and win 76-56. It was a stellar performance, one that Steve Alford had been waiting for all year. Better late than never. The seniors walked off the court at Carver-Hawkeye in their last regular season game as winners, a tumultuous season seemingly years ago.

For Bill Self, the last two weeks of the season were filled with gut-wrenching finishes and important victories. Starting with Penn State at home, the Illini faced four Big Ten opponents and had to win all four to stay in the hunt for another Big Ten title. Against the Nittany Lions, they looked like their preseason ranking, dominating the undersized visitors by getting the ball to Robert Archibald down low. The senior scored a career high 25 points and had 10 rebounds as Illinois won their fifth straight game. The final was 83-56, but it really wasn't even that close. Against Northwestern, a surprise among the Big Ten in 2001–2002, Illinois allowed the Wildcats just 41 points the *entire* game, including just two baskets in the first 17 minutes, en route to a 56-41 win. Northwestern shot 29% from the field and missed all 17 of their three-point attempts. After a slow start, the Illini went on a 17-2 first half run and never looked back in building a 28-point lead. Though Frank Williams had only seven points, there were no postgame criticisms, accusations, or questions surrounding his effort. It's funny how winning seems to solve problems, or at least put them under the rug. (Williams did suffer from another stomach flu, spending time at the toilet before the game and at halftime.)

The six victories in a row set up a showdown with co-leader Indiana in Champaign on February 26. It would be the final home game for the Illini seniors and for the junior Williams, and the packed Assembly Hall crowd understood the emotion. Indiana and Ohio State were both 10-4 in conference, Wisconsin was at 10-5, and Illinois was 9-5. A win over Indiana could move Illinois into a tie for first depending on the outcome of two other games.

On Illinois' first possession, Williams took the ball and drove to the basket for a layup. That was only the beginning. The junior put on a display worthy of early entry to the NBA. He scored 24 points, shot eight of 19 from the field and seven of nine from the free throw line and at one point, scored seven straight points to stave off an Indiana rally, as Illinois won 70-62. Brian Cook also stepped up, scoring 15 points and shutting down Indiana's All-American, Jarred Jeffries, holding him to just three points in 29 minutes. Earlier in the week, in response to a reporter's question, Indiana coach Mike Davis had maintained that no one on Illinois could stop Jeffries, and the junior Cook took it personally. Late in the game, Davis's assistant Ben McDonald was assessed a technical foul, delighting the sold-out crowd. With just moments remaining, Self put injured senior Damir Krupalija in the game, for one last ovation at home.

It was a remarkable turnaround for Illinois, who at one point in the season looked shaky to even play in the postseason. That is why it is a marathon, not a sprint.

22

The Final Days

NOTRE DAME ENTERED ITS LAST TWO REGULAR SEASON GAMES AT 9-5, TIED FOR second with Syracuse in the Big East West. Finishing second would earn the Irish a bye in the first round of the Big East Tournament in New York City. They were 19-8 on the season and had moved to the top of the "bubble teams" with the impressive win over Miami on February 23. It's good to have big wins late in the season and with only St. John's and Providence left, a 20-win season and an NCAA berth seemed in their grasp.

Mike Jarvis' Red Storm were led by Marcus Hatten, Anthony Glover, and Eric King, three guys with NBA potential, who had led St. John's to a 19-9 record. Notre Dame came out strong in the first half at Madison Square Garden, scoring seemingly at will and led at halftime, 47-40. After Harold Swanagan nailed a jumper just moments into the second half, St. John's went on a 22-4 run, fueled by a Hatten point explosion. With seven minutes left, the Irish had rallied back, and a three by Matt Carroll knotted the game at 66. But St. John's went on a 10-3 spurt and a tip-in by Ryan Humphrey with two minutes left pulled the Irish to within one, but that would be as close as they got.

In the 84-81 win, Hatten scored 28 points and had 10 assists while Glover scored 20. For Notre Dame, Humphrey played outstanding, scoring 29 points and grabbing 11 boards. The Irish could muster only eight baskets in the final 20 minutes. The loss kept the Irish win total at 19, one away from the magic number of 20, and dropped them a half a game behind Syracuse for second in their division.

As his team prepared for the regular season finale against Providence, with a bye and a 20-win season on the line, Brey was optimistic about the prospects. "I'm pretty comfortable where we sit," Brey said. "Our RPI is in the thirties, we have some big wins, and if we beat Providence we will win 20 games [with one against a Division II opponent]. We should be a lock."

Fate rested not just with the Irish, however, but with the outcome of the Boston College-Syracuse game. If Notre Dame won and Syracuse lost, the Irish would finish in second place, earning the bye. Villanova had beaten Syracuse earlier in the week, so Syracuse and Notre Dame both stood at 9-6 in the Big East West. Back home in South Bend, Notre Dame lived up to its part, finishing the game on a 19-4 run to beat the Friars 76-68 before a sell-out crowd at the Joyce Center. Though they trailed by three at the half, the Irish got contributions from everyone and erased a seven-point second-half deficit to win. Chris Thomas dished out three assists, bringing his season total to a school-record 217 and Humphrey recorded his seventh straight double-double. Now it was watch and wait time for the Irish, as the Boston College-Syracuse game was not until Sunday afternoon.

Their prayers were answered. Boston College defeated Syracuse 69-65, and the Irish finished second in the Big East West standings, earning a bye in the conference tournament. That sealed the deal for them. Brey had been honest with his team throughout the final few weeks, telling them exactly where they stood with regard to a possible NCAA berth. They did not campaign for it, and neither did their coach. They simply went out and did it, letting their record speak for itself. They could not be ignored any longer.

There was a lot at stake in the last days for UCLA and Steve Lavin as well, as they battled for seeding in the PAC-10 Tournament and an invitation to the NCAA Tournament, while trying to avoid their worst conference finish in history. They hosted Oregon State on February 28, a team that had won just four conference games all season. In what Lavin would call the "most ugly game I've seen in my 11 years at UCLA," his Bruins escaped Pauley with a 65-57 win over the Beavers, to give them 11 conference wins and 19 victories on the season. The game was not decided until the final two minutes, when UCLA sealed it with clutch free throw shooting. Something magical had happened early in the second half. When Lavin became frustrated that his five starters were not hustling and playing well, the coach turned to his bench and put in the future. Freshmen Ryan Walcott, Andre Patterson, and Dijon Thompson joined sophomore T. J. Cummings and veteran Rico Hines. The bench quintet scored 19 points and pulled the Bruins ahead for good. It wasn't pretty but it was a win.

By game time against Oregon in Westwood on Saturday, March 2, the Ducks had little to play for. They had already clinched their first PAC-10 title since 1939 and were the No. 1 seed for the following weekend's PAC-10 Tournament at the Staples Center in Los Angeles. Still, they had not won at Pauley since 1984 and wanted the momentum heading into the postseason. In the locker room before tip-off, on an emotional Senior Day at Pauley Pavilion, Lavin kept it sweet and simple. Instead of the usual numbers, names, and different colored inks on the board, he simply wrote "Together" and "Emotion." He paid respects to the seniors in the room, Matt Barnes, Billy Knight, and Dan Gadzuric, and talked to the team about keeping their emotions in check. He didn't need to tell the team what was at stake. He didn't need to get them fired up or he didn't know what else to try.

In a game that went down to the final buzzer, Oregon got what they wanted and ended their losing streak at Pauley. Like they had against Oregon State, the younger UCLA players excited the crowd and brought the Bruins back from a 45-40 deficit in the second half to take the lead 49-48. In the 65-62 win though, Freddie Jones, who had victimized UCLA in Eugene, scored 22 points. Ryan Walcott missed a potential tying three at the buzzer while Cedric Bozeman watched from the bench. (Lavin was encouraged by the fact that Walcott exhibited confidence in taking the last shot.) As the game ended, Oregon players hugged, celebrated, and donned PAC-10 Champion hats. Coupled with Cal's loss to Arizona earlier in the day, the Bruins' loss was costly, dropping them to sixth in the conference, depending on the outcome of the remaining games. There was a log-jam behind the Ducks in the PAC-10, and any of five teams could finish as high as second or as low as sixth. All the Bruins could do now was sit and wait, at 19-10, 11-7 in conference play with no national ranking.

For Bill Self and Illinois, the season came down to the final game at Minnesota, with a share of the Big Ten Championship at stake. If they won in Minneapolis, they would claim a share of the title with Wisconsin, Ohio State, and Indiana, and would extend their winning streak to eight. If they lost, they would finish with six conference losses, tied for second, and would have failed in their expectations to defend their Big Ten title. In an unbelievably crazy and unpredictable game, the final minutes were almost indescribable. With just over two minutes to play the Gophers held a nine-point advantage, 66-57. But they had been notorious for their inability to hold leads this season, and Illinois smelled blood. Ahead 66-62, Minnesota got trapped underneath their own basket, wilting under the Illinois press, and Illinois got a tie-up. The possession arrow, however, favored Minnesota and the hosts had another chance to extend their lead, but the Gophers' Kevin Burleson lost the ball and Cory Bradford picked it up. Bradford took the ball and nailed a three-pointer to pull Illinois to within one. "Right place at the right time," the senior would say after the game.

Now up by only one, Minnesota worked to get the ball past halfcourt, as Illinois' full-court trapping press went at it again. Hurried by the defense, Burleson again turned the ball over, this time throwing a pass out-of-bounds. It was an unbelievable turn of events for Illinois in the last two minutes. They had trailed by nine, but now had a chance to win it with possession of the ball, down by one, with 6.9 seconds left in the game. Illinois worked the ball in from under Minnesota's basket, and the ball ended up with Frank Williams. The guard made a move and drove to the hoop, hitting a layup with 2.9 seconds left, but injuring his wrist in the process. It was his only basket of the second half. Time ran out on Minnesota, and Illinois earned another Big Ten championship.

Most coaches will tell you that over a long season, to win a championship you need to be good and lucky. The Illini were both. They were able to turn their season around, win their last eight games, and defend their conference title. Along the way, they suffered devastating injuries and losses, but luck found them, particularly in the final game. The win earned them a bye in the Big Ten Tournament the following weekend and gave them 23 wins on the season.

There was a jubilant and relieved locker room after the game and Self focused his postgame remarks on what the group had achieved. "This one is special because we shared it with each other. Don't be mad about people jumping back on our bandwagon now; let them back on. We did it the hard way, but we did it."

Five hundred fans greeted the team at Willard Airport as they charted back from Minneapolis, and already talk turned toward the NCAAs. "I think we should be a five seed or higher," Self suggested, "and if we win the Big Ten Tournament, then certainly a No. 2 seed." But before taking on the Big Ten and the NCAAs, Self had to take on the rumor mill.

Nolan Richardson had threatened to resign his job at Arkansas citing racism, and the controversy heated up in late February, culminating in his dismissal from the university. Speculation immediately began as to his replacement, and one name seemed to come up often—Bill Self. It made sense. He was an Oklahoma guy with great ties to Arkansas; his wife was from the area, and he was certainly a proven winner. But Self knew that his team needed no distractions now that they were on a roll and squashed any talk of an imminent move. "Let's put it to rest right now," Self was quoted in the newspapers on March 5 as saying, "I am not interested in anything other than the job I currently hold." In coaching terms, that may mean, I am interested, but just can't tell you right now.

For Steve Alford and his seniors, the final game at Michigan State was about pride and the future. They were not playing for seeding in the postseason, with their only hope of the NCAAs being a sweep of the Big Ten Tournament, and it looked like they may not even get an NIT bid. As they took the floor at a hostile Breslin Center on March 2, the players and coaches seemed thankful it was coming to an end. A challenging and frustrating season for Alford was almost complete, yet he never gave up on coaching the team.

Things did not look good early on for Iowa, falling behind 36-16 with 7:43 left in the first half. But they stayed hungry, and after a barrage of three-pointers, a 9-1 run, and some free throws, they had cut the lead to 11 at halftime. The Hawkeye defense was not impressive in the first half, giving up 10 offensive rebounds and letting MSU shoot seven of 12 from three-point land. In the second half, Iowa came out with a minirun and trailed 55-50 with 15:38 left, but allowed the Spartans a run of their own to push the lead to 65-54 with just over 11 minutes remaining. For the next minute, Iowa put on a clinic. Duez Henderson hit a three and Chauncey Leslie hit two threes, and the lead was suddenly only 65-63. But that was as close as the Hawkeyes would get, as Michigan State regrouped and built the lead back up to eleven, closing out the game for a 93-79 win. Alford's protests with the officiating reached a fevered pitch late in the game, and the coach was assessed a technical. In their final regular season games, Luke Recker scored 20 and Reggie Evans had 13.

Now they had to regroup and look to repeat history.

23

96 Hours

THE GRANDDADDY OF ALL OF THE POSTSEASON CONFERENCE TOURNAMENTS HAD BEEN the Big East Tournament in Madison Square Garden. It was this eastern conference that really elevated college basketball to the forefront with its teams, marquee players, and conference tournament in the early 1980s. Guys like Ewing, Mourning, and Mullins all became bona fide stars playing in the Big East. What made their conference tournament so great was the location and the unknown. Playing on perhaps the most famed court in the world, The Garden, was something special. With the intense New York crowds, the big city, the bright lights, and many Big East schools within 100 miles of the city, the rivalries took on a new dimension. But in recent years the conference, and its tournament, have taken a back seat on the national stage. The crowds are smaller, the facilities dated, and the teams not as dominant.

With their late-season surge and some help, Notre Dame earned a bye in the first round on Wednesday, March 6, but still arrived in New York on Monday. They would play the winner of St. John's–Seton Hall on Thursday night, so the Irish would prepare and also enjoy their time in New York City. Mike Brey had been to many conference tournaments and numerous Final Fours, and knew that the experiences were like no other, so he wanted his young men to have fun. On Tuesday morning, however, their trip took on a powerful tone, one that was far from enjoyable.

Earlier in the fall after the September 11 attacks, the Notre Dame community embraced the police and firemen of New York City, inviting them to South Bend for football games, concerts, and banquets. When some of the cops and firemen came to a Notre Dame football game in October, they spoke briefly at the pregame pep rally at the Joyce Center. Brey and his players got friendly with the officers, and on a return visit for a U-2 concert at the Joyce, the NYPD and NYFD officers extended an invitation to Brey and his team for a tour of Ground Zero on their next trip to New York.

The Irish spent two hours that March morning visiting history. The cleanup had been underway for six months, but the destruction was still visible. The players and coaches were silent as their guide gave them skyscraper views and ground-level walking tours. Like most Americans, the images on television were not real for the Irish contingent, too hard to imagine. But walking along the dirt among the debris, it became all too real. The visit to the devastated sight was profound for the team and for Brey and his assistants. Not only was it a stark reminder of the world in which they now lived, but it put the game of basketball into proper perspective. Ryan Humphrey was visibly emotional as were many of his teammates.

"One thing that stuck out," Brey recalls, "was that so many policemen and firemen named O'Malley and O'Leary just came over and shook our hands. It was kind of like a bond we had with the New York Irish."

The players had a shootaround on Wednesday and spent the afternoon relaxing at their hotel, walking the city streets, and sleeping. Assistants Lewis Preston and Sean Kearney were at MSG watching the first round games, scouting potential opponents. The team and Brey headed out to the ESPN Zone on Times Square for dinner and then retreated to their hotel for the night.

Game day was a different mood and attitude for the players and coaches. Things were intense; it was time to focus. After breakfast in the hotel, the team gathered in a banquet room to listen to a scouting report on St. John's, their opponent that night. They were very familiar with the Red Storm, having played them eight days earlier in the same building. It would be a decidedly home-team crowd advantage for St. John's, but Brey felt confident his team could get the win. The coaching staff went over the personnel again and showed the players some tape of St. John's win over Seton Hall the previous night. There was a shootaround for the Irish around noon, and the team spent the rest of the day as they would any other road game day. Sleep, television, family visits, Mass, and the pregame meal. They boarded the bus around 6:30 P.M. and headed over to the Garden.

Teams enter Madison Square Garden through an entrance on 33rd Street, at the bottom of the arena. After being searched by security, the team, coaches, trainers, and managers gathered on a freight elevator that held 40 people. The elevator stopped at the third floor and the team exited, walking a few yards into their assigned locker room. The Irish had arrived an hour before their scheduled tip time, and after getting dressed, the players had little to do as the Connecticut-Villanova game ran late, a game decided by two points in the end. Some of the players walked out into the arena and took seats to watch part of the game, some stayed behind in the locker room and stretched while listening to their Walkmans. Chris Thomas grabbed a ball and dribbled in the hallway. Mike Brey found his peace. He found it in a maintenance hallway adjacent to the locker room area, where he sat in a red folding chair reserved for a security guard. But there was no guard, and very little commotion in the hallway. Brey sat, hands clasped together, thinking. As game time approached, he gathered his troops in the locker room and gave them a message.

"It's time for this program to take the next step. To get to that next step, we need to start by winning this one. It's tournament time."

The Irish came to play and there was little doubt who the better team was on this night. Notre Dame scored the first seven points of the game and shot 63% in the first half. They hit shot after shot, from inside and out, building a 42-28 halftime lead. The players ran back into the cramped and hot locker room, as the coaches gathered in a makeshift

coaches' room down the hall. There were leftover water and Coke bottles and stale pret-
zels on a table in the room, with five chairs and nothing more. There was really little to say
between the coaches on this day. Notre Dame was playing excellent basketball and there
were few, if any, halftime adjustments needed. The coaches looked over the first-half stats
and then headed into the locker room.

"Great half, men," Brey began, "you took it to them. But we can have no let up. We
must keep playing defense and grabbing rebounds," Brey continued, followed by a recita-
tion of some of the positive first-half stats. He asked the captains if they had anything to
add, but besides a "let's keep it up," there was very little. "Let's take this next step," Brey
ended his talk, as the team huddled for a chant.

The second half was not as dominating for the Irish, as least not at first. St. John's, led
by Marcus Hatten, who had lit Notre Dame up just a week earlier, scored 14 points, 12 of
them on three pointers and the Red Storm clawed back to 53-48. But on this night, Notre
Dame would not be denied. With three-pointers from David Graves, Matt Carroll (2), and
Thomas, the Irish went on a 20-2 run to blow the game wide open. The game was over
before the buzzer sounded, and Brey and his team enjoyed the final minutes, though the
hostile MSG crowd did not.

"That's step one," Brey said afterward. "We took care of business tonight and now
we have UConn. That's about as good as we've seen all season. You seniors should be
proud for leading the way and playing like men."

Back at the hotel, the coaches stayed up late watching tape of Connecticut, a team
they had not faced in the regular season because of the unbalanced Big East schedule.
Brey and his assistants were optimistic. UConn would be tough, but the coaches felt that
their guys were up to the challenge. Connecticut had been the dominant team in the Big
East during the last six years, including four Big East Tournament titles and a national
championship in 1999. They had won seven straight games and were ranked No. 19 coming into the game, carrying a strong contingent from Storrs, just 140 miles away.

The teams matched up well with each other, evident by the early score. For the first
20, the teams traded buckets and miniruns, but neither was able to pull away. Thomas,
Carroll, and Ryan Humphrey led the way for Notre Dame, giving them a balanced scoring attack from inside and outside. At halftime, the score was 41-36, UConn.

The game was still close midway through the second half, tied at 59, when UConn
finally pulled ahead. The Huskies went on a 10-0 run and held Notre Dame scoreless for
close to seven minutes, a fact hard to believe considering the performance a night earlier
by the Irish offense. The lead crept up to 11 with 3:51 remaining, but Notre Dame continued to battle. Thomas scored his team's final 11 points over the last three minutes of the
game and pulled his team to within four, but it was not enough. Connecticut advanced to
the championship game with an 82-77 win. Thomas finished with 24 points and 10 assists.
In the locker room, Brey was positive, pointing out how far this team had come. They had
won 21 games, advanced to the semifinals of the Big East Tournament, and seemed to be
a lock for the NCAAs. It was now just a matter of watching and waiting.

The Staples Center in downtown Los Angeles was rocking and it wasn't because the
Lakers were playing rival Sacramento. On this night, the hometown UCLA Bruins
were taking on No. 25-ranked Cal in an opening round game of the PAC-10 Tournament.
The Bruins sealed the date with Cal after finishing sixth in the conference standings, their
lowest finish in history. There was excitement at Staples this year only because of athletic
politics. The previous year, athletic directors voted to reinstate a postseason tournament

for the first time since 1991. The debate had raged for the past few years, with proponents talking about television ratings, revenue, and positioning for the NCAAs. Detractors thought it would take away from the regular season, hurt the more powerful teams in the conference, and create havoc for conference teams if there were upsets in its own post-season tourney. It was the vote of UCLA's athletic director Peter Dalis that finally gave organizers the necessary majority.

So the tournament returned in style in downtown L.A., and UCLA looked to get its twentieth win of the season, and begin its customary postseason run under Lavin. However, UCLA did not look like a tournament team for much of the first half, fighting back twice from nine-point deficits, to *only* trail by three at the break. Early in the second half, Jason Kapono hit a basket that gave UCLA its only lead of the game 35-34 in a low scoring affair. Cal responded with a 9-0 run to put the Bears in control. UCLA pulled back to within one, going on a 9-2 run with 11:35 left in the game. Ryan Walcott hit a basket with 2:06 left to tie the game at 59 and send the Staples crowd into a frenzy. But over the final 1:39, Cal outscored the Bruins 8-2 and came away with a 67-61 win. UCLA had chances down the stretch, but its best shooters could not connect and UCLA was left with a sour taste yet again. They sat at 19-11 and were confident that their big wins, strong RPI, and strength of schedule would get them a decent seed for the NCAAs. The Bruins were 8-9 over the last two months of the season, not an impressive way to finish.

Indianapolis has been home to many memorable postseason games, including Final Four wins by Louisville (1980), Duke (1991), Arizona (1997), and most recently, Michigan State (2000). In the second week of March, fans in the basketball-crazy state were packed into Conseco Fieldhouse, home of the Indiana Pacers. There is constant debate over which postseason conference tournament is the best in the game today, the ACC's or the Big Ten's, but a basketball fan cannot go wrong at either event. In a wide-open Big Ten race in 2001–2002, four teams shared the regular season title and several more were just a game or two away. This could be anybody's tournament. There was the recent memory of what happened 12 months earlier at Conseco, when Steve Alford's Iowa Hawkeyes won four straight games over four days, upsetting the conference leaders along the way to win the Big Ten Tournament title and the automatic NCAA berth that came with it. Iowa had had a horrible season in 2000–2001 and unless they made a miraculous run, they would have been watching the NCAA Tournament from home. Their remarkable wins in the 2001 Big Ten Tournament gave this year's team hope that they, too, could erase a season of missed opportunities with a memorable four-day trip to Indianapolis.

The Big Ten prohibits teams from coming to the host city more than 24 hours before their scheduled game, a move intended to keep student-athletes in class. Iowa was seeded No. 9, and faced No. 8-seed Purdue in the opening round on Thursday afternoon, March 7. Iowa had lost on the road at Purdue by five in late January, and it was hard to predict which Iowa team would show up to play the early-round game. It took only a few minutes to find the answers.

Purdue opened up the game with an 11-5 lead, but baskets by Luke Recker and free throws by Reggie Evans gave Iowa its first lead, 16-15. The Boilermakers were beset by foul trouble, forcing coach Gene Keady to sit many of his key players, and Iowa made 14 of 24 first-half free throws to lead 46-34 at halftime. The Hawkeyes continued their solid play in the second half, taking a 20-point lead at one point en route to an impressive 87-72 win. They shot 57% from the floor and Recker, alone, made nine of 10 shots. He finished with 25 points and Evans scored 19 and tied a career high with 18 rebounds. The win gave

Iowa some confidence, and around Indy, talk began about last year's run. Recker had not played in last year's tourney due to a season-ending knee injury, and this could be his final showcase for his fans, critics, and NBA scouts, including the Pacers' President Donnie Walsh, on hand for the games.

Next up for the Hawkeyes was top-seeded Wisconsin, co-champion of the Big Ten, a team Iowa had split with in the regular season. One of the beauties of conference tournaments is the short amount of rest and preparation time that coaches and players have between games. Assistant coaches are up 20 hours a day, watching games, scouting opponents, and putting together tape. Players get iced down, rest, and eat, and for Iowa, attend chapel as well. Most teams have faced their opponents at least once during the regular season, so there is some familiarity. But teams and personnel change over the course of the season, so a team may be much different come March.

Very few fans will remember the final score of the Iowa-Wisconsin quarterfinal game at Conseco, but most will never forget the second-half performance put on by Luke Recker. Playing as if his life depended on it, Recker put on a clinic, culminating with a shot for the ages.

After a poor start by Iowa, few fans could have expected how the game would end. The Hawkeyes trailed 8-0 just two minutes into the game. The lead was 18-9, then 18-15, then 21-17 and finally 26-21 Wisconsin at the half. Iowa had not played great, but only trailed by five at the break. Recker had four points in the first half.

At halftime, Alford focused on motivating his team with thoughts of the postseason. It was simple, really. Did the team want to play in the NIT or NCAAs? Their only shot at the big tournament was to go all out in the second half to keep their hopes alive of another four-game sweep. In the second half, Iowa managed to close the gap to six before a memorable run. The Hawkeyes took a 39-37 lead with 10:15 left in the game, but they could not hold it as the Badgers came back with a 7-0 run of their own to build their lead to five with just over nine minutes remaining. And then came the Recker show. He scored 24 points in the second half, including outscoring the entire Badger team 16-12 down the stretch.

With the game tied at 56 and 8.5 seconds to go, Recker dribbled to the foul line, launched a running one-handed floater, and watched it as it went in with 1.4 seconds left. Everyone in the building knew that Recker would take the last shot, but still Wisconsin could not stop it. After a Badger timeout, Chauncey Leslie stole the inbound pass and Iowa had win number two. Now Indy and the college basketball world were *really* talking, as a showdown loomed between Iowa and Indiana, a rematch of the 2001 championship game won by Iowa. Everyone knew the Recker and Alford storylines, and surely the media would play up Recker's hostile treatment and poor performance in Bloomington in February. The Hawkeyes retreated to their hotel and began the preparations.

Meanwhile, after Iowa beat Wisconsin, Illinois arrived at the Fieldhouse for its quarterfinal game against Minnesota, the team it had beaten five days earlier when the Gophers' collapsed at home. Champaign was a mere 90 miles from Indianapolis and the crowd was fervently pro-Illinois. Because the game was scheduled so late on Friday, Self made his team take mandatory walks out of the team hotel on Friday so they wouldn't go stir crazy. As the Illini made their way down the elevators at the Hyatt Hotel two hours before tip-off, they were greeted at the bottom by the Illinois cheerleaders, pep band, and fans, who formed a human tunnel as the team made its way onto the bus. The short ride over to Conseco was quiet. Illinois was on a mission and was focused.

In the pregame locker room, Self was worried that the Gophers would be up for revenge. "We pulled a rabbit out of our hat up there last weekend," he said, referring to the miraculous comeback at Minnesota, "and they need this win to get them into the NCAA Tournament."

This one was over before it began. Illinois made its first seven shots, went on a 15-2 run and led 25-9 ten minutes into the game. Minnesota seemed intimidated and reminded of their earlier collapse as Illinois pounded them. The Gophers did respond with a run of their own and actually cut the lead to 10 at halftime, 46-36. The closest Minnesota got in the second half though was eight, and at one point trailed by 24 after Brian Cook nailed a three. The final was 92-76 as Cory Bradford scored 25 points, including starting the game with three three-pointers in the first three minutes. Frank Williams finished with only four points, but had 11 assists, playing with a sore wrist he had injured against the Gophers earlier that week. The Illini advanced to face Ohio State in one semifinal, with Iowa and Indiana matching up in the other.

By the time the Illinois-Minnesota game concluded, it was well past midnight and Self looked tired but relaxed in the locker room. He told his team how impressed he was with their shooting performance, particularly Bradford, as the team huddled up to do its final chant. "One down and two to go," the coach remarked, a businesslike approach for a team that could win the whole thing.

On Saturday, March 9, Iowa suited up for the Indiana game. There was an electric feeling in the air. Surely it would be emotional for Recker again, but this time, he would be ready for it. In the four-games in four-days format, teams need to put their last game behind them and the emotions that come with it. Recker had been the hero against Wisconsin 24 hours earlier, but that wouldn't help him score against Indiana. Iowa jumped out to an early lead before the Hoosiers responded with a 9-0 run to lead by four just five minutes into the game. Unheralded Brody Boyd, who was the hero for Iowa in their amazing sweep last season, came off the bench to hit two big threes and suddenly Iowa was up 17-11 with 13:51 to go in the first half. Indiana went on another 9-0 run to retake the lead and the battle continued back and forth until halftime, with Indiana leading 33-30 at the break. The second half went back and forth as well and the game seemed headed for a dramatic conclusion. With the score tied at 42 with 10 minutes left, it was anybody's game. Then Indiana went on a 7-0 run, led by super-sub and crowd favorite A. J. Moye and All-American Jared Jeffries. The gap grew to eight with five minutes left. But Recker, Duez Henderson, and Pierre Pierce played instrumental roles in leading the Hawkeyes back to tie the game with three minutes remaining.

Indiana took a 60-57 lead, but with just under a minute to play, Recker hit a three to tie the game. It was unbelievable. Here was the vilified Recker bringing his team back, nailing crucial shots, trying to get payback. But he was not done. With 13 seconds remaining, Recker grabbed a rebound off an Indiana miss and called timeout as he flew out-of-bounds. Pierce brought the ball up after the timeout, beating full-court pressure, and got the ball to Recker on the baseline in the right corner. He faked a shot to get Jeffries in the air, took a quick dribble, and let go a floating one-handed shot. The ball seemed to stay in the air for minutes, and the delayed reaction by Iowa and Indiana emphasized that point. Recker was the hero once again, hitting the game winner as time expired to give Iowa a 62-60 victory and a spot against Ohio State for the Big Ten Championship for a potential berth in the NCAA Tournament.

The term "storybook ending" is probably overused, but is so apt in describing Recker's performance against Indiana. In an emotional postgame locker room, Recker seemed stunned and tearful at what fate had brought him. His journey had been a long and difficult one and his decisions second-guessed by many. But even Indiana fans, the ones who hurled the insults at him in Bloomington, found themselves happy for their home state boy. The next day, Indiana papers were cheering Recker, laying to rest the vitriolic speech and editorials.

Iowa assistants Greg Lansing, Sam Alford, Brian Jones, and Rich Walker stayed to watch the Illinois-Ohio State game, to scout out their potential opponent in Sunday's final. The players and Alford headed back to the team hotel, where the players grabbed some naps and Alford watched the semifinal on television.

Conseco was packed with fans from both schools. As the game began, Illinois took the upper hand, going inside to Robert Archibald, getting Cory Bradford open looks and putting extensive pressure on the Buckeye guards, forcing them into poor shots. But the guards, Brian Brown and Brent Darby, settled down and found their rhythm, combining for 22 points in the first half. Ohio State trailed the entire 20 minutes until Darby's three at the buzzer gave them a 41-40 lead. It was a disappointing end of the half for the Illini, after they had dominated much of the play.

"We need to control this game," Self told his troops. "We are relaxing on defense and letting them make their shots." He went on to explain that tough defense would win the game and that they could have no letup for 20 minutes.

In the second half, the game was tied at 65 before Ohio State built on its momentum and opened up a 10-point lead with just over five minutes to go. Brian Cook hit a three and two quick baskets by Archibald and Sean Harrington brought the lead down to two, 85-83, before Brown and Darby scored to push the lead back to six. Frank Williams hit a layup with 23.4 seconds left, but Ohio State made its free throws down the stretch and won 94-88. Cook had 22, Williams 18, and Archibald 16, yet Illinois lost for the first time since losing at home to Michigan State on February 3. Brown and Darby finished with 50 points and Ohio State made 17 straight free throws down the stretch. Afterward, Self talked to his team about their poor defense, about not playing with enthusiasm and reverting to old habits.

"That loss hurt our seeding for the NCAA," Self said months later, "but it sure was an attention-getter for the players. They needed to refocus." Illinois was done prematurely with its visit to Indianapolis, and headed home to Champaign to wait for Selection Sunday.

It was Saturday night, March 9, and Alford's Hawkeyes were exhausted. They had just played their third game in three days. Back at the Adams Mark Hotel, the team gathered in a seventh-floor banquet room as Alford went over the next day's opponent, Big Ten Co-Champ Ohio State. He was tired, as were his players, but the coach was going on adrenaline and fire. Here was his chance to salvage a miserable season, one that challenged him as a coach. A win the next day would send Iowa back to the NCAA Tournament, and make history, as Iowa would become the only team in NCAA history to win four games in four days *twice*.

The scouting report on the Buckeyes wrapped up and the team headed down to a second-floor room for desserts; most notably ice cream sundaes. The coach sent them to bed around 9:45 P.M. He stayed with his father, and some other Iowa personnel, and was soon joined by Tanya, Kayla, and Bryce. He put Bryce on his lap, kissed his forehead twice, and seemed to cherish the moment. But Alford had things to do. He had to figure out a plan to beat Ohio State. So he reluctantly said goodnight to his kids, told Tanya he would see her later, and headed upstairs to watch film with his assistants. Alford would not go to sleep until close to 3:00 A.M. that night and would be up by 7:00 to start Sunday.

Nothing too remarkable about a coach staying up late at night watching film, especially the night before the conference championship game. What sets Alford apart from other coaches, however, is that he stayed up until 2:00 A.M. five months before watching tape of a *preseason* game—twice. He is a competitor who wants to win, who learned from an early age that hard work is the answer, and the only answer, for success. But the same characteristics that made Alford a great player may make coaching a challenge for him. His insistence and demands on himself are often projected onto his players with consequences. He wants them to want it as bad as he does. He wants them to come in at midnight to shoot 1,000 free throws before going to bed. He wants them to have the internal drive to get up for every game. But in reality, most players do not have what Alford has. So he feels let down, and his players feel that they have let him down, creating a combustible climate for the Hawkeyes. When the team struggled in the 2001–2002 season, digging out of the hole was hard.

On the final day of the Big Ten Tournament, the team gathered in the second-floor banquet room for breakfast and for a pregame chapel led by close Alford friend Rick Nielson, who spoke about finishing and completing goals. The team adjourned to a room across the hall, cleared of chairs and tables, with masking tape on the ground outlining a foul lane and three-point arc. For the next 30 minutes, the team walked through their set plays and defensives against Ohio State. At the conclusion, Alford sat them down against a wall and the coach spoke to his team. "We have a shot at the NCAAs. You need to visualize cutting down these nets like I did last night. We can be the first team in NCAA history to win four games in four days in *two years*. They say we are soft, so let's show them how tough we can be and beat them with toughness. We need to go out, and regardless if we are tired, compete on every play. Let's go out and do what Rick [Nielson] talked about in chapel—finishing. Let's go out and finish this thing."

The Hawkeyes had been through a difficult season, but a win in the championship game later that day would silence many critics. For Alford, just digging out of the hole was the real victory. His team retreated to their rooms and then hopped onto the bus at 2:00 P.M. to ride over to Conseco.

By this point, the national media had turned its attention to the happenings in Indy. Iowa's incredible run had captured the attention of basketball fans everywhere, who were busy predicting who would make the NCAAs and who would be left behind. On this final day, just hours before the NCAA Selection Committee released the brackets, Iowa would attempt to make history. Ironically, the men and women choosing the tournament field were just blocks away, secluded in suites at a hotel in downtown Indianapolis. Much of their work had been done by the time the game started, but still, it was not complete.

Fifteen seconds into the game, Ohio State's Boban Savovic hit a three-pointer and his teammates helped push the lead to 9-0 as Alford took a timeout. As the coach huddled with his assistants on the court, the team huddled on the bench and Recker chastised them for not playing defense and implored them to get focused. The Buckeye lead shrunk to six, 15-9, but another 9-1 run put them ahead 24-10 midway through the first half. Recker and Boyd hit threes to keep Iowa in the game, but by halftime, Ohio State led 37-29, a score that could have been much worse for Iowa. In the locker room, Alford underscored the point of leaving it all on the court as the season wound down. If the Hawkeyes could get some stops, they were right back in this thing. Before the game, he was worried about Recker's potential for a letdown, after the emotions of the Indiana win. His star did not play a great first half, but fatigue also played a role, with two games decided on the last shot in the last 48 hours.

Perhaps inspired by the halftime pep talk, Iowa came out and scored six straight points to cut the lead to two and with 10:07 left in the game, Iowa was hanging tough, trailing by just three. But fatigue set in and Iowa could not keep up with the seemingly fresh legs of Ohio State. The Buckeyes went on a 21-8 run to put the game out of reach. Iowa committed 19 turnovers in the game and allowed Ohio State to shoot 48% from the field. Savovic was the star for OSU: 27 points, five assists, three rebounds, and three steals. Illinois-killer Brent Darby had 14. For Iowa, Recker finished up his impressive four-day outing with 21 points. The team was emotionally and physically exhausted, as was their coach, but they had come to Indianapolis and proved how talented they were.

"For the seniors, your dream is over. We are not going to the NCAAs. But how we prepare for the NIT will be a test, a challenge for us. Good things can happen when you are focused and you prepare properly, which we didn't have in early January. Now we have to go to the NIT." Even though Alford was disappointed, he thought positively. Iowa would be the best team in the NIT field, they could have three home games and a trip to New York City. It would still be a tournament championship, even if it was preceded by only three letters, not four.

24

March Is for Dough

GATHERING AROUND TELEVISION SETS IS A TRADITION ON THE SECOND SUNDAY IN March, as fans, teams, gamblers, television execs, ad pitchmen, promotional staffs, and every other interested party await the announcement of the NCAA Tournament brackets. In recent years, the Selection Show on CBS has drawn huge ratings, and the NCAA has accommodated the network's schedule by completing the brackets by 5:30 P.M. for the 6:00 show. As in past years, CBS sent crews around the country to capture the reaction of coaches and players as they watched and waited for their names to be called. There was no need for Steve Alford to watch the show, and he only caught a moment of it as he prepared to head back to Iowa City from Indy. Illinois gathered in the basement of Bill Self's home to watch as Mike Brey's Irish met in the entertainment room in his basement. UCLA met in their locker room at Pauley Pavilion, ate some pizza, and watched the Selection Show.

The brackets unfolded and UCLA was seeded No. 8 in the West Regional, pitted against No. 9-seed Mississippi in Pittsburgh, with a potential second-round game against top seed Cincinnati. Notre Dame was seeded No. 8 in the East, taking on UNC-Charlotte in Greenville, South Carolina, with an intriguing second-round possibility against No. 1 seed and defending national champion Duke. Notre Dame's freshmen Chris Thomas and Jordan Cornette were the only Irish to leap up when their team was announced, the veterans calmly laughing. Illinois meanwhile got to stay close to home as the No. 4 seed, playing San Diego State in Chicago in the Midwest Region, with Florida a likely second-round opponent, a team that had defeated the Illini in the 2000 Tournament. Kansas loomed in the Sweet Sixteen, a team that Illinois knocked out last year. (The placing of Illinois in Chicago drew criticism from around the country, as it was seen as an unfair advantage for the Illini. A new "pod" system came into play this year with the Selection Committee trying to eliminate long distance travel in the early rounds, allowing higher seeded teams to play close to home. The No. 1 seed in the Midwest was Kansas, despite being beaten by

Oklahoma in the Big 12 Championship game. They had to travel to St. Louis to play its early games. Second-seeded Oregon traveled to Sacramento and No. 3 seed Mississippi State went to Dallas.) When Illinois was announced, there was a subdued reaction from the team, a far cry from last year, when CBS producers and cameras were on hand for the Selection Show and had encouraged the players to jump up and scream.

There are two things that happen immediately after the brackets are announced for teams that make the Dance. First, administrators, with the advice of coaches, get to work on the details of how and when to get to the game site, ticket information, accommodations, meals, etc. For most teams, a traveling party of close to 60 is typical; that is a large group of people to get from Point A to Point B. For coaches, the priority turns to their first and possible second-round opponents. Coaches will tell you, and their teams, that they are only concerned with the first game, but they and their assistants are working on potential second-round matchups. Because the brackets are announced on Sunday and there is travel time to be considered, teams have very little time to gather scouting information and tape on opponents.

Coaches often share information with other staffs, particularly if there are previous friendships between staff members. Rarely is information shared between conference opponents, especially during the regular season, but a staff member from a SEC school may call a buddy at a PAC-10 school for the lowdown on another PAC-10 mate. Not all coaches give up information, but many will do so for friends. Sharing really comes into the play on the day the brackets are announced in March, especially because teams may be facing each other for the first time so staffs try to get all of the information they can from their upcoming opponents' previous opponents. When Notre Dame was bracketed to play UNC-Charlotte, assistants Sean Kearney and Anthony Solomon worked the phones and their connections to find information on Charlotte. "We will find information out from our friends," Brey insists, "but when others call us, we rarely will give information on any conference teams in the Big East but may on nonconference opponents. There is sort of a gentlemen's agreement that you do not share info on conference teams."

In addition, Brey is hesitant about sending the actual scouting reports or game film to other staffs. It's just his philosophy. There are film exchanges routinely between teams in preseason and during the regular season, where each team will provide an equal amount of tapes (usually two) on themselves for their opponents. Come Tournament time, however, most leagues, like the Big East, are much more reluctant to provide information and film on league members.

"A guy would have to be my half-brother for me to help him with information when it comes to the Tournament, if he is looking for information on an opponent," says Bucknell coach Pat Flannery. "During the preseason, it is a lot more relaxed, but some coaches are very paranoid. We're not inventing anything new here, we are just recycling old ideas to fit a style or new rules."

The Iowa coaching staff did prep work and scouting for their first round NIT game at home against LSU, but they didn't have the enthusiasm to go overboard. Despite missing out on the NCAAs, the Iowa faithful packed Carver-Hawkeye Arena to cheer on their team, as they looked ahead to next season. LSU went 18-14 on the season and getting to the NIT was satisfying. For Iowa, it was a consolation prize. Iowa had accepted the invitation, but not every team did. After failing to make the NCAAs, Georgetown decided not to participate in the NIT so the "student-athletes wouldn't miss more class." It probably wouldn't have been a problem for them to miss class for the NCAA Tournament.

So Iowa and LSU met on March 13 in Iowa City. Early on in the contest, Iowa trailed 15-8, but with Pierre Pierce providing some spectacular plays, Iowa stayed in the game. They went on a patented 9-2 run, but gave up some easy baskets on the defensive end of the floor. LSU held a 29-28 lead going into halftime. In the locker room, Alford tried to get his kids going for the final 20 minutes. "We have a great crowd, we're on TV, you guys should be playing at your best."

Iowa played well in the second half, and midway through, held an eight-point lead. But clutch shooting by the Tigers evaporated it. With 3:57 left, the game was tied when LSU's star, Ronald Dupree, scored and the Tigers never trailed again. Only a three at the buzzer by Chauncey Leslie made the score a two-point difference, 63-61. Luke Recker finished his collegiate career with 12 points on four of 16 shooting and Reggie Evans scored 10 points and grabbed nine boards.

"Some of you in this room didn't want the season to continue," the coach said disappointedly to his team after the game, a veiled reference to his seniors. "Well now it's over, and we look forward."

The season had finally come to a conclusion for Alford and his team. In the days and weeks after the NIT loss, fingers were pointed at Recker and Evans for giving up on the team, particularly in the LSU game. They didn't want to be playing in the NIT and their effort showed it. Pierce led the Hawkeyes with 13 points and at least gave Alford and the Iowa fans something to look forward to next season. After the game, when asked about the team's season, the coach said, "We took a step backward this year."

"Things have not gone as well as they were designed for Alford at Iowa," suggests *The Sporting News'* Mike DeCourcy. "It was supposed to be a coronation when he arrived in Iowa City. People wanted to believe that he could win in Iowa." Perhaps some still do.

Notre Dame had not won opening-round NCAA games in consecutive years since 1978 and 1979, when coach Digger Phelps led the program, so the Irish and Mike Brey were looking to tie history against UNC-Charlotte on Thursday, March 14. The 49ers had won four straight opening-round games dating back to 1997 and were a formidable opening game for the Irish. Led by Jobey Thomas, No. 9 seed Charlotte played in Conference USA and faced a difficult schedule during the year. Brey assumed that they would be a challenge for Notre Dame and prepared his team as such. The night before the game, Notre Dame got a break when Jobey Thomas fell ill and was unlikely to contribute much the following day.

The first half was about as even as a half could be, ending in a tie at 35. At halftime, Brey was calm and businesslike. "We are playing a very good game," he began, "but we need to slow the pace down. If we do that, we will have a better chance. I know you guys are excited to play in the NCAAs, but now the first half is behind us, so let's just settle down."

Opening the second half on a 33-12 run put the game out of reach, as the Irish turned to their big guns for offense. Matt Carroll, David Graves, and Ryan Humphrey hit shot after shot and before the 49ers knew it, they trailed by 19 with seven minutes remaining. The final was 82-63. Carroll hit four of five three-point attempts to finish with 20 and Humphrey got 20, from inside and from shooting 10 for 10 from the foul line. Graves added 19. It was an impressive win for Notre Dame and for the second year in a row, they were headed to the second round. Their next opponent would be Duke, first-round winners over Winthrop. The No. 1 seed, defending national champion, and former employer of Mike Brey.

"I'll talk to you all day tomorrow about who we play next," Brey said at his postgame press conference, deflecting the multitude of questions about his matchup with Duke.

In the 2000–2001 tournament, Mike Krzyzewski had faced another former assistant, Quin Snyder in the second round and talked openly about how difficult that was. Since the moment the brackets were announced March 10, it was no secret that the Brey-Krzyzewski meeting would be a media frenzy. In response to a reporter's question about facing Brey, Krzyzewski said, "I hate it. It's not even like or dislike. I hate it. I would think Mike doesn't look forward to it, either."

As Brey and his team studied up on Duke on Friday, Steve Lavin's players took the floor at the Mellon Arena in downtown Pittsburgh for a first-round game against Mississippi and their coach, Rod Barnes. Coming into the game as the No. 8 seed, UCLA had lost four of its last six games and had not strung together two impressive performances since the winning streak in December. If history is a predictor, fans should have known that Lavin's team would advance. Outside of a 1999 first-round upset loss to Detroit Mercy, Lavin's teams had all advanced to at least the Sweet Sixteen in his five seasons as coach. Regardless of how they played during the season or how they finished it, UCLA made a run in March. The run this year started against Ole Miss, and the spark came from an unlikely source.

The Bruins struggled out of the gate as the five starters, Matt Barnes, Cedric Bozeman, Billy Knight, Jason Kapono, and Dan Gadzuric appeared out of sync. Knight eventually got hot, but not before Lavin made the decision to bench his starters midway through the first half. Like he had done in previous games, Lavin brought on Ryan Walcott, T. J. Cummings, Dijon Thompson, Andre Patterson, and senior Rico Hines. Thompson scored 10 points and Patterson added five as the fresh five went on a 15-0 run that put UCLA in the driver's seat. The young guys were playing so well that Lavin actually called back his starters from the scorer's table as they were about to re-enter the game. It was the decision after the first USC game back in January that allowed for the success on this night. The coach decided back then to get his young guys playing time throughout the conference season, regardless of the struggles they might endure. Lavin knew it was all about March, and knew that in the NCAAs, it was time for the freshmen to be seasoned enough to perform.

By halftime, UCLA held a 36-26 lead and never looked back. "We need to capitalize on the momentum," Lavin told his team at the half. "We are playing well and we are wearing them down. We have used 10 guys and everyone is helping out." The coach had learned about his team as the season progressed. He realized that his quicker underclassmen provided a new dimension to the team that was missing for most of the season.

Knight hit three straight three-pointers to start the second half and the Bruins cruised from there, winning 80-58 over Ole Miss. Knight finished with 21 points and Thompson had 16. In fact, Thompson and his benchmates outscored the Bruin starters 42-38 in the game. Amazingly Kapono, the Bruins leading scorer on the season, finished with just two points. Hines had his best game of the year, scoring seven. The win moved UCLA into a second-round game against top-seeded Cincinnati, a team that many experts predicted would win the national title.

At the United Center in Chicago (a "second home court" according to Robert Archibald), Bill Self's Illini crushed San Diego State in an opening-round game before 20,850 pro-Illini fans. The Aztecs hadn't been to the NCAAs since 1985 and they showed it, making just 39% of their shots and getting pushed around by the bigger and more experienced Illini, who were favored by 11 points. Frank Williams had a career high five three-pointers to finish with 25 points. Freshman Luther Head was splendid, scoring a career high 19. The final was 93-64, and the game was as lopsided as the score. Illinois had now won 10 of its last 11 and sat at 25-8 on the season. Up next for the No. 4 seed was Creighton, a double-overtime upset winner over Florida.

A ll eyes were on Mike Brey as he walked toward center court in front of the scorer's table at the BiLo Center in Greenville, South Carolina, before his team's second-round game against Duke. Usually, the pregame handshake between coaches is a non-event, a three-second exchange of niceties and best wishes. But as Brey stuck out his arm on this day, he was greeted by his friend and mentor. He had been an assistant to Mike Krzyzewski for eight seasons and won two national championships with the Blue Devils. It was Krzyzewski who gave Brey his start, plucking him from DeMatha High School and bringing him to the big leagues. It was "Coach K" that gave him career advice, recommendations, and ultimately, approval. He knew Brey and his family well, and once a Dukie, always a Dukie. Still, this was a difficult moment for both coaches. But don't get too caught up in the sentiment of that moment. Make no mistake, both Brey and Krzyzewski would do everything they could to beat each other.

They first saw one another in Greenville at the coaches' meeting the day before the first-round games, Duke against Winthrop and Notre Dame against UNC-Charlotte. They were genuinely happy to see one another. Krzyzewski congratulated Brey on the great season, and began to pump him up about beating Charlotte—even though it might set up a showdown between the two friends. Brey asked about Krzyzewski's ailing hip and his family. They had a 10-minute conversation.

After both teams disposed of their Thursday opponents, things changed. Brey and Krzyzewski wanted to beat each other, rip the other's heart out, and would do everything to make that happen. At the press conferences on Friday, Brey passed Krzyzewski in the press room and the younger coach noticed a change in his friend's behavior. "He seemed a little more bothered and agitated. It was a little forced humor. I am sure that it was tough on him going up against me."

So the traditional coaches' handshake before tip-off took on added significance since these men were more than just opposing coaches. Krzyzewski grabbed Brey's hand, put his other arm on Brey's elbow, and told him how proud he was of the job that Brey had done with his team. Krzyzewski was classy, Brey appreciated the gesture, and the two men wished each other luck and headed to their respective benches.

"We need to be steady emotionally," Brey told his team just moments before tip-off. "We are older and wiser, so let's take a businesslike approach. If we keep our emotions in check, we can beat these guys."

It was clear to the Notre Dame coaching staff how you beat Duke: stop the inside game of Carlos Boozer, contain Jason Williams, and hope that no one else beats you—easier said than done. In its last three games, Duke had jumped out to leads of 27-7, 21-7, and 39-9 and with a penchant for starting poorly, Brey was concerned about his team falling behind. The day before the game, the coaching staff taught the players a triangle-and-two defense, intended to contain the penetration from the Duke guards.

From the tip, it seemed the ugly head of poor starts would not surface on this day for Notre Dame. On offense, the Irish went down low, getting the ball to Humphrey and challenging Boozer to stop him. "Hump" had nine first-half points and eight rebounds. The Irish seemed to be able to get to the basket at will, scoring nine of their 11 baskets on layups or short follow shots. On the defensive side of the ball, Brey wanted the Irish defense to force Duke to shoot from the outside, keeping them away from the basket, and Notre Dame did just that, including two great blocks by Humphrey on Boozer and Williams.

In the closing moments of the first half, Humphrey was called for a hard foul on Duke's Mike Dunleavy and was assessed a technical for hitting Dunleavy in the head as the two became tangled up on the floor. Players from both teams gathered and talked trash, but the officials quickly stepped in. Referee Tim Higgins called both coaches to the middle of the scorers' table to explain his call. "It was kind of weird," Brey reflected later. "I mean, it wasn't us, it was our kids, but we were both pissed off. Of course, my kid got the technical foul. But at the end of the discussion, we both kind of just said, you know what, let's just play ball." Dunleavy hit his two free throws from the original foul and the two from the technical to give Duke a 45-37 lead.

At halftime, Brey reiterated his pregame theme. "You see, just like I have been telling you, these guys are human. If anybody should know, it's me. We are a better team than them right now." And then turning to tactical changes, "Let's get the ball down low more to Swanny and Hump."

Things started ominously for the Irish in the second half, as Dunleavy drilled a three on Duke's first possession. But the usually composed and experienced Blue Devils collapsed. They turned the ball over five times and allowed Notre Dame to score 14 straight points. A timeout by Krzyzewski could not stop the bleeding and by the time Duke found its legs, they trailed by seven. With six minutes left in the game, Notre Dame had built a 71-64 lead and with the way Duke had been playing, an upset seemed in reach. But there was a reason Duke was No. 1, and it would not relinquish its crown easily. Helped by turnovers and missed shots by Notre Dame, Duke went on a run to even the game up. The game was tied at 71 with 4:28 left and tied again at 75 with 90 seconds remaining. Williams and freshman Daniel Ewing hit free throws down the stretch and the outcome was decided, an 84-77 Duke win. The Blue Devils hit 13 of 14 free throws in the final five minutes. David Graves went out in style scoring 20 points and Matt Carroll hit for 20.

The Duke mystique had kicked in and they had put the game out of reach. Brey took a seat on the bench with 45 seconds remaining and kind of smiled. They almost had it. Brey knew that there were very few windows of opportunities, and the Irish may have missed theirs. As the buzzer sounded, Brey walked toward Krzyzewski, shook his hand, gave him a hug, and wished him well in the next round. Brey then pulled aside Jason Williams and told him, "I was there the last time Duke went back-to-back and it is special. There is nothing like it, so go out and do it." In the postgame frenzy, many Duke staffers, assistants, SIDs, and trainers, many of whom knew Brey when he coached at Duke, came over and wished him well, congratulating him on a tremendous season with the Irish. Brey returned to the Notre Dame locker room and the emotions caught up with him.

After the game, it was a sense of sadness, relief, and frustration for Mike Brey. His feelings on this day were a lot different from what they were after the previous season's final loss to Ole Miss in the second round of the tournament. After that loss, Brey was more relieved and exhausted than anything else. After being hired in July, he and his staff went nonstop for eight months, traveling, living in hotel rooms with their families, and trying to coach the team. Since Brey was new to the Irish, he never felt quite as connected to that first team. At the end of the Ole Miss game, Brey took a deep breath, and looked forward to time away.

Flash forward to 2002, as the Irish assembled in their locker room at the BiLo Center after their loss to Duke. In the locker room after the game, Brey had to pause a few times as he spoke to his team. He is not an emotional man, but could not help himself. As he talked about his three key seniors, Harold Swanagan, David Graves, and Ryan Humphrey, Brey felt lost, like a father letting his kids go.

"This is the goal of every team," Brey told his team. "To finish the season playing a game when you know you gave it everything that you had and left it all on the floor." Later, Brey reflected on the moment, understanding that his emotions that day meant that he had a real connection with this team. As the team left the arena that Saturday, Brey walked down the tunnel and into the South Carolina sunshine. It was 70 degrees, his team had just finished a hell of a season, and it was spring. *We have achieved* he thought to himself; we can head into the offseason being proud of what we have accomplished. It wasn't the relief he had felt a year earlier, but it was a sense of satisfaction nonetheless.

He felt more confident in his decisions, determining that indeed, he had grown as coach and was a better one. As things settled down, Brey met with athletic director Kevin White to discuss the future. The coach was in a pretty good spot. He was comfortable at Notre Dame, his family liked it, and he was peaking in terms of marketability. He trusted White to "do the right thing," meaning make Brey's contract more lucrative and give the basketball program more attention. "He has always been fair to me," Brey thought to himself. (At the end of the Duke game, in the locker room, White had grabbed Brey, pulled him aside and told him what a great year the coach had had. He then added, "We will talk about next year.") "That late season run in the Big East Tournament and here in the NCAAs, really was an endorsement for our program and coaching staff, the idea that I can get it done," said Brey.

In the warmup lines before taking on top-seeded Cincinnati, Rico Hines was talking a little trash and was getting it back from the Bearcat players. On his sneaker, Hines had written "Final Four," a reminder for him and his teammates of their ultimate goal. Whether that instigated the crosscourt conversations or not, Hines got into a jabfest. Official Mike Kitts warned the Bruin to quit the trash-talking or face a technical. It was a precursor to the battle that was to come. Two storied basketball programs, UCLA and Cincinnati, the homes to Lew Alcindor and Oscar Robertson, unbelievably had not met on the basketball court since 1965. The Bearcats had been a powerful force in college basketball for the past 10 years under coach Bob Huggins, but had only made it to one Final Four. This season, Cincinnati was led by All-American Steve Logan and a cast of junior college players and transfers that made them a formidable team. UCLA was a strong No. 8 seed, as their inconsistent play during the regular season had given the Selection Committee little reason to seed them higher.

Steve Lavin knew going into the game that stopping Logan would be a key and the coaching staff designed a myriad of defenses designed to contain the speedy guard. The Bruin staff had gotten some help preparing for the Bearcats from former UCLA guard Cameron Dollar who, at the time, was an assistant to Lorenzo Romar at St. Louis, a conference mate of Cincinnati. The defense on Logan worked in the first half, as the guard took five minutes just to get his first shot off and scored only one basket in the half on a layup. He went one for six in the first 20 minutes. UCLA was effective in shutting down Logan, but not the other Bearcat players. Leonard Stokes scored 18 points in the first half, hitting four three-pointers. Cincinnati took a 47-37 lead into the halftime locker room.

"We know we can play with these guys," Lavin began, "if we calm down and play smart, this is our game." In noting that the Bruins were giving up too many second-chance points, Lavin emphasized rebounding and boxing out during the 15-minute break. "They are getting dunks and layups off of their second shots, just like 'SC' did against us at the Forum. Keep your poise and play tough-nosed defense."

The lead held steady for the first 10 minutes of the second half and with 9:20 remaining, it looked like the Bearcats were in control, leading by 11. But then things got interesting. Barnes scored six points in three seconds. He took a three-point shot and made it, and there was an off-the-ball foul called on Cincinnati so UCLA retained possession. On the inbounds, Barnes got the ball again, and again, hit a three-pointer. After forcing a turnover, UCLA got the ball down low to Dan Gadzuric for a monstrous dunk, and the lead was suddenly just three, 65-62. The Bruins continued to battle and Jason Kapono's three in transition with 5:09 left evened the score at 71. As the clock wound down to the final seconds, the teams were deadlocked at 80 and UCLA had the last possession. Lavin called a timeout and designed a play in the huddle with Kapono as the first option. But once the ball was inbounded to Barnes, he decided to do it himself and took an ill-advised shot, which missed, and the game was headed to overtime.

The first overtime was heated and physical, but the teams ended up where they had started—tied. Cincinnati actually had a chance to win the game at the end of the first overtime, but missed several short shots. Tied at 90, the teams headed to a second overtime. In the second five minutes, the Bruins scored the first four points, then Cincinnati hit some shots and after a three-point play by Knight, UCLA led 97-93 with 1:27 remaining. Dijon Thomspon hit a jumper to take the lead to six, Cincinnati missed on its possession, and the Bearcats quickly fouled UCLA. After Barnes hit one free throw, Cincinnati scored, but Thomspon hit two more free throws to put UCLA up 102-95. The Bearcats' Field Williams and Logan hit threes to cut the lead to 103-101 with 1.6 seconds left. Cincinnati fouled Ryan Walcott and the redshirt freshman nailed both free throws to seal the win. UCLA committed only nine turnovers the entire game and incredibly, the freshmen, Bozeman and Walcott, who shared point guard duties, had none. Rico Hines injured his knee and played only four minutes. He would be out for the next round with a cartilage tear, a blow to the Bruins. Hines may not have led the team in scoring, but he was their leader, on and off the court.

It was an amazing game for college basketball fans, as both teams truly left everything on the court. Both had chances to win the game but, ultimately, it was the mix of experience and youth that propelled UCLA into yet another Sweet Sixteen. There was a sense of relief for Lavin, but also a calm expectedness. Somewhere inside, he knew that he had the ingredients to go deep in the Tournament. Of course, he and his team had been written off months earlier, but he had built a foundation with the little things during the season that would prepare them for these types of games. They were on their way to San Jose.

The Creighton Bluejays had been the darlings of the NCAAs before, with stunning first-round upsets over the years. This March, the victim was Billy Donovan's Florida Gators, who the Bluejays beat in double overtime on a Terrell Taylor three-pointer with 0.2 seconds left in the second extra period. Bill Self worried about the play of Creighton's big men and of the toughness of their guards. If they could knock off Florida, with big men and good guards, Illinois could be vulnerable.

Self's biggest concern in the pregame locker room was that his players would think that Creighton's win over Florida was a huge upset. In reality, the Bluejays were a very tough team and it was only a mild surprise that they had beaten the higher-seeded Gators.

Brian Cook caught fire from the get-go, scoring from inside and out, and Illinois jumped to a quick 17-6 lead just six minutes into the game. Creighton struggled from the outside and couldn't seem to get the ball to the post against Cook and Robert Archibald. But with just over 13 minutes remaining in the first half, Cook picked up his second personal foul and Self had no choice but to sit him on the bench. Without the versatile Cook in the lineup, Creighton was able to go inside and finally got hot outside, going on a 16-6 run to pull within five, 31-26, heading into halftime. Despite sitting on the bench with two fouls, Cook scored 14 points in the first half on six of seven shooting. Illinois star Frank Williams disappeared in the first half, taking just two shots and missing them both. His coach was not happy. In the locker room, Self was infuriated at the play of many of his go-to guys, particularly Williams. The coach singled him out for his lack of effort and took him to task for not being aggressive enough on the floor.

Creighton's Kyle Korver hit a three early in the second half to get his team to within two. But Williams began a barrage with a reverse layup and followed that up with a three. Williams had gotten the message, like he had against Arizona in early December. Illinois went on a run before Creighton rallied to get it to 46-44, holding Illinois scoreless for four minutes. Williams then ignited a 12-0 Illinois run and his team led 64-49 with 4:15 remaining. The Illini held on for the 72-60 win. In the second 20 minutes, Williams scored 20 points on seven of 10 shooting, dished out five assists, and grabbed five boards. Surprisingly, the Bluejays outrebounded Illinois 34-27. But it didn't matter, Illinois was back in the Sweet Sixteen.

"That was a great job out there tonight," the coach told his team. "We went out there and did what we were supposed to do. Now we get to play Kansas, the No. 1 team. Let's be responsible as we work toward the game."

25

A Week in Tournament Life

AVING STRUGGLED THROUGH THE REGULAR SEASON WITH AN 11-7 CONFERENCE record, and having earned the dubious distinction of finishing the lowest for a UCLA team in PAC-10 history, Steve Lavin and his Bruins felt the heat. The coach had heard the criticism before, the calls for his head, the attacks on him and his coaching abilities by the press and the fans. Throughout the difficult regular season and into March, the coach talked about resiliency; a term Lavin had come to know the meaning of well.

The coaches lucky enough to still be playing in late March face increasing distractions to the task at hand. Five days in Lavin's life, smack in the middle of the Tournament, reveal as much about him as they do about the challenges of coaching today. From facing the media pressure and ticket requests, to quelling rumors about the future and keeping players' egos in check, a coach must find a way to get results on the floor while doing everything else his job demands.

Sunday, March 17, 2002. The final seconds of the second overtime moved very slowly for Lavin. His team fought back from a 10-point second-half deficit and was on the verge of defeating No. 1 seed Cincinnati. The final horn sounded sending his exhausted players into hugs of relief. Lavin gave Jason Kapono a hug and walked past the scorer's table and shook hands with Bearcat coach Bob Huggins. Though not close friends by any means, the two coaches respected one another, and both understood what the win meant for Lavin. The UCLA coach had almost universal empathy from coaching colleagues around the nation, as they read and listened to the accounts of coaching in the shadow of John Wooden.

In the Bruin locker room, there was a calm celebration. Yes, the team won to advance to yet another Sweet Sixteen; yes, in the process they stuck it to all of the pundits who left them for dead back in February; yes, Lavin again showed the world that he could coach. But there was more work to be done by this team, and as they had during the regular season, they took each victory in stride. Success for this team was not defined by the final

16; success meant a trip to Atlanta for the Final Four. "We wanted to get to the West Regional [San Jose] and we did that. We just took a longer route," Lavin told his team after the game. "This was truly a team effort."

In his postgame press conference, Lavin gave credit to a hard-playing Cincinnati team and to the leadership from his veterans, notably Matt Barnes, Rico Hines, Billy Knight, and Dan Gadzuric. He talked about resiliency once again; the fact that now is when wins count, not in December. When his players took the podium, they were confident with an edge when they spoke, but who could blame them after beating the No. 1 seed.

The team headed through the Mellon Arena tunnels on their way to their bus, but it took Lavin a little longer, as he accepted congratulatory handshakes and posed for pictures with interested fans. Unbeknownst to him, his cell phone was "blowing up," with calls from friends, family, and coaches from around the country. Lavin was in a good mood and, as he does most times, obliged the autograph- and picture-seekers. The traveling party all finally made it on to the bus. Lavin sat in the first row with his girlfriend and his parents, grabbing a few private celebratory moments as the bus headed for the airport, where a chartered flight awaited to take the team home from Pittsburgh.

They arrived back in Los Angeles around 8:15 P.M. local time, boarded a bus right off the tarmac and headed to Westwood and the UCLA campus. By the time they landed, the bandwagon was growing. Impatient and critical fans who previously were calling for Lavin's firing were now rooting for the Bruins and remarkably even for Lavin. There would always be the diehard Lavin-haters, but it's amazing what a win can do, especially a win in March. Lavin stopped in his second-floor office in the J. D. Morgan Center, turned on his cell phone, picked up a few items from his desk, and then headed home to Marina del Rey.

Monday, March 18. The phone in the UCLA basketball office started ringing at 7:00 A.M., when no one was there to answer it. Alumni, fans, and friends of Lavin called to offer their congratulations and some looked for tickets. When is the team going up to San Jose? Where are they staying? Can Lav leave some tickets for me? These were the typical questions that continued throughout the day (and the week for that matter), leaving Lavin's assistant, Dana Martin, a very busy man. Downstairs in the Morgan Center, basketball Sports Information Director Bill Bennett frantically tried to get work done to no avail. In a three-hour period on Monday morning, he received 50 voice mail messages on his office phone.

For Lavin, it was a busy Monday as well. He woke up around 7:30, had breakfast, made calls, and watched video before heading into the office. He had been this far in the Tournament before and he knew the distractions that awaited him at work. He spent his first hour in his office just listening to more phone messages, returning some calls, and reading a few press clippings for recruit mailouts that Martin had left on his desk. Dressed in a pair of black slacks and a white collared short-sleeved shirt, he was comfortable but not too casual. He cleaned up part of his desk, signed letters awaiting his signature and at around 1:00 P.M. ate lunch with his staff. They had gathered in his office to talk about the Sweet Sixteen matchup with Missouri. Lavin, assistants Jim Saia, Gerald Madkins, and Patrick Sandle, director of basketball operations Jamie Angeli, and intern and former player Brandon Loyd sat around the spacious office going over the details.

The phone was also busy that Monday for Saia, one of the top assistants on many "short lists" for job openings. He was not only helping the team prepare, but was on the lookout for a head coaching opportunity at a time when many were becoming available. The farther UCLA advanced, the more interest in Saia there was, and the more he fielded calls from headhunters about potential moves. It is hard as an assistant to simply blow off these calls during Tournament time and solely focus on your upcoming opponent, as one call could change your life.

On this day, there would be no team meeting, no practice, and no film session. The players had just played Friday–Sunday games and flown across the country Sunday night. It had been a long five days and with the Missouri game scheduled for Thursday, it would be a very short practice week. Lavin decided to give the players the day off, realizing that they could use the rest. The coach and his assistants used Monday to prepare a game plan for Missouri, which they would share with the team at practice on Tuesday. (Lavin decided the team would take the hour flight up to San Jose after classes and practice on Tuesday, leaving around 7:00 P.M.) Lavin stayed in the office late, watching tape of the Tigers with his assistants, returning phone calls, and doing media interviews. Around 10:00 P.M., he grabbed some game tapes of Missouri and headed home. He managed to watch only a bit more of the Tigers at home before crashing in bed at 12:30 A.M.

Tuesday, March 19. The phone kept ringing in the UCLA basketball office and on Lavin's mobile phone. He woke up at 7:30 A.M. read the *Los Angeles Times* over coffee and Cornflakes. In the day's edition, sports columnist Bill Plaschke wrote a fairly positive piece on Lavin and the Bruins, going so far as to acknowledge that perhaps Lavin was a decent basketball coach. It was a refreshingly upbeat piece in the often-critical hometown paper, but Lavin didn't take it as a turn for the better. He learned the hard way, to cast a cold skeptical eye at the L.A. media. He packed his bags for the trip to San Jose, including enough for five days—if he needed clothes for that long.

As he headed to the office in his Lexus up the 405 Freeway, he talked on the cell phone with friends and tried to arrange tickets, while staff members Doug Erickson, Martin, and Angeli worked feverishly to comply with the ticket requests back in the office. A player's father needed two tickets; a friend of the program needed a hotel room; an old coaching buddy wanted to come to San Jose, and everyone wanted to talk with Lavin.

The coach arrived in the office around 12:40 P.M. His plan for the day was simple. Return some phone calls, meet the media, practice, and then, immediately after practice, head with the team to the airport. He was dressed nicely in a pin stripe suit, white dress shirt with no tie, and with a dash of informality, a yellow UCLA baseball hat. It seemed out of place with the suit, but he didn't care. His cell phone was on and attached to his waist, though he didn't answer the continuous stream of calls. He took a seat at his desk and was immediately surrounded by various staff members with questions, reminders, and letters to sign. As he worked his way through the items, he ate a turkey sandwich, a bag of chips, and a bottle of water followed by a Diet Coke. Former UCLA player Sean Farnham stopped in to say congratulations, just as Lavin's cell phone rang again. He looked at the Caller ID and saw a 206 area code. Curious, he answered the call. It was Earl Watson, his four-year star player, his "coach on the court," and at the time, a Seattle Supersonic calling from Washington. (Watson would sign with Memphis in the offseason.) His former player was checking in on his old coach, like a son calling his father to see how things were going. In the course of the 15-minute call, Watson passed on his thoughts about a potential UCLA recruit.

Lavin was still on the phone when Martin came in and gave him the signal that it was time to move. The coach was to meet with the media on the floor of Pauley Pavilion at 1:00 P.M., and as usual, Lavin was pressed for time. He made his way down to the floor where he was immediately swamped by a horde of 40 reporters. There were numerous television crews and reporters, fighting each other to get their microphones near Lavin's mouth. The coach waited for the mass to settle down and began to answer questions, many of which had nothing to do with UCLA's next opponent, Missouri.

"Steve, how are you always able to turn it on come Tournament time?"

"Talk about the resiliency of you and this team."

"What impact does John Wooden still have over you and this program?"

"Would you be the coach today if Tyus Edney did not hit the game winner in 1995?"

The coach handled the questions comfortably with smiles, laughter, and soundbites. He was quite patient with the media, putting reporters at ease, and answered every last question from the local and national reporters. Bill Bennett grabbed Lavin by the arm and walked him to the other side of the floor where a *CNNSI* crew and reporter Tom Rinaldi waited. He conducted a 10-minute interview, focused on Lavin's job and his critics, rather than on the Sweet Sixteen, and in the process, allowed the coach a chance to allude to Rodney Dangerfield getting no respect. Lavin encountered more reporters on his way to the coaches' locker room, and again stopped to give them some time—something he really didn't have.

The players arrived and dressed, and handled the media's full-court press. Sandle gathered them on the court to stretch around 2:00 P.M. (close to 30 minutes late). Lavin finally made his way to the court and Pauley was cleared of most onlookers and media. He gathered the team at center court and talked in a hushed tone. "It kind of worries me that we will be playing near home," the coach began, referring to the Bruins playing in San Jose, just an hour flight away. "There will be more distractions, more ticket requests. We can lose our edge very quickly. Forget about the bandwagon and the pats on the back, we need to play with an edge and take the next step, with better defense and intensity. Practice today, and in fact this whole week, will be about staying in a routine. Same routine in practice. We worked hard this year to play in the West [Regional] and now we are here. But we know we want to get to Atlanta. That starts right now in practice."

And with that, the scheduled 60-minute practice got underway. The players knew the routine by now, quickly assuming their positions for the Flanker drill, a three-man full-court passing and shooting drill, with an emphasis on rebounding and outlet passes. Lavin yelled "pop the cork," among other encouraging phrases, wanting his players to step it up a notch. Flanker moved into Peer Pressure, the intense, variety of full-court passing and catching drills with a lot of talking and even more sprinting. As the drill moved forward, the count was reset for travels, missed catches and, ultimately, for a lack of intensity. On the third reset, Lavin sent the team for a Gatorade break and seniors Rico Hines (sitting out injured) and Matt Barnes gathered the players together under one basket and gave them a message about busting their asses in practice and staying focused. The drill resumed.

Peer Pressure was followed by a full-court 3-on-2 drill, with an offensive player (one of the threes) getting back on defense for a 2-on-1. The team shot free throws after the drill before heading into a halfcourt passing drill with an emphasis on cuts and backdoors. Team managers kept track of the team's passes on the scoreboard. More free throws were followed by 5-on-5 full court, with Lavin and his assistants occasionally stopping the action to make points about how to play Missouri. "They can score," Lavin told his troops. And then in a defensive stance, "We always need to have a hand in their face even way out here [three-point arc]. Every Missouri catch we have to be up in their face."

Former UCLA coach Walt Hazzard arrived at practice and took a seat with his son, Rasheed, in folding chairs next to the court. Lavin and his assistants made their way over to the coach and paid their respects. Practice continued with more full-court work on UCLA's defensive and offensive sets. Practice ended, the team showered and boarded the bus for the Los Angeles International Airport, joined by the UCLA traveling party of close to 60.

They flew American Airlines and arrived in San Jose near 9:15 P.M. They were bused to the Santa Clara Marriott, grabbed a late snack, and headed off to bed. Lavin settled into his hotel suite, talked with his assistants and went to bed.

Wednesday, March 20. The Marriott is located just minutes from the offices and training facilities of the NFL's San Francisco 49ers. Earlier in the week, 49er scout Jim Abrams had stopped by the UCLA offices to wish the coaches good luck. Abrams was a graduate assistant football coach at Purdue the same time Lavin was working under Gene Keady. After their brief encounter, Lavin had the idea of arranging for legendary 49er coach and team executive Bill Walsh to talk to the Bruins. With a few phone calls and help from Abrams, the talk was set. Before they headed out to the 49er facility, the team met for breakfast in a first-floor banquet room and then went to a mandatory study hall, where many of the players took final exams, as UCLA was on the quarter system. Meanwhile, Lavin relaxed in his hotel room, reading the paper and working on his practice plan for the day.

The team was to be on the bus at 12:15 P.M., to go to the 49er practice facility and then to the Compaq Center for practice. But the bus was not full at 12:15. In fact, the bus waited an extra 20 minutes as five players finished up their exams, proctored by Academic Advisor Mike Casillas. Casillas then FedExed the exams back to campus.

The bus arrived at the 49er facility around 1:00 P.M., where the team was greeted by Walsh and a trophy case containing five Super Bowl trophies. Some of the players were in awe; others were not. Walsh gave the team a brief tour of the facility, including the locker room, weight room, and indoor pool, and then led them to the assembly room where the championship coach gave some championship advice.

"You have had the perfect season to win it all," the 70-year-old Walsh began. With his intense glare, silver hair, and legendary status, he was an imposing figure. "You have had ups and downs, and some embarrassing losses. Your season runs parallel to my third Super Bowl team, when we had gone 6-5, the media were after me and then we won every other game to win the championship. The playoff games we were at our best. Your situation is ideal. You are coming together at the right time. The embarrassing losses and coaching decisions are behind you," he said with a smile.

The UCLA players and coaches listened intently and the room was dead silent. The man before them had won at the college and pro level and had won five Super Bowls, something no other coach had done. What he had to say had meaning.

"What you are playing with is the skills you learned at an early age. You don't have to play better and don't think you need to do that extra thing. If a NASCAR driver decides he needs to go faster to win, he ends up in the hospital. If Tiger Woods decides he needs just a little more length in his drives, he loses his rhythm. You just have to focus on these two games. And who do you play for? The coaches? No, I don't think so. Your school? Maybe, but probably not. You play for each other, your teammates, that's what makes this so special. You will never forget these experiences and in 20 years, you will all have been All-Americans—because you told everyone that you were."

Walsh concluded his 10-minute remarks by encouraging the team to trust one another, to keep the "machine" going with good momentum, playing as a unit. "There is no better team right now than UCLA. You must be focused. How much more lucky can you be? You are not 25-2 or 28-3 like Kansas who is sweating it out. Depend on the work you have put into this and you will be successful." And with that, the powerful pep talk was over. Walsh took the team upstairs to the executive offices and before sending the Bruins on their way, posed for a picture with the group.

The Compaq Center is a state-of-the-art arena in downtown San Jose, a 15-minute drive from the 49er complex and Marriott Hotel. The UCLA bus pulled up to the delivery entrance and once inside the arena tunnel, the team was escorted to their locker room, just a few feet from Missouri's. Lavin was brought to the CBS television room where he did an interview with CBS producers. As he walked in, he bumped into Missouri coach Quin Snyder. The two coaches had a mutual respect for each other, and both of them had "underachieved" on the season according to the critical eye of intense fans and media. Lavin and Snyder have known each other for many years, getting to know one another well when Lavin spent time in Durham visiting Mike Krzyzewski. "It's been a hell of a season," Lavin said to the coach three years his junior, and they talked about the frenzy surrounding their programs.

As Lavin made his way back to the locker room, he was immediately swamped by the camera crews in the hallway. The crunch of reporters stopped Lavin just 10 feet from where Snyder was holding court. It was a weird juxtaposition. The two coaches answered many of the same questions about failed expectations, resiliency, and about one another. Even more remarkable, in between the two packs of media, Lavin's father, Cap, was surrounded by four or five print guys, asking him about the game and his son. Cap Lavin was a legendary player in the Bay Area, so many of the local media had an interest in his thoughts.

One by one, the TV crews pulled away from the coaches and the press made its way into the UCLA locker room where the players relaxed, watching ESPN's *Pardon the Interruption* on a TV. Matt Barnes, Jason Kapono, and Rico Hines were in the CBS interview room, and on their way back to the UCLA locker room, encountered Snyder in the hallway. Kapono and Snyder hugged, Barnes shook Snyder's hand, and Hines gave him a brief hug after which Snyder wished him well. As the players talked to the press about how excited they were to be there, Lavin was at the microphone in the press room, answering the usual questions with his reliable sense of humor.

By 3:10 P.M., the team hit the floor for their shootaround. The practice sessions the day before NCAA Tournament games are open to the public and for this session, there were close to 500 people in the stands. The team stretched a bit on their own before practice, then opened up with 10 minutes of free shooting, five minutes at each end of the court. Lavin then gathered his troops, and they quickly moved into the Flanker drill for six minutes, Peer Pressure for 10 minutes, and half-court work on offensive sets. The team scrimmaged full court for six minutes before ending the 50-minute session with free throws.

By the time the team arrived back at the Marriott it was dinnertime. They gathered in a first-floor banquet room and gobbled up chicken, vegetables, corn bread, and ice cream. As dinner ended, the team pushed the tables back and arranged themselves in a semicircle of chairs, facing a television set and assistant Gerald Madkins, who was about to go over the Missouri scouting report. Missouri was a tough 12-seed, having defeated No. 5 Miami and No. 4 Ohio State en route to the Sweet Sixteen. They were such a good team that at one point in the season they were ranked as high as No. 2 in the country. As usual in the scouting session, each player was given a packet of information detailing Missouri's personnel tendencies, offensive and defensive sets, out-of-bounds plays, keys for UCLA at both ends of the floor, and the Tigers' statistics on the season.

Before Madkins began, Lavin made it clear to the team that Missouri would come out playing hard, especially two California kids to whom UCLA did not offer scholarships: Long Beach, California, products Wesley Stokes and Travon Bryant. "They feel that we dissed them," Lavin told his players, "making a big deal about it in the press. This isn't T-ball where everybody gets a chance to bat and nobody gets out. We only have so many scholarships—so tough."

Madkins went through the information in the packet, pointing out how best to defend each Missouri player and what to expect the following night. Madkins had stayed back at the hotel preparing the scouting report, watching and editing tape while the team went to the 49er complex and the practice and media sessions. Some of the information on Missouri he had gotten from the Georgia and Alabama coaching staffs, two schools with strong coaching ties to UCLA.

As with most teenagers, the Bruins' attention span was short, but as the assistant continued for 30 minutes, they tried their best to stay focused. After wrapping up the scouting report, Madkins played the edited tape he had put together on Missouri. First, there were personnel highlights, eight or nine plays by each of the Tiger players, showing their offensive moves. Then there were Missouri offensive sets, against zone and man defenses, followed by the Tigers' defenses and out-of-bounds plays. The entire tape lasted about 15 minutes. At the conclusion, Lavin huddled his team together, hands in the air, and gave them their instructions for the night: they were to be in their own rooms by midnight.

The coach headed out to downtown San Jose for dinner at *Il Fornaio* with some out-of-town friends and for Lavin, it was a great way to relax before game day. Even as late as 11:00 P.M. the night before the game, the coach continued to get ticket requests from friends and family, and his administrative assistants worked on getting more. Lavin was given 20 tickets as part of UCLA's allotment, but anything over that number he had to buy on his own. With tickets scarce, it was even more than the usual chore for Dana Martin and Doug Erickson to accommodate the requests and their boss didn't help by promising tickets to so many family and friends. After dinner, the coach made his way back to the Marriott, where he was immediately engaged in conversation by some UCLA supporters in the lobby. He made a brief stop in the hotel restaurant to say hello to some friends and walked back to his room at 12:30 A.M.

Thursday, March 21. Lavin looked refreshed as he entered the team meal room on the first floor of the Marriott. It was game day, and you could see the difference in his demeanor. Although he was still light-hearted and shook hands with fans as usual, he was more focused in his approach. He sat down at a table to talk with Madkins while the players finished breakfast—a meal of pancakes, eggs, potatoes, and fruit. UCLA's scheduled shootaround was at 11:00 A.M., and the team was on the bus by 10:30 for the drive to the Compaq Center.

Shootarounds on Tournament game days are closed to the public and the media, so the atmosphere inside the arena was more intense than it was on Wednesday, with fewer eyes on the coach and the team. They walked through offensive sets, and Lavin and his assistants demonstrated to the team how to play defense against Missouri's sharpshooters. The players ran some shooting drills and took free throws and then left the floor.

As the team arrived back at the hotel, the lobby was a sea of UCLA supporters and parents who awaited their arrival. As the players and coaches made their way back to their rooms, Lavin was inundated with requests as usual. Some fans wanted to shake his hand and wish him luck while others wanted a photo—or two. He obliged all comers, taking the time to sign shirts and balls for little kids and schmoozing with some Bruin donors and longtime friends. He finally made his way back to his suite to relax before changing for the game. His suite on the first floor was really two adjacent rooms. One, a large room with a bar, sofa, dining table, and entertainment center, connected to a typical hotel room with beds, bathroom, and so on. There were cookies on the table in the suite, a gift from a former player's mother. Lavin grabbed a few moments of solitude before getting dressed.

The UCLA bus left the hotel at 5:15 P.M. for the approximate tip-off at 7:15 P.M., and with heavy traffic en route to the arena, it was a good thing they gave themselves two hours. Upon arriving at the Compaq Center, the team made its way to the locker room as the assistants took seats to watch part of the Oklahoma-Arizona game from the stands. Lavin did his pregame interview with the home broadcasters and waited patiently in the locker room. At the conclusion of the first game, the Bruins hit the floor for warmups and returned to listen to some final instructions. "Missouri has an explosive offense," the coach reminded his players, "and we have to watch [Ricky] Paulding, [Kareem] Rush, and [Clarence] Gilbert," a trio he had previously warned the Bruins about. "We can't get beat off the dribble and we need to get hands in their faces when they shoot."

The first half was some ugly basketball, as both teams struggled to get it going on offense. UCLA led the entire first half until Paulding hit a jumper in the closing seconds to give Missouri its first lead. As was his custom, Lavin never took a seat, walking the sidelines, protesting some calls to the refs, squatting at the end of the bench. The Bruins shot only 31% in the first half. Missouri turned the ball over 10 times in the first 20 minutes. At halftime, Missouri was up by two, 30-28.

"There are no easy baskets out there," Lavin began his halftime talk. "They are getting behind Dan and pushing him out from the block, even after he gets the ball. We need to be patient on offense and make the extra pass." Lavin was not getting any contributions from his bench in the first half, with Dijon Thompson, Andre Patterson, T. J. Cummings, and Ryan Walcott combining for zero points.

The second half was emblematic of the entire Bruins' season. Great runs, amazing hustle, and dunks along with major defensive breakdowns and shooting slumps. At one point, UCLA had an eight-point lead, spurred by nine straight points from senior Matt Barnes. (The senior would finish the game with 23 points and 11 rebounds.) But then the walls came down. Missouri got hot. Rush and Gilbert caught fire, hitting short-range jumpers and deep threes. By the time UCLA stopped the bleeding, they trailed by nine with just under two minutes remaining. Though they fouled to stop the clock, the lead remained too big to overcome, and with 43 seconds remaining, Lavin replaced his starters and seniors with his bench, many of whom had seen minutes earlier in the game. As Gadzuric, Barnes, Knight, and Kapono left the floor, Lavin gave them each a hug, knowing that it was over for his seniors, and perhaps for Kapono, who was considering leaving for the NBA. In place of them on the court was a mix of freshmen and sophomores, a glimpse into next season. Thompson, Patterson, Cummings, Walcott, and Cedric Bozeman. Afterward, Lavin said he "watched the passing of the baton to the next generation of UCLA players."

The postgame locker room was not as emotional as one might think, especially considering the Bruins had lost a lead and a core group of seniors had played their last game. Lavin gave each player a hug, talked to the freshmen about staying positive for next year, and told the team that they had fought back over a long season, having overcome injuries and setbacks, and should be proud of their accomplishments.

Lavin answered questions from the imposing media presence in the press conference and locker room. The game ended around 9:20 P.M. PST, but the team did not return to the hotel until 11:20 P.M. Though it was late, and though their season had ended on a loss, the Marriott lobby was again filled with Bruin fans and family members. The hotel bar *Characters* was packed with the Bruin faithful, eating, drinking, and watching *SportsCenter* on large screen televisions. As the players and coaches entered the lobby, spontaneous applause broke out by the hundred or so mingling around. Parents gave hugs to players, players gave kisses to girlfriends. Gerald Madkins got kisses from his wife and two kids, and headed back to his room. Jim Saia walked around in a slight daze before joining assistant Patrick Sandle in the hotel bar.

As for Lavin, he was still the favorite son and the main attraction with this crowd. Moving from one group to another, he shook hands, received hugs and congratulations "on a fine season," commented on the Missouri loss and otherwise was animated in defeat. There was some discouragement in his face, but also some relief. For most coaches, the finality of the last loss doesn't hit until days after the final whistle. Lavin's older brother, John, was in the lobby, as was his girlfriend, Treena, and they watched Lavin finish one conversation before being engaged in another. As the lobby cleared, Sandle came out to grab his boss and bring him into the bar. As Lavin entered, he got applause again from the two hundred or so patrons, and again shook hands, smiled, and accepted congratulations. Still dressed in his dark suit, white shirt and tie, he stood out among the blue jeans and UCLA sweatshirt crowd. Lavin stayed in the bar until 1:00 A.M. with friends and family, before heading back to his room.

UCLA had a charter flight for the trip back to Los Angeles on Friday morning and it would be another early wakeup call for Lavin. But this day would be different. The season was over. The speculation about his future was muted after another Sweet Sixteen run. Lavin was proud of the way his team had battled to the end; of how they had learned from their mistakes during the season. The losses of Bozeman and Hines to injuries, the failure of the press early on, the balancing act between the young and the old players made it an interesting season for the coach. The only problem with making the Tournament is the realization that all but one team goes home a loser.

Bill Self knows all about that. He took Tulsa to the Elite Eight two years ago and last season took Illinois to the Elite Eight. His experiences in those previous trips helped prepare him for the onslaught and distractions of Tournament week. On Monday, March 18, the day after Illinois beat Creighton to advance to the Sweet Sixteen, Self arrived at his Illinois office at 9:00 A.M., earlier than usual, and began to take care of the distractions. There were the fans stopping in to sing his praises, friends and family calling for tickets, and media phone interviews. But Self had another distraction to deal with. With well-respected assistants, Norm Roberts, Billy Gillispie, and Wayne McClain, and at the time of year when jobs opened up, Self had to devote time to working the phones on behalf of his assistants. He made calls to athletic directors and fellow coaches, guys who might be able to help one of his assistants land his first Division I head coaching job. Gillispie was interested in TCU, McClain in Bradley, and Roberts was considering four or five schools. Self made the calls, even though his help could lead to the breakup of his staff. But that's what head coaches do, and this was the time of year to do it.

Self continued to deny being in contact with Arkansas and publicly stated that he had no interest in their opening. Self fought off the rumors and innuendoes as his staff prepped for No. 1 seed Kansas on Monday afternoon.

He didn't plan on doing anything basketball related until 12:30 P.M. or so. He had watched tape of Kansas at home on Sunday night, and would watch a lot more on Monday. He decided to do a walk-through with his team at 3:00 P.M. on Monday, not a full practice. He wanted to begin to make his players aware of some Kansas sets and plays and noted to the team that the Jayhawks ran so many different sets that the staff needed more time to prepare. The university was on Spring break, so there were few on-campus distractions. The Illinois coaching staff prepared scouting reports and film on Kansas, Oregon, and Texas, so they would be prepared for an Elite Eight opponent if they got by Kansas. But getting by Kansas would not be easy.

Kansas was as deep as Illinois, and had the size to match up. Big 12 Player of the Year Drew Gooden was 6'10", and Nick Collison and Wayne Simien were 6'9". The Jayhawks had steady guard play from Aaron Miles and Kirk Hinrich and throw in the deadly three-point shooting of Jeff Boschee and you can understand why Kansas was the No. 1 seed. For Self and Kansas coach Roy Williams, the meeting was déjà vu. In the Sweet Sixteen just a year earlier, Illinois defeated Kansas 80-64 to advance to the Elite Eight. Frank Williams lit the Jayhawks up for 30 points in the victory. It was no secret that this time around, Kansas had to find a way to stop the All-American. That job fell to the freshman guard Miles, who seemed eager for the assignment. Miles would get many minutes filling in for the injured Hinrich, who had hurt his ankle in Kansas' first-round game. Illinois was averaging 77.3 ppg and Kansas was scoring 91.2, tops in the nation, and both coaches expected a high-scoring affair.

The team flew up to Madison, Wisconsin, on Wednesday after practice to prepare for the late Friday night start. They did the typical shootarounds, walk-throughs, media interviews, and scouting sessions over the next 48 hours. Self found time to watch more tape on Kansas and even take an afternoon nap.

In the days leading up to the game, Self was honest in his assessment of Kansas to the media, telling them that Kansas was the best team in the country over the course of the season and deserved to be the No. 1 seed in the Midwest. In the pregame locker room at the Kohl Center, before the scheduled 9:20 P.M. start, the coach gave his team a caveat to that statement. "Kansas has been the best team throughout the season and we have had our struggles. But we need to just be better than them one night. We didn't perform well during the regular season and that is why we are meeting the No. 1 seed."

Self implored his team to have confidence, which the coach felt they had, and Self himself was confident that they would beat the favored Jayhawks. (Personally, he thought if they got past the Jayhawks they had a good shot at the national title.) "We have gone over our keys to the game before. Let's relax and take this game one possession at a time."

Hinrich hit a three 10 seconds into the game but didn't score again, spending time on the bench with foul trouble and the sore ankle. Kansas staked a 17-11 lead, as Illinois shot just one of 10 from the floor in the opening minutes. In the first half, Miles did his job, preventing Williams from breaking out for a huge game and keeping the Illinois guard from penetrating. Of course, it helps when you have the size presence inside to discourage a small guard from going to the rim. On offense, Kansas was on fire, with Gooden scoring down low (though Collison could not manage a point), as the Jayhawks shot 54% in the first half. By halftime, the No. 1 seed was up 40-34, despite Boschee's having an off game, Hinrich's spending a lot of time on the bench, and Collison's going 0 for the half.

"We had a few bad possessions, guys, that's all that is keeping us out of this game," Self told his team at halftime. "We missed some shots and had too many lapses of concentration. We certainly gave it everything we had."

The second half was full of drama, clutch shots, and missed opportunities. Kansas controlled the lead throughout the half, and led by 10 with just over five minutes to play. But each Jayhawk run was answered by Illinois, who, sparked by the inside play of Robert Archibald, closed to within two with 1:15 to play. Illinois could not hit on three attempts to tie or take the lead in the final 90 seconds (Cook missed two threes and Williams missed a jumper) while Kansas converted its free throws en route to a 73-69 win.

"It's more sadness than relief," Self remarked privately after the game.

A difficult year for the team and their coach had come to a sudden end, as most seasons do. But Self was proud of the way they had fought until the end, giving maximum effort over the course of the Tournament. Still, the team took the loss fairly hard and there were tears in the locker room. Self kept his remarks to his players short, reminding them of how hard they had played and how proud he was of the way they got back on their feet at the end of the season. "Win or lose, I could not have been prouder of you guys. You know in life, there are winners and losers. Winners are rewarded and losers are not seen in the same light. But I could not have asked for anything more."

For the coach, the loss to Kansas ended a year filled with distractions, from key injuries to the players' thoughts of the NBA, from coaching rumors to the highest of expectations. After things settled down, he had time to reflect. "It was a unique year that required a lot of energy on all of our parts. This was not the most difficult year that I have had as a coach, but it certainly was the least enjoyable. But you know, that is what coaching is. Dealing with those distractions and still being able to get your team to play hard."

The hurt and pain from the Sweet Sixteen loss for Self was doubly hard, considering how close to the Final Four he had been the past three seasons. Sometimes it is harder to get close to the goal and fail to reach it, then it is to fail miserably. Even though the season ended, there was still one more tough challenge. Like most coaches, Self and his wife were headed down to Atlanta for the Final Four, a week of fun, rekindling friendships, and looking ahead. But this visit would be especially difficult for the Illinois coach.

"It is going to be very hard to be down there and it certainly won't be as fun. To come so close the last few years, knowing that we had a shot this year makes it very difficult."

26

The Season Never Ends

THE LOBBY OF THE ATLANTA HILTON, THE FINAL FOUR COACHES' HOTEL, WAS PACKED. From the atrium between the sliding glass doors to all the way back near the bathrooms. There were people everywhere. As you walk through the front doors, all eyes turn to you. It's rather unsettling. Look to your left and you see Jerry Tarkanian leaning against a wall, with a group of four or five men paying their respects. Nolan Richardson, who had lost his job at Arkansas, walks through and gets handshakes and condolences. There is Gonzaga's Mark Few, Oregon's Ernie Kent, and Alabama's Mark Gottfried slowly making their way from one end of the lobby to the other. There are hundreds of coaches in the lobby. Some are JV high school coaches while others are the top names in the game.

As you make your way through the lobby, there are the ticket scalpers who try to be subtle, but subtly is not in their personality. "You got tickets?" they attempt to ask in a hushed tone. They move fast without really hearing the answer, eager for the next piece of fresh meat.

What is the most common question asked in the thousands of conversations in the lobby over the course of six days? "So, what do you hear?"

As much as the Final Four week is about the Tournament, the National Association of Basketball Coaches annual meeting, and carousing with longtime friends, it is really a job fair like no other. Coaches flock to the coaches' hotel lobby every year looking for jobs. There are the unrealistic high school or junior college guys, wearing their school's warmups, looking to introduce themselves to any coach who will listen. There are the Division I assistants, reintroducing themselves to one another and letting it be known they are looking for the next gig. Throw into the mix the fact that most ADs come to the Final Four. It is chaos that goes on from 7:00 A.M. to 5:00 A.M. No joke.

Coaches and ADs know that the Final Four is a career fair and, thus, those that want to avoid it do not make an appearance in the lobby. If you are a newly hired coach—stay away. A coach rumored to be up for a job—stay away. An AD conducting a search—stay away. Perhaps that is why at the Hilton you didn't see newly hired Arkansas coach Stan Heath or Missouri's Quin Snyder, rumored to be up for the Washington job. Washington AD Barbara Hedges was also a no-show, though she was in town.

Remember the children's game "Pass It Down the Line" or some called it "Telephone"? The one in which one person starts a rumor, whispers it to someone sitting next to him, starting a chain of whispers between kids? By the time it reaches the end, it is much different from how it started. The lobby of the Hilton is one big Pass It Down the Line. A coach will ask you what you have heard and before allowing you to answer, he will interject what he has heard. Within moments, that information, fact or fiction, has spread like the chicken pox. There are more rumors in the lobby than at a prom.

In fact, the hotel lobby at the Final Four has taken on a life of its own. A top coach like Illinois' Bill Self cannot get from the elevator to the front door in 20 minutes. Stopped by job-seekers, AAU coaches, ticket scalpers, former assistants, and friends, one will find the short trip to feel more like a marathon. But the lobby is just a part of the business of coaching.

Self came to Atlanta despite his disappointment of coming so close yet again, and brought his wife, Cindy. They arrived on Thursday and watched Illinois players Robert Archibald and Cory Bradford participate in the All-Star game and three-point shootout, respectively. They had dinner with the Illinois staff, Cindy got some shopping in, and Self caught up with friends for generous Southern cooking. He attended the variety of coaches meetings, noting that "Now that I am at a bigger program, I need to be on top of changes and issues affecting the game." They sat in the Nike suite at the semifinal games on Saturday night and headed home on Easter Sunday.

Steve Alford brought along his son, Kory, and his father and assistant coach, Sam, and avoided the crowds and lobby as much as possible. They took in a Toronto Raptors-Atlanta Hawks game and went to the Hoop Jam festivities where Kory could enjoy the games. They, too, got out of town early, leaving Sunday morning for Iowa City.

Mike Brey came solo to the Final Four, his wife and kids having been to so many over the years. Brey spent some time schmoozing in the lobby and made appearances at the Adidas and Intersport parties. The Adidas party at the Final Four is always a highlight, an extravagant cocktail party with the who's who of college basketball. All three of Brey's assistants joined their boss in Atlanta, as did his boss, athletic director Kevin White, with whom they dined on Friday night. At the semifinal games on Saturday night, Brey sat with the Notre Dame provost and headed home early Sunday morning.

One no-show at the main event was Steve Lavin. The UCLA coach came down with a viral infection the day before heading to Atlanta and spent the weekend in bed in Marina del Rey. Jim Saia, Patrick Sandle, and Gerald Madkins all came to Georgia and represented Lavin well.

J ust because the NCAA Tournament comes to an end does not mean that coaches get to vacation for the next three months. In fact, with the new recruiting calendar in effect in 2002, many of the coaches hit the road the day after the title game when the NCAA allows contact between coaches and recruits. Head and assistant coaches spread out across the country, making home visits, eating meals with high school coaches, and planning ahead for 2003–2004. As Lavin says, "There is no off-season for coaches."

May and August had been the times when coaches could grab a week or so with their family on a tropical island. But now with sophomores and juniors coming to campus on unofficial visits and phone work to be done, finding time for a get-away is difficult. Lavin heads to Cancun, Mexico, every May with Treena, and this year he brought along his parents for their fiftieth wedding anniversary. The coach and his family spent eight days on the Mexican coast and came back tan and well-rested. Brey and his family made their annual trip to Rehoboth Beach, Delaware, the first week of July, while Alford, Tanya, and the kids stayed in Sarasota, Florida, for a week in the end of June and spent time at their lake home in Indiana in August. (Self could not take a family trip due his health.)

The end of June is a big time for the programs and the coaches, as the NBA holds its annual draft from Madison Square Garden. Each coach had high hopes for their stars: Self had a sure first-rounder in Frank Williams, despite his "down" year and big man Robert Archibald could be a sleeper in the late second round; Brey had no illusions that David Graves or Harold Swanagan would be drafted, but after impressive performances at the predraft camps, Ryan Humphrey looked like a draftee; Lavin had Matt Barnes and Dan Gadzuric as potential picks; Alford had Luke Recker and Reggie Evans, two players who at the start of the year seemed like lottery picks, but now were projected to be late second-rounders—if at all.

Surprisingly, Humphrey was the first to go, selected by the Orlando Magic with the 19th pick in the first round, shocking some experts but not his coach, who believed that Humphrey's work ethic and intensity impressed the NBA scouts. With the drafting of Humphrey, Notre Dame became only one of four teams to have a first-round pick in the past two years, joining Indiana, Duke, and Stanford. The lock lottery pick from the preseason, Williams was drafted by Denver with the 25th pick and then traded to the Knicks. His drop from the top seven to No. 25 was clearly a reflection of his up and down season. With the third selection in the second round, the 32nd pick overall, the Memphis Grizzlies took Archibald and two picks later, the Milwaukee Bucks selected Dan Gadzuric. Both big men deserved the shot, but experts thought Gadzuric's quick feet would earn him a higher pick—perhaps *his* down season cost him. With a strong showing at the predraft games in Portsmouth and Chicago, Barnes made himself an NBA draft pick, taken as the 46th pick overall, 17th in the second round, by the Cleveland Cavaliers.

As the draft neared its conclusion, Evans watched from his mother's home in Pensacola and Recker watched with his fiancée from a suite at the Venetian Hotel in Las Vegas. They waited. And waited. The two preseason All-Americans and Wooden Award candidates did not hear their names called on draft day. Recker had worked hard since the end of the season to get into shape and work on his shot—something his college coach thought he should have done before the season. Evans continued his tireless work but did not do enough to impress the general managers. Both players caught on with summer pro teams and entertained the possibility of making an NBA roster; Recker with the Miami Heat and Evans with the Seattle Supersonics. (Recker would not make that roster while Evans became a Seattle starter by the beginning of the NBA season.)

Self watched the NBA draft at home with some Illinois players. He continued to battle his intestinal tear, or diverticulitis, and doctors urged the coach to have surgery to rectify the problem. Self was to leave for Germany in August for 10 days as the coach of the Big Ten All-Stars, and doctors wanted him to have time to fully recover. Right before the start of the July recruiting season, on June 28, Self underwent surgery and had 12 inches of his intestines removed and 36 large staples put into his stomach. He lost 20 pounds in two weeks. Self recovered at home and was able to go into the office for the first 10 days of the recruiting season, but couldn't travel far. He felt good enough to fly in late July to the Adidas Big Time Tournament in Las Vegas, but after only one day, fell ill and returned to Champaign. There was some good news for Self, as he got a verbal commitment from rising high school senior Brian Randle, a coveted recruit who Duke, North Carolina, and Notre Dame were all pursuing.

There were two major changes for coaches in the July 2002 evaluation period. One was the dates, with the month now split into two 10-day evaluation periods separated by a four-day dead period. Second, coaches could no longer talk with recruits, parents, or their AAU coaches during tournaments. No more 10-deep lines waiting to shake hands with an AAU coach; no more trying to corner parents to find out which way their son was leaning. The new rule left coaches guessing until late July or early August.

All four coaches hit the road in July, but took different paths around the nation as they evaluated recruits at camps and AAU tournaments. Lavin first hit Indy for the Nike camp and then the Adidas ABCD camp in New Jersey, and ran into former boss and current Georgia coach Jim Harrick. Considering what Lavin had endured since taking over for Harrick in 1996, the older coach joked, "I never thought that you would outsurvive Pete Dalis," the now-retired UCLA athletic director. "It's unbelievable! You outlived the S.O.B. Congratulations." (Harrick knowing that Dalis played a role in the ouster of the previous three head coaches.) After ABCD, Lavin went to Philadelphia, Seattle, Las Vegas and Miami before taking the path less traveled, heading to Caracas, Venezuela, for the World Games, where he watched prized recruit Aaron Brooks lead the USA team. Lavin was so hot on Brooks that he spent days simply following the recruit around the world. Lavin spent five days in Venezuela, but caught a stomach infection and barely made it back home (after a stop in a Miami hospital).

Mike Brey was all over the map, from the Nike camp in Indianapolis to the AAU Nationals in Orlando to the Big Time Tournament in Las Vegas to the month-ending event in Los Angeles; with stops in Teaneck for ABCD, Augusta for the Peach Jam, and Chicago for individual evaluations along the way. Brey was well versed in the July recruiting period, but this summer, he earned a bit more respect from fellow coaches and recruits after his impressive year at Notre Dame. Steve Alford also hit Indy, New Jersey, Augusta, Las Vegas, and Orlando.

For Alford, it was a difficult summer. In a span of eight weeks, he had one player cited for marijuana possession, one cited for underage drinking, one current player and one recruit failed to meet academic requirements, and one incoming recruit got homesick and left Iowa City for good. Then, just days before the start of classes in August, sophomore Marcellus Sommerville announced he was transferring. Things got worse. In early October, Chauncey Leslie was charged with a "disorderly house" and perhaps most devastating, Pierre Pierce was charged with third-degree sexual assault. By the time practice started in October, Alford was down to eight scholarship players. There was one bright spot for Alford, however, and it occurred in the first week of August.

The coach had gotten back in touch with his college coach, Bobby Knight, in late January, in the midst of Iowa's losing streak. The men continued conversations throughout the spring and Knight invited Alford down to Lubbock for a few days to talk basketball and life. So in the first week of August, Alford flew down and spent what he called "an amazing" two and a half days with The General.

"I took probably 40 pages of notes on things that he talked about," Alford said, his eyes wide open like a boy's in a candy store. They watched film together, talked about recruiting, fund-raising, the best uses for assistants and, of course, offensive and defensive sets. They rehashed old Indiana stories over meals and even did a joint appearance on Fox Sports Net's *The Best Damn Sports Show Period*, co-hosted by Iowa native Tom

Arnold. "I sensed I had a relationship with Coach Knight again," Alford said a week later. "It feels good."

Steve Lavin also got bad news as the summer wound down. Sophomore-to-be Andre Patterson, who figured heavily in Lavin's plans for 2002–2003, became academically ineligible and would have to sit out at least the first part of the season and star recruit Evan Burns failed to qualify for admittance to UCLA. Aaron Brooks, the big-time recruit Lavin followed throughout the world during the summer, committed to Oregon.

In August, the coaches mixed relaxation with preparation. There was still recruiting work to be done and unofficial visits to host. Self took his staff with him as he coached the Big Ten All-Star team in a 10-day trip to Germany, where the team finished 4-1. Illinois players Sean Harrington and Roger Powell performed well for Self going up against professional clubs.

By the end of August, all of the coaches were preparing for the start of classes, not for the return of their players. The NCAA now allows scholarship athletes, including incoming freshmen, to take classes in the summer and live on campus, so all of the programs had their teams pretty much assembled and playing together every day. When classes began in late August (late September for UCLA), the coaches met with their teams, organized conditioning and individual workouts, and geared up for another season. It was early fall, but already their thoughts were on March. Who will get their teams there? What challenges may lie ahead for the coaches? Will 2002–2003 bring success or failure?

The 2001–2002 season was a long one for the four coaches, as is every season. There were player injuries, academic problems, player family troubles, fund-raisers, interviews, health issues, recruiting wins and losses, and yes, upsets. The season was typical in many respects for all coaches, who deal with these issues every year. It is their job.

For Steve Lavin, his preseason mantra of stability did not hold true. With key injuries, particularly to Cedric Bozeman and Rico Hines, a lack of team speed, the early-season upset losses to Ball State and Pepperdine, the challenge of managing the younger and older players, the early failures of the full-court press and the inconsistent play, Lavin struggled to find consistency in performance all season long. Yet, happily, there were no off-the-court distractions, suspensions, investigations, job threats or death threats to contend with, and the UCLA coach could handle everything that came to him. He remains an enigma to some UCLA fans, proving that in adversity, there can be triumph. His sixth-place finish in the PAC-10 was virtually erased from memory by the wins over Mississippi and Cincinnati in the NCAA Tournament, and the close loss to Missouri in the Sweet Sixteen.

As he enters his seventh season as the head coach at UCLA, a feat no one could have predicted, Lavin seems to be resolved that nothing that he can do at UCLA will ever be enough. No Tournament wins, upsets over top-ranked teams, players to the NBA, great recruiting classes, or even a potential national championship will ever be sufficient— something it has taken him a few years to learn and accept. He will be back for the 2002–2003 season, working under a new boss, athletic director Dan Guerrero, and welcomes back a core of performers including Bozeman, Dijon Thompson, T. J. Cummings, and All-Conference player Jason Kapono. Throw in the addition of Michael Fey, and redshirts Jon Crispin and Ray Young, and UCLA could vie for the PAC-10 title.

Like *they* say every year, this could be Lavin's last, though he has a six-year contract. Something the coach himself acknowledges. How much can he take in pursuing his avocation? Perhaps he will move to another college program, far away from Los

Angeles; perhaps the NBA will come calling or a television network eager to land the personable coach will offer him a chance to critique others. But for now, he prepares to do it all over again.

It was an enjoyable year for Mike Brey, finally getting comfortable at Notre Dame. His house was completed, his offices redone, his staff was now working like clockwork, he had a boss who believed in him, and a group of seniors to lead the way. Of course, having Chris Thomas step in and be the Big East Rookie of the Year helped. The Irish came close to the Sweet Sixteen, losing to Duke in a heartbreaker, and again had a 20-win season. Brey continued to hone his coaching skills, many of which deal with the mental game. He had to keep his freshman star poised, senior David Graves, calm and Harold Swanagan focused. There were injuries and a three-game losing streak to contend with, but he managed to pull the Irish through.

Brey heads into the new season with Chris Thomas and Matt Carroll headlining the squad, and Brey expects to get contributions from Maryland transfer Dan Miller and incoming freshmen Torin Francis and Chris Quinn. There will be no Hawaii trip this season, but there is a nonconference matchup against defending national champion Maryland.

The success of Notre Dame and Brey in his first two years has created a level of expectations in South Bend. With the price of success comes the expectation that you can do it again, a pressure that coaches feel the weight of all the time. Notre Dame basketball was back on the map, but can Brey take the team a step further? With the resurgence of the Irish football program under new coach Tyrone Willingham, will Brey's progress go unnoticed?

Illinois was expected to play in Atlanta in late March. Bill Self was there but only as a spectator. His team reached the Sweet Sixteen, something most schools would be gleeful about. But at Illinois, expectations of a Final Four did not materialize to the disappointment of many fans. On closer inspection, just getting to the round of 16 was an accomplishment for Self and the Illini. He had lost his team leader, Lucas Johnson, to injury before the season even started. His injury was followed by setbacks for Damir Krupalija and Robert Archibald. His freshmen did not grasp things as quickly as the coach would have liked, and he struggled to keep star Frank Williams motivated. After Illinois lost three in a row in late January and early February, the season looked like an utter failure. But the coach and team battled back, and with hard work, a new attitude, and a little bit of luck, they shared a piece of the Big Ten title.

For the coach, it was his most challenging year in the profession. Dealing with the injuries and roster management, as well as with the expectations, made for a pressure-packed season. Still, he was proud of the way his team fought back and, though they fell one possession short against Kansas in the final game, Self deemed the season a success. Illinois' season did not play out the way he had envisioned it back in October, but then again, most seasons don't. Coaches must routinely adjust, finagle, and manage their teams to get the most out of them as the season progresses, and certainly in March. What fans and alumni may see as seasons of failure, may actually be seasons of success.

On top of the challenging season, Self also dealt with his health. His ongoing battle with colon pain from late November resulted in a difficult physical state for parts of the season and eventual surgery in June, forcing him to sit out the important July recruiting period. There were also the rumors of a potential move to Arkansas at the worst possible time, as the coach was preparing his team for the Tournament. But the distractions were par for the course for high-profile coaches.

Though Illinois lost Robert Archibald, Frank Williams, and Cory Bradford, among others, Self welcomes Deron Williams, Dee Brown, James Augustine, and Aaron Spears for the 2002–2003 season, with the freshmen expected to get plenty of playing time. The centerpiece of the Illini will be Brian Cook, who finally will get his chance to shine in the spotlight, and who will, hopefully, get help from Sean Harrington, Luther Head, and a much-improved Roger Powell. In the 2002–2003 season, Self will be without assistant Billy Gillispie, who was named head coach at UTEP in early November.

Perhaps none of the four coaches had a more difficult year than Iowa's Steve Alford, who questioned himself, and his team, on so many occasions. A squad led by two preseason All-Americans and ranked in the Top Ten did not even make the NCAA Tournament. A midseason losing streak, humiliating losses, and internal strife were barely offset by another impressive run in the Big Ten Tournament. Players sat on the bench because of injuries and academics, because of a lack of effort and poor leadership. Alford's family and faith kept him grounded and comforted when times were troubling, but it was only after reestablishing a relationship with Bobby Knight that Alford was able to get refocused on what he needed to do and how he was going to do it.

After three years in Iowa City, the pressure has started to mount on the coach, even from the Iowa faithful. With a move to Indiana now unlikely, Alford's home is Iowa City. The new million-dollar home that he and his family will move into in November, complete with a half-court indoor basketball court, suggests that he is there to stay. Despite the off-season headlines, Alford is excited about the new season, as he has a strong freshmen class arriving in Iowa City, including Jeff Horner and Greg Brunner, two Iowa boys looking to make an immediate impact.

Coaching is more than a career choice or an avocation—it is a way of life. At the highest levels of collegiate basketball, the twenty-first-century coach is no longer beholden to a whistle and clipboard. The responsibilities have grown as the game has been reshaped by the money, television, and the NBA draft. The impact is felt all the way down to youth leagues, where every player wants to be the next Mike and every coach thinks he is Dean Smith. It is clear that coaching is now vastly different from previous decades.

Should we ask our coaches to do more than draw up plays and win ballgames? Should we ask our coaches to fund raise for the universities, to spend their days writing letters and calling recruits, to keep daily track of students' academic progress, to give repeated interviews to the media, to fill in as fathers and brothers, and to sacrifice their own families? Shouldn't coaches simply be asked to just coach? The problem, as it is in so many professions, is money. The money made from television contracts, ticket sales, sneaker companies and, most importantly, NCAA Tournament appearances has changed the game, and the men leading it, forever. When we pay coaches large amounts of money, we should demand that they go beyond drawing up plays. Unfortunately, too many fans and administrators see the large contracts as a promise to win—and win fast. They neglect to see the sacrifices that coaches make on a daily basis; they don't see the bonds forged between coach and player that last a lifetime; they don't see the midnight staff meetings or the hours a coach sits at home breaking down film; they don't see how much coaches truly care about their players and their futures. All they see is the record and the Tournament brackets.

At some point in the next decade, coaches may no longer be asked to do so much. They may no longer be held accountable for unrealistic expectations and for the academic progress of their students. They may not be hired or fired as quickly as they are today, and the goal of every coach may not simply be to make the NCAA Tournament. Most coaches, but not all, enter the profession because they love to teach and they love young minds. When those people stop becoming coaches, the world will take notice and things will change. School presidents and athletic directors will stand up for the coaches that "do it right," regardless of the wins and losses.

There are hundreds, if not thousands, of excellent basketball coaches at all levels, from elementary teams to the NBA. Some are well-known, while others toil in obscurity. Just because a coach gets publicity, fame, and riches does not mean he must be a better coach than a no-name. Some assistants never get the chance to run their own programs, but that does not mean they are not qualified to do so. Some coaches work a lifetime at a Division III school, junior college, or high school, but that does not mean that they are any less of a coach than one in a power conference.

Coaches return each year, reenergized by the "offseason," ready to take on the peaks and valleys of their chosen profession. No one forces them to do it. They do it because they love the game and they love teaching and shaping young minds. They are the men of college basketball. The Men of March.

Index

About the Author

A s a journalist, coach, educator, and fan, BRIAN CURTIS brings considerable experience in television and sports to his latest project. Most recently, Curtis was a sports reporter and broadcaster for Fox Sports Net, based in Los Angeles, primarily covering college basketball and college football. He was nominated for two Los Angeles Emmy Awards in 2001. Curtis also has worked as a sports reporter and anchor for a local television station in Ohio, covering basketball and football in the Mid-American Conference. He hosted a sports radio talk show, *Sports Conversation*, in Virginia and covered ACC basketball on radio.

In addition to his work in broadcasting, Curtis has been a soccer coach at the collegiate and high school levels and has worked in the athletic departments at three Division I schools. He is a member of the United States Basketball Writers Association. Curtis gives his time to the Special Olympics as well.

He holds a masters degree from Ohio University in sports administration and a bachelors degree from the University of Virginia in government. He currently resides in Los Angeles, California, with his wife, Tamara.